LEGAL NURSE
CONSULTING
PRINCIPLES
and
PRACTICE

LEGAL NURSE CONSULTING
PRINCIPLES
and PRACTICE

 AMERICAN ASSOCIATION OF
LEGAL NURSE CONSULTANTS

Edited by
Julie Brewer Bogart, RN, MN
Prairie Village, Kansas

Associate Editors:
Shirley Cantwell Davis, RN, BSN
Atlanta, Georgia
Deborah H. Dlugose, RN, BA, CCRN, CRNA
Hagerstown, Maryland
Jill D. Holmes, RN, MSN, FNP
La Jolla, California
Patricia W. Iyer, RN, MSN
Flemington, New Jersey
Barbara Oberg Blake, RN, MS
Houston, Texas
Doreen James Wise, RN, MSN, EdD
Houston, Texas

CRC Press
Boca Raton   London   New York   Washington, D.C.

Library of Congress Cataloging-in-Publication Data

Legal nurse consulting : principles and practice / American
    Association of Legal Nurse Consultants ; edited by Julie Brewer
    Bogart...[et al.].
        p. cm.
    Includes bibliographical references and index.
    ISBN 1-57444-123-X (alk. paper)
    1. Nursing—Law and legislation—United States. 2. Nursing
consultants—Legal status, laws, etc.—United States. I. Bogart,
Julie Brewer. II. American Association of Legal Nurse Consultants.
KF2915.N8L35 1997
344.73′0414—dc21

                                                   97-50089
                                                      CIP

© 1998 by American Association of Legal Nurse Consultants

No claim to original U.S. Government works
International Standard Book Number 1-57444-123-X
Library of Congress Card Number 97-50089
Printed in the United States of America   5 6 7 8 9 0
Printed on acid-free paper

Acknowledgments

I wish to recognize the many authors who enthusiastically accepted the role of risk takers to write a chapter for this first-edition textbook. Their willingness to present their experience and scholarship for critique by peers is one measure of their professionalism.

I wish to thank the reviewers who greatly enriched the book and provided information and insight to the risk takers.

The editors of this textbook performed brilliantly. Often it was under trying circumstances and in the context of extremely busy professional lives. They worked both as editorial team members and leaders of the authors in their sections. They were superb in both roles.

I am grateful to Ann Cordes and Karen Nason and other staff members of AALNC for their unwavering support, guidance, and expertise.

Thanks to all current and previous AALNC Board of Directors for their vision which directed the creation of this textbook.

I would like to acknowledge the original Core-Curriculum development-committee members who laid the foundation for the content outline of the book.

I am especially grateful to my long-distance friends in AALNC for their no-nonsense good sense, patience, and unequivocal support for this project.

Julie Bogart, RN, MN
Editor

Preface

Legal nurse consulting (LNC) is a rapidly growing specialty practice of nursing. There has been a lack of literature or comprehensive textbooks devoted to the skills, processes, and information requisite to quality LNC practice. AALNC publishes the *Journal of Legal Nurse Consulting* and now a core curriculum, *Legal Nurse Consulting: Principles and Practice* to meet the need for relevant and essential information. The content contributes to defining the knowledge base of the speciality, reflects the current scope of practice, and provides an authoritative resource for practicing LNCs. Though comprehensive in scope, it is not intended to be the sole source of information for an LNC practice. It is, however, a primary source book for legal nurse consultants.

Legal Nurse Consulting: Principles and Practice is a key reference textbook for the neophyte and advanced as well as the generalist and specialist LNC. It is valuable to the LNC in a law firm, health care system, insurance company, or independent practice. Educators will use it as a core textbook for LNC programs, for legal and ethical issues courses, and for risk management topics in undergraduate or graduate nursing programs. Employers will purchase it as a reference text for the LNC's bookshelf. Nurses working in roles as diverse as health care risk managers, life-care planners, expert nurse witnesses, crime scene investigators, health care licensing agency investigators, and administrators of government injury reimbursement programs will include this textbook in their own reference libraries.

The authors are a diverse group of talented LNCs, attorneys, and other professionals. They bring to the book a wide breadth of practice experience and represent almost every state in the country. Their pioneering and voluntary contributions deserve our gratitude. In many cases in this first edition, there was no previous chapter from which to build content. They started from scratch and created content based on expertise developed from years of practice and study.

The reviewers acted as the quality controls in the process. Two to three reviewed each chapter. They not only critiqued but often went a step beyond the traditional reviewer's role to contribute content or examples to enrich the chapter. The end result is a truly collaborative, contributed textbook.

Editing a contributed textbook is a complex task. It requires balancing content, format, style, integration, and innovation. It requires special people who are willing and able to work as a team and who trust and respect one another. I am personally grateful to the authors, reviewers, and editors who took time from their very busy schedules and personal lives to contribute to this book. Their patience, attention to detail, professionalism, enthusiasm, and dedication far exceeded my expectations. Within the shared responsibility for this book lies its value and validity.

The process of preparing for the second edition begins with the publication of the first. Subsequent editions will revise and build on this effort to document what LNCs do and how they do it. As you read this first edition, I encourage you to write your suggestions and constructive criticisms to the editors of the second edition. Your feedback is important to ensure the second edition exceeds the first. The process of revision, refinement, and evolution of this textbook will be continuous.

I am proud to have been associated with this first edition, and present it to you on behalf of the contributors.

Julie B. Bogart, RN, MN
Editor

About the Editors

Editor

Julie Brewer Bogart, RN, MN
Prairie Village, Kansas

Ms. Bogart has 12 years of experience as an independent legal nurse consultant and expert witness and is currently a risk management specialist for two hospitals. She has authored several articles on the role of the nurse in presenting medical-record evidence at trial. In addition to her editing responsibilities for *Legal Nurse Consulting: Principles and Practices,* she also co-authored several chapters. She frequently makes presentations to a wide variety of nursing specialty groups on legal issues of practice. She has served on the national board of AALNC as Treasurer and President (1997-98). Ms. Bogart received a Bachelor of Science degree in Nursing in 1970 and a Masters in Nursing degree in 1980 from the University of Kansas Medical Center. She has 21 years clinical nursing experience in medical-surgical and critical-care units. She is an adjunct and consulting faculty member at two university schools of nursing.

Associate Editors

Barbara Oberg Blake, RN, BSN, MS
Houston, Texas

Ms. Blake has been a Legal Nurse Consultant for over 10 years in the Houston, Texas law firm of Franklin, Cardwell and Jones, assisting in the defense of physicians, hospitals, and nurses in medical malpractice lawsuits. Her masters degree is in nursing with an emphasis in nursing education. She served on the Program Committee for the 1994 National AALNC Conference in Houston, Texas, was a Director-at-Large and is current President-Elect for the Greater Houston Chapter of AALNC. She has published three articles in the field of nursing and has given lectures to various groups of nurses on the role of the legal nurse consultant, including a presentation at the 1997 AALNC National Conference. In addition, she was editor for two general readership monthly publications in Houston, Texas.

Shirley Cantwell Davis, RN, BSN
Atlanta, Georgia

Ms. Davis is the owner of Davis and Associates, a consulting firm in Atlanta, Georgia. She has gained extensive experience over the past 15 years working in many areas of medical-legal litigation. Ms. Davis has worked as an in-house consultant for both defense and plaintiff firms in the field of medical malpractice. Her independent consulting practice has also included national cases of pharmaceutical and medical-products liability litigation. Additionally Ms. Davis has written and lectured nationally on various topics of interest to legal nurse consultants. She is a founding member of AALNC and was its first president in 1990. Since that time, she has played an active role in the advancement of legal nurse consulting in the areas of education, standards, and certification. Presently, Ms. Davis serves as an editor for the *Journal of Legal Nurse Consulting*.

Deborah Dlugose, RN, CCRN, CRNA
Hagerstown, Maryland

Deborah Dlugose is President of Wright Professional Associates. PC of Chapel Hill, North Carolina and Hagestown, Maryland. She blends clinical expertise with her background in communications. She is nationally recognized as a speaker, writer, and editor in nurse-anesthesia, critical care nursing, quality assurance, and legal nurse consultant practice. She maintains an active clinical practice in nurse-anesthesia along with her commitments to nursing education and literature.

Jill Holmes (Fisher), RNCS, MSN, FNP
La Jolla, California

In 1987 Ms. Holmes answered an ad ("Wanted: Nurse to assist attorneys with medical records") and joined Gray, Care, Ames & Frye (now Gray, Care, Ware & Freidenrich), a large law firm in San Diego. She consulted in cases for both plaintiff and defense attorneys in personal injury, product liability, and medical malpractice areas with occasional assistance given to the trusts & estate department. She was a founding member of the American Association of Legal Nurse Consultants and served as San Diego Chapter President in 1990-91. In 1995 she left the law firm to pursue a post-master's nurse practitioner certificate and currently practices as a Nurse Practitioner in the Senior Behavioral Health Program at UCSD Medical Center - La Jolla, Thornton Hospital. She continues to practice as a legal nurse consultant on occasional cases for two area attorneys. Ms. Holmes authored two chapters in addition to acting as an editor for this text.

Patricia Iyer, RN, MSN
Flemington, New Jersey

Ms. Iyer is president of an independent legal nurse consulting practice, located in central New Jersey. Med League's staff of nurses and support personnel provide national consulting services for personal injury, medical malpractice, and products liability cases. Ms. Iyer has 10 years of experience as a medical surgical nursing expert witness and 8 years of experience as a legal nurse consultant. She is co-author of seven nursing textbooks. She also served as the editor of a book on nursing malpractice, published by Lawyers and Judges Publishing Company. It is one of the only books that has been written for attorneys solely on nursing malpractice. Along with Nancy Camp, RN MSN LNC, Ms. Iyer co-authored a Mosby Year Book text on nursing documentation which is being revised for its third edition.

Doreen James Wise, RN, MSN, EdD
Houston, Texas

Dr. Wise received a Bachelor in Nursing from Vanderbilt University, a Masters in Nursing from Cal State Los Angeles, and a Doctoral at Baylor College of Medicine and University of Houston. Her clinical career has included pediatrics and mental health nursing in which she was certified for 10 years by the ANA during her tenure as a psychotherapist in private practice. The skills learned there have served her well in 15 years of legal nurse consulting as an independent practitioner and as President of Medical Research Consultants, Inc. Dr. Wise is a recent past president of AALNC. In addition to her editing responsibilities, she contributed two chapters and co-authored a third for this publication.

Contributors

Tonia Dandry Aiken, RN, JD
President
RN Development
Metairie, Louisiana

Julie Anderson, BSN, MSN, JD
Attorney
McFall, Sherwood & Sheehy, PC
Houston, Texas

Kathleen Woods Araiza, RN, BA
Frederick, Maryland

Gretchen Aumann, RN, BSN, Doctoral
  Candidate
Houston, Texas

Mary T. Baldwin, RN, BSN, MRA, PHN,
  CCM, CRRN
Rehabilitation Nurse Consultant
Baldwin Consultants
San Diego, California

Sue Barnes, RN, MSN, MSHCA
CEO, Legal Nurse Consultant
Sue Barnes Medical Consulting Services, Inc.
Phoenix, Arizona

Jenny R. Beerman, RN, MN
President
Beerman & Associates
Kansas City, Missouri

Julie Brewer Bogart, RN, MN
Risk Management Specialist
Prairie Village, Kansas

Adrienne Bond, JD
Attorney at Law
Houston, Texas

Judith L. Bragdon, RN, MN
Silver Spring, Maryland

Karen Cepero, MSN, CCRN, CEN, CS
Director of Cardio-Pulmonary Services
Jersey City Medical Center
Jersey City, New Jersey

Tracye L. Chovanec, RN, BS
Legal Nurse Consultant
Dushman, Friedman, and Franks, PC
Fort Worth, Texas

April Clemens
Legal Nurse Consultant
Venice, California

Patricia A. Costantini, RN, MEd
Rehabilitation Consultant
Costantini Rehab Incorporated
Pittsburgh, Pennsylvania

Doug Davis, RN, BSN
Legal Nurse Consultant
Davis & Associates
Arlington, Texas

Shirley Cantwell Davis, RN, BSN
Owner
Davis and Associates
Atlanta, Georgia

Nathan Dean, MEd, CRC, CDMS
Vocational Consultants, Incorporated
Phoenix, Arizona

Kevin Dubose, BA, JD
Partner
Holman, Hogan, DuBose, & Townsend
Houston, Texas

Janet G. Foster, RN, MSN
Adjunct Faculty
College of Nursing, Houston Baptist
  University
Houston, Texas

Karen S. Fox, RN, BSN
President
The Medical Resource Nework, Inc.
Portland, Oregon

Gail N. Friend, RN, JD
Friend & Associates, LLP
Houston, Texas

Agnes M. Grogan, RN, BS
Co-owner
V/G Associates
Running Springs, California

Kathy A. Gudgell, JD
Owner
Health Care Law Consultants
Lexington, Kentucky

Julianne Hernandez, RN, MPH
Legal Nurse Consultant
Stewart, Tilghman, Fox & Bianchi, PA
Miami, Florida

Jill D. Holmes, RNCS, MSN, FNP
Nurse Practitioner
Senior Biohavioral Health Unit at
  Thornton Hospital
La Jolla, California

Rosanna L. Janes, RN, BSN
Legal Nurse Consultant
Luce, Forward, Hamilton, & Scripps, LLP
San Diego, California

Betty B. Joos, RN, BSN, MEd
Legal Nurse Consultant
Sautee, Georgia

Janet G. Kremser, RN, MN
Windhorst, Gaudry, Ranson & Higgins
Gretna, Louisiana

Mary L. Lanz, RN
Legal Nurse Consultant
Harris & Palumbo
Phoenix, Arizona

Barbara J. Levin, RN, BSN
Independent Legal Nurse Consultant,
  Massachusetts General Hospital
  Orthopedic Trauma Unit
Hingham, Massachusetts

Barbara L. Loecker, RN, BSN, MSEd
Owner
Medical Litigation Resources
Olathe, Kansas

Melanie P. Longenhagen, RN, MSN, CCM
Southhampton, Pennsylvania

Joan K. Magnusson, RN, BSN
Legal Nurse Consultant
McMillen & Reinhart, PA
Orlando, Florida

Sue Mahley, RNC, MN
Assistant Professor of Nursing
Research College of Nursing
Kansas City, Missouri

Kathleen Martin, MSN, MPA, CCRN, CS
Director of Nursing
Jersey City Medical Center
Jersey City, New Jersey

Joseph R. McMahon, JD
Houston, Texas

Thomas B. Méndez, RN
Houston, Texas

Joan E. Miller, RN, MS, CRRN, CCM
Owner
Miller Medical Consulting Services, Inc.
Phoenix, Arizona

Phyllis, F. Miller, RN
Senior Legal Nurse Consultant
Medical Malpractice
Robins, Kaplan, Miller & Ciresi, LLP
Minneapolis, Minnesota

Barbara R. Noble, RN, BSN
Legal Nurse Consultant
Watson, Caraway, Harrington, Nelson,
  Midkiff & Luningham
Fort Worth, Texas

Maureen Jane Orr, RN, BS, CIRS, CCM
Supervisor
AIG Health Care Management Services, Inc.
Miami, Florida

Marva J. Petty, RN, MSN
Legal Nurse Consultant
The Medical Resource Network, Inc.
Vancouver, Washington

Patricia L. Pippen, RN, BSN
Legal Nurse Consultant
Dallas, Texas

Jennifer L. Rangel, JD
Attorney
Friend & Associates, LLP
Houston, Texas

Sherri S. Reed, RN, BSN
Legal Nurse Consultant
Wilson, Kehoe, & Winingham
Indianapolis, Indiana

Judy A. Ringholtz, RN, BSN
Legal Nurse Consultant
McFall, Sherwood & Sheehy
Houston, Texas

Paula Schenck, RN, BSN
Legal Nurse Consultant
Sidley & Austin
Glen Ellyn, Illinois

Suzanne D. Schutze, RN, BS
Independent Legal Nurse Consultant
Austin, Texas

Kathleen M. Spiegel, RN, MSN
Risk Management Consultant
Medical Inter-Insurance Exchange (Miix)
Pittsburgh, Pennsylvania

Patricia Ann Steed, RN
Legal Nurse Consultant
Allen, Weathington & Reeves
Atlanta, Georgia

Barbara A. Stilwell, RN, MSN
Brown & Kelly
Niagara University
Buffalo, New York

Brett A. Storm, JD
Attorney
Friend & Associates
Houston, Texas

Adella Toepel, RN, BA
Legal Nurse Consultant
Robins, Kaplan, Miller, & Ciresi
Minneapolis, Minnesota

Karen L. Wetther, RN
Owner
Medical Legal Resources
Carsbad, California

Doreen James Wise, RN, MSN, EdD
President
Medical Research Consultants, Inc.
Houston, Texas

Mona G. Yudkoff, RN, MPH, CRRN, CCM
Consultant
Bala Cynwyo, Pennsylvania

Reviewers

Candace M. Addlesperger, RN, BSN,
    CCM, CLCP
Matrix Rehabilitation Consultants
Englewood, Colorado

Linda Alweiss, RN, BSN
Masana, Cathcart & McCarthy
Los Angeles, California

Jeannie L. Autry, RN, BSN
Cooper, Aldous and Scully
Dallas, Texas

Judith A. Avery, RN, BSN
Mitten, Goodwin & Raup
Phoenix, Arizona

Joanne M. Behymer, RN, MSN, C-CHN,
    C-PHN
Behymer Medical Legal Consulting
Carlsbad, California

Alice Bevans, RN, PhD
Genesee, Idaho

Beverly J. Botchlet, RN, MSN
Discovery, Incorporated
Oklahoma City, Oklahoma

Kathryn M. Caraway, JD
Weiss & Eason
New Orleans, Louisiana

Michael S. Cardwell, MD, JD, MPH
Riverside Hospital,
Maternal-Fetal Medicine
Toledo, Ohio

Linda L. Carter, RN, BSN
Medical Legal Consulting
Newcastle, California

Sandra S. Carter, RN, BA
Wagstaff & Cartmell, LLP
Kansas City, Missouri

Doreen R. Casuto, RN, MRA, CRRN, CCM
Resources in Rehabilitation
San Diego, California

Cynthia L. Chalu, ARNP, BSN, MN, C-WHNP
Medilex, Inc.
Clearwater, Florida

Shirley Cantwell Davis, RN, BSN
Davis & Associates
Atlanta, Georgia

Ellen Smith Davis, RN, MSN
Vinson & Elkins, LLP
Houston, Texas

Marilyn Dymer, RN, BSN, MNEd, JD
Dymer Medical-Legal Consulting
Kansas City, Missouri

Beverly Ann Tedder Essick, RN, BSN, MSN
Risk & Insurance Management at
NC Baptist Hospitals, Inc.
Winston-Salem, North Carolina

Bonnie Faherty, RN, PhD
Los Angeles, California

Michele Frazer Feldman, RN, MSN
Michael J. Galligan Law Firm, PC
Des Moines, Iowa

Sylvia Franklin, BSN, ARNP, MS
Pinellas Co. SAVE, Pasco Co. SAVE,
    Hillsborough Co. Crisis
Pinellas Co., Pasco Co.,
    Hillsborough Co.,Florida
Clearwater, Florida

Judith A. Gic, RN, BS CRNA JD
Law Office of Judith A. Gic
New Orleans, Louisiana

Eileen Glass, MA, CRC, CDNS, CCM
Pinder Rehabilitation Services
Altamonte Springs, Florida

Liz Nader Hahn, RN, BSN
Davis & Wilkerson, PC
Austin, Texas

Cynthia A. Haseley, RN, CCM, CLCP
Matrix Rehabilitation Consultants
Englewood, Colorado

Amy Heydlauff, RN
Medical Discovery
Chelsea, Michigan

Marjorie J. Hickey, RN, MSN, CCM, CIRS
M.J. Hickey & Assoc.
Missoula, Montana

Lenore S. Holland, RN, MS
Treon, Strick, Lucia, and Aguirre
Phoenix, Arizona

Deanna L. Holm, RN
Independent Legal Nurse Consultant
Livermore, California

Janet K. Huff, RN, MEd, CCRN
Salinas, California

Mark J. Katzman, RN, MS
Mandell, Schwartz & Boisclasr, Ltd.
Providence, Rhode Island

Paul F. Kavanaugh, JD
Bartimus, Kavanaugh, Frickleton
 & Presley, PC
Kansas City, Missouri

Laurie J. Kelfer, RN, MSN, CNA
Shannon, Gracey, Ratliff & Miller, LLP
Fort Worth, Texas

Janice M. Kern, RN, BA, BSN
Amgen, Inc.
Thousand Oaks, California

Kathie L. Kochanowsky, RN, MSN
Vinson & Elkins LLP
Houston, Texas

Jo Anne Kuc, RN, BSN
Midwest Medical Legal Resources, Inc.
St. John, Indiana

S. W. Longan, III, JD
Longan & Associates
Leawood, Kansas

Junie Maggio, RN, BSN, CCM, CDMS
Independent Legal Nurse Consultant
Overland Park, Kansas

Sue Mahley, RNC, MN
Research College of Nursing
Kansas City, Missouri

Mary Angela Meyer, JD
Franklin, Cardwell & Jones
Houston, Texas

Denise Novakoski, RN, BSN
Fisher, Gallagher & Lewis, LLP
Houston, Texas

Elaine Olive, RN, MSN
Hartline, Dacus, Dreyer & Kern
Dallas, Texas

Flora Ann Pinder, EdD, CVE, CRC,
 LMHC, CDMS
Pinder Rehabilitation Services
Altamonte Springs, Florida

Mary Watt Polak, RN, MS, CEN, TNS
CNA Insurance Companies
Chicago, Illinois

Mary Kathryn Sadler, RN BSN MBA
Medical-Legal Consulting
Charleston, West Virginia

Mary Ann Shea, RN, BS, JD
Midwest Medical/Legal Services
St. Louis, Missouri

Sharon G. Slifko, RN, JD
Treon, Strick, Lucia & Aguirre, PA
Phoenix, Arizona

Connie B. Sunday, RN, MS, JD, CLCP
Medical Litigation Management
Houston, Texas

Christine Ernst Taft, MS, MA
Archie Dykes Library, University of
  Kansas Medical Center
Kansas City, Kansas

Diana L. Tershakovec, RN, MSN
Wicker, Smith, Tutan, O'Hara, McCoy,
  Graham & Ford, PA
Miami, Florida

Marlene R. Vermeer, RN, BAN
Office of Marlene Vermeer, RN
Irvine, California

Mary A. Woodbury, RN, BSN, MPH
Dow Corning
Midland, Michigan

Deborah M. Wright, RN, MPA, CRM
Landels, Ripley and Diamond
San Francisco, California

Contents

SECTION VIII: BUSINESS PRINCIPLES FOR THE LEGAL NURSE CONSULTANT

SECTION IX: THE LEGAL NURSE CONSULTANT AS EXPERT WITNESS

SECTION X: THE LEGAL NURSE CONSULTANT'S ROLE IN THE INSURANCE INDUSTRY

SECTION XI: THE LEGAL NURSE CONSULTANT'S ROLE IN HEALTH CARE RISK MANAGEMENT

Section I
The American Association of Legal Nurse Consultants

Chapter 1

The History and Evolution of Legal Nurse Consulting

Rosanna Janes, Julie Bogart, Joan Magnusson, Betty Joos, and Jenny Beerman

Contents

1-57444-123-X/98

Early Legal Nurse Consultant Practice

It is difficult to determine when nurses gained recognition as Legal Nurse Consultants (LNCs), since attorneys have sought nurses to answer questions for many years regarding medical–legal matters. Nurses have been recognized as consultants to attorneys and have been compensated for their expertise and contribution for at least 25 years if not longer.

Nurses' earliest and most common experiences in the legal arena have been as expert witnesses in nursing malpractice cases. As the courts began to recognize that nurses, rather than physicians, should define and evaluate the standard of nursing practice, nurses were sought to review cases and offer opinion testimony about nursing care. During the 1980s, nursing malpractice litigation expanded along with medical malpractice. Nurses became more interested and educated about the legal issues impacting health care. The role of expert nurse witness came to be recognized as an essential professional function. Articles featuring the nurse as expert witness appeared with more frequency in a wide variety of nursing journals. Through the process of serving as expert witnesses, nurses evolved independent legal consulting practices that thrived in response to demand. It was clear to both nurses and attorneys that nurses were uniquely qualified to aid attorneys in their medical–legal practices.

During the same period, attorneys in both plaintiff and defense law firms searched for resources to help them understand medical records, medical literature, hospital policies and procedures, and medical testimony for an increasing case load. Nurse consultants came to be valued as cost-effective alternatives to physician consultants, who were often unavailable as a result of practice demands. Law firms began to seek and employ nurses for their expertise, creating a new position on the litigation team. Attorneys began to value their input on a broad scope of personal injury and criminal cases. With growing demand and opportunities for nurses in the legal community, the numbers of practicing LNCs began to increase.

Today, nurses also consult as health care risk managers and as case managers. Some develop life-care plans for legal purposes. Others locate and qualify health care expert witnesses for attorney clients. The scope of practice of LNCs has broadened to include not only medical malpractice, personal injury, and product liability areas of law, but also employment law, administrative law, and criminal law.

The title "Legal Nurse Consultant" was not commonly used until the National Steering Committee for the American Association of LNCs (AALNC) formally adopted it in July 1989. Prior to 1989, LNCs were identified with a number of titles, such as medical litigation consultant, medical–legal nurse consultant, medical litigation analyst, medical support specialist, medical paralegal, or nurse paralegal. Regardless of the title, they were all pioneers of new roles for nurses in the legal environment.

AALNC Founding

During the 1980s in three separate areas of the country, groups of nurses practicing as consultants to attorneys formed local professional associations for the purpose of educating the legal profession about the effectiveness of the nurse consultant as liaison between the legal and medical communities, as well as to provide a network for members to share expertise. These three groups became the founders of the national association. They were the Arizona Nurse Consultants in Law established in Phoenix in 1983, the Georgia Association of Legal Nurse Consultants founded in Atlanta in 1986, and the San Diego Association of Medical Legal Nurse Consultants founded in 1987. Interestingly, all three organizations formed independently with the same visions, goals, and objectives for what became known as legal nurse consulting.

In April 1988 the *American Bar Association Journal* featured the Arizona Nurse Consultants in Law in an article entitled "Law Firms Branch Out." It chronicled the founding of the group of 50 nurse members in Arizona. The focus of the article described the ways in which nurses assist attorneys prepare for personal injury and medical malpractice cases. Rosanna Janes, founder and first president of the San Diego association, unaware of the Arizona group, discovered the article and contacted Carolyn Ehrlich. Carolyn related that attorneys in Arizona had been utilizing the expertise of nurses in law firms for 12 to 14 years. Rosanna and Carolyn shared their common dream and vision of forming a national association.

In September of 1988, Rosanna Janes and Paula Schenck, another San Diego group member, met with Carolyn Ehrlich and the board members of the Arizona group in Phoenix to open discussions regarding forming a national association. In October, the San Diego association reciprocated by hosting a luncheon meeting for Carolyn Ehrlich. In addition to San Diego group members, Nancy Grace from San Francisco and Lisa Morgan from Santa Barbara also attended. Discussions focused on common interests and goals, the feasibility and barriers to creating a national association, and the structure necessary to found such an organization. Experience with founding of other professional nurses associations provided models for the group. Following the meeting, efforts to locate other LNCs across the country began.

A Dream Becomes Reality

On July 29, 1989, a national steering committee composed of representatives from all three groups met in San Diego and the American Association of Legal Nurse Consultants was founded. In addition to the members of the steering committee, 33 other LNCs attended, representing: San Diego, Oakland, Bakersfield, and Los Angeles, California; Phoenix, Arizona; Minneapolis, Minnesota; and Atlanta, Georgia.

National Founding Steering Committee Members

Carolyn Ehrlich, Chairman
Mary Beth Sloan, Secretary
Judy Guerin, Treasurer
Jane Hanford, Phoenix Chapter National Steering Committee Chairman
Paula Schenck, San Diego Chapter National Steering
    Committee Chairman
Shirley Cantwell Davis, Atlanta Chapter National Steering
    Committee Chairman.

During that first working meeting, the name of the association was determined, the mission statement written, and goals for the association identified. The founding members also discussed various issues, such as membership categories, qualifications, dues, and commenced planning for a national conference. A conference program committee was appointed, chaired by Cindy Spofford, and charged with organizing the first annual educational conference to be presented in early 1990. Following the meeting, a major project was launched to locate potential members across the U.S. to join the new association and attend the conference. Carolyn Ehrlich volunteered to compile a national mailing list, which became the first AALNC membership directory.

The National Steering Committee met again in San Diego in September and Phoenix in November. Many long hours, intense debate, and discussion among the founding members were spent creating the foundation structure of AALNC.

National Founding Members

Elise Alpert	Rosanna Janes
Ingrid Angelini	Dorothy Kenny
Judy Brklacich Avery	Marilyn Mason-Kish
Mary Baldwin	LuAnn Klein
Cynthia Ballard	Joy Lawson
Joanne Behymer	Kathleen Loeffler
Jean Buechsenstein	Catherine McCaig
Marlene Vermeer-Campbell	Debra McGinty
Denise Castillon	Marcia Haston McMichael
Shirley Cantwell Davis	Sally Moshier
Carolyn Ehrlich	Georgine Paulin
Deena Ferris	Mareen Phalon
Nancy Grace	Nancy Reed
Paula Griess	Patricia Reigers
Patricia Griffin	Paula Schenck
Agnes Grogan	Mary Beth Sloan
Judy Guerin	Ellen Smith
Barbara Hampe	Cindy Spofford
Jane Hanford	Adella Toepel
Lynne Harris	Myrene Treick
Carol Herring	Claudette Varanko
Charlotte Hildenbrand	Karen Wetther
Jill Denison Holmes	Paula Woo
Janet Huff	James Zuffoletto
Anne Hughes	

The National Steering Committee was replaced as the decision-making body of AALNC when the first Board of Directors was elected in March 1990. Shirley Cantwell Davis from Atlanta became its first president. (See Appendix 1.1.) The first national conference was held in Phoenix in March, 1990. AALNC's mission of promoting the professional advancement of registered nurses practicing in a consulting capacity in the legal profession was inaugurated.

Membership grew rapidly to over 2000 by the end of 1996, as did the complexity of organizational structure and function. There were nine chapters in 1990. By 1996 there were 31 chapters (see Appendix 1.2). AALNC took a major step in its evolution with the decision to hire an association management firm in 1993. After a difficult year with the first management company, AALNC contracted with Association Management Center (AMC) of Glenview, Illinois in 1994. As a result of that partnership, AALNC has been able to undertake multiple complex projects such as development of a core curriculum textbook and a certification program for LNCs.

Educational Conferences

The first national conference in Phoenix, March 14 to 17, 1990 was attended by 180 nurses from around the country. It was the first conference of its kind focused on legal nurse consulting. The first five conferences were planned and presented by a volunteer committee. Attendance grew yearly, as did the variety of educational opportunities through general and concurrent sessions. The fifth conference was the first in which the new association management company assisted the volunteer committee. As the organization matured and evolved, levels of expertise developed in the membership with novice and expert LNCs attending the same conferences. Conference committees responded by offering cutting-edge topics and high-profile speakers as well as sessions for the less-experienced LNC. The annual conference is the major networking and educational opportunity for the membership and in 1996 attracted over 400 attendees.

AALNC Annual Conferences

1990	Phoenix, Arizona
1991	Atlanta, Georgia
1992	San Francisco, California
1993	Chicago, Illinois
1994	Houston, Texas
1995	Orlando, Florida
1996	San Diego, California
1997	Pittsburgh, Pennsylvania
1998	Dallas, Texas
1999	Reno, Nevada

Network News and the *Journal of Legal Nurse Consulting*

The first newsletter for the organization was published in April of 1990 and was called *AALNC News* for the first two issues. Joanne Behymer submitted the winning name in a contest, and it was thereafter called *Network News*. Kathy McCaig was the first chairman of the publication committee and first editor serving through

April 1993. Rebecca Dawson followed and served as editor through July 1995. From October 1995 through July 1996, Mary Watt Polak was editor, followed by Jenny Beerman. The first publication committee was responsible for publication of the newsletter as well as the membership directory. The newsletter evolved into a peer-reviewed journal with a three-person manuscript review panel by July 1993. By the January 1995 issue, the publication was called the *Journal of Legal Nurse Consulting* (*JLNC*), the cover was changed, and the contents were divided into three sections: "Inside This Issue" contained lead and feature articles; "Departments" contained repeating columns such as References and Resources, and Legalese; "Network News" continued to present news of the organization. An annual index was first published at the end of 1994. Application was made and an ISSN number assigned by the Library of Congress. The official publication of AALNC, the *JLNC* expanded from a few pages in a simple newsletter to a professional, refereed journal and is considered one of the most-valued benefits of membership.

Scope of Practice, Standards of Practice, and Professional Performance

At the request of several members, in October 1990, the AALNC Board of Directors established the *ad hoc* Standards Committee. The purpose of the committee was to define the various aspects of legal nurse consulting. Nine board members volunteered to serve on the committee and seven general members were appointed. In 1991, a 17th member was added to the committee. The committee represented 9 states with 12 independent consultant members and 5 members employed by law firms. Committee membership was relatively stable for the next 4 years. By 1993, 4 members had resigned for various reasons. At the time of the disbandment of the committee in January 1995, there were 11 members remaining.

The committee completed its mission statement in February 1991. It stated the purpose of the AALNC Standards Committee was to define the scope of practice for nurses consulting within the legal profession. In addition, standards defining a minimum level of competence were to be established consistent with standards already defined by the American Medical Association, the American Bar Association, and other professional nursing and legal associations.

In 1990, the American Nurses Association (ANA) had just published recommendations defining a structure for rewriting standards of practice for clinical nursing. The then AALNC Standards Committee believed the ANA model was not applicable to the practice of legal nurse consulting since delivery of patient care was not involved.

Before standards could be written, the committee set out to define the scope of practice of legal nurse consulting. During the next 12 months, the committee developed a questionnaire that became the "1992 Role Delineation Study." It contained 108 questions divided into categories dealing with biographical data; professional activities; medical review, analysis, and research; document preparation; client/expert liaison activities; and specialized activities as an expert witness or life-care planner. The role delineation study was sent to 400 randomly selected members in March 1992. The committee wrote the first scope of practice statement from the data. After a few revisions, the AALNC published the final version in January 1994. This document described the practice environment and role of the LNC as it existed at the time.

The committee then turned its attention to development of the standards. After discussion of the various formats used for writing standards, the committee agreed to adopt a format similar to the nursing process. The members felt it would illustrate how the specialty practice of legal nurse consulting fit into the nursing profession. Furthermore, it would strengthen the acceptance of AALNC's standards of practice by nursing colleagues and other professions.

By October 1994 the committee had drafted standards for board review. The document identified four essential components of legal nurse consulting: Practice, Professionalism, Education, and Research. The committee believed no single category was mutually exclusive and some standards related to more than one area. They recommended the purposes of the standards were:

1. To assist in evaluation of quality of legal nurse consulting practice
2. To provide a common base for LNCs to coordinate and unify efforts in development of quality practice
3. To assist other professions in understanding what to expect from LNCs
4. To support and preserve the rights of those served by LNCs

After reviewing the first standards draft, the board asked the committee to address certain terminology and phraseology. In addition, the board requested that standards be written to allow measurement criteria to be added to each standard in the future. The committee was provided with the ANA Standards of Professional Performance and encouraged to contact the AALNC staff director of education to assist them in revising the structure of the draft.

After the first draft of standards was submitted to the board, questions arose regarding AALNC's philosophy of the professional identity of LNC. In January 1995, the board met to discuss whether legal nurse consulting was a profession in its own right, a specialty practice of nursing, or a specialty practice of law.

A review of the characteristics of a "profession" led the board to conclude legal nurse consulting could not be defined as such. Legal nurse consulting lacked its own body of knowledge that was not dependent on other professions. Furthermore, it did not have a formal education process that was commonly accepted by society, or any research to validate the body of knowledge and prove quality of service. A review of AALNC's bylaws, scope of practice, and code of ethics reinforced the board's conviction that the nursing profession was the basis for the practice of legal nurse consulting. While these documents acknowledged the need for acquiring certain knowledge and skills from the legal profession, they clearly stated that legal nurse consultants did not practice law.

After much discussion, the board voted to affirm the position that legal nurse consulting was a functional specialty practice of nursing. In order for AALNC's projects to proceed credibly, efficiently, and economically, it was decided that standards, core curriculum, and certification would be developed on that basis. The board requested that the current draft of standards be integrated into the framework of nursing standards promulgated by the ANA in 1991. The Standards Committee chairperson reminded the board this was a direction contradictory to the conclusions made by the committee in 1990.

To facilitate the completion of the standards and allow work to begin on the core curriculum, the board retired the original Standards Committee and appointed a Standards Task Force, charged with completing the standards and presenting the draft to the membership in May 1995. The task force originally consisted of two board members, three members of the original Standards Committee, and one general member. They were assisted by the AALNC staff director of education.

The document presented to the board at their next meeting was entitled, "Scope and Standards of Practice for the Legal Nurse Consultant." It included a revised version of the original scope of practice, which had been adopted in January 1994. Minor changes were made to support the board's affirmation that legal nurse consulting is a functional specialty practice of nursing. The Scope of Practice reflects the diversity of practice settings and services performed by LNCs nationwide (see Appendix 1.3).

In keeping with the ANA model, Section I of the standards (see Appendix 1.4) contained six standards of practice: Assessment, Analysis, Resolution Identification, Planning, Implementation, and Evaluation. Section II consisted of the eight standards of professional performance: Quality of Practice, Performance Appraisal, Education, Collegiality, Ethics, Collaboration, Research, and Resource Management. Key indicators or measurement criteria were listed under each standard. The board made a few minor revisions and approved it for presentation at the May 1995 annual membership meeting. Over the next few months, members were asked to submit their comments and questions for review.

By October 1995, all comments submitted by members had been reviewed and discussed by the task force, the board, and legal counsel. Based on those discussions, the task force made the following modifications. They changed the term, *Resolution Identification*, to *Outcome Identification*. The stem statement was rewritten to emphasize the LNCs role in identifying the desired outcome of his or her own work in the larger context of a case or claim in a legal process. Other stem statements in Section I were reworded for clarity. The key indicators under each standard of practice had been written broadly to cover the wide range of legal nurse consulting activities dependent on practice settings and experience levels. However, this made them more difficult for some members to apply specifically in their own practices. Recognizing legal accountability for adherence to the standards, the board decided to publish Section I without key indicators in the first edition. In Section II, Standard 5, Ethics, the key indicator concerning compensation was deleted because it could have been construed as unnecessarily restricting financial terms of a consulting arrangement.

The first official AALNC "Scope and Standards of Practice for the Legal Nurse Consultant" was published in October 1995. The board retired the task force and appointed a new standards review committee to monitor information supplied by members on application of the standards to their practices. The board recognized that this document will undergo evaluation and revision as the specialty practice of legal nurse consulting evolves.

Code of Ethics

An ethics committee was formed in 1991 and AALNC's Code of Ethics was adopted and copyrighted in April 1992 (see Appendix 1.5). The AALNC's Code of Ethics for LNCs provides the guidelines for professional performance and conduct for practice and affirms the values and practices of the ANA and the American Bar Association.

NFSNO Membership

In January 1994, AALNC applied for membership in the National Federation of Specialty Nursing Organizations (NFSNO), to strengthen AALNC's relationship with other nursing specialty organizations and to validate its identity as a professional nursing association. The NFSNO consists of more than 40 nursing organizations representing over 400,000 nurses. NFSNO promotes specialty nursing practice and its contributions to the nation's health through collaborative efforts of member organizations. NFSNO's goals include promoting nursing education and research, supporting efforts to improve nursing practice, and participating in legislative activities relevant to health care. Membership eligibility is limited to nursing organizations with national scope and in existence for at least 2 years. Member organizations must also include a majority of registered nurses, governed by an elected body with bylaws defining purpose and function, and have goals compatible with those of NFSNO. There are two classifications of membership: regular and affiliate. Regular member organizations must have a body of knowledge and skills in a defined area of clinical practice with a patient client base focused on a specific condition, disease, or practice environment. Affiliate members must meet the general requirements, but may not meet the specific requirements of regular members.

On July 21, 1994, AALNC was seated as an affiliate member of NFSNO at their annual meeting. AALNC continues to support the mission and goals of NFSNO through its membership and by regular delegate attendance at the annual meeting.

NOLF Participation

In November 1996, representatives of AALNC's board audited the Nursing Organization Liaison Forum (NOLF) meeting in Washington, D.C. NOLF provides a forum for interaction among national nursing organizations to increase unity in the nursing profession. To participate, organizations must meet certain qualifications, such as that the majority of the Board of Directors must be nurses and be approved by the ANA Board of Directors. Attended by representative leadership of the boards of nursing organizations, the annual forum of nursing organizations addresses issues of mutual concern across nursing specialties. Participation provides increased visibility for AALNC and access to information about issues and trends in nursing, and political and marketplace forces that impact a broad range of nursing practice. In December 1996, AALNC applied to become a regular participant in NOLF.

Appendix 1.1
AALNC Presidents

1989–90	Carolyn Ehrlich, MSN (Founding Steering Committee Chairman)
1990–91	Shirley Cantwell Davis, BSN
1991–92	Paula Schenck, BSN
1992–93	Marlene Vermeer-Campbell, BA
1993–94	Marilyn Mason-Kish, BA
1994–95	Doreen James Wise, EdD
1995–96	Joan Magnusson, BSN
1996–97	Karen Fox, BSN
1997–98	Julie Bogart, MN
1998–99	Patty Costantini, MEd

Appendix 1.2
AALNC Chapter Listing

Contact the chapter president in your area for information on local meeting dates and locations. If you are interested in organizing a chapter, please call the national office at 847/375-4713.

ARIZONA
Phoenix Chapter
Sue Barnes
602/992-2374
P.O. Box 13441
Phoenix, AZ 85002

CALIFORNIA
Bay Area of Northern California
Sheryl Picco
510/687-5657
P.O. Box 3300
San Leandro, CA 94578-0300

Los Angles Chapter
Susan Brandlin
310/285-0807
P.O. Box 9222
Whittier, CA 90608

Orange County Chapter of Southern California
Linda Stempel
714/502-8106
5405 Alton Pkwy., Suite 5A450
Irvine, CA 92604

Greater Sacramento Area Chapter
Ruth Swiggum
916/783-7213
P.O. Box 660011
Sacramento, CA 95866-0011

San Diego Chapter
Nancy Blevins
619/687-7766
P.O. Box 2822
San Diego, CA 92112-2822

DELAWARE
Diamond State Chapter
Linda Swartley
302/888-1461
P.O. Box 4265
Greenville, DE 19807

FLORIDA
Greater Fort Lauderdale Chapter
Lucy Guadalupe
954/979-5711
P.O. Box 698
Fort Lauderdale, FL 33302

Miami Chapter
Josephine Vella
305/764-7155
P.O. Box 110134
Miami, FL 33111-0134

Greater Orlando Chapter
Paula DeMott
407/898-5577
P.O. Box 3201
Orlando, FL

Greater Tampa Bay Chapter
Patricia Breen
813/943-0066
P.O. Box 22874
Tampa, FL 33622-2871

GEORGIA
Atlanta Chapter
Martha Morris
404/885-6357
P.O. Box 55438
Atlanta, GA 30308

ILLINOIS
Greater Chicago Chapter
Barbara Nihill
847/604-1442
P.O. Box A-3913
Chicago, IL 60690

INDIANA
Greater Indianapolis Chapter
Judy Krimmel
317/290-6400
P.O. Box 1702
Indianapolis, IN 46206-1702

KENTUCKY
Lexington Kentucky Chapter
Donna Hunter-Adkins
606/252-0233
P.O. Box 22535
Lexington, KY 40522-2535

LOUISIANA
Baton Rouge Chapter
Sharon Duvernay
504/367-6169
3216 W. Esplanade, A4-288
Metarie, LA 70005

MARYLAND
Greater Baltimore Area Chapter
Kathy Araiza
410/296-9502
P.O. Box 342112
Bethesda, MD 20827-2112

MICHIGAN
Greater Detroit Chapter
Debbie King
313/533-6610
P.O. Box 1
Chelsea, MI 48118

MINNESOTA
Minneapolis Chapter
LeaRae Keyes
612/349-8241
P.O. Box 2843
Minneapolis, MN 55402

MISSOURI
St. Louis Chapter
Tina Bruce
314/991-6177
P.O. Box 50166
St. Louis, MO 63105

NEW JERSEY
Hackensack North New Jersey Chapter
Linda Lajterman
201/236-0723
P.O. Box 4521
Warren, NJ 07060

NEW YORK
Rochester New York Chapter
Claudia Egan
716/889-5559
P.O. Box 92204
Rochester, NY 14692

NORTH CAROLINA/SOUTH CAROLINA
Columbia Chapter
Jane Mihalich
803/779-8080
P.O. Box 1866
Columbia, SC 29202-1866

OHIO
Cleveland/NEO Chapter
Wanda Burns
330/652-5827
P.O. Box 455
Chesterland, OH 44072

Youngstown Ohio Chapter
Rebecca Lucas
216/385-2781
7110 Lockwood Blvd., Suite 183
Youngstown, OH 44512

OREGON
Greater Portland/Valley Chapter
Mary Lou Hazelwood
503/494-0915
1500 Gossamere Lane
Stayton, OR 97383

PENNSYLVANIA
Philadelphia Chapter
Linda Crompton
610/975-4574
175 Strafford Avenue, Suite One
Wayne, PA 19087

Pittsburgh Chapter
Linda Fowler
412/835-1657
P.O. Box 97104
Pittsburgh, PA 15229-0104

RHODE ISLAND
Greater Providence Chapter
Barbara Levin
617/740-1515
8 Country Drive
Hingham, MA 02043

TEXAS
Austin Chapter
Francine Fleming
512/327-7684
P.O. Box 5294
Austin, TX 78763

Dallas Chapter
Patricia Pippin
214/824-6551
P.O. Box 50394
Dallas, TX 75250

Fort Worth Chapter
Janis Roberts
817/274-2511
P.O. Box 866
Fort Worth, TX 76101

Greater Houston Chapter
Ginny Stegent
713/952-3620
7500 San Felipe, Suite 600
Houston, TX 77063

Appendix 1.3
Scope of Practice for the Legal Nurse Consultant*

Introduction

The legal nurse consultant is a licensed registered nurse who performs a critical analysis of health care facts and issues and their outcomes for the legal profession, health care professions, and others, as appropriate. With a strong educational and experiential background, the legal nurse consultant is qualified to assess adherence to standards of health care practice as it applies to the nursing and health care professions.

This Scope of Practice for the Legal Nurse Consultant has been developed from data gathered by the American Association of Legal Nurse Consultants. The results reflect the diversity of practice settings of and services performed by legal nurse consultants nationwide. The American Association of Legal Nurse Consultants acknowledges the *American Association of Legal Nurse Consultants Code of*

---

* Reprinted from *Network News,* October 25, 1995. With permission.

Ethics for legal nurse consultants, which provides the guidelines for professional performance and conduct for practice and affirms the values and practices of the American Nurses Association and the American Bar Association.

Practice Environment

The legal nurse consultant practices the art and science of his or her nursing specialty in a variety of settings, including law forms, government offices, insurance companies, hospital risk management departments, and as self-employed practitioners. The legal nurse consultant is a liaison between the legal and health care communities and provides consultation and education to legal, health care, and appropriate other professionals in areas such as personal injury, product liability, medical malpractice, workers' compensation, toxic torts, risk management, medical professional licensure investigation, and criminal law.

Role of the Legal Nurse Consultant ∖

The primary role of the legal nurse consultant is to evaluate, analyze, and render informed opinions on the delivery of health care and the resulting outcomes. While the practice of each legal nurse consultant varies with respective practice opportunities and experience levels, certain commonalities prevail. Parameters of the practice may include, but are not limited to

- Facilitating communications and thus strategizing with the legal professional for successful resolutions between parties involved in health care-related litigation or other medical–legal or health care–legal matters
- Educating attorneys and/or others involved in the legal process regarding the health care facts and issues of a case or a claim
- Researching and integrating health care and nursing literature as it relates to the health care facts and issues of a case or a claim
- Reviewing, summarizing, and analyzing medical records and other pertinent health care and legal documents and comparing and correlating them to the allegations
- Assessing issues of damages and causation relative to liability within the legal process
- Identifying, locating, evaluating, and conferring with expert witnesses
- Interviewing witnesses and parties pertinent to the health care issues in collaboration with legal professionals
- Drafting legal documentations in medically related cases under the supervision of an attorney
- Developing collaborative case strategies with those practicing within the legal system
- Providing support during discovery, depositions, trial, and other legal proceedings
- Supporting the process of adjudication of legal claims

Summary

This document identifies the legal nurse consultant as a specialist unique in the profession of nursing and as someone whose practice is of value in the legal field. The intent of this document is to conceptualize the legal nurse consultant's practice as it exists today; it is limited only by the depth and breadth to which the nursing specialty has currently developed. It is anticipated that future studies will indicate expanded roles and practice environments for the legal nurse consultant.

Adopted by the American Association of Legal Nurse Consultants, January 1994; amended April 1995.

Appendix 1.4
Standards of Legal Nurse Consulting Practice*

Section I: Standards of Practice

The legal nurse consultant has the knowledge and capability sufficient to conduct his or her practice in accordance with each of the standards set forth below.

Standard 1. Assessment

The legal nurse consultant collects data to support the systematic assessment of health care issues related to a case or claim.

Standard 2. Analysis and Issue Identification

The legal nurse consultant analyzes collected data to identify the health care issues related to a case or claim.

Standard 3. Outcome Identification

The legal nurse consultant identifies the desired outcome of his or her work product as related to the health care issues of a case or claim.

Standard 4. Planning

The legal nurse consultant formulates a plan of action to achieve the desired outcome.

Standard 5. Implementation

The legal nurse consultant implements the plan of action.

---

* Reprinted from *Network News*, October 26, 1995. With permission.

Standard 6. Evaluation

The legal nurse consultant evaluates the effectiveness of the plan of action in achieving the desired outcome.

Section II: Standards of Professional Performance

Standard 1. Quality of Practice

The legal nurse consultant evaluates the quality and effectiveness of his or her practice.

Key Indicators

1. The LNC participates in quality of practice activities as appropriate to the individual's role, education, and practice environment.
2. The LNC uses the results of quality of practice activities to initiate changes in practice.

Standard 2. Performance Appraisal

The legal nurse consultant evaluates his or her own practice in relation to professional practice standards and relevant statutes and regulations.

Key Indicators

1. The LNC engages in performance appraisal, identifying areas of strength as well as areas for professional practice developments.
2. The LNC seeks constructive feedback regarding his or her own practice.
3. The LNC takes action to achieve goals identified during performance appraisal.
4. The LNC participates in peer review, as appropriate.

Standard 3. Education

The legal nurse consultant acquires and maintains current knowledge in nursing and health care issues.

Key Indicators

1. The LNC participates in ongoing educational activities pertaining to the health sciences and the law relevant to his or her practice areas.
2. The LNC seeks experiences necessary to maintain current licensure as a professional registered nurse.
3. The LNC seeks the knowledge and the skills that are appropriate to the LNC's practice setting.

Standard 4. Collegiality

The legal nurse consultant contributes to the professional development of peers, colleagues, and others.

Key Indicators

1. The LNC shares knowledge and skills with colleagues and others.
2. The LNC provides peers with constructive feedback regarding their practice.
3. The LNC contributes to an environment that is conducive to the education of nurses entering the field of legal nurse consulting.
4. The LNC contributes to an environment that is conducive to the health science education of legal team members, as appropriate.
5. The LNC contributes to an environment that is conducive to the education of health care professionals regarding legal issues applicable to the health sciences.

Standard 5. Ethics

The legal nurse consultant's decisions and actions are determined in an ethical manner.

Key Indicators

1. The LNC's practice is guided by the ANA's *Code for Nurses with Interpretive Statements* (1985) and the AALNC Code of Ethics.
2. The LNC's practice affirms the values, standards, and practices of the profession of nursing.
3. The LNC maintains confidentiality commensurate with the attorney–client privilege.
4. The LNC practices in a nonjudgmental and nondiscriminatory manner.
5. The LNC evaluates all cases and clients for potential conflicts of interest and declines when conflicts are evident.
6. The LNC seeks available resources to help formulate ethical decisions.
7. The LNC who testifies as an expert witness confines testimony to his or her area of expertise.

Standard 6. Collaboration

The legal nurse consultant may collaborate with legal professionals, health care professionals, and others involved in the legal process.

Key Indicators

1. The LNC consults with legal professionals, health care processionals, and others, as appropriate.
2. The LNC makes referrals as needed.

Standard 7. Research

The legal nurse consultant recognizes research as a methodology to further the legal nurse consultant's practice.

Key Indicators

1. The LNC takes action substantiated by research as appropriate to his or her role, education, and practice environment.
2. The LNC participates in research activities as appropriate to his or her role, education, and practice environment.

Standard 8. Resource Management

The legal nurse consultant considers factors related to ethics, effectiveness, and cost in planning and delivering client service.

Key Indicators

1. The LNC selects expert assistance based on the needs of the case or the claim.
2. The LNC assigns tasks based on the knowledge and skill of the selected provider.
3. The LNC assists legal professionals and others in identifying and securing appropriate services available to address issues pertaining to the case or the claim.

Glossary

Analysis: Judgment following investigation and study of health care issues related to a case or a claim in the legal process that results in identification of relevant issues.

Assessment: A systematic, dynamic process by which the legal nurse consultant through interaction with legal professionals, health care professionals, and appropriate others collects and interprets data about the health care issues of a case or claim.

Attorney–client privilege: An evidentiary rule that confidential communications in the course of professional employment between an attorney or the attorney's representative and the client may not be divulged by the attorney or his representative without the consent of the client.

Case: A general term for an action, cause, or suit at law or equity, a question contested before a court of justice.

Claim: A demand for compensation or retribution.

Client: One who employs, uses, or contracts the service of the legal nurse consultant and may be, for example, an attorney, claims manager, or a company, agency, or institution involved in the investigation or processing of a case or claim.

Confidentiality: State or quality of being confidential; reliance on another to keep secrets; relation of trust.

Evaluation: Process of determining the progress of legal professionals, health care professionals, and appropriate others toward the attainment of desired outcomes and the effectiveness of practices.

Health care issue: A matter that pertains to one or more of the following: a professional's, institution's, or organization's responsibility to provide for another's physical and psychological well-being; adherence to standards, guidelines, or policies, and the provision of reasonable health care; disputes that arise from the relationship between adherence to established standards, accepted guidelines, or validated scientific or technological knowledge and the claimant's outcomes; and the evaluation and assessment of a claimant's damages.

Health care providers: Individuals with special expertise who provide health care services or assistance to clients. They may include nurse, physicians, psychologists, social workers, nutritionists or dietitians, and various therapists. Providers also may include service organizations and vendors.

Implementation: May include any or all of these activities: intervening, delegating, and coordinating. Legal professionals, health care professionals, and others, as appropriate, may be designated to implement the steps, components, and intervention identified in the plan of action.

Key indicator: A measure, gauge, or sign that there is compliance with and achievement of a standard.

Plan: Comprehensive outline of actions to attain the expected or desired outcome.

Standard: Authoritative statement enunciated and promulgated by the profession by which the quality of practice, conduct, and education can be judged.

Standards of practice: Authoritative statements that describe a competent level of legal nurse consulting demonstrated through assessment, analysis and issue identification, outcome identification, planning, implementation, and evaluation.

Standards of professional performance: Authoritative statements that describe a competent level of behavior in the professional role, including activities related to quality of practice, performance appraisal, education, collegiality, ethics, collaboration, and resource management.

Work product: The expression of opinions, conclusions, and materials developed at the request of the client that will assist the client in carrying the case or claim to completion.

References

American Nurses Association. (1985) *Code for nurses with interpretive statements.* Washington, DC: Author.

American Nurses Association. (1991). *Standards of clinical of clinical nursing practice.* Washington, DC: Author.

Appendix 1.5
AALNC Code of Ethics and Conduct with Interpretive Discussion* **

Preamble

The Code of Ethics and Conduct of the American Association of Legal Nurse Consultants is based on beliefs about the nature of individuals and society. The code of professional and ethical conduct provides guidelines to its members for professional performance and behavior. The success of any professional organization results from the competence and integrity of its members. Our goal to those we serve is that they be assured of our accountability.

We recognize a responsibility to other professional organizations with which we are aligned, in particular, the American Nurses Association and the American Bar Association. We accept and abide by the principles of their codes of ethics and conduct. By our support of the Code of Ethics and Conduct of the American Association of Legal Nurse Consultants, we affirm that the rights and trust placed in us will not be violated.

1. The legal nurse consultant does not discriminate against any person based on race, creed, color, age, sex, national origin, social status, or disability and does not let personal attitudes interfere with professional performance.

   Individual differences do not influence professional performance and practice. These factors are understood, considered, and respected when performing activities.

2. The legal nurse consultant performs as a consultant or an expert with the highest degree of integrity.

   Integrity refers to uprightness, honesty, and sincerity. The legal nurse consultant directs those attributes to the requirements of the profession. Integrity is a personal and sacred trust and the standard against which the legal nurse consultant must ultimately test all decisions. Honest errors and differences of opinion may occur, but deceit, poor judgment, or lack of principles must not be tolerated.

3. The legal nurse consultant uses informed judgment, objectivity, and individual competence as criteria when accepting assignments.

   The legal nurse consultant does not purport to be competent in matters in which he or she has limited knowledge or experience. Only services that meet high personal and professional standards are offered or performed.

---

* Adopted and copyrighted © April 1992 by American Association of Legal Nurse Consultants. Reprinted with permission.
** Updated January 16, 1997.

4. The legal nurse consultant maintains standards of personal conduct that reflect honorably upon the profession.

   The legal nurse consultant abides by all federal and state laws. The legal nurse consultant who knowingly becomes involved in unethical or illegal activities negates professional responsibility for personal interest or personal gain. Such activities jeopardize the public confidence and trust in the nursing profession.

5. The legal nurse consultant provides professional services with objectivity.

   The legal nurse consultant provides services free of personal prejudice and conflict of interest. The legal nurse consultant reflects on all current assignments and commitments before accepting assignments, making decisions, rendering opinions, or providing recommendations. Personal prejudices and conflicts of interest must be recognized, as they may interfere with objectivity and adversely affect performance.

6. The legal nurse consultant protects client privacy and confidentiality.

   The legal nurse consultant uses confidential materials with discretion. The legal nurse consultant respects and protects the privacy of the client. The legal nurse consultant does not use any client information for personal gain.

7. The legal nurse consultant is accountable for responsibilities accepted and actions performed.

8. The legal nurse consultant maintains professional nursing competence.

   The legal nurse consultant is a registered nurse and maintains an active nursing license. The legal nurse consultant is knowledgeable about the current scope of nursing practice and the standards of the profession. The legal nurse consultant does not practice law.

Conclusion

Each individual's personal commitment to the Code of Ethics and Conduct of the American Association of Legal Nurse Consultants is the ultimate regulator of his or her behavior. By adopting this Code of Ethics and Conduct, we affirm to those with whom we serve that they have the right to expect us to abide by this code.

As members of the American Association of Legal Nurse Consultants, we pledge to demonstrate to the public this commitment of integrity and professional excellence.

Section II
Legal Theory for the Legal Nurse Consultant

Chapter 2

The Law

Tonia Dandry Aiken

Contents

Objectives

- To discuss the definition of law
- To discuss the types of law

1-57444-123-X/98
© 1998 by American Association of Legal Nurse Consultants

- To define the elements of negligence
  Duty
  Breach of duty
  Proximate cause/casual connection
  Damage
- To discuss quasi-intentional and intentional torts

Introduction

In today's legal environment, the legal nurse consultant (LNC) must be knowledgeable in many aspects of law, nursing, medicine, and the social influences controlling and affecting patient care, legal claims, and litigation. It is extremely important that the LNC be well read on such topics as managed care, case management, health care administrative concerns and issues, advanced practice issues, and health care policy. These are the legal "hot" buttons that are being "pressed" in today's judicial arena.

The law over the centuries has evolved into a quagmire of rules, statutes, regulations, case law, codes, and opinions that in many instances will vary from state to state, state to federal, and jurisdiction to jurisdiction. Laws are used to control and guide people and entities in relationships, unions, and interactions. Laws are used to resolve conflicts involving people, corporations, countries, and states. Laws have evolved through the ages and have resulted in major changes in the way people live and work.

Sources of Law

The word *law* originates from the Anglo-Saxon term *lagu* meaning "that which is fixed." There are several sources of laws that affect individuals, society, and the medical arena. The sources of laws include

1. Constitutional law
2. Statutory law
3. Administrative law
4. Common law

Constitutional Law

Constitutional law is a compilation of laws, principles, and amendments that are used to govern and guide federal and state governments, corporations, society, and individuals. The constitutional laws and amendments guarantee individuals certain rights such as the right to privacy, freedom of speech, and equal protection (see Appendix 2.1). The Constitution grants certain powers to the federal government and agencies. The Constitution is the supreme law of the land and takes precedent over state and local laws. Constitutional law is the highest form of law in the U.S. If not adressed in federal law, then the issue is "given" to the state government. In some instances laws are codified at both the state and federal level for different circumstances.

An example of a federal act that affects health care providers is OBRA. The Omnibus Budget Reconciliation Act (OBRA), enacted in 1987, regulates the manner in which nursing homes deliver care, monitor quality of care, supply staff, train assistants, and protect the patient's rights.

Federal and state governments have the constitutional authority to develop and create laws. In addition to creating laws, they also have the ability to enforce the laws that have been established.

Statutory Law

Statutory laws are laws enacted by federal, state, and local legislative bodies. Many health care providers, special interest groups, legal groups, and attorneys are involved in lobbying for certain bills or amendments to pass, promote, or protect their specific interests. An example of statutory law in many states is the law outlining the statute of limitation for bringing a medical malpractice, wrongful death, or personal injury claim. For example, Louisiana's Revised Statute 9:5628 Actions for Medical Malpractice is as follows:

A. No action for damages for injury or death against any physician, chiropractor, nurse, licensed midwife practitioner, dentist, psychologist, optometrist, hospital duly licensed under the laws of this state, or community blood center or tissue bank as defined in R.S. 40:1299.41 (A), whether based upon tort, or breach of contract, or otherwise, arising out of patient care shall be brought unless filed within one year from the date of the alleged act, omission, or neglect, or within one year from the date of discovery of the alleged act, omission, or neglect; however, even as to claims filed within one year from the date of such discovery, in all events such claims shall be filed at the latest within a period of three years from the date of the alleged act, omission nor neglect.

B. The provisions of this Section shall apply to all persons whether or not infirm or under disability of any kind and including minors and interdicts.

Administrative Law

Administrative laws originate from administrative agencies that are under the arm of the executive branch of the government. For example, state boards of nursing are state administrative agencies. These agencies then promulgate rules and regulations to guide nursing practice in the state and to enforce the Nurse Practice Acts. Such nursing board regulations are considered administrative laws that are legally binding. The state boards of nursing conduct investigations and hearings to ensure enforcement of the Nurse Practice Acts. Nurses can have their licenses limited, revoked, suspended, probated, or they can receive a reprimand and fines in violation of the Acts. For instance, in Louisiana, the State Board of Nursing has designated the following as violations that affect a nurse's license:

1. To sell, or attempt to sell, falsely obtain, or furnish any nursing diploma, license, or record, or aid or abet therein

2. To practice nursing under any diploma, license of record illegally obtained, signed, or issued unlawfully

3. To practice nursing unless duly licensed to do so under the provisions of this Part

4. To use in connection with his name any designation tending to imply that he is a registered nurse or advanced practice registered nurse unless duly licensed to practice under the provisions of the Part

5. To practice nursing during the time the license issued under the provision of the Part is suspended or revoked

6. To knowingly practice nursing during the time his license has lapsed for failure to renew license

7. To conduct any programs or curriculum of nursing, preparing students who are seeking licensure as registered nurses under the provision of this Part unless such programs or curriculum is approved by the Board

8. To aid or abet anyone in the violation of any provision of this Part

9. To violate any provision of this Part

(*Source:* The Louisiana State Board of Nursing, Law Governing the Practice of Nursing, § 925. Violations; penalty.)

It is important for any LNC working on a matter involving nursing practice, medical practice, or the practice of any health care provider to have access to the statutes which regulate that practice.

Attorney general's opinion is a second type of administrative law. The attorney general provides an opinion, regarding a specific interpretation of the law since it cannot be found in a statute of regulation. The opinion is based on statutory and common law principles.

Common Law

Common law derives from the judiciary branch of government. It is based on judicial decisions. Court cases that are resolved through the judicial process act as a data bank for those seeking information in various types of cases whether it is a case on personal injury, medical malpractice, workers' compensation, admiralty, bankruptcy, or domestic cases. LNCs and attorneys search for cases similar to the ones that they are evaluating, mediating, arbitrating, settling, or trying. The case information gives valuable insight into the value of the case, damages and injuries suffered, experts used, and the "mind set" of the judge or jury on deciding for or against plaintiff and awarding damages.

Common law interprets disputed legal issues, statutes, and regulations and is created by the various courts. For example, if a nurse feels that there has been an error made by the State Board of Nursing in a disciplinary action, the nurse can file a court action.

Legal doctrines also affect cases. For example, *the doctrine of res judicata* ("a thing or matter settled by judgment") prevents the same parties from trying a case based on the same issues. The doctrine of *stare decisis* ("to stand by things decided") applies to previously tried cases with similar fact patterns. The courts will review similar cases and arrive at usually similar decisions.

Types of Law

Several types of law that the legal nurse consultant may encounter are

1. Common law
2. Civil law
3. Criminal law
4. Contract law
5. Tort law

Common Law

Common law rules and legal principles developed in England are followed by 49 states and the federal courts. Louisiana is the only state that has adopted the Napoleonic Code, developed from a compilation of civil laws of the French, Spanish, and Romans. The Civil Code is a compilation of rules and regulations authorized by the legislatures. For example, Civil Code Article 2315.2 Wrongful Death Action in part states:

A. If a person dies due to the fault of another, suit may be brought by the following persons to recover damages which they sustained as a result of the death

1. The surviving spouse and child or children of the deceased, or either the spouse or the child or children

2. The surviving father and mother of the deceased, or either of them if he left no spouse or child surviving

3. The surviving brothers and sisters of the deceased, or any of them, if he left no spouse, child or parent

B. The right of action granted by this Article prescribes one year from the death of the deceased.

    C. The right of action granted under this Article is heritable, but the inheritance of it neither interrupts nor prolongs the prescriptive period defined in this Article.

    D. As used in this Article, the words 'child,' 'brother', 'sister,' 'father,' and 'mother' include a child, brother, sister, father, and mother, by adoption respectively.

Civil Law

Civil law is law that applies to the rights of individuals, whereas criminal law deals with offenses against the general public. With *civil law* the remedies for a person or entity involve money or compensation, or perhaps "specific performance" may be required of the defendant. If a defendant has breached a contract, the court may order the completion of the work or reimbursement of money.

Criminal Law

Criminal law is created to provide guidance and protection to those injured by offenses against society. The criminal justice system has been created to deter, punish, and/or rehabilitate persons who perform criminal acts. Criminal conduct can include forgery, burglary, murder, assault, battery, theft, rapes, and false imprisonment. An action by an individual is considered a criminal act even if it is directed solely at an individual. For example, with a charge of assault and battery, the criminal justice system is set up so that the offense is seen and viewed as an act against society as a whole.

> If, for example, a person is practicing medicine without a license, is that considered a civil or criminal offense? (Criminal — because it is viewed as an offense against the general public and society)
>
> If the state statute requires that child or elder abuse be reported and a nurse or physician refuses to report the abuse, is this considered a civil or criminal action? (Criminal)
>
> If a patient receives too much of a medication because the nurse fails to properly administer the correct dose, which causes respiratory arrest, anoxia, and brain damages, is this considered a criminal or civil matter? (Civil)

See Chapter 5 on Criminal Law: Procedure and Evidence.

Contract Law

Contract law involves agreements between parties, individuals, and/or entities. The three requirements for a contract include: offer, acceptance, and consideration. Contracts can be in oral or written form depending on the subject matter and the reason for the contract. Today, health care providers are faced with many opportunities for employee/employer contracts and for other types of contracts with HMOs, suppliers, and facilities.

Tort Law

Tort law is an area of *civil law* that encompasses negligence, personal injury, and medical malpractice claims. A tort is a wrongful act that is committed by someone and causes injury to another's person or property. Tort law remedies attempt to make someone whole again usually with compensation in the form of a monetary award. This is in contrast to criminal law which usually imprisons and/or fines the defendant.

Negligence is a failure to act as an ordinary prudent person or "reasonable man" would do under similar circumstances. There are four elements of negligence that must be proved in order for there to be a viable medical malpractice claim.

1. A *duty* must be owed to the patient. This duty usually occurs when the health care provider accepts responsibility for the care and treatment of that patient.
2. The *breach of duty or standard* of care by the professional. The standard of care for that type of specialty and that particular type of treatment must be determined to see if there has been an act of omission or commission that has caused damage to the patient.
3. *Proximate cause/or causal connection* must be evident between the breach of duty and the harm or damages that have occurred to the patient/plaintiff.
4. *Damages or injuries* suffered by the plaintiff. Damages or injuries can take the form of any of the following including but not limited to: loss of love and affection; pain and suffering; mental anguish; emotional distress; loss of chance of survival; disfigurement; past, present, and future medical expenses; past, present, and future loss of wages; premature death; and loss of enjoyment of life.

In *Gordon v. Willis Knighton Medical Center,* 661 So.2d 991, La (1995), the court awarded $350,000 for wrongful death damages and $60,000 for the patient's pain and suffering. Breaches of the standard included:

1. Patient should have been classified as an "urgent cardiac patient" upon arrival.
2. Patient should have been evaluated immediately by a nurse and physician within fifteen minutes.
3. The patient should have been given oxygen. The emergency room nurses removed the oxygen that had been placed on the patient by the paramedics when transferring.
4. Emergency room nurses failed to notify the emergency room physician of the patient's arrival.

The myocardial infarct was caused by lack of oxygen to the heart. Also, the patient's medical records were altered and lost.

Quasi-Intentional Torts

"Quasi-intentional" torts protect an individual's interest in privacy, the person's reputation, and freedom from legal action that is unfounded. In contrast to the malpractice cases based on negligence, quasi-intentional and intentional torts are not based on the negligence theory. These torts are intentional, in that the person or entity is reasonably certain that harm will result from his actions.

For example, defamation (libel and slander) is a *quasi-intentional tort*. It is the false communication of information to a third party that in some way causes harm to the person (e.g., economic loss, loss of esteem/reputation in the community). Truth is a defense in such a claim. Breach of confidentiality is another quasi-intentional tort. For example, a health care provider talks about the HIV results of Patient Smith in the elevator. Smith's neighbor hears this information and "spreads the news" that the patient is HIV positive. Suit may be brought against the facility and health care provider for breach of confidentiality.

Intentional Torts

The following are intentional torts. *Assault* is an intentional act that causes fear or apprehension that a person will be touched in an injurious or offensive manner. *Battery* is the actual unpermitted touching. *Medical battery* is the unpermitted touching of a patient associated with the lack of informed consent to perform the procedure or treatments. For example, a surgeon has an informed consent to amputate the right foot because of gangrene but actually amputates the left foot. The patient could file a tort claim based on medical negligence along with an intentional tort claim of medical battery for amputation of the wrong foot.

Other intentional torts include:

1. *Invasion of privacy* is when a person's privacy right has been violated through public disclosure. Disclosure is such that a reasonable person would object to such an intrusion or disclosure.
2. *False imprisonment* is another intentional tort that is defined as: The unlawful intentional confinement of a person through physical, chemical, or emotional "restraints" so that the person is conscious of being confined and harmed by it. Areas of health care where there are more likely to be claims include emergency room and psychiatric facilities.
3. *Trespass to land* can be both an intentional tort or a negligent act that occurs when a person refuses to leave a place, places something on the property, or causes another person to enter that property. For example, a visitor absolutely refuses to leave the hospital after visiting hours and is asked to leave by facility personnel.
4. *Intentional infliction of emotional distress* is the intentional invasion of the patient or person's peace of mind by the defendant's behavior.

Law is not an "exact science." LNCs will enter an arena that is constantly changing. It is filled with challenges and controversy and will allow LNCs to grow and reach their potential.

Discussion Questions

1. The four elements of negligence include all but
   a. Breach of the standard
   b. Damages
   c. Duty owed
   d. Proximate malpractice
   (Answer: d)
2. The different sources of law are
   a. Administrative and constitutional
   b. Statutory and substantive
   c. Procedural and common
   d. Substantive and procedural
   (Answer: a)
3. Battery
   a. Is a quasi-irregular tort
   b. Is unpermittted touching
   c. Is based on the *stare decisis* theory
   d. Is only a criminal offense
   (Answer b)
4. All of the following are intentional torts, except
   a. Battery
   b. Defamation
   c. Assault
   d. False imprisonment
   (Answer b)

Bibliography

Aiken, T. D., Ed., *Legal, Ethical and Political Issues in Nursing,* Philadelphia, F.A. Davis, 1994.

Guido, G. W., *Legal Issues in Nursing, 2nd ed.,* Stanford, Appleton and Lange, 1997.
   Northrop, Cynthia E. and Kelley, Mary E., *Legal Issues in Nursing,* St. Louis, C.V. Mosby, 1987.

Appendix 2.1
U.S. Constitutional Amendments 1 to 10 and 14

1. Congress shall make no law respecting an establishment of religion, or prohibiting the free exercise thereof; of abridging the freedom of speech, or of the press; or the right of the people peaceably to assemble, and to petition the Government for a redress of grievances.
2. A well-regulated Militia, being necessary to the security of a free State, the right of the people to keep and bear Arms, shall not be infringed.

3. No soldier shall, in time of peace, be quartered in any house, without the consent of the Owner, nor in time of war, but in a manner to be prescribed by law.

4. The right of the people to be secure in their persons, houses, papers, and effects, against unreasonable searches and seizures, shall not be violated, and no Warrants shall issue, but upon proper cause, supported by Oath or affirmation, and particularly describing the place to be searched, and the persons or things to be seized.

5. No persons shall be held to answer for a capital, or otherwise infamous crime, unless a presentment or indictment of a Grand Jury, except in cases arising in the land or naval forces, or in the Militia, when in actual service in time of War or public danger, nor shall any persons be subject for the same offense twice put in jeopardy of life or limb, nor shall be compelled in any criminal case to be a witness against himself, nor be deprived of life, liberty, or property, without due process of law; nor shall private property be taken for public use, without just compensation

6. In all criminal prosecutions, the accused shall enjoy the right to a speedy and public trial by an impartial jury of the State and district wherein the crime shall have been committed, which district shall have been previously ascertained by law, and to be informed of the nature and cause of the accusations; to be confronted with the witnesses against him; to have compulsory process for obtaining witnesses in his favor, and to have the Assistance of counsel for his defense.

7. In Suits at common law, where the value in controversy shall exceed twenty dollars, the right of trial by jury shall be preserved, and no fact tried by a jury, shall be otherwise reexamined in any Court of the U.S. than according to the rules of the common law.

8. Excessive bail shall not be required, nor excessive fines imposed, nor cruel and unusual punishments inflicted.

9. The enumeration in the Constitution, of certain rights, shall not be constructed to deny or disparage others retained by the people.

10. The powers not delegated to the U.S. by the Constitution, nor prohibited by it to the States, are reserved to the States respectively, or to the people.

and

14. Section I. All persons born or naturalized in the U.S., and subject to the jurisdiction thereof, are citizens of the U.S. and the State wherein they reside. No State shall make or enforce any law which shall abridge the privileges of immunities of citizens of the U.S.; nor shall any State deprive any person of life, liberty, or property, without due process of law; nor deny to any persons within its jurisdiction the equal protection of the laws.

Chapter 3

Standards of Care

Tonia Dandry Aiken

Contents

Objectives

- To define standards of care
- To discuss sources of standards of care
- To discuss standards of professional performance
- To define the steps in a trial process

1-57444-123-X/98
© 1998 by American Association of Legal Nurse Consultants

Reasonable Standards

The *standard of care* is a term used to designate what is accepted as "reasonable" under the circumstances. It is a "measuring scale." In a malpractice claim, legal nurse consultants (LNCs) must determine what the standard of care was at the time of the alleged act or omission that caused damage to the plaintiff. The standard of care is that degree of skill, care, and judgment used by an ordinary prudent health care provider under similar circumstances. The standard of care may encompass more than one "reasonable" action in a given situation.

When a plaintiff seeks the advice of an attorney regarding a possible medical or nursing negligence claim, the first documents that must be obtained are the medical records. The attorney or LNC can then review the care and treatment rendered to the patient by examining the records. Routinely, a time line or chronology of events is done so that it is easier to put things in perspective. Medical records are read "across the board" meaning that the records are read day by day. In other words, all tests, treatments, medications, and care given are put in chronological sequence for each day.

A chronology of events can be placed on a minute-by-minute evaluation of the record or day-by-day evaluation depending on the allegations of the specific acts of medical negligence. If the LNC is dealing with a product liability case or toxic tort, the standards applicable to the specific set of circumstances must be determined to see if breaches occurred. *Product liability* claims involve cases where medical products such as a Lugue rods and wires used in spinal surgeries or birth control devices have caused damage or injuries to a patient. The suit is against the manufacturer of the product (see chapter on toxic torts).

Experts

In most jurisdictions an expert witness in the same field of practice as the defendant is required to testify to what is the standard of care and whether or not the standard was breached. In addition, an expert witness provides the necessary testimony on proximate cause and damages. If the records must be sent to an expert, then the records should be organized in a binder with individual sections noted (e.g., Dr. Smith's record 12/97–2/98). Each page should be numbered, if it has not been numbered by the facility. A copy of the Complaint or Petition for Damages should be included, if it has been filed. A table of contents indicating what records are being sent to the expert must be included. A duplicate set should be maintained for the attorney so that the expert can talk to the attorney and refer to pertinent pages, information, or entries.

In the letter to the expert, the attorney or LNC usually requests an objective medical or nursing opinion on whether or not liability exists on the part of the defendant based on the appropriate standards of care. The expert may be asked to provide cites, references, and/or copies of the appropriate supporting documents for the standards of care. A written report may be required but the expert should be instructed to call first to discuss his or her findings prior to writing a report.

Sources for Standards

If the legal nurse consultant or expert is requested to obtain the standards of care for a case (e.g., skin care for a diabetic patient) numerous sources can be found. For example, the American Nurses Association has standards of care manuals for nurses in all aspects of nursing (e.g., neurosurgical, perioperative, and school nursing; see Appendix 3.1). National professional organizations have standards of practice pertinent to their areas. (See Appendix 3.2 for a list of many of the national nursing specialty organizations.)

Statutes and regulations also provide standards for how health care providers practice. For example, in most states, health care providers are required by law to report child and elder abuse, or fines and penalties can be imposed.

Authoritative textbooks are also used as standards. Many times the authors of these textbooks are also retained as experts by the parties. It is presumed that the textbooks have the most current information on the conditions, treatments, and standards in a particular field of medicine or nursing, although some experts say that by the time a textbook is published the information is outdated.

The *State practice acts* are also used as a standards of care. For example, the act may state that a nurse may not render a diagnosis because this would be considered practicing medicine.

State practice guidelines are also used as standards. Boards determine if certain treatment, actions, and/or functions can be performed and/or delegated.

Facility and unit policies and procedures may also establish standards of care for the health care provider. Many times, health care providers are informed that there are policies and procedures, but fail to take the time actually to review and understand them. Policies and procedures are commonly used in negligence claims. Examples:

1. Decubitus Ulcer Claims — Policies and procedures maintaining skin integrity of a diabetic patient
2. Heating Pad Burn Claims — Policies and procedures on monitoring and documentation of the skin condition at specific intervals (e.g., to prevent burns) may be important to show that the patient was not monitored properly and in a *timely* fashion
3. Fetal Distress/Brain Damage Baby Claim — Policies and procedures on assessments, monitoring, and reporting distress to prevent injuries

In the above examples, the policies and procedures are usually requested by plaintiff's counsel in a Request for Production of Documents. *Requests for production of documents and things* are requested by the plaintiff or defendant for items from the other party, which pertain to the issues of the lawsuit and that may lead to discoverable information. A *subpoena duces tecum* may also be issued by the court to obtain the necessary documents. It is served on an entity or person who is in control of specific documents and other material relevant to facts in issue.

Equipment manuals are also used to establish the standard of care. For example, an intravenous infusion set requires a special filter to be used to prevent an air embolism. If the nurse fails to set up the system properly by omitting the filter, a breach has occurred. It is important that the LNC request personnel files to see if the staff have received in-service instruction and education on equipment that is the focus of the lawsuit, either before or after the malpractice claim has been made. The attorney and LNC must also decide if there is the possibility of a medical product liability claim against the manufacturer of the equipment. It may be determined that the medical product is defective in design, use, or in the materials used to manufacture it.

Job descriptions can also be used as standards of care. For example, an operating room nurse is required to do three counts in a surgical procedure. If the nurse fails to do the required number of counts for whatever reason, a breach may be alleged because the nurse failed to perform the requirements of her job resulting in injury to the patient (e.g., lap pad left in the abdomen that caused sepsis).

Critical pathways or guidelines are not mandatory. If a critical guideline is treated as a standard of care, then it *must* be followed.

Administrative code regulations, both state and federal, play an important role in certain health care settings (e.g., home health and nursing homes). Such regulations establish standards to be met.

Court decisions and administrative rulings are also used as standards. Case law may set out certain guidelines and standards involving malpractice, personal injury, contract, and other areas of laws. A review of case law should be done to determine how the courts have decided on such issues. This generally is not a duty for the LNC but usually falls to the attorney or paralegal.

The *Joint Commission on Accreditation of Healthcare Organizations* (JCAHO) also sets out standards for health care professionals.

Standards of Professional Performance

Standards of professional performance are described in terms of competency and not in terms of reasonable care. Technological advancements provide new and better aids and equipment to treat patients. The criteria to measure compliance with the use of such new technology will also change. Criteria to determine the standards of practice are being developed by the specialty areas of medicine and nursing. (See Appendix 3.2 for a list of specialty organizations.)

The Use of Standards

Standards may be used for different reasons, as evidence for or against a plaintiff or defendant in medical malpractice cases, disciplinary actions, custody matters, workers' compensation claims, committment proceedings, and personal injury claims.

Errors in Judgment

If the health care professional makes an error in judgment, he or she is not liable for negligence. Two factors must be present for an action to be called an error in judgment:

1. The health care provider's care must have conformed to the current professional standards of care

2. The health care provider must possess knowledge and skills similar to those of an average member of the profession

Standard of Care: Case Discussion

In *Flanagan v. Labe,* the Superior Court of Pennsylvania held that a nursing expert was not competent to testify on legal causation. Also, the state laws forbade nurses from formulating medical diagnoses. The plaintiff presented a *nursing* expert to prove that the nurse's failure to treat properly led to the development of progressively worsening subcutaneous emphysema. The court would not allow the nurse expert to testify to a "reasonable degree of *medical* certainty" regarding causation. The nursing expert, however, testified as to the breaches of the standard by the nurses who should have provided reasonable *nursing* care with a patient who had complaints of pain and breathing problems.

The Lawsuit

Prelitigation Panels for Malpractice Claims

If a lawsuit is instituted, based on a breach of the standard of care, several steps are involved in the trial process. In some states, there is a statutory requirement that forces the plaintiff to go through a prelitigation or medical review panel process. The process varies as to the length of time it takes to complete along with the composition of the panel members. The panel members may consist of health care providers, lawyers, and/or judges depending on the state. Documents and materials are submitted to the panel members who then determine if malpractice occurred.

Arguments for prelitigation panels include: that the panels decrease the number of frivolous lawsuits filed and allow attorneys to get rid of cases if it is determined through the panel process that the cases have little or no merit. Those opposing the use of prelitigation panels argue that they simply delay the plaintiff from entering the judicial arena and add to the costs of pursuing and defending a case. However, if the panel determines that malpractice has occurred, this sometimes facilitates settlement.

The Procedural Process

Initiation of a Lawsuit

1. Client interview
2. Review and evaluation of pertinent medical/physician records and other documents
3. Determination if any breaches (acts and/or omissions) have caused damages to the plaintiff
4. Determination of damages (e.g., lost wages, medical expenses, pain and suffering, loss of chance of survival, disfigurement, loss of society, loss of consortium, loss of love and affection, emotional distress, mental anguish, and diminution of the enjoyment of life)

5. Filing of the necessary documents to institute the prelitigation panel process if applicable in that state
6. Filing the Petition for Damages or Complaint in the appropriate court after the panel process; if there is no prelitigation process, this is the first step to instituting the lawsuit
7. Answer by defendant
8. If not answered in a timely way, possible entering of a default judgment by the court
9. Possible filing of Motion to Dismiss
10. Possible filing of counterclaims
11. Possible filing of amended and/or supplemental pleadings by either party

Discovery Stage

1. Various types of discovery are done to determine all of the facts surrounding the allegations of the Petition for Damages or Complaint.
2. Several types of discovery are used.
   a. Physical exam
   b. Interrogatories
   c. Request for Production of Documents
   d. Admission of fact or request for admission
   e. Depositions

Trial Process

1. Prelitigation conferences may be held
2. Settlements may be proposed
3. Mediation or arbitration may be done to avoid trial
4. Trial of lawsuit
5. Selection of the jury if it is a jury trial — (*voir dire*) questioning of potential jurors
6. Opening statements by plaintiff and defendant
7. Plaintiff presents his or her case
8. Motion for Directed Verdict against plaintiff
9. Defendant presents his or her case
10. Rebuttal
11. Closing statements by plaintiff and defendant
12. Jury instructions
13. Jury deliberations
14. Verdict
15. Appeal (optional)

Discussion Questions

1. Standard of care
   a. Is based on the highest level of care at the time
   b. Is used only in cases involving malpractice
   c. Is based on the current standards for when the suit is filed
   d. Is used to designate what is reasonable under the circumstances
   (Answer: d)
2. Sources of standards
   a. Are only determined by the experts
   b. Include authoritative texts and consensus opinions
   c. Include statutes and policies
   d. Are found in the medical records
   (Answer: c)
3. Critical pathways/guidelines
   a. Are only medical opinions on how to render care
   b. Are mandatory
   c. Are treated as standards of care
   d. Are not required to be followed
   (Answer: d)
4. Standards of care
   a. Must be breached in a malpractice claim
   b. Are based only on medical criteria
   c. Do not change
   d. Are viewed as having little weight in a case
   (Answer: a)

Bibliography

Aiken, T. D., Ed., *Legal, Ethical and Political Issues in Nursing,* Philadelphia, F.A. Davis, 1994.

American Medical Association and National Health Lawyers Association, *Physician's Survival Guide — Legal Pitfalls and Solutions,* The Associations, 1991.

Carroll, M. M., "Nursing malpractice and corporate negligence: how is the standard of care determined?" *Journal of Nursing Law,* Vol. 3/Issue 3, 1996.

Tammelleo, D., Ed., *Reagan Reports, Flanagan v. Labe,* 666 A. 2d 333, 1995.

Standards of Clinical Nursing Practice, MO, American Nurses Association, 1991.

Appendix 3.1
Standards of Care Manuals for Nurses

1. Standards of Clinical Nursing Practice
2. Standards for Nursing Professional Development: Continuing Education and Staff Development

3. Standards of Community Health Nursing Practice
4. Standards of Nursing Practice in Correctional Facilities
5. Scope of Practice for Nursing Informatics
6. Standards of Home Health Nursing Practice
7. Standards of College Health Nursing Practice
8. Orthopedic Nursing Practice: Process and Outcome Criteria for Selected Diagnoses
9. Standards and Scope of Hospice Nursing Practice
10. A Statement on the Scope of College Health Nursing Practice
11. A Statement on the Scope of Home Health Nursing Practice
12. Standards and Scope of Gerontological Nursing Practice
13. Standards of Practice for the Perinatal Nurse Specialist
14. Standards of Perioperative Nursing Practice
15. Standards of Cardiovascular Nursing Practice
16. Standards of Neurological and Neurosurgical Nursing Practice
17. A Statement on the Scope of Medical-Surgical Nursing Practice
18. Outcome Standards for Rheumatology Nursing Practice
19. Neuroscience Nursing Practice: Process and Outcome Criteria for Selected Diagnoses
20. Standards of Oncology Nursing Practice
21. Statement on the Scope and Standards of Respiratory Nursing Practice
22. Statement on the Scope and Standards of Otorhinolaryngology Clinical Nursing Practice
23. The Scope of Practice of the Primary Health Care Nurse Practitioner
24. Standards of Practice for the Primary Health Care Nurse Practitioner
25. The Scope of Nursing Practice
26. The Scope of Cardiac Rehabilitation Nursing Practice
27. Standards for Organized Nursing Services and Responsibilities of Nurse Administrators across All Settings
28. Standards of Addiction with Selected Diagnoses and Criteria and Statement on the Scope and Standards of Psychiatric Mental Health Clinical Nursing Practice

Appendix 3.2
National Nursing Specialty Organizations

1. American Academy of Ambulatory Care Nursing (AAACN)
2. American Association of Critical-Care Nurses (AACN)
3. American Association of Diabetes Educators (AADE)
4. American Association of Neuroscience Nurses (AANN)
5. American Association of Nurse Anesthetists (AANA)
6. American Association of Occupational Health Nurses (AAOHN)
7. American Association of Spinal Cord Injury Nurses (AASCIN)
8. American College of Nurse-Midwives (ACNM)
9. American Nephrology Nurses Association (ANNA)
10. American Psychiatric Nurses' Association (APNA)
11. American Society of Ophthalmic Registered Nurses, Inc. (ASORN)

12. American Society of Plastic and Reconstructive Surgical Nurses, Inc. (ASPRSN)
13. American Society of Post Anesthesia Nurses (ASPAN)
14. American Urological Association Allied, Inc. (AUAA)
15. Association for Practitioners in Infection Control (APIC)
16. Association of Operating Room Nurses, Inc. (AORN)
17. Association of Pediatric Oncology Nurses (APON)
18. Association of Rehabilitation Nurses (ARN)
19. Association of Women's Health, Obstetric, and Neonatal Nurses (AWHONN)
20. Dermatology Nurses' Association (DNA)
21. Emergency Nurses' Association (ENA)
22. International Society of Nurses in Genetics, Inc. (ISONG)
23. Intravenous Nurses Society, Inc. (INS)
24. National Association of Nurse Practitioners in Reproductive Health (NANPRH)
25. National Association of Nurse Massage Therapists (NANMT)
26. National Association of Pediatric Nurse Associations and Practitioners (NAPNAP)
27. National Association of School Nurses, Inc. (NASN)
28. National Flight Nurses Association (NFNA)
29. National Nurses Society on Additions (NNSA)
30. Oncology Nursing Society (ONS)
31. Society of Gastroenterology Nurses and Associates, Inc. (SGNA)
32. Society of Otorhinolaryngology and Head-Neck Nurses, Inc. (SOHN)
33. Academy of Medical-Surgical Nurses (AMSN)
34. American Holistic Nurses Association (AHNA)

Chapter 4

Liability of Health Care Providers

Tonia Dandry Aiken

Contents

Objectives

- To define common areas of liability in the health care arena
- To discuss the implications of a malpractice claim on a health care provider's license
- To discuss common documents/materials requested and used to pursue or defend claims

Introduction

Liability requires that the party or person responsible for injuries or damages be held accountable. Legal accountability requires that the health care provider be held responsible for the action taken when providing care and treatment to patients. *Vicarious liability* occurs when the law, in certain limited instances, imposes liability on a principal for the acts or omissions of an agent. *Ostensible authority* is a doctrine of law whereby a hospital is liable for the negligence of an independent contractor if the patient has a rational basis to believe that the independent contractor is a hospital employee, for example, a physician in the emergency department.

Diagnostic Errors

Allegations of diagnostic errors are common in medical negligence claims. Some of the reasons for errors include physician's expertise, knowledge base, and experience may vary depending on the medical problems presented; diagnostic studies are not perfect; diseases can present in numerous and sometimes vague ways that are not the typical textbook manifestations.

Legal nurse consultants (LNCs) should review the records to determine if the physicians utilized any of the following strategies in assessing the patient.

1. A careful history is important. Is communication with the patient difficult because of a language barrier? Other factors to be considered are the patient's mental status, or his or her inability to understand the physician's questions — a red flag should go up as a potential area for liability.
2. Careful physical exams can demonstrate evidence of the presence or absence of a disease entity or medical condition.
3. Diagnostic tests have limits. If the clinical picture of the patient warrants additional testing even with a previous negative finding, did the physician order additional diagnostic testing? Could the additional testing have discovered that the patient had, e.g., a subdural hematoma or embolism?
4. Did the physician consider all working diagnoses so that all possible tests and evaluations could be done?

In *McRee v. Perry County General Hospital,* the patient went to the emergency room complaining of chest and arm pain. He was discharged and diagnosed as having mild hypertension and high cholesterol. He later suffered a fatal cardiopulmonary arrest. Diagnostic studies indicated abnormalities; however, the physician failed to do additional testing in light of the abnormalities. He also failed to diagnose coronary artery disease. The defendant settled.

In *McCann v. Lee,* a pathologist issued a report that a tissue specimen was from a malignant tumor in the patient's rectum. The patient underwent surgery for removal of his rectum. The pathology report stated "atypical mucus hyperplasia," not cancer. The jury awarded $1 million in compensatory damages and $1 million for the patient's wife for loss of consortium. The circuit court ordered remittitur of $750,000, resulting in a total of $1.25 million.

Treatment Issues

Treatment issues are seen in areas for the health care provider, such as hospital settings, long-term care facilities, and home health settings. Treatment issues involve a wide variety of potential breaches. For example,

1. Failure to treat in a timely fashion
2. Failure to treat properly
3. Failure to perform the treatment
4. Failure to use equipment properly
5. Failure to treat in a timely way when signs and symptoms of a deteriorating condition are evident
6. Failure to diagnose

In *Rice v. Skyline Nursing Home,* a 79-year-old patient was dropped while being transferred to a wheelchair. He fractured a hip that required surgery. The patient then developed three decubitus ulcers which became infected. He became comatose and was hospitalized and required additional surgery and 5 months of therapy. The parties mediated a $550,000 settlement.

Communication Issues

Communication is crucial today because of all of the different "players" that are involved in the care and treatment of the patient. Communication lines must be open between

1. The health care provider and patient
2. The health care provider and other health care providers
3. The health care provider and social services
4. The health care provider and administration
5. The health care provider and risk management
6. The health care provider and the case manager
7. The health care provider and the insurer

With managed care and case management, communication lines must be open and direct. Otherwise, the patient may suffer injuries, and facilities and insurers may be sued and held liable for damages. Common types of communication failure allegations include

1. Failure to communicate
2. Failure to communicate in a timely fashion
3. Failure to document communication with patient, patient's family, and/or other health care providers
4. Failure to communicate the appropriate information
5. Failure to act based on the communication received

In *Ramsey v. Physician's Memorial Hospital, Inc.,* a nurse failed to communicate to the physician that ticks had been removed from the two children's bodies. The physician diagnosed measles instead of Rocky Mountain spotted fever. One child died and the other suffered injuries.

Monitoring

Monitoring a patient involves all levels of health care providers from physicians to nursing assistants. Policies and procedures which set out monitoring responsibilities are important sections in the facility's policy and procedure manuals. Monitoring breaches include some of the following:

1. Failure to properly monitor the care, treatment, and condition of the patient
2. Failure to monitor in a timely fashion
3. Failure to report to the appropriate person deviations (changes in the patient's status when monitoring)
4. Failure to document monitoring
5. Failure to use the proper equipment to monitor the patient
6. Failure to instruct and teach the patient properly about monitoring their condition (e.g., sugar level to determine insulin needed)
7. Failure to use the equipment properly when monitoring a patient (e.g., turning off the alarm button on an infusion pump or telemetry monitor)
8. Failure to monitor and check equipment and use of equipment

Supervision

Supervisory issues have always been an area of great interest whether they involve the physician in an operating room or a clinical instructor with a student. The common areas of potential liability vary. For instance, with unlicensed assistant personnel, there is great concern over the issue of who is actually supervising the patient.

Supervisory liability focuses on the failure to supervise properly and also the failure to delegate properly. For example, if a supervisor knows that the staff does not possess the knowledge, experience, and expertise to perform a delegated task, but delegates it anyway, legal liability may result if the patient is injured.

Additionally, if the supervisor fails to supervise properly or gives the incorrect instructions, liability may occur. For example, a nurse asks a supervisor to show her how to z-track because she has forgotten. The supervisor uses her forearm, because she is in a hurry, and demonstrates. The nurse goes into the patient's room and z-tracks on the forearm causing severe necrosis and disfigurement. Both the supervisor and nurse may be held liable for their breaches.

Supervisory breaches include

1. Failure to supervise properly
2. Failure to delegate properly
3. Failure to evaluate properly the health care provider rendering treatment
4. Failure to educate properly and "check off" that the staff has demonstrated the required skills

5. Failure to document that the staff has been orientated, evaluated, and/or trained
6. Failure to use good judgment

Medication

Medication errors are high on the list of potential areas of legal exposure. Errors can be acts of omission or acts of commission. Breaches involving medication may include such things as

1. Failure to administer the correct drug
2. Failure to administer medication in a timely fashion
3. Failure to administer the drug properly using the correct route
4. Failure to give the medication to the correct patient
5. Failure to check intravenous sites (e.g., for infiltration or infection)
6. Failure to administer any drug
7. Failure to administer the correct dosage
8. Failure to confirm or clarify a medication order
9. Failure to detect signs and symptoms of drug toxicity
10. Failure to order or request an order for drug levels
11. Failure to recognize adverse reactions and/or side effects
12. Failure to recognize and/or check the chart for drug allergies resulting in administration of the wrong drug and a potentially dangerous reaction
13. Failure to document the injection site
14. Failure to use the proper size needle for the specific drug administered and the required site
15. Failure to use aseptic technique

Case example: An injection is given in such a way that the sciatic nerve is stuck and causes "drop foot syndrome" in the patient.

Falls

Patient falls are extremely common problems and the reason for numerous lawsuits. Geriatric patients, medical-surgical patients, and pediatric patients are all potential fall victims. Patients with the following conditions are more susceptible to falls than others:

1. Heavily sedated patients
2. Patients with mobility problems
3. Patient with mental conditions (e.g., Alzheimer's, dementia, organic brain syndrome)
4. Patients who wake up to go to the bathroom or get out of bed for some other reason
5. Patients on numerous medications that combined may cause problems with drowsiness, balance, coherence
6. Patients who have fallen before
7. Noncompliant patients

Sometimes it is difficult to predict which patient will fall. Falls can result in injuries that range from minor bruising to subdural hematomas and death. Documentation of what was found at the time of the fall must be examined by the LNC.

1. Was there an order for side rails?
2. Did the health care providers follow hospital policies and procedures?
3. Was the patient properly managed and treated after the fall? Were there any protocols for monitoring?
4. What injuries did the patient suffer?
5. Did the fall exacerbate an already preexisting condition or cause a new injury?
6. Was the policy and procedure with regard to notifying the physician and family followed?
7. If the side rails were not used as ordered, were the policies and procedures followed regarding notification of the appropriate parties?
8. If the patient fell, was an incident report written?
9. What were the conditions of the surroundings (e.g., the floor where the fall took place)?

All of the above should be considered by LNCs when working on a fall claim whether it is for a plaintiff or a defendant. Also, LNCs should talk to the risk manager and interview those involved in the fall if they are working with the defendant. Obtaining an IME (independent medical exam) should be considered if the damages claimed are not consistent with documented damages.

In *Hooker v. Crystal Park Nursing Home,* an 85-year-old woman fell and fractured her hip. She developed pneumonia and died approximately 3 months later. The plaintiff claimed that the nursing home negligently failed to prevent falls and train its employees properly in the safe care of geriatric patients. The parties settled for $150,000 plus a waiver of a $14,000 debt for services rendered.

Restraints

Restraints can cause circulatory damage or nerve damage, brain damage, and death. It is important that the policies and procedures be requested or subpoenaed to determine if they were in fact followed. For example,

1. Was the patient properly monitored and in a timely way?
2. Was the patient abandoned for a period of time wherein he or she suffered injuries?
3. Were all of the alternatives to restraints used?
4. Were body system checks done (e.g., neurological, respiratory, circulatory, etc.)?

Documentation must be evaluated carefully along with an analysis of policies and procedures.

Independent Contractors

An *independent contractor* is an individual who contracts to perform services with another party (e.g., facility). The independent contractor is not "controlled" or supervised by the other party except as to the end results. Cases vary as to the liability for facilities for the actions or omissions of independent contractors. If the facility holds itself out to the public as offering, for example, emergency care, the patient has no choice in choosing a physician. Also, the "public" reasonably perceives that such services were rendered by facility employees. Courts have held if the above scenario occurs, the facility can be held liable. With *an employee*, the facility has a right to control method, time, and the manner of accomplishing the task or services.

Disciplinary Actions

If a health care provider violates his or her Practice Act, the license may be probated, suspended, or revoked. A probated license will usually allow the person to work with certain stipulations such as quarterly evaluations from the supervisor or a certain number of continuing education hours, etc. A suspended license will not allow the health care provider to work during the suspension time unless the suspension is stayed based upon certain stipulations that must be followed. A revoked license prohibits the health care provider from working in his or her professional capacity.

As indicated in Chapter 2, there are violations indicated in states' practice acts. If a health care provider is negligent and a malpractice claim is filed against the health care provider, this may or may not have implications on the professional license. Sometimes, the professional may be reported to the state board due to circumstances arising out of the alleged incident of malpractice. This could result in an investigation by the board and possible repercussions. Some state boards may not investigate the matter until the malpractice litigation is completed. This is a decision made by the Board.

Sources of Information

Potential sources of information that will aid the LNC in gathering facts about the case include

1. Ambulance run reports
2. Emergency department records
3. Emergency department logs
4. Coroner's report
5. Death certificate
6. X-ray department
7. Code logs
8. Switchboard operator's log
9. Nursing supervisor shift reports

10. Laboratory logs
11. Fetal monitor strips
12. EKG strips
13. Telemetry strips
14. Holter monitor strips
15. Patient census sheets
16. Long-distance phone bills to show calls to physicians or patients
17. Employee time cards
18. Medication wastage records
19. Surveys for long-term care facilities (to determine if cited for deficiencies)
20. Laboratory computer tapes and records
21. Employee personnel files
22. Police report
23. Insurance policies
24. Medical records
25. Pharmacy bills
26. Physical therapy records/bills
27. Client's uninsured policy (if applicable)
28. Psychiatric records
29. Lost wage information
30. Other bills (e.g., traction units, cervical collars)
31. X-ray diagnostic studies that show injuries (e.g., MRI, CT scan)
32. Toxicology screens (if drugs/alcohol suspected)

LNCs are in an excellent position to review, evaluate, and analyze potential liability and damage claims. Medical negligence claims, personal injury, workers' compensation, product liability, toxic torts, and automobile cases are all areas of law to which the LNCs can apply their skills to assist the attorney in pursuing or defending the claims.

Discussion Questions

1. Legal accountability
   a. Applies only in accounting
   b. Refers to being responsible for a party's damages
   c. Refers to legal aid and financing
   d. Applies only to health care issues
   (Answer: b)
2. Communication
   a. Involves patient, family, attorneys, and coroner
   b. Liability is rare in product liability claims
   c. Breaches involve documentation and failure to act
   d. Is not an important part of patient care
   (Answer: c)
3. Supervisory issues
   a. Involve the areas of delegation and education
   b. Are not pertinent in today's legal claims

    c. Do not involve the unlicensed assisted personnel

    d. Is not an area of liability

    (Answer: a)

4. Two or more common areas of potential legal exposure include all, except

    a. Falls and X-rays

    b. Monitoring nursing students

    c. Medications and restraints

    d. Breast implants and enemas

    (Answer: d)

Bibliography

Aiken, T. D., *Legal, Ethical and Political Issues in Nursing,* Philadelphia, F. A. Davis, 1994.

Beckman, J. P., *Nursing Malpractice — Implications for Clinical and Nursing Education,* Seattle, University of Washington Press, 1995.

Guido, G., *Legal Issues in Nursing,* 2nd ed., Stamford, Appleton Lange, 1997.

Hooker v. Crystal Park Nursing Home, Kansas, settled before filing, December 22, 1995.

Iyer, P., Ed., *Nursing Malpractice,* Tucson: Lawyers and Judges Publishing Company, 1996.

McCann v. Lee, 679 So2d. 658, 1996.

McRee v. Perry County General Hospital, Mississippi, Perry County, Cir Ct., No. 95-0083, April 3, 1992.

Ramsey v. Physician's Memorial Hospital, Inc., 373 A2d 26 (Md. App. 1977).

Rice v. Skyline Nursing Home, Texas, Dallas County 44th Jud. Dist. Ct., No. 95-6785-B, March 19, 1996.

Staiger, T. and Paaur, D., Strategies for reducing diagnostic errors, *Resident Staff Physician,* July 1996.

Chapter 5

Criminal Law: Procedure and Evidence

Joseph R. McMahon, III

Contents

Objectives

- To provide an overview of specific areas of criminal law, procedure, and evidence
- To review the basic constitutional protections afforded to those accused of criminal offenses in connection with the collection and admission of evidence
- To address the admissibility of scientific evidence in criminal proceedings

1-57444-123-X/98
© 1998 by American Association of Legal Nurse Consultants

Introduction

Criminal law is a field which is by itself extremely broad and which continues to grow broader with each passing legislative session or appellate decision. The practice of criminal law encompasses the application of law, procedure, and evidence. It would be impossible to provide a complete analysis of each of these areas of the law within the constraints of this chapter. Therefore, this chapter will attempt to meet the above objectives.

Criminal Law

Criminal law is the body of law by which all human conduct is judged. Although laws which make conduct criminal vary widely from community to community, state to state, and country to country, each system of laws is based upon the social mores and values of the society that establishes them. Laws are the enactment of social, political, and moral viewpoints of a society.

Unlike civil law, rarely are criminal consequences attached to negligent acts. Although some jurisdictions have enacted statutes which penalize the consequences of a negligent act, these damages are more commonly than not addressed in the civil courts of our country where monetary damages are at issue. In the rare incidences where criminal law considers the effects of negligence, wanton disregard of human safety is a general issue which must be considered and prosecutorial discretion has great leeway.

Although each of us is familiar with a variety of terms used within the context of criminal law and evidence from entertainment and the media, our understanding of the topic is generally flawed by inaccuracies inherent in these media. For instance, many of us have heard the television prosecutor argue that the murder was premeditated; however, in most jurisdictions, there is no requirement that the prosecutor prove that a killing was premeditated to support a conviction for murder. Several of the everyday inaccuracies in criminal law will be addressed while exploring criminal law, procedure, and evidence in this chapter.

Violations of criminal law generally require some level of intent to commit the crime charged. General criminal intent is present whenever there is specific intent and also when the circumstances indicate that the offender, in the ordinary course of human experience, must have expected the prescribed criminal consequences as reasonably certain to result from his or her act or failure to act. In a general intent crime, the criminal intent necessary to sustain a conviction is shown by the very doing of the acts which have been declared criminal. Specific criminal intent is that state of mind which exists when the circumstances indicate that the offender actively desired the prescribed criminal consequences to follow his or her act or failure to act.

An example of a general intent crime is simple possession of narcotics. The prosecutor in Louisiana who seeks to convict a defendant of simple possession of narcotics must prove that the defendant possessed a narcotic substance which has been classified as illegal. There is no need for the prosecutor to prove specific intent; general intent to commit the crime is sufficient to support the conviction under Louisiana law.

An example of a specific intent crime under the common law is burglary. Burglary requires the breaking and entering into a dwelling of another, but in addition to the general intent to commit the trespass, it must also be established that the defendant acted with intent to commit a felony within the premises. Therefore, the prosecutor is required to establish that the offender had "specific intent" to commit a felony in addition to the breaking and entering in order to secure the conviction.

Louisiana law defines *second degree murder* as the killing of a human being when the offender has the specific intent to kill or cause great bodily harm; L.R.S. 14:30.1. In order to prove successfully the elements of this crime and obtain a conviction, the prosecutor must prove to the jury that the defendant killed the victim and that the defendant possessed the specific intent to kill or inflict great bodily harm upon the person of the victim. If the prosecutor is unable to prove that specific intent existed, the jury should not find the defendant guilty of second degree murder.

Criminal Procedure

The prosecutor is required to prove the level of intent along with each and every element of the crime to support a conviction for any crime, whether it be a felony or misdemeanor. The criminal defense attorney is not required to prove anything in a criminal prosecution, whereas the defense attorney in a civil trial has an equal and opposite responsibility to present evidence supporting the defense position. The Fifth Amendment to the U.S. Constitution grants the accused the right to be silent and not to testify against or incriminate himself or herself. Specifically, the amendment provides that "No person...shall be compelled in any criminal case to be a witness against himself." The prosecution bears the entire burden of proof. After the prosecution has presented its case, the accused may present witnesses on his or her own behalf or rest upon the presumption that a person is innocent until proved guilty. If a defendant elects to present a defense in a criminal case, generally his or her counsel will seek to disprove the facts presented by the prosecution which support the elements of the crime or the attorney will attempt to create doubt in the minds of the judge or jury. For example, a person charged with the crime may present alibi witnesses who place the person in a different location at the time of the offense or may attack the reliability of evidence used by the prosecution.

The prosecution in a criminal case bears the burden of proof. Just as in a civil case, the party bringing the action is required to prove the case. Civil and criminal cases differ in the standard by which they are to be judged. Civil cases are generally judged by the preponderance of the evidence standard. This standard requires finders of fact to listen to the evidence and render their verdict based upon a finding of which side presented the best evidence to support their position. In criminal law, the prosecutor is required to prove his or her case beyond a reasonable doubt in the eyes of the trier of fact. This standard has been defined numerous times by numerous scholars and practicing members of the criminal bar across the country. While no two will agree what the definition of reasonable doubt is, suffice it to say that it is generally agreed that reasonable doubt is doubt based on reason and common sense. Triers of fact are called upon to listen to the evidence as presented by the prosecution or defense to determine if the facts as presented are logical, credible, and worthy of belief. If the facts are such, they should be used as a basis for reaching a verdict. If they are not logical, credible, and worthy of belief, then they should be used to reach the opposite verdict.

Should the prosecution fail to prove the allegations beyond a reasonable doubt in the eyes of the trier of fact and an acquittal or not guilty verdict is rendered, the prosecution may not subject the accused to another trial. The Fifth Amendment to the U.S. Constitution further provides that "Nor shall any person be subject for the same offense to be twice put in jeopardy of life or limb." This provision, commonly referred to as "Double Jeopardy," is more far-reaching than the amendment or its name implies. Not only is the prosecution barred from bringing an action against an accused who has been acquitted for the same offense, it is also barred from pursuing criminal charges against an accused for crimes which require proof of the same elements. For example, although an accused may be charged with theft and possession/receiving stolen things, the accused may not be tried nor convicted of both offenses in most jurisdictions under Double Jeopardy.

The Sixth Amendment to the U.S. Constitution provides that in addition to the right to a speedy trial, an accused has the right to confront his or her accusers and to be represented by counsel. This amendment allows the accused to take advantage of the subpoena power of the court to require witnesses to appear and to testify. It also secures for an accused competent counsel to assist in his or her defense. The test for determining whether or not counsel was competent was outlined in *Strickland v. Washington,* 466 U.S. 668, 693, 104 S.Ct. 2052, 2068, 80 L.Ed.2d 674 (1984). In order to prove ineffective assistance of counsel the defendant must show that the counsel's performance was deficient and that this deficiency prejudiced the outcome of the trial. To show that counsel was deficient, the defendant must demonstrate that counsel failed to meet the level of competency normally demanded of attorneys in criminal cases. The U.S. Supreme Court has held that the benchmark for judging a charge of ineffectiveness is whether or not the attorney's conduct so undermined the proper functioning of the adversarial process that the trial cannot be considered to have produced a just result, *U.S. v. Cronic,* 466 U.S. 648, 104 S.Ct. 2039, 80 L.Ed.2d 657. Decisions of counsel regarding trial strategy are generally not considered as the basis for an ineffective-assistance-of-counsel claim under the Sixth Amendment and the holding of *Strickland v. Washington.*

Evidence

In criminal law, prosecutors and defense counsel rely on three types of evidence. These types of evidence include testimonial evidence, physical evidence, and scientific evidence. Within each of these three types of evidence, there is direct and indirect evidence. Before discussing the three types of evidence, direct and indirect evidence should be defined. Direct evidence is evidence which taken alone is designed to establish a fact or element. For example, a witness can testify that he observed a defendant point a gun at a convenience store clerk and demand money or a videotape could be introduced which shows the scene as the robbery took place. This would serve as direct evidence that an armed robbery had occurred. Indirect evidence is competent evidence which establishes a fact or element by reference. This evidence, although competent, must be viewed by the trier of fact to eliminate all other reasonable explanations. For example, as a trial progressed evidence was presented that revealed that a search of the defendant's residence uncovered a handgun similar to that described by the clerk. Although this is competent evidence and should be considered by the jury, it does not conclusively establish that the defendant committed the armed robbery. Equally true is the following, when the jurors walked into the courtroom it was a sunny spring day; during the trial a man wearing a wet raincoat and carrying a wet umbrella walks into the courtroom. This is indirect evidence that it may be raining outside. If there are no other reasonable explanations or evidence presented, indirect evidence can be used to establish that it is or has been raining.

Testimonial Evidence

Testimonial evidence is best defined as that evidence which is presented through the words of victims, witnesses, and parties to a criminal case. This evidence amounts to the words of those who were present when a crime was committed, those who investigated the crime after it took place, or those who dispute the accused's involvement. Although not required to testify at trial, the words of a defendant prior to trial may be used against him or her. In *Miranda v. Arizona*, 384 U.S. 436, 86 S.Ct. 1602, 16 L.Ed.2d 694 (1966), the court held that before the State may introduce into evidence what purports to be a confession or statement of a defendant, it must first affirmatively show that it was freely and voluntarily given and was not made under the influence of fear, duress, menaces, threats, inducements, or promises. In addition, if the statement was made during custodial interrogation, the State must prove that the accused was advised of his or her *Miranda* rights and intelligently and voluntarily waived those rights. It is not sufficient for the words to be read to an accused; officers and prosecutors looking to use an accused's words against him or her must prove to the court that the accused understood the rights as explained and voluntarily waived the rights.

Physical Evidence

Physical evidence consists of objects or tangible items which are used to demonstrate or establish facts or elements of the crime charged. Physical evidence generally consists of drugs, money, guns, photographs, or other objects found or discovered in conjunction with the investigation of the crime. Objects which are taken from the person or control of a defendant are subject to constitutional protections. The Fourth Amendment to the U.S. Constitution provides that

> The right of the people to be secure in their persons, houses, papers, and effects, against unreasonable searches and seizures, shall not be violated, and no Warrants shall issue, but upon probable cause, supported by Oath or affirmation, and particularly describing the place to be searched, and the persons or things to be seized.

This amendment seeks to protect individuals against unreasonable search and seizure. The prosecution is required to prove that items seized from an accused were done so in a manner so as to enforce the constitutional protections granted to the defendant. Property which is abandoned by a defendant is not constitutionally protected. Therefore, the subject who flees from the police discarding narcotics does not enjoy constitutional protections over the narcotics; however, officers must meet constitutional safeguards when serving search warrants or taking property from an accused's person. These safeguards include those provided by the amendment. Police officers must provide to the court by affidavit or oath sufficient facts to establish probable cause for the issuance of the search warrant. Probable cause exists when the facts and circumstances within the officer's knowledge and of which the officer has reasonably trustworthy information are sufficient to warrant a person of reasonable caution in believing that an offense has been or is being committed.

Evidence may also be seized by officers without the necessity of a warrant under certain jurisprudentially approved circumstances. For instance, officers may seize evidence from the person of an accused when the search is performed incidental to a lawful arrest. Property may be seized from a vehicle when that vehicle is being impounded. Evidence may be seized when it is in the plain view of an officer. For example, a police officer walking through a neighborhood observes a marijuana plant growing in the front room of a home. The officer may seize the plant as evidence. Equally true, an officer conducting a traffic stop who observes a weapon or narcotics on the floorboard of the stopped vehicle may seize the evidence. The officer may not, however, shuffle through the vehicle to uncover the contraband or place it in plain view. These are a few examples of issues common to the constitutional questions involved in searches and seizures by law-enforcement officers. This area of the law is extremely broad and cannot be completely covered here.

Scientific Evidence

Scientific evidence is that field of expertise where physical objects and technology merge to establish facts or elements or to disprove facts or elements. Scientific evidence includes fingerprint analysis, ballistics, blood testing, and DNA testing in blood, saliva, and semen.

Admissibility of Scientific Evidence

The Federal Rules of Evidence provide the basis for most rules of evidence that have been adopted by individual states and that determine the admissibility of scientific evidence. As such, Federal Rule of Evidence 702 provides

> If scientific, technical, or other specialized knowledge will assist the trier of fact to understand the evidence or to determine a fact in issue, a witness qualified as an expert by knowledge, skill, experience, training, or education may testify thereto in the form of an opinion or otherwise.

Subsumed in the requirements of Rule 702 is the premise that expert testimony must be reliable to be admissible, *State v. Cressey,* 628 A.2d 696, 698 (N.H.1993). A recent U.S. Supreme Court case, *Daubert v. Merrell Dow Pharmaceuticals, Inc.,* 509 U.S. 579, 113 S.Ct. 2786, 125 L.Ed.2d 469 (1993), set forth a means for determining reliability of expert scientific testimony and answered many questions as to proper standards for admissibility of expert testimony. The standard for admissibility of evidence in criminal cases is equally applicable to civil litigation and should not be thought of as a separate or distinct standard.

In *Daubert,* the Court was concerned with determining the admissibility of new techniques as bases for expert scientific testimony. Formerly, the test for admissibility of expert scientific testimony was based on a short, citation-free 1928 decision of the District of Columbia Court of Appeals, *Frye v. United States,* 54 App.D.C. 46, 293 F. 1013 (1923). In *Frye,* the rule for admissibility of expert testimony was delineated as requiring "general acceptance" of a technique in its respective scientific field before the technique would be considered admissible. Finding that "a rigid 'general acceptance' requirement would be at odds with 'the liberal thrust of the Federal Rules'," the Court in *Daubert* concluded that *Frye's* "austere standard, absent from and incompatible with [this liberal thrust] should not be applied in federal trials."

The Court replaced *Frye* with a new standard that requires the trial court to act in a gatekeeping function to "ensure that any and all scientific testimony or evidence admitted is not only relevant, but reliable." This requirement stems from a belief that the rules on expert testimony serve to relax "the usual requirement of first-hand knowledge" to ensure reliability on the part of a witness. This relaxation is justified so long as "the expert's opinion has a reliable basis in the knowledge and experience of his discipline."

The reliability of expert testimony is to be ensured by a requirement that there be "a valid scientific connection to the pertinent inquiry as a precondition to admissibility." This connection is to be examined in light of "a preliminary assessment" by the trial court "of whether the reasoning or methodology under-lying the testimony is scientifically valid and of whether the reasoning or meth-odology properly can be applied to the facts in issue." The Court went on to make some suggestions as to how a court could fulfill its gatekeeping role. These involve whether or not the technique had been subjected to peer review and/or publication, the "known or potential rate of error," the existence of "standards controlling the technique's operation," the technique's "refutability," or, more simply put, testability, and, finally, an incorporation of the *Frye* general acceptance in the scientific community as only a factor in the analysis.

The Court also stated that other rules of evidence govern this testimony, mainly Federal Rule of Evidence 403's balancing test that will exclude probative evidence if outweighed by its potential for unfair prejudice. The Court noted the possibility that the expert's testimony can be quite misleading and prejudicial if this gate-keeping role is not properly satisfied, requiring a flexible approach and a careful evaluation of the methodology surrounding the testimony and its conclusions. Conjectures that are probably wrong are of little use, however, in the project of reaching a quick, final, and binding legal judgment — often of great consequence — about a particular set of events in the past. In practice, a gatekeeping role for the judge, no matter how flexible, inevitably on occasion will prevent the jury from learning of authentic insights and innovations. That, nevertheless, is the balance struck by rules of evidence designed not for the exhaustive search for cosmic understanding but for the particularized resolution of legal disputes.

This raises the question of the admissibility of the latest scientific evidence to be commonly used in criminal law and civil law, DNA testing. Both federal and state courts have found that, in general, DNA profiling is a reliable technique and is admissible, for example, *United States v. Jakobetz,* 955 F.2d 786 (2nd Cir.1992); *Hayes v. State,* 660 So.2d 257 (Fla. 6/22/95); *Commonwealth v. Rodgers,* 413 Pa.Super. 498, 605 A.2d 1228 (Ct.1992); *Trimboli v. State,* 817 S.W.2d 785 (Tex.App. Waco 1991), aff'd, 826 S.W.2d 953 (Tex.Cr.App.1992); *Caldwell v. State,* 260 Ga. 278, 393 S.E.2d 436 (1990). Courts have agreed that the principles of DNA profiling and restriction fragment length polymorphism analysis are both relevant and reliable and are thus admissible.

In DNA analysis, as with any type of scientific evidence, it is of utmost importance that the party wishing to introduce such evidence be able to show a "chain of custody." Chain of custody relates to the handling of evidence from the time of retrieval up to testing and until presentation before the trier of fact. The chain of custody is a requirement for admissibility because it substantiates reliability of the evidence by seeking to prevent altering of or tampering with evidence. Although different methods are used from jurisdiction to jurisdiction to protect the chain of custody for different types of evidence, the most common method used for medical evidence is to place the evidence in sealed containers. The containers are sealed with tape upon which identification information is written. As the evidence travels from one individual or agency to another, records are kept of the date, time, and person who handled the evidence. At trial, these persons are called to testify as to when and how they received the evidence, and what they did with it while it was in their possession. This procedure is necessary to illustrate to the court that the evidence is reliable and has not been tampered with or altered in any way.

Last, when attempting to present scientific evidence, the presenter is required to prove that the witness is qualified to render an expert opinion in the field for which the witness has been called. This requires the party calling the witness to show that the witness has knowledge, experience, and training which is sufficient to support his or her statements and conclusions. Generally, courts will look to the educational background, work experience, and training of a potential witness when considering allowing him or her to testify as an expert. Additionally, the court will consider whether or not the potential expert has published any materials on the topic and whether or not the witness has been qualified or refused qualification in any other court. Only after a witness has been qualified as an expert will the court allow a witness to render opinion evidence; otherwise, witnesses are limited to factual testimony only.

The effect of scientific evidence on a criminal case can best be illustrated by the following example. In a rape case, there are generally only two defenses available to defense counsel. The first is consent of the victim. This is tantamount to the defendant admitting to engaging in sexual intercourse with the victim but denying that it was against the victim's will. The second defense is one of faulty identification. In a trial where the first defense was employed the prosecution would seek to introduce evidence to show that the sex act was not consensual. This evidence would include the victim's testimony, photographs of her physical appearance shortly after the incident, and medical evidence of bruising or tearing.

Scientific evidence is not especially useful in this situation because of the defendant's admission that he engaged in sexual intercourse with the victim. However, scientific evidence, in particular DNA testing, becomes especially relevant under the second defense. When an accused claims incorrect identification, the case hinges upon the prosecution's ability to establish that the victim's identification is not incorrect. If the physician who examines the victim shortly after the rape is able to locate semen or other bodily fluids, DNA can be used to link the accused to the crime. The availability of DNA testing has resulted in convictions of sex offenders who in the past would have escaped conviction.

Further Information

This is a brief summary of criminal law, evidence, and procedure. It consists of generalizations which attempt to make it flexible for a diversified group of readers. For a more-detailed explanation of these topics, readers should consult the federal and state laws and cases within their jurisdiction.

Chapter 6

Informed Consent

Julie Anderson

Contents

1-57444-123-X/98
© 1998 by American Association of Legal Nurse Consultants

Objectives

- To define and describe the legal concept of the duty to obtain informed consent
- To state the majority rule for the standard used to measure whether a physician or health care provider has met the legal obligation for obtaining informed consent
- To state who must obtain informed consent
- To list four situations where informed consent must be obtained
- To describe the elements a patient/plaintiff must prove in order to prevail on an informed consent theory
- To identify the resource(s) in a jurisdiction in which to find the law on informed consent

Definitions and Terminology

Informed Consent

Informed consent is a process that involves *disclosure* of information by health care professionals to a competent patient who is presumed to have the capacity to understand it and a *decision* by that patient based on the information received. This is usually thought of in the context of a patient making a decision whether to consent to or refuse a proposed treatment, such as a surgical procedure or medical therapy.

Duty

Duty in this context arises out of the relationship between a patient and a health care provider, wherein the provider has a responsibility to make *reasonable disclosure* to the patient of the risks incident to medical diagnosis and treatment, based on the patient's right to determine what shall be done to his or her own body.

Reasonable Person

The hypothetical "reasonable person" is a means by which to measure a duty to be performed objectively. The reasonable person with respect to informed consent law is a hypothetical objective person in the same or similar circumstances as the patient/plaintiff. The measurement is whether or not this hypothetical objective person would be influenced in his/her decision-making process by disclosure of risks in the same or similar circumstances.

Inherent Risk

Inherent risk is one of the factors considered in determining how much information must be disclosed. This is a risk of a complication that is existent in and inseparable from the procedure contemplated. For example, bleeding or hemorrhage is a possible complication of every surgical procedure, and is thus an inherent risk. Other examples of inherent risks include brain damage or death during anesthesia; allergic sensitivity reactions to blood transfusions, contrast media, or drugs such as antibiotics; and swelling, pain, tenderness, or bleeding at the puncture site of blood vessel perforation for invasive procedures such as radiographic studies or cardiac catheterization that use contrast media.

Something that is done to correct a complication that has occurred is not considered an inherent risk. An example of this would be when intervention is necessary to correct a condition or complication that occurred as a result of a procedure or treatment, such as surgical reexploration to locate and repair bleeding vessels within the abdomen after abdominal surgery.

Material Risk

Materiality of the risk is the other factor that is considered in determining how much information must be disclosed. Materiality involves the relative *importance to the patient* of the specific risk at issue, or whether or not knowledge of the risk could influence the patient's decision to consent. This becomes a balancing test, whereby the court will consider factors such as remoteness of the risk, the probability of the risk occurring, and the severity of the risk. Thus, even a statistically remote risk may be considered material if its severity is such that a patient could consider it in his decision to undergo the proposed therapy or reject it.

An illustrative case involved a patient who developed tardive dyskinesia while on psychotherapeutic medications. Expert testimony at trial was that the statistical risk of this side effect was "small to extremely small," but the court held that the incidence of occurrence, along with evidence of the seriousness of the condition, its permanence, its presentation, the lack of known cures, and its overall effect on the body, was sufficient evidence that the risk was material enough to influence a reasonable person.*

Standards

Standards are the measuring stick by which compliance to a duty is measured. There are essentially three standards or tests by which to measure a health care provider's fulfillment of the obligation to disclose risks inherent in contemplated

---

* *Barclay v. Campbell,* 704 S.W.2d 8 (Tex. 1986).

medical procedures to the patient. The standard used depends on the particular jurisdiction.

> *Subjective test* — This standard considers what inherent risks the *patient/plaintiff believes* were material to his decision to undergo treatment and thus should have been disclosed.

> *Objective standard* — This standard considers what inherent risks a *reasonable patient* in similar circumstances to the patient/plaintiff *would have believed* were material and thus should have been disclosed. Also known as the "reasonable person" rule, this is the majority rule in the United States.

> *Professional standard* — This test considers what risks a *reasonable medical practitioner* of the same school and same or similar community and circumstances would have disclosed to the patient.

Scope of the Duty

A health care professional responsible for a patient's medical care should inform the patient of his or her assessment of the patient's needs, alternative treatment options, the risks attendant to those options, any expectations relevant to those options, and the potential consequences if the patient chooses to forego treatment altogether. Obviously, health care professionals strive to involve patients in their care, and to that extent share information at many different levels. However, certain types of care give rise to a legal duty to share information, and that is where informed consent law comes in. The questions become when is it necessary, who has the duty, and to whom is the duty owed?

When Must Informed Consent Be Obtained?

It is necessary to obtain informed consent whenever a patient is faced with alternative treatment choices and needs information to make an informed decision. The more common situations are those where the patient is faced with a choice involving surgery, anesthesia, blood transfusions, diagnostic invasive procedures such as cardiac catheterization or intravenous pyelogram, radiation treatment for conditions such as cancer or leukemia, or chemotherapy for certain disease states. Other situations that call for informed consent to be obtained from the patient before embarking on the proposed treatment plan include experimental treatments or studies, sterilization, or certain immunizations. Additionally, federal law requires that patients who are to be transferred (or who have refused recommended transfer) to another facility for health care treatment under emergency circumstances must be informed of the risks and benefits of transfer as opposed to staying in the original facility.* These are all situations which require written documentation of consent. A commonly litigated informed consent issue which does not necessarily require formal written documentation is when medications have been prescribed that result in an untoward side effect to the patient, and

---

* See 42 U.S.C. 1395dd (West Supp. 1996), known as the "anti-dumping" statute.

the patient claims he or she would have been influenced *not* to take the medication if the side effect had been known.

Who Performs the Duty?

The Patient's Personal or Attending Physician

Traditionally, the treating physician has the responsibility to explain to patients the alternatives, risks, and benefits to any proposed treatment plan or option. However, medical treatment and surgical procedures often require the involvement of additional health care personnel. In some jurisdictions such as Texas and Washington, the duty has been expanded by statute to include "health care providers." Such statutory language usually includes nurses, hospitals, dentists, podiatrists, pharmacists, and nursing homes as well as physicians. Whether or not this broader language will be held to mean that every entity and every individual has equal informed consent obligations will depend on case law construing such language in the particular jurisdiction. Practically speaking, however, such a construction would present an undue burden and an administrative nightmare for the various medical and health care personnel. Case law in those jurisdictions continues to hold the physician primarily responsible.

One exception to the general rule that the physician is responsible for obtaining informed consent is patient transfer pursuant to the federal anti-dumping statute discussed above. This law specifically mandates that the *hospital*, not the physician, take reasonable steps to obtain a patient's informed consent both for transfer under emergency conditions and for refusal of transfer if transfer is deemed medically appropriate.*

Primary or Referring Physician vs. Specialist or Consultant

The vast majority of jurisdictions are quite clear that the responsibility to obtain informed consent rests with the patient's own attending physician. However, if someone other than the attending physician, such as a specialist or consultant, actually performs a specific treatment or surgery, it then becomes that person's duty to inform the patient of the risks. For example, the anesthesiologist must discuss with the patient possible anesthetic complications during a planned surgery, and the gastroenterologist consulted by the attending physician must discuss risks and hazards of the endoscopy procedure he or she proposes.

Courts generally have been reluctant to impose upon a referring physician a duty to obtain informed consent for a procedure that is to be performed by a specialist who presumably is most familiar with the procedure and its risks and alternatives. However, several jurisdictions have held that a physician who actually prescribes the specific diagnostic procedures to be performed by another physician could be held liable for failure to obtain the patient's informed consent.** These courts reason that the patient's personal physician bears primary responsibility for

---

* 42 U.S.C. 1395dd. .
** See *Bowers v. Talmage,* 159 So.2d 888 (Fla. App. 1963); *Prooth v. Wallsh,* 432 N.Y.S.2d 663 (Sup. Ct. 1980); *Berkey v. Anderson,* 1 Cal.App.3rd 790, 82 Cal.Rptr. 67 (1969); *Jacobs v. Painter,* 530 A.2d 231 (Me. 1987).

all phases of treatment, including procedures performed by specialists to assist in the patient's diagnosis. However, this is not the general rule.

Who Can Give Consent?

The Patient or Authorized Agent

There is a legal presumption that any person who has reached the age of majority (usually 18 years) is competent and may therefore make decisions about medical care. For informed consent, competence refers to decision-making capacity, or the patient's ability to engage in rational decision making, rather than the patient's clinical condition.

Many people have executed health care directives which authorize another person, usually a spouse or significant other, to make health care decisions when and if the person becomes incapacitated and unable to do so. (See section on treatment decisions.) Sometimes a person will have a legal guardian, in which case that person is authorized to give or withhold consent to treatment for the patient. However, health care providers who communicate medical information to a third person who is *not* authorized by the patient to make health care decisions for the patient expose themselves to liability for breach of statutory privileges, for invasion of privacy, or for breach of contract.

Minors

In the case of minors, parents must give consent. If parents are unavailable in a given situation, certain others, usually next of kin in a hierarchical fashion, may be authorized under the jurisdiction's Family Code. Sometimes minors can consent independently. For example, some Family Codes provide that a minor does not have to have parental consent in order to obtain treatment for venereal disease, drug addiction, or pregnancy. In addition, emancipated minors (for example, minors that are married or have been legally adjudicated as emancipated) can consent to treatment without parental participation. What constitutes an emancipated minor differs from state to state, and each state's Family Code should be consulted for those laws.

Mentally Incompetent Persons

Finally, the Family Codes or the Mental Health Codes of a particular state may contain provisions allowing procedures to be performed without the usual consent, where the patient is mentally incompetent or committed to a mental institution and cannot give informed consent because of that mental condition. In Texas, this exception allows for the performance of surgery or other treatment in these circumstances under the advice and consent of three licensed physicians, without consent of the patient's guardian.*

---

* See Tex. Health & Safety Code § 551.041 (Vernon 1992), but these laws will vary from state to state. Refer to each state's Mental Health statutes.

Exceptions to the Duty

There are certain situations when it is not possible or feasible to obtain informed consent, and when those circumstances occur, the duty is suspended.

No Need for Treatment

When a physician determines that a patient is not in need of medical treatment, the physician is not required to inform the patient of possible risks and benefits of nontreatment. Courts have held that the informed consent doctrine cannot be extended to require disclosure of the risks of a recommendation of nontreatment, when the physician, in the exercise of his or her best judgment, believes no treatment is necessary. This has been litigated in the context of alleged failure to diagnose certain conditions, where the patient/plaintiff alleges the physician should have performed further testing.*

Emergency Situations

Consent is implied if a patient is unconscious or otherwise unable to give express consent, immediate treatment is necessary to save the life of the patient, and the harm from failure to treat is imminent and outweighs the harm threatened by the proposed treatment. In such cases, the rule is suspended and the physician is not held liable for failing to obtain informed consent, even if complications occur which would be considered both inherent and material. In this context, the rule requiring parental consent for a minor is suspended, if the minor needs emergency treatment and the parents are not available to give consent.

Therapeutic Privilege

This is a rare exception which allows a physician to withhold information which he/she reasonably believes could hinder treatment or prove harmful to the patient. Also called "not medically feasible," the concept has been employed in an attempt by the defendant physician to justify nondisclosure on the basis that it is in the best interests of the patient not to do so. For example, in the above case involving the psychotherapeutic drug which resulted in the side effect of tardive dyskinesia,** the doctor argued that the patient's schizophrenia rendered him unable to have the reactions of a reasonable person which justified nondisclosure of the risk. The court disagreed, holding that the patient's right to disclosure was not negated just because his doctor did not believe his patient was reasonable. Situations that fall under this category should be extremely rare.

---

* *Scalere v. Stenson,* 211 Cal.App.3rd 1446, 260 Cal.Rptr. 152 (1989).
** *Barclay v. Campbell,* 704 S.W.2d 8 (Tex. 1986).

Practical Considerations

Documentary Requirements

Informed consent, as a process resulting from dialogue between the patient and the physician or health care provider, does not refer simply to a signature at the bottom of a form. However, in all cases where informed consent is required, it should be documented that such consent was in fact obtained by the person who has the duty to obtain it. Sometimes oral disclosure will be sufficient, but the proof becomes problematic if the only witnesses to the conversation were the doctor and the patient.

Executed consent forms should be a part of the patient's permanent medical record. Consent forms can be *general,* such as the broad form a patient signs consenting to medical care and the release of certain information on admission to a hospital, or *specific,* such as the consent form for the administration of blood or blood products. The forms must be signed by the patient or authorized agent, and witnessed, which is usually done by a nurse or other person who must ascertain that the patient has in fact had a discussion with the physician and has given informed consent based on that discussion. If a patient does not speak English, a translator must be involved in the process, and should also sign the consent form. If no form is required or used in a particular facility, narrative notes by the health care provider in the chart should suffice.

In some jurisdictions, specific language is required by statute for certain forms. In Texas, for example, the legislature has determined what constitutes the inherent and material risks for a large number of procedures, and has developed a list of procedures with their attendant risks which is used verbatim by hospitals and health care providers.* If this form is used for disclosure of risks, it is admissible in court and creates a rebuttable presumption that the health care provider has complied with the statutory standard and is not negligent. The Health Codes of a jurisdiction should be consulted for the applicable law in each state.

List A procedures require full disclosure of risks by the physician or health care provider to the patient or person authorized to consent for the patient. Two examples:

Cholecystectomy with or without common bile duct exploration:

1. Pancreatitis
2. Injury to the tube between the liver and the bowel
3. Retained stones in the tube between the liver and the bowel
4. Narrowing or obstruction of the tube between the liver and the bowel
5. Injury to the bowel and/or intestinal obstruction

Myelography:

1. Chronic pain
2. Transient headache, nausea, vomiting
3. Numbness
4. Impaired muscle function

---

* Tex. Rev. Civ. Stat. Ann. Art. 4590i (Vernon 1997).

List B procedures require no disclosure. Examples include local anesthesia, hemorrhoidectomy, myringotomy, needle biopsy or aspiration, lumbar puncture, many invasive radiologic procedures, and others.

Proof in Court

Informed consent as a theory of liability on which a plaintiff tries to obtain a money judgment is most frequently combined with a medical negligence theory rather than being the sole theory in a claim. The elements of the plaintiff's case in an informed consent action are the same as in general medical negligence: duty, breach of duty, and proximate cause of the injury.

Under the majority rule, plaintiffs asserting informed consent claims must prove (1) that the complication or condition in question was a risk *inherent* in the procedure performed, (2) that a reasonable person fully informed of all inherent risks would *not* have consented to the treatment in question, and (3) that the patient/plaintiff was in fact *injured* by the occurrence of this complication or condition about which he or she was not informed. The nexus between the failure to disclose a particular risk and the later occurrence of that complication must be shown in order for the patient/plaintiff to prevail in the lawsuit.

Generally, expert medical testimony is necessary to prove the plaintiff's case in a negligence action based on informed consent (and to defend a physician's actions in this regard). The expert must testify regarding the inherency of the risk complained of and all other facts concerning the risk which show that knowledge of the risk could influence a reasonable person in making a decision to consent to the procedure.

Viability of the Cause of Action

Practically speaking, an informed consent claim is often difficult to sell to a jury, especially if the procedure or treatment in question is lifesaving, curative, or necessary for a serious medical condition. Often it becomes a swearing match between patient and physician whether or not discussion of risks was actually held, even if there is documentation. In cases where the defendant physician or health care provider has proven compliance with a statutory or common law duty, and a properly executed consent form is part of the record, the patient/plaintiff must resort to claiming that the *scope* of the disclosure was inadequate, or that the *validity* of the consent is in question. In that regard, the patient may claim that he or she did not have the capacity to give consent, or that he or she did not sign the form. Contract defenses such as fraud, mutual mistake, accident, or undue influence are typically employed in such situations.

On the other hand, the reasonable person standard increases the difficulty of a physician obtaining summary judgment, because the defendant must negate that knowledge of a particular risk of injury could influence a reasonable person in making a treatment decision. This typically is a question of fact for the jury rather than a question of law for the court. (Summary judgment is the process by which a court decides, based on evidence presented by the defendant doctor, that there is no genuine issue of material fact for a jury to consider, and in essence dismisses the case against the defendant as a matter of law.)

Resources

There are a variety of resources in every jurisdiction that can be consulted to determine the law and to research the issue.

External Sources

These sources include institutional and individual licensing provisions, accreditation standards, and federal and state statutes and regulations. The state hospital licensing laws and the medical, dental, podiatric, chiropractic, and nurse practice acts of each state are excellent sources, and should be consulted at the outset. While there is no universal federal law specific to informed consent in general, the previously mentioned federal anti-dumping statute speaks to the specific issue of patient transfers and the consent required therein. Also, because of Medicare or Medicaid requirements for those entities receiving federal monies as providers, a health care facility may be indirectly affected in this area. Federal courts will follow state law when faced with this issue in a federal lawsuit. State statutes and regulations that might address informed consent issues include tort reform laws or statutes regulating the insurance industry. Besides statutes addressing informed consent requirements, the Joint Commission for the Accreditation of Healthcare Organizations (JCAHO) requires a hospital or health care facility to have a policy on informed consent which is developed by the medical staff and governing body of the hospital that is consistent with any legal requirements, and, for the facility to be accredited, every patient medical record must contain evidence of informed consent for any procedures and treatments that are covered by such policy.* Finally, legal literature such as law review articles and legal practice guides can be consulted for guidance on the applicable law.

Internal Sources

These resources include hospital policies and procedures, individual job descriptions, and possibly other hospital documents such as contracts, that might identify or define certain responsibilities with respect to informed consent. Medical staff bylaws, rules, and regulations are required to address the issue. Local custom (practices within other hospitals in the community) may also be informative for the purposes of comparison.

Conclusion

The law of informed consent is fairly simple and straightforward, being based on negligence principles. Variations among jurisdictions in the standards for proof of the elements are not extreme, and can easily be found by consulting the appropriate authorities.

---

* See the *Accreditation Manual for Hospitals,* published by the Joint Commission, for the exact language in a given year.

Discussion Questions

1. The duty to obtain informed consent prior to a medical procedure is the responsibility of
   a. The attending physician
   b. The nurse obtaining the patient's signature on the consent form
   c. The physician who is to perform the medical procedure
   d. The patient
   (Answer: c)

2. Most jurisdictions follow which rule for measuring whether or not a health care provider has met the obligation for obtaining informed consent:
   a. The reasonable professional standard
   b. The reasonable person standard
   c. The subjective patient standard
   d. The rational expectations standard
   (Answer: b)

3. A physician must obtain the patient's informed consent for
   a. Administration of blood or blood products
   b. An elective cholecystectomy
   c. Voluntary sterilization
   d. Transfer to another hospital at the patient's request
   e. All of the above
   f. None of the above
   g. A, b, and c only
   (Answer: g)

4. In order to prove a case, a plaintiff relying on an informed consent theory must present testimony showing that
   a. The condition about which the plaintiff is complaining is an inherent risk attendant to the procedure the plaintiff underwent
   b. The plaintiff in fact developed this condition
   c. The plaintiff would not have consented to the procedure had he/she been informed of the risk
   d. All of the above
   e. A and b only
   f. A and c only
   (Answer: e)

Glossary

Informed consent: The process of disclosure of information, usually regarding proposed medical treatment, by health care professionals to a competent patient who is presumed to have the capacity to understand the information, and a decision by that patient based on the information received.

Inherent risk: A risk of a complication or condition that is existent in and inseparable from the medical procedure or treatment.

Material risk: A risk that, if the patient was informed of it, could influence his or her decision to consent to the proposed treatment or procedure.

Summary judgment: The process by which a court decides, based on evidence presented by the defendant doctor, that there is no genuine issue of material fact for a jury to consider. Therefore, the court dismisses the case against the defendant as a matter of law, the case does not go to trial, and the patient/plaintiff recovers nothing from the defendant.

Chapter 7

Treatment Decisions

Gail N. Friend, Jennifer L. Rangel, and Brett A. Storm

Contents

1-57444-123-X/98

> Every human being of adult years and sound mind has a right to determine what shall be done with his own body.
>
> *Schloendorf v. Society of New York Hosp.*
> 105 N.E. 92, 93 (N.Y. 1914)

Justice Cardoza's statement in 1914 has been quoted by numerous courts in determining a person's right to make the treatment decisions affecting his or her own person. As discussed in the preceding chapter, every patient has the "right" to give informed consent before medical treatment is rendered. The corollary to this is the "right" of a patient to refuse medical treatment, even lifesaving medical treatment. The law in the U.S. is generally settled regarding a competent patient's ability to refuse treatment. However, many issues arise in regard to the rights of an incompetent patient.

Origin and History of the Right to Refuse Medical Treatment

The right to refuse medical treatment did not reach center stage in the courts until recently. The majority of the law concerning this issue has been created in the last 10 years. The reason for this recent abundance of court and legislative interest is the advances in medical technology that make it possible for a patient's life to be sustained by machines and artificial means on the brink of death. Patients may not desire that their lives be extended if the quality of life has dissipated. Consequently, the legislatures and the courts must carve out guidelines for the termination of life-sustaining medical treatment when patients or their legal representatives refuse to consent to the treatment or seek withdrawal of current treatment.

The U.S. Supreme Court recognizes that a person has a constitutionally pro-tected liberty interest in refusing unwanted medical treatment. In *Cruzan v. Missouri Department of Health*, the Supreme Court held that this liberty interest arises from the Fourteenth Amendment to the Constitution. An individual's liberty interest in the refusal of medical treatment must be balanced against a state's interests in preserving life, preventing suicide, protecting the integrity of the medical profession, and protecting innocent third parties. Thus, this "right" to refuse medical treatment is not absolute. However, the courts generally hold that a competent person's interest in refusal outweighs the state's interests. The balancing test customarily becomes a serious obstacle only when a patient is incompetent.

In addition to the U.S. Constitution, the right to refuse treatment has been found to be guaranteed by the common law in the states. This means that courts have held that the case law in individual states grants patients this right. The common law right flows from the Informed Consent Doctrine which requires a patient's informed consent before treatment is rendered. For example, in 1989, the Illinois Supreme Court held that Illinois common law provides a person the right to reject medical treatment. The court in *In re Estate of Longeway* determined that this right encompassed all treatment including life-sustaining treatment such as artificial hydration and nutrition.

Other state courts have relied on their own constitutions or state statutes in concluding that a person has the right to decline medical care. In the wake of suits brought by patients and their families or guardians, state legislatures have enacted various statutes to address the mechanics of refusal of treatment. Courts may find that these statutes enunciate such a right. For example, the Illinois Living Will Act expressly states that, "[t]he legislature finds that persons have a fundamental right to control the decisions relating to the rendering of their own medical care, including the right to have death delaying procedures withheld or withdrawn in instances of a terminal condition." Further, many state courts have held that their state constitutions create a privacy right which encompasses the right to refuse treatment. Consequently, many state constitutions are stronger than the U.S. Constitution in providing a basis for the right to refuse treatment as opposed to merely establishing a liberty interest.

Categories of Refusal

Refusal of medical treatment can include refusal of a specific medical procedure like surgery, refusal of medications, or refusal of artificial treatment such as a respirator or nutrition and hydration through a tube. Refusal might also take the form of a "do not resuscitate" (DNR) order. This is a physician's order that a patient is not to be resuscitated by any means if his heart should stop or he stops breathing spontaneously. Thus, cardiopulmonary resuscitation (CPR) should not be administered.

All states empower parents with the right to consent to medical treatment for their minor child. Along with this responsibility comes the right to refuse treatment for their child. However, when a parent refuses to consent to lifesaving treatment for a child, the state may intervene to save the child's life. In most states, the state agency responsible for protecting children may petition a court to take temporary guardianship of a child for the purpose of consenting to treatment. This frequently occurs in cases where a parent refuses medical treatment for religious reasons. Thus, the parent's right to refuse medical treatment for a child may be limited by the state. In such a situation, the state's interest in preserving the child's life outweighs the parent's rights because the child is too young to legally express what his or her wishes would be.

A Competent Patient's Right to Refuse

The law has principally determined that a competent patient has the "right" to refuse any medical treatment. This right is recognized regardless of the potential outcome of the refusal. In acknowledging this prerogative, courts have upheld an individual's right to refuse blood transfusions, resuscitation, and artificial life-sustaining measures such as hydration and nutrition intravenously or through a nasogastric or other tube. A competent person's right to reject medical treatment has been challenged by physicians and hospitals but the patient's wishes usually prevail.

In *Bouvia v. Superior Court of Los Angeles County,* a California appellate court held that a competent patient had the right to refuse life-sustaining medical treatment and the state and her physicians must abide by her refusal. In this case, Elizabeth Bouvia was a 28-year-old woman who suffered from severe cerebral palsy and, as a result, was a quadriplegic. Ms. Bouvia was in severe pain, bedridden, and completely immobile except for the ability to move a few fingers on one hand and some slight head and facial movements. Ms. Bouvia, who was mentally competent and college educated, expressed her desire to die and requested the removal of the nasogastric tube supplying her with hydration and nutrition. She dictated her wishes regarding removal of the tube to her assistant who wrote them down and she then signed the paper with an "x" made by holding a pen in her mouth.

The court held that Ms. Bouvia had the right to control her own medical treatment and, thus, required the withdrawal of the nasogastric tube. The right to have life-support equipment disconnected is not limited to terminally ill patients or patients in a persistent vegetative state. After stating that it was immaterial that the removal of the tube might hasten Ms. Bouvia's death, the court commented: "[b]eing competent she has the right to live out the remainder of her natural life in dignity and peace," *Bouvia v. Superior Court of Los Angeles County,* 225 Cal. Rptr. 297, 305 (Cal. Ct. App. 1986). According to this court, Ms. Bouvia's right to decide for herself what treatment she received outweighed any state interests in preserving her life. Most courts, although not employing as strong language as the California court, hold that a competent patient has a right to refuse medical treatment which must be respected by the state.

Religious Motivation for Refusal of Lifesaving Treatment

The right to refuse medical treatment is further strengthened when the patient refuses on the basis of religion. The most well-known cases involve patients of the Jehovah Witness religion who refuse the administration of all blood products even when such treatment is necessary to save or extend their lives. The courts customarily respect an individual's First Amendment right to freedom of religion even if the exercise of this right places the individual's life in jeopardy. Regardless, hospitals and physicians are trained to save lives and tend to feel an overwhelming obligation to at least attempt to administer the lifesaving treatment. For this reason and to avoid potential liability from failure to provide medical care, the health care providers of an individual refusing treatment tend to seek court guidance when dealing with this issue.

In *Fosmire v. Nicoleau,* the New York Court of Appeals held that a competent adult has a right to refuse a blood transfusion. The patient lost a substantial amount of blood following a cesarean section to deliver her child. She refused the transfusions because her religion, Jehovah's Witness, prohibited this treatment. The hospital sought a court order to administer the transfusion. The court signed an order without notice to the patient or her family granting authorization for the hospital to administer blood products to the patient to save her life. The patient appealed the decision even though she had already received two transfusions. The appellate court vacated the court order and held that the court should never have granted permission for the transfusion to occur because the patient had the right to refuse even lifesaving treatment and the state's interests do not override this right.

Despite the body of law to the contrary, many lower-level state courts have and continue to order blood transfusions over the patient's strong objections in order to save the individual's life. As illustrated above, the orders which have been appealed are usually overruled by the courts holding that the patient's refusal must be respected. However, in most cases, the damage has already been done. For example, a U.S. district court in Connecticut granted permission to a hospital to administer blood to a patient who refused the transfusion on the ground that the treatment was against his Jehovah Witness religion. In *United States v. George,* the transfusion was administered immediately following the court's order and the patient had no time to appeal the ruling. An appeal could potentially nullify the court's order but could not undo the transfusion. Thus, the main purpose of an appeal is to protect the patient against future transfusions.

A few courts have considered limiting an individual's right to refuse when the individual has minor children. In a Supreme Court of Massachusetts case, a competent adult was hospitalized for a bleeding ulcer and her physicians believed that a blood transfusion was necessary to save her life. In *Norwood Hospital v. Munoz,* the patient, a Jehovah Witness, refused the transfusion on religious grounds. The hospital sought a court order to administer the transfusion in order to protect the patient's child from abandonment by his mother. The court held that the state's interest did not override the individual's right to refuse medical treatment absent compelling evidence that the child would be abandoned if the mother died and only the father was left to raise the child. In this case, there was no evidence that the father with the support of his family could not raise the child. It would be very rare that compelling evidence would exist on this issue. The majority of the states hold that an individual with a minor child has the same right to refuse medical treatment as any other competent adult.

However, if the patient is a minor, the right of the minor and their parents to refuse is not nearly so absolute. Because a minor lacks the capacity to consent or refuse medical treatment, this right advances to the minor's parents. Generally, a parent has the right to make medical decisions for a minor child. Nevertheless, this right is not unconditional. If a patient's refusal of treatment endangers the child and, thus, amounts to neglect, virtually all states allow a temporary guardian to be appointed or the state to intervene in order to consent to the treatment. The courts reason that such patients lack the capacity to decide what their beliefs are for themselves and, thus, should not lose their life based on the parent's beliefs.

The issue becomes more complicated when the minor is mature. The Illinois Supreme Court held that a 17 year old was a mature minor and, thus, had the right to refuse medical treatment. In the case of *In re E.G.,* the minor suffered from leukemia and needed blood transfusions to extend her life. The state filed a petition seeking an order stating that the minor was neglected because her parents would not consent to the transfusion and further that the court appoint a guardian to consent. The juvenile court granted the order but the family appealed and the appellate court and Supreme Court vacated the order. The Illinois Supreme Court determined that if the evidence is clear and convincing that a minor is mature enough to appreciate the consequences of her actions, the minor has the same right as an adult to refuse medical treatment. This right has generally been conferred only on minors between the ages of 16 and 17 on a case-by-case basis. A hospital faced with a minor's refusal of medical treatment would be wise to seek state intervention and court guidance.

The courts have also grappled with a pregnant patient's right to refuse lifesaving treatment which will affect the birth/life of the unborn child. An Illinois appellate court determined that a competent adult patient has the right to refuse treatment regardless of pregnancy. In the case of *In re Baby Boy Doe,* a pregnant woman's fetus was diagnosed as receiving insufficient oxygen in the womb and her physicians recommended an immediate cesarean section or induced labor. The patient refused both treatments on the basis of her religion. She had complete faith in God's healing powers and chose to await natural childbirth. The physicians and hospital contacted the state's attorney who petitioned a court to appoint the hospital as custodian of the fetus for immediate delivery. The court denied the petition and upheld the patient's right to refuse treatment. This decision was affirmed by the appellate court holding that the potential impact on the fetus from the patient's refusal was legally irrelevant because under Illinois law a fetus has no rights separate from the mother while *in utero.* In this case, no harm resulted from the patient's refusal as she delivered a healthy baby naturally. Nonetheless, positive results such as these do not always occur.

In contrast to Illinois, a minority of courts have limited the rights of a pregnant woman in regard to refusal of medical treatment. In 1981, the Supreme Court of Georgia affirmed a court order authorizing the performance of a cesarean section and the administration of any necessary blood transfusions to a pregnant patient refusing the treatment on the basis of her religion. The patient and her husband believed that the Lord had healed her body and that whatever happened would be the Lord's will. In *Jefferson v. Griffin Spalding County Hospital Authority,* the patient was in her 34th week of pregnancy and due to deliver any time. Her physicians discovered that she suffered from complete placenta previa and, therefore, the child could not survive natural childbirth. The mother had only a 50% chance of surviving childbirth. According to the doctors, a cesarean was necessary to save both the mother and the fetus. Due to the viability of the child and the nearness of the patient's due date, the court granted temporary custody of the fetus to the Department of Human Resources with the authority to make all medical decisions. The court ordered the patient to submit to a sonogram and if the sonogram showed placenta previa, to submit to a cesarean. The Supreme Court of Georgia upheld this order finding that the fetus had the right to the state's protection. This decision is in the minority as most states do not recognize the rights of a fetus especially as superior to the mother's right to refuse treatment. However, many states have established that CPR may not be withheld from a pregnant woman regardless of her wishes.

Consequently, the law is relatively settled that a competent adult has the right to refuse medical treatment on the basis of religion. In most states, this right extends to a pregnant woman irrespective of the effect of the refusal on the fetus. The only absolute limitation on this right is if the patient is a minor, in which case, the state will normally appoint a temporary guardian to consent to the treatment in order to protect the child's life.

The Right of an Incompetent Person to Refuse Medical Treatment

In general, the courts realize that the right to refuse medical treatment extends to incompetent patient. In *Brophy v. New England Sinai Hospital, Inc.,* the Supreme Judicial Court of Massachusetts reasoned incompetent patients as well as competent individuals must have this right because the "value of human dignity extends to both." Nevertheless, the issues concerning an individual's right to refuse medical treatment become further complicated when the individual is incompetent. A few examples of incompetent patients are persons who are minors, in comas, mentally deteriorated, or mentally ill. Pursuant to law, such persons cannot legally consent to medical treatment or make decisions for themselves. A surrogate decision maker, usually a parent, spouse, other family member, or an appointed guardian, makes decisions for the patient. However, the law limits a surrogate decision maker's right to refuse lifesaving or life sustaining medical treatment for an incompetent individual. The courts and legislatures fear abuse if surrogates are allowed the unrestricted right to withdraw or refuse treatment. In response to these concerns, a number of means have been developed by states to determine the legality of a surrogate's refusal of treatment.

A Person is Incompetent But Made Desires Known When Competent

The individual states provide varying methods through which a competent person may memorialize his desires regarding medical treatment in the event the person becomes incompetent. In order to encourage individuals to execute such directives, the Federal Patient Self-Determination Act requires hospitals, nursing homes, hospices, home health agencies, and other specified entities to provide written information to each individual receiving medical care regarding the individual's rights under state law to make decisions regarding medical treatment including the right to accept or refuse treatment and to execute advanced directives. The health care provider must document in the patient's medical record whether or not the patient has executed an advanced directive. In addition, the health care provider must ensure compliance with the requirements of state law regarding executed directives.

The National Conference of Commissioners on Uniform State Laws proposed the Uniform Rights of the Terminally Ill Act. This act established uniform provisions regarding powers of attorney for health care, living wills, and other directives. Most states have adopted at least portions of this act. This section discusses three specific types of directives and the statutory guidelines for each. These directives include DNR orders, living wills, and durable powers of attorney for health care.

Do-Not-Resuscitate Orders

A patient's consent to administer emergency care including CPR is presumed in an emergency medical situation. Thus, due to the urgency of the patient's condition, health care professionals are compelled to initiate emergency care without inquiring into the patient's wishes. However, the majority of the states have enacted legislation authorizing and prescribing guidelines for the use of DNR orders. This is a statement that resuscitation methods should not be attempted on a patient if the need arises. DNR orders are different from written directives because they are executed by a physician with the patient's or his representative's consent when the physician believes that a situation requiring resuscitation is anticipated. Ordinarily, the patient has already been diagnosed with a terminal condition or is in a persistent vegetative state when the order is issued. In contrast, written directives are executed by the patient, when he is competent, in anticipation of the need to make important medical decisions when the patient becomes incompetent. Most written directives expressly consent to a DNR order when the circumstances support its issuance.

Most statutes regulating the use of DNR orders specifically apply to medical emergencies which occur either (1) in a health care facility such as a hospital or nursing home or (2) outside of a facility, for example, in a patient's home. Many states authorize the use of a DNR identification device which the patient wears so the emergency medical technicians will be aware of and honor the DNR order. Although the statutes generally allow for the issuance of DNR orders for competent and incompetent patients, a few states' legislatures require that DNR orders only be issued upon a competent patient's consent. The statutes also vary in regard to who may consent for an incompetent patient, whether witnesses are required, and if the patient must have a terminal condition. A limited number of statutes expressly require that the patient's condition be terminal while other states' statutes are silent on this issue apparently relying on the physicians to only issue DNR orders in appropriate circumstances. Even though they vary slightly on the specific requirements for issuing a DNR order, the state statutes have the same general purpose. Following is a sampling of the specific requirements in a few states in order to provide an overview of the law in this area.

Georgia has enacted a statute providing that an adult competent patient with decision-making capacity may consent to a DNR order and its implementation at a later time. This consent may be oral or in writing. A physician may issue the DNR order after the patient has provided consent. In the event that the patient is incompetent, an authorized surrogate decision maker may consent based upon what the patient would have wanted under the circumstances. In addition, the parent of a minor patient may consent. However, if the physician determines that the minor is of sufficient maturity to understand the nature and effect of a DNR order, the order will not be valid unless the minor patient's consent is obtained. If the patient is incompetent and no authorized decision maker exists, the attending physician may issue an order provided that a second physician concurs in writing in the patient's medical record that the order is appropriate; an ethics committee or similar panel concurs in the physicians' opinions; and the patient is receiving inpatient or outpatient treatment or is a resident of a health care facility other than a home health agency or hospice.

Similarly, the Texas statute that governs out-of-hospital DNR orders states that a competent person may execute a written DNR order directing health care professionals to withhold CPR provided that the patient has been diagnosed by a physician as having a terminal condition. The order must be signed by the attending physician, the patient in the presence of two witnesses, and the two witnesses. The fact that an order exists and the reasons it was executed should be noted in the patient's medical record. A standard form for out-of-hospital DNR orders has been prescribed by the Texas statute. In addition, Texas allows for the issuance of a DNR order by nonwritten communication. In this situation, a competent adult patient must consent in the presence of the attending physician and two witnesses. The order must be signed by the witnesses and the doctor and the issuance of the order noted in the patient's medical record.

The Texas statute also provides for issuance of an out-of-hospital DNR order when the patient is incompetent and, thus, cannot provide consent. If the patient is a minor, the patient's parents, legal guardian, or managing conservator may consent. For adult incompetent patients, the patient's legal guardian, proxy, or agent designated by durable health care power of attorney may consent to the issuance of the DNR order. In the event that the adult does not have an agent, proxy, or guardian, the attending physician and at least two qualified relatives may executive the DNR order. A qualified relative means a person in the following order of priority: (1) the patient's spouse; (2) a majority of the patient's reasonably available children; (3) the patient's parents; and (4) the patient's nearest living relative. The decision to consent to a DNR order for an incompetent patient must, if possible, be based on knowledge of what the person would desire. The order must be executed in the presence of at least two witnesses.

In California, a succinct statute establishes only that a DNR order must be a written document signed by the patient or a legally recognized surrogate decision maker, a physician, and a surgeon. In contrast, Kansas has enacted a statute requiring that DNR orders only be issued by a physician upon the consent of the patient. Further, the order must be in writing, signed by the patient or another at the patient's expressed direction, dated, and signed in the presence of a witness. New York's statute requires the consent of an adult with capacity. If the patient is in the hospital, consent may be expressed orally in the presence of a physician associated with the hospital and another witness. A patient may also express consent in writing, dated, and signed in the presence of two witnesses. If the physician determines in writing that, to a reasonable degree of medical certainty, a discussion of resuscitation would cause the patient to suffer immediate and severe injury, he may issue an order without consent after receiving the written concurrence of another physician, ascertaining the wishes of the patient to the extent possible, listing the reasons for not consulting the patient in the medical records, and obtaining the consent of the patient's agent or a surrogate decision maker.

The majority of the statutes provide immunity for health care professionals acting in good faith based on reliance on a DNR order. Professionals either providing or withholding CPR pursuant to a DNR statute are protected from civil, criminal, or professional liability. This means that disciplinary action may not be taken by a licensing board and they may not be sued by the patient or his family. In addition, the state may not criminally prosecute a professional. This immunity generally applies if the professional withholds resuscitation pursuant to a DNR order or provides resuscitation because he is reasonably unaware of the order or believed it to be revoked.

When a statute requires that a witness sign the DNR order certifying that the patient or another qualified person consented to the order, the witness generally must fulfill certain requirements. Texas provides a basic example of these requirements. In Texas, a witness may not be related by blood or marriage to the patient; entitled to any part of the declarant's estate pursuant to a will or by operation of law; an attending physician; an employee of the attending physician; an employee of the health care facility in which the declarant is a patient if the employee is providing direct patient care to the patient or is directly involved in the financial affairs of the facility; another patient in the health care facility; or a person who has a claim against any part of the patient's estate after the patient's death. Most states attach similar limitations to who may serve as a witness. As illustrated, the statutes regulating DNR orders vary only minimally from state to state. Nevertheless, nurses should consult the statute in the state in which they practice.

Living Wills

Living wills, another type of directive, are recognized and respected by health care professionals in most states. Also known as advanced directives to physicians, living wills must adhere to specific statutory guidelines in order to be honored in many jurisdictions. Customarily, the statutes governing living wills are called Natural Death Acts. A living will is generally defined as a written expression by a competent adult of his desires regarding life-sustaining treatment in the event of a terminal illness or injury. Because the statutory guidelines regarding living wills vary among the states, a sampling of state statutes will be discussed in this section. These statutes generally provide that a directive does not apply if or when the patient is pregnant.

In Texas, the Natural Death Act declares that a competent adult may execute a written directive at any time provided that the directive is signed in the presence of two witnesses who also sign the directive. The declarant must notify his attending physician of the existence of the directive. However, if the patient is unable to communicate, another person may notify the physician. The directive should be placed in the declarant's medical record. Customarily, the directive provides that the declarant does not wish for life-sustaining procedures to be used to artificially prolong life if the declarant has an incurable or irreversible condition caused by an injury, disease, or terminal illness as certified by two physicians and the attending physician determines that death is imminent without the application of life-sustaining treatment. In addition, the directive may name a proxy who the declarant authorizes to make treatment decisions if the declarant is comatose, incompetent, or incapable of communication. The directive may be revoked by the declarant at any time and the patient's current communicated desires always outweigh the force of the directive. For example, if the patient has executed a living will, but requests a life-sustaining procedures after being certified as having a terminal condition, the current wishes must be respected.

Pursuant to the Texas statute, a competent adult may execute a directive orally if it is issued in the presence of the attending physician and two witnesses. The witnesses must meet the requirements set out above under DNR orders. The physician must make the existence of the directive an entry in the declarant's medical record and the witnesses must sign the entry. In addition, a directive may be executed on the behalf of a minor, under the age of 18, by the patient's adult spouse or, if none, the parent or legal guardian.

The Texas Natural Death Act states that a physician, health care facility, or health professional that causes or participates in the withholding or withdrawal of a life-sustaining procedure in accordance with a patient's directive and the statute is not civilly, criminally, or professionally liable as a result of that action unless he or she was negligent. Thus, a nurse would not be subject to a civil suit, criminal charges, or an action by the licensing board for unprofessional conduct if the nurse acted pursuant to a living will which meets the requirements of the statute. A professional is potentially liable only if he or she is proven to have acted negligently. For example, if a valid living will exists but there is a later dated physicians progress note stating that patient has revoked the living will, the nurse may be negligent if the nurse fails to read the note and as a consequence, the patient is not resuscitated.

In Texas, a directive is not honored until the patient is certified as having a terminal condition which will lead to death within a relatively short period of time absent life-sustaining treatment. Illinois has enacted an analogous statute. A directive executed pursuant to the Illinois Living Will Act may only be given effect when the patient has a terminal condition defined as "an incurable and irreversible condition which is such that death is imminent and the application of death delaying procedures serves only to prolong the dying process," Illinois Living Will Act, Ill. Rev. Stat. ch. 755 para. 35/2(h) L(1966). Arguably, a directive will not be followed if a patient is in a persistent unconscious state but is expected to live for years and, thus, is not in a terminal condition. Nevertheless, Illinois courts have construed the definition of terminal to include persons in a persistent unconscious state if death would be imminent upon withdrawal of the life-sustaining treatment. The guidelines for executing a directive and immunities provided for following a directive are identical to the Texas statutory requirements.

In contrast, California's Natural Death Act provides that a directive may be given effect when a patient is either in a terminal condition or a persistent unconscious state. The California statute is virtually identical to the Texas statute in the requirements for the execution of the directive. The directive becomes operative when it is communicated to the attending physician. In addition, the attending physician along with another physician, who examined the patient and confirmed the diagnosis, certify in writing that the patient is in a permanent unconscious condition or has a terminal condition and is no longer able to make medical decisions. However, a living will has no force in California if it was executed while the patient was a patient in a skilled nursing facility or a long-term care facility unless one of the witnesses was a patient advocate or ombudsman designated by the State Department of Aging.

As with the Texas law, a provider honoring a directive or acting in accord with reasonable medical standards is immune from civil, criminal, or professional liability. A physician or other provider may presume that a declaration is valid in the absence of contrary knowledge. Regardless of these immunities, California has enacted strict penalties for failure to comply with the Natural Death Act. A number of other states have adopted this approach. Under this section of the statute, a physician or provider who is unwilling to comply with the directive must transfer the individual to another physician or health care provider who will honor the directive. Failure to do so constitutes a misdemeanor. In addition, a physician who willfully fails to record a determination of terminal condition or permanent unconscious state or the terms of the directive in the patient's medical record commits a misdemeanor. An individual who willfully conceals, defaces, or obliterates another person's directive without the declarant's consent, falsifies a revocation, or coerces or fraudulently induces an individual to execute a directive is guilty of a misdemeanor, Also, a person who requires or prohibits a directive as a condition of providing insurance or receiving health care services has committed a misdemeanor. California attaches an even more severe penalty for an individual who falsifies or forges another person's directive or willfully conceals personal knowledge of a revocation with the intent to cause the withholding or withdrawal of life support. Such conduct constitutes unlawful homicide if life-sustaining treatment is withheld or withdrawn and death hastened as a direct result.

The Illinois Living Will Act also imposes a series of penalties for violating the statute. The Illinois penalties are not as severe as the California penalties but still serve to protect patients from the desires of others overriding their wishes regarding life-sustaining treatments. The willful concealing, obliterating, defacing, or damaging of another's directive or the falsifying of a revocation creates civil liability. This means that the patient or his representative may bring a civil suit against the wrongdoer. Further, a physician who willfully fails to notify the health care facility or fails to comply with the statute is guilty of unprofessional conduct under the Medical Practice Act. If a physician willfully fails to record the determination of a terminal condition in the medical record without giving notice to the patient or the patient's representative of the physician's refusal to follow the directive so that the patient could have been transferred is also guilty of violating the Medical Practice Act. The Living Will Act provides that a physician who records a determination in the medical record is presumed to be acting in good faith unless it is proven that the physician violated the standard of reasonable medical care. In addition, the statute follows California in providing that requiring or prohibiting the execution of a directive is a misdemeanor. Illinois adopts California's section regarding criminal homicide calling such a crime involuntary manslaughter.

As illustrated, the majority of state Natural Death or Living Will Acts follow the same basic rules regarding the execution and use of directives. The states vary mainly on the determination of when a patient has a qualifying condition allowing for the use of the directive. Some states require the patient be certified as having a terminal condition, while other states allow directives to be utilized when a patient is in a persistent vegetative state, also. Many states enforce serious penalties against providers and other persons who refuse to comply with a directive, prevent the use of a valid directive, or knowingly cause an invalid or revoked directive to be followed causing a patient's death. However, all of the statutes provide immunity from civil, criminal, or professional prosecution for following the statutes and a directive in good faith.

Durable Health Care Powers of Attorney

A Durable Health Care Power of Attorney is a document executed by a declarant which delegates to an agent the authority to make health care decisions if the declarant becomes incompetent or incapable of communication. Many states have enacted legislation creating rules for the execution and use of a durable power of attorney for health care. However, some states rely on older established statutes regulating general powers of attorney. Following is a representative sample of the durable power of attorney for health care statutes.

The Texas Durable Power of Attorney for Health Care Act provides that a competent adult may execute a document appointing an agent to make health care decisions for the person in the event the person becomes incompetent. The principal may not designate as an agent his or her health care or residential care provider or an employee of the provider unless the employee is a relative. The power of attorney must be signed by the principal (the person executing the document) in the presence of two witnesses. The witnesses must meet the same requirements as set out above in the DNR order section of this chapter and they must attest that the principal appears to be of sound mind to make a health care decision, stated in the witnesses' presence that he or she was aware of the nature of the durable power of attorney, voluntarily signed the document free from any duress, and requested the witnesses to serve as witnesses. If the principal is physically unable to sign, another person may sign for the principal in the principal's presence and at the principal's express direction. The power of attorney may designate an alternative agent should the first designatee be incapable of acting as an agent. The power of attorney is not effective unless the principal asserts and signs that the principal has received and understood the contents of a statutorily prescribed statement disclosing the effect and requirements of a power of attorney. The document is effective indefinitely but may be revoked at any time.

A designated agent may exercise decision-making authority only if the principal's attending physician certifies in the medical record that the principal lacks the authority to make medical decisions. The agent must make health care decisions in consultation with the attending physician and according to the principal's wishes including religious or moral beliefs. If the principal's wishes are not known, the agent must base his or her decision on the principal's best interests. The physician does not have a duty to verify that the agent's decision is consistent with the principal's wishes or beliefs. As with other directives, if the physician refuses to comply with the agent's decision, the physician must inform the agent who may select another physician. An agent may request, review, receive, authorize the release of, or consent to the disclosure of the principal's medical information. An agent may not, under any circumstances, consent to voluntary inpatient mental health services, convulsive treatment, psychosurgery, abortion, or the omission of comfort care for the principal.

Even though the agent becomes the decision maker, the attending physician must make a reasonable effort to inform the principal of any proposed treatment or of any proposal to withdraw or withhold treatment. Treatment may not be given nor withheld if the principal objects regardless of whether a durable power of attorney is in effect or the patient has been certified as incapable of making health care decisions. In the event that a petition for appointment of a guardian is filed or a guardian is appointed, the guardian may file a motion asking the probate court to determine whether or not to suspend or revoke the power of attorney. The court must consider the preference of the principal as expressed in the power of attorney. A health care provider, residential care provider, managed care organization, or insurer may not discriminate against a person because the person has or does not have a durable power of attorney for health care.

Pursuant to the Texas statute, an agent is not criminally or civilly liable for a health care decision made in good faith under the terms of the power of attorney and the statute. In addition, a physician or other health care provider is not subject to criminal, civil, or professional liability for an act or omission if done in good faith pursuant to the power of attorney and was not negligent. A provider is not liable for failure to comply with a durable power of attorney if the provider was not provided a copy of it or had no knowledge of the directive. Providers are also not liable if they act as directed by a power of attorney which has expired or been revoked without their knowledge. The existence of a power of attorney does not alter the liability for health care costs. Thus the patient and any responsible party remains liable for treatment costs. A near relative of the principal, a guardian, social worker, physician, clergyman, or another responsible adult directly interested in the principal may bring an action to request that the power of attorney be revoked because, at the time it was signed, the principal was not of sound mind to make a health care decision or was under duress, fraud, or undue influence.

The majority of the state statutes regarding durable health care powers of attorney are comparable to the Texas statute. The California Durable Power of Attorney for Health Care is virtually identical to the Texas act and only varies in a few minor areas. For example, in California the power of attorney may either be signed by two witnesses or acknowledged before a notary public. In addition, if the document is signed by witnesses as opposed to a notary, only one witness must meet requirements similar to those discussed above regarding DNR orders. The witnesses must attest that the principal is personally known to them or that the principal's identity was proved by convincing evidence. Convincing evidence means that the witness has no knowledge that would lead a reasonable person to believe that the principal is not who he or she claims to be. The agent may rely on a valid identification card or driver's license, a passport, or a similar document containing a photograph and description of the principal, signed by the principal, with an identifying number, and which is current or issued within the last 5 years. California places a penalty which Texas does not recognize on any person who alters or forges a durable power of attorney for health care or willfully conceals or withholds knowledge of a revocation intending to cause the withholding or withdrawal of life-sustaining health care. If these acts or omissions directly cause such treatment to be withheld, thus hastening the death of the principal, that person may be prosecuted for unlawful homicide.

The Illinois Power of Attorney for Health Care Act is in harmony with the Texas Act. However, Illinois places a duty on the agent to notify the health care provider of the existence of the power of attorney or its revocation if the patient is unable to or fails to do so. Illinois places the same penalty as California on a person who acts or omissions cause the withholding or withdrawal of life-sustaining treatment. Illinois labels this as involuntary manslaughter. Additionally, the Illinois Act provides that a person is civilly liable if he or she willfully conceals, cancels, falsifies, forges, or alters a power of attorney or an amendment to revocation without the principal's consent. A person is civilly liable and commits a Class A misdemeanor if he or she requires or prevents the execution of a power of attorney as a condition of insuring or providing any type of health care services. Illinois allows for nonstatutory health care powers of attorney to be recognized provided they are executed by the principal, designate the agent and the agent's powers, and the agent is not a person prohibited from being named as an agent, such as the principal's health care provider. A nonstatutory power of attorney need not be witnessed to be valid.

These statutes illustrate the various attempts by the states to provide a means for individuals to make health care decisions or appoint another to do so in the event the person becomes incompetent and is ill or injured. The state statutes are generally similar, but nurses should become familiar with the specific provisions applying to the state in which they consult.

A Person is Incompetent and Failed to Provide Prior Written Directions

The majority of states that have confronted the issue of the withdrawal or withholding of life-sustaining medical treatment in the absence of a directive have done so through the courts and not the legislatures. Thus, the rules produced by the courts tend to be more restraining than if the state legislatures were to enunciate guidelines. Without legislative guidance, the courts tend to examine each case on its own facts and are reluctant to set forth any broad guidelines. In spite of strong urging by the highest courts in many states, the state legislatures have rarely responded by passing relevant statutes.

The Forms of Substitute Decision Making

This section discusses the various standards set out by the courts in order to illustrate the differences and similarities. The highest courts in approximately half of the states have decided cases regarding surrogate decision makers along with a handful of federal courts including the U.S. Supreme Court. In general, the courts adopt one of two basic theories in deciding these cases. The courts either employ the surrogate-decision-making standard or the best-interests-of-the-patient standard.

The Legal Standard of Surrogate Decision Making

Courts that utilize the surrogate-decision-making standard require that the surrogate make the treatment decision based on evidence of the patient's desires and beliefs. In some states, this is a very rigorous test that very few cases meet and which generally requires the surrogate to apply to a court for permission to withdraw or withhold treatment. A few states have developed differing standards depending on whether the patient has a terminal condition or is in a persistent vegetative state. The tests are typically stricter for coma patients as opposed to terminally ill patients. A cross section of the court decisions regarding withholding or withdrawing life-sustaining medical treatment is provided.

In *Cruzan v. Director, Missouri Department of Health,* the U.S. Supreme Court approved the Missouri Supreme Court's test regarding the withdrawal of life-sustaining treatment from a patient in a persistent vegetative state. In this case, the family of Nancy Cruzan, a 30-year-old victim of an automobile accident, petitioned the court to allow Ms. Cruzan's health care providers to remove the feeding tube providing her with nutrition. The case progressed to the Missouri Supreme Court, and the court denied the family's plea holding that the family had failed to present clear and convincing evidence that Ms. Cruzan would have wanted the feeding tube withdrawn. The U.S. Supreme Court affirmed the Missouri decision determining that the state's interest in preserving life was strong enough to allow it to require clear and convincing evidence of the patient's wishes before withdrawing life-sustaining treatment. Although the court affirmed the Missouri Supreme Court, other states are not required to adopt this stringent standard of proof. The U.S. Supreme Court merely held that it is permissible for a state to do so.

The Supreme Court of New Jersey has developed separate tests for the withdrawal or withholding of life-sustaining medical treatment depending upon the condition of the patient. In one of the earliest cases decided regarding this issue, the court established guidelines for patients in persistent vegetative states. The court reiterated and expanded on the *In the Matter of Karen Quinlan* decision in the *Jobes* case. *In the Matter of Nancy Ellen Jobes* involved a 31-year-old patient who had degenerated into a persistent vegetative state as a result of an automobile accident. The court determined that although evidence of Ms. Jobes's wishes was presented, this evidence was not clear and convincing. Thus, the court relied on the *Quinlan* test. In order for treatment to be withheld or withdrawn, the patient's family must consider the patient's personal value system, prior statements about and reactions to medical issues, the patient's personality, and religious, ethical, and philosophical values in order to determine what course of medical treatment the patient would choose. The patient's close family members' substituted judgment will be relied upon unless the health care professionals are uncertain about whether or not family members are protecting the patient's interests. If the professionals are concerned, treatment should not be terminated absent the appointment of a guardian by a court. Generally, judicial review of the family's decision is not required. However, the family must obtain statements from two independent physicians knowledgeable in neurology attesting that the patient is in a persistent vegetative state and without a reasonable chance of recovery. The patient's attending physician must also submit a similar statement. However, if the patient is in a hospital setting, the prognosis committee's review should be substituted for the statements of two independent physicians.

In 1985, the New Jersey Supreme Court created guidelines for the withdrawal of life-sustaining medical treatment from a terminally ill elderly patient in a nursing home. In *In the Matter of Conroy,* the patient suffered from organic brain syndrome, arteriosclerotic heart disease, hypertension, and diabetes mellitus. She could not speak, was unable to move from a semifetal position, was incontinent, and her ability to swallow was limited. However, Ms. Conroy exhibited some level of consciousness and was not comatose. The court determined that life-sustaining treatment could only be withheld if a specific procedure was followed. First, the patient must have been determined to be incompetent by a court and a guardian must have been appointed. A person who believes that withholding or withdrawal of life-sustaining treatment would realize the patient's wishes or be in the patient's best interests must notify the Office of the Ombudsman. The ombudsman should investigate the situation and report to the Commissioner of Human Services and any other agency that regulates the facility. The attending physician and nurses should furnish evidence concerning the patient's condition. Two unaffiliated physicians should be appointed by the ombudsman to confirm the patient's diagnosis and prognosis. Treatment may then be withheld or withdrawn if the guardian, physicians, and ombudsman concur that one of the following tests has been met. In order to meet the *subjective test,* evidence must be presented to clearly show that the patient would have refused treatment under the circumstances involved if able to choose for herself. This evidence may be drawn from, but not limited to, a living will; an oral directive to a family member, friend, or health care provider; statements made by the patient regarding medical treatment administered to others; the patient's religious beliefs; or consistent patterns of conduct in prior medical decisions. In addition, medical evidence regarding the patient's condition, treatment, and prognosis is an essential prerequisite. This evidence must establish that the patient is elderly, incompetent, resides in a nursing home, has severe and permanent mental and physical impairments, and has a life expectancy of approximately 1 year or less. Treatment may also be withheld if one of two *best interest tests* are met. These tests will be discussed in detail in the next section.

Two years later, the New Jersey Supreme Court, in *In re Peter*, considered this issue in regard to an elderly patient in a persistent vegetative state. The court rejected the best interests test for patients in persistent vegetative states but held that the subjective surrogate-decision-maker test discussed in the *Conroy* case controlled. Thus, treatment may be withheld or withdrawn if clear and convincing evidence exists to show that if the patient were competent, the patient would decline treatment. The surrogate decision maker must first notify the Office of the Ombudsman and the ombudsman must secure two independent medical opinions to confirm the patient's condition and prognosis. If clear and convincing evidence exists that the patient has designated a family member or close friend to make medical decisions, the ombudsman should then defer any decisions regarding life-sustaining treatment to that person. If, however, no such designation has been made, the ombudsman may defer decisions to a close family member or must request that a guardian be appointed.

The Illinois Supreme Court has developed a slightly different test for withdrawal of treatment. The court initially determined that a patient must be terminally ill and in a persistent vegetative state or in an irreversible coma before artificial sustenance may be withdrawn. In *In re Estate of Longeway,* the court required the patient's attending physician and two other consulting physicians to concur in this diagnosis. If this factor is met, the patient's guardian or family must utilize the substituted judgment test to determine what decision the patient would make if competent. The decision maker may rely on relevant statements made by the patient while competent and the patient's personal value system, religious beliefs, ethical beliefs, life goals, attitudes toward sickness, and any other relevant information regarding the patient. In addition, a court must review this evidence and if the evidence is clear and convincing the court may order that the treatment be withdrawn or withheld.

In a later decision, *In re Greenspan*, the Illinois Supreme Court provided some slight latitude in the definition of terminal illness. The court determined a patient was in a terminal condition when death would be imminent if the life-sustaining procedure were absent. Pursuant to this broader definition, virtually any patient in a persistent vegetative state who requires a feeding tube for nutrition is in a terminal condition because, without food and water, the patient will die within a short period of time. However, the Illinois decisions continue to allow the withdrawal of treatment only if the patient is comatose. Thus, an incompetent patient with a terminal illness who has some level of consciousness could not have treatment withheld or withdrawn. The remainder of the guidelines established in *Longeway* are still in effect.

The highest court in Massachusetts also allowed the removal of a feeding tube from a patient in a persistent vegetative state pursuant to substituted decision making. In *Brophy v. New England Sinai Hospital, Inc.,* the family provided evidence regarding the patient's prior statements about life-sustaining treatment, his religious beliefs, the impact on the patient's family, the probability of adverse side effects; and his prognosis with and without treatment. However, the court upheld the right of the health care facility to refuse to withdraw the treatment. The family was allowed to transfer the patient to a facility that would comply with their decision to discontinue treatment. Similarly, in *Guardianship of Jane Doe,* the court utilized the substituted judgment test in analyzing the removal of a feeding tube from an incompetent, mentally retarded adult in a persistent vegetative state. The court enunciated a procedure for such cases in which a judge must hold a hearing to identify the choice the patient would have made if competent. The lack of evidence of prior statements regarding medical treatment does not bar the use of the substituted judgment test because the court may additionally look to the factors discussed in *Brophy.*

The Arizona Supreme Court has established simpler guidelines for withdrawal or withholding of life-sustaining treatment from an incompetent patient. In *Rasmussen v. Fleming,* the court held that judicial intervention is not necessary unless the interested parties conflict regarding the decision. In situations where the parties concur, the family and/or guardian should conduct substituted decision making. However, if no reliable evidence of the patient's wishes exists, the best interests test should be conducted.

The Pennsylvania Supreme Court adopted the substituted judgment standard in determining whether to allow the withdrawal of a gastronomy tube from a 43-year-old patient in a persistent vegetative state. In *In re Fiori,* the patient had been in this state since the age of 24. His mother who was also his legal guardian petitioned the court to allow the tube to be removed. The court determined that life-sustaining treatment for a patient in a persistent vegetative state with no chance of recovery could be terminated even though the patient had never expressed any opinions regarding termination of treatment provided that a close family member utilizes the substituted judgment test and two qualified physicians certify that the patient is in a persistent vegetative state without reasonable possibility of recovery. Court involvement is not necessary unless a dispute exists or no close family member exists in which case a guardian should be appointed and court direction must be sought before treatment is terminated.

Although most states rely on court decisions regarding surrogate decision making, Texas provides a unique provision in its Natural Death Act regarding the withdrawal or withholding of life-sustaining treatment when a patient has not executed a living will or a power of attorney for health care. The Texas Natural Death Act allows the attending physician and at least two persons to make this decision. The consenting persons must be chosen from the following list in the given order to priority: (1) the patient's spouse; (2) a majority of the patient's reasonably available adult children; (3) the patient's parents; or (4) the patient's nearest living relatives. The decision must be based on what the patient would desire, if known, and must be made in the presence of two qualified witnesses. If the patient has a legal guardian, the attending physician and the guardian may make this decision.

These cases and statutes illustrate the broad interpretations of the substituted judgment standard which has been adopted in various states. Some states require court intervention whenever a decision to withdraw or withhold life-sustaining treatment from an incompetent patient is made, while other states allow intervention by a judge only in a dispute between the interested parties. The states employing this standard also differ on the burden of proof applicable to the determination. A few states require clear and convincing evidence of the patient's desires. This is a much higher burden than the one used in most civil suits although it does not rise to the level of a criminal trial which requires proof beyond a reasonable doubt.

The Legal Standard of Best Interests of the Patient

The standard of best interests of the patient is an easier burden for families to meet. Under this test, the decision maker must decide, not what the patient would have wanted, but what is best for the patient. This involves consideration of the patient's suffering, prognosis, the invasiveness of the treatment, and the patient's quality of life. Although the majority of states have not adopted this standard and, instead, rely solely on the substituted judgment test, a growing minority of states are utilizing the best interests standard in situations in which no evidence of the patient's intent exits.

The Supreme Court of Washington adopted the best interests standard in determining whether or not artificial nutrition could be withdrawn from a patient with Batten's disease. In *In the Matter of the Guardianship of Barbara Grant*, Ms. Grant was 22 years old and in an almost vegetative state due to a terminal genetic degenerative condition of the central nervous system. Her parents sought an order from the court providing that certain life-sustaining treatments not be initiated should they be indicated including CPR, the use of an artificial respirator, or the insertion of nasogastric tube. Ms. Grant resided in a state-operated school with a policy to use all measures necessary to sustain and individual's life. However, the attorney general agreed to follow the parent's wishes if the court agreed. In response to the Grants' petition, the court established a standard for withholding life-sustaining treatment from an incompetent patient. First, the attending physician and two other qualified physicians must determine with reasonable medical judgment that the patient is in an advanced stage of a terminal and incurable illness and is suffering severe and permanent mental and physical deterioration. The patient's legal guardian, if one has been appointed, or, if not, the patient's family must then determine that if the patient was competent she would choose to refuse treatment or, if this is not possible, that withholding treatment would be in the patient's best interests. No members of the patient's family may object to the decision and the physicians and health care facility may likewise not object. In determining the patient's best interests, the guardian or family should examine evidence regarding the patient's present level of physical, sensory, emotional, and cognitive functioning; degree of physical pain from the medical condition, treatment, and termination of treatment; degree of humiliation, dependence, and loss of dignity; life expectancy and prognosis; treatment options; and the risks, side effects, and benefits of each treatment option. Under these circumstances, court intervention is not required.

Similarly, the Wisconsin Supreme Court utilized the best interests standard for a persistent vegetative patient with a history of schizophrenia. In the decision, *In re Guardianship of L. W.*, the court pronounced guidelines for allowing a guardian to consent to the withdrawal of life-sustaining treatment when a patient was never competent or whose conduct when competent was not sufficient to allow the use of the substituted judgment standard. In order to terminate treatment, the attending physician and two independent neurologists must conclude that the patient is in a persistent vegetative state with no reasonable chance of recovery and the guardian must determine in good faith that the withdrawal of treatment is in the patient's best interests. The guardian must look to certain factors in determining the best interests of the patient. The factors given by the court are the same as those enunciated by the Washington Supreme Court in the *Grant* case. In addition, if a health care facility has a bioethics committee, it should also be consulted. However, court involvement is not necessary without a dispute among the interested parties.

In the *Conroy* case, discussed above, the New Jersey Supreme Court allowed treatment to be withdrawn from an elderly, nursing home patient with a life expectancy of less than 1 year if the substituted decision making or one of two best interests tests was demonstrated. Pursuant to the first best interests test, some trustworthy evidence must exist that the patient would have refused treatment and the decision maker must be satisfied that the burdens of the patient's continued life with the treatment outweigh the benefits. In other words, the patient's suffering with the treatment greatly exceeds any physical pleasure, emotional enjoyment, or intellectual satisfaction that the patient still derives from life. Under the second test, treatment may be withheld absent evidence of the patient's wishes if the net burdens of the patient's life with the treatment clearly outweigh the benefits the patient derives from life. To meet this test, the administering or continuing of life-sustaining treatment must reach the level of being inhumane. The mere fact that a patient's prognosis is poor or his functioning is limited is insufficient to meet this last test. In either of the best interests tests, the patient's family must also concur in the decision to withdraw or withhold treatment.

Similarly, in the *Rasmussen* case which was discussed in the previous section, the Arizona Supreme Court held that the best interests test should be adopted whenever the substituted judgment test is inapplicable, such as when patients were never competent or no evidence of their wishes exists. The court provided that, in the best interests test, the decision maker assesses the patient's suffering, preservation or restoration of functioning, and the quality and extent of sustained life.

In regard to minors, the Illinois Supreme Court, in *Curran v. Bosze,* utilized a best interests analysis in holding that the testing of minor twins' bone marrow to determine their suitability as donors should not be ordered when one parent, the primary caretaker and sole custodian, refused consent and the other parent consented. In this case, although the parents had never married, they had entered into an agreed order stating that the mother had the sole care, custody, and control of the children but that in matters relating to health, the mother was required to consult and confer with the father. Another of the father's children, the twins' half-sibling, suffered from acute undifferentiated leukemia and needed a bone marrow transplant. The father requested that the twins be tested to determine if they were compatible donors. However, the mother refused to consent to the test and harvesting procedure. The court determined that the procedure was not in the twins' best interest. The court emphasized three factors in determining the child's best interest: (1) the parent who consents on behalf of the child must be informed of the risks and benefits inherent in the procedure; (2) there must be emotional support available to the child from the child's primary caretakers; and (3) there must be an existing, close relationship between the donor and the recipient. In *Curran*, the court stated that no close relationship existed between the children especially since the twins did not know that the patient was related. Further, the mother would not be able to support the twins fully during the procedure because of her opposition to the donation.

These cases illustrate that a few states have adopted the best interests standards when the patient's wishes could not be ascertained. Most of the states adopting this standard do not require court involvement and allow the family or guardian and the physicians to make the decision after considering a number of relevant factors.

Active Euthanasia or Assisted Suicide

When a physician or other person assists a terminally ill patient in ending his or her life, this is termed assisted suicide or euthanasia. The most well-known method of assisted suicide is a physician prescribing drugs that will effectively and painlessly terminate the patient's life. Although the majority of states prohibit any act which assists another to die, some health care providers strongly believe that a patient has the right to die with dignity and end intolerable suffering and, thus, occasionally violate these statutes privately. No physician has been convicted of assisting a patient's suicide due mainly to the public's sympathy and support of their actions in extreme cases. In light of the public's support, a few states have attempted to enact statutes legalizing physician-assisted suicide under specific guidelines and two state statutes prohibiting assisted suicide have been invalidated in the courts.

State Statutes That Prohibit Assisted Suicide

Although no state currently prohibits suicide or attempted suicide, approximately 43 states have statutes prohibiting assisted suicide. However, two recent federal appellate cases have found two such state statutes unconstitutional. In *Compassion in Dying v. Washington,* the Ninth Circuit sitting *en banc* held that a terminally ill person has a right to die. Specifically, the court determined that a person with a terminal condition has a liberty interest in determining the time and manner of one's death pursuant to the due process clause in the Fourteenth Amendment to the U.S. Constitution. The court emphasized that

> A competent terminally ill adult, having lived nearly the full measure of his life, has a strong liberty interest in choosing a dignified and humane death rather than being reduced at the end of his existence to a childlike state of helplessness, diapered, sedated, incontinent.
>
> *Compassion In Dying v. Washington,* 79 F.3d 790, 813–814, 1996 U.S. App. Lexis 31944, at 78 (9th Cir. 1996)

However, the court provided that some regulation by the state would be permissible to protect the state's interests. This decision is limited to a physician providing a patient with the means to commit suicide when the patient commits the suicidal act himself or herself. The court reserved its ruling on situations in which a patient could not self-administer the lethal dose of medications prescribed by the physician. On July 3, 1996, the Supreme Court entered a stay on the Ninth Circuit's invalidation of the Washington statute after a petition for *certiori* was filed. It is probable that the Supreme Court will accept *certiori* in order to resolve the issue.

Shortly after the Ninth Circuit's decision, the U.S. Court of Appeals for the Second Circuit held that New York's state statute prohibiting assisted suicide was also unconstitutional. However, in *Quill v. Vacco,* the court relied on the equal protection clause of the U.S. Constitution instead of following the Ninth Circuit's reasoning which relied on the due process clause. Thus, although the cases achieve the same result, their opinions differ and create a conflict which only the U.S. Supreme Court can resolve. The Second Circuit held that a right to assisted suicide cannot be found in the Constitution. However, the court determined that the statute was unconstitutional because competent, terminally ill patients were treated differently. Competent adults with terminal conditions on life support have a right to withdraw treatment and utilize their physician and a surrogate decision maker to assist. In effect, this is a hastening of death and equates to suicide. However, a competent, terminally ill adult not on life support is prohibited from gaining assistance from a physician or other person to hasten death. According to the court, this violates the equal protection clause of the Constitution because the differentiation between terminally ill patients is not rationally related to a valid state interest.

In contrast, the Michigan Supreme Court held that the state's statute prohibiting assisted suicide was validly enacted and does not violate either Michigan's constitution or the U.S. Constitution. *Michigan v. Kevorkian* was decided prior to either the Ninth or Second Circuit opinion regarding assisted suicide statutes. The Michigan Supreme Court decided that no right to commit suicide existed and, as a consequence, a person has no right to the assistance of others in committing suicide. According to the court, a person only has a right to withdraw or withhold life-sustaining treatment and not a general right to die. The U.S. Supreme Court has denied a petition for *certiori* on this case, and, therefore, the Michigan Supreme Court opinion defines the law in Michigan.

In spite of the numerous state statutes prohibiting physician-assisted suicide, there is no reported case of a criminal conviction against a physician. For example, a grand jury refused to indict a physician who intentially prescribed barbiturates to a patient for the patient to use to end her life. The physician was arrested after admitting his actions in an article in the *New England Journal of Medicine.* The most widely publicized trials have involved Dr. Kevorkian who has had the cases dismissed or been found not guilty in numerous indictments involving his acts assisting terminally ill patients to commit suicide.

Despite this trend to invalidate state assisted suicide statutes and the lack of prosecution under existing statutes, one state has recently enacted strong legislation prohibiting such assistance. On August 5, 1996, Rhode Island enacted legislation making it a felony for an individual or licensed health care professional to provide the physical means by which another person can commit or attempt to commit suicide with the purpose of helping someone commit suicide. A health care professional includes a physician, nurse, nurse anesthetist, podiatrist, physician assistant, pharmacist, and dentist. This statute excepts from prosecution the legal withdrawal or withholding of life support and the prescription or administration of medications or procedures to relieve a patient's discomfort even if it hastens death. This is one of the few statutes that is specific to physician-assisted suicide. The American Civil Liberties Union has expressed interest in challenging the constitutionality of this legislation in federal court.

State Statutes That Legalize Assisted Suicide

At this time, three states have held referenda on proposals to permit physicians to assist terminally ill, competent adults to commit suicide. The proposals in Washington and California failed probably due to the fact that the measures contained few safeguards. Nevertheless, these votes were very close and a more protective proposal could potentially be passed in the future. Various public-opinion polls have indicated the growing support for physician-assisted suicide in proper circumstances.

In the other state election, in Oregon, the proposal was passed. The Oregon statute contains numerous guidelines designed to protect patients when assisted suicide is chosen. However, a federal district judge has entered an injunction keeping the statute from taking effect. In *Lee v. Oregon,* the judge ruled that the statute is unconstitutional because it fails to ensure that only competent adults with terminal conditions will choose assisted suicide. According to the court, the statute contains no procedures for determining that the patient is competent to make such a decision and is not under the influence of any other person. The attending physician makes the determination of whether or not the patient is qualified to decide to die. In *Compassion in Dying,* The Ninth Circuit indicated that the district judge's reasoning in *Lee v. Oregon* directly conflicted with the Ninth Circuit's opinion. Thus, the injunction may be overturned on appeal to the Ninth Circuit and the statute placed in effect, barring any future Supreme Court opinions.

The conflict among the federal and state courts regarding the constitutionality of statutes both prohibiting and legalizing assisted suicide will only be resolved if the U.S. Supreme Court accepts *certiori* in one of the cases where petitions for review have at present been filed. Due to the stay which the Supreme Court placed on *Compassion in Dying*, it is likely that this issue will be decided in the near future.

A Health Care Provider's Potential Liability Resulting from the Right to Refuse

Health care providers are placed in a precarious position when faced with a patient who is refusing medical care. Although the statutes and the courts attempt to protect providers, failure to respect a patient's right to refuse medical treatment may give rise to a civil suit by the patient for damages. In addition, withholding or withdrawing treatment pursuant to a patient's alleged wishes can also lead to liability if the family disagrees or claims that the patient did not want treatment withdrawn. Court intervention prior to withholding treatment might not always protect a provider, either. Nevertheless, if a health care provider is in doubt as to the proper course of action, involving the court is a prudent step. This area of the law is just beginning to develop and cases are still relatively rare in many states. However, a few intrepid courts have found liability against providers.

Wrongful Life

A cause of action for wrongful life has not been recognized by the majority of states. In the minority of states that have recognized this action, the action has arisen because of the birth of a child. For instance, a mother may have an aminocentesis to determine the health of her fetus. She is informed by her physician that the results are normal, but the child is born with birth defects. A wrongful life cause of action is brought on behalf of the child against the doctor and it will normally allege that the doctor has negligently given the child life. In this situation, the child's parents, in some jurisdictions, have a claim for wrongful birth asserting that they would have aborted the fetus if they had known of the serious birth defects. Another cause of action, wrongful pregnancy may be alleged when a person undergoes a medical procedure for sterilization and later becomes pregnant or impregnates.

A cause of action similar to wrongful life may theoretically be used when a person on life support is kept alive against his wishes. A claim by a person on life support will differ from a child's claim because life is only being extended and not given as in the case of a child. However, both the patient on life support and the child complain because they are alive. Courts generally have not favored this action possibly due to the disturbing ethical problems it raises in valuing life. For example, the Ohio Supreme Court recently held in *Anderson v. St. Francis-St. George Hosp., Inc.,* that "there is not [a] cause of action for wrongful living." As noted by the concurring opinion, the furthering of life cannot be considered a damage under the confines of present negligence law.

Wrongful Death

In contrast, most states recognize wrongful death as a viable cause of action. In these states, the cause of action usually arises statutorily; i.e., it is created by the state legislature rather than by the state courts. Generally, these actions are allowed to be brought when a person has died because of the tortious or criminal act of another person or entity. For instance, in *Easterbrook Health Care Center v. Spilman,* the Florida Court of Appeals found that Easterbrook had caused Mr. Spilman's death by allowing him to contract fatal infections. The court reasoned that Mr. Spilman was a person covered by the Florida wrongful death statute and that Mr. Spilman's injury occurred because Easterbrook tortiously deprived Mr. Spilman of his rights as a nursing home resident.

For purposes of this chapter, a wrongful death action may arise when a patient is not competent to consent to withdrawal of treatment or an unqualified person consents to withdrawal of the patient's life support. For example, a patient's family may sue for wrongful death if a patient does not consent to a DNR order, but a perceived spouse or common law spouse consents to no resuscitation. If one patient's children prove that the person who ordered no resuscitation was not a spouse, the children have a potential claim for wrongful death. These cases all have a common characteristic in that the person bringing suit alleges that the patient has not legally refused treatment. A potential wrongful death action may occur each time life support to a patient is withdrawn not in accordance with the statutes which govern its removal. As seen, state statutes regarding withdrawal of life support differ. Therefore, in these areas, determination of a wrongful action must begin with the statutes and case law which determine when it is legal to remove life-sustaining devices.

Violation of Right of Bodily Self-Determination

A recent case in Connecticut has created a new potential cause of action against providers who fail to respect a patient's refusal of treatment. In *The Stamford Hospital v. Vega,* Ms. Vega was admitted to the hospital for the birth of her child. After delivering a healthy baby, Ms. Vega began to hemorrhage. She was a Jehovah's Witness and had signed a form refusing all transfusions. The doctors tried a number of alternatives but realized that a blood transfusion was necessary. Both Ms. Vega and her husband continued to refuse the transfusion. The hospital sought an injunction from a court allowing a transfusion to be administered. After holding an emergency hearing, the court ordered the transfusion. After receiving transfusions, Ms. Vega recovered and was discharged. She then initiated an appeal of the court's order authorizing the transfusions.

The Connecticut Supreme Court held that the case was not moot even though Ms. Vega had already received the transfusion of which she was complaining. The court reasoned that the issue was one which would arise in the future when other Jehovah's Witnesses refused blood transfusions and, thus, the court should resolve the issue now. According to the court, Mrs. Vega's common law right of bodily self-determination had been violated by the court's injunction and the administration of the transfusions. Pursuant to the court's opinion, the hospital had no right or obligation to administer unwanted medical care on a patient who competently declined the care after having been fully informed of the consequences of her decision. The court held that both the hospital and trial court were obligated to respect Ms. Vega's choice to refuse a blood transfusion. The case was then remanded by the Connecticut Supreme Court to the trial court for judgment to be rendered for Ms. Vega. This is an important case to be aware of because it unequivocally states that the hospital should not have questioned Ms. Vega's refusal.

Battery

When medical treatment is rendered to a person without informed consent, a court may hold that a battery was committed. A battery is an unwelcome touching. This cause of action has generally been applied when a person consents to a medical procedure such as surgery but the physician failed to provide the patient with all of the necessary facts for the patient to make an informed decision regarding the treatment. Although this claim has been infrequently made in the context of an expressed refusal of treatment which was not respected by a provider, it is a potential area which a patient may rely on in bringing suit against a hospital or other health care provider.

Violation of Due Process

If the hospital is managed by a governmental unit such as a county, municipal district, or the state, a patient could potentially bring suit against the facility for violation of due process. In this type of claim, the patient alleges that the facility failed to provide notice and a hearing prior to obtaining a court order and administrating medical treatment in spite of the patient's express refusal. This type of suit has customarily been brought when patients refuse treatment which their physicians believe is necessary to save their life.

For example, in *Novak v. Cobb County Kennestone Hospital Authority,* a 16-year-old Jehovah's Witness patient and his mother refused a blood transfusion. The hospital petitioned the court for the appointment of a guardian *ad litem* for the patient. The court considered the petition and appointed a guardian without notice to either the patient or his mother. The following day, due to the patient's deteriorating condition, the court held an emergency hearing at the hospital. Although the physicians and the guardian attended and testified, neither the patient nor his mother were given notice. At the conclusion of the hearing the court ordered the transfusion which was then promptly administered. The patient and his mother brought suit against the hospital for violating their due process. The U.S. Court of Appeals for the Eleventh Circuit dismissed the patient's claims holding that the court independently held a hearing and ordered the transfusion. The court has judicial immunity and cannot be held liable for its order. The hospital could only be held liable if the patient proved that the hospital and the physicians conspired with the judge to administer the transfusion. This is a relatively high burden which few patients could prove. However, if the hospital had acted without a court order in administering the transfusion, the patient's claims may have been successful.

Violation of Federal Constitutional Rights

Even if a hospital is not managed by a governmental entity, the hospital and physicians may be liable for violating a patient's constitutional right to freedom of religion. If the health care providers act pursuant to a court's order, they are acting under the color of state law. In *McKenzie v. Doctors' Hospital of Hollywood, Inc.,* a U.S. District Court in Florida held that a patient had jurisdiction to assert this claim. The patient was hospitalized and her physicians recommended a blood transfusion. When the patient and her husband refused on the basis of their religion, the hospital obtained a court order authorizing the transfusion. Upon learning of the order, the patient left the hospital and sought treatment elsewhere. The court dismissed the patient's claims holding that because the patient left the hospital of her own free will without receiving the transfusion, the hospital had not prevented the patient from executing her constitutional rights. Although this claim has not been actively pursued by injured patients, it is a potential claim which may be brought by persons refusing medical treatment on the basis of religion.

Refusal of Family to Pay Further Medical Costs

In *Grace Plaza of Great Neck, Inc. v. Elbaum,* a patient's family refused to pay the patient's future medical costs due to the long-term facility's refusal to remove the patient's feeding tube. The patient's husband successfully petitioned the court to allow removal of the feeding tube. However, due to the facility's continued refusal, the husband was forced to remove the patient from the facility. He refused to pay for the patient's treatment from the time of the facility's first refusal of his request to withdraw artificial nutrition before he had sought court authorization. The facility brought suit against the husband to recover the past-due costs of the patient's care. The court determined that the husband was required to pay for the services because the facility had not acted in bad faith in refusing to withdraw treatment. Pursuant to the court's opinion, a facility that is uncertain about the discontinuance of treatment is within its rights to refuse to terminate the care until the issue is legally determined.

This is one of the first cases regarding who must pay for treatment which the patient and/or the family have decided should be withdrawn. Although the outcome in this case protected the facility, health care providers should be aware of this potential cause of action because it may become a more familiar argument due to the expense of life-sustaining treatment and in cases where life-sustaining treatment is extended without cause.

Conclusion

Nurses and other health care providers should familiarize themselves with the law in the state in which they practice. The issues of refusal of medical treatment and right to die have gained national attention and support in recent years, thus yielding an onslaught of litigation. To protect themselves, providers must follow the statutory and court guidance in their state in order to respect a patient's right to refuse treatment. Many potential causes of action exist which patients or their families may utilize to bring suit against providers who do not adhere to these state guidelines.

Glossary

Cardiopulmonary resuscitation: A restoration of cardiac output and pulmonary ventilation following cardiac arrest and apnea, using artificial respiration and closed chest message.

Common law: In general a body of law that develops and derives through judicial decisions, as distinguished from legislative enhancements.

Competent: Duly qualified; answering all requirements; having sufficient capacity, ability, or authority; possessing the requisite physical, mental, natural, or legal qualifications; able; adequate; sufficient; capable; legally fit

Declarant: A person who makes a declaration; one who makes a sworn statement.

Do-not-resuscitate order (DNR): An order by a physician(s), following discussion with and informed consent by a legally competent patient or the patient's legal representative, which orders health care providers NOT to perform resuscitation procedures on this patient when these procedures are necessary for sustaining the patient's life; a DNR order is frequently initiated by the patient's living will or the legal representative's medical power of attorney.

Euthanasia: The act, by commission or omission, of painlessly ending the life of persons suffering from incurable and distressing disease as an act of mercy.

Guardian: A person lawfully invested with the power, and charged with the duty, of taking care of and managing the property and rights of another person, who, for defect of age, understanding, or self-control, is considered incapable of administering his or her own affairs.

Incompetency: A relative term which may be employed as meaning disqualification, inability, or incapacity, and it can refer to lack of legal qualifications or fitness to discharge the required duty and to show want of physical or intellectual or moral fitness.

Informed consent: A person's agreement to allow something to happen (such as surgery) that is based on a full disclosure of facts needed to make the decision intelligently, i.e., knowledge of risks involved, alternatives, etc. Informed consent is the name for a general principal of law that a physician has a duty to disclose what a reasonably prudent physician in the medical community in the exercise of reasonable care would disclose to a patient as to whatever grave risks of injury might be incurred from a proposed course of treatment, so that a patient, exercising, ordinary care for his or her own welfare, and faced with a choice of undergoing the proposed treatment, or alternative treatment, or none at all, may intelligently exercise judgment by reasonably balancing the probable risks against the probable benefits.

Liberty interest: An interest recognized as protected by the due process clauses of state and federal constitutions.

Life-sustaining medical treatment: Medical treatment which sustains a person's life functions, including respiratory and cardiopulmonary functions, preventing the person's body from reaching that state where it is declared legally dead.

Living will: A document executed by a competent person which governs the withholding or withdrawal of life-sustaining treatment from an individual in the event of an incurable or irreversible condition that will cause death within a relatively short time, and when such person is no longer able to make decisions regarding his or her medical treatment.

Negligence: The failure to use such care as a reasonably prudent and careful person would use under similar circumstances; it is the doing of some act which a person of ordinary prudence would not have done under similar circumstances or failure to do what a person of ordinary prudence would have done under similar circumstances.

Ombudsman: An official or semiofficial office or person to which people may come with grievances connected with the government. The ombudsman stands between, and represents, the citizen before the government.

Persistent vegetative state: Denoting especially an enduring state of grossly impaired consciousness, as after severe head trauma or brain disease, in which an individual is incapable of voluntary or purposeful acts and only responds reflexively to painful stimuli.

Power of attorney: An instrument in writing whereby one person, as principal, appoints another as his agent and confers authority to perform certain specified acts or kinds of acts on behalf of principal.

Terminal illness: A medical practitioner's term for a disease that is incurable or irreversible and which will, with a high degree of probability, cause the death of a patient, within a relatively short period of time.

Wrongful death: Type of legal theory argued on behalf of a deceased person's beneficiaries that alleges that death was attributable to the willful or negligent act of another.

Wrongful life: Refers to a type of medical malpractice claim brought on behalf of a child, alleging that the child would not have been born but for negligent advice to, or treatment of, the parents.

Chapter 8

Complex Litigation

Adella Toepel

Contents

Objectives

- To define complex litigation and related concepts that require judicial management
- To describe the tools of complex litigation (class action and multidistrict litigation) established by the courts to deal with multiple claimants
- To identify the differences and parallels between toxic tort and product liability
- To define toxic tort
- To define the concept of strict liability as it relates to product liability

Introduction

One of the defining characteristics of complex litigation is the need for judicial management. Complex litigation usually involves many parties in numerous related cases, often in different jurisdictions, involving large numbers of witnesses, documents, and extensive discovery. The term *complex litigation* refers as much to the need for management by the court as to the resolution of difficult or challenging questions of law. The purpose of judicial management is to bring about "the just, speedy, and inexpensive determination" of the litigation (*Manual for Complex Litigation*, 1995, p. 3).

Role of the Court in Complex Litigation

Complex litigation frequently involves two or more separate but related cases. All related cases pending or which will be filed in the same court will generally be assigned to the same judge. Counsel informs the assigned judge of any pending related cases, and the judge also attempts to ascertain if related cases are pending. This is to improve efficiency and coordination in the consolidation of related cases. Consolidation may be possible even when cases are filed in different courts. Cases from other districts may be transferred under 28 U.S.C. Statute 1404(a) or 1406 to the consolidation court, and cases brought in state court may be removed to the federal court and transferred or refiled in the consolidating district court. (*Manual for Complex Litigation*, 1995). Coordination of proceedings is accomplished by counsel with appropriate communication to the judge. Often a lead case is designated in the consolidated litigation. Rulings in lead cases may apply to other consolidated cases.

The transfer of cases to the consolidating court is for case management purposes. Effective management requires the judge to be active, to have substantive involvement, to make timely dispute decisions, to monitor the progress of the litigation continuously, to be fair and firm on time limits and other controls, and to be carefully prepared (*Manual for Complex Litigation*, 1995). The attorneys, who may be more familiar than the judge with the facts and issues in the case, play a significant part in developing the litigation plan and its execution. Often cases with multiple plaintiffs, where there is common law and fact, are assigned a class action status or multidistrict litigation status (M.D.L.).

Class Actions

To file and maintain a class action, a plaintiff or plaintiffs must file a Motion for Class Certification. Federal Rule 23(a) states that the following requirements must be met for a class to be certified:

> One or more members of a class may sue or be sued as representative parties on behalf of all, only if (1) the class is so numerous that joinder of all members is impracticable, (2) there are questions of law or fact common to the class, (3) the claims or defenses of the representative parties are typical of the claims or defenses of the class, and (4) the

representative parties will fairly and adequately protect the interests of the class (*Federal Civil Judicial Procedure & Rules*, 1996, p. 93).

The court reviews the motion and other documents filed in support of and in opposition to the motion in the context of relevant case law and the legal and factual issues raised by the Class Action Complaints. After a class is certified, the court typically sets a deadline as to when one may opt not to participate in the class (opt-out). After that date passes, the plaintiffs who have not opted out will be bound by the decisions of the court and class counsel. Except for a few well-defined exceptions, the court requires notice to the class and provides a voluntary opt-out for claimants who do not wish to participate in the Class (*Manual for Complex Litigation*, 1995).

Litigation in which claims are made by or against a class tend to be complex and will require judicial management (complex litigation). It calls for closer judicial oversight than other types of litigation because it imposes unique responsibilities on the court and on counsel. Once class allegations are made, various otherwise routine decisions are no longer within individual litigant's control. The attorneys and parties seeking to represent a class assume fiduciary responsibilities, and the court bears responsibility to protect the interests of the class members, for which Rule 23(d) gives the court administrative powers (*Manual for Complex Litigation*, 1995).

Multidistrict Litigation

M.D.L. is another tool established by the court to deal with multiple claimants who have at least one significant issue in common but have filed separate law suits. The goal of M.D.L. case management is to bring about just, speedy, and inexpensive determinations, avoiding unnecessary and unproductive activity in litigation that may involve large numbers of witnesses and documents and extensive discovery. The certification of an M.D.L. by the federal court allows for judicial management of complex cases where the litigation involves many parties in numerous related cases, especially if pending in different jurisdictions. Related cases pending in different federal courts may be consolidated in a single district and assigned to one federal judge by a transfer of venue. (Consolidation may be done in state court on a more informal basis, depending on the state rules of court.)

The Federal Judicial Panel of Multidistrict Litigation is authorized to transfer civil actions pending in one or more than one federal district, involving one or more common questions of fact for coordinated or consolidated pre-trial proceedings. No single factor determines the selection of the district to which the actions are transferred. Numbers of cases pending, where discovery has occurred, the site of occurrence of common facts, and the district where cost and inconvenience would be minimized are considered in the selection of the district. The panel will also consider the experience and skill of the available judges. Based on its consideration of these factors, the panel will designate a judge to whom the cases are transferred for pre-trial proceedings. Counsel in various cases may agree with the judge to try a "lead" case. Rulings in lead cases may be the basis for opinions or rulings, although not conclusive, in other courts.

The power of the court enables the judge to exercise extensive supervision and control of the litigation under the Federal Rules of Civil Procedure, particularly Rules 16, 26, 37, 42, and 83. Fed. R. Civ. Pro. 16 (12) specifically addresses complex litigation, authorizing the judge to adopt special procedures for managing difficult or protracted actions that involve complex issues, multiple parties, difficult legal questions, or unusual proof problems (*Manual for Complex Litigation,* 1995, p. 10). Such management allows the judge to use judicial time wisely and efficiently, especially early in the litigation. Therefore, pre-trial conferences are held even if some parties have not yet appeared or even been served. The assignment of a single judge serves to satisfy these special judicial needs through-out, and the judge's role is crucial in developing and monitoring an effective plan for orderly conduct in pre-trial and trial proceedings. The attorneys may be more familiar than the judge with the facts and issues of the case and play a significant part in developing a litigation plan and case management order (CMO). The judge may decide to refer pre-trial control to a magistrate judge or may appoint a special master (for limited purposes that require special expertise) and must order what is being referred to the magistrate or special master. The *Manual for Complex Litigation,* published by the Federal Judicial Center, is an important reference for the management of complex litigation.

An M.D.L. is not a class action, although a class can be included in an M.D.L., along with other similar claims. The common issues could involve facts regarding product liability, negligence, breach of warranty, fraud, adequate warning, breach of express or implied warranties, and whether the product was defective. These claims may arise from the same event, the same product, or the same course of conduct and are based on the same general legal theories. The resolution of common issues in separate suits reduces considerable expense by avoiding redundant evidence in endless repetition of those common issues at individual trials. The courts have utilized trial techniques that include not only deciding common liability issues, but determining compensatory and/or punitive damages as well. The court may try to identify common issues and reserve remaining issues, such as proximate (individual) causation and damages for individual suits based on medical history, general health, and extent of injury. For example, in mass tort actions, there are many separate issues relating to individual claimants, such as proof of injury, proximate causation, and damages. Certain issues may not be common to all who have filed a claim but are predicated on the defendant's liability for injuries from the same product or the same course of conduct by the manufacturer with respect to testing, research, manufacture, promotion, and marketing.

Mass Torts

Courts have recognized the need for special procedures in litigation involving multiple tort claims arising from a mass disaster, such as a plane crash of a commercial airliner, hotel fire, or chemical explosion. These injuries occur at a single site and usually manifest themselves immediately. In mass toxic tort or defective product litigation, injuries may occur in numerous, widely dispersed locations at different times, and the full impact of injury may remain hidden for years. All three types of litigation require courts to deal with multiple personal injury and damage claims, but management of mass toxic tort and defective product litigation is significantly more complex and demanding (*Manual for Complex Litigation*, 1995, p. 308). Management of mass tort litigation can be complicated by many factors and falls in the realm of complex litigation. Related cases may be filed in different courts, both federal and state, often with multiple plaintiffs and defendants. Cases may be governed by different state laws regarding issues of liability, the measure of compensatory damages, the standards for punitive damages, the statute of limitations, and insurance coverage. Conflicts among defendants may arise and third-party complaints may be filed, resulting in numerous additional parties. Highly technical expert testimony is usually needed and sometimes its admissibility is disputed. This requires the judge to play the role of gatekeeper in reviewing novel scientific evidence. The judge may also need to assume the role of managing the litigation because of the sheer number of cases.

Consolidation of cases in a single court for joint trial may not be feasible because of individualized causation and damage issues. If M.D.L. treatment of the federal cases is not possible and/or if consolidation treatment in a single court is not possible, state and federal judges may try to coordinate proceedings and will preside at joint hearings and conduct other court proceedings. Coordination between state and federal courts reduces duplicate efforts, aids in scheduling discovery plans, appoints special masters and lead counsel, and creates document depositories. Some states have developed comprehensive legislation to deal with product liability cases, while other states have statutes that are issue specific, such as statutes of limitations, strict liability, evidence, limitations of liability of nonmanufacturers, and defenses. The U.S. Department of Commerce has developed a Model Uniform Product Liability Act for voluntary use by the states in an effort to stabilize product liability law. It was published in the *Federal Register* on October 31, 1979.

Product Liability

The term *product liability* applies to the liability of a manufacturer, nonmanufacturer seller, or processor to a buyer or third party for injury caused by a product which has been sold. Product liability includes negligence and claims such as breach of implied warranties and breach of express warranties. Previously, such matters were dealt with under the legal classifications of negligence or sales. However, product liability became a legal heading in its own right with the development of the doctrine of strict liability in tort. Within the strict liability formula, the one who sells any product in a defective condition deemed unsafe to the user or consumer or to their property is subject to liability for physical harm or property damage. To support a strict liability cause of action, the plaintiff must prove that the product was in a condition not contemplated by the ultimate consumer which would make the product unreasonably dangerous.

Theories of product liability had their origins in tort and contract law. For years, the most common ground for recovery for personal injury or other damages was negligence. Recovery for product-caused injury was also sought under the theory of breach of warranty. This caused difficulty for the injured party who had no direct dealing with the manufacturer. Beginning in 1963, a new basis for liability emerged — the principle of strict liability in tort — which is embodied in the Restatement (Second) of Torts and was first clearly applied by the California Supreme Court. Product liability, including strict liability, grew out of a public policy that people needed more protection against dangerous products than was currently afforded by the law of warranty. However, various theories of liability may apply to product cases, including breach of express or implied warranty, negligence, fraud, strict liability, alternative remedies, or other theories. It should be kept in mind that product liability cases share the basic characteristics of other lawsuits, and many legal techniques in litigating other kinds of cases may apply in litigating a product liability case.

The product may be defective because of a manufacturing flaw, a defective design, or a failure to warn of dangers in the use of the product within the meaning of the Restatement of Torts provision. The restatement formula requires proof that the product is both unreasonably dangerous and defective. Some jurisdictions do not require proof that the product was unreasonably dangerous to permit the plaintiff to recover damages under the strict liability theory. Some jurisdictions, under the Restatement provision, substitute the term *not reasonably safe*. The consumer-expectation test adopted by the courts for determining whether or not a product is in an unreasonably dangerous condition is that the product sold must be dangerous to the extent beyond which the ordinary consumer who purchased it would have contemplated, with ordinary knowledge, common to a community, the characteristics of the product. To establish that an allegedly defective product was unreasonably unsafe, the plaintiff must prove that the product was more dangerous than the ordinary consumer might expect when the product was used as it was intended or used in a foreseeable manner. Proving the product was defective generally requires showing not just that the product was defective for its intended use, but also that the product was so dangerous that a prudent manufacturer would not market the product knowing the product's condition.

When the consumer-expectation test is inapplicable because the ordinary consumer would not form an expectation as to the safety of a product, the courts often apply risk/benefit factor analysis, that is, the utility of the product measured against the danger-in-fact associated with the use of a product. A product is not unreasonably dangerous or defective if it is inherently and obviously dangerous, or if its defect is one of which the user should be aware. Some products are incapable of being safe for their intended and ordinary use, but if properly prepared with proper instruction and warning, they are neither defective nor unreasonably dangerous. Such cases may involve prescription drugs, vaccines, blood, and medical devices, and are provided for under the Restatement (Second) of Torts Section 402A, Comment K. Comment K provides that two classifications of drugs are exempt from the doctrine of strict liability — drugs with a known but reasonable risk of injury and drugs which are new and experimental and the risk is unknown. The manufacturer bears the burden of proving that its product is unavoidably unsafe.

The term *product liability* does not include action against one's employer for injury covered by workers' compensation. However, an employer may be held liable in product liability contexts where the employer is also the manufacturer or seller of a defective product causing injury to the employee. Such an action would fall under the so-called dual capacity doctrine. The more common experience is that a third-party manufacturer is sued, even though the injury occurred in the workplace.

There are common issues present in every product liability case, regardless of the theory on which it is brought. The plaintiff must prove that he or she suffered injury or loss because the product was defective, and must also prove that the defect was the proximate cause of such injury or loss. It is also necessary for the plaintiff to show that the product was defective when it left the control of the manufacturer or seller who is being sued, not merely that a defect existed at the time of injury. The burden of proof remains with the plaintiff, therefore, even where the action is grounded on a theory, such as breach of warranty or strict liability in tort, which negates the need for proving a specific act of negligence or breach of duty on the part of the defendant (*American Law of Product Liability*, 1987).

Toxic Torts

Toxic torts are defined as civil actions asserting a demand for recovery of damages where there was exposure to a chemical substance, emission, or product that allegedly resulted in physical and/or psychological harm. In a toxic tort case, the defining event is exposure to the toxin. The defining consequence is some adverse health effect on the individual(s) such as illness or reproductive problems. The typical toxic tort case involves a plaintiff with cancer suing for damages against an industrial site allegedly responsible for chemical releases, runoffs, or ground seepage that has affected the plaintiff's residence. The parties in toxic torts often know each other and this familiarity can breed hostility because of personal outrage along with a serious illness. Often a toxic tort case involves multiple parties or could involve an employee in the absence of workers' compensation, or in addition to workers' compensation, where a third party has manufactured and/or released the toxic substance.

A familiar subset of plaintiffs in toxic tort litigations is older, male, blue-collar workers with lung disease from asbestos exposure. Another example of a subset of plaintiffs includes those with concerns and fears about future illness from exposure to cancer-causing materials. The defense counsel will be experienced with chemical and environmental defenses and will represent insurers or companies. Typically, the plaintiff's attorney will be working on a contingent-fee basis. The litigation is considered expensive, and expert witnesses and pre-trial proceeding costs are so high that they are usually borne by fairly experienced plaintiff lawyers in large firms.

Some key terms in toxic tort cases include *acute risks* which arise immediately from a brief contact with a chemical substance; *air toxics* which is the general name for chemicals released into the air as vapor, smoke, or airborne chemicals. The federal air pollution regulations determine what chemicals are toxic and what levels of exposure over a period of time of sustained contact are believed to have effects harmful to humans. There can be rare, sudden explosions such as the Bhopal tragedy in India, but, typically, long-term releases causing chronic health effects are the usual sources of toxic tort litigation. The term *air toxics* includes many invisible airborne chemicals that may cause adverse health effects. *Air pollution* is a broader term and includes visible elements such as haze, smoke, and smog. *Carcinogenicity* is the scientifically demonstrated potential of a chemical to cause cancer, e.g., tobacco smoke, radiation. *Chemical substances* is a generic term which covers basic elements and complex chemical compounds. *Chronic risks* arise from repeated contact with a chemical substance over a sustained period of time. *Citizen suits* are statutory actions brought by persons other than a federal agency against defendants to enforce the penalty provisions of federal environmental laws. *Environmental releases* are liquids, solids, or gases that exit into a facility's external environment, e.g., sewers, landfills, bodies of water, etc. (O'Reilly, 1992).

Except for asbestos and Agent Orange, toxic tort cases lack specific statistics kept in one national database. The tort system classifies toxic torts as a subset of complex litigation. The litigants generate considerable motions practice and extensive pre-trial maneuvers, often with an overlay of government environmental enforcement action. The cases are often highly publicized, which can generate considerable pressure on the court as the case is being administrated.

Parallels between Product Liability and Toxic Torts

The product liability system intersects with the law of toxic torts cases to the extent that some exposures can best be remedied under strict liability in tort. Although a toxic tort typically involves exposures to potentially hazardous chemicals, it can look like a product liability action. Some of the chemical exposures occur through products with which the plaintiff has worked or to which he has had exposure at work. Product liability theories include traditional remedies of negligence and warranty, as well as the recent concept of manufacturer strict liability. Under strict liability, plaintiffs need not prove fault or intent of the manufacturer, but they must prove there was a defect that made the product unreasonably dangerous, that the defect was present when the product left the manufacturer's control, and that the injury was proximately caused by the defect (O'Reilly, 1992).

Glossary

Complex litigation: Usually involves many parties, in numerous related cases, often in different jurisdictions, involving large numbers of documents, witnesses, and extensive discovery that will require judicial management generally assigned to the same judge.

Opt-out: After a class action is certified, a deadline is set, typically by the court, as to when one may voluntarily decide to not participate in a class action; after the date passes, plaintiffs who have not opted-out will be bound by the decisions of the court.

Strict liability: Doctrine by which the one who sells any product in a defective condition deemed unsafe to the user or consumer or to their property is subject to liability for physical harm or property damage; the plaintiff must prove the product was in a condition not contemplated by the ultimate consumer which would make the product unreasonably dangerous.

References

Federal Civil Judicial Procedure and Rules, 1996.

Federal Judicial Center, Ed., Part II: Management of complex litigation. Part III: Class actions, *Manual for Complex Litigation*, 3rd ed. (1995), Aspen Law & Business, Englewood Cliffs, NJ, 3–32, 211–246, 308–330.

Order and Findings on Class Certification, MDL No. 95-1060R, U.S. District Court, Central District of California. Filed February 21, 1996.

Order Approving Plaintiffs' Class Notice Plan and Forms of Notice, MDL No. 95-1060R, U.S. District Court, Central District of California. Filed February 21, 1996.

O'Reilly, J. (1992). *Defining Toxic Torts. Toxic Torts Practice Guide*, 2nd ed., McGraw-Hill, New York, 2-1–2-7; 5-1–5-8.

Travers, T., Ed., *American Law of Products Liability*, 3rd ed. Part I (1987). The Lawyers Co-Operative Publishing Co. Bancroft-Whitney Co., Rochester, NY, chap. 1, 5–106.

Chapter 9

Access to Medical Records

Kathy Gudgell

Contents

1-57444-123-X/98

Objectives

- To identify the sources of law governing the content and preservation of medical records
- To explain the reasons for the confidentiality of the medical record
- To discuss the appropriate times for disclosure
- To describe the process for accessing medical/health records, agency records, and/or other pertinent records
- To delineate the rules of evidence for introducing medical records at trial

Introduction

Legal nurse consultants (LNCs) spend many hours reviewing, analyzing, and preparing medical records for litigation. This task will often include identifying and obtaining records that are missing. In order to know what is missing, the LNC must first know what is supposed to be in the record and why. The LNC must then know if a record is obtainable and how to obtain it. Last, the LNC should be aware of some basic rules of evidence controlling the admissibility of the record in a court of law in order to ensure that the record meets these requirements.

Medical Records

Standards/Regulations Governing the Content of the Medical Record

What the medical record must contain is dictated by federal, state, and local regulations, accrediting organizations, institutional policy, and the professional standards of the practitioner who enters data in the record. The statutory requirements most often reflect the standards of health information management that one of the largest accrediting bodies in the United States, the Joint Commission on Accreditation of Healthcare Organizations (JCAHO) requires of its members.

JCAHO

JCAHO is a private, nonprofit organization that was founded in 1951 in order to provide a minimum level of quality in the medical care setting. The commission publishes separate annual manuals for different health care settings, with a fairly universal requirement for all settings that the medical record contain "sufficient information to identify the patient, support the diagnosis, justify the treatment, document the course and results, and promote continuity of care among health care providers" (JCAHO, 1996, p. 173).

According to JCAHO guidelines, the hospital record should consist of two categories of information — administrative data and clinical data. The administrative data should contain

1. An admission/discharge sheet with basic identification data
2. An attestation statement that indicates primary and secondary diagnoses, the final diagnosis, and the major procedures that were performed during the hospital stay
3. Conditions of admission that include a statement of consent by the patient to receive basic care
4. Consent forms for release of information to research groups and special consents for operative procedures

Clinical data should include

1. History and Physical (H&P) — A concise summary of past medical problems, familial history, social and personal data, as well as the present illness or chief complaint that led to the hospitalization. This summary, along with the physical exam described below should be completed within 24 h of admission and be readily available if the patient must undergo a surgical procedure. The physical examination should include a review of systems (ROS) assessment followed by the physician's impression/conclusions with a plan of care.
2. Physician Order Sheets — All orders must be written in the chart, dated, and authenticated or confirmed by authors that entries are correct which is usually accomplished by a valid signature. Verbal orders are acceptable only in emergency situations and must be signed and dated by the physician at the earliest possible time. Fax orders and authentication by computer key may be acceptable in some states.
3. Physician Progress Notes — Notes should be entered daily or with any change in the patient's condition or according to hospital policy.
4. Diagnostic Studies/Special Reports
5. Surgical Reports
6. Discharge Summary Report — The attending physician should make a timely note summarizing the major events during the hospitalization along with a discharge plan and follow-up care. A transfer note must accompany a patient who is transferred to another facility.
7. Nurses Notes/Data
8. Graphic Sheet
9. Medication Administration Record
10. Consult Reports
11. Records of Donation and Receipt of Transplant or Implants
12. Discharge Instructions to the Patient or Family
13. Autopsy Results

Federal

For those institutions participating in federal reimbursement programs, federal regulations regarding the content of the medical record will apply. These regulations are issued by a governmental agency, Health Care Financing Administration (HCFA) and published in the Code of Federal Regulations (CFR). Generally, the federal requirements coincide with those of JCAHO. They, too, require that the record include "information to justify admission and continued hospitalization, support the diagnosis, and describe the patient's progress and response to medications and services" (42 CFR 482.24(c), 1994). Like JCAHO, the federal agency has published specific regulations for different health care settings.

State

State regulations governing the content of the medical record vary greatly. Some states have promulgated a very detailed regulatory scheme that is based on JCAHO guidelines and/or federal Conditions of Participation rules, while others have only general requirements that would allow the institution to form its own guidelines as long as the guidelines conform to other controlling regulations. See Appendix 9.1 for information on ways to research state statutes.

For those states with more comprehensive regulations, the regulations will most likely be found in the state's administrative code rather than the statutes. Again, there will usually be specific regulations for different health care facilities with an underlying universal requirement that the record "contain sufficient information to identify the patient clearly, to justify the diagnosis and treatment and to document the results accurately" (Kansas Hospital Regulations 28-34-9a(d)(5), 1993).

Institutional

Institutional policies may further define the content of the facility's records. If institutional policies are more stringent than JCAHO or federal guidelines, the institution can be held to the higher standard by the JCAHO. The institution should therefore strive to be consistent with whatever policy it has implemented.

Institutional policies mostly dictate only the actions of its employees. However, some courts have found that an institution has an independent duty to monitor whether or not the physician, who is most often a nonemployee, is in compliance with federal record-keeping regulations. If the physician is not in compliance with these regulations, the physician's privileges to use the facility may be revoked or suspended.

Professional Standards

The American Medical Association (AMA) has published several policy statements concerning medical records (AMA, 1991). These have been fairly general statements that do not dictate the content of the record other than Policy #315.996 that addresses the use of scientific accuracy in racial, ethnic, and religious designations. It is expected, however, that the physician follow the JCAHO or other statutory record-keeping guidelines and that progress notes be legible, factual, relevant, and pertinent.

The content of physicians' office records is not generally mandated by regulation. In certain areas of practice, there may be record-keeping regulations if the physician is participating in certain federally controlled programs. For example, the federal Controlled Substance Act has a record-keeping requirement for the physician who "regularly engages in the dispensing or administering of controlled substances and charge patients, either separately or together with charges for other professional services, for substances so dispensed or administered" (21 CFR 1304.03(d), 1995).

The standards of nonphysician health care professionals may require certain information to be timely recorded. The *Standards of Clinical Nursing Practice* published in 1991 by the American Nurses Association (ANA) require that an assessment be "documented in a retrievable form," and a diagnosis be "documented in a manner that facilitates the determination of expected outcomes and plan of care" (ANA, 1991, p. 9–11). Other required recordings include measurable outcomes, the plan of care, interventions, and revisions of care (ANA, 1991). The standards of practice for physical therapists as published by the American Physical Therapy Association recommend the documentation of an initial evaluation to include identifying information plus provision of "sufficient data to establish time-related goals" and "objective measures to establish a baseline" (Scott, 1994, p. 210).

Retention of Records

Once the record is in existence, the holder or "custodian" of the record has the responsibility to safeguard the record and the information therein. The specific question that will be addressed in this section is the length of time the record must be preserved.

As with the content of medical records, retention of medical records is controlled by JCAHO recommendations, federal, state, local regulations, institutional policies, and professional organizational standards. Other factors such as space available and cost of storage may also influence a health care facility's retention-of-records policy.

According to JCAHO, the "hospital determines how long medical record information is retained, based on law and regulation and the information use for patient care, legal, research, and educational purposes" (JCAHO, 1996, p. 180). Federal law requires that institutions participating in federal reimbursement programs preserve records for a minimum of 5 years (42 CFR 482.24(b)).

As expected, state regulations vary. Some states mandate extensive retention policies such as North Dakota that requires that patient record be retained for 25 years, while some states do not address the issue (Hirsch, 1995). Other states require a 10-year retention period which exceeds federal law requirements but coincides with the recommendations of the American Hospital Association and the American Health Information Management Association (AHIMA) (Roach, 1994). In some states, there may be special rules that apply to the records of deceased patients that would allow destruction of the record earlier than the mandated period. Some rules mandate preservation of the whole record for a certain number of years and then permanent preservation of only specific parts thereafter (Roach, 1994).

The state record-keeping requirements and individual institutional policies are or should be heavily influenced by the state statute of limitations that controls tort and/or contract actions. A state may require that a medical malpractice case be commenced within 5 years of date of the injury. In that state, the record retention period would most likely be at least 5 years (Roach, 1994). Many states observe the "discovery" rule in determining the statute of limitations for tort actions. This generally means that the statute of limitations is not triggered until the patient has discovered an injury that was caused by someone's negligence. In these jurisdictions, the statute of limitations for tort actions is extremely variable as it may be many years before an injury due to negligence is discovered. It would therefore be prudent for a facility in a jurisdiction that follows the discovery rule to retain records indefinitely (Kingsolver, 1995).

Similarly, rules for the retention of records of minors are influenced by the statute of limitations for tortious actions against minors. Since a legal action can be commenced up to 1 or 2 years after the minor turns 18 in most states, the records of minors should be retained at least this long. Some states mandate that minor records must be kept until the age of majority plus 3 years (Roach, 1994). For those states following the discovery rule (see above), indefinite retention of records may be necessary.

The mission of the facility may have an impact on an institution's record retention policies. Educational and research facilities may have special needs for long-term preservation of records as they may wish to perform retrospective reviews or monitor long-term effects of drug trials. For these reasons, this type of facility may choose to retain records for 75 years or for an indefinite period (Roach, 1994). Businesses that keep exposure records as mandated by the Occupational Safety and Health Administration (OSHA) must retain the exposure record for 30 years (OSHA, 1993). Medical records mandated by OSHA must be kept by the business for the duration of employment plus 30 years (OSHA, 1993).

Whatever the retention policy may be, the custodian has the added duty to preserve the record in good order. Microfilming or computer storage is generally acceptable. If and when a document is destroyed, a record should be made of the name of the patient, the date of destruction, and the records destroyed (Hirsch, 1995).

Confidentiality/Privacy/Privilege

Patients reveal many details of their private and personal life to their physician. This disclosure of private information is expected and encouraged so that a physician is in possession of all pertinent information needed to make a diagnosis and treat the patient appropriately. In turn, it has been the ethical duty of the physician to maintain the details of the patient's illness and communications arising thereof in confidence. This confidentiality between physician and patient has been an accepted practice since the time of Hippocrates who said:

> Whatsoever things I see or hear concerning the life of men, in my attendance on the sick or even apart therefrom, which ought not be noised abroad, I will keep silence thereon, counting such things to be as sacred secrets.

This tradition to maintain communications confidential between physician and patient has been extended to the information contained within the written record.

In fact, in the U.S., it is not just an ethical and moral duty to protect the confidential information in the patient's file but a legal obligation that is imposed upon the custodian of the record. The U.S. Supreme Court has determined in recent decisions that the right of privacy is guaranteed by the U.S. Constitution. Privacy is defined as the right to "have peace of mind regarding the exposure and revelation of [one's] body, or depictions thereof, to unauthorized persons" (Hirsch, 1995, p. 312). The right to confidentiality or protection from the unauthorized release of information stems from this right to privacy.

Besides court decisions, there are also laws that protect the confidentiality of medical records. Those institutions that are agents of the federal government are compelled by the Privacy Act of 1974 to maintain medical records confidential. This Act requires that the collection of data by federal agencies must be relevant to the agency's authorized purpose and can be released only with permission. A more recent law, the Americans with Disabilities Act requires that all information obtained about employees during medical examinations be maintained as confidential information (Gosfield, 1996).

On the horizon is a Medical Records Privacy Act that was proposed in 1995 (S. Bill 1360, 104th Cong., 1st Session) that would supersede state laws that are inconsistent with its provisions. Besides establishing access of medical records to patients who are termed "subjects of the Protected Health Information (PHI)," this act outlines restrictions on use and disclosure of the PHI otherwise. The Act would provide for civil and criminal sanctions against the health information trustee (HIT) who violates the disclosure provisions.

An evidentiary rule that goes hand in hand with confidential communications between physician and patient is the concept of "privileged" communication between certain professionals and other individuals. Many states recognize communications between physician and patient and betweeen psychotherapist and patient as privileged. The patient is the one who holds the privilege, which means that the professional may not reveal the details of the communication unless the patient allows the professional to do so. There are some exceptions to this rule of disclosure which are discussed below.

In order for the communication to be privileged, it must have occurred in a confidential setting. Discussing one's medical condition to one's physician outside of a professional setting in the presence of acquaintances destroys the privilege. The relationship must also be one that society seeks to foster and confidentiality must be necessary to maintaining a full and satisfactory relationship between the parties. Last, the injury that would inure by disclosure must be greater than the benefit gained in litigation (Hirsch, 1995).

If the above conditions are met, a physician/patient communication is considered privileged and immune to discovery absent waiver of the privilege by other circumstances. This privilege may extend to physicians' office staff if they are functioning as agents of the physician. In a recent case in Georgia, *Plunkett v. Ginsburg*, 456 S.E. 2d 595, the Court of Appeals found that a psychiatrist/patient privilege granted by statute in Georgia did not extend to nurses who were acting outside of their capacity as agents of the physician.

State laws governing confidentiality of medical records and privileged communications differ greatly in their protection. Some provide strong sanctions against offenders; others are very lenient. The laws usually attempt to balance the individual's "right to privacy" and the public's "right to know" according to the policy of the various states. For example, a person who sought medical treatment in an Oklahoma hospital had wounds that fit the description of a man suspected of rape. The treating physician disclosed the man's identity to the police. After the man was arrested and convicted for rape, he sued the physician for breach of confidentiality. The Supreme Court of Oklahoma in *Bryson v. Tillinghast,* 749 P.2d 110 (Okla. 1988) found that public policy favored disclosure without permission in this instance (Roach, 1994). The breach of confidentiality suit against the physician was unsuccessful.

Access by the Patient

It is now almost universally acknowledged that ownership of the physical medical record, which includes radiographs and all other reports, resides in the facility or the health care practitioner who made the record subject to the patient's interest to the information contained therein. In the past, the custodian has argued that the subject of the information did not have the right of access to the record. Many states have since conferred a statutory right of access to patients. Other state courts have recognized a common law right to access.

As mentioned above, a proposed federal law would provide for universal access by a patient to his or her medical records. OSHA mandates that an employee have access to his/her record of exposure to toxic substances and/or any relevant medical records held by the employer (OSHA, 1993). If no exposure record exists, the employee has the right to review records of other employees with similar job duties without the other employees' permission. Access to medical records of other employees with similar job duties requires specific written consent from the other employee (OSHA, 1993).

The right to request the records of a minor patient resides in the parent or the legal guardian. In the case of divorced parents, the custodial parent is the one with the right to access for a minor child. For a deceased patient, the administrator of the estate may request medical records (*KMA Journal,* 1995) or as otherwise designated by state law.

Access is defined as reasonable access. The patient or a person authorized by the patient may review the record in the medical records department of a health care facility under supervision at a time that is convenient for the facility. Or, a notarized request identifying the specific records the patient desires may be sent to the facility. The institution then has the responsibility to reproduce the record in a timely fashion. The facility cannot refuse to reproduce the record despite nonpayment of other outstanding bills. Most states allow the facility to charge a reasonable fee for the copying services (Roach, 1994). This "reasonable fee" should reflect the actual costs to the hospital for record duplication and may range from $0.10 to $1.00 per page.

Access is not guaranteed to all records in all states. A few state laws restrict access to the mental health record. In New York, if a patient requests his or her mental health records, the patient's physician is notified of the request. The facility may refuse or approve access based on the physician's opinion that release of the record will or will not be damaging to the mental health of the client. Some states restrict access to the medical record to inpatients and require that the patient be released from the facility's care prior to review of his or her record (Roach, 1994).

Whatever policies the holder of the record institutes in order to accommodate patients' access to their records, there must be controls in place to maintain the confidentiality of the record during copying or reviewing of the record at the facility. For example, the original record should not be removed from the facility for copying purposes and there should be an area for reviewing the record that may be supervised by hospital personnel.

Access by Third Parties without the Patient's Express Consent

There are instances in which confidential information will be released to third parties without the express permission of the patient. In fact, there are times when the confidential information must be disclosed to governmental agencies in order to protect a public interest.

Information may be released to a third party when the actions of the patient have implied consent or waiver. It is generally assumed when a spouse, family member, or significant other is present during a discussion of the patient's medical condition that the health care practitioner may speak freely concerning private information. If there are questions concerning which family members should have access to information at a later date, the health care practitioner should consult with the patient. Ascertaining which family members may receive information would be particularly important for the health care practitioner in a federal facility treating alcohol and substance abuse patients where confidentiality requirements are stringent.

In some states, the filing of a lawsuit which brings the plaintiff's physical or mental condition into issue acts as consent to examine the relevant portions of the individual's medical records by the opposing side (Hirsch, 1995). Consent of a patient to store information in a clinical data bank that would be accessible to several health care practitioners may be construed by some state courts as a waiver of the physician/patient privilege making those records no longer confidential (Gosfield, 1996).

The information in the medical record is available to quality assurance personnel in the health care facility, researchers (Roach, 1994), auditing committees, and billing departments (Feutz-Harter, 1989). Insurance companies may have access to confidential records in order to determine third-party payments. In many instances, the patient signs a general waiver allowing the above collections of data upon admission to a health care facility.

The type of information that is not readily accessible to third parties without very specific consent of the patient depends on federal and state statutes. A federal law severely restricts access to alcohol and drug abuse records (42 CFR 2.1 et seq.). The facility may not even acknowledge the presence of the client in the facility without the client's permission. The consent form for release of information is highly specific and includes an expiration date for the consent. The disclosure must be accompanied by a statement that the receiving facility does not have the right to redisclose without redisclosure authorization (Feutz-Harter, 1989).

Access to information regarding nonparties to a lawsuit that would be used to prove recurring negligence or some other issue may or may not be allowed. If the identity of the other patients can be redacted from the record and the litigant can show good cause, the court may allow discovery of such information

(Hirsch, 1995). In criminal cases, patient records are generally obtainable when investigating charges of Medicaid fraud or when the patient is a victim of a crime (Pozgar, 1996).

Access to sensitive information such as HIV results or information indicating a diagnosis of AIDS may be denied to nonauthorized individuals. In Kentucky, a request for "all" medical records does not include release of information about sexually transmitted disease (*KMA Journal*, 1995). Rather, a very specific request outlining the exact information that the patient is willing to release must be included. A specific request may also be necessary in some states for genetic screening and testing information (Gosfield, 1996).

Two other areas of very sensitive information are sperm donor and adoption records. In both instances, strict confidentiality laws were designed partially to protect the identity of the natural parents. Access to both types of records has undergone major changes in the last 20 years. Although the federal courts have upheld the constitutionality of the older statutes that refuse to break the seal of secrecy of donor/adoption records, many states have changed those restrictive laws to allow disclosure of relevant medical information to the child or child's representative. However, the disclosure is, most often, not automatic and falls within the discretion of a governing body or the court that will release the information only upon the showing of good cause (Roach, 1994).

Mandatory Disclosure

Some types of confidential medical record information must be disclosed. The specific reporting requirements may vary from state to state but every state has mandated the reporting of suspected child abuse. Different contagious diseases are also reportable in different states. All states require the reporting of AIDS. Some states allow the health care practitioner to disclose a patient's HIV status to the patient's partner although it may not create a duty to do so (Roach, 1994).

Other mandatory disclosures include the reporting of births and deaths, certain wounds, accidents and/or other violently incurred injuries, fatalities due to blood transfusions and/or certain medical devices, workers' compensation claims, seizures, certain congenital diseases such as the inborn error of metabolism PKU, and/or occupational diseases.

Most states have Open Records Acts that would operate to make medical records at a state hospital mandatorily available to the general public except for an exemption protecting the confidentiality of the record. The Freedom of Information Act (FOIA) is the federal counterpart to the states Open Records Acts. Like the Privacy Act, however, it applies only to true federal agencies and not to those agencies merely receiving federal funds. The FOIA also exempts disclosure of medical records if it would "constitute a clearly unwarranted invasion of personal privacy" (Hirsch, 1995, p. 322). Other business records from public institutions, however, including minutes of board meetings, are subject to disclosure under the state or federal open records law (Kingsolver, 1995).

In a famous California case, *Tarasoff v. Board of Regents,* 7 Cal. 3d 425, the court imposed a duty on health care practitioners to warn third parties of a credible threat against them. In this case, a patient informed his psychiatrist of his intent to harm a third person. Considering himself bound by confidentiality, the psychiatrist did not reveal the danger to the third party. The third party was injured and died by the patient's hand. In litigation brought by the victim's parents, the court found that the psychiatrist had not only been released from the bonds of confidentiality but had a duty to warn the third party of the impending danger.

Computerized Records

Not all record-keeping guidelines have kept pace with computer technology. For example, some states still require that records be written or signed in ink. This requirement is clearly inconsistent with computer-created records and calls into question the legality of the computerized record in that state. The trend toward computerized records, however, is clear. The use of computerized records has been investigated by the Department of Health and Human Services as a way to reduce governmental health care administration costs (Minor, 1996). Many private health care facilities are in the process of implementing or have implemented some form of medical record computerization.

With the growing acceptance of computer technology revolutionizing the management of information, the health care practitioner/facility must adjust to the new problems caused by the integration of computerized data. Maintaining restricted access to confidential records is becoming more and more difficult as innumerable unauthorized persons gain access to the record-keeping system. The risk of loss or destruction of computerized data must also be addressed.

The issue of confidentiality is further confused by the fact that information is instantly transmitted from one state to another. Since state confidentiality laws may be inconsistent, it becomes unclear which state law is controlling when there are rapid transmissions to successive locations.

Security measures will not completely protect computerized information, but some reasonable measures must be taken to show a good faith effort to preserve confidentiality and to protect the data from inadvertent loss. These efforts should include technical features such as passwords, procedural approaches such as security training and periodic risk assessments, physical safeguards such as restricting access to terminals, and personnel safeguards such as hiring appropriate staff who can abide by confidentiality requirements (Lawrence, 1994).

There should be a well-designed user-identification system. Encryption of the data and use of digitalized signatures may be used to ensure that data have not been altered during transmission. Dial-back modems that check the identify of the person calling for access is a method of authenticating a request for data. Backup programs and virus detection programs will protect the computerized data from destruction or loss.

Whatever system is instituted, it should balance the right of privacy and the need for quick access to the data (Gosfield, 1996). The method of generating computer records must also be trustworthy enough to meet the evidentiary rules for admission of the medical record into evidence during litigation (see below).

Nondiscoverable Information

Other than sensitive health care information cited above that cannot be released without express authorization, there are records pertaining to patient care that may not be accessible. These include peer review records and incident reports.

Medical staff of health care facilities are generally charged with the responsibility to ensure the quality of care of patients and to oversee the ethical and professional practices of staff members. Part of this responsibility is carried out by peer review which entails the evaluation of "professional performance, ethical behavior, quality of care, utilization patterns, or selected aspects of the performance" of the medical staff and other health care professionals (Cronan, 1995).

In order to promote open and frank discussion during peer review evaluations, communications revealed during these conferences are usually privileged and immune to discovery (Neil, 1994). This means that participants cannot be sued for statements made during an evaluation conference that might otherwise be considered defamatory nor will the record of the meeting be made available for a patient pursuing a legal action against the subject of the peer review.

The extent of nondiscoverable items is usually restricted to the notes/minutes/reports made by the committee itself. It does not apply to the medical record. What may fall in the gray area of things that are discoverable or not are recommendations made by the committee concerning the continuing or revocation of staff privileges based on a finding of the board (Neil, 1994).

Incident reports are not granted the same privilege as peer review evaluations, but they may be just as inaccessible. An incident report is a report of an unusual event "not consistent within the routine operation of the hospital or the routine care of a particular patient ... it may be an accident or a situation which could result in an accident" (Hirsch, 1995, p. 301). If the incident report is filed as part of the medical record, it may be discoverable and admissible into court under the business records exception to the hearsay rule (see below).

If the incident report is directed to the legal department of the facility, it may be undiscoverable as the facility will argue that the report was made in anticipation of litigation. Documents that are prepared with "an eye toward litigation" are considered the attorney's work product which is generally undiscoverable. Even work product such as the incident report in this instance can be discoverable, however, if a record of the incident is otherwise unavailable and the fact witnesses have no recollection of the event. Alternatively, the incident report may be undiscoverable if it can be characterized as part of the peer review process, in which case, statutory immunity to discovery may apply.

Using the Legal Process to Obtain Access

Medical records may be obtained from health care facilities and practitioners by the client's representative after a release form has been properly signed. It may be necessary to involve the court to obtain records if one of the parties refuses to allow the other party access to the documents in his or her possession. If a party refuses to disclose medical records, the statute of limitation may be tolled based on the theory of fraudulent concealment (Feutz-Harter, 1989). In those states with access guaranteed by statute, a private cause of action may arise against the custodian if access is refused.

After a lawsuit is filed, whether in federal or state court, the parties begin investigating the facts/issues of the case through formal discovery processes. One method of discovery is the request for production of documents. If the document is not produced, the party seeking the document can file a motion with the court to compel production. If the motion is granted, the opposing party must produce the document or face the possibility of sanctions including a charge of contempt of court (Lobe, 1995).

Another method of discovery is the subpoena which would require attendance of a party or witness to court or to a deposition. This may be accompanied by a subpoena *duces tecum* which requires that certain documents be brought to the deposition (McHugh, 1995). If the witness at trial or deposition is asked to reveal privileged or confidential information, the witness should consult an attorney before responding. The attorney may file a motion for a protective order asking the court to allow the witness to refuse to answer. In the case of substance abuse records, under federal law, there must be a court order accompanying the subpoena finding that disclosure of this confidential information "is more important than the purpose for which Congress mandated confidentiality" before disclosure should occur (Hirsch, 1995, p. 330).

Health Care Practitioner Information that must Be Requested

In 1990, a national data bank called the National Practitioner Data Bank (NPDB) (45 CFR 60.1–60.14, 1994) was created pursuant to the 1986 Health Care Quality Improvement Act. The NPDB established reporting requirements from health care entities to the bank whenever an adverse licensure or professional review action or a payment occurred as a result of a medical malpractice action. A query to the NPDB must be made by a health care facility whenever a health care practitioner applies for clinical privileges at the facility. Since JCAHO requires a practitioner to apply for clinical privileges at a health care facility every 2 years, the hospital must request information from the NPDB upon the initial application for privileges and every 2 years thereafter. If a subsequent legal action arises, the hospital is deemed to be in possession of the information in the data bank. "Knowledge of an adverse action is imputed to the hospital whether the hospital makes the inquiry or not" (45 CFR 60.11(5), 1994).

The NPDB will only disclose information of the adverse action or payment of a claim to those health care groups that qualify under the law. These include health care practitioners making queries about themselves, health care facilities granting privileges, professional societies, state licensing boards, and some federal agencies (Antoine, 1995). There is one instance whereby the information will be disclosed to an attorney. In the event that an attorney has filed suit against an institution and requests information from the NPDB concerning a defendant party, the NPDB will release the information "only upon submission of evidence that the hospital failed to request information from the Data Bank as required by 60.10(a), and may be used solely with respect to litigation resulting from the action or claim against the hospital" (45 CFR 60.11(5) 1994).

Evidentiary Rules

Introduction

Just as there are federal and state rules of civil and criminal procedure controlling the process of a legal action, there are federal and state rules controlling what information and witnesses can be used in the courtroom. Since state rules vary, the emphasis of this discussion will be on the Federal Rules of Evidence (FRE).

Hearsay Rule

Part of the job of the trier of fact in the courtroom, whether a judge or jury, is to evaluate the witness's perception, memory, and narration of events. The court system attempts to promote these three factors by requiring the witness to take an oath and testify in the personal presence of the judge or jury, but, most importantly, by subjecting the witness to cross-examination (FRE 801, Advisory Committee Notes).

The right to cross-examine adverse witnesses has been considered so vital to the legal process that the FRE does not allow statements into evidence that are offered to prove the truth of the matter asserted unless the declarant is present at trial. This is the hearsay rule of evidence. There are many instances, however, where the court has found the out-of-court statement to be so reliable and trustworthy that cross-examination of the declarant who made the statement is not necessary to test its truthfulness. These instances have been incorporated into the Rules of Federal Evidence as exceptions to the hearsay rule.

Business records fall into the category of reliable and trustworthy evidence that is admissible whether the declarant is available or not when it meets the requirements of 803(6):

> A memorandum, report, record, or data compilation, in any form, of acts, events, conditions, opinions, or diagnosis, made at or near the time by, or from information transmitted by, a person with knowledge, if kept in the course of a regularly conducted business activity, and if it was the regular practice of that business activity to make the memorandum, report, record, or data compilation, all as shown by the testimony of the Custodian or other qualified witness, unless the source of information or the method or circumstances of preparation indicate lack of trustworthiness.

Therefore, according to the rule, the four indicators of reliability of business records are that they were made as a part of a regularly conducted business, they were made close in time to the event, the events were observed and recorded by a person with knowledge, or transmitted to the recorder by a person with knowledge (Egan, 1994).

Medical records usually fall into the category of business records as they are made by persons under a "business duty" to record accurate information to assist in the diagnosing and treating of patients (the ordinary course of business for a health care practitioner/facility). The information is further authenticated by the responsible individual with a signature. The record is made close in time to the event so that the record is not skewed by lapses in memory. It is made by persons with firsthand knowledge or by those with information transmitted by persons with firsthand knowledge, again ensuring accuracy.

If the record can be contested on any one of these grounds, it may not be accepted as a reliable enough piece of evidence to allow admission under the business rule exception to hearsay. Computerized printouts will generally qualify as a business record as FRE 803(6) is fairly broad in its description of what a record is (report, memorandum, or "data compilation"). However, if a computerized record does not provide an acceptable legal signature, it may be contested. If there are not safeguards in place within the computerized system to protect against modifications without erasing the original entry, the accuracy and reliability of the record can be contested (Waller, 1995). Another problem with the computerized record is the inability to determine whether the record is complete or not, a necessary requirement to be admissible under another evidentiary rule (Mauet, 1996).

In order to prove to the court that the medical record is reliable and trustworthy, it must be introduced at trial in such as way that it fulfills the four requirements of 803(6). A witness must be able to identify the record and verify that it was made at or near the time of the event by a person with knowledge in the regular course of business. In the case of computer records, the witness should also be familiar with the safeguards that were/are in place to protect the reliability and accuracy of the record including ways that the data was gathered, stored, and can be retrieved (FRE, 1992). The FRE no longer requires that the custodian of the record be the one through whom the evidence is introduced as long as the witness is qualified to testify how the record was made. Many state rules of evidence are consistent with the federal business records exception to hearsay (Mauet, 1996).

There are other grounds upon which the medical record can be contested to prevent admission of the document into evidence. There may be instances in the record whereby the statement that is recorded is hearsay — the "double hearsay" problem. For example, the health care practitioner may have recorded statements concerning the immediate cause of injury or assertions about fault. Unless those statements fall within an exception to the hearsay rule, it cannot be admitted into evidence to prove the cause of injury or fault. Most often, however, the admission of medical records is not an issue at trial as the parties will generally resolve any disputes concerning the medical records at a pre-trial conference.

Public Records Exception

The public records exception is another exception to the hearsay rule that is very similar to the business records exception. Like the business records exception, its reliability for accurateness depends on the recording of data by persons with firsthand knowledge under a duty to make the report. The public records exception, however, applies only to records made by public offices or agencies and so would be useful only for public health care facilities.

Best Evidence Rule

The "best evidence" rule calls for the best evidence of the contents of the original document whenever the contents of the document are at issue. The contents of medical records may be an issue when/if a party is attempting to prove spoliation of the evidence or tampering of the document. In that instance, the original record may need to be produced rather than a copy of the record.

In most other cases, "a duplicate is admissible to the same extent as an original unless (1) a genuine question is raised as to the authenticity of the original or (2) in the circumstances it would be unfair to admit the duplicate in lieu of the original" (FRE 1003). The authenticity requirement is met when there is sufficient evidence "to support a finding that the matter in question is what the proponent claims" (FRE 901).

Federal Rule of Evidence 1006: Summaries

Medical records are often voluminous. FRE 1006 allows the preparation of summaries of writings, recordings, or photographs which cannot conveniently be examined by the court as long as the originals are available. The parties must have notice of the use of summaries at trial and an opportunity to compare the summaries to the record for accuracy. The preparer of the summaries must be available for cross-examination in order to explain how the summary was made and why it is an accurate and relevant representation of the records.

The federal rule, however, does not specifically state that the summary must be made available to the opposing party at pre-trial conference, although it has been argued that "the framers of the Rule clearly contemplated a pre-trial resolution of any issues that may be raised concerning the use of summaries" (FRE 1006). Some states do require exchange of proposed summaries prior to trial.

Exhibits

A summary is essentially an example of an exhibit as it is an aid in the presentation of the case to the trier of fact. An exhibit can be "anything, other than testimony, that can be perceived by the senses and be presented in the courtroom" (Mauet, 1996). There are, however, some restrictions as to the information that will be acceptable for admission. The exhibit cannot be so prejudicial or inflammatory that it outweighs its probative effect. For example, graphic pictures of a deceased motor vehicle accident victim with multiple injuries must have some evidentiary relevancy to the case. An attempt to sway the jury by provoking certain emotional responses alone should not be allowed. The determination of admissibility is made by the court.

There is also a particular sequence of questions/actions that must be followed in order to meet the foundation requirements for admissibility. These requirements are that the witness is competent to introduce the evidence, the evidence is relevant, and authenticated. The exhibit must reasonably depict the place/device it represents and in some courts, be helpful in the witness's explanation of the events to the trier of fact.

References

American Medical Association, *Policy Compendium*, AMA, 1991, 225–231.
American Nurses Association, *Standards of Clinical Nursing Practice*, ANA, 1991.

Antoine, M. P., Protecting peer review and hospital committee records, in *Health Care Facility Records: Confidentialilty, Computerization and Security.* Loyola University, Chicago, 1995, 27–46.

Cronan, C. J., Credentialing and peer review, *Kentucky Health Law*, Continuing Legal Education Department, University of Kentucky, 1995.

Release of patient medical records, *KMA Journal*, 93, 297–300, 1995.

Egan, T. P. et al., Admission of business records into evidence: using the business records exception and other techniques, *Defense Law Journal*, 677, 1994.

Federal Rules of Evidence, West Publishing Co., St. Paul, MN, 1992.

Feutz-Harter, S., *Nursing and the Law*, 5th ed., PESI, 73–84, 1989.

Gosfield, A., *Health Law Handbook*, 1996 ed., Deerfield, IL, 145–173.

Hirsch, H., Medical records, in *Legal Medicine,* Mosby, St. Louis, 1995, 297–311.

Hirsch, H., Disclosure about patients, in *Legal Medicine,* Mosby, St. Louis, 1995, 312–342.

JCAHO, *1996 Accreditation Manual for Hospitals,* Vol. 1, *Standards,* JCAHO, 1996, 171–186.

Kingsolver, J., Information and access issues in the health care environment, *Kentucky Health Law*, University of Kentucky, 1995.

Lawrence, L. M., Safeguarding the confidentiality of automated medical information, *Journal of Quality Improvement*, 20, 639, 1994.

Lobe, T. E., *Medical Malpractice: A Physician's Guide*, McGraw-Hill, New York, 1995.

Mauet, T., *Trial Techniques*, Little, Brown, Boston, 1996, 139–213.

Minor, B., The impact of information technology on medical records privacy, *Medical Trial Technical Quarterly*, Summer, 87–105, 1996.

Neil, B. A., Medical records committees: should they tell us what they know? *Trial Dip. J.,* 17, 11–15, 1994.

Nolfi, E. A., *Basic Legal Research,* Macmillan/McGraw-Hill, New York, 1993.

OSHA, *Access to Medical and Exposure Records,* U.S. Department of Labor, 1993, 1–18.

Pozgar, G., *Legal Aspects of Health Care Administration*, Aspen Publications, Gaithersburg, MD, 1996.

Roach, W. H., *Medical Records and the Law*, Aspen Publishers, Gaithersburg, MD, 1994.

Scott, R., *Legal Aspects of Documenting Patient Care*, Aspen Publishers, Gaithersburg, Md, 1994.

Waller, A., Computerized records: legal and security issues, in *Health Care Facility Records: Confidentiality, Computerization and Security,* Loyola University, Chicago, 1995, 47–72.

Bibliography

36 Am. Jur. Trials 695. Obtaining, Organizing and Abstracting Medical Records for Use in a Lawsuit.

Flight, M., The medical record, in *Law, Liability and Ethics,* 2nd ed., Delmar Publishers, 111–133.

Garmer, W. et al., *Medical Malpractice*, University of Kentucky Press, Lexington. In press.

Harney, D., *Medical Malpractice*, 3rd ed., Michie Co., Charlottesville, VA, 485–503.

Hirsch, H., Medical records: everything you always wanted to know, *Medical Trial Technical Quarterly*, 40, 285–326, 1994.

Huffman, E., *Health Information Management,* Physicians' Record Company, Berwyn, IL, 1994.

Jessen, J. H., Electronic evidence discovery opens new doors in litigation, *Medical Malpractice: Law & Strategy*, II., February, 1–2, 1994.

Nagel, D., Medical privacy: technology is eroding confidentiality, *Newsday*, October 27, 1995.

Szekely, D. G. et al., Legal issues of the electronic dental records; security and confidentiality, *Journal of Dental Education*, 60, 19–23, 1996.

Appendix 9.1
Researching State Statutes

The easiest way to search state statutes is through an electronic database such as Westlaw or Lexis. Even the World Wide Web offers some on-line services for state law. This discussion will be a brief introduction to nonelectronic legal research.

If you are unlucky enough to be researching the law the old-fashioned way, you must have access to a law library that has a copy of your state's statutes. If you have a choice between a set of statutes that are annotated or not, use the copy that is annotated. Annotated copies contain case summaries of how the court has interpreted the law. After locating the statutes, search the index which is usually a separate volume for the particular topic in which you are interested. For example, "Confidentiality" may provide you with a cite for the statute controlling confidentiality of medical records in your state, or try "Medical Records." Similarly, you may research the Statute of Limitations in your state for tort actions by looking under "Statute."

After finding the appropriate section and reading the law, read the addendum information after the statute. There may be history notes or research references. In the annotated copy, there may be cites to case law that explain some of the language used in the statute. Next, check the inside covers of the volume. There are often legislative changes to the law that occur between times of publication of hard copies of the statutes. These changes are published in pamphlet form and placed inside the front or back cover of the appropriate volume of the statutes and are called "pocket parts." It is essential that the pocket part be reviewed for the latest version of the law.

The statute may refer to an administrative code. While the legislature mandates broad laws, agencies with greater expertise and knowledge of technical details are empowered to publish rules and regulations that control the specifics on how to carry out the law. These rules and regulations have the effect of law as the legislature voted these bodies into existence and gave them authority to make binding regulations. Most often, it will be the administrative code in which you would find more detailed rules such as what must be included in the medical records.

Statutes are enacted into law by legislative bodies but are subject to interpretation by the courts. Statutes are not always clearly written and may carry ambiguous meanings. To be certain that a court in your state has not found the statute to be unconstitutional or interpreted the wording in a way that is not favorable to your point of view, you may wish to research case law within your jurisdiction. An easy way to check the most recent decisions concerning your statute is to "shepherdize" the statute. *Shepherd's Citations* publications are listings of cases that refer back to other cases or statutes. As with pocket parts, it is essential that any case or statute upon which you plan to rely be shepherdized for the most recent rulings.

For example, in 1990, Kentucky's statute of limitation for medical malpractice actions required that the suit be commenced within 5 years from the date on which the alleged negligent act or omission occurred. The Supreme Court of Kentucky, however, found that this statute interfered with a right granted by the Kentucky State Constitution allowing its citizens to have access to the courts and found the 5-year statute of limitations unconstitutional. The 5-year limitation, however, was still on the books. If a researcher was not diligent in checking the pocket part or shepherdizing the statute to determine if case law had overturned the statute, a grave error could occur. For statutes from other states, the process is exactly the same providing the law library has a copy of the other state statutes.

Case law is published in volumes called "reporters" and can also be found in the law library. Federal case law is reported in federal "reporters" and the states are divided into seven loosely associated geographical groupings. For example, case law from West Virginia, Virginia, North Carolina, South Carolina, and Georgia is published in the South Eastern Reporters and case law from North Dakota, South Dakota, Nebraska, Minnesota, Iowa, and Wisconsin is published in the North Western Reporter, etc.

An excellent resource for legal research is *Finding the Law* by Morris Cohen et al., although the latest edition was published in 1989 and it may provide more detail than you care to explore. As a last (or maybe first) resort, the law librarian should prove to be very helpful.

Section III

Legal Nurse Consultant Practice Environments and Practice Areas

In the last decade of the 20th century, traditional nursing practice — hospital-based — has altered to a degree that would have been hard to imagine just 20 or 30 years ago. Nursing practice has infiltrated all types of community settings. At the same time, nurses have become less bound by tradition, notions of hierarchy, and physical facility restrictions. The motivated nurse with entrepreneur spirit and skills has recognized potential career opportunities and applied nursing education and experience to pioneer new areas of practice.

In the following section, the reader will find a sampling of the areas of practice, positions, and environments in which nurses have applied their expertise in the legal arena. This survey is not meant to be all inclusive or provide detailed information on the topics, but it demonstrates the wide variety of practice opportunities currently available for LNCs. The opportunities are evolving as the medical and legal interface changes as altered by market forces and politics. These descriptions provide the reader an overview of the current broad scope of practice of LNCs and the rich contribution they are making in a wide variety of environments to health care–related legal issues.

by Jill Holmes, RN

Chapter 10

The Legal Nurse Consultant Practice Environment

Sue Barnes, Paula Schenck, Kathleen Spiegel, Jill Holmes,
Suzanne D. Schutze, and Judith L. Bragdon

Contents

1-57444-123-X/98
© 1998 by American Association of Legal Nurse Consultants

Objectives

Upon the completion of Chapter 10, the reader will be able to:

■ Describe the practice environment of the legal nurse consultant in an independent setting, the law firm, an insurance company, and a risk management department
■ Describe the advantages and disadvantages of being an independent legal nurse consultant
■ Describe the pros and cons of working in-house for a law firm
■ Differentiate between the role of the claim representative and risk management consultant in an insurance company
■ List the responsibilities of the legal nurse consultant in risk management
■ Explain how the nursing process is used in investigation of violations of health care statutes

The Legal Nurse Consultant in Independent Practice by Sue Barnes

One of the most-liberating paradigms of nursing practice alternatives is the legal nurse consultant (LNC) in independent practice. The nurse having "the (new) right stuff," as described by Joline Godfrey in her book *Our Wildest Dreams,* can achieve professional satisfaction by starting a business and developing it consistent with personal career goals. There are challenges in the process, new skills that must be learned, and financial considerations that must be addressed in selecting this particular career path.

What does it take to be an independent LNC entrepreneur? It takes most of the same attributes and skills required in other business ventures. A "can do" attitude is one of the most important characteristics. This optimistic outlook enables the individual to look beyond the obstacles and see the possibilities. Carpenito and Neal (1994) conducted a survey of 20 entrepreneurs who responded that an entrepreneur should be creative, flexible, and enthusiastic. Additionally, it takes energy, commitment, persistence, self-confidence, and setting of achievable goals and time lines. Being self-motivated, organized, disciplined, and maintaining high standards are also important for working in an unstructured environment. The Center for Entrepreneurial Management survey (as cited in Carpenito and Neal, 1994) found that successful entrepreneurs have been fired from a job, have a bachelor's or master's degree, are very organized, are extroverts and enjoy people. The "right stuff" to create a business is often not taught but learned through risk taking and failure (Godfrey, 1992). While having worked in a law firm can be an asset for the LNC considering independent practice, it is not a prerequisite for the individual who is self-directed. The key contribution of the LNC to litigation, after all, is health care knowledge and experience; numerous resources are available to learn the less critical but enriching legal aspects of case analysis.

Many nurses find the major motivation for starting an independent LNC business is empowerment. Establishing one's own business parameters that include what, where, when, and how much is the biggest advantage of becoming an independent consultant. The LNC may choose the client, the workload, and work assignments that are consistent with personal values and interests. There are no monthly reports, requisitions for supplies, or endless meetings. Personality conflicts and office politics are eliminated. Feedback is provided on an ongoing basis when the client pays the bill and uses the services again. Rarely do business crises occur. If the client does have a rush job, the price goes up to compensate for the increased workload and rescheduling of priorities. The LNC sets project priority usually based on dollar value or an established due date.

Time flexibility is another advantage of working as an independent LNC. There is no established time to begin and end work, there is no specific number of sick days or allotted days off.

This scenario seems attractive to the overworked clinical practitioner or stressed in-house LNC, physically and emotionally drained by the demands of employment and lack of control. However, it is important to note that most independent LNCs with thriving practices frequently work evenings and weekends in addition to the regular workweek. Although there is no escape for the independent LNC from hard work and long hours, the personal gratification may be great.

For the independent LNC, income has unlimited potential depending on business and personal choices. The amount of work and the business structure are determined by income goals and ambition. Establishing a reasonable fee schedule and building a steady client base is important for meeting the minimum income requirement. A single individual can only generate a limited number of billable hours. Once a business is established, if more income is desired, it can be expanded by delegating work to independent contractors or employees. Income is then limited only by the LNC's business acumen.

There are disadvantages to independent practice which must be taken into careful consideration. Even if the idea of an independent practice is appealing, not everyone has the attributes, skills, or resources to succeed. The income is not stable or predictable, and ceases for the solo practitioner if he or she does not work due to illness or vacation. It can take up to 2 years or more to build a dependable clientele in a small practice. Projects can take 2 weeks to 2 months and billing turnaround time is on the average 30 to 45 days, sometimes more. Marketing, fee negotiation, and bill collection are not skills with which many nurses are proficient or comfortable. Bill collection can be frustrating, as well as time and resource consuming. Efforts may culminate in occasional write-offs or filing suit against a client in small claims court. Large projects can require subcontractors which may mean substantial out-of-pocket expenses paid up-front prior to collection of fees. Other economic considerations are the lack of benefits including health insurance, paid vacations and sick time, and a retirement package. Taxes are not automatically deducted from a paycheck, necessitating payment of estimated taxes. Self-discipline and a plan are necessary to manage income. The services of an accountant are essential. There are expenses for office rent, equipment, books, marketing, support and professional services, and supplies. Many nonbillable hours are spent on marketing, invoicing, and other administrative tasks necessary to keep the business operating. The isolation of an independent practice is also a major consideration for some people. While there is daily contact with the "outside" world via the telephone, the socialization of most large work-places is conspicuously absent for the lone practitioner. These issues must be carefully deliberated when considering independent LNC practice. It is not all glamour and big money!

The best advice for a nurse without LNC experience contemplating independent LNC practice is to find a mentor and "don't quit your day job" until the business is on solid ground. Networking is the best way to find a mentor; AALNC is the best source for mentors. Attending AALNC annual conferences and local chapter meetings offers the best opportunities to develop relationships with seasoned LNCs. For those nurses who have never worked in a law firm, subcontracting work from a mentor is the ideal approach to learning and building LNC skills in an economical manner. It provides an introduction to the work in a mutually beneficial and supervised learning environment. It is important to approach this form of apprenticeship as a business and take steps to become invaluable. It is essential to follow assignment directions carefully, to be thorough, professional, and to complete the project in a timely and cost-efficient manner. It is unwise as a subcontractor to submit 20 hours for payment on a project that would take an experienced LNC 10 hours.

The essential foundation of a successful independent LNC practice is the business plan. The independent LNC does not fail to thoughtfully write business goals and a concrete action plan annually. (See Chapter 30: Business Principles for the Independent LNC, for details on the components of a business plan.) The business plan is evaluated regularly throughout the year, and is directly tied to the financial goals of the business.

Marketing is continual for the successful independent LNC. Business is primarily based on networking and referral. To obtain and retain clients requires some business and political savvy, anticipating client needs and making adjustments when necessary, but mostly by being available and at the right place, at the right time. Regular attendance and networking at local trial lawyers association meetings and continuing legal education (CLE) seminars (by buying booth space or paying the fee to attend the program) almost always yields new business or contacts. A course in marketing and sales techniques is highly recommended for the independent LNC. Most nurses have not been schooled in "selling" their services. Tips for ways to market independent LNC services can be found in the *Journal of Legal Nurse Consulting* articles and through experienced colleagues.

Negotiation skills are also valuable for establishing and collecting fees, and setting assignment deadlines. Fees are negotiated consistent with community standards and based on well-thoughtout criteria which can include expected deadlines, volume of work, and the potential of a consistent ongoing working relationship with the client. The tasks of obtaining an oral or written agreement and a retainer are completed before work is begun. The independent LNC also negotiates contracts for office space, equipment, services and supplies of subcontractors, employees, and vendors. Almost everything in business is negotiable.

What is the typical independent practice like? Referrals from satisfied attorneys and other LNCs are the largest source of new clientele. Requests for services range from complete nurse consulting services from medium or small law firms or from insurance companies to overflow work from large law firms with in-house LNCs. Large projects and last-minute deadlines in law firms are common reasons to outsource work to the independent LNC. The more flexible and diverse the experience of the independent LNC, the more attractive and usable the service. The LNC's practice can be very busy, demanding, and the work heterogeneous. Some independents specialize in a single service, such as life-care planning or expert location, while others diversify. Services may include summary, chronology, and analysis of medical records, literature research, location of qualified experts, witnessing independent medical examinations, assistance with preparation of trial exhibits, investigation of allegations against health care practitioners or facilities, determination of damages, preparation of life-care plans, trial consultation, and expert testimony. Cases in which independent LNCs are involved vary widely from medical/nursing malpractice to product liability, toxic torts, personal injury, and criminal cases, the commonality being medical- or physical-related evidence.

Medical records for review and analysis are usually received via regular mail or a delivery service unless the attorney wishes to meet face-to-face to discuss the case and expectations. Case review and analysis is accomplished in the most-efficient and cost-effective manner. While some nurses opt to write their own reports using a word-processing program, dictation and the services of a good medical transcriptionist may be a better use of time and resources. Detailed chronologies are time intensive. Scanning documents such as operative reports or consultations, and dictating hand-written progress notes, significantly reduces the amount of time to complete a chronology. Finding the right transcriptionist has its own set of challenges. Utilizing new business technology, techniques, and resources is important to maintaining a competitive edge. Presenting the most professional work product possible fosters business growth. It is helpful for the independent LNC to attend local business support and equipment shows annually to keep abreast of ways to improve work product and efficiency.

After completion of a case, the method of presenting the work product depends on the complexity of the case and the attorney's preference. The purpose of meeting with an attorney is not only to present case findings but to discuss and develop a plan of action for the case. The attorney's and the LNC's time is limited so presentations are concise and well organized. All such meetings are viewed as marketing opportunities.

Ongoing communication with attorney clients is critical for business success. The independent LNC must make special efforts since there is no daily contact with the case attorney as there is for the in-house LNC. Regular, nonintrusive follow-up calls to inquire about the status of ongoing cases keeps the LNC "fresh" in the attorney's mind and often results in new work assignments or cases. Faxing a status update report on an assignment is another effective way to keep the lines of communication open.

Collegial contact with other LNCs is a very critical part of being a successful independent LNC. Information and resource sharing enhances the practice and is accomplished among defense and plaintiff LNCs without violating confidentiality and avoiding conflicts of interest. LNC peers are excellent sources for problem solving as well as for business referrals. There is no substitute for networking with colleagues and opportunities to do so are built into the business plan and nurtured.

The use of subcontractors presents some interesting challenges which some independent nurse consultants choose to avoid. Problems with some part-time subcontractors or employees are that they lack the insight of the experienced consultant, they take longer to complete a project which can reduce profit margin, and reports require review and sometimes extensive edit. (Lack of writing skills is one of the principal barriers to successful independent LNC practice.) Dealing with subcontractors requires transformational leadership which empowers colleagues and makes followers into leaders (Swansburg, 1996). Not all independent LNCs are blessed with these leadership skills. They are, however, vital for economic survival when subcontractors are necessary to complete large projects or for a growing LNC practice. Subcontracting has constraints imposed by federal employment laws and economic considerations. A business attorney and an accountant should be consulted to select the best work delegation method, and to assure adherence to legal and tax requirements.

In conclusion, making a decision to pursue a career as an independent LNC requires an honest inventory of one's strengths and weaknesses. As in other kinds of new businesses, the failure rate is high. Business skills, including marketing, negotiation, leadership, delegation, financial management, written and oral communication, and business planning must be acquired, practiced, and perfected. Until recently, nursing education curricula did not begin to prepare nurses for entrepreneurship. Older graduates have had to educate themselves in the school of "hard knocks." Those who have been successful have paved the way and are mentors for growing numbers of independent LNCs. There are new and diverse challenges, personal satisfaction, and potential financial rewards for the nurse with the right stuff for independent legal nurse consulting.

References

Carpenito, L. J. and Neal, M. C. (1994). Nurse entrepreneurs, in J. McCloskey and K. Grace, Eds., *Current Issues in Nursing,* 4th ed, St. Louis, MO, Mosby, 43–48.

Godfrey, J. (1992). *Our Wildest Dreams,* New York, Harper Collins.

Swansburg, R. C. (1996). *Management and Leadership for Nurse Managers,* 2nd ed., Sudbury, MA, Jones and Bartlett.

Other Resources

Flanagan, L. (1993). *Self-Employment in Nursing: Understanding the Basics of Starting a Business,* Washington, D.C., American Nurses Publishing.

Godfrey, J. (1996). Been there, doing that, *Inc.,* 18(3), 21–22.

O'Connor, L. (1990). *Working at Home: A Dream That's Becoming a Trend,* Eugene, OR, Harvest House Publishers.

Roberts, R. (1994). Marketing savvy, *Network,* 5(3), 25.

Vogel, G. and Doleysh, N. (1994). *Entrepreneuring: A Nurse's Guide to Starting a Business,* 2nd ed., New York, National League for Nursing.

Zagury, C. S. (1995). *Nurse Entrepreneur: Building the Bridge of Opportunity,* Long Branch, NJ, Vista Publishing.

The Legal Nurse Consultant in the Law Firm
by Paula Schenck

The law firm offers a myriad of opportunities to the LNC and a work experience that is unparalleled (see Table 10.1 for the advantages and disadvantages). Working in a law firm provides unique insight into how a case proceeds from start to finish. The close day-to-day interaction with attorneys and the local legal community is one component often missed by the independent LNC. However, law firms have their own set of challenges that must be met in order to succeed in this environment. In the midst of busy and often intense law firm activity, the LNC has an opportunity for concentrated learning. The LNC is often the lone representative of all medical professionals and, as such, must learn to present scientifically based information quickly and accurately, often accessing and learning new information in a short period of time. Adaptability and flexibility are keys to success. To be willing to go beyond one's "comfort zone" is a definite asset and more recently is becoming a prerequisite to maintaining a position within a law firm. The reason is simple. Law firms, like most corporate entities, want committed team players. That means that everyone pitches in to get the job done, whether or not the task is within one's job description.

Law firms vary greatly depending on their size and services. Size may vary from one attorney with a secretary to a large multinational firm with many attorneys and support staff. The LNC's role in each of these environments depends on the structure and needs of the firm and its attorneys. While a sole practitioner may need the LNC to fill multiple roles, some of which may be outside the LNC's expertise, a large firm may limit what the LNC does to a single task such as summarizing and analyzing medical records. In most instances there are no steadfast rules as to how best to utilize an LNC. In one respect, this is fortunate. It allows each individual LNC to develop his or her role in creative ways that benefit both the firm and the LNC. The role of an LNC within a law firm is continually evolving, and is limited only by the nurse's ambition and ingenuity.

Table 10.1   Pros and Cons of Law Firm In-House Employment for the LNC

Pros	*Cons*
Regular salary	Salary potential limited
Benefit package may include paid vacation, sick days, holidays, health insurance package, retirement program	Lack of control of daily schedule; inflexibility due to trial/deposition schedules
Extensive support staff and resources (secretary, researcher, computer and software, library, etc.)	Little or no choice of case or task assignments
Case involvement from beginning to end	High stress to meet billable hour requirements
Day-to-day close professional/collegial relationship with attorneys, LNCs, paralegals, and others	

Opportunities

While it is true that the LNC is hired for health care knowledge and experience, it is always a good idea to gain experience in a wide variety of legal areas whenever the opportunity arises. The ambitious LNC with job security in mind should not limit work experience to one attorney or one area of practice. The LNC should seek assignments in a variety of practice areas which may include product liability, toxic torts, employment law, probate, health care administration, environmental law, workers' compensation issues, personal injury, and medical malpractice. The LNC may be the first to recognize an area in which his or her expertise and skills could contribute to the case's success. It is up to the LNC to initiate approaches and strategies to demonstrate how the LNC's specialized skills could augment team efforts.

The first LNC hired by a law firm is often thrust into the role of a pioneer. The LNC may find it necessary to explain his or her role and to continually prove themselves to attorneys, legal assistants, law clerks, secretarial staff, etc. Even if the LNC works with attorneys who are familiar with the LNC role, not every attorney will understand or comprehend the breadth of what LNCs have to offer. It is effective to develop a short, concise, and clear statement of competencies and deliver it regularly with confidence and authority. This technique helps reinforce the LNC as an invaluable member on a variety of litigation teams. Meeting with the paralegal staff and discussing complementary strengths and abilities helps avert unfortunate turf battles.

Medical Record Review

Often, the very first assignment given to an LNC in a law firm is to review a set of medical records and provide a quick summary of injuries. With this type of assignment, the LNC is wise to provide anatomic pictures of the injuries and make a list of the key health care providers for future depositions. The LNC could also recommend the areas of specialty for expert witnesses and provide expert names. The LNC might list possible independent medical examinations (IME), if on the defense, or offer to attend the defense IME, if working for the plaintiff. If appropriate, the LNC should always follow through with the suggestions as efficiently and expeditiously as possible. Most attorneys will welcome a proactive approach as it provides them with answers to questions not yet considered. This also keeps them one step ahead, which is always appreciated.

Communication

In a large firm, the LNC works with law clerks, new associates, senior associates, junior partners, and partners. Courtesy and professionalism extended to all members of the legal team will earn respect. Interfirm communication is often accomplished by an interoffice memorandum or e-mail. One easy, unassuming way to remind all firm members of the LNC's source of value is to use the RN credential after his or her name in all correspondence. It lends credibility to opinion memos and summaries and reminds everyone of the LNC's uniqueness on the legal team. Law firms may send the LNC's work product, typically opinion memos, to the client. The "RN" reminds clients that they have hired a law firm with a nurse, whose health care expertise is invaluable to the case.

Expert Witnesses

A good knowledge of the local medical community is important to the in-house consultant. The best recommendations for physician or nurse expert witnesses come from firsthand knowledge of their reputations as clinicians and expert witnesses. Networking with other LNCs in the community can be helpful in locating qualified expert witnesses. LNCs involved in locating and engaging expert witnesses are familiar with both the local health care professional community and the requirements for an expert witness; current and competent clinical practice as well as an articulate professional, capable of explaining the health care issues clearly to the jury.

Billable Hours

The legal nurse consultant needs to be ambitious and productive to maintain a position in a law firm. Small law firms may have their own hourly or salary-based system, but most large defense firms have an annual billable hour requirement for their attorneys, nurse consultants, and paralegals. Billable hours are the justification for the LNC position. If the billable hours for the current nurse are over and above what is required, another LNC position may be created. In general, administrators of moderate-to-large law firms will evaluate the billable hours as a measure of the LNC's contribution to the firm. This eventually may translate into pay raises and/or bonuses! The way to increase billable hours is oftentimes left up to the nurse. Some firms will have enough work to keep one or even two full-time nurses busy; however, if the LNC is in the position of needing more hours, the LNC should approach attorneys for additional assignments. Once the attorney understands the LNC's capabilities are not limited to summarizing medical records, the attorney will more than likely ask the LNC to do much more on assigned cases.

Summary

The experience gained by working in a law firm is invaluable. Unlike an independent LNC, the in-house LNC is often involved in a case from the time it is screened and accepted through settlement or a trial verdict. The in-house LNC is available immediately and involved in regular strategy, planning, or problem-solving meetings. The LNC is able to contribute to case progress in a proactive and ongoing way. Having daily, direct access to attorneys, files, and oftentimes the client offers unique learning and role development opportunities within the law firm environment. The outside independent consultant usually has only intermittent and limited contact with the case attorney, and is not privy to the broad scope of information about the case. The LNC in a large law firm has resources available such as research librarians, informational systems experts, paralegals, and computer databases to enhance work efficiency. Such resources allow the LNC to maximize use of his or her expertise and talents to, for example, review and evaluate the literature rather than researching the databases and retrieving the articles. The law firm is a rich and rewarding work environment for the LNC.

The Legal Nurse Consultant in the Insurance Company by Kathleen Spiegel

The professional liability insurance company practice setting provides a highly cherished degree of autonomy for the LNC. The insurance industry typically divides its market into geographical areas. Frequently, two nurse consultants service a geographical region. One manages claim activity and the other does risk management consultations. Although titles vary and may include *Representative, Consultant,* or *Analyst,* the titles used typically are Claim Representative and Risk Management Consultant.

Some LNCs employed in these roles work within the company headquarters or a regional office. Since some companies cannot support offices in every region, many LNCs work out of their homes. The insurance company provides the necessary equipment and supplies, an expense account, and usually, a company car. Although working from the home setting has some obvious advantages, LNCs who work within the insurance company office have the advantages of clerical support, daily collegial interaction, and a clear separation between home and work life. In either setting, however, the LNC is at liberty to self-manage time and activities which allows a high degree of independence and autonomy.

Insurance carriers provide liability coverage for hospitals and physicians. The LNC, therefore, deals with a myriad of risk issues facing health care institutions and physician office practices. Consulting for a professional liability insurance carrier requires a strong experiential base. It is definitely not a setting for "on-the-job training." The background of the LNC is often as a hospital risk manager with several years of experience.

The Role of the Claim Representative

When an adverse event has occurred and there is reason to believe that a claim may be filed, the insured, whether a hospital or a physician, contacts the Claim Representative. The Claim Representative provides guidance and direction to the insured on how to immediately proceed. The Claim Representative then painstakingly reviews the medical records and other pertinent documents, and schedules interviews with appropriate witnesses and other personnel. Many times, a small claim is negotiated to settlement between the Claim Representative and the injured party or attorney. Careful negotiation of a claim may avert a potential lawsuit. In the event a claim is substantial, or a lawsuit filed, direct settlement negotiation may not be undertaken. The Claim Representative contacts assigned defense counsel and collaborates closely with the attorney to develop the case strategy. Assisting defense counsel in selecting and evaluating potential witnesses and experts to provide testimony is an important aspect of the Claim Representative's role.

There are specific skills that are essential for a Claim Representative to possess. A solid working knowledge of the technical aspects of the legal process is critical. Claim and litigation management skills can be honed by studying the body of literature available on these topics. Effective interviewing and negotiating skills are also necessary.

The Role of the Risk Management Consultant

The LNC as a Risk Management Consultant provides proactive or preventative risk management support activities to the insured health care provider or facility. A major component of the LNC's role is to provide educational programs and seminars for health care personnel. The LNC also performs physician office practice surveys and hospital department audits to determine areas of risk. Review of policies, procedures, and medical records may be conducted separately, or in conjunction with audits and surveys. On a daily basis, the Risk Management Consultant provides telephone consultations to various insureds. Often, even experienced hospital risk managers require a "second opinion" on unusual events that can occur in some of today's specialized health care settings.

An important attribute of the Risk Management Consultant is common sense. Nurses with education and experience focused on a problem-solving process are particularly gifted with a sense of logic necessary in this field. A strong knowledge of federal and state statutes and regulations and Joint Commission on Accreditation of Healthcare Organizations standards is key to success in providing meaningful consultations to insureds.

The Legal Nurse Consultant in Risk Management by Jill Holmes

The mission of those LNCs who practice in the area of risk management for both health care providers and hospitals/clinics is to identify and control those conditions and behaviors which may expose the individual or the organization and its staff to the possibility of risk or financial loss.

The accountability or duty of the health care provider to his or her patient is not a new concept. The Code of Hammurabi (2250 B.C.) made it clear to the intervening surgeon what penalties he would suffer should he cause a man's death during wound repair.

> *If a physician operates on a man for a severe wound with a bronze lancet and causes a man's death...they shall cut off his fingers.*

Today, health care providers do not face the prospect of physical mutilation due to a bad outcome, but there has been an increase in malpractice lawsuits. This is due to a number of events such as higher patient expectations, managed care with its impact on the physician/patient relationship, reduction of professional staff in hospital or clinic settings, a rise in the degree of morbidity in patients admitted to hospitals, and innovations in civil law. It is the risk management department's responsibility to manage medical and general liability exposure when incidences occur as well as to initiate preventative risk management education for faculty and staff.

There are a number of LNCs who either assist or manage the risk management activities for a medical entity. Size of the medical organization ranges from a free-standing clinic to a large medical center. Some LNCs work in this capacity for a company that serves as third-party administrators for a hospital or consortium of hospitals.

In general, the LNC's duties and activities center around several key areas that are described in the next three sections.

Incident Reporting

The LNC may oversee or manage the initial investigation of all reported incidents/accidents/events that could endanger patients, visitors, or staff and ultimately lead to financial loss. Such incidents may include failure to diagnose; delay in diagnosis; unanticipated death; reaction to medication, blood products, or any other substance; unplanned surgery, return to surgery; excessive blood loss leading to transfusion; wound dehiscence; incorrect instrument, needle, or sponge count; patient, staff, or visitor falls; medication errors; equipment failures or malfunctions, loss of valuables, and behavior problems. The LNC initiates collection of all pertinent information in anticipation that a claim will be filed as well as informing the facility's senior management and legal counsel of the actions taken. The LNC also identifies the high risk areas within the facility and helps management target and initiate changes in policies and/or procedures to reduce that risk. The LNC maintains the data collected from all incident reports, notes the action(s) taken in response, and records outcomes. In those cases where there may be a conflict of interest between physician and the hospital, the LNC proceeds cautiously during the investigation.

Based on identification of incident reports which require action, the LNC assists in the development of appropriate in-service programs to alert and educate the staff to potential problems and solutions. The LNC also promotes early proactive reporting by staff in the event of a reportable incident so that corrective steps may be taken in a timely manner.

Policy Development

Regardless of size, every medical facility is subject to a myriad of codes, laws, rules, and regulations that direct how patient care is delivered. The LNC must be familiar with all manner of regulatory and legislative directives in order to assist with development of compliant facility policies and procedures.

Internally, as situations and problems arise, the LNC identifies policies that require changing and assist staff to alter behavior to reduce risk. The LNC reviews all proposed changes with hospital legal counsel and policy committees.

Legal Process

The LNC assists and coordinates the release of appropriate records and other claim-related information to the requesting attorney(s), court(s), or investigative agencies as appropriate, working closely with the custodian of medical records and legal counsel.

The LNC in the hospital or clinic setting contributes scientific knowledge base together with a grasp of how hospitals function. The LNC works closely with legal counsel, providing the attorney with an overview of the medical facts, the particular medically related issues of the prospective claim, and the status and results of the investigation.

The risk management position requires that the nurse be intelligent, discrete, flexible and assertive, yet tactful. Communication skills should be of the highest caliber since the nurse is often involved with highly charged issues involving a number of individuals. It is a rewarding career for the right person.

Reference

Harpster, J. D. and Veach, M. S., Eds. (1990). *Risk Management Handbook for Health Care Facilities,* American Hospital Publishing, Chicago.

The Legal Nurse Consultant in State Agencies by Suzanne D. Schutze

Nurses in State Government

LNCs in state government work in diverse settings, using their medical knowledge to assist government in its function of providing or evaluating health care delivery to citizens. These settings can be divided into four groups:

1. Traditional or clinical nursing, i.e., the public health nurse who immunizes children against communicable diseases, a nurse working in a state hospital, penal system, rural health or indigent care clinics.
2. Civil litigation defense involving state universities, prisons, schools, and hospitals.
3. Utilization review in the state welfare health system, and evaluation of crime victims' injuries to determine if financial compensation is appropriate.
4. Regulatory agencies such as professional licensing boards and the department of health and human services.

The focus of this section will be the nurse working for a licensing board whose job title is *Investigator*. See Appendix 10.1 for the use of the nursing process in investigations.

The organization of regulatory agencies varies from state to state. Some states combine regulatory agencies under one umbrella agency, and the nurse investigator may have cases involving any profession involved in medical care or medical insurance fraud. Other states have separate licensing boards for each profession.

In the role of investigator, the nurse may,

- Evaluate allegations that a nurse has violated the state's Nurse Practice Act and/or investigate similar complaints against physicians;
- Determine whether hospitals, nursing homes, lay midwives, massage therapists, X-ray technicians meet state standards, usually promulgated by the Department of Health;
- Evaluate the severity and duration of work-related injuries, complaints about the quality of a physician's care, or an employer's lack of cooperation as defined in the state's workers' compensation system, and participate in dispute resolution of these issues; and/or
- Monitor health care fraud perpetrated by or on insurance companies regulated by the Department of Insurance.

The LNC Investigator

The LNC investigator conducts complex investigations of alleged violations of state laws which relate to health care. This requires knowledge of state statutes and regulations, which have the effect of law, specific to the licensee's profession, and any other law which may impact the practice of that profession. The state's Medical Practice Act may not contain a provision about a physician dispensing medications in the office setting, but the Pharmacy Act or other laws regulating drugs cover such a circumstance. Administrative statutes and regulations also cover civil and criminal activity of professional licensees. Failure to consider these laws and regulations and the Health and Safety Code can result in an improper or incomplete investigation.

Investigators may be certified as peace officers so they can serve subpoenas. Since documentary evidence requires an affidavit, some investigators are notaries. In the course of an investigation, the LNC educates complainants and licensees about state laws and regulations related to professional practice. Other work includes reviewing and analyzing records, preparing reports, assisting at depositions and in court, testifying at hearings, and acting as liaison with other state and federal regulatory and enforcement agencies. The nurse investigator uses the nursing process to organize and conduct an effective investigation.

At the conclusion of the investigation, if violations of regulations or statutes are identified, legal action will be necessary. The nursing process is again implemented as the LNC assists the attorney's preparation for conferences and hearings with licensees or entity representatives. Some agencies have only one attorney and rely heavily on the LNC to draft restrictive orders on the violations for the attorney's review. Other agencies' attorneys use their own legal assistants for such tasks, and the LNC may be consulted for specific medical information or asked to testify to the medical facts or medical evidence. The LNC may be present at depositions or accompany the attorney to hearings.

If a state allows the subject of an investigation in which violations are identified to work out a settlement, that subject may or may not be represented by an attorney during the process. The Agreed Board Order, which results from a settlement conference, is a legal document which contains Findings of Facts and Conclusions of Law and places restrictions on the subject's license and/or imposes monetary penalties on the subject. The licensee is advised to have legal counsel review this before signing it.

State agency attorneys usually have extensive experience or certification in administrative law. It is not uncommon for them to employ LNCs who also specialize in this area. It is less common, however, to find an independent LNC consulted in these cases.

The administrative hearing is a less formal court procedure than civil trial and may last a day or two, but seldom more than a week. The agency attorney and the LNC, and the opposing attorney and licensee client, are often the only parties before the judge. Even though the hearing is open to the public, spectators are rare. If present, they could include family of the licensee, agency representatives, or a newspaper reporter in cases involving sex, drugs, or multiple deaths.

Ethics

The inclination and opportunity to give legal or medical advice may be greater for the investigator LNC than for LNCs in civil or criminal areas because of the narrow focus on violations of health care statutes pertaining to the case. For the complainant and subject of the investigation, the LNC investigator may be the sole resource for information, and interpreter of whether violations of these statutes have occurred until the final report is written. The LNC is often asked for legal advice from the subject. "You just tell me what to do, and I'll do it," and the complainant, "Do you think I should file a lawsuit?" Medical advice may be requested by either "Next time I treat a patient like this, should I...," and "Should I have another operation?" The LNC must be cautious in phrasing answers to such questions. A complainant might obtain more satisfaction by filing a lawsuit, but an investigator cannot ethically give advice to do so, nor refer a complainant to an attorney with information about what is in the medical records that may constitute negligence.

Conflict of interest issues can arise when the investigator knows the complainant or the subject of the investigation. It could be very easy unconsciously to gather only the facts which support a particular point of view, or be accused of doing so. A wise investigator will return this case to the supervisor for reassignment.

Bias presents an ethical problem less easily discerned. An investigator may unknowingly harbor an opinion about allegations which involve an egregious act, such as the physician who supplies drugs to a patient in exchange for sex, or an impaired nurse who has been responsible for two infant deaths. The ensuing investigation is neither fair nor objective, and the case outcome is incomplete or improper. The LNC must examine and understand personal biases and conflicts of interest and should make a firm commitment to the impartial collection and objective analysis of evidence so that case outcomes are proper and equitable.

References

Vernon's Texas Civil Statues, Art. 4495b, the Medical Practice Act.

Board Rules and Regulations, Texas State Board of Medical Examiners, Ch. 161–191, June 14, 1996.

Rules of Practice and Procedure, Title I, Part VII, Ch. 155–173, April 1996. Austin, Texas, State Office of Administrative Hearings.

Taylor, S. B. (1996), *Administrative Law—Overview of the Contested Case Process Under the Administrative Procedure Act,* Austin, Texas, State Office of Administrative Hearings.

Job Descriptions for Nurses, Office of the Texas State Auditor, 206 East 9th Street, #1900, Austin, TX 78701.

The Legal Nurse Consultant in the U.S. Department of Justice
by Judith L. Bragdon

The U.S. Department of Justice (DOJ) hired the first nurse consultant in 1991 in the Radiation Exposure Compensation Unit of the Constitutional and Specialized Torts Branch of the Civil Division. The principal responsibility of the nurse in this position involves conducting an assessment and verification of medical documentation submitted in support of claims under the Radiation Exposure Compensation Act (RECA) of 1990. RECA directs the Attorney General of the U.S. to provide lump-sum compensation payments to individuals who have contracted compensable diseases such as lung cancer and other nonmalignant respiratory diseases identified in the RECA. The LNC in this position:

- Responds to Congressional inquiries
- Plans the process of identification of informative medical records
- Secures information-sharing agreements with universities, tumor registries, and community hospitals
- Develops the structure and process of case review
- Assists somewhat confused potential claimants in understanding the medical and legal terminology of the claim process
- Develops new guidelines for interpreting the RECA
- Researches and writes new regulations
- Reports on statistical findings of quality assurance reviews
- Abstracts clinical information

Other responsibilities include serving as principal liaison between Justice Department attorneys and other federal agencies, such as the National Institute of Occupations Safety and Health (NIOSH), the National Institutes of Health (NIH), the National Cancer Institute (NCI), universities, community hospitals, state and local tumor registries, and, of course, the claimants and their attorneys.

An especially high profile opportunity for the LNC in this position is to present testimony to the RECA committee of President Clinton's Task Force on Human Radiation. As principal medical analyst, the LNC is charged with providing the committee an overview of the medical aspects of the Radiation Program as well as suggestions for potential changes to the RECA itself.

Possibly the most fascinating aspect of the position involves the interactions with the principal population, the Navajo uranium miners and their families. For many of the Navajo claimants, there are cultural, language, and geographical barriers to resolve, testing the LNCs understanding of regulations, challenging nursing problem-solving skills, and demanding a balance between creativity and compliance with the regulations. It is not uncommon for the LNC to travel across remote areas of the Navajo reservation to present public education sessions regarding the regulatory criteria and requirements for compensation eligibility. Given that the program goals are to provide compassionate compensation to individuals injured as a result of their own government's nuclear weapons' testing program, frequent phone calls come from legislative staffers and distressed citizens who have lost yet another family member to a cancer which, the claimants held, was a direct result of radiation exposure. Fortunately, the RECA does not require that claimants prove causation. Counseling and therapeutic communication skills are often pressed as claimants recite frequent, tragic stories of the demise of entire Utah families, exposed to radioactive fallout in the 1950s.

While the position description for the LNC at the DOJ cites a Bachelor of Science in Nursing as a requirement, it also demands a history of extensive clinical experience in oncology, certification in Oncology Nursing, knowledge of nonmalignant respiratory diseases, previous medical legal experience, and prior research and publication background. The complexity of the work ranges from rather straightforward claim evaluation to in-depth analysis of complex medial legal policy issues of intense political interest.

Opportunities abound at the DOJ to provide advice and guidance to unit attorneys to solve clinical and research questions. On occasion, members of the Radiation Program team find themselves "using the law to force the science." For example, when a recommendation was made for changes in the regulation which would permit submission of a particular kind of diagnostic test for which there are not yet any published and generally accepted diagnostic findings, the LNC was called upon to identify national experts in the field of radiology to form a panel of advisors. Serving as the project manager, the LNC charged the panel to pool their collective research findings and expertise to develop a set of realistic, reproducible diagnostic findings consistent with the particular compensable disease under evaluation. In the space of 2 months, the panel developed a test protocol and a diagnostic framework for identifying subclinical disease in a large portion of claimants who would otherwise have been unable to demonstrate eligibility utilizing standard testing.

The role of the LNC at the DOJ has been a trailblazing role. Attorneys there are still unaware of the unique talents and skills nurses can bring to the legal arena as educators, researchers, counselors, and when appropriate, patient advocates. The role of the LNC at the DOJ has expanded greatly. Attorneys in government agencies involved in areas of litigation, such as commercial, environmental, antitrust, and criminal, have begun to appreciate the great potential contributions the LNC can make to their legal teams.

Appendix 10.1
The Nursing Process in Investigations

The investigator's job description is compatible with the nursing process.

The Problem

Receive assigned and prioritized cases

Cases contain written allegations suggesting one or more possible violations of health care statutes. These come from the public, other health care professionals, legislators, other state agencies, or are generated by the investigator or the agency itself.

Assessment

Analyze assigned cases to develop an investigative plan.

A case is opened by reviewing the allegations. Do the allegations relate to a violation of a statute or regulation. Is there more than one violation? Should this case be made a high priority. If so, why? How much more information is needed? Who must be contacted? What is the potential for information or evidence being lost through death or destruction, withheld because of other legal actions, or witnesses changing their minds about cooperating? How long will the case take to reach completion? Will a consultant (an expert witness) be needed to testify to the standard of care?

Outcome Identification

Recommend appropriate case disposition to the Director of Investigations

A case is closed with a written report containing proof that a violation does, or does not, exist. All allegations in a complaint must be answered to the satisfaction of the final decision makers of the case, i.e., the agency attorneys, executive director, and/or the board members. An agency's board members are generally political appointees. They are licensees of the agency and lay people with varying life experience, occupational, and cultural backgrounds. The report must be written with their levels of understanding and expertise in mind. If the report is forwarded to the executive director and an attorney for legal action, it must relate allegations to specific violations of the law, and enumerate supporting evidence and witnesses. A poorly written report may be returned for additional work or cause a case to be dismissed.

Planning

Prepare release forms or subpoenas for relevant records

- Prepare witness and document affidavits.
- Make appointments for interviews with involved parties.
- Determine need for consultant to address standard of care.
- Liaison with other divisions or agencies as appropriate.

Some investigations can be handled by phone or mail requests for information. Others require travel to inspect a site, equipment or drugs, or to interview a complainant or the subject of the investigation. A high-priority investigation, such as a report of an impaired physician or a nursing home death, may consume many hours and disrupt the progress of other ongoing cases. The LNC uses all available resources to complete the investigation as efficiently as possible. If the case involves a physician already being monitored by a compliance officer, the LNC and compliance officer may share information or combine the investigation effort. Agency attorneys may have other cases on the same individual or facility awaiting legal action. Conferring with them can supplement evidence already available, uncover a pattern of substandard practice, or change the investigation's priority by combining the case with others.

The case may require a consultant opinion to determine whether the standard of care has been breached in a way which speaks to a particular violation of the state's professional practice act. The LNC may be responsible for finding this expert, or participate in the search under the aegis of the attorney. Thereafter, the LNC may act as liaison with the expert through testimony and case resolution.

If criminal activity or health care fraud is suspected, the investigator contacts appropriate authorities, from local police to the FBI. States may allow the release of confidential files only to law enforcement agencies when a criminal act is involved. Documents would not be released if the criminal acts by the subject were not related to their professional practice.

Implementation

> Conduct on-site investigations as needed, interview witnesses, identify documentary evidence; prepare reports and documentation of investigative activities

Evidence accumulated is certified by affidavit. It must be checked for completeness, the pages numbered and collated in a logical order. Each investigative activity, such as facility inspection, interviews, record reviews, drug audits, or discussions with a consultant, is documented in a written report for the investigative file.

Throughout the investigation, the LNC is in contact with the complainant and other witnesses. The LNC must understand the law regarding what information can and cannot be given to these individuals. In Texas, the investigative file is confidential, not subject to the state's Open Records Act. Divulging information gathered in an investigation could nullify the file's confidentiality. On the other hand, some information may be necessary to gain a witness's cooperation, explain events to a consultant, or involve another agency or law enforcement body in the investigation. Consulting with the attorney assists the investigator in handling these matters without tainting witnesses and evidence, or destroying the case.

Evaluation

> Evaluate work performed using the following criteria

1. Cases completed cover the range of perceived violations and reach the appropriate conclusion.
2. The time limit set for completing the investigation was met.
3. The investigator's recommendation for disposition of the case was accepted.
4. There was no need for additional investigation or evidence after the final report was submitted.

Chapter 11

The Legal Nurse Consultant Practice Areas

Sue Barnes, Jill Holmes, Adella Toepel, Patricia A. Costantini, and Doug Davis

Contents

Objectives

Upon the completion of Chapter 11, the reader will be able to:

- Describe the role of the legal nurse consultant as part of the litigation team
- Explain the services provided by the legal nurse consultant
- List the components of a life care plan
- Describe the goal of a criminal investigation and the legal nurse consultant's role
- State the purpose of case management

Medical Malpractice
by Sue Barnes

Briefly stated, medical malpractice is the failure of a health care provider to meet the prevailing standard of care. In a cause of action for medical malpractice, the burden of proof rests with the plaintiff who must establish all four elements of proof, which include duty, breach of duty, causation, and damages. While this description of medical malpractice seems simple, the true nature of proving a medical malpractice case is an extremely lengthy and complex process described in detail in other chapters.

It has been estimated that medical therapy in the U.S. results in unintended injuries that affect 1.3 million people each year (Leape et al., 1995). Although many are unavoidable, as many as two thirds may be secondary to errors in patient care management (as cited by Leape et al.). It is the LNC's role to assist the litigation team in the process of substantiating or refuting that an adverse event is medical malpractice.

According to the National Practitioner Data Bank (1996) there were 116,883 disclosable malpractice payment reports by insurers in 1996. These reports, on an average, reflect incidents that occurred sometime in 1991 or 1992. Payments do not accurately reflect malpractice incidents since some are based on allegations only (Birkholz, 1995). The payments are a result of a written claim of clinical malpractice and claims filed in court. It does not reflect information on individual practitioners making payments directly to clients or practitioners affected by the "corporate shield" effect in which the settlement included an agreement not to name the individual practitioners. Physicians represented 77.8% of the practitioners, dentists 14.1%, and all others 7.9% which includes podiatrists, pharmacists, chiropractors, and nurses, etc. (National Practitioner Data Bank, 1995). Malpractice categories, mean payment, and mean delay between reporting and the date of the incident are as shown in Table 11.1. For copies of the latest *Annual Report* and information on the National Practitioner Data Book, contact the Data Bank Help Line at 1-800-767-6732.

The layperson often equates a bad patient outcome with malpractice which is an erroneous presumption of negligence (Shandell and Smith, 1996). The LNC plays an extremely pivotal role on the medical malpractice team for either the defense or plaintiff side. To ferret out the facts of a case from either perspective, the LNC needs a solid foundation of medical knowledge, an understanding of legal principles, and exceptional analytical skills. Given a "perfect world," if every

Table 11.1 Mean and Median Malpractice Payment Amount, Mean Delay between Incident and Payment, and Number of Malpractice Reports by Malpractice Reason

Malpractice Reason	Number of Reports	Mean Payment	Median Payment	Mean Delay between Incident and Payment (years)
Diagnosis related	31,651	190,181.20	98,904.00	4.94
Anesthesia related	3,727	199,777.50	60,000.00	3.59
Surgery related	27,907	136,943.30	60,000.00	4.29
Medication related	7,379	123,346.80	29,999.00	5.24
IV & blood products related	561	154,066.40	40,000.00	4.79
Obstetrics related	8,357	335,315.30	166,625.00	6.57
Treatment related	32,744	95,929.62	25,000.00	4.40
Monitoring related	1,583	179,753.60	65,000.00	5.16
Equipment or product related	547	59,726.08	15,000.00	3.71
Miscellaneous	2,427	91,102.03	25,000.00	5.16
All Reports	**116,883**	**1,566,141.83**	**585,528.00**	**4.78**

Data compiled by National Practitioner Data Bank, September 1,1990 through December 31, 1996.

plaintiff firm used a professional LNC to review cases for merit, the number of unwarranted lawsuits could be significantly reduced. If an experienced LNC reviewed every claim or case referred to an insurer or defense law firm, meritorious cases would be expeditiously settled.

Each case that goes forward requires extensive, detailed medical record review and analysis; investigation of applicable standards, policies, and procedure records and other documents; literature research and evaluation; and location of qualified experts for case review. The LNC may provide these services as an employee of the insurance company or law firm, or as an independent consultant. LNCs with current clinical practice may also serve as expert witnesses in cases of nursing negligence. In addition to these functions, the in-house LNC may act as an intermediary between the attorney and client, experts, and other witnesses. The LNC often provides client education and psychological guidance. The emotional strain in the form of either grief or anger for either plaintiff or defendant(s) is enormous. It is within the purview of the in-house LNC to refer the client to community resources for aid and counseling as needed. The independent LNC or nurse expert generally has little direct contact with the client, whether plaintiff or defendant, working instead on an intermittent consultant basis with the attorney.

In any capacity, medical malpractice cases constantly challenge and expand the professional knowledge and resources of the LNC. Analogous to the high drama of life and death situations in the clinical hospital environment, medical malpractice cases in the legal arena may have hundreds of thousands, if not millions, of dollars and years of emotional anguish invested in case outcome for all parties involved. Involvement in such cases is undertaken by LNCs with the same reverence, commitment, and dedication as direct patient care in the clinical setting.

References

Birkholz, G. (1995). Malpractice data from the National Practitioner Data Bank. *Nurse Practitioner* (20), 32–35.

Leape, L. L., Bates, D. W., Cullen, D. J., Laird, N., Petersen, L. A., Small, S. D., Servi, D., Laffel, G., Sweltzer, B. J., Shea, B. F., Hallisey, R., Viet, M. V., & Nemeskal, R. (1995). Systems analysis of adverse drug events. *JAMA* 274(1), 35–43.

Shandell, R. E. & Smith, P. (1996). *The Preparation and Trial of Medical Malpractice Cases.* New York: Law Journal Seminars-Press.

U.S. Department of Health and Human Services. (1995). *National Practitioner Data Bank* (Annual report). Rockville, MD: Author.

U.S. Department of Health and Human Services. (1996). *National Practitioner Data Bank* (Annual report). Rockville, MD: Author.

Other References

Lobb, M. L., Riley, G. C., & Clemens, A. M. (1994). The legal nurse consultant's role on the defense team in a medical malpractice lawsuit. *Network* 5(4), 3–7.

Mayberry, A. & Croke, E. (1966). Issues leading to malpractice show little change: A review of the literature. *Journal of Legal Nurse Consulting* 7(2), 16–19.

Personal Injury
by Jill Holmes

Personal injury cases involve some injury to a person(s) caused by the negligence of another, others, or an entity. Medical malpractice, product liability, toxic tort, and even criminal cases are all personal injury cases. The types of personal injury cases referred to in this section specifically relate to a wide variety of accidents such as those involving automobiles, boats, fire and explosions, slips and falls, etc.

The LNC's contribution to litigation of these cases, as in-house employee or independent consultant, centers primarily around identification, assessment, and presentation of the injuries/damages consequent to the accident. The plaintiff may have fully recovered from minor to serious injuries (but with large hospital bills and pain-and-suffering damages) or have sustained catastrophic and permanently disabling injuries. Evaluation of alleged negligence is generally left to others.

The LNC working on such a personal injury case for a defense firm may never see the plaintiff physically until deposition or trial, although via testimony of others and thorough review of medical records may "know" the plaintiff very well. Based on analysis of the medically related documents, the LNC prepares the defense attorney for depositions and trial by advising about

- The plausibility of the injuries being a direct result of the accident or event at issue
- The likelihood of hospital and medical care being related to preexisting conditions, rather than the injury caused by the accident
- The reasonableness of the plaintiff's requests for ongoing treatment and future rehabilitation

The LNC may draft deposition outlines and questions related to these issues for depositions of treating physicians or other care providers, and plaintiff experts. The LNC may also find or custom-produce pertinent medical illustrations to be used by defense experts or treating physicians to explain the precise degree and extent of injury and treatments.

The LNC working for plaintiff's counsel may meet the plaintiff early on during the initial interview and actively collaborate with the attorney to determine whether or not to take the case. During screening evaluation, the LNC tests the validity of the accident causing the injuries claimed, the sincerity of the plaintiff's attempt(s) to ameliorate the injuries by seeking appropriate and consistent treatment, and outlines current and future consequent disabilities. The next step is to obtain and carefully review all medical records. An initial medical record summary and analysis may be in memo form and often serves as a plan for the legal team during case development. The case is often accepted or rejected by the attorney based substantially on the LNC's analysis and recommendation.

If the case is accepted, and during subsequent case development, the in-house LNC regularly interacts with both plaintiff and family members, providing emotional support as needed during the long legal process. The LNC also acts as liaison between the plaintiff's treating medical care providers, medical/nursing damage experts, and the legal team. As the case proceeds, the LNC remains alert to future medical developments which may arise as a result of the initial injuries to plaintiff. Anticipating new or protracted medical complications is the responsibility of the LNC since no other member of the legal team possesses the same level of medical knowledge and expertise.

In these personal injury cases, the LNC may encounter assignments out of the ordinary, such as collaborating with experts such as accident reconstructionists, mechanical engineers, or combustion and fire experts. These experts work with the LNC to understand and explain how injuries suffered by plaintiff could have occurred or to discover plausible alternative explanations. The LNC may serve as a film consultant during creation of a videotape of "A Day in the Life" of a catastrophically injured plaintiff, taking care to preserve the plaintiff's dignity while demonstrating the full extent of the injuries.

The independent LNC may be hired as an expert by plaintiff's attorney to present the medical record evidence to the jury at trial. In this capacity, the LNC educates the jury about the damages by describing injuries and treatments, defining medical terminology, explaining procedures, and summarizing and presenting evidence supporting pain and suffering found in the medical records.

On either the plaintiff or defense side of the case, the LNC provides ongoing support to the legal term at time of trial. Special assignments such as evidence location, exhibit creation such as storyboards, time lines, and medical illustrations are challenging and interesting. Disclosures during the trial itself about key medical issues lead to "emergency" research to refute or support testimony. Such research is best conducted by the LNC who is familiar with medical literature and terminology.

In personal injury cases as defined above, the LNC serves as an expert in the area of injury/damage analysis. The LNC provides critical evaluation of medical records, coordination of and assistance to experts and witnesses, testimony regarding injuries and treatments, and, for the plaintiff, emotional support and occasional medical care referrals. Given the high volume of personal injury cases evaluated and litigated by attorneys today, the LNC experienced in these types of cases is an invaluable asset, saving time and money for both plaintiff and defense counsel.

References

Bogart, J. and Beerman, J., Expert fact witness: a testifying role for the legal nurse consultant, *Journal of Legal Nurse Consulting*, 6(4), 22–28, 1995.

Faherty, B. L., The nurse legal consultant and disabling injuries, *Rehabilitation Nursing*, 16, 30–33, 1991.

Davis, S. C., Maximizing effectiveness in retaining expert witnesses, *Journal of Legal Nurse Consulting*, 6(3), 9–10, 1995.

Turner, N., The legal nurse consultant as a court appointed expert, *Journal of Legal Nurse Consulting*, (6)1, 12–14, 1995.

Role of the Legal Nurse Consultant in Complex Litigation: Product Liability and Toxic Torts
by Adella Toepel

Product liability and toxic tort cases usually involve multiple clients with injuries from the use of the same product or toxic exposure. They usually fall under the scope of complex litigation, often within a multidistrict litigation (M.D.L.) or class action. The LNC must study and understand the global issues of liability and injury related to such groups of cases. In addition to grasping the common facts of the group as a whole, the LNC may evaluate each case separately for (individual) proximate causation that may include evaluation of the individual's prior medical history, documentation of injury to support the claim, alternative causation issues, damages related to past and future medical care, and proof of product identification or toxic exposure.

There may be supporting medical literature to help establish or refute causation. Literature searches for this purpose are often the responsibility of the LNC. Medical issues in these cases may be cutting edge or controversial in the medical community with few studies to support or refute the claim of damages. Because studies may be ongoing, medicine may change through the life of the case. The search for and retention of medical experts may change accordingly.

Retrieval and review of all appropriate medical records, bills, and other key documents to prepare for settlement or trial may be part of the LNC's role in case management. It may be the duty of the LNC to locate and consult with medical experts, draft correspondence and reports, assist with court fillings, maintain client contact, remain up to date on the health status of each client, prepare exhibits, assist at depositions, and draft and answer interrogatories in preparation for resolution of the cases by settlement or trial.

There may be instances in which product liability and toxic tort cases do not involve an M.D.L. or class action. Each such individual case must also be evaluated for proximate causation and damages. The facts of the case and legal theories must be established the same as for the large-group cases, along with planning for specific case management. The individual case does not have the advantage of the multiple resources or central repository of information of the large-group cases.

The collection, management, and efficient retrieval of data in cases that involve multiple plaintiffs (hundreds or thousands) and defendants is critical and accomplished with the use of computers and other technology. The LNC must become proficient with databases developed to track massive amounts of data throughout the litigation.

The LNC specializing in product liability or toxic tort cases usually does so as an employee of a law firm. Such cases consume an LNCs full attention for years and require expensive technology and support staff. Only law firms with single or small-group cases may contract with the more-expensive independent LNC for medical record summary and evaluation, and damage assessment. The transition for the independent LNC used to working on diverse personal injury cases one at a time to the world of complex mass litigation is challenging.

References

Federal Civil Judicial Procedure and Rules, 1996.

Federal Judicial Center, Ed., Part II: Management of complex litigation. Part III: Class actions, *Manual for Complex Litigation,* 3rd ed. (1995), Aspen Law & Business, Englewood Cliffs, NJ, 3–32, 211–246, 308–330.

Order and Findings on Class Certification, M.D.L. No. 95-1060R, U.S. District Court, Central District of California. Filed February 21, 1996.

Order Approving Plaintiffs' Class Notice Plan and Forms of Notice, M.D.L. No. 95-1060R, U.S. District Court, Central District of California. Filed February 21, 1996.

O'Reilly, J. (1992). *Defining Toxic Torts. Toxic Torts Practice Guide,* 2nd ed., McGraw-Hill, New York, 2-1–2-7; 5-1–5-8.

Travers, T., Ed., *American Law of Products Liability,* 3rd ed. Part I (1987). The Lawyers Co-Operative Publishing Co. Bancroft-Whitney Co., Rochester, NY, chap. 1, 5–106.

Workers' Compensation
by Patricia A. Costantini

Workers' compensation laws were developed as systems which would provide income and medical benefits to workers injured in the course of employment, while also reducing personal injury litigation. Despite this fact, many aspects of workers' compensation cases focus on the legal issues related to causality, aggravation of preexisting conditions, compensability, and impairment ratings (Clifton, 1996).

Workers' compensation laws exist in every state, although they differ in scope, administration, and benefits (Weed and Field, 1994). There are also federal workers' compensation laws limited to federal employees and those workers employed in some aspect of interstate commerce.

LNCs provide a variety of services in consultation on cases involving workers' compensation issues. These nurses usually work for insurance carriers, third-party administrators, and private rehabilitation companies. In this role the LNC may

- Participate in providing medical and/or disability case management services
- Conduct medical research regarding appropriate treatment alternatives
- Identify medical experts for second opinions or independent medical evaluations
- Audit medical bills for relationship of charges to the injury
- Complete life-care plans to assist insurance companies with setting financial reserves for long-term care

The LNC frequently acts as a liaison between treating physicians or other health care providers and the employer to provide information and education which will assist with determining job modifications necessary to accommodate a safe return to work. This involves completing job analyses (U.S. Department of Labor, 1991), which outline essential tasks and physical demands of specific positions. A working knowledge of the Americans with Disabilities Act is essential.

Workers' compensation hearings are often held to resolve disputes relating to medical or return to work issues. The LNC who has provided services in a case may be called as a fact witness to testify about the injured worker's cooperation in seeking appropriate medical care or participation in prescribed therapies.

The LNC's involvement with workers' compensation cases requires unique medical, legal, insurance, and employment knowledge as well as advanced skills to assess, investigate, organize, communicate, teach, and document (Marcinko, 1995).

References

Clifton, D. W. (1996). Managed workers compensation. Case review, *The Journal of Case Management Professionals,* 2(3), 20–24.

Marcinko, D. (1995). Career alternatives for the legal nurse consultant: rehabilitation nursing in private practice, *The Journal of Legal Nurse Consulting,* 6(1), 11.

U.S. Department of Labor (1991). *Revised Handbook for Analyzing Jobs,* Washington, D.C., The Department.

Weed, R. and Field, T. (1994). *The Rehabilitation Consultant's Handbook,* Athens, GA, Elliot & Fitzpatrick.

Life-Care Planning
by Patricia A. Constantini

LNCs frequently function as life-care planners. In this capacity, they prepare life-care plans on behalf of attorneys or insurance carriers, in order to provide detailed information about future complex service needs and costs resulting from catastrophic injury and/or illness. They may also be asked by an attorney to critique the life-care plan of a colleague submitted by opposing counsel. The role of the life-care planner is one which has evolved out of the practice of medical and disability case management.

Life-care planning was first mentioned in the legal literature in 1981 (Deutsch and Raffa, 1981), and in rehabilitation literature in 1985 (Deutsch and Sawyer, 1985). Since that time, a variety of professionals have engaged in this practice, including registered nurses, rehabilitation counselors, clinical therapists, and physicians. In general, qualifications for the role of life-care planner include knowledge about the medical aspects of disabilities and experience with the coordination of related services.

A life-care plan is a comprehensive document and educational tool, which delineates an individual's needs created by an injury or illness, and details the costs of services required to meet those needs. An objective and professional life-care plan emphasizes quality care, cost-effectiveness, and prevention of complications. The life-care plan is created to convey complex future care/cost details to all parties involved in an injury case. The plans are useful when evaluating damages related to catastrophic conditions such as spinal cord injuries, head injuries, amputations, birth-related impairments (e.g., cerebral palsy, mental retardation, static encephalopathy), burns, seizure disorders, organ transplants, etc.

A thorough life-care plan usually includes specific components (Weed and Field, 1994), all of which relate to service needs:

- Projected nonmedical evaluations
- Projected therapies
- Wheelchair needs
- Orthotics/prosthetics
- Independent function aids
- Home equipment/accessories
- Medications/supplies
- Home care/facility care
- Future routine medical care
- Transportation
- Architectural renovations
- Leisure/recreation equipment
- Future medical/surgical care
- Aggressive, potential complications
- Vocational assessment

In order to complete a life-care plan, it is usually necessary to first review and assess the available medical information, interview the injured individual and/or family members, communicate with treating health care professionals, and conduct research regarding diagnosis, treatment, services, and costs. The life-care plan is then written and finalized.

Life-care plans are frequently requested by insurance carriers and attorneys. Insurance companies use the life-care plan in workers' compensation case management or managed care planning, primarily to set aside financial reserves appropriately to pay for long-term care. Attorneys utilize the information provided by the life-care plan to address damages in personal injury, medical malpractice, product liability, motor vehicle accident, and workers' compensation cases.

While some life-care planners may be hired by the attorney in a consulting capacity only, most often, the life-care planner involved in litigation will be identified as an expert witness. The LNC preparing a life-care plan in such cases must be prepared to testify in court to educate the jury and to defend the plan submitted. This role requires appropriate educational and employment credentials, and excellent communication skills. (See Section IX The Legal Nurse Consultant as Expert Witness.)

References

Deutsch, P. M. and Raffa, F. (1981). *Damages in Tort Actions,* Vol. 8, New York, Matthew Bender.

Deutsch, P. M. and Sawyer, H. W. (1985). *A Guide to Rehabilitation,* New York, Matthew Bender.

Weed, R. and Field, T. (1984). *The Rehabilitation Consultant's Handbook,* Athens, GA, Elliott & Fitzpatrick.

The Legal Nurse Consultant's Role in Criminal Law
by Doug Davis

The increase in numbers of victims of violent crimes throughout the U.S. has provided a new dynamic role for the LNC in the area of criminal law. Criminal cases require the expertise of professionals from different disciplines in and out of the criminal justice system. Prosecutors and defense attorneys are beginning to recognize the importance and significant role the LNC can play as part of the litigation team. The nurse's experience and clinical knowledge provides attorneys with a previously untapped source when handling criminal cases that involve medicolegal issues. The LNC specializing in criminal cases becomes a medical investigator, exploring and evaluating data gathered during the investigation of crimes against persons.

During the course of a criminal law practice, attorneys are confronted with a wide variety of assaults and deaths. The most common cases are those associated with gun shot wounds, cutting wounds, stabbing wounds, and blunt-force injuries. In these types of cases the prosecutor and defense attorney utilize the LNC to provide a basic understanding of the pathology of wounds and injuries. This information allows them to address the medicolegal issues in the case in a manner that can be readily understood by a judge and jury.

The LNC/Medical Investigator

The ultimate objective of a criminal investigation is to present to a court of law both the physical evidence and the suspect. The success or failure of the effort is related closely to the actions initiated by law enforcement at the time the crime is brought to their attention. What law enforcement does or fails to do in the critical early stages may well determine the course of the investigation. The facts that are obtained and the evidence that is uncovered and protected are instrumental in directing the prosecution or defense attorney to a successful conclusion of the case. Investigations, regardless of type of ultimate purpose, involve the task of gathering and evaluating information. It is important that the investigation process be thought of in terms of gathering information rather than of gathering evidence. During the review of a criminal investigation, the LNC plays a significant role in evaluating crime scenes, medical reports, and evidence-collection protocols related to medicolegal issues in a criminal case.

Assault and Death Investigations

The investigation of assaults and deaths requires the greatest effort on the part of law enforcement. During an investigation, a vast amount of information and evidence may be collected from a variety of sources such as witnesses, police officers, and forensic pathologists. A significant amount of information gathered during the investigation may be related to medicolegal issues in the case.

Certain characteristics of wounds such as gunshots, stabbing, cutting, and blunt-force injuries may provide clues to the circumstances under which they occurred. There are also a number of factors that will affect the characteristics of the wound and change its appearance, for example, the type of weapon, the distance, the passage through clothing, the passage through the body, and the body part affected. Stabbing and cutting wounds vary according to the type of weapon and how it is used in the attack, such as a thrusting, slicing, or twisting motion. Blunt-force injuries may be evident by outward signs such as lacerations and bruising. However, a lack of external injuries does not mean that blunt force was not applied. In many instances, internal damage to organs occurs without any external signs of violence. The LNC with a working knowledge of the pathology of wounds can provide attorneys with valuable information about the nature and extent of various types of wounds and injuries.

The LNC and the Medicolegal Autopsy

The purpose of an autopsy is to establish the cause of death and make a medical determination of all the other factors which may have contributed to death. From an investigative point of view the cause of death is considered the pathological condition which produced the death; the manner of death; the instrument or physical agent that was used; the mode of death; the intent when the instrumentality was employed; and by whom. The complete medicolegal autopsy or postmortem examination involves the examination of the crime scene, identification of the body, external examination of the body, internal examination of the body, and the toxicological examination of body fluids and organs.

The LNC may be utilized to witness and/or review the autopsy report and translate the findings into simple, layperson's terms. The LNC's knowledge of human anatomy and physiology, wound pathology, and laboratory test interpretation is invaluable to prosecutors and defense attorneys reviewing the results of a medical autopsy.

Summary

Criminal cases are complex and require the coordinated effort of all persons involved on the litigation team. The LNC becomes a facilitator and coordinates the efforts of scores of people associated with the various elements of the case as it pertains to the medicolegal issues. With a solid foundation of medical knowledge and health care experience, and through extensive study of forensic evidence and criminal investigative experience, the LNC develops an expertise in the appraisal of criminal evidence. The LNC becomes a valuable resource to the litigation team helping to solve the mysteries and discover the truth during a criminal investigation and trial.

References

DiMaio, V. (1992). *Gunshot Wounds. Practical Aspects of Firearms, Ballistics, and Forensic Techniques,* CRC Press, Boca Raton, FL.
Eckert, W. (1996). *Introduction to Forensic Sciences,* CRC Press, Boca Raton, FL.
Jerath, B. and Rajinder, J. (1993). *Homicide. A Bibliography,* CRC Press, Boca Raton, FL.

Case Management
by Patricia A. Constantini

Case management is "a collaborative process which assesses, plans, implements, coordinates, monitors and evaluates options and services to meet an individual's health needs through communications and available resources to promote quality, cost effective outcomes." (CMSA, 1995, p. 8). This process is carried out in numerous settings, by a variety of professionals, including LNCs.

The practice of case management involves primarily the coordination of services. While case management has been around since the early 1900s (CMSA, 1995), it has grown dramatically in the last 20 years. This is especially true since it is increasingly recognized as an essential component in managing workers' compensation cases, and in managed care in the changing health care industry (Van Genderen, 1996).

Case managers practice in a variety of environments including hospitals, government agencies, independent case management companies, insurance companies, and health care facilities. It is key that the case manager has basic knowledge of the medical aspects of disease and disability, as well as service systems, and community resources. The case manager's role includes the implementation of service plans. How those plans are carried out will be partly based on the source of the referral and the setting in which case management takes place. The practicing case manager will be required to learn and understand the policies, contracts, and regulations associated with each case, in order to coordinate the most cost-effective care. For example, knowledge of specific health insurance guidelines, government agency regulations, or state workers' compensation laws will be necessary in order to carry out service plans in accordance with the coverage an individual patient or client has.

There is no one body of knowledge which defines case management (Toran, 1996); it is usually recognized as an area of practice involving a number of disciplines, including nursing, social work, and rehabilitation counseling. The Commission for Case Manager Certification has established six essential activities and five core components of case management (CCMC, 1996). The activities include assessment, planning, implements, coordination, monitoring, and evaluation. The core components of case management are coordination and service delivery; physical and psychological factors; benefit systems and cost–benefit analysis; case management concepts; and community resources.

Depending on the work environment, case managers conduct research regarding diagnosis and treatment alternatives, coordinate independent medical evaluations, and may be called upon to testify as fact witness in workers' compensation cases. Those with advanced experience frequently develop life-care plans as part of comprehensive rehabilitation management (Deutsch, 1994). The case manager as life-care planner may also be asked to testify as expert witness about the life-care plan in civil litigation cases.

References

CCM (1996). *Update*, Rolling Meadows. IL: Commission on Case Manager Certification.

CMSA L(1995). *Standards of Practice for Case Management*, Little Rock, AR, Case Management Society of America.

Deutsch, P. M. (1994). Life-care planning: into the fusture. *NARPPS* (National Association of Rehabilitation Professionals in the Private Sector) *Journal*, 9(2, 3), 79–84.

Toran, M. R. (1996). Case management in a changing world, *The Case Manager*, 7(1), 69–73.

Van Genderen, A. (1996). How to develop and manage a case management department, *The Journal of Care Management*, 2(4), 30–41.

Section IV
Ethics

Chapter 12

Ethics and the Legal Nurse Consultant

Gretchen Aumman

Contents

Objectives

- To discuss the moral basis of nursing
- To identify and distinguish between two basic moral positions
- To identify the primary principles underlying the moral positions
- To discuss resources available to the LNC regarding ethical issues in nursing

1-57444-123-X/98
© 1998 by American Association of Legal Nurse Consultants

- To discuss the moral foundations underlying legal nurse consulting
- To identify and discuss some major ethical issues in legal nurse consulting

Introduction

Until recently, many nurses assumed that ethical decision making was the sole province of other professionals; physicians predominantly, in health care, were seen as holding and exercising sole control in ethical decision making, whatever the problem was at hand. Because physicians claimed ownership of patients, nurses frequently yielded accountability for such decisions under the mistaken impression that was as it should be. Today, however, as nursing has come of age, nurses individually and collectively are coming to realize the value of nursing practice in health care and other fields as well.

Solutions to moral problems many times are not arrived at easily or readily. Competence in ethical decision making must accompany nursing's new-found accountability if the profession is to survive and prosper as a credible and important part of health care in all its aspects. Such competence is acquired through the study of ethics, the understanding of one's own values and moral underpinnings, and the development of a reasoned approach to moral problems that reflects both knowledge and understanding and that documents one's moral position. It is only when these steps are taken and applied that a nurse, in whatever forum she is practicing, can behave as a truly accountable practitioner.

Definition of Ethics and Morals

Ethics is defined as "the philosophical inquiry into the principles of morality, of right and wrong product, of virtue and vice, and of good and evil as they relate to conduct" (Ladd, 1978, p. 400). Ethics has to do with thinking and acting on our thoughts regarding what is right or wrong, good or bad. Most of us recognize an ethical dilemma when confronted with one. Such dilemmas have to do with different understandings of what is right or wrong, or how one ought to be or act.

While ethics involves the study of how we deal with differences in understandings of good, morality is the reflection of those decisions in everyday life. When speaking of morals, we refer to the standards of right and wrong in the communities in which we live and practice. Thus, one might feel moral distress when confronted by a dilemma, but one undertakes an ethical evaluation by studying the underlying differences, and attempting to discern a resolution to the problem.

Morality therefore consists of the studied judgments of a society regarding how one should act toward others within that society. More often than not, moral consensus in American society is arrived at through public discussions or hearings, for instance, on topics such as abortion, health care, and gun control. When a society feel strongly about a particular view such that documentation of that view is deemed important, that "institutionalization" frequently takes the form of a law, act, code of laws, and so forth. The laws of a society are therefore a reflection of its moral stance on particular issues held to be of special import in that society. It is clear, because of the amount of time it takes to formulate, discuss, and pass laws, that legislation in many areas will reflect the societally held view from several to many years before. It is rare for the laws to be contemporaneous with society's views on current "hot" issues.

Nursing as a Moral Enterprise

Nursing is an essential moral enterprise, involving caring for and treating the sick, comforting and protecting those who suffer. Nursing derives its moral worth from the work that it does, and documents its moral position in a variety of ways. As a profession, it has developed a code of ethics that holds nurses accountable for ethical decisions and behavior within nursing practice. Moreover, it is from the view of nursing as a profession that further shape and direction is found regarding ethics.

Concern for moral standards is not unique to the field of nursing. Many groups of working people holding a common goal consider themselves as professionals in their fields, and seek to establish their positions by developing codes of ethics. Consequently, there are numerous types of ethical codes published, from varying associations, including, for example, lawyers, teachers, physicians, accountants, flight attendants, and so forth. Not all groups who develop codes of ethics are professionals, however. A profession involves several characteristics not held by all groups claiming such status. This is important, because it is from its position as a profession that nursing derives much of its moral stance and authority.

A profession primarily entails a particular view or attitude toward the work it encompasses. A profession includes a calling to do specific work; this attitude frequently involves a dedication to the work and people that goes beyond the usual 8-hour-per-day job. Professionals feel responsibility for the quality of their work and identify with others who share their perspectives. Professionalism goes beyond attitude, however. The social dimensions of being a professional shape the member's relationships with co-workers and the organizations they join. Professionals frequently are held in a position of regard in their communities and, as such, are held to a higher level of accountability in their practices.

Along with their dedication and position in the community, professions further include three common criteria that serve to distinguish the work and people who perform it, and their consequent interest in ethics. The first of these criteria is competence at a high level of expertise. A professional may not solely claim an ability to perform the services involved; a profession requires a claim to and requirement of maximal competence, based on extensive education, experience, continued learning, and mastering the underlying principles, all of which are based on an underlying theory of practice, scientific foundation, or distinct body of knowledge.

A second criteria of a profession is that of social value. Professionals claim to perform work that has significant value to the people in the society in which it is practiced. Their competence is linked to something that holds special value to those in the society, such as health, education, justice, or religion.

Autonomy in their work is the third criterion of a professional. The distinguishing feature between a profession and a craft, job, or other type of endeavor frequently hinges on the criterion of the practitioner's ability to control various aspects of his or her work, such as how the work is done, the goal of the endeavor, conditions of employment, and so forth. Professionals maintain their claim to autonomy in part through the claim to special competence, because the professional, for instance, the nurse, is the only individual who has the unique training, education, experience, knowledge, and judgment to perform nursing work. Therefore, in order to continue to claim professional autonomy, the practitioner has an obligation to pursue further training, education, and so forth in the area of practice.

Nursing has struggled long and hard to achieve recognition of its claim for autonomy, in the steps toward recognition of nursing's place as a separate and distinct profession. Establishment of a code of ethics is a primary method of stating the autonomous goals, distinct body of knowledge, and special competence in a field holding significant value in the society. The American Nurses Association (ANA) Code of Ethics is the statement of such claims for nursing. (See Appendix 12.1.)

When an individual undertakes the practice of nursing, he or she makes a moral commitment to uphold and support the values and obligations expressed in the code. Accountability in individual practice is a hallmark of a professional and is the keystone of nursing as a profession. Nurses are accountable for their practice, including the decisions and judgments they make regarding clients or patients. The question then arises regarding how nurses can make responsible judgments in their practice, particularly in difficult cases, unusual circumstances, or emerging subspecialties. While the Code of Ethics for Nurses offers some insight, an exploration into ethical decision making and the principles that underlie the practice of nursing may prove more fruitful and provide some further direction.

Basic Moral Positions

Before a concrete ethical problem can be resolved, it is necessary to understand the conflict between moral views. Ethical positions are derived from several ethical theories, including consequence-based theories, and those based on a view of duty or obligation. It is within these frameworks that nurses struggle, address specific issues such as privacy and confidentiality, and truth telling. Reflection on and resolution of ethical problems in nursing frequently go on without any formal consideration of ethical theory. Nurses make ethical decisions daily, frequently without any thought, consideration, discussion, or justification regarding their basic moral positions or principles. The fact that two people have different foundations for their views is often irrelevant to resolution of the problem at hand. For instance, a nurse may come to the conclusion that a particular course of action should be followed because not doing so would cause untold and unnecessary harm to others. Another nurse may decide for the same course of action, but may have come to the decision through an analysis of her own obligations as a nurse to this particular patient, regardless of outcome. Each has come to the same resolution of the problem, but from vastly different conceptions of what constitutes right or good. Ethical problems do not always work out this way, however, particularly when the concepts of right are based on differing views. In these situations a discussion of the nature and justification of the theories and principles involved can perhaps shed some light on possible resolutions.

Theories of ethics serve several purposes: they provide a general overview of the conception of the good held by the theory; they delineate individual rights and duties held by the framework; and they set the ordering or priorities of the elements within the framework. Whether certain goals, duties, or rights are basic or subordinate to something else is important in determining the structure of an ethical theory.

By definition, theories are general in nature. They provide a framework and some direction for moral activities and questions; theories are incapable of providing specific direction in particular cases. This type of direction is found through an exploration of the basic principles that emerge from the ethical theories. Although there are many important ethical principles, those addressed here are specific to nursing and to legal nurse consulting.

Consequence- or Outcome-Based Views

A consequence-based theory of ethics locates the rightness or wrongness of actions in the outcome of those actions. Thus, in this view, no action is in and of itself inherently right or wrong. The outcome determines how the action can be judged. In this view, for instance, whether or not one should tell the truth to a client or patient will be decided by what happens, by the outcome of the action. For instance, if telling a patient that he or she has cancer would result in that patient being harmed through great psychological distress, then in the consequence-based theory of ethics, telling such a patient the truth would not be the right thing to do. While this is a very bad example, nurses and other professionals use consequence-based reasoning frequently in their analyses of ethical problems, as in, for example, risk–benefit analysis: do the benefits of a particular action outweigh the risks involved?

A formulation of a consequence-based ethical theory is utilitarianism (Arras and Rhoden, 1990). Articulated by Jeremy Bentham (1748–1832) and John Stuart Mill (1806–1873), the premise of utilitarianism is that the combined good of all those involved in a situation has greater importance than the good of a single individual. "The greatest good for the greatest number" is the common formulation of this premise. An action is right or wrong according to its usefulness in promoting the good of all concerned.

In this view, actions such as saving a life or ending a life are neutral, intrinsically neither right nor wrong. Their rightness depends only on their *consequences,* the good or harm that results for everyone involved. Thus utilitarianism is termed a *consequentialist* position, in contrast to positions in which actions are believed intrinsically right or wrong regardless of their results. For the utilitarian, actions are morally inseparable from their results.

When presented with a moral dilemma, the person reasoning through utilitarian arguments first must identify potential outcomes of actions. The moral criterion for action in the utilitarian framework is that it produce the greatest balance of good over harm for all concerned. The first difficulty or problem for the utilitarian is deciding how large to make the circle of people whose good should be taken into account. The number of people affected must remain a matter of judgment for the utilitarian. Not only will the number vary with the situation, but it will increase or decrease according to the action chosen.

The second problem for the utilitarian is deciding how to define good in tallying the amount of it that each possible action would achieve. How is the good to be defined? Is it whatever each person in the situation desires? Can death be a good outcome in one case but not in another? Can release from suffering count as a greater good than continued life? Can the pleasure of two persons outweigh the pain of one? How can individual goods be combined to produce a "general" good?

General good is difficult to define. Any situation involving several individuals consists of several discrete individual goods. Averaging those different goods together to calculate the overall good masks the most important thing about them, their individual character. Physical pain for one person will represent a greater harm than for another; continued life will represent a greater good for some than for others. For a general good to be conceptualized, it would be necessary to regard harms and benefits as comparable for everyone. For example, it would be necessary to decide that a particular good such as preservation of life is the highest good for everyone. There is no way, however, in which such an objective scale could be devised. Definitions of harm and benefit are by nature personal, determined subjectively by each individual.

Closely related to utilitarianism, and held as the primary principle in that theoretic framework, is the principle of beneficence. Beneficence is the position in which the right action is the one that prevents harm and produces the greatest amount of good for the individual. The patient's well-being is the sole criterion for a good outcome.

Based on that premise, beneficence involves not only acting to promote the patient's best interest, but doing so even when the nurse's view of the patient's good conflicts with the patient's view. Thus, beneficence turns into paternalism when a patient disputes the professional's view.

Paternalistic acts and attitudes are those that limit the liberty of individuals for their own good. In nursing, paternalism involves the use of some form of coercion to benefit a patient who does not regard the intended outcome as a benefit, or does not regard it as a great enough benefit to outweigh the suffering required to attain it. The coercion need not take overt form. Failing to obtain explicit consent counts as limiting patients' liberty, as does failure to provide patients with adequate information on which to base their consent.

Critics of paternalism claim that only patients themselves can determine what is in their best interest, since that judgment must be based ultimately on subjective, personal values.

Patients cannot know what is best for them without first knowing all of the options available and the objective reasons for and against each one. That information must be provided by the professional. But the professional cannot know which of the options is most consistent with an individual patient's values. That subjective dimension only the patient knows. Objective information itself cannot be the basis for a decision, because it does not take into account a particular patient's fear of anesthesia, fear of blood transfusion, willingness to live with only partial recovery, dedication to following the medical regimen, and so on. These are matters of personal evaluation that only the patient can determine.

A second criticism of paternalism rests on the belief that competent patients have the right to decide what will be done to them. Their freedom of self-determination includes the right to make decisions others consider mistaken or harmful, the right to base decisions on factors others would judge insignificant or irrelevant, and even the right to value an outcome no one else may consider good, namely, death.

The paternalist assumes that illness diminishes the capacity for rational decision making and that the right of self-determination therefore applies only to healthy persons. A person's autonomy definitely is altered by the emergence of physical limitations such as pain or immobility, and the seeking of professional help reflects an awareness of one's own limited understanding. That does not, however, negate the possibility of competent decision making. Patients may be overwhelmed by pain or devastated by a disability, but their limited perspective can be enlarged by access to the different perspective provided by the professional.

Obligation-Based Theory

As noted earlier, utilitarianism is primarily concerned with raising the quality of life; it holds that persons are morally obligated to increase well-being and to decrease the amount of pain and suffering in the world (Arras and Rhoden, 1990). These are among the goals of every practicing nurse. Considerations of utility are very important in ethical problems in health care. Who can imagine discussing chemotherapy or surgical procedures, for example, without pondering the risks and benefits involved? Utilitarianism, however, cannot provide a completely adequate moral philosophy. Other ethical viewpoints, based on conceptions of duty or obligation, emerged in response to the inadequacies of utilitarianism. A duty-based theory of ethics locates the rightness or wrongness of actions in principles that govern behavior. Such theories take some particular duty or set of duties as fundamental. Examples of duty- or obligation-based theories include those based on a duty to obey God's will, as in the Ten Commandments; the principles set down in the ANA Code of Ethics for Nurses (see Appendix 12.1); and traditional medical morality rooted in the Hippocratic Oath.

One major ethical viewpoint, known as Kantianism (Immanuel Kant, 1724–1804), holds that consequences do not make an action right or wrong. Rather, the moral rightness of a person's actions is dependent upon whether or not those actions uphold a principle, regardless of outcome (Arras and Rhoden, 1990). For instance, a nurse may administer a drug properly and with the appropriate preparation, and yet, because of some rare and unforeseeable complication, the patient dies. Did the nurse act wrongly because the patient died? Most individuals would think it unfair to judge the moral worth of the nurse's action solely on the basis of its outcome if the result were unintended and not due to negligence. Common sense says that the nurse's motive, that is, the principle behind the action, should determine any judgment regarding the morality of the action.

Kant believed that nothing is good in itself except a "good will," by which is meant the uniquely human capacity to act according to the concept of law, i.e., principles. In estimating the total worth of one's actions, Kant believed that a good will takes precedence over all else (Macklin, 1976). Contained in a good will is the concept of duty. According to Kantianism, only when persons act from a notion of duty do their actions have moral worth. For instance, nurses have a duty to tell patients the truth. However, merely because a nurse tells a patient the truth does not necessarily mean that the action was morally worthy. Perhaps the nurse told the truth to prevent further difficulties later on, or perhaps the nurse did so to avoid legal problems. Although this nurse may be acting in *accordance with duty,* the nurse is not acting *from duty.* For Kant, actions have true moral worth only when they arise from a recognition of a duty and a choice to perform that duty.

Kant also held that an absolute moral truth had to be consistent and free from internal contradiction. Thus, in order for a rule of conduct to be a moral rule, it had to hold universally, in all situations, without exceptions. Further Kantianism also posits that, in keeping with the idea that humans are rational beings, humans should treat each other as ends in themselves, not as mere means to an end (Beecher, 1966). Thus, medical researchers, no matter how lofty their goals, may never use human beings in research without first obtaining their truly informed consent (Englehardt, 1982).

A duty-based framework of ethics such as Kant's contains several appealing elements that are applicable to health care. First, Kant's ethics takes much of the "guesswork" out of moral decision making in health care. To act morally is to act on principle. No matter what the consequences or situational nuances, some actions are always wrong. Second, Kant's ethics recognizes humans as intrinsically worthy of respect. Unlike consequentialist ethics, Kant's mandate to treat persons as ends in themselves and not only as means to an end places the individual at the center of moral decisions. In health care, this serves to bring a much needed humanism to care dominated by machines and technology (Bursztain et al., 1984). Third, Kant's concept of duty implies the moral obligation to act from a respect for rights and a recognition of responsibilities. According to Kant, people act morally when they behave according the concepts of law. Subscribing to this theory necessitates defining and specifying rights and responsibilities clearly and then following the moral imperative in acting with respect to them. Since each individual participating in a nurse/patient relationship has equal claims and duties, Kant's ethics implies a mutuality in relationships between patients and nurses that is not seen in the utilitarian frameworks.

Criticisms of Kant arise from several areas. First, there is no clear method to resolve conflicts of duties. For instance, suppose that by lying to a patient, the nurse knows he or she can spare that patient emotional turmoil and pain. The nurse presumably has a duty to tell the truth and a duty to refrain from causing pain to others. Which of these obligations takes precedence when they conflict? Second, how does one resolve the question of who qualifies as a rational autonomous being? Kant is quite clear that duties are owed to beings who are rational and autonomous (Katz, 1984). Where, though, no children fit in? Or senile adults? How should nurses consider their duties to nonrational, nonautonomous persons? Third, there is no compelling reason that certain actions should hold without exception (Ramsey, 1973). In Kant's view, truth telling in nursing practice, therefore, would mean that all patients should be told all the truth all of the time. Clearly, this flies in the face of what nurses experience in their day-to-day practice, as well as contradicting common sense. The rigidity of Kant's rule, which allows no exceptions, precludes it from being accepted totally as the basis for nursing practice. However, despite its obvious shortcomings, Kantianism holds an appeal for nursing practice precisely because of its recognition of the nature of nursing as more than the scale on which one balances risks and benefits, and because of the humanity necessary in health care.

From Kant's view of ethics emerges its primary ethical principle, respect for autonomy. Respect for a person's autonomy denotes a moral position based on the individual claim to self-determination. It is the position in which patient autonomy is the primary value governing the nurse's actions. This means that the nurse, although still concerned with acting in the patient's interest, does not define that interest in any way contrary to the patient's own definition. In this view, it is not the professional, but the patient, who determines what "best interest" means.

Respect for autonomy is not a form of consumerism in which the nurse's role is merely to clear a path and stand guard so patients can exercise their autonomy single-handedly. Such respect recognizes the real limitations imposed by illness and recognizes patients' need for assistance in exercising autonomy in a situation that may be both unfamiliar and frightening. The nurse helps patients with decision making. In consumerism the nurse has no desire to participate in decision making; nurses merely supply patients with the facts, then withdraw, leaving the decision in the patient's hands. The nurse is detached from the decision making, just as in paternalism the patient is removed from decision making. One ethical view, consumerism, dispenses with the nurse just as the other view, paternalism, dispenses with the patient.

In an obligation-based framework, the relationship between nurse and patient is a partnership, in contrast to consumerism and paternalism. It assumes that patients can be more fully and freely self-determining if they are actively assisted in that endeavor than if they are left to their own devices. The purpose of the partnership is for patients' own values ultimately to be the deciding ones, since only patients can know their personal criteria for health.

Even professionals disagree on the definition of health. The reason for disagreement is the value component of any definition. No concept of health (or disease) is simply a descriptive statement about the presence or absence of a particular condition. Every concept of health includes an evaluation of certain conditions as either desirable to undesirable, worthy of being preserved or calling for a change. In different cultural groups, as in different individuals, the same condition may be evaluated in opposite terms, depending on whether or not it is consistent with the culture's overall values and goals. Witness, for example, the controversy in the deaf community regarding the questions of teaching deaf children to lip-read and to speak; as well as the use of cochlear implants.

Because health is not a final goal in itself but a means to other ends, a concept of health depends on the specific physical and mental requirements of those ends. Sterility may be a defect in some persons, a treatment for others. A sculptor may not need the same degree of visual acuity as a painter. Loss of a limb may mean insurmountable disability for an athlete, or minimal impairment for a teacher. In each of these cases, a personal or cultural goal provides the framework for a definition of health.

In addition to the goals that health serves for an individual, a concept of health is personal because it involves a determination of the part of the self that will receive care in preference to other parts. In a physiological concept of health, the physical has priority over the emotional, intellectual, and spiritual aspects of the self. Some patients may assign a higher value to caring for a nonphysical aspect of the self. The health of that part of the person may be attainable only at the expense of the physical self. For example, a paraplegic woman, whose profession as a family therapist requires many hours of sitting, discovers that decubiti develop if she does not lie down every 2 hours, but she may choose to give less priority to physical health to maintain more-intense professional involvement. Decisions expressing a personal concept of health reflect the way in which a person values the different aspects of the self. Expression of that individual self-concept is the aim of the nurse/patient partnership.

Principles Underlying the Moral Positions

Theories of ethics are necessarily broad and general. They are meant only to provide an underlying philosophy or way of thinking about the ultimate goals of ethics. Such theories are only minimally helpful in day-to-day situations, when one tries to think and reason through some of the dilemmas that arise in nursing practice. Each of the ethical theories has at its foundation a number of underlying principles. There are many ethical principles, but presented here are several that apply particularly to nursing practice. These are *respect for autonomy, beneficence and nonmaleficience,* and *justice.*

Respect for autonomy refers to others' respect for the right and claims of each individual for self-determination, for thinking about, arriving at decisions about, and acting on those decisions that the individual finds serve his interests. This issue emerges frequently in health care, most typically as a difference in opinion between what the patient wants and what the provider sees is best for him or her. Autonomy is not an absolute right that cannot ever be overridden. It is a very strong claim, however, that warrants very strong arguments to be overridden.

Beneficence and nonmaleficence refer to the duties of health care providers to protect the patient and to provide positive treatment or help. There are many times that a health care professional must actually do harm to a patient in order to provide a benefit; a common example of this is performing surgery, which involves incising a patient's body in order to (presumably) provide a benefit, such as removing a ruptured appendix, etc. Beneficence taken to the extreme degenerates into paternalism, which essentially says to a patient that the health care provider knows what is in the patient's interests better than the patient does. There may be times that this is true, such as in comatose or clearly incompetent patients. However, the process of deciding on a patient's competence to make health care decisions for himself is rigorous, and cannot be arrived at whimsically. Clearly, the health care provider's duty to provide a benefit to the patient can conflict with the patient's view of his or her own best interest. Ethical reasoning provides a method for thinking through those dilemmas.

Justice as a principle of ethics involves the obligation to be fair to all persons. While there are several types of justice, including retributive (punishment) and procedural (the process of law), justice here is meant as *distributive*. By this we mean that the distribution of a good, such as health care, legal assistance, and so forth, will be performed as fairly as is societally possible. Thus, the "good" will not be distributed on the basis of race, sex, marital status, financial status, or even merit. The good of health care is distributed on the basis of need, which means that some people will get more than others because their need is greater.

Society struggles daily with this concept, particularly when trying to decide on both basic minimum standard health care that should be available to all, and the "ceiling" or maximum amount of health care that all people have a right to (and therefore a right to expect government support in acquiring) as members of the society. The principle of justice underlies the first statement in the ANA Code of Ethics as well as the AALNC code.

The majority of nurses in clinical practice involving patients on a day-to-day basis typically are presented with ethical dilemmas involving clashes between trying to respect patient autonomy and their duty to provide a benefit and prevent harm to the patient. LNCs, however, more often than not deal with the principle of justice as the underlying principle they struggle to uphold in their practice. Obviously, justice is the primary principle undergirding the legal profession, and this translates to LNCs as well. Justice as fairness to the individual emerges in conflict with justice to society and societal values in this arena. Whether they work as independents or are employed by either a plaintiff or defense attorney, LNCs have as their guiding principle the duty to be fair and to support fairness to the clients and others involved in their cases.

Justice as the Basis for Legal Nurse Consultant Practice

Legal nurse consulting as a subspecialty of nursing thereby derives its moral agency from the nursing profession, with recognition and incorporation of aspects of legal professional ethics. LNCs work within the framework of the legal system, primarily with lawsuits. The goal of a lawsuit has been described as, and should be, to discover the truth in the particular situation, and to arrive at a just and equitable solution. LNCs need to remind themselves of this goal as it frequently becomes easy to get caught up in a "win at all costs" mentality that supports outcomes that may be unfair and unjust, not only to the clients but also to the legal and medical systems, as well as society in general. While nurses are urged to become advocates for their clients, advocacy for any nurse, including LNCs, includes supporting the patient/client's interests within the boundaries of honest and fair analysis and consequent judgments. Therefore, for instance, for the same reason that a nurse caring for a patient should never give a lethal dose of medicine even if the patient desires it, an LNC who advocates for his or her client must do so objectively, with fairness to all in mind. Some LNCs, for instance, refuse to work for tobacco company defense firms, and cannot see that an ethical LNC could possibly do so. While it is wholly the LNC's choice whether or not to work for such companies, it is also entirely defensible for LNCs to undertake such positions with no risk to their ethical practice, as long as LNCs remain honest and fair in their judgments. It is possible that some companies may be sued by plaintiffs who have not been damaged by the company's product. The LNC has a place in ferreting out the reasonable cases from the unwarranted ones. The same reasoning holds true for LNCs who work for aggressive plaintiff's attorneys or criminal defense attorneys, for instance. The principle of justice is served when people who have not been damaged by a company's product are prevented from collecting that to which they are not entitled. The principle of justice is also served when a medical malpractice case is settled reasonably and fairly based on analysis and judgments made by an objective and honest LNC (Hussey, 1996).

The primary ethical responsibility of the LNC is that of professional integrity, which encompasses professional behavior and attitudes, as well as a continuing dedication to maintain excellence in the profession. This is approached through continuing professional education in both professional matters specific to legal nurse consulting, such as legal seminars regarding the legal process and the LNC's part in that process, as well as keeping up with changes in nursing and medicine in order to stay current with contemporary health care practice (Aiken, 1994).

Professional conduct in an LNC may involve the requirement to advise the proper authorities of any action which clearly demonstrates deceit, dishonesty, fraud, or misrepresentation by another LNC, or even by an expert witness. Further, LNCs are required by their ethical code to maintain the highest standards of *personal* conduct that reflect honorably on the LNC and nursing professions (Fiesta, 1994).

Other ethical issues that arise frequently in LNC practice involve questions regarding confidentiality, conflicts of interest, and expert witnesses.

Confidentiality refers to keeping private all information provided by the client or acquired from other sources before, during, and after the course of the professional relationship (Thomas, 1996). While privacy deals with the person, for instance, with issues of intimacy, confidentiality refers to sharing of information about the client that he or she holds as private. This includes, in the LNC's practice, information from or about the client such as medical records and so forth (Simpson, 1996). Confidentiality requires that an LNC may not use privileged information either to the advantage of the LNC or to the disadvantage of the client. Further, confidentiality also requires that an LNC should not engage in any unnecessary or indiscreet communications concerning clients. Such communications would be analogous to the "elevator consults" that occur in many hospitals, during which a patient's confidentiality may be violated extensively and repeatedly (Warr, 1996). An LNC may not disclose any information regarding a client to anyone who is not directly related to the workup of the case. Violation of this ethical rule is not only an ethical violation, it may be a legal issue.

A *conflict of interest* refers to information about a client held by a member of the legal team (an attorney, paralegal, LNC, etc.) that, if revealed to other members of the legal team, may cause some harm, injury, or prejudice to the client. The information does not have to be privileged or include actual documented facts about the client's legal matter. An LNC possesses information about a client, about the attorney's strategies, thought processes, work product and other privileged information. Conflicts of interest in the LNC's practice frequently result from personal or business relationships outside the legal environment or from legal matters at the LNC's former place of employment.

In order to respect a client's autonomy, conflicts of interest that exist within the LNC's relationships with the client or the attorney must be revealed to the client, who then retains the prerogative of staying with the firm/attorney or finding someone else. Not to reveal a recognized conflict of interest constitutes a significant violation of both ethical and legal principles. Even the appearance of a conflict of interest must be recognized and reported by the LNC to the attorney who in turn must report it to the client.

Examples of a conflict of interest may include

- When an LNC changes jobs: an LNC may move from one firm that is handling a legal matter for a client to another which is handling the same matter on behalf of the opposition.
- Family or personal relationships: an LNC may be related to or close friends with a party, client, or someone involved in a legal matter on whom the LNC has been asked to work.
- Business and personal relationships outside their employment: an LNC may have knowledge of or relationships with others through business, organizations, and so forth that may lead to or be perceived as leading to a conflict of interest.

Each time a new case comes in, or whenever an LNC moves from one firm to another, serious consideration of actual or potential conflicts of interest needs to be pursued. If there is either an actual or even perceived conflict of interest, the LNC should report it to the attorney immediately. The LNC may continue to work in that firm, provided the client is informed of the conflict, gives consent for continued representation, and an "ethical wall" (also known as a "Chinese wall") is erected around the LNC and adhered to by all who continue to work on the matter. In adversarial matters, the attorney may also be required to obtain the adversary's consent.

Independently contracting LNCs are at greater risk for conflicts of interest than LNCs employed in the more traditional setting, that is, an attorney's office. Any new case that comes in should be scrutinized carefully for conflicts before any substantive work takes place on it. Any conflicts must be reported to the referring attorney, and a plan developed to deal with the conflict, such as referral to another LNC. It should also be clear by now that one of the ethical practicalities of LNC work is scrupulous record keeping.

LNCs who also work as expert witnesses face several unique ethical questions, including those involving confidentiality and conflicts of interest. Additionally, experts must be objective, honest, and fair in their reports and opinions, resisting any pressure from attorneys or others working on the case to change or modify their opinions. If the expert reviews the case and has a helpful opinion on it, that expert may then be engaged and named. Should an expert find that his or her opinion is not supportive of the client's case, the expert's involvement should end at that point. If the point of a lawsuit is discovery of truth and redress of injustices, it is clear that those goals can never be met by dishonest or biased opinions from an expert more interested in making money than living up to the ethical standards of the profession. LNCs working with experts also must be scrupulous in their efforts to allow for honest differences of opinion and to work to find and retain ethical experts.

Experts at times are approached by attorneys to work on a contingency-fee basis. It is never appropriate for any LNC to work on a contingency basis, for reasons that involve conflicts of interest and an inability to render objective or fair opinions when "going along" could drastically improve one's finances. It is unethical for either an expert or other LNC to work on contingency, and in most states it is illegal. Other billing practices of both LNCs and expert witnesses/LNCs are also suspect. Billing at LNC/expert rates for work that is substantially clerical constitutes unethical practice, as does billing for work that the expert *would have* performed (but did not), such as reading depositions and so forth, had the matter not settled.

Identifiying and Handling Ethical Dilemmas in Legal Nurse Consulting

Ethical dilemmas for LNCs arise in the form of differences of opinion regarding the conduct of a case, including intake, review, forming an opinion, billing, and working with or as an expert. Identifying such problems at times is easy, because of the sense of unease or discomfort the LNC has when dealing with a particular case or client. At such times, the LNC needs to review seriously what ends or goals are being addressed, and whether those are in keeping with the ethical directives of LNCs. Reviewing the ANA Code of Ethics for Nurses as well as the AALNC code may help shed some light on the source of the LNC's moral discomfort. (See Appendix 1.5.)

Further help can be found in reviewing the codes for ethical behavior of related professions, such as the legal and paralegal codes. Other sources for ethical problems solving include discussing the issue, in confidence, with another LNC, or the State Board of Nursing or State Bar.

LNCs, as all health professionals, deal with ethical issues every day. More often than not, the process by which a decision is made is not explicit, as in those situations where the ethical conflict is clear. The purpose of learning about ethics is to help develop an understanding of those cases and situations that are especially problematic, that are not clear or familiar, and that are not addressed in the codes. Such problems should be approached systematically and appropriately.

1. The first step in such an analysis is data collection. Information relevant to the case/problem should be identified and reviewed. From this, a problem statement should be articulated, and the specific dilemma described.
2. Second, the LNC needs to identify his or her personal biases regarding the issues at hand. This can be approached by the LNC identifying who he or she most identifies within the situation. Once that "sympathy" is elucidated, further work can address whether or not the personal or professional biases involved tend to hold undue sway over the situation or those involved in it.
3. Third, the LNC should identify all other possible points of view relevant to the problem. This is another way to ensure that personal or professional biases do not influence the decision-making process. Other possible points of view could also be elucidated through discreet consultation with the appropriate individuals. These could include, for example, another LNC if the issue is between LNCs, an attorney, medical or nursing personnel, social worker, and so forth.
4. Fourth, the LNC should analyze all the issues in light of the principles and rules of ethics and the appropriate codes of ethical behavior, some of which are presented herein. Such analysis is more helpfully conducted with others, such as LNCs or legal professionals, rather than a solitary

debate by a lone LNC. All of this clearly should be undertaken with fitting seriousness and confidentiality.

5. Finally, a decision should be arrived at by those involved in the discussion. The LNC should then act on that decision to the best of his or her ability.

The best method of addressing ethical dilemmas is prevention, through self-knowledge, scrupulous work to identify and handle appropriately any conflicts of interest before a case is accepted, and professional integrity. LNCs as both nurses and legal professionals have a unique place in both the legal and health care systems, working toward justice for individuals and society through their efforts to address and redress inadequacies in each arena. An LNC can only be effective in this work only when he or she adheres to the moral high ground. Such work then benefits all in the long term.

Glossary

Beneficence: The ethical view that the right action is that which promotes the good of the individual patient as that good is understood by the professional.

Ethics: The systematic investigation of questions about right and wrong. It involves critical analysis of different views of right and wrong, with particular attention paid to the underlying values of each view, its coherence and consistency, and its implications in actual situations.

Kantianism: An ethical viewpoint based on Kant's categorical imperative: "Act only on those rules which you can *will* to be universal law." All specific moral duties are derived from this principle.

Morality: Refers to the common conceptions of what is right and what is wrong. Our morality and morals are reflected in how we live, the decisions we make, and what we hold as valuable.

Paternalism: An extension of beneficence. It is the view that professionals understand patients' best interests better than patients and thus are entitled to act so that a patient's well-being (as professionally defined) is promoted, even when the patient does not agree.

Utilitarianism: The ethical view that the right action is that which promotes a greater balance of good over harm for everyone concerned in a situation.

References

Aiken, T. D. (1994). What nurses need to know about legal, ethical, and political issues, *Revolution,* 4(2), 72–75.

Arras, J. and Rhoden, N., Eds. (1990). *Ethical Issues in Modern Medicine,* 3rd ed., Palo Alto, CA, Mayfield Publishing.

Beecher, H. J. (1966). Ethics and clinical research, *New England Journal of Medicine,* 274(24).

Bursztain, H. J. et al. (1984). The technological target: involving the patient in clinical choices, in *The Machine at the Bedside: Strategies for Using Technology in Patient Care,* Reiser, S. J. and Anabar, M., Eds., New York, Cambridge University Press.

Englehardt, H. T. (1982). Bioethics in pluralist societies, *Perspectives in Biology and Medicine,* 26(1).

Fiesta, J. (1994). Failing to act like a professional, *Nursing Management,* 25(7), 15–17.

Hussey, T. (1996). Nursing ethics and codes of professional conduct, *Nursing Ethics,* 3(3), 250–258.

Katz, J. (1984). Respecting autonomy: the struggle over rights and capacities, in *The Silent World of Doctor and Patient,* New York, Macmillan.

Ladd, (1978). *Encyclopedia of Bioethics,* 400.

Macklin, R. (1976). Moral concerns and appeals to rights and duties, *Hastings Center Report,* October.

Ramsey, P. (1973). The nature of medical ethics, in *The Teaching of Medical Ethics,* Veatch, R., Ed., Hastings-on-Hudson, NY, The Hastings Center.

Simpson, R. L. (1996). Ethics and privacy in a technologically driven health care network, *Nursing Administration Quarterly,* 21(1), 81–84.

Thomas, B. (1996). Duty of confidence, *Nursing Times,* 92(39), 53.

Warr, T. (1996). Breaking patient confidentiality, *Nursing N. Z.,* 2(8), 12.

Appendix 12.1
American Nurses Association: Code for Nurses

Preamble

A code of ethics makes explicit the primary goals and values of the profession. When individuals become nurses, they make a moral commitment to uphold the values and special obligations expressed in their code. The Code for Nurses is based on a belief about the nature of individuals, nursing, health, and society. Nursing encompasses the protection, promotion, and restoration of health; the prevention of illness; and the alleviation of suffering in the care of clients, including individuals, families, groups, and communities. In the context of these functions, nursing is defined as the diagnosis and treatment of human responses to actual and potential health problems.

Some clients themselves are the primary decision makers in matters concerning their own health, treatment, and well-being, the goal of nursing actions is to support and enhance the client's responsibility and self-determination to the greatest extent possible. In this context, health is not necessarily an end in itself, but rather a means to a life that is meaningful from the client's perspective.

When making clinical judgments, nurses base their decisions on consideration of consequences and of universal moral principles, both of which prescribe and justify nursing actions. The most fundamental of these principles is respect for persons. Other principles stemming from this basic principle are autonomy (self-determination), beneficence (doing good), nonmaleficence (avoiding harm), veracity (truth telling), confidentiality (respecting privileged information), fidelity (keeping promises), and justice (treating people fairly).

In brief, then, the statements of the code and interpretation provide guidance for conduct and relationships in carrying out nursing responsibilities consistent with the ethical obligations of the profession and with high quality in nursing care.

Code for Nurses

1. The nurse provides services with respect for human dignity and the uniqueness of the client unrestricted by considerations of social or economic status, personal attributes, or the nature of health problems.
2. The nurse safeguards the client's right to privacy by judiciously protecting information of a confidential nature.
3. The nurse acts to safeguard the client and the public when health care and safety are affected by the incompetent, unethical, or illegal practice of any person.
4. The nurse assumes responsibility and accountability for individual nursing judgments and actions.
5. The nurse maintains competence in nursing.
6. The nurse exercises informed judgment and uses individual competence and qualifications as criteria in seeking consultation, accepting responsibilities, and delegating nursing activities to others.
7. The nurse participates in activities that contribute to the ongoing development of the profession's body of knowledge.
8. The nurse participates in the profession's efforts to implement and improve standards of nursing.
9. The nurse participates in the profession's efforts to establish and maintain conditions of employment conducive to high-quality health care.
10. The nurse participates in the profession's efforts to protect the public from misinformation and misrepresentation and to maintain the integrity of nursing.
11. The nurse collaborates with members of the health professions and other citizens in promoting community and national efforts to meet the health needs of the public.

Section V

Professionalism, Standards of Practice, and Standards of Professional Performance

Chapter 13

Professionalism and Standards of Practice and Professional Performance for Legal Nurse Consulting Practice

Maureen Jane Orr, Julie Bogart, and Joan Magnusson

Contents

Objectives

- To identify the key elements that define a profession relative to nursing practice
- To discuss the relationship of the specialty practice of legal nurse consulting to the profession of nursing
- To define the nursing process as it applies to legal nurse consulting
- To define the Standards of Professional Performance as they apply to legal nurse consulting
- To explain by example how the LNC can apply the Standards of Practice to a typical case
- To explain by example how the LNC can apply the Standards of Professional Performance to consulting in the legal arena

Introduction

How we define ourselves as a specialized area of nursing practice is the heart of what distinguishes legal nurse consultants (LNCs) from other nursing professionals. In order for attorneys, judges and juries, risk managers, insurance adjusters, nurses and other health care providers, and the public to understand who we are and what we do, we must clearly define our practice in the legal arena, and clarify our similarities and differences with other nursing specialties. We are also obligated as professionals to define and ensure our ethics and quality of practice. In practice, our actions must meet criteria that can be measured. Standards provide that basis for practice accountability. The standards of practice and professional performance were written by the American Association of Legal Nurse Consultants (AALNC) to meet these professional goals.

Chapter 13 is designed to provide an overview of the broad scope of the standards of practice and professional performance for legal nurse consulting. Because the standards are based on the American Nurses Association (ANA) model of standards and the nursing process, many of the terms in this chapter will be familiar to nurses who have been in active clinical practice. Utilization of the nursing process occurs as second nature to the experienced nurse. With care and thought, that same process is adapted and applied by LNCs to all aspects of their work.

Definition of a Professional

"A butcher, a baker, a candlestick maker...," so goes the nursery rhyme. All of us can think back to jobs we have had — babysitter, waiter, salesperson, etc. There are many occupations, not all are considered professions.

Endeavors have been made to define a profession by identifying various common characteristics. Five attributes generally accepted as essential for an "occupation" to attain recognition as a profession are (Quinn and Smith, 1987; Chaska, 1990; Oermann, 1991; Moloney, 1992):

- A high status granted by society because of altruistic motivation and commitment to serve society

- A systematic unique body of theory, obtained through a university-based education with practical experience to master the knowledge base
- An authority to define the profession and autonomy in its practice
- A code of ethics
- A professional culture that embodies certain values and norms

Whether or not nursing qualifies as a "true" profession has been debated for decades. The debate and discussion itself has promoted recognition of inconsistencies and movement toward solutions, most notably in the areas of educational preparation and control over professional practice. Nursing continues to evolve toward full attainment of these attributes but today is generally accepted as a profession.

One of the concepts used to define a profession is that its services are vital to the viability of a society. It is generally accepted that nurses provide a valued service based on altruistic motivation. The public assumes the title of "nurse" carries with it a certain level of expertise and commitment, and accepts nurses as providing essential services desired and needed by society. It is this assumption which, in part, sets the legal precedent of professional "duty." Many of the current changes in health care delivery may further validate nursing as a profession because of its increasing responsibility and authority in public health maintenance as well as illness management.

While nursing may have various levels of education as entry into practice, a commonality is the knowledge base of health sciences and the nursing process coupled with a minimum of experience necessary to prepare one for licensure and practice. It is the continued application of this theory in practice which supports the premise of a profession. It is the one common bond all nurses share.

The concept of autonomy in practice has also been an area of challenge for nursing as well as for many other professions. It is probably true that no single health care professional, with the complexities in providing health and illness care, can claim absolute autonomy. However, changes in today's health care system have actually propelled nurses into more-autonomous roles (nurse practitioners, case managers) as cost-effective providers of health care services.

Professionals have codes of ethics to help regulate their relationships with clients as well as each other. The ANA developed a formal written Code for Nurses in 1985 which all nurses honor regardless of specialty. Formal codes of ethics are usually based on a set of values and norms which represents the philosophy and practice of the profession.

Professionals have strong values pertaining to their "occupational identity." This identity impacts on all aspects of the professional's attitude and behavior toward work and lifestyle. The values established by the profession become the rules of expected behavior among the members of the profession with expectations of loyalty and adherence.

Could legal nurse consulting be considered a profession absent association/consanguinity with the profession of nursing? Would LNCs want to abandon the professional affiliation with nursing to attempt creation of a new "profession" which merely applies nursing education and experience to legal tasks. (Wouldn't such a path eventually lead to elimination of the need for formal nursing education or practice? Perhaps a specialized year or two of study of health sciences and law would suffice.) Are LNCs not performing nursing services if they do not provide hands-on traditional clinical bedside care in their work?

Legal nurse consulting has no unique body of knowledge or theory as yet thoroughly published, debated, or researched. Legal nurse consulting has no accepted standardized educational preparation nor is assigned prestige and value by society (or as yet by many potential clients). The majority of LNCs do not have control or autonomy over their practice. The value of LNCs as professionals to society and clients is rooted in the common professional identity, nursing. The question is then, are LNCs practicing nursing in the legal arena?

Direct patient care is no longer the defining parameter of what makes a nurse a nurse. How nurses apply health science education and expertise to the ultimate benefactor of the service is the defining parameter. The broad application of the nursing process, nursing education and practice experience, and professional ethics and standards to the benefit of the health care system and the patients it serves more aptly defines the scope of the practice of nursing.

Nursing in the legal arena seeks to right a wrong, to prevent untoward events, to manage injuries resulting from such events when they occur. LNCs provide direct and indirect services to that end for patients and the health care system within the legal environment. For example, whether an LNC is working on the plaintiff or defense side of a professional negligence case, the goal is defense of the standard of care. The standard of care directly affects patient care and is defined in the legal as well as the health care practice arena.

Legal Nurse Consulting as a Specialty Practice of Nursing

Following years of discussion and debate, the Board of Directors of the AALNC resolved in 1995 that first and foremost, the professional foundation of legal nurse consulting is nursing. In applying that foundation in a consulting capacity in the legal arena, a new specialty practice of nursing is defined. LNCs are valued in the legal arena for their health care education and experience, rather than knowledge of the law. They apply this special expertise in legal environments that previously did not have the benefits of their services. In so doing, the quality of the application of the law to health care–related cases, issues, projects, or practices is improved. Clients may be patients, attorneys, insurance companies, hospitals, government agencies, or a variety of others. Although knowledge of the law enriches the LNCs contribution, the client depends on the LNC's health care expertise. The ultimate benefactor of the LNC's work is the quality of health care.

A duty of any profession is to promulgate standards by which the quality of practice of its members can be assessed. As in other nursing specialties, the AALNC has written a scope of practice, and standards of practice and professional performance to meet its professional responsibility to its clients and society (see Appendixes 1.3 and 1.4).

The Scope of Practice for Legal Nurse Consultants was based on a role delineation study, adopted in 1994, and amended in 1995. It emphasizes the knowledge and skills that are unique to nursing and that are useful in the critical analysis of health care issues involved in various legal processes (see Appendix 1.3).

Standards of practice provide common ground for basic practice accountability (Litwack, 1996, p. 8). They are authoritative statements by which the profession describes the responsibilities for which its practitioners are accountable. The Standards of Practice for Legal Nurse Consulting are based on the ANA model and incorporate the nursing process with adjustments for the context of legal nurse consulting practice (see Figure 13.1).

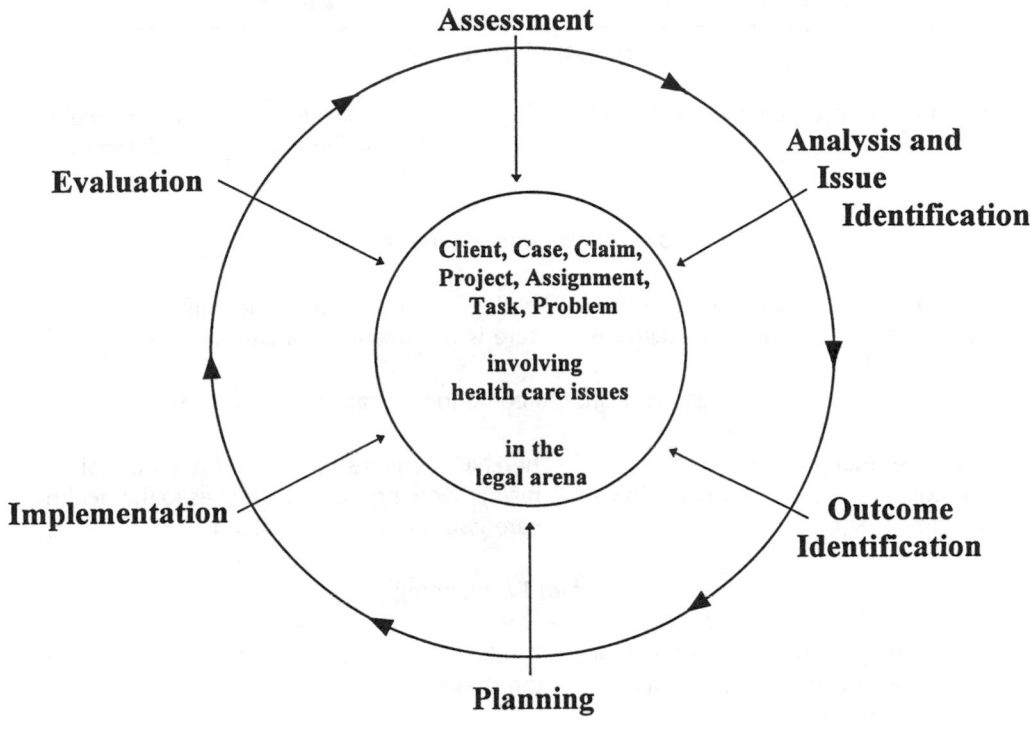

Figure 13.1 Standards of Practice for LNCs.

The Nursing Process as It Applies to Legal Nurse Consulting

The nursing process consists of actions that are logical, interdependent, sequential but cyclic: *assessment, diagnosis, outcome identification, planning, implementation, evaluation.* This is a basic problem-solving process or approach to any assignment. Nursing diagnoses are derived from an analysis of the assessment data. All of these actions require critical thinking, the use of clinical experience, and health science education.

In adapting the nursing process to the practice of legal nurse consulting, the following actions are identified: *assessment, analysis and issue identification, outcome identification, planning, implementation, evaluation.* The concept of nursing diagnosis is interpreted to mean those opinions formulated by the LNC from analysis of the data to determine health care issues important to resolution of legal claims or cases. Those opinions are called issue identification. The anticipated or hoped–for outcomes of the process are then identified and listed.

Planning, implementation, and evaluation of the plan of action follow. (See Table 13.1 for comparison of clinical nursing standards and LNC practice standards.)

Table 13.1   Comparison of Standards of Clinical Nursing Practice of the ANA and the Standards of Practice of the AALNC

Clinical Nursing Standards	LNC Practice Standards
Standard I: Assessment	
The nurse collects patient health data	The LNC collects data to support the systematic assessment of health care issues related to a case or claim
Standard II: Analysis and Nursing Diagnosis	
The nurse analyzes the assessment data and makes a nursing diagnosis	The LNC analyzes data to identify the health care issues related to a case or claim
Standard III: Outcome Identification	
The nurse identifies expected outcomes which are individualized to the patient	The LNC identifies the desired outcome of his/her work product as it relates to the health care issues of a case or claim
Standard IV: Planning	
The nurse develops a plan of care that prescribes interventions to attain expected outcomes	The LNC formulates a plan of action to achieve the desired outcome
Standard V: Implementation	
The nurse implements the interventions identified in the plan of care	The LNC implements the plan of action
Standard VI: Evaluation	
The nurse evaluates the patient's progress toward the attainment of expected outcomes and alters the plan accordingly	The LNC evaluates the effectiveness of the plan of action in achieving the desired effect and alters the plan accordingly

The purpose of the nursing process is to provide the LNC with a framework or consistent problem-solving approach for meeting the needs of the particular case, client, task, or role. This framework also gives the LNC the skills to work with various colleagues in the legal realm so that a successful outcome can be achieved. It also provides the means of measuring whether or not and how well standards are met by practitioners.

While the Standards of Practice spell out how LNCs problem-solve and manage assignments, the Standards of Professional Performance constitute the guidelines for the LNC's professional performance. Adherence to these guidelines will bring a consistency to the practice, so the person engaging the services of an LNC is assured quality of practice.

Incorporation of the LNC Standards of Practice and Standards of Professional Performance into one's practice aids in the development of a consistently high standard of practice, job satisfaction, as well as peace of mind that all aspects of an assignment are covered from every possible angle. Meeting the needs of the client generates good will and additional work. Having a plan of action to guide the LNC through every assignment results in significant savings of time and energy and assures a consistent quality product.

The LNC works with a client to obtain the information necessary to make an assessment. After analysis of the case, the issues are discussed jointly. The client often assists with issue identification and outcome identification. Implementation of the plan often occurs in partnership, and evaluation is an ongoing process.

Summary

A plan of action needs thoughtful preparation and a consistent guideline in order to aid professionals in their work. These standards can be adapted and used as such a guide for the LNC. Purposeful thought should be applied to any case or assignment. The steps of assessment, analysis and issue identification, outcome identification, planning, implementation, and evaluation will assist LNCs in achieving the best possible outcome of their work.

Application of the Standards of Legal Nurse Consulting Practice and Standards of Professional Performance creates a foundation for the practice of the LNC. LNCs can build on that sound foundation in their own practice based on their individual education, experience, and enthusiasm.

Glossary

Analysis and issue identification: As an LNC standard, analysis of data to identify the health care issues related to a case or claim.

Assessment: As an LNC standard, a collection of data to support the systematic assessment of health care issues related to a case or a claim.

Collaboration: As it applies to the LNC, the LNC collaborates with legal professionals, health care professionals when necessary.

Collegiality: As it applies to the LNC, the LNC shares knowledge and contributes to the development of peers, colleagues, and others.

Criteria*: Variables known to be relevant, measurable indicators of the standards of clinical nursing practice.

Education: As it applies to the LNC, educational activities are ongoing and pertain to the LNCs practice area.

---

* These definitions have been taken from the American Nurses Association Task Force on Nursing Practice Standards and Guidelines Working paper.

Ethics: As it applies to the LNC, the LNC is guided by the ANA Code for Nurses with Interpretive Statements and the AALNC Code of Ethics.

Guidelines*: A process of client care management which has the potential of improving the quality of clinical and consumer decision making: includes assessment and diagnosis, planning, intervention, evaluation, and outcome.

Implementation: As an LNC standard, implementation of the plan of action.

Outcome identification: As an LNC standard, the identification of desired activities as related to the health care issues of a case or claim.

Performance appraisal: Evaluation of the practice of the LNC in relation to professional standards and relevant statutes and regulations.

Planning: As an LNC standard; formulation of a plan of action.

Procedures: A series of recommended actions for the completion of a specific task or function. Procedures may be either specific to an institution or applicable across settings.

Professional: A person with a specialized training in a field of learning, art or science.

Properties of the nursing process: Purposeful, systematic. dynamic, interactive, and flexible.

Quality of practice: Evaluation of the quality and effectiveness of practice.

Resource management: As it applies to the LNC, the LNC selects expert assistance on the needs of the case or the claim.

References

Aiken, T., *Legal Ethical and Political Issues in Nursing*, F. A. Davis, Philadelphia, 1994, 57–71.

American Nurses Association, *Standards of Clinical Practice*, Kansas City, MO, American Nurses Association, 1991.

Andrews, M., Goldberg, K., and Kaplan, H., *Nurse's Legal Handbook*, Springhouse Corp., Springhouse, PA, 1996, 2–39.

Atkinson/Murray, *Fundamentals of Nursing*, Macmillan, New York, 1985, 3–77.

Brunner, L. and Suddarth, D., *The Lippincott Manual of Nursing Practice*, 4th ed., J. P. Lippincott Co., Philadelphia, 5–7.

Chaska, N. L., *The Nursing Profession. Turning Points*, C. V. Mosby, St. Louis, MO, 1990.

Dolan, J., Fitzpatrick, M., and Herrmann, E., *Nursing in Society, A Historical Perspective*, 4th ed., W. B. Saunders, Philadelphia, 1983, 1–5.

Emergency Nurses Association, *Emergency Nursing Core Curriculum*, 4th ed., W. B. Saunders, Philadelphia, 1996, 687–695.

Iyer, P., Taptich, B., and Bernocchi-Losey, D., *Nursing Process and Nursing Diagnosis*, 3rd ed., W. B. Saunders, Philadelphia, 1994, 1–33.

Litwack, K., *Core Curriculum for Post Anesthesia Nursing Practice*, 3rd ed., W. B. Saunders, Philadelphia, 1996, 8–14.

Moloney, M. M., *Professionalization of Nursing. Current Issues and Trends*, 2nd ed., J. B. Lippincott, Philadelphia, 1992.

Oermann, M. H., *Professional Nursing Practice. A Conceptual Approach*, J. B. Lippincott, Philadelphia, 1991.

Quinn, C. A. and Smith, M., D., *The Professional Commitment: Issues and Ethics in Nursing*, W. B. Saunders, Philadelphia, 1987.

Rosedahl, C., *Textbook of Basic Nursing*, 5th ed., J. B. Lippincott, Philadelphia, 1991, 3–30.

Appendix 13.1
Application of the Standards of Practice for the Legal Nurse Consultant

The following are examples of activities pertaining to the Standards of Practice. It is important to emphasize that legal nurse consulting is more than a group of isolated activities, but rather a process. Properties of the process are listed in Table 13.2. Examples are by no means comprehensive. Not all activities will be undertaken in all assignments. Certain activities may be listed under different headings depending on assignment or points in time in case progress. Preparation of a chronology, for instance, may be part of assessment in one case, and implementation in another. The examples are meant to give the reader further explanation of how the Standards of Practice can be applied in various situations.

Table 13.2   Properties of the Nursing Process for Legal Nurse Consulting

1.	Purposeful	Goal oriented
2.	Systematic	Uses an organizational approach to achieve a purpose or solve a problem
3.	Dynamic	Involves continuous change and adaptation
4.	Cyclic	Steps are sequential, interdependent, and recurrent
5.	Interactive	Based on a reciprocal relationship between LNC and client
6.	Flexible	Can be adapted to any LNC field; phases are used sequentially and cyclically

Example 13.1

The family of a resident of a long-term care facility who has died unexpectedly after undergoing multiple surgeries notified the facility they are considering filing suit. The LNC has been engaged by an attorney client to evaluate the claim for merit. (The "client" in this instance may represent either the family or the facility.)

Assessment

Data collection as basis for further activities

The LNC reviews medical records from the hospital where the surgeries were performed, the nursing home facility, and the hospital where the patient was taken prior to her death.

The LNC requests and reviews a copy of the death certificate and autopsy report to determine the cause of death.

The LNC reviews the literature pertaining to the applicable state regulations for medical care rendered in a long-term care facility.

The LNC obtains and reviews medical references regarding the indications for, risks of, and known complications of the surgeries.

The LNC prepares a time line summary (chronology) of the hospital and nursing home care from the records obtained.

The LNC consults with decedent's family members to gain more information regarding the decedent's condition and interaction with the health care providers prior to death.

Analysis and Issue Identification

Analysis of the data to determine the health care issues related to the claim

Based on the time line summary and the state's requirements for documentation, the LNC determines that a portion of the records pertaining to the care in the nursing home is missing.

Based on the information from the autopsy report and medical research information, the LNC determines that the decedent's cause of death was *not* an expected or known risk of the surgical procedures.

Comparison of interviews with family members and analysis of the time line of events, the LNC identifies long periods of time without patient assessment of the decedent by nursing personnel.

The LNC determines that based on current information available, the decedent's death may have been due to lack of appropriate care in the nursing home.

Outcome Identification

Results hoped for related to analysis and issue identification

The LNC determines that the missing records may contain information to support (or refute) the alleged negligence and should be obtained if they exist.

The LNC determines that medical and nursing experts in the care of patients in long-term care facilities be consulted and retained to review records and testify regarding the standard of care.

Planning

Plan of action to achieve the desired outcome

The LNC recommends the client request additional records and forward them to the LNC for review.

The LNC recommends the client retain medical causation and nursing standard of care experts to review the case and render opinions.

Implementation

Actions taken to implement the plan

The client requests the missing records and informs the LNC that the facility responded that no such records exist.

The LNC interviews three nursing experts in long-term care, and a medical expert published in the literature on pertinent causation issue, verifying qualifications and clinical experience, availability, testimony experience, and fees.

The LNC consults with the client regarding approval to retain the experts at an agreed-upon fee.

The LNC organizes material to be sent to experts and sends a memo to the client concerning when to expect a response from the reviewer.

Evaluation

Determine effectiveness of plan in achieving desired outcome

The LNC and the client review the response of the experts to determine whether the issues initially identified were correct.

Based on the experts' opinion, the client determines the case has merit.

The LNC and the client revise the plan of action to begin pursuit or defense of the claim.

Example 13.2

An LNC working as an investigator for the state licensing board receives a case involving an allegation of sexual misconduct by a psychologist.

Assessment

Data collection as basis for further activities

The LNC reviews the allegations and pertinent state statutes.

The LNC searches in-house database and reviews files of two similar previous complaints.

Analysis and Issue Identification

Analysis of the data to determine the health care issues related to the claim

The LNC determines the case is a high priority due to seriousness of the charge and previous similar complaints.

The LNC determines that confidentiality is especially critical to all parties due to the nature of the allegations.

Based on the complexity of the case, the LNC determines an expert is needed for consultation and to testify as to the standard of care if necessary.

Outcome Identification

Results hoped for related to analysis and issue identification

The LNC determines that a completed report should be submitted to the Director of Investigations within 30 days.

Planning

Plan of action to achieve the desired outcome

With two other new cases pending, the LNC identifies the need to arrange for reassignment of the cases to other investigators.

The LNC identifies and plans to interview involved parties and witnesses: accused, accuser, and office personnel.

The LNC plans to obtain and review medical records.

The LNC plans to obtain expert opinion.

Implementation

Actions taken to implement the plan

The LNC transfers one pending case to another investigator, and places the other on hold per supervisor direction.

Due to short time frame, the LNC immediately schedules interview appointments with the accused, office personnel, and the individual making the accusation.

The LNC prepares witness and document affidavits.

The LNC interviews all parties and prepares summary reports of each interview.

The LNC reviews and summarizes findings in medical records.

The LNC locates and retains expert psychologist, organizes and submits materials for review, interviews and summarizes expert's opinions.

The LNC writes and submits a summary report to the Director concluding that the evidence supports the allegations, and makes recommendations for further action.

Evaluation

Determine effectiveness of plan in achieving desired outcome

The LNC reviews the case with the Director to determine if recommendations for disposition of the case were followed.

The LNC determines if further information or evidence is needed.

Example 13.3

An independent LNC is hired by a plaintiff attorney to determine the long-term damages for the adolescent victim of a drunk-driving moving vehicle accident. The child suffered a closed head injury.

Assessment

Data collection as basis for further activities

The LNC reviews the medical records before and after the accident.

The LNC researches normal growth and development of adolescent girls.

The LNC reviews school records and testing.

The LNC visits and evaluates the child and family in their home.

Analysis and Issue Identification

Analysis of the data to determine the health care issues related to the claim

The LNC determines that the child has gone from above average to below average in school.

The LNC determines that the child requires long-term cognitive and physical rehabilitation.

Outcome Identification

Results hoped for related to analysis and issue identification

The LNC will develop and document a long-term plan of care, detailing costs of care, with the goal of returning the child to the highest level of function possible.

The plan and costs for care and services will be accepted by defendants in settlement or supported by award from jury at trial.

A video of the child's rehabilitation will favorably impress the defendants at settlement and the jury if the case goes to trial.

Planning

Plan of action to achieve the desired outcome

The LNC recommends to the plaintiff attorney that the rehabilitation video be produced.

The LNC plans to request and review medical records discovered missing during original review.

The LNC plans to interview current caregivers and consult a neuropsychologist .

The LNC plans to interview the child's teachers in the local brain injury program.

Implementation

Actions taken to implement the plan

With attorney approval, the LNC arranges and supervises videotape production of the child's daily rehabilitation program in consultation with various rehabilitation caregivers.

At the request of the LNC, the attorney obtains missing medical records for review.

The LNC solicits recommendations for future care from current caregivers and a neuropsychologist.

Based on multiple sources of information, the LNC writes the plan of care and obtains and calculates costs for all care and services.

Evaluation

Determine effectiveness of plan in achieving desired outcome

The LNC seeks feedback from the attorney regarding the plan and costs of care report.

The LNC successfully defends the plan in deposition.

The case is settled for an amount that supports the plan.

Defense attorneys call the LNC 3 months later requesting review of a life-care plan submitted to them in another case.

Self-Test: Application of the Standards to a Typical Case

Instructions: Match the situation with the appropriate standard:

1. Assessment   4. Planning
2. Analysis and Issue Identification   5. Implementation
3. Outcome Identification   6. Evaluation

Situation:

A. The LNC schedules a trip to the library to obtain information on the applicable standard of care.

B. The LNC determines deposition questions should be revised to explore anesthesia standards.

C. The LNC copies pertinent records for the attorney, highlighting specific events.

D. The LNC determines that deposition questions should expose the anesthesiologist's breach of the standard.

E. The LNC gathers data on the case by reviewing the operative report and anesthesia record.

F. The LNC determines that the key issues in the case are whether or not the standards of care were followed.

Key To Answers: A = 4. Planning; B = 6. Evaluation; C = 5. Implementation; D = 3. Outcome Identification; E = 1. Assessment; F = 2. Analysis and Issue Identification.

Appendix 13.2
Standards of Professional Performance as It Applies to Legal Nurse Consulting

Standard I. Quality Of Practice

The LNC evaluates the quality and effectiveness of his or her practice as an LNC.

Key Indicators

1. The LNC participates in quality of practice activities as appropriate to the individual's role, education, and practice environment. Examples:

   The LNC develops a job description for his or her role in a law firm using the AALNC Standards of Practice for Legal Nurse Consultants.

   The LNC collects data on the volume, type, and results of the activities performed for each of his or her clients.

   The LNC reviews various software programs used to organize medical information for case chronologies.

   The LNC develops policies and procedures for LNCs working in an insurance claim department to provide consistency in the method of data collection and report writing.

2. The LNC uses the results of quality of practice activities to initiate changes in the practice. Examples:

   The LNC recommends revision of the firm's current LNC job description to include activities identified in the AALNC Standards of Practice not previously utilized.

Based on an analysis of client activity, the independent LNC sets meetings with those clients who show a decline in use of his or her services to discuss what services may be improved.

The LNC purchases a new computer software program which will allow more flexibility in preparation of individualized chronologies and reports.

Based on implementation of new policies and procedures, the LNC makes recommendations for changes to facilitate processing of insurance claims.

Self-Test

Give an example of how you have applied Standard I, the Quality of Practice to your own practice. Also list at least one example of how you may have initiated any change in your practice, as a result of your role and education.

Standard II: Performance Appraisal

The LNC evaluates his or her own performance in relation to professional practice standards and relevant statutes and regulations.

Key Indicators

1. The LNC engages in performance appraisal, identifying areas of strength as well as areas for professional development. Examples:

   The LNC who has developed a business with five employees establishes a review board of one attorney and one LNC to meet with her on a quarterly basis to review the business plan, progress of the business, and the goals and direction for the future.

   The LNC employed by a law firm meets on a regular basis with the employer or senior LNC for performance appraisal.

   The independent LNC establishes a mentoring relationship with another LNC who works in a similar setting to assist in quality of performance evaluation without breaching client confidentiality.

   The LNC in any setting reviews and reflects candidly on personal performance and plans to attend continuing education for self improvement.

2. The LNC seeks constructive feedback regarding his or her own practice. Examples:

   The LNC conducts an annual survey of clients to determine how well the work product and selected experts met the goals of the client.

   The LNC serving as an expert witness seeks feedback from the client to determine how style of presentation of information to the jury could be improved.

   The LNC asks a co-worker LNC to review a life-care plan for accuracy and completeness before it is submitted to the client.

The LNC working for an insurance company reviews the potential questions for deposition that have been developed with the supervisor prior to a meeting with the defense attorney.

3. The LNC takes action to achieve goals identified during performance appraisal. Examples:

Based on client survey results, the LNC revises the format used to submit summary reports so that the LNC's conclusions are more easily identified

The LNC discontinues recommending medical experts who were not able to meet client deadlines and searches for new qualified experts to replace them.

The LNC providing expert witness testimony plans for more preparation time with the client prior to trial in the future.

The LNC elaborates on the potential complications and their expenses in the life-care plan to better provide the information the client is seeking.

4. The LNC participates in peer review, as appropriate. Examples:

The LNC volunteers to be a member of the quality assurance team for a national insurance company. Responsibilities include evaluation of reports generated by LNCs and generation of recommendations for improvement.

Self-Test

List one area in which you participate in self-appraisal. How do you obtain feedback regarding your work product?

Standard III: Education

The LNC acquires and maintains current knowledge in nursing and health care issues.

Key Indicators

1. The LNC participates in ongoing educational activities pertaining to the health sciences and the law relevant to his or her practice areas. Examples:

The LNC working primarily with environmental and toxic tort claims attends university courses pertaining to public health.

The LNC working in the area of insurance management attends seminars on workers' compensation law and case management.

The LNC attends professional continuing education programs pertaining to clinical nursing and medical practice most relevant to his or her LNC practice.

The LNC reads professional health care and law journals applicable to his or her LNC practice.

2. The LNC seeks experiences necessary to maintain current licensure as a **professional registered nurse**. Examples:

The LNC seeks information regarding the requirements to maintain licensure in each state in which he or she is licensed and obtains all necessary knowledge and skills.

The LNC keeps accurate records for the maintenance of his or her license and renews it prior to expiration.

3. The LNC seeks the knowledge and the skills that are appropriate to the LNC's practice. Examples:

The LNC attends courses designed specifically for legal nurse consulting practice.

The LNC participates in AALNC chapter educational meetings and seminars.

The LNC attends the annual AALNC educational conference.

The LNC reads the Journal of *Legal Nurse Consulting* and other similar publications.

Self-Test

Give two examples of ways in which you have increased your knowledge base in the course of your work as an LNC.

Standard IV: Collegiality

The LNC contributes to the professional development of peers, colleagues, and others.

Key Indicators

1. The LNC shares knowledge and skills with colleagues and others. Examples:

The LNC obtains medical information regarding a new federal requirement for long-term care facilities and takes a copy of it to the local chapter meeting.

The LNC participates in roundtable discussions with other LNCs on selected topics pertaining to development and organization of work product information.

The LNC participates in the AALNC mentoring program.

The LNC shares information requested by colleagues on the internet.

The LNC agrees seeks an opportunity to present at a local or national AALNC conference.

The LNC submits an article to the *Journal of Legal Nurse Consulting.*

2. The LNC provides peers with constructive feedback regarding their practices. Examples:

The LNC acts as a mentor to a less-experienced LNC by answering questions regarding the clarity and accuracy of work product, the importance of client confidentiality, and the potentials for and definition of conflict of interest.

The LNC reviews the marketing plan of a colleague and suggests ways to increase visibility among clients.

The LNC evaluates billing procedures for a less-experienced colleague and advises changes to improve fee collections.

3. The LNC contributes to an environment that is conducive to the education of nurses entering the field of legal nurse consulting. Examples:

The LNC welcomes interested nurses who attend the local chapter meetings and encourages them to join AALNC.

The LNC participates in a program on "What Is Legal Nurse Consulting?" presented to the local chapter of another nursing specialty group.

The LNC writes an article on legal nurse consulting for another nursing specialty's publication.

The LNC participates in the AALNC mentoring program.

4. The LNC contributes to an environment that is conducive to the health science education of legal team members, as appropriate. Examples:

The LNC determines the legal team members lack information about the appropriate use of CPR in a case in which CPR was used inappropriately. The LNC arranges for an educator to come to the firm to teach the staff about the latest techniques of when, where, why, and how to use CPR.

The LNC presents a program on medical terminology for the legal secretaries and paralegals at his or her firm.

The LNC collects medical literature on shoulder dystocia, with accompanying illustrations, and presents it to the attorney client to assist in the evaluation of a case.

The LNC obtains a Groshong catheter and demonstrates its use to the attorney in a case of professional malpractice in which a home health nurse allegedly misused it, causing a severe infection.

5. The LNC contributes to an environment that is conducive to the education of health care professionals regarding legal issues applicable to the health sciences. Examples:

The LNC participates in an educational program for home health nurses on the most common areas of liability in their clinical practice.

The LNC coordinates seminars for medical groups on risk management activities for their practices to minimize medical malpractice claims.

The LNC assists in the preparation of a nurse who will be giving testimony as a defense witness in deposition.

Self-Test

How have you contributed to the development of your peers and colleagues?

Standard V: Ethics

The LNC's decisions and actions are determined in an ethical manner.

Key Indicators

1. The LNC's practice is guided by the ANA Code for Nurses with Interpretive Statements (1985) and the AALNC Code of Ethics.

2. The LNC's practice affirms the values, standards, and practices of the profession of nursing. Examples:

   The LNC bases opinions and recommendations on the published theory and practices of the health sciences, as well as his or her own knowledge gained through clinical experience.

   The LNC acting as expert nurse witness provides an objective opinion regardless of the whether engaged by defense or plaintiff attorney.

3. The LNC maintains confidentiality commensurate with the attorney/client privilege. Examples:

   The LNC adheres to ethics of confidentiality by refraining from discussing any issues pertaining to the merits of a case with anyone except the client who engaged him or her, the client's employees, or the party whom the client represents.

   The LNC providing expert witness testimony clarifies with the client when the LNC's communications and opinions may become discoverable and prepares written reports only on the request of the client.

4. The LNC practices in a nonjudgmental and nondiscriminatory manner. Examples:

   The LNC avoids using defamatory language in writing or in speaking when talking about any case. Stereotypes are never used, nor slang terms that reflect a casual approach to serious matters.

   The LNC acting as expert nurse witness remains objective in his or her analysis of the health care issues in a claim and does not alter testimony solely to satisfy the needs or goals of the client.

5. The LNC evaluates all cases and clients for conflicts of interest and declines when conflicts are evident. Examples:

   The LNC begins the review of a hospital claim and recognizes that one of the potential defendants is a personal friend. The LNC notifies the client, declines the case, and recommends the services of another LNC with commensurate expertise.

   The LNC in independent practice keeps accurate records of all cases he or she has reviewed or is working on for plaintiff's attorneys. The LNC cross-checks each new file for conflicts of interest before accepting a case from a defense attorney.

The LNC has been asked to review a claim in anticipation of providing expert witness testimony. The nursing care in question was rendered at a facility where the LNC was once employed in a supervisory capacity and served on the Nursing Policy and Procedures Committee. The LNC declines the case on the premise that the attorney for the facility may use information from the LNC's personnel file to discredit his or her testimony, thus putting the client's case in jeopardy.

An attorney who does a high volume of personal injury claims and potentially could be a good source of revenue for the independent LNC asks the LNC to review a backlog of several potential claims and prepare a summary of each claim. However, the attorney will only pay for a maximum of 1 hour on each claim, regardless of the amount of medical information reviewed. The LNC declines to accept the assignment on the basis that an adequate and valid review cannot be made with those restrictions.

6. The LNC seeks available resources to help formulate ethical decisions. In each of the examples given in all of the previous key indicators, the LNC could use the following resources to assist him or her in making an ethical decision:

   The ANA Code for Nurses

   The AALNC Code of Ethics

   The applicable state's Bar Association Rules of Ethics

   The ABA's Code of Ethics

   The AALNC Board of Directors

   The AALNC local chapter's Ethics Committee chairperson

   Experienced colleagues

7. The LNC who testifies as an expert witness confines testimony to his or her area of expertise. Examples:

   An LNC is testifying as an expert witness based on her experience as head nurse in a pulmonary unit of a large teaching hospital. Prior to that experience, she taught aerobics part-time. The opposing counsel asks her questions about exercise, obesity, and nutrition. She declines to speak about those issues from an expert point of view, as her primary purpose in the case is to testify about the nursing responsibilities in observing blood gas levels in a patient with chronic obstructive pulmonary disease.

   An LNC working in a perinatal setting is asked to review the standard of care rendered by the nurses at the delivery of a baby with severe shoulder dystocia. The attorney asks the LNC to give an opinion on the cause of the child's brain injury. The LNC limits his testimony to the nursing care issues and defers causation issues to the perinatologist expert.

Self Test

Give one example of how a conflict of interest might occur in the work of an LNC and explain how it could be avoided. Explain why the source of information is important in coming to an ethical conclusion.

Standard VI: Collaboration

The LNC may collaborate with legal professionals, health care professionals, and others involved in the legal process.

Key Indicators

1.   The LNC consults with legal professionals, health care professionals, and others as appropriate. Examples:

The LNC confers with a toxicologist and a pulmonologist about the medical consequences of inhalation of toxic fumes in a case of inhalation of a combination of burned chemicals.

The LNC seeks information from a client regarding who he or she represents in the claim and what access the LNC will have in gaining information from the party or providing information to the party.

The LNC discusses the issues pertaining to standards of care, injuries, and causal relationships with the expert witness reviewing the claim to assist the client in evaluating the merits of a claim.

The LNC consults with an IV therapy nurse specialist to inquire about standards of care for central lines.

2.   The LNC makes referrals as needed. Example:

An obstetrical case has been assigned to the LNC with primary expertise in mental health. He feels reasonably sure that he can obtain the necessary information for the attorney on the case, but it will involve days of research and hours of billable time. Instead, he refers the case to an LNC whom he knows has the background in obstetrics and the research material at her fingertips. Not only is time and money saved for the client, but the reputation of the LNC will be enhanced as one who is highly ethical.

Self-Test

Describe two ways in which you have collaborated with other professionals while working as an LNC.

Standard VII: Research

The LNC recognizes research as a methodology to further the LNC's practice.

Key Indicators

1.   The LNC takes action substantiated by research as appropriate to his or her role, education, and practice environment. Example:

An LNC has a strong background in oncology and nursing home administration. She is working as an in-house LNC for a large firm that is involved in obtaining patents for new pharmaceuticals. Her work entails development of spreadsheets that detail the results of the clinical trials with physicians. Her expertise enables her to interpret the data and inform the attorneys of the implications of the results.

2. The LNC participates in research activities as appropriate to his or her role, education, and practice environment. Examples:

The LNC develops a database of claims activity for his or her employee in order to identify trends in the successful resolution of claims for the company.

The LNC completes and returns a salary survey questionnaire developed by his or her professional association.

The LNC in risk management conducts a survey study to determine the reasons critical care nurses are sued and, based on results, develops risk mangement activities targeted to reduce the risks in her facility.

Self-Test

How has research affected your role as an LNC? Are there any research activities you have participated in since working as an LNC?

Standard VIII: Resource Management

The LNC considers factors related to ethics, effectiveness, and cost in planning and delivering client service.

Key Indicators

1. The LNC selects expert assistance based on the needs of the case or claim. Example:

The LNC has been asked to assist on a case in which a patient developed paralysis after an anterior thoracic diskectomy. A review of the surgical reports indicates that the team of physicians included an anesthesiologist, an orthopedic surgeon, and a thoracic surgeon. After numerous inquiries, however, the LNC determined that one physician was a vascular surgeon instead of a thoracic surgeon. In searching for expert physicians to assist in the case, the LNC located an expert orthopedic surgeon who then assisted her in locating a vascular surgeon and an anesthesiologist. Background information was then obtained and confirmed on all the experts, including confirmation of education, board certification, and publications.

2. The LNC assigns tasks based on the knowledge and skill of the selected provider. Examples:

An LNC working in-house for a firm that adjusts auto claims supervises the national team of LNCs. A case has arrived on her desk that demands a response in 3 days and requires an LNC with pediatric intensive care experience. The LNC reviews her database of personnel to locate a consultant who has recent pediatric ICU experience and who also works well under the pressures of a deadline.

The LNC is responsible for obtaining an illustration of a surgical procedure to be used as demonstrative evidence. The LNC selects a company with an in-house medical illustrator with proven ability to make visually complex subjects simple and understandable for the jury to produce the product.

The LNC receives a large stack of medical records which need to be organized, paginated, and indexed for use as a trial exhibit. The LNC uses the services of a legal assistant with trial experience to assist in the project.

3. The LNC assists legal professionals and others in identifying and securing appropriate services available to address health care issues pertaining to the case or claim. Examples:

There has been a leakage of nitrous oxide from an overturned railroad car in a large metropolitan area. There are 2000 claimants. The LNC has been requested by the insurance company to assist in locating expert physicians who can assist in defending the multiple claims. Potential side effects of exposure to the chemicals are researched and the LNC determines that medical experts should include toxicologists, pulmonary specialists, gastroenterologists, neurologists, dentists, and ophthalmologists. Experts are contacted and assigned to the appropriate cases.

The LNC is working on a catastrophic brain injury case with the workers' compensation attorney. The LNC reviews the life-care plan and conducts a survey to locate a suitable rehabilitation facility which will meet the injured persons needs.

Self-Test

List ways in which you have managed your resources. How do you keep track of your case information once you have closed a file? Are you able to pull information from previous cases to use on new work?

Section VI
Legal Writing

Chapter 14

Legal Writing

Kevin Dubose

Contents

Objectives

- To describe the philosophical reasons for clearer, crisper writing
- To give four principles of clearer, crisper writing
- To write more clearly and concisely
- To provide clients with a more valuable work product

1-57444-123-X/98
© 1998 by American Association of Legal Nurse Consultants

Why "Legal Writing" Is a Misnomer

Using the label "legal writing" suggests that writing by and for lawyers is different from other writing, and that it comes with its own rules, stylistic conventions, and expectations. Accepting a different mind-set for legal writing probably contributes to the stilted, convoluted, jargon-laden prose that we have come to accept as legalese.

Legal writing does not have to be different from any other good writing. The only thing that distinguishes legal writing from other writing is the subject matter — not the style. Writers who assume a different and unnatural voice in an attempt to "sound like a lawyer" rarely write with clarity and grace. Writers should strive to communicate clearly and concisely, not to sound like a lawyer.

Writers Should Consider Their Audience and Their Purpose

The sole goal of writing is communication. Communication is not a self-indulgent process in which writers merely disgorge information. Rather, communication must involve transmission and reception. Writing without regard for the audience is like shooting an arrow into the air and hoping that someone will run underneath it with a bull's-eye. Good communicators always present information with the audience and the purpose of the communication firmly in mind.

When Writing Consider:

The audience
The purpose

Potential Audiences for Legal Nurse Consultants

Legal Nurse Consultant Writing Audiences

Expertise in law and medicine	Attorneys experienced in health care claims
	Exert witnesses with legal experience
	JD–MDs
	RN–JDs
Expertise in law, not medicine	Judges
	Attorneys without health care claim experience
	Legal assistants without health care claim experience
Expertise in medicine, not law	Doctors, nurses without legal experience
No expertise in law or medicine	Nonmedical clients
	Family members
	Nonmedical fact witnesses

Legal nurse consultants (LNCs) should pay particular attention to the sophistication of their audience in two areas: law and medicine. Some audiences have expertise in both law and medicine. This category includes attorneys who handle health law claims, expert witnesses with experience in the legal system, JD–MDs, JD–RNs, and other LNCs. Other audiences are familiar with the legal system, but ignorant about medical matters. That group includes judges, attorneys, and legal assistants without experience in health law claims. Other audiences are well versed in medical matters, but naive about legal proceedings. That group includes doctors or nurses without experience in the legal system. Finally, some audiences lack knowledge and sophistication in both law and medicine. This category includes nonmedical clients (usually plaintiffs), family members, and other nonmedical fact witnesses.

The writing style appropriate for these audiences varies considerably. The writer must assess the audience, and write on a level that is understandable to the audience, without talking down to it.

Potential Purposes for Writings by Legal Nurse Consultants

Purposes of Legal Writing

Purpose	Examples of LNC Legal Writings
Informative	Chart analysis, literature summary, compilation of injuries caused by a defective product
Commemorative	Client intake interview, conference with expert
Inquisitive	Interrogatories, requests for documents
Persuasive	Settlement brochures

Writers also must consider the purpose of the writing. Writing about legal matters serves one of four purposes:

- *Informative* writing transmits information to the reader. For LNCs, informative writing includes reports, memoranda, chart analyses, literature summaries, and reports evaluating the standards of care.
- *Commemorative* writing records events. Medical chart notations and memoranda to document conversations are commemorative writings, as are summaries of client intake interviews and conferences with potential experts.
- *Inquisitive* writing poses questions. Inquisitive writings include interrogatories and requests for production.
- *Persuasive* writing tries to persuade. In litigation, persuasive writing includes briefs, motions, and correspondence intended to induce settlement.

Writing style and substance vary tremendously depending on the purpose. For example, informative writing should be an objective, fair presentation of both sides; persuasive writing should be slanted in favor of the writer's position. Persuasive writing should be brief; inquisitive writing should be extremely thorough so that unasked questions do not create loopholes through which critical information can be withheld.

No single method of writing is universally preferable. Rather, writers should be mindful of both audience and purpose, and choose a writing style that is appropriate for the circumstances.

For All Audiences and All Purposes, Writers Should Strive for Reader-Friendly Writing

Regardless of the purpose of the writing, the purpose cannot be achieved unless writers communicate to their readers. Communication is a difficult and uncertain art. However, writers greatly enhance the chance of communication when they make the reader's job easier.

Reasons for Reader-Friendly Writing

All readers engage in two activities: deciphering and comprehension. The deciphering function consists of determining what is being said and how it can be structured in a logical, absorbable framework. The comprehensive function consists of digesting what has been deciphered and responding to it. Readers have a fixed amount of time and energy. More time and energy spent on one activity reduces the time and energy for the other activity. Writers should want readers to spend their time and energy on comprehension. Accordingly, the goal of writers should be to minimize the time and energy required for deciphering, so that more time and energy can be devoted to the comprehension function.

Practically speaking, writers want to make a good impression on their readers, whether they are employers, expert witnesses, judges, or opposing counsel. Positive impressions are more likely if the reader does not have to spend time trying to glean the meaning of what has been written. Readers who have to work hard are not favorably disposed to writers who place that burden upon them. Accordingly, the goal of writers should be to make the reader's job easier.

Attributes of Reader-Friendly Writing

Attributes of Reader-Friendly Writing	
Brevity	Use short words, sentences, paragraphs
	Omit unnecessary words
Clarity	Clear communication of the data
Simplicity	Avoidance of complexity
Structure	Prepare detailed outline
	Use headings, subheadings of outline in text

Brevity

Most readers would rather do something other than read legal writing. Judges, lawyers, doctors, and LNCs are all human beings with busy schedules, short attention spans, and limited tolerance for boredom. Readers appreciate writers who reduce the time required for reading.

Necessary information should not be sacrificed for brevity. However, unnecessary and redundant information should be ruthlessly trimmed so that the product is as short as possible.

1. *Use short words, short sentences, and short paragraphs* — Not only should the entire product be brief, so should each of its components:

   Short words. Writing as if you have a thesaurus in one hand and a dictionary in the other is pointless. Readers do not read that way. If writers use words that are unfamiliar to their readers, the readers must either look them up in the dictionary (creating more work for readers, which makes them cranky toward the writer), guess about their meaning (perhaps incorrectly), or just skip them without understanding them. Each of those consequences is unfavorable. Although the medical and legal professions are full of long, unfamiliar words that have no short, familiar substitute, shorter words should be used when possible.

   Short sentences. Although it is possible to write clear sentences that happen to be lengthy, the possibilities for confusion and awkwardness increase when sentences get longer. Additionally, reading a sentence creates dynamic tension between writer and reader; if the tension is sustained for too long, the reader becomes uncomfortable and the ending is often disappointing. Sentences that exceed three or four lines should be carefully examined.

   Short paragraphs. Dynamic tension also applies to reading paragraphs. People like to receive information with an end in sight. When we read a book, we check to see how many pages it has. When we watch a television show, we check to see how long it lasts. When we read a paragraph, our eyes scan the left-hand column for the next indention. Readers are disheartened when they see an entire page without paragraph breaks. Long paragraphs abuse the reader's patience and dissipate dynamic tension. Generally, shorter paragraphs are preferable.

2. *Omit unnecessary words,* including

   Series of synonyms. Avoid expressions like

ordered, adjudged, and decreed	if and when
null and void	save and except
each and every	aid and abet

   Several words when one will do:

Instead of:	*Use:*
in the event that	if
on or about	on
prior to	before
subsequent to	after
for the reason that	because

   Two-word expressions when one word necessarily implies the other. For example:

past history	reason why
mutual agreement	as to whether
sum total	

Meaningless modifiers. Avoid adverbs used for effect, which add nothing to the sentence's meaning. This list includes "actually," "basically," "essentially," and "generally." These words can be used meaningfully, but often are not.

Statements of personal belief. Avoid beginning sentences with phrases like "I believe...," "it is my feeling that...," "it is our position that..." First, it goes without saying that these statements are the writer's belief, feeling, or position. Second, the prefatory phrases weaken the statements that follow, making them sound tentative and uncertain. If writers are sure about their statements, they should be made directly, not qualified or watered down by statements of personal belief. On the other hand, LNCs sometimes are asked to provide personal impressions. In those situations, using a qualification of personal belief is appropriate. Nevertheless, statements of personal belief are overused and always should be scrutinized to determine whether they are necessary and appropriate.

Clarity

Written communication is a miraculous process, even in the best of circumstances. Writers initially formulate ideas, and then articulate them. Words are assembled and arranged on paper. Readers read those words, and formulate ideas. The goal of writers should be for their original idea to be a close as possible to the idea ultimately formed in the mind of the reader. Most words in the English language have more than one meaning; when used in combination the possible meanings increase geometrically. The fact that writers' ideas and readers' perceptions ever coincide is phenomenal.

The likelihood of similarity between beginning and ending ideas is maximized when writers communicate ideas as clearly as possible. Writers should strive to eliminate the potential for multiple meanings, misleading impressions, and confusion. Style and elegance should be sacrificed in favor of clarity.

Most writers are poor judges of the clarity of their own writing. They cannot fairly judge the mental impressions their words generate in others, because they are unavoidably reminded of their original ideas. The best way to evaluate writing clarity is to ask someone else to read it. Putting the work aside for a few days helps somewhat, but there is no substitute for a fresh pair of eyes brought to a writing effort.

Simplicity

Although simplicity is often related to clarity, the two are not synonymous. Complex ideas may be communicated clearly, and simple thoughts may be communicated in a manner that is unclear. However, as a general proposition, simple is more likely to be clear, and vice versa.

Complex and sophisticated concepts have no value if they cannot be communicated clearly to the most simpleminded member of the potential audience. At best, they are a waste of time. At worst, an unfathomable concept may frustrate and alienate the audience, and be counterproductive.

Complex writing makes the reader's job more difficult by making the reader spend more time and energy on deciphering, leaving less time and energy for comprehension. Writing should be so simple that the reader should be able to read it once, put it down, and be able to explain what the writing was about.

There are no stupid readers; there are only foolish writers who are unable or unwilling to communicate appropriately with their audience.

Structure

The human mind is incapable of processing and retaining unstructured information. If writers do not provide a structure that makes the information accessible, the reader must do the work required to structure the information. Readers who do that extra work are resentful of the writer, and the opportunity to make a good impression has been squandered. Readers who are unwilling to do the work necessary to process the information allow it to pass quickly through their mind without being perceived or retained. The worst thing that a writer can do to a reader is to wander off in a rambling stream of consciousness, with no structure, order, or direction.

Effective structure requires two steps. First, writers should prepare a detailed outline before beginning to write. An outline forces writers to organize thoughts, and is probably a more important step in the creative process than translating those thoughts into prose after the outline has been completed. Although modifications may be necessary during the writing process, some form of structure must be maintained rigorously.

The second step to effectively structured writing is communicating the outline to the reader. There is no reason to be subtle or secretive about the outline. It should be communicated to the reader with headings, subheadings, bold-faced type, underscoring, enumeration, or any other type style conventions to enhance the visual accessibility of the outline.

Reader-Friendly Writing Requires Rigorous Editing

Most writers do not write with brevity, clarity, simplicity, and structure in a first draft. These qualities are developed through rigorous editing, by primary writers and by others. Every paragraph, sentence, phrase, and word should be scrutinized to determine whether it is necessary, whether it is clear, and whether it could be stated in another manner that is clearer or more concise. The timing of drafts and deadlines should allow ample time for editing, with as much time devoted to editing as the writer spent on the first draft. Good editing is hard work, which takes a long time. However, it can make the difference between tolerable writing and great writing.

Reader-Friendly Writing Has Been Endorsed by the Bar

Suggestions for more user-friendly legal writing are not the pipe dreams of a few eccentric legal scholars who have fallen under the spell of the plain language movement. Rather, organized bar associations have endorsed these concepts. For example, the Board of Directors of the State Bar of Texas unanimously passed a resolution urging the members of that state to follow a "Charter for Plain Legal Writing," which contained the following suggestions:

1. Write simply. Never use a long word when a short one will do. Never use a Latin or French word when an English one will do. Avoid legal jargon and technical terms unless they are necessary.
2. Omit needless words.
3. Provide clear transitions from one idea to another.
4. Generally, write sentences with an average of fewer than 20 words. Include only one main idea in a sentence.
5. Prefer the active voice; that is, make sure the subject of the sentence performs the action of the verb.
6. Use concrete, specific words instead of abstract, general words.
7. Make sure each paragraph has a clear purpose, progresses logically, and contains one main thought.
8. Use headings, lists, bullets, and ample spacing for appeal and clarity.
9. Make sure your documents are well organized, logical, accurate, and immediately comprehensible to the intended reader.
10. Break a rule rather than say something silly.

Similarly, the Canadian Bar Association and the Canadian Banker's Association have drafted "The Ten Commandments for Plain Language Drafting."

1. Consider your reader and write with that reader's viewpoint in mind.
2. Write short sentences.
3. Say what you have to say, and no more.
4. Use the active voice.
5. Use simple, "everyday" words.
6. Use words consistently.
7. Avoid strings of synonyms.
8. Avoid unnecessary formality.
9. Organize your text:
    a. In a logical sequence;
    b. With informative headings; and
    c. With a table of contents for long documents.
10. Make the document attractive and designed for easy reading.

These rules provide specific suggestions for achieving the qualities of reader-friendly writing articulated in this chapter: simplicity, clarity, brevity, and structure. Writing with those qualities in mind, and writing with an awareness of the audience and purpose, will make writing more reader-friendly, and will increase the likelihood of communication.

Discussion Questions

1. The most important goal of legal writing is
    a. To provide as much information as possible to the reader

b. To entertain the reader with colorful language and imaginative prose

c. To make the product easy for the reader to read and understand

d. To provide tangible evidence of the work you've done

(Answer: c)

2. Which of the following phrases does not contain needless repetition

    a. Each and every

    b. Dilation and curettage

    c. Aid and abet

    d. Past history

    (Answer: b)

3. Which of the following statements accurately describes the relationship between the purpose of a piece of writing and the appropriate writing style?

    a. Informative writing should provide an objective, fair presentation of both sides

    b. Commemorative writing should be as brief as possible

    c. Inquisitive writing should be careful not to offend by asking for too much

    d. Persuasive writing should be lengthy and thorough to cover every possible angle

    (Answer: a)

4. Effective legal writing always requires

    a. A complex structure subtly embedded in the prose

    b. A liberal sprinkling of legal jargon so that if sounds like a lawyer

    c. Long words, long sentences, and long paragraphs

    d. Rigorous editing

    (Answer: d)

Bibliography

Garner, B. A., *A Dictionary of Modern Legal Usage,* 1987. Oxford University Press, Oxford.

Garner, B. A., *The Elements of Legal Style,* 1991. Oxford University Press, Oxford.

Goldstein, T. and Lieberman, J. K., *The Lawyer's Guide to Writing Well,* 1989. McGraw-Hill, New York.

Strunk, W. and White, E. B., *The Elements of Style,* 3rd ed., Macmillan, New York, 1979.

Williams, J. M., *Style: The Lessons in Clarity and Grace,* 3rd ed., 1989. Scott, Foresman and Co.

Wydick, R. C., *Plain English for Lawyer,* 2nd ed., 1985. Carolina Academic Press.

Section VII

The Legal Nurse Consultant's Role in the Litigation Process

Chapter 15

Communication with Plaintiff Clients

Sherri S. Reed

Contents

1-57444-123-X/98

Objectives

- To define communication, interview, and the reciprocal nature of interpersonal communication as it applies to the client-attorney relationship
- To define the purpose of the client interview in a legal setting
- To describe two areas that make the nursing practice a discipline
- To describe three components of interviewing skills nurses acquire through their practice and education
- To identify three skills LNCs possess as an interviewer that give them an advantage over in-house office staff specializing in plaintiff's work

Introduction

This chapter addresses the in-house legal nurse consultant's (LNC's) key role in the initial and ongoing communication with plaintiff(s) in civil tort litigation. Discussion will be directed toward the advantages of utilizing LNCs, as responsible and proficient communicators, with broad health care education and experience, to assist the attorney to litigate the plaintiff's claim effectively and successfully.

The nursing process provides a systematic means for nurses to demonstrate accountability and responsibility to the law firm's clients during the lititgation process. Responsible communication conveys to clients that their feelings are respected, which leads to commitment and compliance on the clients' part (Balzer-Riley, 1996). Commitment and compliance lead to successful implementation of strategies in a legal case.

Communication Defined

As defined by *Webster's Dictionary*, communication is "a sending, giving, or exchanging of information, ideas, etc." (Webster's, 1989, p. 198). The primary purpose of communication is the conveyance of information. Interviewing is "a meeting of persons face to face especially for formal discussion or to meet with someone to examine his qualifications or to get information from him" (Webster's, 1989, p. 506). Communication through interviewing is a fundamental component of the LNC and client relationship. Interviews are always goal directed (Balzer-Riley, 1996, p. 84). They may be formal or informal. In order for the attorney and his or her team to represent the client effectively, they must engage in full, open, and honest communication.

Purposes of Client Communications

- Establish and maintain rapport
- Collect data
- Educate client
- Support client

Barriers to Communication

It is important to recognize the potential barriers to effective communication between a plaintiff and attorney or LNC. Such barriers can be numerous and are unique to each client/case. Barriers may include, but are not limited to, language, age, ethnic background, socioeconomic status, and religion. The client's prior legal experience, as well as the attorney and LNC's previous experience with similar clients/case may also present barriers. The natural tendency to judge, to evaluate, to approve or disapprove the statement of the client based on one's own value system or preconceived notions can be a major barrier to interpersonal communication. Once perceived by the client, this potential barrier may inhibit the client's freedom to provide information, or to make choices appropriate to his or her situation and value system. It may also become a source of dissatisfaction with legal representation if the outcome of the case is not successful. An accepting, nonjudgmental attitude is essential to an effective relationship with the client.

> **Potential Barriers to Communication with Client**
>
> - Language
> - Age
> - Socioeconomic status
> - Ethnic background
> - Religion
> - Client's previous experience with legal system
> - Legal team's previous experience with similar cases/clients

Communication in the Context of a Legal Case

The object of the attorney/client relationship is a mutually satisfactory resolution of the business which the client brings to the attorney. In terms of the process, the object is a comfortable working relationship between the attorney and the client (plaintiff). The process affects content. The legal problem is evaluated in terms of whether or not the client will follow the course of action agreed upon in collaboration with the attorney and other members of the legal team. The client's actions and attitude depend in part on how the client feels about the attorney and support staff. The LNC plays a key role in the communication process as the one person on the legal team with both health care and legal experience. A special bond is often forged between the LNC and client for this reason. The LNC becomes a resource for the client and a liaison with other members of the legal team.

The essence of an interviewing and counseling relationship is movement toward choice. To this end, there must be a proper balance of information and freedom (Shafer, 1976). Freedom means giving the client options from which to choose and allowing the client to make informed decisions. Information helps the client understand the risks and benefits of the options. Ultimately, the attorney needs to ensure that decisions of his client are made only after the client has been informed of relevant considerations. It is often desirable for an attorney to point out those factors which may lead to a decision that is morally just as well as legally permissible. The plaintiff's desires in the matter have to be carefully elicited and his choices made with adequate legal information.

A client's decisions in litigation will proceed from relatively more emotional factors, love, hate, fear, and anger, than will the decisions by the attorney. The client who has been injured or who has lost a loved one often seeks financial retribution but may primarily want a public admission of fault from the defendant. Clients may be unable to see the facts of the case beyond the injuries sustained. It may be inconceivable to them that the defendant may not have been negligent or that the negligence may not have caused the injuries. Or they may be shocked to discover that even if found negligent, the defendant's license to practice may not be at risk. The client's goals must be accurately identified. Education and emotional support can then be appropriately directed at those goals. It is crucial for the LNC to obtain the facts of the client's situation from an objective perspective, in order to help the client, or to help the client help himself.

Purpose of Client Interviews in a Legal Setting

Establishing Rapport through Effective Communication

The rapport established between the plaintiff/client and the attorney or the LNC at the time of the initial interview can have far-reaching consequences in terms of the accuracy and completeness of information obtained. It will also affect the attorney's ability to counsel the client effectively when alternative courses of action arise (Nelken and Schoenfield, 1983).

The initial client interview often creates lasting impressions for both client and attorney and his or her team. The client will often deal with the legal support staff such as the LNC, paralegal, or secretary more often than the attorney throughout a lengthy litigation process. The fact-gathering process can be easily sidetracked or blocked if the client is suspicious of the attorney, resents the attorney as an authority figure, or for any other reason does not have a good rapport with the attorney or members of the team.

Nurses learn communication and interviewing skills as part of their interpersonal and assessment skills requirements. The skill of active listening means that the interviewer becomes engaged in the client's thought processes. It requires considerable energy on the part of the nurse interviewer (Balzer-Riley, 1996). Nurses are trained to attend carefully to the patient's conversation flow and analyze it as the client is speaking. The nurse then directs the client into appropriate problem-solving modes based on the assessment.

Successful interviewing skills include a balance of verbal and nonverbal behavior, empathy, and assertive responses, and client-centered techniques, each chosen specifically to promote trust (Lindberg et al., 1994). In turn, these skills assist in preparing the client for deposition testimony or the negotiation process. A trusting client will be open and receptive to ideas and take the LNC and/or attorney seriously when discussing these areas. Successful interviewing solicits and provides pertinent information, influences the client to effect some change or to respond appropriately to a request for medical care compliance, and encourages attitudes that allow the client to consider settlement alternatives.

Client contacts will take place throughout several years of litigation. The LNC is the appropriate contact person for the client since these contacts often include obtaining updated medical information and answering questions or discussing the medical aspects of the case. Clients will remain more cooperative and receptive to advice or counsel if they feel that they have been listened to attentively. Clients need to believe that the attorney and the support staff are advocates, working on their behalf in order to maintain a trusting and amenable relationship through the conclusion of the case.

The LNC can assist in initiating a working relationship with the plaintiff in an open, reflective, and supportive atmosphere in the law office, on the telephone, or in the client's home. The LNC understands the use of devices, such as: active listening, empathic regard for the client's feelings, and acceptance. Legal professional ideals, the dynamics of interpersonal relationships, and a respect for the individual require that clients remain active in the resolution of their own legal problems.

Data Collection

With every client, the attorney must gather sufficient facts to enable the attorney to conduct the appropriate research and further factual investigation, and also enough information about the client's attitude toward those facts to help the client choose an appropriate course of action. The initial stage of the interviewing/counseling process should conclude with a clear understanding between attorney and client of the future course of action: what steps will be taken, when, and by whom. The attorney should be comfortable with the facts presented as accurate and complete, including preexisting medical conditions, in order to determine what, if any, role these conditions may play in the liability or causation issues.

LNCs are skilled in the nursing process which provides a systematic means to collect and assess health care data accurately and thoroughly. LNCs are able to use their knowledge and expertise in assessment to take a detailed, accurate clinical health history from the client. They identify damages resulting from the alleged negligence of the defendant. They identify information concerning influences of past medical history and care (preexisting conditions). LNCs identify factors which will influence compliance with future medical therapy. They identify the need for future medical care or evaluations related causally to the incident, such as coagulation studies for monitoring anticoagulation or periodic abdominal series for gastrointestinal conditions (Appendix 15.1). This information can then be added to the damage profile.

The assessment process also enables the nurse to determine a person's strengths that promote health behaviors and wellness. It focuses on the whole person rather than just the signs and symptoms of disease so the LNC elicits information regarding social and cultural background, support systems, value systems, or health perceptions. These additional elements contribute significantly to the pursuit of a successful lawsuit.

Assessment of the client's reaction to loss can help the LNC evaluate the plaintiff's psychological status. The LNC is aware that a loss can include loss of body parts, functions, independence, or any type of physical, emotional, or intellectual loss whether real or perceived. Identification of the client's coping skills contributes to an understanding of how the client will deal with the stress of a lengthy lawsuit. The client may need to be referred to a psychologist or others for help in dealing with unresolved issues related to loss. These needs are a significant part of the damages in a plaintiff's claim. They also may affect the client's ability to withstand the rigors of a stressful legal process.

In ongoing contacts with the plaintiff, the LNC must obtain updated medical information and records in order to supplement information to defense counsel and update the profile of damages. These contacts also serve to determine the plaintiff's compliance with subsequent medical treatment recommendations and provide ongoing support to the client. The LNC, as an educator, understands that assessment through interviewing and questioning is a continuous, ongoing process lasting as long the claim lasts and that this process should clearly identify strengths and weaknesses in the plaintiff's case. The LNC working for the plaintiff in civil tort litigation is uniquely qualified to interview clients initially and to perform the subsequent client interviews.

The Initial Interviews

The initial (potential) client interview may take place over the telephone, in the attorney's office, at the client's home, or in a health care facility. The LNC should begin the interview with the client with introductions and an explanation of his or her role as a nurse on the litigation team. The client is asked to explain *briefly* what happened or why the client is calling the law firm. It may be clear early on that the client does not have a case. He/she may be angry because the call light continually went unanswered but without resultant injury. The LNC may provide a brief explanation to the caller and terminate the interview. If the incident merits further inquiry, the LNC obtains the client's full name, addresses, and phone numbers, and those of the client's close relatives. The LNC should ask the client what his or her goals and objectives are for contacting the attorney office. What is it that the client wishes to accomplish by filing a lawsuit? The LNC may discover that the client does not necessarily want to file a lawsuit but only to know what happened that caused an injury. The client may want financial compensation or to "prevent this from happening to someone else."

Early in the interview, the LNC must identify any conflicts of interest that would prohibit involvement in the case. Names of all potential health care defendants should be solicited. The LNC should also inquire about any previous involvement with the legal system and names of attorneys' or defendants. If a conflict is evident, the interview can be terminated until the conflict can be resolved in discussion with the attorney.

If no conflict is evident, the interview should proceed to solicit more-detailed information again by asking the open-ended question of "What happened to you?" Most clients are eager to tell their story to a nurse who understands the medical issues of their claim. The LNC must efficiently direct the interview to sort the irrelevant from the pertinent information by guiding the story with specific questions or requests for additional details. However, the LNC must listen carefully to the client and not allow previous experience with similar cases to color the client's story. Allow the client to tell the story in his or her own words. The LNC's notes should include dates, times, and location of events described, and the names of all potential defendants or fact witnesses. Were any police or other reports were filed? Did the client or any family members keep logs or diaries of the events in question? Does the client have any pertinent documents such as discharge instructions or other written instructions from medical personnel? Did the client comply with instructions? The LNC should determine and record the statute of limitation date for the alleged negligence.

After the client has told the story, the LNC and the client should discuss the impact of the injury on health, lifestyle, or job, i.e., identify the damages. The complete health history covering all body systems is elicited and reviewed to determine preexisting conditions. Specific questions about current medical problems caused by the injury and the effect of the injury on the preexisting medical problems are included. The LNC also gathers available data relative to medical expenses and wage loss. It is important to obtain names, addresses, phone numbers of all past and current treating physicians or other health care providers and caregivers who may provide information about future medical problems and care related to the injury.

The interview should conclude with a brief explanation of the next step of the litigation process and a reminder to the client to notify the LNC or attorney of any change in his or her medical condition. The client should also be cautioned not to discuss the lawsuit with anyone outside his or her family. Key office staff may be introduced to the client and contact phone numbers provided.

Key Elements of Initial Interviews with Client

- Listen carefully to the client
- Allow client to tell the story in his or her own words
- Be empathetic
- Determine statute of limitations
- Obtain names, addresses, phone numbers of client and close relatives
- Determine conflicts of interest
- Identify client goals/objectives
- Obtain accurate and complete medical information using assessment tool
- Obtain names, addresses, phone numbers of current and past treating health care providers
- Describe current compared with previous lifestyle
- Solicit brief occupational history and effects of injury
- Estimate medical expenses
- Estimate lost wages
- Introduce key office staff
- Provide client with office phone numbers

Education of Client

Legal Issues

Often, the client's perception of the nature of a legal problem will differ from that of the attorney, particularly in a medical malpractice action. For example, the client must understand that the defendant health care provider's license may not be suspended or revoked in the event of a successful outcome. Monetary compensation may be the only effect suffered by the defendant health care provider. The attorney and LNC may use the initial and ongoing interviews with the client to educate him or her about the legal process. The LNC may prepare educational materials such as a booklet containing this information that can be provided to all clients. Clients should be instructed that their role in the litigation process is an active one and they must respond to requests for subsequent information promptly and fully.

Educate Client Regarding Legal Issues

- Elements of proof required for successful case outcome
  - Liability
  - Proximate cause
  - Damages
- Process of litigation
  - Interaction with defendant and insurance carrier
  - Medical releases
  - Expert case review
  - Petition/complaint
  - Discovery
        Interrogatories
        Requests for production
        Depositions
  - Arbitration, mediation, settlement
  - Trial
- Potential length of process
- Importance of compliance with current medical treatment
- Future course of action related to litigation
- Potential outcomes
  - Monetary damages
  - No loss of license or public admission of wrongdoing

Medical Issues

Clients often view the LNC as a resource person who can answer questions about their injury, ongoing medical problems, and care. They want to know what happened to them to cause their injury and why. The LNC plays a vital role in educating the client about the reasons for continuing therapies and the importance of compliance with the medical plan of care.

Conclusion

LNCs, as client educators and skillful communicators, are critical to the litigation process. Their health assessment skills help them to obtain data that describes a person's responses to potential or actual health problems. This assessment enables the LNC to determine a person's strengths that promote health behaviors and wellness. Since the LNC's assessment focuses on the whole person rather than just the signs and symptoms of disease or injury, the LNC elicits information about social and cultural background, support systems, values, and health care perceptions. In turn, this information enables the attorney to build a solid and complete case or, in the alternative, to decide that it is not a case which should be filed.

The LNC working for the attorney who represents a plaintiff in civil tort litigation is uniquely qualified by virtue of specialized communication and interviewing skills, systematic data collection and organizational skills, and the nursing process to assist the attorney in the initial interviews and subsequent client communications.

Effective communication is important during advocacy for clients and one of the LNC's most effective tools for assisting persons to adapt to life changes and the ongoing stress of litigation. Beyond the nurse/client relationship, learned and familiar communication skills can be used with other health care providers (subsequent treating physicians and medical experts) and the public (attorneys/employers) to litigate a client's claim successfully (Lindberg et al., 1994).

Glossary*

Assessment: The first step of the nursing process, during which data are gathered and examined in preparation for the second step, diagnosis.

Damages: A pecuniary compensation or indemnity, which may be recovered in the courts by any person who has suffered loss, detriment, or injury, whether to his person, property, or rights, through the unlawful act or omission or negligence of another. A sum of money awarded to a person injured by the tort of another.

Diagnosis: The second step of the nursing process, during which data are analyzed and pulled together for the purpose of identifying and describing health status (strengths, and actual and potential health problems).

Evaluation: The fifth step of the nursing process, during which the extent of goal achievement is determined; each of the previous four steps is analyzed to identify factors that enhanced or hindered progress, and the plan of care is modified or terminated as indicated.

Implementation: The fourth step of the nursing process, which involves putting the plan of care into action.

Litigation: A lawsuit. Legal action, including all proceedings therein. Contest in a court of law for the purpose of enforcing a right or seeking a remedy. A judicial contest, a judicial controversy, a suit at law.

Malpractice: Professional misconduct or unreasonable lack of skill. This term is usually applied to such conduct by doctors, lawyers, and accountants. Failure of one rendering professional services to exercise that degree of skill and learning commonly applied under all the circumstances in the community by the average prudent reputable member of the profession with the result of injury, loss, or damage to the recipient of those services or to those entitled

---

* Definitions from Black, 1979, and Alfaro, 1992.

to rely upon them. It is any professional misconduct, unreasonable lack of skill or fidelity in professional or fiduciary duties, evil practice, or illegal or immoral conduct.

Nursing process: An organized, systematic method of giving individualized nursing care that focuses on identifying and treating unique responses of individuals or groups to actual or potential alterations in health.

Plaintiff: A person who brings an action; the person who complains or sues in a civil action and is so named on the record. A person who seeks remedial relief for an injury to rights; it designates a complainant.

References

Alfaro, R. (1992). *Applying Nursing Diagnosis and Nursing Process: A Step-by-Step Guide,* Philadelphia, J. B. Lippincott.

Anderson, C. (1990). *Patient Teaching Communication on Information Age,* Philadelphia, J. B. Lippincott.

Balzer-Riley, J. W. (1996). *Communications in Nursing,* Philadelphia, J. B. Lippincott.

Black's Law Dictionary (1979). St. Paul, MN, West Publishing.

Lindberg, J. B., Hunter, M. L., and Krusqewski, A. Z. (1994). Introduction to Nursing Concepts, Issues, and Opportunities, Philadelphia, J. B. Lippincott.

Nelken, M. L. and Schoenfield, M. K. (1983). Problems and cases in interviewing, counseling and negotiation, St. Paul, MN, National Institute for Trial Advocacy.

The New Lexicon Webster's Dictionary of the English Language (1989). New York, Lexicon Publications.

Reilly, D. E. and Oermann, M. D. (1992). *Clinical Teaching in Nursing Education,* New York, National League for Nursing.

Shafer, T. L. (1976). *Legal Interviewing and Counseling,* St. Paul, MN, West Publishing.

Sundeen, S. J., Stuart, G. W., DeSalvo Rankin, E. A., and Cohen, S. A. (1994). *Nurse–Client Interaction Implementing the Nursing Process,* St. Louis, Mosby.

Suggested Readings

American Nurses Association (1990). *Survival Skills in the Workplace: What Every Nurse Should Know,* Kansas City, MO, Author.

Lisnek, P. M. (1992). *Effective Client Communication. A Lawyer's Handbook for Interviewing and Counseling,* St. Paul, MN, West Publishing.

Appendix 15.1
Sample Questionnaires

PERSONAL INJURY INQUIRY CALLS

_____

Name of Caller:_____

Address:_____
      Street

      _____
      City, State, Zip Code

Telephone:_____(home)
               _____(work)

Was call for a specific attorney? If so, name of attorney.
_____

Was caller referred by another person? If so, name and address of person.
_____
_____

Is caller currently represented by an attorney? If so, name and address of attorney
_____
_____

Date of incident giving rise to injury.
_____

Place of incident.
_____

Brief summary description of incident.
_____
_____
_____
_____
_____
_____

Brief description of injury.
_____
_____
_____
_____
_____

Approximate amount of medical, hospital and related expenses incurred.

Medical and hospital bills_____

Insurance Carrier_____

Wage loss_____

Date:_____   _____
                                            Person receiving call

Malpractice Questionnaire
Page 1

Name: M___. _____   ___. _____

Address:_____

City/St:_____

Home Ph: (__) ___ - ____ Wk (__) ___ - ____ Alt (__) ___-____:_____

*** Date of Injury/Occurrence ____/____/_____ Statute Problem ___(Y/N) ***
*** Suspected Statute of Limitation ____/____/_____ REJECT __ ACCEPT__ ***

LED's OFFICE ONLY

Date started ___/___/___ First knowledge ___/___/___ Surgery ___/___/__

Problem_____
_____
_____
_____
_____

Family Medical History_____
_____
_____
_____
_____

Personal Medical History_____
_____
_____
_____
_____

Personal Surgical History_____
_____
_____
_____

Malpractice Questionnaire
Page 2

Medications (Past and Present)

From	To	Dosage	Medication Name:

___/___/___ : ___/___/___ : _____ _____
___/___/___ : ___/___/___ : _____ _____
___/___/___ : ___/___/___ : _____ _____
___/___/___ : ___/___/___ : _____ _____
___/___/___ : ___/___/___ : _____ _____
___/___/___ : ___/___/___ : _____ _____
___/___/___ : ___/___/___ : _____ _____
___/___/___ : ___/___/___ : _____ _____
___/___/___ : ___/___/___ : _____ _____
___/___/___ : ___/___/___ : _____ _____
___/___/___ : ___/___/___ : _____ _____
___/___/___ : ___/___/___ : _____ _____

List all doctors seen concerning condition   Hospital (if any)

___ _____ _____ ph (~~~) ~~~~~ : _____
___ _____ _____ ph (~~~) ~~~~~ : _____
___ _____ _____ ph (~~~) ~~~~~ : _____
___ _____ _____ ph (~~~) ~~~~~ : _____
___ _____ _____ ph (~~~) ~~~~~ : _____
___ _____ _____ ph (~~~) ~~~~~ : _____
___ _____ _____ ph (~~~) ~~~~~ : _____
___ _____ _____ ph (~~~) ~~~~~ : _____
___ _____ _____ ph (~~~) ~~~~~ : _____
___ _____ _____ ph (~~~) ~~~~~ : _____
___ _____ _____ ph (~~~) ~~~~~ : _____
___ _____ _____ ph (~~~) ~~~~~ : _____
___ _____ _____ ph (~~~) ~~~~~ : _____
___ _____ _____ ph (~~~) ~~~~~ : _____
___ _____ _____ ph (~~~) ~~~~~ : _____

Name, ph #, of other med care   Type (RN, Phy. Ther.)

___ _____ _____ ph (~~~) ~~~~~ : _____
___ _____ _____ ph (~~~) ~~~~~ : _____
___ _____ _____ ph (~~~) ~~~~~ : _____
___ _____ _____ ph (~~~) ~~~~~ : _____
___ _____ _____ ph (~~~) ~~~~~ : _____
___ _____ _____ ph (~~~) ~~~~~ : _____
___ _____ _____ ph (~~~) ~~~~~ : _____
___ _____ _____ ph (~~~) ~~~~~ : _____

Malpractice Questionnaire
Page 3

Chronological list of events leading to present condition:

Page 1

___/___/___ : _____
___/___/___ : _____
___/___/___ : _____
___/___/___ : _____
___/___/___ : _____
___/___/___ : _____
___/___/___ : _____
___/___/___ : _____
___/___/___ : _____
___/___/___ : _____
___/___/___ : _____
___/___/___ : _____
___/___/___ : _____
___/___/___ : _____
___/___/___ : _____
___/___/___ : _____
___/___/___ : _____
___/___/___ : _____
___/___/___ : _____
___/___/___ : _____
___/___/___ : _____
___/___/___ : _____
___/___/___ : _____
___/___/___ : _____
___/___/___ : _____
___/___/___ : _____
___/___/___ : _____
___/___/___ : _____
___/___/___ : _____
___/___/___ : _____
___/___/___ : _____
___/___/___ : _____
___/___/___ : _____
___/___/___ : _____
___/___/___ : _____
___/___/___ : _____
___/___/___ : _____

Malpractice Questionnaire
Page 4

Chronological list of events leading to present condition:

Page 2

___/___/___ : _____
___/___/___ : _____
___/___/___ : _____
___/___/___ : _____
___/___/___ : _____
___/___/___ : _____
___/___/___ : _____
___/___/___ : _____
___/___/___ : _____
___/___/___ : _____
___/___/___ : _____
___/___/___ : _____
___/___/___ : _____
___/___/___ : _____
___/___/___ : _____
___/___/___ : _____
___/___/___ : _____
___/___/___ : _____
___/___/___ : _____
___/___/___ : _____
___/___/___ : _____
___/___/___ : _____
___/___/___ : _____
___/___/___ : _____
___/___/___ : _____
___/___/___ : _____
___/___/___ : _____
___/___/___ : _____
___/___/___ : _____
___/___/___ : _____
___/___/___ : _____
___/___/___ : _____
___/___/___ : _____
___/___/___ : _____
___/___/___ : _____
___/___/___ : _____
___/___/___ : _____
___/___/___ : _____
___/___/___ : _____
___/___/___ : _____
___/___/___ : _____

Malpractice Questionnaire
Page 5

Sign any releases __ Explain_____

_____

_____

_____

Reason for procedure_____

_____

_____

_____

Complications/risks prewarned of_____

_____

_____

_____

Complications/risks existing that you were not warned of_____

_____

_____

_____

Suspected negligence_____

_____

_____

_____

Types experts needed_____

_____

_____

_____

Items brought_____

_____

_____

_____

_____

List all places medical records need to be obtained

1 _____   6 _____
2_____   7 _____
3_____   8 _____
4_____   9 _____
5_____   10 _____

Malpractice Questionnaire
Page 6

Possible Defendants

Def 1 _____ Ph (__) __-___

Addr_____City_____

Action: _____

Def 2_____ Ph (__) __-___

Addr_____City_____

Action: _____

Def 3_____ Ph (__) __-___

Addr_____City_____

Action: _____

Def 4_____ Ph (__) __-___

Addr_____City_____

Action: _____

Def 5_____ Ph (__) __-___

Addr_____City_____

Action: _____

MALPRACTICE INFORMATION SHEET

INJURED OR DECEASED PERSON

Name _____ Date of Birth _____
        Last   First   Middle   Maiden   Month / Day / Year

Address _____
        Street   Apt. No.   City   State   Zip

Home Telephone _____ Social Security No. _____
                Please Include Area Code

Work Telephone _____ Occupation _____
                Please Include Area Code

Employer _____ How Long at this job _____

Is this injury related to a Workman's Compensation Claim _____
                                                    Yes   No

Estimated time lost from job as a result of this injury _____

Estimated total loss of earnings as a result of this injury __$_____

PERSON COMPLETING FORM
(If Different)

Name _____ Date of Birth _____
        Last   First   Middle   Month / Day / Year

Address _____
        Street   Apt. No.   City   State   Zip

Home Telephone _____ Social Security No. _____
                Please Include Area Code

Work Telephone _____ Relationship _____
                Please Include Area Code

If Injured Person Is Deceased _____
                              Date of Death   Place of Death - City, County, State

Cause of Death _____

Was Autopsy Performed _____ Where _____
                    Yes   No

Person with Power of Attorney/Executor/Executrix _____
                                    Attach Copy of Document Denoting Legal Representative

---

Referring Attorney _____
                    Name   Address

Date of Alleged Injury/Malpractice _____

Date you Suspected Malpractice _____

Alleged Defendant Physician(s) _____

Hospital Where Malpractice Occurred _____
                                    Name of Hospital   City   State

MEDICAL HISTORY OF INJURED/DECEASED PERSON

	Yes / No	Detail Positive Remarks Include Date and Treatment		Yes / No	Detail Positive Remarks Include Date and Treatment
Diabetes			History of Transfusion		
Hypertension			HIV (AIDS)		
Heart Disease			Street Drugs		
Rheumatic Fever			Tuberculosis		
Kidney Disease/UTI			Asthma		
Nervous and Mental			Anes. Complications		
Epilepsy			Drug Allergies		
Seizures			Cancer		
Hepatitis/Liver Disease			Major Accident		
Varicosities/Phlebitis			Other		
Thyroid Dysfunction			Other		

Use of Tobacco	_____ # Cigs/Day _____ Age Began Smoking _____ Age Stopped Smoking	Use of Alcohol	_____ # Drinks/Wk _____ Age Began Drinking Alcohol _____ Do Not Drink Alcohol

Height _____   Weight _____ lbs.   Weight change in the last year _____ lbs.

Name of Family Physician _____

Address of Family Physician _____

Please list all hospitalizations **before** the injury occurred, including all surgical procedures

Date	Hospital	Reason for Admission
_____	_____	_____
_____	_____	_____
_____	_____	_____
_____	_____	_____
_____	_____	_____

FAMILY HISTORY OF INJURED/DECEASED PERSON
Includes Injured/Deceased's Mother, Father, Siblings (Brothers or Sisters)

	Yes	No		Yes	No
Cancer			Diabetes		
Hypertension			Heart Disease		
Seizures/Epilepsy/Neurological Problem			HIV (AIDS)		
Genetic or Chromosomal Disease			Other		
Other			Other		

Comments _____

PLEASE ANSWER THE FOLLOWING QUESTIONS WITH RESPECT TO THE INCIDENT INVOLVING THE ALLEGED MALPRACTICE AND THE INJURED PERSON'S SUBSEQUENT CARE

List **ALL** medications you (the injured person) are taking routinely, including all pain medications

Medication	Date Prescribed	Doctor	Condition	Pharmacy (Drug Store)

List **ALL** physicians and therapists who are treating or have treated you (the injured person) <u>since</u> the date of injury

Name & Location of Health Care Provider	Date(s) Treated	Condition

List **ALL** hospitals that you (the injured person) have been treated at <u>since</u> the time of the injury

Name & Location of Hospital	Physician	Date	Condition

What is your (the injured person's) current condition _____

_____

What physical and/or mental problems do you (the injured person) believe were directly caused by the injury

_____

_____

Are you (the injured person) currently using any braces, canes, crutches, or other devices _____   _____
                                                                      Yes   No

    If yes, please describe _____

Are you (the injured person) currently able to work _____   _____ Date returned to work _____
                                              Yes   No

If you (the injured person) are working, are there any limitations _____   _____ Describe _____
                                                                 Yes   No

_____

Give an <u>estimate</u> of the medical expenses you have incurred since the date of injury __$_____
              (Please include all expenses paid by insurance, Medicare and/or Medicaid)

_____

Have you been involved in any previous lawsuits or claims _____   _____
                                              Yes   No

If yes, please explain _____

_____

_____

THIS PORTION OF THE FORM MUST BE COMPLETED TO FAIRLY EVALUATE YOUR CLAIM

IN YOUR OWN WORDS, PLEASE GIVE A DESCRIPTION OF THE EVENTS THAT TOOK PLACE BEFORE, DURING, AND AFTER THE ALLEGED INJURY/MALPRACTICE, DETAILING THE INCIDENTS OR EVENTS, THE PERSONS INVOLVED, AND WHAT YOU OR YOUR FAMILY WERE TOLD REGARDING THE ALLEGED INJURY/MALPRACTICE. CONTINUE ON THE BACK OF THIS PAGE OR ATTACH A SEPARATE SHEET.

OBSTETRICAL INFORMATION SHEET

<u>MOTHER</u>   Name _____   Date of Birth _____
                        Last   First   Middle   Malden   Month / Day / Year

               Address _____
                        Street   Apt. No.   City   State   Zip

               Home Telephone _____   Social Security No. _____
                               Please Include Area Code

               Work Telephone _____   Occupation _____
                               Please Include Area Code

<u>FATHER</u>   Name _____   Date of Birth _____
                        Last   First   Middle   Month / Day / Year

               Address _____
                        Street   Apt. No.   City   State   Zip

               Home Telephone _____   Social Security No. _____
                               Please Include Area Code

               Work Telephone _____   Occupation _____
                               Please Include Area Code

<u>CHILD</u>   Name _____   Date of Birth _____
                        Last   First   Middle   Month / Day / Year

               Address _____
                        Street   Apt. No.   City   State   Zip

               Home Telephone _____   Social Security No. _____
                               Please Include Area Code

If Injured Person Is Deceased _____
                               Date of Death   Place of Death - City, County, State

               Cause of Death _____

               Was Autopsy Performed _____ _____   Where _____
                                      Yes   No

               Name of Person with Power of Attorney _____
                                                     Attach Copy of Document Denoting Legal Representative

Referring Attorney _____
                    Name   Address

Date of Alleged Injury/Malpractice _____

Date You Suspected Malpractice _____

Alleged Defendant Physician(s) _____

Hospital Where Malpractice Occurred _____
                                     Name of Hospital   City   State

Obstetrical Information Sheet (page 2)

MOTHERS MEDICAL HISTORY

Total Times Pregnant	Full Term Deliveries	Premature Deliveries	Abortions Induced	Abortions Spontaneous	Ectopic Pregnancies	Multiple Births	No. of Living Children

PAST PREGNANCIES

Date of Delivery	Weeks of Gestation	Length of Labor	Birth Weight	Type of Delivery	Anesthesia Used	Place of Delivery	Child Living Yes / No	Treatment for Preterm Labor Yes / No

PAST MEDICAL HISTORY

	Yes / No	Detail Positive Remarks Include Date and Treatment		Yes / No	Detail Positive Remarks Include Date and Treatment
Diabetes			RH Sensitized		
Hypertension			Tuberculosis		
Heart Disease			Asthma		
Rheumatic Fever			Drug Allergies		
Mitral Valve Prolapse			GYN Surgery		
Kidney Disease/UTI			Operations		
Nervous and Mental			Hospitalizations		
Epilepsy			Anes. Complications		
Hepatitis/Liver Disease			Abnormal Pap		
Varicosities/Phlebitis			Uterine Abnormality		
Thyroid Dysfunction			Infertility		
Major Accidents			DES Exposure		
History of Transfusion			Street Drugs		
HIV (AIDS)			Hepatitis B		
Genital Herpes			Rash/Virus Since LMP		
Chlamydia/Syphilis			Other		

Use of Tobacco _____ # Cigs/Day Prior to Preg.
_____ # Cigs/Day During Preg.
_____ Age Began Smoking

Use of Alcohol _____ # Drinks/Wk Prior to Preg.
_____ # Drinks/Wk During Preg.
_____ Age Began Drinking Alcohol

Obstetrical Information Sheet (page 3)

SCREENING STUDIES

Includes Baby's Mother, Baby's Father, Siblings (Brothers or Sisters), or Anyone in Either Family

	Yes	No		Yes	No
Mothers Age Greater Than 35?			Neural Tube Defect		
Downs Syndrome (Mongolism)			Tay Sach's Disease		
Sickle Cell Disease or Trait			Hemophilia		
Muscular Dystrophy			Cystic Fibrosis		
Huntington Chorea			Mental Retardation		
Other Genetic or Chromosomal Disease			More than 3 Spontaneous Abortions		
History of Stillbirth			HIV (AIDS)		
Learning Disability			Hydrocephalus (Water on the Brain)		
Seizures/Epilepsy/Neurological Problem			Cerebral Palsy		
Heart Defects			Other Birth Defects		
Comments					

PLEASE ANSWER THE FOLLOWING QUESTIONS WITH RESPECT TO THE PREGNANCY INVOLVING THE ALLEGED MALPRACTICE

	Yes/No	Detail Positive Remarks Include Date and Treatment		Yes/No	Detail Positive Remarks Include Date and Treatment
Vaginal Bleeding			Vaginal Discharge		
Nausea/Vomiting			Constipation		
Headaches			Abdominal Pain		
Urinary Complaints			Fever		
Exposure to Chemicals			Anemia		
Prenatal Vitamins			Diabetes		
Hypertension			Epilepsy/Seizures		
Swelling of Hands/Feet			Supplemental Iron		
Colds/Flu			Any Type of Infection		
Exposure to X-rays			Blurred Vision		

Was a Home Pregnancy Test Done _____ _____ Date _____ Result _____
　　　　　　　　　　　　　　　　　Yes　　　　No

Were Birth Control Pills Being Used at the Time of Conception _____ _____ Brand _____
　　　　　　　　　　　　　　　　　　　　　　　　　　　　Yes　　　　No

Before Pregnancy Weight _____ lbs. Height _____ Weight at the Time of Delivery _____

Last Menstrual Period _____ Definite _____ Approximate _____ Unknown _____

Obstetrical Information Sheet (page 4)

Date of First Prenatal Examination _____   Pregnancy Confirmed by Physician ____Yes____   ____No____

Name of Doctor _____   Address _____

Did you continue to see this doctor for the entire pregnancy until delivery ____Yes____   ____No____

If other doctors were seen, please list them _____

What was the original estimated date of confinement (due date) established by the physician _____

If the due date changed during the pregnancy, please list here _____

Did you work at any time during this pregnancy ____Yes____   ____No____   Type of work _____

Date you stopped working _____   Were you exposed to chemicals/ toxic substances ____Yes____   ____No____

When did you first feel the baby move _____   Was the baby active during pregnancy ____Yes____   ____No____

How often did you see the physician for prenatal visits _____

List **ANY** medications, including prescription, non prescription, or street drugs taken during this pregnancy

Medication	Date Prescribed	Doctor	Condition
_____	_____	_____	_____
_____	_____	_____	_____
_____	_____	_____	_____
_____	_____	_____	_____

Was an ultrasound done during the pregnancy ____Yes____   ____No____   Date _____

Who performed the ultrasound _____   Result _____

If subsequent ultrasound done, list date performed and who performed _____

Was an amniocentesis done during the pregnancy ____Yes____   ____No____   Date _____

Who performed the amniocentesis _____   Result _____

Was a glucose tolerance test (GTT) done during the pregnancy ____Yes____   ____No____   Date _____

Who performed the GTT _____   Result _____

Describe any problems the physician anticipated during the pregnancy or with the birth of the baby

_____

_____

Were you ever admitted to the hospital or seen in the emergency room during this pregnancy ____Yes____ ____No____

Hospital	Date	Doctor	Condition
_____	_____	_____	_____
_____	_____	_____	_____
_____	_____	_____	_____

Did you attend childbirth classes ____Yes____   ____No____   Where _____

Obstetrical Information Sheet (page 5)

Date labor began _____ Time _____ a.m./p.m.

What were the first symptoms of your labor _____

_____

When did the membranes (bag of water) rupture (break) _____

Did your membranes rupture spontaneously ____Yes____ ____No____ Was the fluid clear in color ____Yes____ ____No____

Did the physician rupture the membranes ____Yes____ ____No____ Was the fluid clear in color ____Yes____ ____No____

If the fluid was not clear in color, please describe _____

Was there any bleeding at the time the labor ____Yes____ ____No____ If yes, when did it start _____

How long did the bleeding last _____ Was it spotty, mild, moderate, or severe _____

What time was the physician notified you were in labor _____ Physician's name _____

What were his instructions _____

Were his instructions followed ____Yes____ ____No____ If not, why _____

What time did the mother go to the hospital _____ Hospital name _____

Was an electronic fetal monitor used at the hospital ____Yes____ ____No____

How long was the labor _____ Did the mother receive any medication for pain ____Yes____ ____No____

Did the mother receive any medication to increase contractions (labor pains) ____Yes____ ____No____

Did the mother receive epidural anesthesia ____Yes____ ____No____ What time _____

BIRTH OF THE INJURED INFANT

What time was the baby born _____ a.m./p.m. What physician delivered the infant _____

Was the baby born by vaginal delivery or cesarean section _____

If a cesarean section was performed, what were you told as the reason _____

Was the father in the delivery room ____Yes____ ____No____ What was the baby's weight _____ lbs. _____ oz.

Does the mother or father remember hearing the baby cry in the delivery room ____Yes____ ____No____

Did the mother or father see the baby in the delivery room ____Yes____ ____No____

What was the baby's color _____ Was the baby moving ____Yes____ ____No____

Name of the baby's pediatrician _____ Was the pediatrician at the delivery ____Yes____ ____No____

When did you first learn there was a problem with the baby _____

Who told you there was a problem _____

What were you told _____

Obstetrical Information Sheet (page 6)

Was the baby treated in the Intensive Care Nursery _____ _____ How long _____
_{Yes} _{No}

Was the baby on a ventilator (machine to assist the baby's breathing) _____ _____
Yes No

Did the baby have problems sucking _____ _____   Did the baby have seizures _____ _____
Yes No Yes No

How long was the baby in the hospital _____   Discharge date _____

Was the baby transferred to another hospital _____ _____   Date of transfer _____
Yes No

Name and address of hospital _____

Why was the baby transferred _____

Primary physician caring for baby at the second hospital _____

Please list ALL physicians caring for the baby at the time of birth or at the hospital the baby was transferred to

_____   _____

_____   _____

_____   _____

_____   _____

What have you been told is the diagnosis of the child's condition _____

_____

_____

What have you been told caused this child's condition and who informed you of this _____

_____

_____

_____

CHILD'S PRESENT CONDITION

What is the child's age today _____   Who is the child's general pediatrician _____

Please check the items that apply to your child at the present time

_____ Able to move his/her arms and legs normally
_____ Able to speak normally
_____ Recognizes Mommy
_____ Recognizes Daddy
_____ Problem with seizures
_____ Blind   Right eye ____   Left eye ____   Both eyes ____
_____ Hearing problem   Right ear ____   Left ear ____   Both ears ____
_____ Heart problem
_____ Microcephaly
_____ Hydrocephalus   Does the child have a shunt: Yes ____   No ____
_____ Feeds himself
_____ Sits without assistance
_____ Walks
_____ Attends school   Name of school: _____
_____ Allergies _____

Obstetrical Information Sheet (page 7)

Please list the names of the hospitals that the child has been treated at <u>since</u> the time of birth

Name & Location of Hospital	Physician	Date	Condition
_____	_____	_____	_____
_____	_____	_____	_____
_____	_____	_____	_____
_____	_____	_____	_____
_____	_____	_____	_____

List the names of <u>all</u> physicians, dentists, and therapists who are treating or have treated the child <u>since</u> birth

Name & Location of Health Care Provider	Date(s) Treated	Condition
_____	_____	_____
_____	_____	_____
_____	_____	_____
_____	_____	_____
_____	_____	_____
_____	_____	_____
_____	_____	_____
_____	_____	_____
_____	_____	_____
_____	_____	_____

Has the child had any psychological testing _____ _____   When _____
                                           Yes   No

Who performed the psychological testing _____
                                                           Name and Address

Has the child had any genetic testing _____ _____   When _____
                                 Yes   No

Who performed the genetic testing _____.
                                               Name and Address

List all medications the child is currently taking

Medication	Date Prescribed	Doctor	Condition
_____	_____	_____	_____
_____	_____	_____	_____
_____	_____	_____	_____
_____	_____	_____	_____
_____	_____	_____	_____

Obstetrical Information Sheet (page 8)

Does the child use any type of braces or special equipment _____ _____ Describe _____
                                                                 Yes   No

Is the child cared for at home or at a special facility _____

Name and address of the special facility _____

_____

Have you initiated any previous lawsuits or claims _____ _____
                                                    Yes   No

If yes, please explain _____

_____

_____

THIS PORTION OF THE FORM MUST BE COMPLETED TO FAIRLY EVALUATE YOUR CLAIM

IN YOUR OWN WORDS, PLEASE GIVE A DESCRIPTION OF THE EVENTS THAT TOOK PLACE BEFORE, DURING, AND AFTER THE BIRTH OF THIS CHILD DETAILING THE INCIDENTS OR EVENTS YOU BELIEVE ARE A BASIS FOR THE ALLEGED INJURY/MALPRACTICE. CONTINUE ON THE BACK OF THIS PAGE OR ATTACH A SEPARATE SHEET.

Chapter 16

Interacting with Defense Clients

Karen Fox

Contents

Objectives

- To state three roles in which the LNC may interface with health care provider defendants
- To describe the role of the LNC in interviews with health care provider defendants

1-57444-123-X/98
© 1998 by American Association of Legal Nurse Consultants

- To demonstrate how to participate as a defense team member
- To explain the importance of understanding the philosophy of the company insuring the health care provider or health care system

Introduction

Legal nurse consultants (LNCs) play a vital role in the defense of professional negligence cases and other litigation involving health care issues. Today, many professional liability insurance carriers have integrated LNCs into their companies in roles such as claim specialists, adjusters, health care consultants, or loss prevention/risk management consultants. Insurance carriers or self-insured companies retain defense law firms to represent health care providers and health care systems, such as large health maintenance organizations. These defense law firms also utilize LNCs, either as in-house employees or in a contractual capacity. In the defense arena the health care provider defendant (HCPD) is often referred to as the client, particularly in the context of a law firm setting. However, LNCs currently find themselves in more-expansive roles, with their defense clients including attorneys, insurance companies, third party administrators, and self-insured companies. Although many of the principles are similar, there are some additional considerations for the LNC working within the context of a larger defense system, rather than with an individual HCPD. This chapter will look at defense clients in several contexts.

The Health Care Provider as a Defense Client

The LNC as a Liaison

In the defense arena, one of the most important roles of the LNC is that of liaison between the HCPDs and their attorneys and liability insurance carriers. Many HCPDs find the prospect of litigation very daunting; the concepts of law and the process of discovery and trial are as foreign to them as the practice of health care is to most attorneys. Fortunately, LNCs provide the bridge between these two disciplines by offering health care and health science education to attorneys and insurance professionals, and legal process education to health care providers. On a daily basis, LNCs assist with many aspects of the litigation process including: processing or composing complaints, responding to allegations, preparing answers, composing or responding to discovery requests, preparing or responding to interrogatories, scheduling of and preparing for depositions, seeking and retaining medical experts, and other aspects of discovery. Most of these terms and processes are unfamiliar and anxiety producing to HCPDs who may be exposed to them for the first time (Louisell and Williams, 1994). Explaining the legal jargon is a crucial part of assisting the HCPD through the legal process. Describing the expected time frames for the process also helps to prepare the HCPD who is used to a faster course of events. Explaining from the outset that "the wheels of justice grind slowly" may help change unrealistic expectations and decrease apprehension in the HCPD.

The LNC as a Facilitator

LNCs are knowledgeable about health care issues and "safe" in the sense that they are most often perceived as non-threatening by HCPDs. Thus, another role the LNC performs is that of facilitator for the HCPD in the legal process. Lawyers, even those on the defense team, are often perceived as threatening simply based on the adversarial nature of our justice system (Louisell and Williams, 1994). The pairing of an LNC with a lawyer for initial client interviews provides countless rewards for the defense team. During the initial interview, the LNC has the opportunity to facilitate for HCPDs at times when they may not be able to adequately express an opinion or question adequately. An LNC is usually intuitively aware of difficult issues for the HCPD and may be able to intervene with therapeutic communication techniques. The LNC can also be useful in identifying areas that need further clarification for either the HCPD or the attorney. Thus, the LNC serves as translator between the two, asking questions of clarification to be certain that meanings of words are clearly understood and comprehended by all.

The LNC as a Support Person for the HCPD

An HCPD's anxiety can be dramatically reduced by the presence of another health care provider, someone who "speaks their language." Sharing commonalities is a highly effective stress-reducing, team-building technique. The LNC's involvement in the initial interview can serve to build trust between the defense team and the HCPD. The LNC can initiate this connection by sharing stories about previous successful outcomes. Further, the LNC can explain the defense team's role, including a general chronology of case development and a description of what will be expected of the HCPD. When the HCPD views the LNC as an advocate, initial apprehension is eased. Most health care providers who are calm, appropriately assertive, and equipped with knowledge of the legal process are able to participate fully and effectively in their own defense. Those who are paralyzed with fear or who are suffering damaged self-esteem because of the allegations against them create an extra burden for the defense. Just as providing explanations and information to patients helps decrease anxiety and improves self-care, providing information and guidance when working with HCPDs can be equally effective. Helping them see their role in the context of the whole of the litigation process while alerting them to the need to persevere, despite the inherent stress of the litigation process, will improve the HCPD's ability to be a highly functioning defense team member.

Additional intervention by a trial consultant, with psychological or communication expertise, may be beneficial to help assess and prepare the HCPD witness. If the status of the HCPD warrants, the assistance of a mental health professional may be necessary. A physician defendant, whose wife had died shortly before the malpractice action began, found a therapist very helpful in sorting out his grief related to the loss of his wife from the anger and anxiety produced by the malpractice allegations. The physician was able to participate more fully in his own defense once his mental health issues were addressed.

The LNC as Educator and Researcher

LNCs also function as educators and researchers. Videotapes describing the litigation process are frequently available from the HCPD's insurance carrier or from the medical/legal or risk management departments of the health care organization. State and local medical and nursing associations are also good resources for state-specific legal information for health care providers. Discovery rules vary considerably from state to state. The LNC must be familiar with the rules in the state where the litigation is filed in order to accurately explain the rules to the HCPD. A simple chart of the legal process, as it relates to a medical malpractice lawsuit, can also be a helpful teaching tool (Rabinow, 1989). The LNC may recommend role-playing or using a videotape so HCPDs can watch their own testimony to develop confidence when testifying. Creating and providing a list of the available resources to HCPDs early in the litigation process helps HCPDs recognize and anticipate their own needs, thereby making it easier for them to request assistance.

HCPDs are often valuable resources for pertinent medical information related to the medical or nursing care issues in the case. They may have extensive literature collections, bibliographies, articles, or monographs on subjects pertinent to the litigation. They may have diagrams or anatomic models which can serve as cost-effective trial exhibits. Additionally, they are often knowledgeable about the local and national experts which will be needed for evaluation of the standard of care and, potentially, testimony. They may also direct the LNC to pertinent standards published by professional associations. Such information is readily accessible and serves as an avenue for the HCPD to participate in his or her own defense.

The Initial Interview with the HCPD

To evaluate the HCPD's background and effectiveness as a witness, the LNC should begin the interview process by focusing on questions about education, work experience, certifications, and publications. Most people feel comfortable talking about themselves, and, in this way, the interview process starts out in a nonthreatening manner. The LNC and attorney (if present) can use this opportunity to observe and evaluate the HCPD's demeanor, communication style, credibility, and jury appeal (Harney, 1993).

Depending on the practice setting, an LNC may perform the initial interview alone or through a team approach, working with the defense attorney and/or an insurance professional. If conducting the interview alone, an LNC must take detailed notes in order to prepare a memorandum to the defense attorney summarizing findings and recommendations. Providing such documentation is important to keep all the defense team members apprised of the status of the work in progress, and to avoid duplication of effort and increased defense costs.

In preparation for the initial interview with an HCPD, the LNC should prepare a list of questions covering such areas as

- Clarification about the defendant's charting
- Independent recollection of the issues
- Chronology of events
- Meetings/discussions with others

- Names of other witnesses
- Additional documents needed
- Theories/ideas for the defense
- Suggestions for experts

Having the health care provider go over each and every chart note helps interpret handwriting and idiosyncratic abbreviations. This review also helps refresh the HCPD's memory about the case. It is also a perfect time to seek information about routine care that may have been provided, but not charted; specific independent recollections about care can also be elicited. The LNC should arrive prepared with a chronological summary of the chart with annotated page numbers. This assists in expediting the interview, and targeting information needed to complete any unreadable portions of the chart. A list of page number citations specific to the individual HCPD's chart entries will also help guide and speed the interview process. During the initial interview, the LNC helps the HCPD to identify any pertinent documents not in the chart or office record, that will be important to the case. Considerations may include

- Any additional medical records in the defendant's possession
- Case-specific hospital or office policies and procedures
- Hospital credentialing materials
- Handwritten personal notes made at the time of incident, but not included in the medical record
- The health care providers *curriculum vitae*
- Any diaries, calendars, logs, or appointment books
- Transcripts of previous deposition or trial testimony given in other cases

Throughout the case, the LNC serves as the medical–legal case manager of sorts, the conveyer of case status reports and a reservoir of resources and legal process information for the HCPD. The LNC's practice setting and working relationship with the other members of the defense team will be important factors to consider when planning the participation of various team members. As an example, an LNC employed in a law firm may be expected to call the HCPD as soon as he receives a verbal report from an expert witness. The LNC may find it necessary to consult with the involved attorney and convey the meaning of the expert review to the HCPD in the context of the case development. Independent LNCs will usually provide a summary of an expert witness review to their attorney client, but often the independent LNC will not have the opportunity to interact with the HCPD.

The principles discussed here are useful for all subsequent interactions with HCPDs such as preparation of interrogatories, deposition preparation, trial preparation, assistance at trial, and coping with the outcome of the case.

The Attorney, Insurance Company, Third-Party Administrator, and Self-Insured Company as Defense Clients

Depending on the practice setting of the LNC, the term *defense client,* rather than referring to the HCPD, may refer to the defense attorney, an insurance company, a third-party administrator, or a self-insured company. It is crucial that the LNC understand the various relationships and coverage issues, as well as the timing and context of his or her role when working with such clients (see Figure 16.1). Clearly defining performance expectations and identifying the parameters of desired involvement are key elements in creating a successful working relationship (Katzenbach and Smith, 1994).

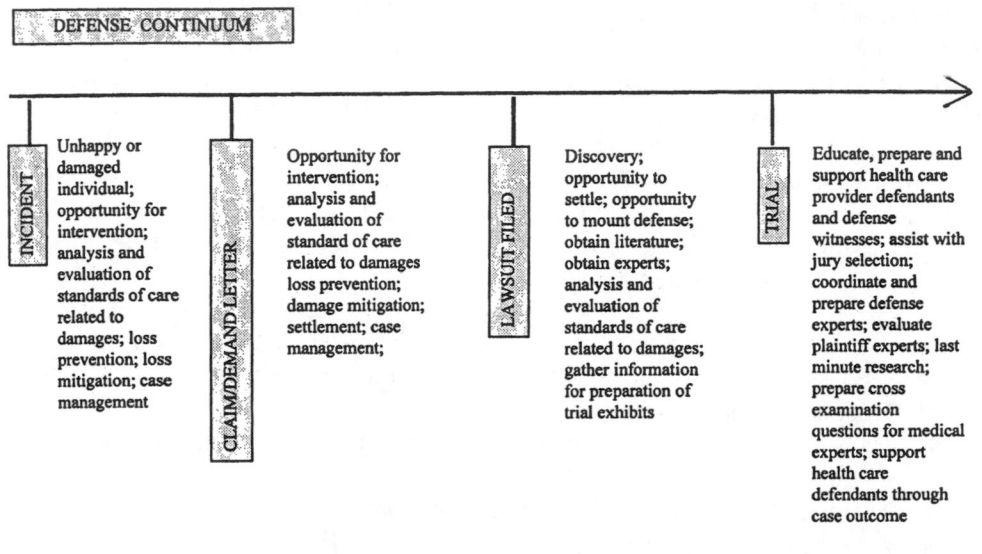

Figure 16.1   Defense continuum.

Understanding the Defense Philosophy of the Client

Experienced LNCs frequently develop their own defense philosophies which they may erroneously believe are representative of all defense clients. There are numerous considerations that contribute to the defense philosophy of the party (i.e., the insurance company, the third-party administrator, the claims resolution committee of a physician-owned company, etc.) who controls the monies spent on the defense of a case or any settlement or award. Past loss experience, economic influences, ethical considerations, religious affiliations, and/or health care provider ownership are just a few of the variables influencing the overall defense philosophy of a health care organization or an insurance carrier. An LNC must have an appreciation and respect for these factors in order to understand the client and appropriately offer services within the greater defense context.

A self-insured health maintenance organization may choose to spend limited funds on early intervention and loss prevention, while applying the greater share of its defense budget to claims containing dollar demands and filed litigation. Another health care organization with a religious affiliation may have a mission to undertake early analysis and intervention in any untoward patient outcome, instituting loss prevention measures and case management for damage mitigation, even in the absence of medical negligence. It is paramount that the LNC understand and accept the differences in these defense approaches. Tailoring one's work product to the client's philosophies and goals is probably the most important and challenging task an LNC must undertake.

Defense philosophies may be elicited during a tactful interview with the client before work is ever undertaken. The LNC's personal philosophies must be identified, isolated, and separated from those of the client for successful meshing of work styles and goals. Attending to the client's needs rather than personal preferences or beliefs is client-centered service at its best (Spector and McCarthy, 1995).

Economic considerations are always important to defense clients. Identifying priorities with the client will help with cost containment. Spending hours on projects which are not perceived as important or valuable to the client is pointless, even though the project may be relevant to the case as a whole. Preparation of a detailed time line chart may be appropriate prior to trial for use as an exhibit, but an insurance carrier may not consider it valuable or cost-effective during their preliminary stages of claim evaluation.

Another consideration to discuss with the defense client is the degree of detail or depth that is expected on a project. Some clients may want every medical word in a report defined parenthetically. Others may be medically sophisticated, and request only an explanation of new procedures or treatments. Some clients want extensive medical research with copies of all pertinent articles reviewed and highlighted. Others will want the results of medical research simply summarized in memorandum format until trial preparation begins. If in doubt about the parameters of a project, it is imperative to clarify one's understanding of the client's expectations prior to undertaking the work. With some clients it may be necessary to do this in writing; other clients may prefer a verbal agreement. Learning to ask the right questions of the client before undertaking the work is a very important part of successful LNC practice (Browne and Keeley, 1994).

The LNC's application of this chapter will vary according to the practice setting, the timing of the work related to the defense continuum, the relationship with the other defense team members, and the defense philosophy of the health care organization or insurance carrier. Whether working with individual health care providers, defense law firms, insurance companies, third-party administrators, or self-insured companies, the LNC will find his or her health science education and clinical experience serves as a firm foundation for broadened roles as liaison, facilitator, support person, educator, researcher, and legal case manager.

Glossary

Allegations: The claims, statements, or assertions made by a party to a legal action or a potential legal action. These assertions may be incorporated in the complaint or the answer.

Answer: The pleading or formal written response of the defendant to the plaintiff's complaint. This response may consist of allegations of facts, including defendant's grounds of defense.

Chronological chart summary: A written document which consists of a verbatim summary of pertinent information from medical records. The summary includes the date and the page number of the referenced information.

Claims specialist/adjuster: The independent agent or insurance company employee who investigates claims, sets insurance reserves, and settles claims against the insured.

Complaint: The original or initial pleading by which a party initiates a legal action.

Damage mitigation: Actions or steps that reduce or limit the damage resulting from an event.

Defense client: Any of the entities which may be referred to as the defense client of the LNC. The LNC may work with one or more entities in assisting the defense in a professional liability case. These entities may include the HCPD, the defense attorney, an insurance company, a third-party administrator, or a self-insured company.

Defense team member: The individuals working on behalf of the defense. The team may include the trial attorney, associate attorneys, LNCs, expert witnesses, and other consultants.

Deposition: A proceeding whereby the testimony of a witness or a party is taken under oath for the purpose of discovery or in order to preserve the testimony in the event that the witness or party is unavailable at the time of trial. During the proceeding, the witness or party orally answers questions presented by the opposing party's attorney.

Discovery: Pre-trial proceedings or devices used by either party to litigation in order to obtain facts and information from the other party as part of trial preparation.

Health care provider defendants: Any of the individuals involved in providing care for the plaintiff who are alleged to have fallen below the standard of care, resulting in the claimed damages. These defendants may include physicians, nurses, therapists, pharmacists, and similar care providers.

Interrogatories: A discovery device or tool in the form of a series of written questions submitted by one party to another party prior to trial for the purpose of gathering information.

Requests for production: A device whereby one party in litigation requests another party to produce or present documents, typically prior to trial, for examination and review.

Self-insured companies: Companies or businesses which set aside a fund to cover potential business liability losses instead of insuring against such a loss through a separate insurance company.

Third-party administrator: A person or company hired to oversee and resolve claims and actions. Third-party administrators, known as TPAs, are often utilized by large self-insured companies such as health maintenance organization or large health care conglomerates to handle claims against the company.

Trial consultant: A consultant employed or hired to assist with trial preparation, typically through the preparation of witnesses and parties for testifying at trial. Trial consultants may also assist in jury selection, through the creation of a profile of desirable jurors. Trial consultants often have background education in psychology and/or communication.

References

Browne, M. K. and Keeley, S. (1994). *Asking the Right Questions: A Guide to Critical Thinking*, Englewood Cliffs, NJ, Prentice-Hall.

Harney, D. M. (1993, 1996 Cumulative Supplement). *Medical Malpractice*, 3rd ed., Charlottesville, Michie Law Publishers.

Katzenbach, J. R. and Smith, D. K. (1993). *The Wisdom of Teams*, New York, Harper Collins.

Louisell, D. W. and Williams, H. (1994). *Medical Malpractice*, New York, Matthew Bender Co., Inc.

Oregon Law Institute (1992). *Trying the Medical Negligence Case*, Portland, Oregon Law Institute.

Rabinow, J. (1989). Where you stand in the eyes of the law. *Nursing 1989*, Feb., 34–40.

Spector, R. and McCarthy, P. (1995). *The Nordstrom Way*, New York, John Wiley & Sons.

Chapter 17

Medical Record Analysis

Shirley Cantwell Davis

Contents

Objectives

- To list three different types of medical records which may not be produced in response to a request for complete medical records and discuss why this may occur
- To outline the key points to be assessed in a complete review of an operative record
- To identify two types of altered records and five ways the LNC can detect alterations
- To discuss the various kinds of medical record summaries which can be performed by an LNC and the advantages for each type of summary
- To describe two examples of common pitfalls in medical record analysis

Introduction

The American Association of Legal Nurse Consultants (AALNC) has defined the primary role of the legal nurse consultant (LNC) to be the evaluation, analysis, and rendering of informed opinions on the delivery of health care and the resulting outcomes. This is accomplished in part by reviewing, summarizing, and analyzing medical records and other pertinent health care and legal documents and comparing and correlating them to the allegations of the complaint (AALNC, 1995b). As such, medical record analysis has been the foundation of legal nurse consulting practice since the profession first emerged.

Attorneys have no formal training regarding medical record analysis and rely heavily on LNCs to review and interpret medical records. Due to the complexity of medically related litigation today, it is essential that thorough medical record analysis be accomplished by all LNCs. Small but highly significant details can be overlooked by attorneys and LNCs with potentially disastrous results during discovery and at trial.

Compilation of Complete Medical Records

Determine Allegations of Case and Disputed Medical–Legal Issues

The *AALNC Standards of Legal Nurse Consulting Practice* state that assessment of the issues is the first step in approaching any medical–legal case. The LNC collects data to support the systematic assessment of health care issues related to a case or claim (AALNC, 1995c, Standard I).

It is essential, before beginning to collect data and review any medical records, that the LNC understand the plaintiff's complaints regarding the subject injuries and his or her perception of how a particular injury occurred. If the case is in litigation, it is important to understand the specific allegations of the complaint.

Case Example 17.1: In reviewing a potential brain-damaged baby case caused by beta streptococcal disease in a preterm infant, the LNC may ascertain the plaintiffs' allegations to be that

- The hospital negligently failed to admit the mother without signs of labor despite prolonged preterm rupture of membranes and a temperature
- The physician negligently failed to respond to fetal distress in a timely manner
- The nurses negligently failed to interpret the fetal heart monitor strips appropriately and notify a physician in a timely manner

Once the disputed medical–legal issues have been determined, it will become clear which medical records are needed to make a thorough and complete evaluation of the case.

Case Example 17.2: In the aforementioned case, the LNC, at a minimum, would then collect the medical records related to the birth of the baby, including the obstetrical records of the pregnancy with the baby in question; all hospital records related to all hospital admissions for pre-term complications and the actual labor and delivery; all fetal monitor strips (including nonstress and stress tests) for all admissions; the initial hospitalization of the baby; any EMS transport records of the baby to a tertiary institution; the hospital records of the tertiary institution together with the office records of the baby's pediatrician, pediatric neurologist, and rehabilitation practitioners. An additional interview with the mother may reveal that several phone calls were made to the obstetrician which were not returned, that the mother had a history of positive beta *Streptococcus* cultures at 26 weeks and that she had preterm labor with her previous children. This would prompt the LNC to follow up by obtaining the medical records from the obstetricians and hospitals concerning her previous deliveries. Once litigation is pending, the LNC would advise the attorney to serve a request for production of documents to include copies of the logs of the physician's phone-answering service.

Compile Complete Medical Records

The medical record must be complete, accurate, and authenticated before it can be introduced into evidence in most instances. All states have statutes regarding medical record maintenance and failure to comply can be grounds for loss of hospital accreditation. Civil liability may also be found against a hospital for breach of duty to maintain accurate records (Pozgar, 1996). The Joint Commission on Accreditation of Healthcare Organizations (JCAHO) regulations require prompt completion of records not to exceed 30 days after the discharge of patients. This time period is spelled out in the medical staff's rules and regulations (JCAHO, 1996, p. 185). Persistent failure to complete records by hospital staff members may be used as a basis for suspension of that staff member (Pozgar, 1996).

When requesting medical records, it is always wise to ask for a certified copy of the medical record. Hospitals and other health care organizations ideally should have a health information management administrator who is licensed by the American Health Information Management Association as a registered record administrator (RRA) in charge of the medical records (Pozgar, 1996, p. 375). The RRA will certify the accuracy and completeness of the copies of the original records. Often, the LNC will have to supply a physician or other health care provider with a "fill in the blank" certification when requesting medical records since many health care providers do not have an official records administrator and are not used to certifying copies of their medical records. See Appendix 17.1.

Records That May Not Be Produced as Part of the Medical Records

There are a number of additional types of medical records which may or may not be included in a response to a request for medical records. The LNC should specifically request the following types of records by name to ensure their production:

Fetal Heart Monitor Strips

Fetal heart monitor strips are electronic transcriptions of medical information and are considered to be part of the medical record of the mother of the fetus. Failure of a health care provider to be able to produce fetal heart monitor strips can be considered destruction of evidence.

The LNC should be sure to specifically request fetal heart monitor strips for all admissions in obstetrical cases since their bulky configuration and odd size necessitates that they often be stored separately from the medical records. This is particularly true of antepartum testing strips which usually remain in the labor and delivery suite for comparison when the patient returns for delivery at a later date.

X-Rays

When evaluating any case involving critical X-rays, the LNC should always obtain copies of those X-rays early on in the litigation, preferably prior to litigation in a plaintiff's case, in the event that original copies are misplaced or lost. Loss of original films does not always imply that there was harmful intent to cover up or obscure evidence. It is important to remember that many types of X-ray films, such as CT and MRI scans, are stored on computer disks. Real-time echocardiograms, angiograms, and ultrasounds are also kept on tape and copies can be obtained.

The LNC will find that often radiograph copies are of insufficient quality to provide an accurate interpretation by an outside radiologist. Health care facilities may provide original X-rays to patients if certain conditions are met, but infrequently to LNCs and attorneys. If a case is in litigation, original films may be produced by agreement of counsel or subpoena.

Also of note is the fact that there may be medical records generated as a result of a radiological procedure which may be very helpful in determining facts about a patient's care but which are kept separate from the permanent medical record. A good example would be the history and physical (H&P) exam done by a radiologist and/or radiology technician during a breast exam. The LNC will have to specifically request copies of this information directly from the radiology department.

Videotapes or Photographic Documentation of Surgical Procedures

It is important to look for evidence in the medical records (or specifically ask whether it exists in interrogatories if the case is in litigation) that such evidence even exists since videotapes or photographs are often kept by the surgeon and not the hospital. The plaintiff may have possession of such documentation, e.g., a videotape of an exploratory laparoscopy, even though there is no written evidence that videotapes or photographs exist.

Emergency Medical Services Transport Records

Many states now require that health care providers only release medical records made as a result of care and treatment at that particular facility. As such, emergency transport or ambulance records may not be released as part of the hospital medical record and will have to be requested separately from the emergency medical service.

Autopsy Records

Even if a patient has died during a hospitalization, the hospital record may be considered complete by the medical records department without the autopsy results, especially if the autopsy occurred outside the hospital at the medical examiner or coroner's office. If the death is unexplained or occurs within 24 hours of admission, it may automatically become a "coroner's case." Be sure to request the original microscopic slides or re-cuts of the originals for outside pathological interpretation when the cause of death is in question, or if the patient had recent surgery.

Billing Records

Billing records are helpful in determining the type of equipment used in a patient's care, what medications were actually given, and many other details of the care and treatment. Billing records can be of extreme importance especially when the LNC suspects there is an unfavorable laboratory result removed from the medical record. One should check the billing records to determine if the charge for laboratory test was ever billed to the patient.

Records from Reference Laboratories

Occasionally, a specimen is sent to an outside laboratory for testing and the test result will be sent back to the hospital after the patient is discharged. As a consequence, the results may not be contained in the chart for a variety of reasons.

Drugstore Pharmaceutical Records

Most drugstores selling pharmaceuticals to the public keep track of all medication records by computer, usually in chronological order. These records are invaluable when drug history is an essential part of a case, as it is in pharmaceutical products liability cases.

The following information, while not specifically part of the medical record, is part of the hospital or health care documentation but will only be available to the plaintiff or third-party defendants by request for production of documents after a case is in litigation.

Operating Room Logs

Operating room (OR) logs often have vital information concerning not only the plaintiff, but other types of operations which were occurring simultaneously in the OR suite during the time period of the plaintiff's operation. Additionally, they may contain clues as to the staffing that was available. For instance, if the plaintiff alleges that an anesthesiologist was overseeing too many operations during the subject time period, the OR logs may be able to clarify the situation for both sides. Understandably, the hospital or institution will insist that the names of the other patients be omitted for patient confidentiality prior to releasing the OR logs to the plaintiff or the defendant.

Emergency Room Logs

Emergency room (ER) logs are very similar to OR logs. Such information as the time the patient came into and was discharged from the ER will be recorded. Like the OR log, they can provide vital information regarding the plaintiff and the other types of patients and their diagnoses on the date in question. For example, in a case where the plaintiff alleges damages due to delay in treatment by the emergency department staff, the hospital defense team may be able to use the ER log to prove the existence of an unusual patient acuity situation, i.e., several trauma patients or full cardiopulmonary arrests during the time period in question.

Laboratory Logs

Most laboratories keep track by computer when certain tests were run and when the results were available to the health care providers. Laboratory logs will often have information regarding nonroutine test results which may not be contained in the medical records because the results were not available prior to the final cumulative laboratory summary results being printed. Sometimes when the results become available, the cumulative summary will not be reprinted or an updated report will not be sent to medical records.

Pharmaceutical Records

In cases involving narcotic administration where there is a dispute over amounts of drugs given, copies should be obtained of the controlled substances records kept by hospital pharmacies as required by law.

Records of HIV Testing

The physican's order for an HIV test and the result of the testing itself are confidential and cannot be obtained with a standard medical release (see Access to Medical Records, Chapter 9.)

Other Types of Medical Records

Visiting Nurse or Home Care

Home care has expanded rapidly in the wake of managed care, and, thus, home care records have consequently become more sophisticated because they encompass specific plans for treatment and documentation of those plans. These records should not be overlooked in cases involving long-term outpatient care between acute hospitalizations or following hospitalization.

Mental Health or Substance Abuse

Records pertaining to mental health or substance abuse usually require specialized consent forms to be obtained due to the confidential nature of their contents (see Access to Medical Records, Chapter 9.) In most cases, the defense will have to prove that the records are essential to the defense of the case before access to them will be allowed by a judge.

Nursing Home Records

As part of the Omnibus Budget Reconciliation Act of 1987 (OBRA 1987), Congress passed the Nursing Home Quality Reform Act requiring substantial changes in nursing home care with more vigorous and more punitive regulatory enforcement (Sartwelle, 1994). As a result of OBRA, there is increasing awareness of negligence occurring in nursing homes. Nursing home records should be obtained and inspected carefully for noncompliance with OBRA as well as for other general negligence.

Outpatient Therapy or Rehabilitation Records

The LNC should not disregard physical, occupational, and speech therapy records in either the prosecution or defense of medical malpractice, personal injury, or workers' compensation cases. There may be admissions by the plaintiff or observations by the therapists which would not appear in the physician's records and could be damaging or supportive of the plaintiff's case. The therapists' observations are usually detailed, precise, and legible. Furthermore, the therapists themselves can be excellent witnesses when deposed and at trial.

In medical negligence cases involving inpatient admissions, therapists' assessments of patient behavior and clinical well-being can be used to compare and contrast effectively the nurses and physicians' observations of the patient during the same period of time.

Computerized Medical Records

Increasingly, health care facilities are moving toward greater use of computerized medical records. Most hospitals have computerized laboratory, pharmacy, radiology, EKG, and EEG reporting as well as computerized invasive monitoring in the ICU and electronic fetal monitoring in the obstetrical unit. Computerized medication records are being seen much more frequently because they have the advantage of diminishing the possibility of medication transcription and administration error. In many areas of the country, operating rooms are experimenting with computerized anesthetic records.

Computerized records decrease the length of time it takes to convey information to all members of the health care team and improve the quality of the medical record. Advantages also include the fact that it is difficult, if not impossible, to lose or misplace a computerized record on a permanent basis due to the internal backup programmed into all computer systems. Potential problems directly related to use of computers in the creation and management of medical records involve the loss of confidentiality and unauthorized disclosure of information.

In terms of medical–legal review, computerized nurse's notes and physician order transcriptions are often voluminous when finally printed. Additionally, the LNC may find the information hard to access due to the nature of the programming of the system. However, one is much more likely to be able to determine exactly when a physician ordered medications or tests and when the order was transcribed in a computerized record than on many standard physician's order sheets.

Incomplete Medical Records

The usual reason for receiving what appears to be incomplete medical records from a hospital or other health care facility is that the page or pages in question are not in the expected chronological or sequential order in the chart. Therefore, it is important to organize the medical records properly before further action is taken. Often one will find the critical "missing" consultation in the middle of the physician's progress notes or some other unlikely place. Sometimes the records will be released from the health care facility prior to being completed by the attending physicians or before final laboratory compilations have been forwarded to the medical records department. This may happen when records are requested soon after the discharge or death of a patient.

It is usually safe to assume that the medical record department is not deliberately trying to thwart the LNC's efforts to get a complete record. Sometimes, the missing records may be the result of an error on the part of the copy technician or the records in question may not have been included as a result of that error. Often a letter to the medical records administrator outlining the exact missing record(s) will be all that it takes to procure them. If the hospital denies the existence of portions of the record which, in the LNC's opinion, must have been created and should be in existence, the medical record administrator should be asked to document the absence of the subject portion in writing.

When dealing with a health care practitioner's office, the LNC may find that the custodian of the medical records is often not a trained medical records administrator and thus missing records may simply occur because of a misunderstanding on the part of the person who responded to the medical records request as to what was wanted. The correspondence or laboratory and radiology reports may be left out entirely because the custodian assumed that they were not necessary to comply with the request. The prudent LNC will specifically delineate all portions of the medical record contemplated by the request when dealing with a health care practitioner's office. Specifically request all handwritten notes, memos, and telephone conference notes. Most health care providers will not send out copies of records received from other treating physicians unless specifically asked; however, some states have laws which prevent this from being done at all. Once the records are received, make certain that the handwritten database or medical history form that the patient filled out on the first visit has been included.

The LNC should be aware of whether or not the law of the state in which the case resides permits an adverse inference to be drawn against a person or facility who is unable to produce a document or study, whether it has been innocuously lost or not (Janulis, 1990, p. 12) since this may have great impact on the status of a case with incomplete records of any kind.

In all cases of missing records, the LNC should advise the attorney of the specific records which are missing as soon as possible and the reason why collection of those records is essential for thorough case review. Many LNCs working for attorneys in law firms will have ongoing authority to request whatever records are necessary; however, LNCs working outside an attorney's office will either advise the attorney regarding which records to obtain or obtain them on the attorney's behalf with a consent form which encompasses the LNC working on behalf of the attorney. Obviously, it is impossible for the LNC to analyze the medical records thoroughly and accurately and make assessment of a particular case if complete medical records are not available.

Organization of the Medical Records

In order to review medical records in the most complete manner possible, it is essential to organize the records into an easily comprehensible format. As nurses, LNCs have a more comprehensive understanding of medical records than any other litigation professional. Therefore, it is critical that LNCs oversee the organization of medical records. Most often, this will consist of organizing all hospital and physician office records into chronological order and a logical order for ease in review. For the purposes of litigation, it is wise to apply this philosophy to all medical records. If, however, the task at hand is to review a potential case involving the possible fracture of a Bjork–Shiley heart valve, and a simple review of the final hospitalization and autopsy reveals that the patient died of a ruptured abdominal aortic aneurysm instead, it may well be a waste of the LNC's time, and the client's money, to spend time organizing ten different hospitalizations in chronological order. However, the attorney should make the decision about whether or not the attorney wants more work done with the medical records, since there may be conferences, hearings, or other situations involving the client where detailed organization of the medical records is still necessary. In a potential plaintiff's case, such as the previously mentioned one, it is still possible that other issues have been overlooked, such as a timely diagnosis and treatment of the abdominal aortic aneurysm.

Several logical sequences of various types of hospital records are suggested in Appendix 17.2. Health maintenance organization (HMO) and physician's records encompass different types of information and necessarily require a different organization. A logical sequence for these types of records is suggested in Appendix 17.2. It is suggested that a progression such as this be followed for all medical record organization in order to place the records in a sequence that lends itself to ease of medical–legal review as opposed to the "52-card pickup" approach that some medical record departments take when releasing records. Often the records are released in a progression that facilitates ease of patient care, but not medical–legal review. A common presentation is to have the physician's orders section as one of the first parts of the chart. While critical in a few cases, the physician's orders are generally not of importance for the majority of medical–legal cases and therefore may be placed further back in the indexed chart. It should be stressed that there is no "right" way to organize and sequence medical records. Obviously, there are a number of ways the LNC can sequence medical records and the type of case may suggest the most logical sequence for ease of review or the LNC or attorney may have a specific format which suits their practice style. It is imperative, however, that all persons on the same side of the litigation team have medical records which are indexed in the same manner.

If there is an abundance of medical records which are not critical to the investigation or litigation of a case, e.g., long-term nursing care due to brain damage resulting from an anesthesia accident, the LNC may want to divide the "excess" records into file folders and label them so that the information can be easily retrieved and accessed when necessary in the future.

Copies of fetal heart–monitoring strips can be difficult to interpret correctly on multiple separate sheets of paper. The LNC may want to take the extra time to meticulously line up and tape together all the pieces of the fetal heart monitor strips so that the panel numbers correlate chronologically. The same principle applies to ICU flow records, when the original encompasses several different folding sheets, so that the times for all the data match and can be easily read and interpreted. The LNC would only want to spend the time doing this in a case where the ICU flow sheets were of central importance to the alleged negligence.

Indexing and Paginating Medical Records

Once the medical records are complete, all medical records should be placed in a loose-leaf binder for ease of review with subsections of each record tabbed and labeled "Progress Notes," "Medications," etc. Formulation of an index, such as is seen in Appendix 17.3 can be a valuable and time-saving aid. An index identifies the exact nature of the medical record contents including the dates of treatment and the types of physicians who have treated the patient. This index is helpful not only to the LNC in their continuous dealings with the medical records, but also to the attorney during discovery so that a comprehensive assessment of the obtained records can be made at any time. Additionally, when medical records are being sent to expert witnesses, an index gives a concise record of exactly what information the expert has received and reviewed in order to arrive at his or her opinion. The index is updated by the LNC as further medical records are collected during the course of case evaluation or litigation.

If the medical records are extensive but complete and certified, pagination may be tremendously helpful in later discovery and at trial. Copies of the complete, certified, and paginated records can be used as invaluable "working copies" during discovery with the advantage of knowing that all the attorneys, experts, and LNCs are referring to the exact same information. Additionally, complete, certified, and paginated records will ensure expeditious review of medical records by expert witnesses which in turn will keep client costs to a minimum. The reader is cautioned not to paginate records that are not complete and not certified, since the numbering system will only cause confusion once the remainder of the records are incorporated. Alternatively, if medical records arrive from another law firm or a copy service with an outside pagination number, the records may be stamped a second time with a different type of pagination system which perhaps incorporates letters with the numbers, e.g., A001, A002, etc.

Medical Record Analysis

The *AALNC Standards of Legal Nurse Consulting Practice* state that once the appropriate data (medical records) has been collected, the LNC must analyze the data and identify the health care issues related to the case or claim (AALNC, 1995c).

A quick assessment of the medical records should be done while the initial record organization is being accomplished. This assessment can be used to get an overview of the issues of the case and to make a mental note of who treated the plaintiff when and where. More importantly, this overview can be used to determine if there are missing records.

> Case Example 17.3: In a case involving alleged failure to diagnose an ascending aortic aneurysm during an emergency visit, one would want to make sure that the reports of the chest X-ray and CT scan which were ordered by the ER physician were in the chart and that copies of those films were complete when ordered from the radiology department.

> Case Example 17.4: In a product liability case involving a prescription of the drug Prozac, a review of all pharmaceutical (drugstore) records would be essential to determine properly all the drugs that the plaintiff was taking during the time of the alleged negligence, since it is common for physicians not to list in their office records on each and every visit the complete list of all the medications the patient takes on an ongoing basis.

The LNC may find it helpful in complicated cases to make an outline of important events during the initial review of the medical records. The outline can be used as a guide for a more in-depth and systematic review of the medical records.

Systematic Review of Hospital Medical Records

Face Sheet and DRGs

Diagnosis-related groups (DRGs) are the basis for the Department of Health and Human Services' prospective payment system (contained in the 1983 Social Security Amendments) for reimbursing inpatient hospital costs for Medicare beneficiaries. The key source of information for determining the course of treatment of each patient and the proper DRG assignment is the medical record (Pozgar, 1996, pp. 375–376).

Consent Forms

The LNC should be familiar with the state statutes regarding the specific informed consent laws for the state in which the case rests. The consent should be properly witnessed, dated, and signed by the patient and the physician. It should also delineate the expected usual, unusual, and rare adverse consequences of the operation or procedure and the risks of nonperformance of the procedure, including the need for and risk of, and alternatives to, blood products (JCAHO, 1996, TX.5.2.2). Additionally, the alternative treatment options which are available to the patient in the event of nonperformance of the procedure should be listed (JCAHO, 1996). The consent form must be completed before the patient is given preoperative medication which could impair his ability to give competent consent (Janulis, 1990, p. 43). Determine if the patient or his representative agreed to the particular operation or procedure performed and if any exceptions to that consent were noted.

> Case Example 17.5: A 42-year-old woman undergoing exploratory laparoscopy for pelvic pain signs a consent form for the laparoscopy and also for laparotomy and hysterectomy with the caveat that her uterus is to be removed only if the surgeon determines there is cancer or severe endometriosis. The surgeon finds an ovarian cyst and a few other mild abnormalities but removes the uterus anyway. The woman sues the surgeon for battery due to lack of consent as well as negligence.

Autopsy

Ascertain whether the autopsy report is a complete protocol or reflects only the preliminary results. Determine if all the microscopic examinations have been performed and whether the results of any toxicology results or special consultations to outside agencies have been received. Autopsy evidence can be critical not only in confirming a diagnosis causing death, but in disproving certain diagnoses.

> Case Example 17.6: In a case alleging that the plaintiff died of a myocardial infarction shortly after being seen for chest pain in the ER, the autopsy may *not* be critical in proving the existence of an acute myocardial infarction since it takes many hours for microscopic and gross evidence of myocardial infarction to manifest itself; however, it will be invaluable in ruling out other causes of death such as stroke, aneurysm rupture, etc.

Discharge Summary

This document can be reviewed as an overview of the hospitalization: the dates of the hospitalization, reason for admission, complaints upon admission, course of treatment and significant findings, response to procedures and treatment, any complications which occurred, the status of the patient at discharge, and the instructions to the patient and family, if any (JCAHO, 1996, p. 182). One should look carefully for details such as when the discharge summary was dictated since it can have bearing on the subjectivity of the content of the discharge summary. Determine if there are handwritten additions, deletions, or changes to the original document, when those changes were made, and their relevance to the subject of the lawsuit.

> Case Example 17.7: A 60-year-old man had exploratory laparotomy to rule out appendicitis but no acute findings or appendicitis were determined intraoperatively. The plaintiff had postoperative fever, increased WBC counts with a shift to the left, but was discharged only to be readmitted several days later with severe draining abscesses from a ruptured appendix. The discharge summary for the initial hospitalization was dictated several days after the admission for the second admission. One would want to look closely at the fact scenario in the discharge summary of the first hospitalization since the surgeon may have been tempted to downplay the severity of the patient's illness prior to the first discharge, after he learned of the patient's subsequent problems.

The discharge summary can also be used as a barometer against which the effects of any treatments which occurred during the admission can be measured. This is important in terms of damages. Did the patient suffer harm or injuries? To what extent was he injured? How permanent are the injuries?

Emergency Medical Services

Compare the patient's admission status with the emergency transport records. This may be important in cases where the patient's condition prior to arrival and/or resuscitation efforts and response prior to admission are critical elements of the case (Janulis, 1990).

> Case Example 17.8: A 38-week-gestational-age baby is delivered precipitously at a rural hospital without an NICU. The infant immediately begins to manifest respiratory difficulties and has severe hypoglycemia. The baby is intubated but oxygen saturation levels indicate still indicate hypoxemia. Sepsis is suspected. An emergency medical transport team transports the baby to a tertiary care institution but the baby dies shortly after admission. Suit is brought against the rural hospital and the pediatrician for failure to transport the baby in a timely manner. The pediatrician claims that he called the tertiary-level hospital immediately after the baby was born, however, the EMS records indicate that the transfer was not requested until the baby was eight hours old.

Emergency Department

Common problems resulting in litigation in the ER include (1) not seeing patients in a timely manner, (2) failing to diagnose the real cause of the plaintiff's problems as a result of inadequate assessment and testing, and (3) discharging patients who should be admitted for further observation and treatment. Knowing this, the LNC should review the time that the patient was admitted, the presenting complaints, and vital signs. Look at the assessment made by the triage nurse and determine if the appropriate triage classification was made. What time was the patient first seen by a physician? Compare the nurse's assessment of the patient with that of the emergency physician. Were the appropriate diagnostic studies ordered by the physician and were they performed in a timely manner? Is there evidence that the plaintiff was under the influence of any alcohol or drugs? Did the patient respond to the treatment rendered? If a patient receives emergency, urgent, or immediate care, and leaves against medical advice, the medical record is required to make a note of this (JCAHO, 1996, IM.7.5.1). Did the patient sign a form to that effect?

History and Physical Examination

JCAHO requires that a patient's H&P exam, nursing assessment and other screening assessments are complete within 24 hours of admission as an inpatient (JCAHO, 1996, PE.1.6.1). The physician may elect to do this in writing or by dictation. Determine the date that the typed history was dictated. The information in a history dictated several days after an admission with complications may be suspect. The name of the person dictating the H&P may also have significance. A physician's assistant (PA) or resident may not have the knowledge base or the clinical expertise to detect or follow up on subtle findings that an experienced physician would. Because the PA works under the supervision of the physician, the physician must still take legal responsibility for the PA's actions. Likewise, a physician covering for a patient's regular physician may not be able to evaluate the patient's current situation in the light of a complex medical history because the physician does not know the patient well.

History. The LNC should look at the patient's chief complaint and past history, looking for clues to the present illness. Evaluate the complaints of the patient for validity as well as for the patient's perception of his own illness and for the prior treatment he has received (Janulis, 1990). Sometimes, the patient will give a history that is slightly or radically different during separate admissions. Compare the histories from all hospitalizations and those from physician's records checking for consistency. Often an error on a history becomes a self-perpetuating "fact" as each subsequent consulting physician obtains the history information from the chart instead of the patient. The LNC should be aware of this and look carefully for the origin of all information. Look for historical information regarding medications, drug allergies, drug and alcohol problems. The history of prior surgeries, illnesses, and injuries can be of extreme importance to the current picture. Failure of a physician to ask proper questions necessary to elicit an adequate history may constitute negligence (Janulis, 1990, p. 23).

Physical Examination. A physical examination record can be important as much for what is omitted from the documentation as it is for the positive and negative (nonexistent) findings that are written about the patient's presenting clinical situation.

Case Example 17.9: A general surgeon examines a woman who is hospitalized for severe right upper quadrant abdominal pain. During the previous year, the woman has been to several gynecologists and radiologists for a breast mass which has not gone away and has not been biopsied. The surgeon makes no mention of breast examination in his physical examination. When it is determined that the woman has infiltrating ductal carcinoma the following year, suit is brought against the surgeon, in addition to the gynecologist and radiologist, for failing to do a complete physical exam during the hospitalization for abdominal pain. The plaintiff alleges that the surgeon would have performed a biopsy to determine the nature of the mass if an appropriate physical examination had revealed its presence.

The physician may often respond "if I didn't write anything about it, then it must not have been a problem" (Janulis, 1990, p. 24). But the corollary to this is "if I didn't write it down, then I did not examine or address the area or problem." Credibility in this type of situation is left for the jury to decide at trial and may depend on the remainder of the physician's examination and the physician's other charting practices or simply on whether or not the physician makes a good expert witness on his or her own behalf, i.e., is the physician believable? As with the history, compare the physical examination findings with those noted by the nurses or physical therapists or any other member of the health care team. The physician's observations are dependent upon patient cooperation and patient reactions which may be entirely spurious and misleading (Janulis, 1990, p. 25).

Provisional Diagnosis. Since the provisional diagnosis reflects the physician's preliminary opinions regarding the patient's condition and is the basis for initial treatment, look closely at his/her conclusions. Were the appropriate conclusions made? Does the treatment plan encompass an appropriate diagnostic workup or treatment for the diagnoses made?

Operative Records

Operative records consist of numerous types of documentation, including consent forms (see above), preoperative and intraoperative nursing records, preoperative, intraoperative, and postoperative anesthesia records, surgical notes, pathology, and postanesthesia care unit records.

Preoperative Nursing Records. Preoperative nursing records are important in determining whether the appropriate preoperative preparation of the patient took place. Documentation of the patient's vital signs, preoperative testing, last food or drink, and signing of the consent form may have important implications for a case. For example, there may be serious implications if the patient aspirates during intubation but the preoperative documentation fails to note that the patient was mistakenly given breakfast.

Intraoperative Nursing Records. Nursing notes can be invaluable in documenting exactly who participated in a surgical procedure and the times that those persons were in the operating room, as well as when the procedure began and was finished. Look for information regarding the skin preparation, the type of preoperative or intraoperative positioning of the patient, the location of the electrosurgical ground pad. The nurses' operative record will contain specifics regarding any devices implanted during the procedure and, often, specialized types of equipment used by the surgeon. Additionally, there will be information regarding drains, sponges, surgical packing, and catheters not found elsewhere. Often there will be clues as to what happened during the operative procedure in the nursing portion of the operative record that will not be contained in the anesthesia charting or the surgeon's operative note.

Anesthesia Preoperative Assessment. The anesthesia preoperative workup should be complete and include a complete history of the patient's response to previous anesthetics, potential problems involving the airway, and current medical illnesses and medications. An assessment of the degree of illness of the patient and his or her risk for anesthetic complications as determined by the American Society of Anesthesiologists (ASA) will be assigned on a scale of I to V and emergencies. The ASA classification can be used as a barometer against which the intensity of intraoperative monitoring of the patient occurred. For example, a Class III patient with diabetic neuropathy and cardiovascular disease should have more-intense monitoring than a Class I patient with no systemic disease. At the conclusion of the preoperative workup, the anesthesiologist should determine an operative plan for the anesthetist (anesthesiologist or anesthetist) that includes the preoperative medication, the type of induction, and the type of anesthesia to be administered.

Anesthesia Records. Determine whether an anesthesiologist, a nurse anesthetist, or a physician's assistant trained in anesthesia delivered the anesthetic agents. Who monitored the patient? Often the induction is performed by an anesthetist with an anesthesiologist present, but the anesthesiologist subsequently leaves the OR suite to oversee another anesthetist. Therefore, it is important to ascertain who actually administered the anesthesia. Depending on the degree of legibility, the actual anesthesia graphic charting and narrative records may be difficult to comprehend. In cases involving intraoperative events, look at the types of inhalation agents (gases) and drugs used for induction, the time of intubation, whether there was any difficulty with the intubation, the number of times it took to intubate the patient, and the patient's vital signs in response to these events. Patient positioning can also have significance in cases involving intraoperative complications or postoperative findings such as neuropathies. Events will often be numbered on the graphic record and correspond to the narrative record. Determine the type of intraoperative monitoring used. An end tidal CO_2 monitor and an oxygen saturation monitor are essential, as recommended by the ASA (ASA, 1995). Look closely at the patient's vital signs and the anesthetist's response to changes in them. It is important to determine whether the patient's condition is due to the effect of the anesthesia or the surgery being performed. Note the length of time that the patient was under anesthetic care and the length of time it took to perform the operation. These times should be compared with those on the intraoperative nurses notes.

Operative Reports. The surgeon is required by JCAHO to dictate or write the operative report immediately after surgery, recording the name of the primary surgeon and assistants, findings, technical procedures used, specimens removed, and postoperative diagnosis. If the operative report is not placed in the medical record immediately after surgery, a progress note should be entered immediately (JCAHO, 1996, IM.7.3.2).

The preoperative diagnosis is sometimes contained in the operative report. In cases where the necessity of the operation is in question, compare all the preoperative diagnosis, the operative findings, and the postoperative diagnosis with the history and physical and the discharge summary for consistency. Be alert for operative reports that are brief and nonspecific, especially in commonly performed surgeries such as hysterectomies.

A good operative report also contains information about the types and locations of drains placed, estimated blood loss, detailed operative findings, and complications encountered during the procedure. Determine the names of any surgical assistants and types of specialized equipment used by the surgeon. Place close attention to the manner in which foreign bodies, such as hip and knee replacements, are described as being inserted. Did the surgeon encounter any unusual bleeding that is not accounted for? Is there mention of distorted or "difficult" anatomy? This is especially important in cases where structures have been encroached upon improperly.

> Case Example 17.10: A 45-year-old woman with right upper quadrant (RUQ) pain, nausea, and vomiting and a positive ultrasound for gallstones has laparoscopy for cholecystectomy. During the course of the operation, the surgeon notes scarring in the gallbladder bed and difficult dissection, yet no intraoperative cholangiogram is done and the surgeon does not convert the operation to a laparotomy. Postoperatively, the patient has additional pain, jaundice, and increasing bilirubin. An esophageal retrograde cholangiopancreatogram (ERCP) and percutaneous transhepatic cholangiogram are consistent with clips on the common bile duct. The plaintiff alleges that the difficult dissection mandated open laparotomy and that the failure to do this resulted in the surgical error.

Surgical Pathology. In cases where biopsies are being done, look at the frozen section diagnosis and compare it with the surgical treatment performed, the follow-up treatment, and the final pathology diagnoses. Sometimes, the frozen section diagnosis will differ from the final pathology diagnosis. Obviously, there are serious implications if a misreading of the frozen section results in unnecessary removal of tissue or body parts. If surgery is being done to remove cancer, make sure that the specimens removed have margins clear of tumor. Note the size of the specimen removed. Is the pathological diagnosis consistent with the surgical diagnosis or the reason the surgery was being performed in the first place? It is important to be familiar with the standard of care in such situations.

> Case Example 17.11: For instance, most general surgeons will tell you that 10 to 15% of all appendectomies are done when there is no microscopic or gross evidence of acute appendicitis. In other words, all the clinical signs and symptoms can indicate a diagnosis of appendicitis without appendicitis being present. Therefore, a negative finding of a normal appendix after an operation for presumed appendicitis does not necessarily mean that the surgeon performed an unnecessary operation.

Postanesthesia Recovery. These records are of vital importance in cases involving immediate postoperative complications which are usually respiratory or cardiac in nature. The LNC should look for trends in vital signs, mental and neurological status, and the timeliness of the response of the nursing staff to those changes.

Postoperative Anesthesia. The anesthesia staff, either an anesthesiologist or a nurse anesthetist, will see the patient postoperatively, usually on the day after surgery and note the patient's response to the anesthetic delivered. In the case of epidural anesthesia, the anesthesiologist or nurse anesthetist will see the patient at least once daily and be available to respond for complications with the epidural until such time as the catheter has been removed and a determination has been made that the patient has not sustained any complications. In cases where the patient received postoperative anesthesia, review the progress notes of the anesthesia staff and the flowcharts corresponding to the anesthesia in question.

Consultations

Determine if the appropriate medical specialty consultations were ordered in a timely manner. Look at the date that the consultant was asked to see the patient and the consultant's response. The consultant should consider all the necessary patient history to draw conclusions. After the consultant has determined a course of treatment for the patient, the consultant should then follow the patient with the attending physician until the problem for which he/she was consulted is resolved. If the attending physician is a family practice physician, the consultant may become the physician in charge of the patient's care while the acute condition is being resolved. Pay close attention to the number of consultants being used in complicated medical and surgical cases. Determine whether one physician was actually looking at the patient as a whole or whether each physician was only looking at the respiratory, gastrointestinal, hematologic, etc. systems individually. Failing to put the entire clinical picture together in complicated cases can result in disastrous consequences for the patient. Consult the hospital medical staff bylaws to determine if there are bylaws governing how the responsibility for total patient care is to be shared or transferred between primary physicians and consultants.

Physician Progress Notes

Progress notes should contain reference to the patient's test results, response to treatment and therapy, and should document objective and subjective signs and symptoms (Janulis, 1990, p. 26). Look at how often the physician(s) charted. Lack of an entry in the progress notes does not necessarily mean that the patient was not seen. When there is no daily note written, check the physician's orders, the nurse's notes, and the notes of other health care providers for clues that the physician actually did examine the patient on a particular day. Does the physician acknowledge other physician's and health care provider's findings as well as the patient's complaints in the notes? As with other narrative parts of the medical record, check the time (if written) and date of all notes for logical sequencing and progression. Look for notes that may not have been written contemporaneously. Does each page have the patient's hospital stamp plate on the corner? Are there notes written with lines drawn through the blank portion of the page so no one else would write on that particular page? Analyze all notes written immediately after an incident, such as an unexpected cardiac arrest, with close scrutiny.

Radiology Reports

As with laboratory reports, compare the times and dates that the X-rays were ordered with the time that the actual films were taken. Many health care facilities do not list this on the radiology report, but the LNC may be able to piece the information together by looking at the remainder of the record, especially the nursing notes. Determine if the X-rays (or any diagnostic tests) were accomplished in a reasonable and timely manner or in the time frame contemplated by the physician when ordering the test. Was relevant clinical information provided with the request as is required for X-ray and clinical interpretation? (JCAHO, 1996, PE.1.4.1). Compare successive radiology reports looking for differences in the findings. Are there reports of air in the abdomen in a postoperative patient? Are there accumulations of fluid noted? Does the report comply with the American College of Radiology Standard for Communication—Diagnostic Radiology? (ACR, 1995.) These standards define the minimum items needed for a diagnostic radiology report and the type of written communication and direct communication which should be transmitted to the ordering physician as a result of such a diagnostic examination. If the technique of the radiology examination is in question, such as in diagnostic mammography, compare the examination with that recommended by the ACR Standard for Diagnostic Mammography (ACR, 1995.)

Laboratory Records

Determine if the appropriate laboratory tests were done for the patient's clinical diagnosis and treatment or as a preoperative workup. Laboratory results can be very meaningful evidence when a physician or other health care provider fails to follow up on abnormal test results. In cases where laboratory results are of importance, ascertain whether or not all the laboratory results are in the chart. A final computerized summary of all the laboratory results gives the best assurance that this is so. Determine the time that the laboratory tests were ordered, the time the samples were obtained, the time that the results were available to the health care providers. Be sure to correlate the physician's progress notes and/or orders regarding specialized tests sent to outside laboratories and make sure those results are on the chart. In cases involving extremes in laboratory values, such as hyperkalemia and hypoxemia, look for "critical" or "panic" values in the laboratory results and the documentation as to who was called regarding those values (usually the nursing staff) and the response to those critical values. Remember that various health care facilities use different normal parameters for various laboratory tests, but that the results are always calibrated to that normal range.

Search for trends in laboratory results:

- Look at the hemoglobin and hematocrit in a surgical case involving postoperative bleeding.
- Ascertain the specifics of the white blood cell count and the differential in a case involving unrecognized infection.
- Determine the result times and trends in cardiac enzymes for a case involving failure to diagnose myocardial infarction.
- Pay close attention to the arterial blood gas results in cases where there are progressive respiratory difficulties and/or respiratory arrest.

■ Look at the culture and sensitivity results for a determination of timely and appropriate management of systemic or local infections.

Transfusion Records

In cases involving transfusion reactions, document the patient and donor's ABO and Rh blood type and cross-matching tests and antibody screening. Establish the events surrounding the blood transfusion including the time the blood product was started and stopped, the amount given, and the documentation of the transfusion reaction. Complete typing and cross-matching may not have been done due to the acute need for blood transfusion; however, technical errors account for most transfusion accidents in nonemergency situations. Improper patient and donor identification remains the leading cause of transfusion errors (Janulis, 1990, p. 48).

Physician's Orders

The orders often provide invaluable clues about communication between the physician and the nurses caring for a patient and the care being rendered. For example, there may be a telephone order for pain medication in the order section of the chart but no mention anywhere else that there was a communication between the physician and the nurse. It is sometimes important to distinguish among orders written directly by a physician, verbal orders, and telephone orders in order to establish the whereabouts of a physician at a certain time. Additionally, the time that orders were written and the time that the order was taken off and countersigned by the nurse should be noted carefully, as well as whether or not the order was transcribed correctly.

> Case Example 17.12: A 55-year-old man who has fallen develops a headache and several hours later develops decerebrate posturing and is minimally responsive to stimulation. The physician orders a number of electrolyte tests and ABGs stat as well as a CT scan. The order for the CT scan is entered as a routine order by the unit secretary and signed off by the nurse in charge of the patient. As a result of this (and several other nonrelated delays) the patient does not have the CT scan done until 8 hours after the original order, by which time he is having apneic spells and one of his pupils is dilated and fixed. The CT scan shows a subdural hematoma which was subsequently emergently evacuated.

Obviously, the physician's orders must be carried out and failure to do so can mean a deviation in the standard of care with only rare exceptions. Standing orders mandate certain actions when specific situations arise, i.e., "O_2 2 liters/by nasal canula for O_2 saturation <93%." Did the health care providers follow these orders? Check the physician's orders for items such as the frequency of vital signs, the patient's prescribed activity level, and other types of required monitoring. Often these are the basis for judging nursing actions in negligence cases. Was the patient monitored with sufficient frequency as contemplated by the physician? For example, did the patient fall while going to the bathroom when he was supposed to be on bedrest?

Medication Records

These records give the LNC a complete picture as to the types of medications being given to the patient and when they were given. JCAHO requires that medication effects on patients be continually monitored (JCAHO, TX.3.9). Look for evidence of patient reactions to medications and the nursing response to those reactions. The patient's medication allergies should be prominently noted. With computerization of medication records, pharmacies will enter allergies in the computer and the computer will alert the pharmacist if a drug is ordered that has cross-sensitivity with a drug that the patient is allergic to, such as antibiotics. This important safety feature may be negated when one-time medications, such as narcotics, are ordered; e.g., administering Tylenol #3 even when the patient is allergic to codeine because the nurse has access to this drug without going through the pharmacy. Of great importance are the "prn" medications since they will occasionally not be mentioned in the nursing documentation. Compare the medications given and the doses of those medications with the physician's orders for discrepancies.

Often when the plaintiff alleges that a drug was not given, or given and not documented, the pharmacy bills can be helpful. Other sources of information to check on the administration of narcotics include the pharmacy narcotic control slips, the pharmacy central narcotic record, and the pharmacy charge slips (Janulis, 1990, p. 34).

Graphics and Flow Sheets

Graphics and flow sheets, such as neurological check sheets, diabetic urine and blood testing, are of importance in cases where there are trends in a patient's condition that are not recognized and no follow-up action is taken. The intake and output sheets may show a progressive positive fluid balance with diminishing urinary output in a patient who has congestive heart failure. Intake and output sheets may be of critical importance in cases involving infants and geriatric patients who are easily subject to dehydration. The vital signs on the graphics sheets may be additional evidence to support the plaintiff's contention that shock was developing and was not recognized in a timely manner. Graphics and flow sheets may be of critical importance to the plaintiff especially when the information required on the graphics and flow sheets has not been entered by the nurses.

Nurses' Notes

As all LNCs know, the nurses' notes are often the most invaluable portion of the medical record, substantiating or contradicting evidence found elsewhere in the patient's hospital chart.

Admission History and Physical. The nursing admission assessment, while not a complete medical history and physical, does assess important considerations for nursing care of the patient while hospitalized. The LNC can determine the patient's physical limitations (and functional status assessment when warranted by the patient's needs or conditions JCAHO, 1996, PE.1.3), mental status, understanding of his or her situation, special feeding problems, and allergies. Often, the most complete list of current medications will be determined by the admitting nurse. Compare the information given in the physician's history with that written by the nurses for differences or contradictions that may have impact for the case.

Nursing Care Plan. The nursing care plan is the basis for rendering care to the patient and should be appropriate for the types of problems the patient is experiencing. The nursing care plan can be used in the legal setting as a barometer of the nurses' understanding of the type of care to be rendered to the patient and a standard by which that care is to be measured.

> Case Example 17.13: The nursing care plan states that close attention is to be paid to monitoring of the respiratory status in a patient who has just undergone tonsillectomy and adenoidectomy, but the nursing notes fail to document such action. The nursing care plan may be used against the nurses to show deviation from the standard of care.

Ongoing Documentation. As all LNCs know, the nurses' notes represent an ongoing account of patient complaints, signs, and symptoms and the nursing response to those complaints, signs, and symptoms and the timeliness of those responses. A determination of the status of the patient before and after diagnostic and surgical procedures can be made, as well as the patient's response to blood products, IVs, and medications. This documentation can be of utmost importance in some medical/legal cases. The nurses' notes may be the definitive clue as to the timing of certain events, such as physician visits as well as untoward events such as adverse reactions, patient injuries, or respiratory and/or cardiac arrest. Look specifically to see if the nurses have followed through with their plan for nursing care of the patient. Did they use appropriate judgment in complying with the standing orders? Look for trends in vital signs, wound problems, pain, and other patient complaints. Did the nurses assess the patient adequately and was the physician notified of adverse conditions and circumstances in a timely manner? The nurses' notes may be invaluable also for what is not written, as much as for what is written.

> Case Example 17.14: Several months postoperatively, a patient alleges that he suffered a stroke as a result of anesthesia administered during a thoracotomy. The anesthesia records do indicate a prolonged period of hypotension during the surgical procedure. However, the patient was hospitalized for several days postoperatively and there is no mention of any cognitive deficits or neurological signs and symptoms during this period of time by the nurses in notes that are extremely detailed and comprehensive.

Charting by exception (PIE charting) can be legally significant due to the information not on the chart. If a hospital's policy is that only exceptions will be charted in the detailed notes, then it is safe to assume that there were no exceptions if none appear. However, problems occur when a nurse does occasionally chart the routine along with the exceptions. If that is the pattern of a particular nurse's charting, it could be argued that he or she failed to observe and document whatever is not written out.

Discharge Instructions. JCAHO requires that hospitals make it clear to patients and their families what their responsibilities are regarding the patient's ongoing health care needs and gives them the knowledge and skills they need to carry out their responsibilities (JCAHO, 1996, PF.1.9). Review these instructions for appropriateness when a posthospital complication is in contention. Was the patient given reasonable instructions applicable to his diagnosis and treatment and did the patient comply with those instructions? For liability purposes, many health care facilities now require that the discharge instructions given to a patient by the nursing staff be documented and signed by the patient and the nurse discharging the patient.

Obstetrical Records

The LNC without special expertise in the field of obstetrical nursing can be at a distinct disadvantage in reviewing obstetrical records, as with anesthesia records. However, certain preliminary information can be determined easily. It may behoove the LNC to review the American College of Obstetrics and Gynecology's Educational Bulletins and Committee Opinions regarding the subject at hand prior to reviewing obstetrical records.

Prenatal Records. The prenatal records are of extreme importance in cases involving progressive problems such as gestational diabetes and others which become apparent or more serious at delivery. The prenatal records should include a good medical history of the mother including any prior pregnancies, family history of systemic diseases such as hypertension or genetic problems, an assessment of pelvic capacity, and progressive monitoring and management of the fetus throughout pregnancy. When the gestational age of the baby is in contention, check the dates of the last menstrual period against the fundal height measurements and any ultrasound testing for size done during the pregnancy. In cases involving complications from preeclampsia, look for trends in blood pressure, urine protein, and edema and how these problems were managed. Was the patient screened between 24 and 28 weeks for gestational diabetes? (ACOG, Dec., 1994.) Look for Group B beta streptococcal screening between 35 and 37 weeks in suspected neonatal sepsis cases. Was the patient seen frequently enough, especially in the last trimester and, if not, was this due to patient noncompliance? Determine if there were problems that became apparent after the record was faxed or sent to the hospital labor and delivery suite. If so, were the hospital nurses apprised of those problems?

Labor Records. The labor records contain graphic flow sheets which chart the numerous variables monitored during labor as well as narrative nurses' notes documenting the progress of labor and the patient's and fetus' response to it. Determine if vital signs were taken with sufficient frequency, especially in cases involving fetal sepsis and preeclampsia. Look at the assessments of uterine contractions, frequency, and quality in cases involving placental abruption and uterine rupture. Assess the manner in which any pitocin was administered. Was it given in a judicial dose and turned off in a timely manner. Judge whether the monitoring of the labor matches the fetal heart monitor strips, looking to see if the nurses made accurate assessments of the type of fetal heart rate patterns they were interpreting. Check the progress of labor on the Friedman curve. Did the station of the fetus and the dilation of the cervix move along the curve at a reasonable rate for a primigravida or multiparous patient? Was the physician or nurse midwife apprised of abnormalities in the labor progress in a timely manner? Did the physician or nurse midwife respond appropriately, given the situation?

Fetal Heart Monitor Strips. The fetal heart monitor strips can be the definitive documentation in an obstetrical case that proves or disproves the plaintiff's case. Special expertise is required to interpret these strips correctly. Fetal heart monitor strip interpretation is almost a science unto itself and the readers are encouraged to educate themselves regarding this prior to attempting independent interpretation. In cases where the labor records in and of themselves reflect a relatively normal delivery without evidence of negligence, the fetal heart monitor strips may have been erroneously interpreted by the health care providers. The initial fetal heart rate pattern should be carefully evaluated for the presence or absence of accelerations, decelerations, and abnormalities of the baseline. The presence of variability or variation of successive beats in the fetal heart rate is a useful indicator of fetal CNS integrity and may serve as an indicator of fetal response to hypoxia in the absence of maternal sedation or extreme prematurity. Prolonged decelerations of at least 60 to 90 seconds are always of concern and may be caused by virtually any mechanism that can lead to fetal hypoxia. When late decelerations become persistent, they are considered a nonreassuring pattern, regardless of the depth of the deceleration. Only when variable decelerations become persistent, progressively deeper, and longer lasting are they considered nonreassuring. A true sinusoidal (regular oscillation of the baseline resembling a sine wave) is always nonreassuring (ACOG, 1995, pp. 2–5). Fetal tachycardia may be an early indicator of maternal fever or it may be an early response to hypoxia.

Delivery Records. Delivery records are especially important in cases where the plaintiff alleges untimely or delayed delivery resulting in an asphyxiated baby or in cases involving birth trauma, such as Erb's palsy. Determine the exact amount of time which occurred between the recognition or appearance of fetal distress and the time of delivery, whether cesarean or vaginal. Was this time period and method of delivery reasonable given the presenting problems? In cases involving cephalopelvic disproportion and birth trauma, determine if the correct sequence of maneuvers was carried out to effect vaginal delivery. Ascertain the type of personnel present at the delivery and their role in the care of the patient and infant. In cases where a compromised infant is suspected, a neonatal nurse and a pediatrician are often necessary. Was the baby resuscitated properly and by whom? It is important to determine who actually made the Apgar assessment and whether or not the assessment was made for 1, 5, 10 minutes of age. In a case where hypoxic ischemic encephalopathy is alleged, the LNC should keep in mind that causation in such a case cannot be proved solely on the Apgar results. ACOG and the American Academy of Pediatrics have determined that profound metabolic or mixed acidemia (pH < 7.00), Apgar score of 0 to 3 for longer than 5 minutes, neonatal neurological manifestations such as seizures, coma, or hypotonia, and multisystem organ dysfunction are all demonstrated in the neonate who has had

asphyxia proximate to delivery which is severe enough to result in acute neurological injury (ACOG, July 1996, p. 2). Was the baby resuscitated appropriately
and by whom?

Review of Other Medical Records

Physician's Office Records

Physician's office records vary greatly from specialty to specialty. An internist who
has seen a patient for many years may have extensively documented medical
records, whereas an ophthalmologist may keep small index cards full of terms
and acronyms unfamiliar to those without ophthalmology training. For maximum
information to be extracted from these records, they, too, like hospital records,
must be logically sequenced.

The LNC should begin a review by determining how and why the patient
came to see the particular physician in question. Was there a referral by another
physician and what problems were specifically to be addressed? Did the physician complete a reasonable H&P examination given the nature of the problem?
Were the appropriate diagnostic studies ordered? Did the physician communicate
effectively with other health care providers concerning previous treatment
regimens or with proposed treatment regimens? Were consultations with other
specialists obtained in a timely manner and were the recommendations of those
specialists followed? Look for evidence of compliance on the part of the patient
with the treatment regimen prescribed? Analyze the types of drugs prescribed
for the patient as well as the amounts, duration, and possible interactions of
those drugs.

Many clues regarding the patient's lifestyle can often be obtained from physician's records that will not be evident in hospital records, e.g., drug abuse,
psychiatric problems, stressful family situations, and aberrant social behavior such
as domestic violence. The LNC should not overlook this type of information
because of its impact on damages for the plaintiff.

HMO Records

The LNC should approach review of HMO records similarly to those of physician's
records, since they are usually composed of a primary care physician's care and
treatment of a patient with consultations being obtained either "in-house" or
outside the HMO or health care network. Given the incentive HMOs have to cut
costs in health care delivery, the LNC should pay particular attention to the manner
in which consultations are managed, i.e., does it appear that a consultation was
obtained in a reasonable period of time? Were the appropriate diagnostic and
health maintenance tests (e.g., mammograms) ordered? Were abnormal diagnostic
test results investigated or followed? Since some HMOs require that their providers
limit the types of treatment for certain diagnoses, determine if the plaintiff was
given all reasonable options or choices for treatment currently available for the
patient's diagnosis.

Comparison of Allegations Made with the Medical Records

After systematic review of the medical records, the LNC should compare the complaints of the plaintiff (where there is no suit filed) or the allegations of the lawsuit to the medical records to determine consistency and/or to detect discrepancies from the medical records. Many well-meaning, but ill-informed, plaintiffs have drawn the wrong conclusions from their care and treatment experiences and the medical records may substantiate this. If the complaint has been filed, the defense LNC should use the medical records to assist in determining the validity of the plaintiff's case. Review of the medical records may indicate that the plaintiff's allegations do not parallel the actual medical negligence that occurred or the allegations may not even be focused on the proper potential defendant.

The LNC working for either the plaintiff or the defendant also identifies all alternative or potential causation theories and investigates the medical records for substantiation of these theories, in order to determine whether a case should be pursued by the plaintiff or, alternatively, vigorously defended or settled by the defendant.

> Case Example 17.15: In the case of the plaintiff alleging that her infant was brain damaged due to undiagnosed and/or untreated Group B beta streptococcal infection, the LNC would review the medical records for other causes of the infant's condition. Common causes of brain injury, such as prematurity, genetic or developmental abnormalies, or even other infections such as those caused by the TORCH organisms, would be looked for to explain the brain injury.

Re-review of the Medical Records

After initial review of the medical records and comparison with the allegations, especially in a complicated case, the central issues of the case will become clearer to the LNC. It is often helpful at this point to clarify some issues with the client, such as the timing of a certain symptom or the effect a surgical complication has had the client's life. A physician defendant could be asked why certain notes were made and their meaning. A preliminary medical literature review may also be helpful in clarifying natural history and pathogenesis of a disease or outlining information necessary to prove causation. In order to conduct a thorough medical records analysis, however, it is often necessary to re-review the medical records a second time, taking note of specific facts relevant to the case. The LNC should use these specifics to generate a written report as detailed later in this chapter.

Altered Medical Records

Altered medical records can be used by the plaintiff to establish liability based on the defendant's conscious wrongdoing. Juries do not respond favorably to intentional record alteration and exposing such actions often leads to punitive damages being awarded. Additionally, falsification of medical records can be the basis for criminal indictment as well as for civil liability for damages suffered (Pozgar, 1996). If the plaintiff can prove that the defendant altered the medical records early on in the case, most insurance companies will negotiate strongly to settle the case.

Numerous types of alterations can be made to medical records. The LNC should be suspicious of any alteration to the medical records and alert the attorney to the suspected nature and validity of the alterations.

Late Entries

The most common alteration is that of the late entry. Hospitals usually have policies and procedures for entering later entries into the record. If the case is in litigation, and if a late entry exists, the LNC should obtain a copy of that policy. Ideally, the entry should clearly state the time and date when the late entry was written and the time and date to which the late entry refers. It is up to the LNC to determine the validity of the entry based on the context.

Case Example 17.16: Late entries are commonly seen on code sheets or narratives concerning codes. A late entry written 1 hour after the fact concerning the administration of several drugs during the course of a code may be considered a legitimate late entry. However, if the late entry occurs several hours or days later and has extreme detail about the patient being monitored closely prior to the arrest when there are other reports in the chart that the patient was cyanotic when found with the pulse oximeter turned off, the LNC should raise questions about the entry.

Falsified Entries

Falsification of records is illegal and physicians and nurses can be indicted and criminally prosecuted for such activity, although this is rarely done. Falsified entries include those that are backdated or changed at a later date. Detecting falsified entries demands a high level of attention on the part of the LNC and requires that the entire record be heavily scrutinized for supporting information if the falsified entries are to be proved to have occurred.

Case Example 17.17: Consider the case of a baby with hypoxic ischemic encephalopathy where the initial Apgar score, recorded by the doctor, was 3, 6, and 7, a finding considered by ACOG and the American Academy of Pediatrics (ACOG, July 1996) not to be consistent with a perinatal insult. The delivery record reflected that no cord blood was sent to the laboratory. Yet, the baby required intubation, had early seizure activity, and multiple organ damage. One might suspect that the Apgar score was fabricated but there would be no way to prove this. The physician, however, came back several months later and entered a cord blood pH form in the chart, listing the cord pH as 7.26. The date of the delivery was 6/15, but the date of the cord pH was listed as 9/15. The discovery of this falsified entry was critical in convincing a jury that the Apgar score had also been falsified.

Fabricated Medical Records

Fabrication of medical records can be equally as damaging as falsifying entries. Fabrication occurs when a physician or other health care provider invents a set of circumstances, usually in retrospect, in order to justify the outcome of some of his or her actions.

Case Example 17.18: In a case involving an unnecessary hysterectomy in a peri-menopausal woman, the physician dictated for the hospital chart a history of hypermenorrhea and dysmenorrhea which had been increasing over a period of many months and had been unresponsive to hormone therapy. This history, with varying degrees of severity was found in several areas of the hospital chart. The physician's diagnosis was severe endometriosis and adenomyosis. However, the referring physician's records revealed that the patient had had no menstrual period for several months and had been referred for left lower abdominal pain. No conservative therapy was even entertained and the patient was taken to the operating room for hysterectomy 2 days after the initial consultation. The operative report and the pathology report showed no evidence of endometriosis or adenomyosis and the uterus was of normal size. The case was settled due to the obvious nature of the fabrication of the medical records indicating the necessity for the operation.

Fabrication of the medical records also includes rewriting and replacing notes in the chart. Physician's office records are the easiest to fabricate. New sheets can be added to the chart or copied over. The dictated notes may be inserted to replace handwritten ones which are then discarded entirely. A whole new chart can be started and the original destroyed. Liquid correction fluid can be used on undesirable content and then the original photocopied. A common fabricated condition in the medical record is that of adhesions. A bowel or bladder perforation will be diagnosed postoperatively and the surgeon will then begin the second operative note discussing the numerous severe adhesions which were present during the first operation (which are not identified in the first operative note) and how the adhesions made the first surgery difficult.

Rewriting and replacing hospital progress or other health care provider notes is most commonly seen in catastrophic situations such as cardiac arrests or acute situations in a hospital, leading to the patient's untimely death, such as acute and severe unrecognized postoperative surgical bleeding or progressive respiratory problems after anesthesia.

Destroyed Records or Medical Evidence

Destruction of medical records or evidence includes loss and concealment of relevant X-rays, laboratory tests, and other evidence such as pathology slides and operative videotapes. The loss or concealment or actual destruction may occur at the time of a potentially legally damaging incident or injury or at some later point when the health care provider feels as though he or she is about to become a defendant.

Omissions

Intentional omission of a true entry or prevention of making a true entry, while not a written act, does constitute an altered record because the record fails to reflect accurately the care given to and the response of the patient.

Illegible Entries

While illegible entries are rarely negligence *per se*, the interpretation of illegible entries may contribute to negligence on the part of others.

Case Example 17.9: A 5-year-old child who was given ten times the dose of a chemotherapy drug because the physician wrote the chemotherapy orders haphazardly. The pharmacist who filled the prescription and the nurses who administered the chemotherapy did not check the mathematics for the appropriate dose per kilogram of that drug prior to administering it. The child suffered an overwhelming bone marrow depression and died of the consequences.

How to Identify Potentially Altered Records

Identification of altered records requires a high degree of attention and a fair amount of skepticism on the part of the LNC. Recognition of the following findings can be the first step in proving record alteration:

- Long defensive narrations of facts that do not appear to be in sequence with the remainder of the medical record
- Pages that are written without the patient's stamp plate in one of the corners
- Notes that are written with the wrong date or time and may not correlate with the remainder of the chart
- Additions to the notes/orders or dictated summaries that are on the edge of the page
- Additions made with a different ink or pen (sometimes this is hard to determine without looking at the original record)
- Laboratory records reflecting tests not done when orders and physician notes reflect that the test was ordered
- Handwritten notes that are written over the top of another previous writing
- A series of separate notes by any health care practitioner that encompass a long period of time but are written one after the other with times in sequence in a seemingly homogeneous handwriting pattern
- Medical bill charges for diagnostic or laboratory tests, medications, or equipment not referenced or seen in the chart
- Pathology or diagnostic findings which do not correlate with the H&P or stated need for a surgical or diagnostic procedure

Minimizing Medical Record Alteration, Loss, or Concealment

When evaluating cases from a plaintiff's perspective and looking for critical evidence, it is often wise to obtain the critical evidence or copies of the same, with a minimum of fanfare at the earliest time possible. It is wise to have the plaintiff obtain a copy of his or her own medical records as opposed to having an attorney officially write for them. This may reduce the possibility of alteration, loss, or concealment of potentially important evidence. The evidence should be conveyed in the safest manner possible, such as hand delivery by courier or another method whereby the package can be tracked.

If the LNC suspects medical record alteration or tampering, the hiring of a document examiner should be recommended to the attorney. Document examiners use a myriad of techniques which can determine, among many things, if all of writing on a page was made at the same time and whether handwritings and pen inks match.

Summary of the Medical Records

Determine Type of Analysis Necessary to Summarize Medical Records

The *AALNC Standards of Practice* require that the LNC identify the desired outcome of his or her work product as related to the health care issues of a case or claim (AALNC, 1995c). When performing medical record analysis, the LNC should identify the type of analysis necessary to convey the most accurate and complete summary of the medical records that the case requires. Obviously, different types of medical/legal cases require different types of analyses.

Chronologies of Events

A chronology should refer the reader to the exact location in the medical records of all the information presented. This can be accomplished by referring to the date and type of entry or by page number of the entry if the records are paginated. As such, an overwhelming amount of information can be simplified into a manageable sequence of events. Chronologies can be extremely useful in outlining a minimum of events to assist an attorney in understanding a sequence of events in a patient's history.

Alternatively, a chronology can encompass a myriad of details concerning the patient's medical history and treatment (see Appendix 17.4) and can be a very useful tool throughout discovery and even in the trial of the case. However, during the course of discovery, additional facts concerning the plaintiff's medical history may become known or additional theories of liability developed which the original chronology does not address. Therefore, it is wise to date the chronology and update it from time to time as additional facts become known. Appendix 17.4 illustrates the medical history of a baby with complex respiratory problems who was being weaned from paralyzing drugs after a tracheotomy and suffered a respiratory and cardiac arrest.

This author has taken chronologies one step further in certain cases to include deposition testimony. This approach works well when the medical records are sketchy on details, yet there is an abundance of deposition testimony reflecting timing (such as in anesthesia-related case) or dates.

Obviously, if done correctly, chronologies such as these prove extremely useful during discovery and at trial in clarifying and delineating sequences of events and actions. The LNC and the attorney, or any other legal professional, should be cautioned in relying on chronologies in place of the medical record itself, since the chronology is useful only to the extent that it includes *all* relevant information regarding the plaintiff's medical records.

Charts and Graphs

In some cases, the most effective summary of medical information can be made in the form of a chart or time line which will immediately communicate important facts of the case. A chart/graph may be as simple as an inventory of laboratory results or it may be more complicated graphic representations of certain facts in a case. Figure 17.1 involves a woman with familial hyperlipidemia who was given subcutaneous estrogen pellets after a hysterectomy and oophorectomy. Her physician then gave her a prescription for Estrace to be taken *prn* in addition to the estrogen pellets, which the plaintiffs alleged to have caused extreme hypertriglyceridemia resulting in severe acute hemorrhagic pancreatitis. Charts such as these can be used to incorporate a modicum of relevant events and actions and illustrate alleged cause and effect on some aspect of the patient's well-being, as in this case with the triglyceride level and the development of pancreatitis.

Summaries

A short summary or outline of the facts of a case may be all that is necessary or wanted by an attorney, especially in a relatively simple medical malpractice or personal injury case. A plaintiff's attorney who is screening a case to decide if the attorney wants to pursue it further will most likely want a brief summary that he or she can use to make decisions regarding the next step. The LNC's recommendations regarding the merits of the case should accompany this summary and will be useful to the attorney in the screening process. Personal injury attorneys usually have a large number of less complex cases and need the basics of who, what, when, where, and how from the medical records instead of meticulous physiological and standard of care detail. Their interest is the effects of an accident or event on the client compared to the client's preexisting condition.

A defense attorney may want to use a short narrative type of summary in planning how to initially approach a case or when communicating with the insurance carrier, but will want an extensive time line or chronology once the case is well in progress. Medical negligence cases usually require more-extensive detail because the focus is on medical and/or nursing judgment and whether or not the professionals involved complied with the standard of care.

Alternatively, the attorney may have a good understanding of the facts of the case but want the LNC's input in determining discrepancies or problem points in the medical records (see Appendix 17.5). In this situation, the LNC may want to provide an objective summary which discusses the facts of the case but adds the LNC's subjective comments, always in parentheses, to assist the attorney in understanding the context of the medical record findings and follow-up recommendations. Appendix 17.5 is an example of such a summary of a case involving a young man who was hospitalized in a small rural hospital after a motor vehicle accident. He was admitted for observation with abdominal pain. Less than 12 hours later, he developed severe septic shock from a ruptured stomach and died the following day.

While there are many different LNC approaches and attorney preferences to medical record summaries, most attorneys want to read an analysis that not only gives a concise overview of the facts and issues, but helps them to understand the bottom line quickly. With this approach, the LNC can begin with a conclusory paragraph followed by substantiation of those facts and opinions. This could include review of the medical records in relationship to the issues in contention in the case, as well as the standard of care (in a medical malpractice case) and the current medical literature on the subject.

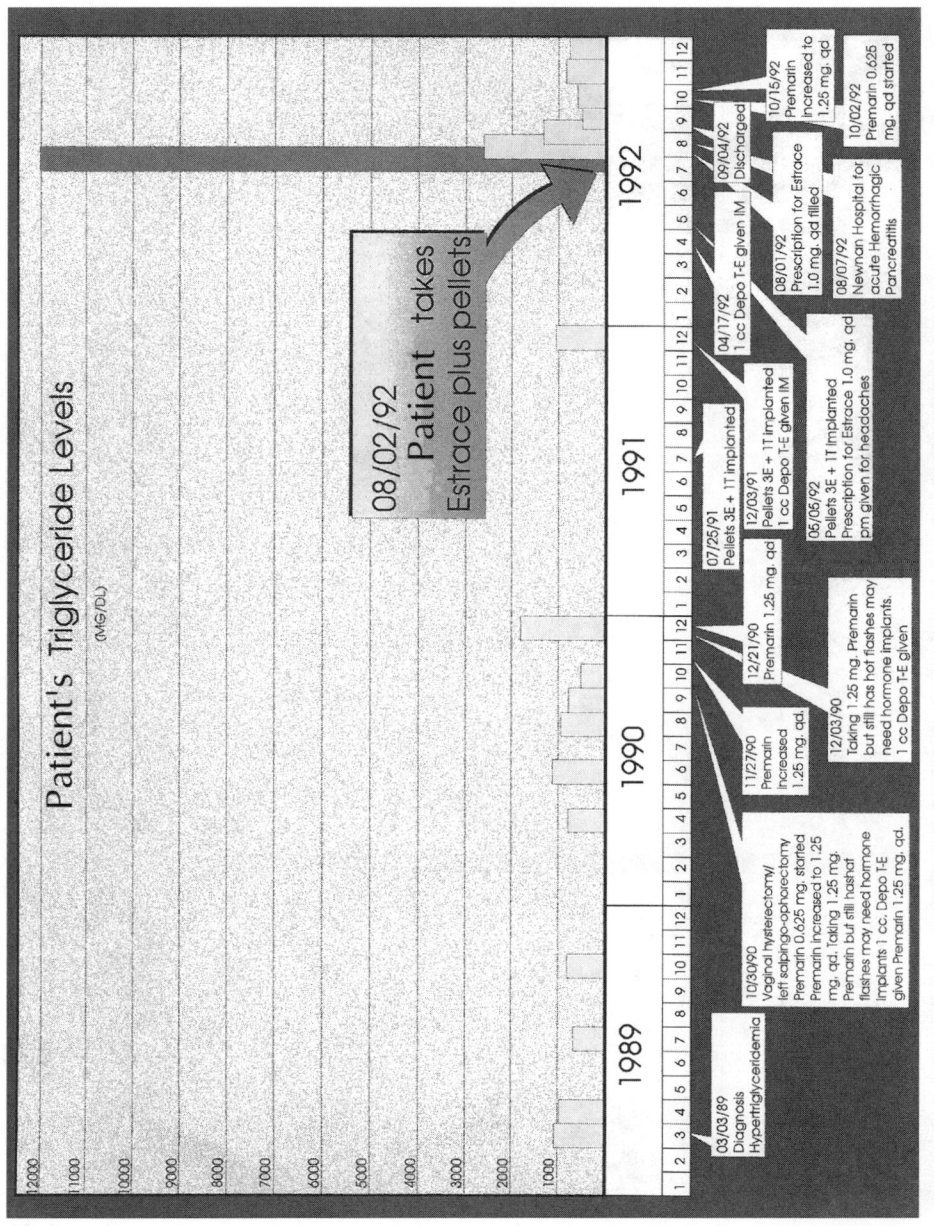

Figure 17.1 Graph illustrating an alleged effect of estrogen on triglyceride levels.

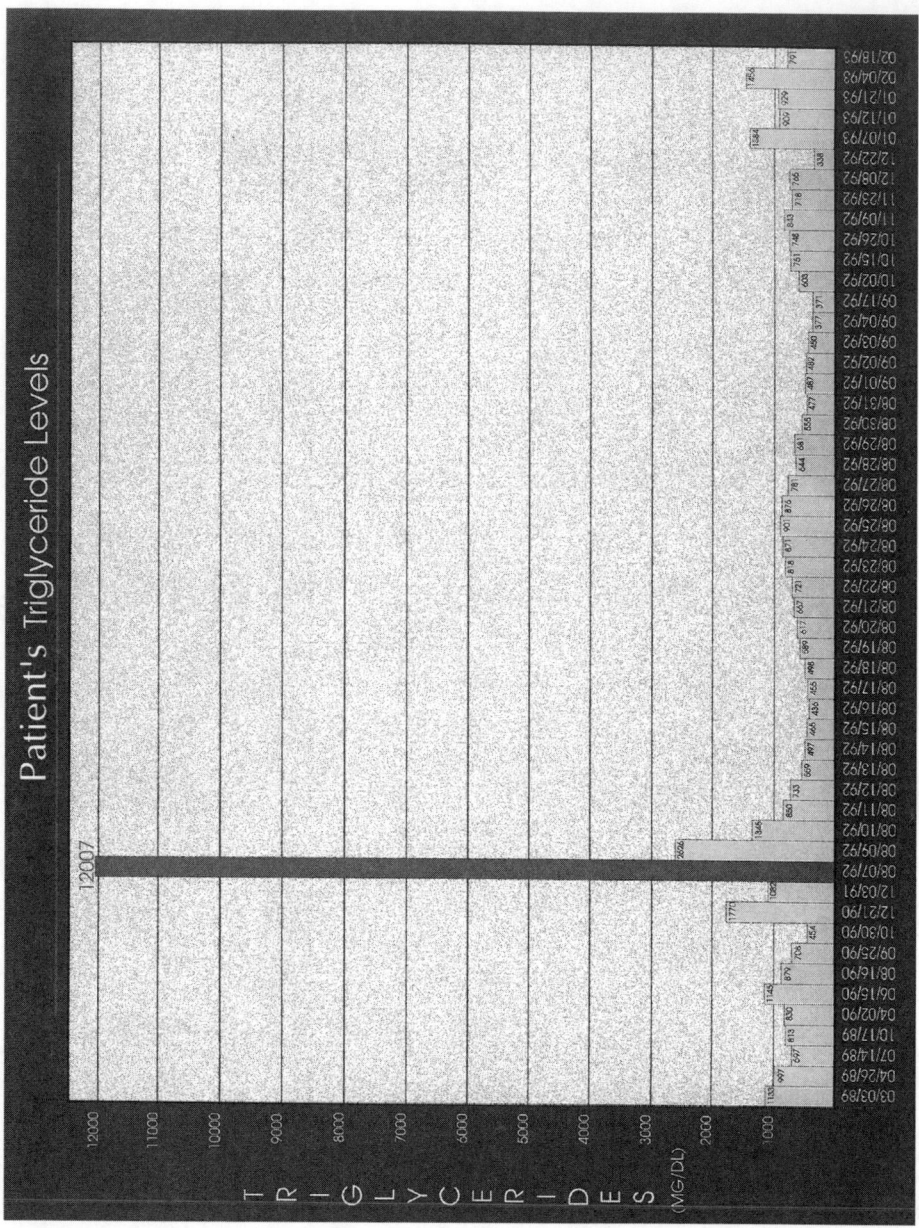

Figure 17.1 (continued)

Some summaries require total adherence to chronological order to understand. In such cases, the date and time of the care provided would be of great importance. Other types of cases require that each health care provider's care be summarized chronologically and separately so that the attorney can see exactly what kind of treatment each health care provider rendered to the plaintiff. Yet another type of summary can be done in cases where there are multiple injuries or trauma. The records can be very briefly summarized by injury so that the attorney can quickly see the progress of each injury from the acute event through rehabilitation and final outcome. Each health care provider's records are reviewed specifically for that portion which addresses the specific injury or diagnosis.

An in-depth summary of the medical records may best be accomplished in narrative style, putting together all the records from various health care providers in chronological order or summarizing each separately. The most comprehensive approach to a medical records summary is a formulation which not only encompasses the facts of the case as reflected in the various medical records, but also an objective analysis of the implications for the attorney and the client and, in a medical malpractice or even a product liability case, an analysis of the standard of care issues involved (see Appendix 17.6).

Whenever providing subjective commentary in any type of medical records summary, the LNC is cautioned to label the summary as "confidential attorney work product specifically requested by (the attorney in question)" so as to minimize the possibility for discovery in an adverse situation. The LNC is also advised to be knowledgeable concerning local discovery rules and recent court rulings regarding LNC work product in his or her state.

Pitfalls in Medical Record Analysis

LNCs must provide professional services with objectivity, free of personal prejudice and conflict of interest (AALNC, 1995a). It is difficult to set aside personal bias in providing analysis to medical records. LNCs who have always participated in litigation from the plaintiff's side may lose their objectivity regarding what constitutes reasonable behavior and standard of care on the part of defendants. On the other hand, many LNCs who have never worked on a plaintiff's case develop a pervasive feeling that plaintiffs are "in it for the money" and are not really injured that badly. These biases must be overcome in order to provide a professional and objective work product.

As the LNC gains experience, bias should become less of a problem. An LNC working for a plaintiff's attorney will always look for the defense of the case as he or she is evaluating the facts supporting the plaintiff's case, even if the negligence is obvious. Were there coexisting factors that contributed to the injury? Did the plaintiff contribute to the injury (important in some states where contributory negligence affects jury awards)? Was the injury a known risk of the procedure? When reviewing a defense case, review the allegations and determine if there is substantiation for them in the medical records and other evidence. Is the defendant's documentation complete and professional? Were all the mandated policies followed? Always look for defenses in a plaintiff's case and for facts supporting the plaintiff in a defense case. The LNC should apprise the attorney of all the known strengths and weaknesses of the case that are evident in the medical record.

The LNC should not purport to be competent in matters in which he or she has limited knowledge or experience (AALNC, 1995a). This is also of great importance in medical records analysis. When analyzing medical records in a case involving complications from a relatively new surgical or diagnostic procedure, the LNC may not have the expertise to evaluate the complications properly, even after consulting standard texts and the medical literature. In cases such as these, the LNC must consult a medical specialist in that field prior to rendering an opinion or inform the attorney of his or her limitations in that area. Providing inaccurate or inadequate medical analysis yields an inferior work product which will ultimately affect the LNC's professional reputation.

Of paramount importance in medical record analysis is the ability to address the central issue of the case in a quick and decisive manner. An LNC may use information collected from the plaintiff or defendant for this purpose. This basic step will prevent the LNC from focusing on issues not central to the reason for the review. Ultimately, this wastes the LNC's time and the client's money and may even lead to the wrong conclusions regarding the case. If a case is in litigation, it is always advisable for the LNC working for either the plaintiff or the defendant to review the allegations of the complaint. The LNC working for the plaintiff may be able to advise the attorney that the attorney missed a major point of the case or did not include all the allegations. An LNC working for the defense may review the medical records based on the allegations of the complaint and immediately determine that the plaintiffs have no actual basis for a case at all.

One of the biggest mistakes an LNC can make is to fail to review the entire record when it is necessary to get a complete overview for causation, liability, and/or damages. One should obviously review as much of the medical records as is necessary to make a determination as to causation, liability, and/or damages, but it takes practice to know how much will be required to be thorough. The LNC may feel constrained by an attorney or insurance company reacting negatively to "excessive" time being billed for such a review, yet, missing critical details will not be beneficial to the attorney's workup and resolution of the case, not to mention the LNC's reputation.

When a medical record is illegible, do not guess regarding its content. It is advisable to leave a "_____" in the summary or a (?) so that the author can be questioned further regarding the entry during a deposition. If the handwriting is legible but the copy is of extremely poor quality, insist that the health care provider or attorney provide a legible copy or permit review of the original medical record.

Overlooking missing or fraudulent records is another pitfall in medical records analysis. Detection of missing and altered records has been discussed previously in this chapter. The fraud may be very skillfully accomplished so as not to be easily determined. A high degree of suspicion must be entertained in order to make such determinations. (See Section on Altered Medical Records.)

Reviewing the records too hastily will also prevent a superior work product by potentially missing important points in the record. Again, there may be pressure to "get through" the material for independent consultants who are being paid by the hour and also for those who bill insurance companies for their work. Ethical principles require that LNCs perform their work with the highest degree of integrity (AALNC, 1995c) and, as such, one must learn to balance the outside financial constraints with the pursuit of a superior work product.

Finally, LNCs must overcome the temptation to tell the attorney/client what he or she wants to hear. Not only would this be unethical and dishonest, it would do undeserved harm to other parties. Instead, a thorough and competent medical record analysis will list the strengths and weaknesses of the client's position. The medical record summary/analysis should always be followed with conclusions and recommendations to assist the attorney in determining how he or she wishes to then proceed.

Summary

Medical record analysis is the cornerstone of LNC practice. The successful and effective LNC will approach the compilation, organization, review, and analysis of the medical records with complete objectivity, providing his or her clients with medical record analyses which are thorough and pertinent to the relevant case.

References

American Association of Legal Nurse Consultants (1995a). *AALNC Code of Professional and Ethical Conduct,* Glenview, IL, American Association of Legal Nurse Consultants.

American Association of Legal Nurse Consultants (1995b). *AALNC Scope of Practice for the Legal Nurse Consultant,* Glenview, IL, American Association of Legal Nurse Consultants.

American Association of Legal Nurse Consultants (1995c). *AALNC Standards of Practice,* Glenview, IL, American Association of Legal Nurse Consultants.

American College of Obstetrics and Gynecology (1994). Diabetes and pregnancy, *ACOG Educational Bulletins,* 200, 1–8.

American College of Obstetrics and Gynecology (1995.) Fetal heart rate patterns: monitoring, interpretation and management, *ACOG Educational Bulletins,* 207, 1–9.

American College of Obstetrics and Gynecology (1996.) Prevention of early-onset group B streptococcal disease in newborns, *ACOG Committee Opinion,* 173, 1–8.

American College of Obstetrics and Gynecology (1996.) Use and abuse of Apgar score, *ACOG Committee Opinion,* 174, 1–3.

American College of Radiology (1995). *Standards,* Reston, VA, American College of Radiology.

American Society of Anesthesiologists (1995). *Standards, Guidelines and Statements,* Park Ridge, IL, American Society of Anesthesiologists.

Dewitt, R. E., (1996). Patient information and confidentiality, in *Treatise on health care Law,* New York, Matthew Bender, 1–131.

Hirsh, H. L. (1995). Medical records, in American College of Legal Medicine, *Legal Medicine,* 3rd ed., St. Louis, MO, Mosby-Year Book, 297–311.

Janulis, D. M. (1990). Medical records, in *Medical Malpractice,* New York, Matthew Bender & Co., 35.1–35.66.

Joint Commission on Accreditation of Healthcare Organizations (1996). *1996 Accreditation Manual for Hospitals: Standards,* Oakbrook Terrace, IL, Joint Commission on Accreditation of Health care Organizations.

Pozgar, G. D. (1996). Information management and health care records, in *Legal Aspects of Health care Administration,* 6th ed., Gaithersburg, MD, Aspen Publishers, Inc.

Roach, W., Jr. (1994). *Medical Records and the Law,* 2nd ed., Frederick, MD, Aspen Publishers, Inc.

Sartwelle, T. P. (1994). Malpractice in nursing homes, in *AALNC Fifth Annual Conference Syllabus,* Chicago, IL, American Association of Legal Nurse Consultants.

Appendix 17.1
Certification

I hereby certify that the attached is a true and complete copy of the medical records pertaining to _____ (patient) kept in the office of _____ (health care practitioner) in my custody and that I am the custodian and keeper of said records.

I further certify that said records were made in the regular course of business of this office and that it was in the regular course of business for such records to be made at the time of events, transactions or occurrences to which they refer or within a reasonable time thereafter.

Signed this ____ day of _____, 199__.

_____
CUSTODIAN OF MEDICAL RECORDS

Sworn and subscribed to before me on this
the ___ day of _____, 199__.

_____
NOTARY PUBLIC
My commission Expires: _____

Appendix 17.2
Sequences of Hospital Records

Adult	*Pregnancy*	*Baby*
Face Sheet	Face Sheet	Face Sheet
Consents	Consents	Consents
Autopsy	Autopsy	Autopsy
Death Summary	Death Summary	Death Summary
Discharge Summary	Discharge Summary	Discharge Summary
Emergency Medical Services	Emergency Record	Labor Summary
History and Physical	Prenatal Record	Resuscitation Record
Consultations	Labor Admission H/P	Emergency Record
M.D. Progress Notes	Labor Record	History and Physical
Code Sheets	Obstetrical Anesthesia Record	Consultations
Anesthesia Reports	Delivery Record	Operative Reports
Operative Reports	Obstetrical Operative Report	M.D. Progress Notes
Radiology	Consultations	Radiology
EEGs	M.D. Progress Notes	EEGs
EKGs	Code Sheets	EKGs
Laboratory	Anesthesia Records	Laboratory
ABGs	Operative Reports	ABGs
M.D. Orders	Radiology	M.D. Orders
Respiratory Therapy	EEGs	Respiratory Therapy
Physical Therapy	EKGs	Physical Therapy
Occupational Therapy	Laboratory	Occupational Therapy
Speech Therapy	ABGs	Speech Therapy
Social Worker Notes	M.D. Orders	Social Work Notes
Dialysis	Respiratory Therapy	Graphics
Graphics	Physical Therapy	Medications
Medications	Occupational Therapy	IV Fluids/Medications
IV Fluids/Medications	Speech Therapy	Nursing Assessment
Nursing Assessment	Social Worker Notes	Nursing Care Plans
Nursing Care Plans	Dialysis	I.C.U. Notes
I.C.U. Notes	Graphics	R.N. Notes
R.N. Notes	Medications	Nursing Discharge Planning
Nursing Discharge Planning	IV Fluids/Medications	Nursing Discharge Summary
Nursing Discharge Summary	Nursing Assessment	
	Nursing Care Plans	
	I.C.U. Notes	
	R.N. Notes	
	Nursing Discharge Planning	
	Nursing Discharge Summary	

Sequence of Physician or HMO Records

Office Notes	Hospital Records
Consultations	Consents
Radiology	General Correspondence
Laboratory	Financial Records
Other Diagnostic Tests	

Appendix 17.3
Sample Index

HARRIET SMITH
MEDICAL RECORDS
VOLUME I OF II

A. Daniel Binder, M.D. (OB/Gyn)
3/6/59–7/5/94
1. Office Notes/mammograms
2. Laboratory

B. John Henry, M.D. (Family Practitioner)
4/17/89–5/30/95
3. Office Notes
4. X-ray/Laboratory
5. Echocardiograms/EKGs

C. Michael Tillman, M.D. (OB/Gyn)
8/1/94–4/3/95

D. Northpointe Breast Care Center
8/3/94

E. Larry Goldstein, M.D. (Surgeon)
9/21/94 –6/29/95

F. Dodge County Hospital
3/2/95

G. Northpointe Medical Center
3/16/95

H. Kevin Robards, Jr., M.D. (Oncologist)
3/23/95–11/27/95

Appendix 17.4
Medical Records Chronology

MEMORANDUM

TO: William A. Todd, Esq.

FROM: Sally H. Davidson, RN, BSN
        Legal Nurse Consultant

DATE: July 21, 1996

RE: MASON v. COATES et al.
        Chronology of the medical records concerning events on 11/19/95 sur-
        rounding the weaning of baby Mason from a ventilator after receiving
        paralyzing agents post tracheotomy

_____
_____
_____
_____

Date/Time	Location (in Records)	Narrative
11/19/95		
0536 am	ABG X-ray	pH 7.45, pCO_2 36, pO_2 51, BE 2.3, O_2 sat 87% CXR Left lower lobe basilar atelectasis persists with no significant clearing compared to 11/18/95. No significant change in the appearance of the chest.
0800	Vent Flow Sht	RR 19, HR 140 Work of breathing easy, breath sounds coarse, chest rise good, color pink FIO_2 0.33, PEEP +4, IMV 17 Pulse oximeter 97%, end tidal CO_2 38 R. Guenther, RRT
1000	MD Notes	Pulmonary: Respiratory stable — pediatric #1 trach On IMV 17, FIO_2 0.33, IMV mode; T 96.4, HR 120–127, RR 17 Good chest excursion, clear breath sounds O_2 sat 96–97%, pO_2 51–56, pCO_2 36–38, pH 7.44–7.45 CXR — diffuse atelectasis left lower lobe Assess: Subglottic/laryngeal obstruction, new tracheostomy Plan: Will lift paralysis following radiological evaluation of femoral catheter. Discussed with Drs. Wilson and Myers. Coates, M.D.
	Vent Flow Sht	RR 18, HR 124; Pulse oximeter 97%; aerosol treatment R. Guenther, RRT
1006	ABG	pH 7.38, pCO_2 45, pO_2 71, BE 1.4, O_2 sat 93.5%
1010	MD Orders	1. Stat AP and lateral view of abdomen — take film directly to Dr. Abre 2. To fluoro as needed to establish location of catheter tip 3. D/C Norcuron when position of catheter tip confirmed. 4. When paralysis lifts, change vent to SIMV, pre____ support, use 10 cm psv level Coates, M.D.

1135	Vent Flow Sht	Pulse oximeter 93%; FIO$_2$ increased to 0.35 R. Guenther, RRT
1145	ICU Notes	Dr. Sink paged per Dr. Coates G. Lillian, RN
1200	ICU Flow Sht	Fentanyl 8 mcg/ml @ 1 cc/hr Norcuron 1 mg/ml @ 1 cc/hr
1230	Vent Flow Sht	RR 20, HR 128; FIO$_2$ 0.35 R. Guenther, RRT
1245	ICU Notes	Dr. Sink here
1300	ICU Flow Sht	Fentanyl 8 mcg/ml @ 1 cc/hr Norcuron 1 mg/ml @ 1 cc/hr
1305	ABG	pH 7.44, pCO$_2$ 38, pO$_2$ 56, BE 2.4, O$_2$ sat 95%
1400	MD Orders	Isovue dye study of central venous catheter position in x-ray department (done) Sink, M.D.
	ICU Flow Sht	Fentanyl 8 mcg/ml @ 1 cc/hr Norcuron 1 mg/ml @ 1 cc/hr
1430	ICU Notes MD Notes	Patient transferred back to ICU. Vital signs stable. Pediatric Surgery: Left femoral venous catheter is in left common femoral vein by Isovue contrast study via catheter proximal and distal ports suitable for medications and dilute HAF. Sink, M.D.
1500	ICU Flow Sht	T 96.2 ax, HR 124, RR 19, BP 94/52, Mean 66, pulses 3+, <2 sec capillary refill Respiratory effort — IMV only; Breath sounds equal and coarse Color pink, warm and dry skin Activity — None; Norc ___ d/c'ed; Glasgow coma scale 10/15 Position — Supine, 2 upper extremity restraints FIO2 33% via trach, tidal volume 115, 4 cm. PEEP, IMV 17/minute, pulse ox 99%
	ICU Flow Sht	Fentanyl 8 mcg/ml @ 1 cc/hr Norcuron 1 mg/ml @ 1 cc/hr
	ICU Notes	Report given to C. Hauten, RN. Pt left attended. G. Lillian, RN

1530	ICU notes	Patient received. __ 9 mo old baby — baby in open crib with sides up. Upper extremities restrained on ____ ____ via trach settings per flow sheet. On cardiac/resp. mon-itor and pulse oximeter with alarms set. Central venous line in left groin with maintenance fluids at 33 cc/hour. Other ports clamped. Fentanyl drip at 0.5 cc/hr via peri-pheral IV (PIV) in right foot. Site without redness or swell-ing. Scalp PIV intact, clamped. Baby remains sedated at this time. No spontaneous respirations riding vent — Foley patent to bedside bag. Nasogastric to LIS. Parents at bedside. C. Hauten, RNC
1526	MD Orders	Decrease Fentanyl to 0.5 cc/hr T.O. Dr. Coates / L. March, RN
1532	ABG	pH 7.48, pCO_2 33, pO_2 65, BE 2.7, O_2 sat 94%
1600	Vent Flow Sht	FIO_2 decreased to 0.30 R. Guenther, RRT
	ICU Flow Sht	HR 122, RR 21/minute, BP 119/80, mean 96, pulses 3+, respiratory effort spontaneous, breath sounds very coarse and rhonchous Skin pink and warm and dry; Glasgow coma scale 10/15 Position — Supine with 2 upper extremity restraints FIO_2 decreased to 30%, TV 115 with PEEP 4 cm. IMV at 17/minute, O_2 saturation 98% Suctioned via ETT tube C. Hauten, RNC
	ICU Flow Sht	Fentanyl 8 mcg/ml decreased to 0.5 cc/hr Norcuron 1 mg/ml turned OFF
	ICU Notes	Baby moving, opening eyes, fussy. IMV decreased to 15 and FIO_2 decreased to 30%. See flow sheet for P.E. C. Hauten, RNC
1630	Vent Flow Sht	RR 22, HR 124 Work of breathing easy, breath sounds coarse, chest rise good, color pink FIO_2 0.30; IMV decreased to 15/minute Pulse oximeter 99%, end tidal CO_2 36 R. Guenther, RRT
1700	ICU Flow Sht	Temp 97.2 ax, HR 122 IMV decreased to 15/minute
	ICU Flow Sht	Fentanyl 8 mcg/ml @ 0.5 cc/hr Norcuron — OFF

1800	ICU Flow Sht	Temp 98.4 ax, HR 155, RR 22
		Skin pink and warm and dry
		Activity ++ 15 (??); Glasgow coma scale 10/15
		Pupils are equal and reactive to light
		Patient supine with 2 upper extremity restraints
		FIO_2 0.30, TV 115 with 4 cm. PEEP. IMV 15/minute
		C. Hauten, RNC

	ICU Flow Sht	Fentanyl 8 mcg/ml @ 0.5 cc/hr
		Norcuron — OFF
	ICU Notes	In process of doing vital signs, respiratory therapist doing respiratory therapy. Baby became extremely agitated. Thrashing head, crying, flailing arms, legs. Sats 88–92 — bagging but no chest rise with manual bagging, unable to auscultate bagged breath sounds. Dr. Coates here, made aware of baby's agitation. Before able to place on trach collar per Dr. Coates, baby began to desat, color became mottled, unable to ventilate; baby became very stiff, dusky to blue. 1810 Dr. Coates in unit — called to bedside; attempted to reinsert trach, then to intubate; 2.5 ETT placed per Dr. Coates, but unable to get chest rise. HR decreased, sats 0. At this time, 1815, other MDs here and other nursing staff and RTs at bedside and CPR begun. Refer to code blue sheet for remainder of code.
		C. Hauten, RNC

1815	Code Sheet	Medication nurse Sallie Wentworth, RN
		Physician in charge Dr.
		Recorder Lisa Pento, RN
		Also attending code: Drs. Peters, Sink, and Coates
		HR 0, BP 0; Pulse strength 0/4
		4 cc. Epinephrine; CPR in progress
	Disch Sum	The child was maintained sedated and paralyzed. He was stable until 11/19/95. At that time, while emerging from the sedation and paralysis, the child had a cardiac arrest and there was a question of displacement of the tracheostomy tube. Other considerations were that the child had a pneumothorax, after severe bronchospasm. The exact etiology of this event never was entirely clear. The child was resuscitated and chest tubes were placed.
		Sedgewick, M.D.

	Consultation	(Scallion — 11/28/95) "At that time, shortly after Norcuron had worn off, the child self-removed the airway. Cardiopulmonary arrest resulted and the child was without heart rate for some 15 minutes...
		Scallion, M.D.

18__	Code Sheet	HR 112, BP 96/36, RR Bagging
		10 mEq NaHCO$_3$
		Pulse strength 0/4 thready; O$_2$ sat 80%

MD Notes

Pediatric ICU Note:
Asked by Dr. Coates to assume care. Joined in code which occurred while I was in ICU at 2–3 minutes into CPR. Child reportedly became cyanotic/agitated after Nor-curon d/c'ed today. No chest movement with bagging. 2.5 ET placed by Dr. Coates with no improvement, trach replaced by Dr. Sink with pull strings retracted, clean visualization of trachea; resp — no improvement.
Jenkins, M.D.

| 1818 | Code Sheet | Pulse strength 1+/4; HR 88 (femoral) |

| 1820 | Code Sheet | No heart rate; O$_2$ sat 87% |
| | | 10 mEq NaHCO$_3$, 4 cc epinephrine, 1.5 cc CaCl$_2$ |

| 1822 | Code Sheet | Pulse strength 1+/4; BP 94/52, 67 mean; no HR without compressions |

| 1824 | Code Sheet | Pulse strength 1+/4; HR only with CPR |
| | | 3.0 OETT per Dr. Peters |

MD Notes

Pulmonary (written at 1940):
Was called to see patient this evening because of acute O$_2$ desaturation. This occurred concurrent with awakening from paralysis/sedation. Within 30 seconds, patient clearly had no airway (i.e., breath sounds absent, cyanosis) and then we attempted to replace tracheostomy tube. This did not improve ventilation — was then intubated with #2.5 ETT which passed with difficulty; however, this did not restore breath sounds, improve chest rise or O$_2$ level... Drs. Jenkins, Sink, and Peters arrived. The tracheostomy tube was preplaced
with an attempt at hand-ventilation. This led to massive dissection of air into the subcutaneous space and abdominal distention. We then inserted a #3.0 ETT transorally.
Coates, M.D.

	Oper Note	The tracheostomy tube was replaced by Dr. James Peters, pediatric anesthesiologist, with ease, noting bilateral aeration to auscultation but continued poor oxygenation and perfusion. Therefore, patient was reintubated with a 3-0 endotracheal tube by Dr. Peters, again, noting bilateral aeration by auscultation but continued poor oxygenation and perfusion. Sink, M.D.
	MD Notes	Pediatric ICU Note (continued): ...Simultaneous placement of new ET 3.0 by Dr. Peters and chest tap by Dr. Sink resulted in restored chest ex-pansion, return of pink color, BP spontaneous heart rate. Jenkins, M.D.
1825	Code Sheet	10 mEq $NaHCO_3$, 4 cc epinephrine
1827	Code Sheet	Pulse strength 1+/4 only with CPR 1.5 cc $CaCl_2$; 16 gauge angiocath right side chest and left side chest per Dr. Sink
	Oper Note	Subcutaneous emphysema on the face and right lateral chest wall quickly developed and the question of bilateral tension pneumothoraces was raised. Therefore, bilateral second intercostal space, 14-gauge angiocaths were placed in the midclavicular line, noting rather prompt improvement in both oxygenation and perfusion and spontaneous return of cardiac rhythm but there was no obvious rush of air from the angiocath to confirm the tension pneumothoraces. Sink, M.D.
1828	Code Sheet	HR 50, BP 126/106, mean 110 Stat CXR
1830(??)	Code Sheet MD Notes	HR 87 spontaneous, RR bagging; O_2 sat 60% Pediatric ICU Note (continued) ...Heart rate returned after 15 minutes CPR. Resumed multiple doses of epinephrine and bicarbonate, 2 of $CaCl_2$. Child started moving again shortly after code. Norcuron given. Arterial line, 3 French arrow placed right several sterile conditions by Seldinger technique. Child well perfused but had no radial pulse, good brachial pulse. Jenkins, M.D.

1831	Code Sheet	HR 108, RR — bagging

1833	Code Sheet	HR 163

1835	Code Sheet	BP 124/30, 87 mean Dopamine 1 cc/hr — 20 mcg/kg/min __ pneumo right; ankle scrotum (??)

1836   X-ray   Portable Chest and Abdomen:
...There is mediastinal emphysema extending into the neck and inferiorly below the diaphragm. There appears to be extraperitoneal air along the right flank extending between the peritoneum and the adjacent abdominal musculature. There is a large amount of intestinal gas and moderate distention of the stomach with air but no definite pneumoperitoneum. As visualized suboptimally, both lungs appear expanded and essentially clear except for minimal left lower lobe and right upper midlung field atelectasis with no definite pneumothorax.
Chandler, M.D.

Oper Note   Pre-op Diagnosis: Right pneumothorax during cardiorespiratory arrest with subcutaneous emphysema and pneumomediastinum.
Procedure:
1.   Bilateral second intercostal space 14-gauge angiocath placement in the midclavicular line for suspected tension pneumothoraces.
2.   Right tube thoracostomy for pneumothorax.
    "...had an acute loss of his effective airway following initial early muscle relaxant weaning in the ICU and required reintubation promptly by Dr. Gerald Coates.
Sink, M.D.

Oper Note   A small persistent air leak was noted from the right angiocath, therefore, prompting placement of a right 4th intercostal space midclavicular line argyle chest tube subsequently.
Sink, M.D.

MD Notes   Pediatric ICU Note (continued)
...Chest tube placed by Dr. Sink after persistent leak through tap catheter (14-gauge angio). CXR showed mediastinal emphysema and probable pneumo-peritoneum. Child had air in scrotum and scalp after code. No infiltrate, good ET position.
Jenkins, M.D.

	MD Notes	Pulmonary (written at 1940 — continued) …The breath sounds were tympanic over the right chest. Bilateral thoracostomy tubes were placed with probable drainage of some free air via the right hemithorax. Concurrent with intubation and the tubes, the chest started to rise and color improved. Coates, M.D.
1840	ABG Consultation	pH 7.14, pCO_2 27.1, pO_2 116.7, BE -17.5 (Scallion 11/28/95 — continued) With reestablishment of heart rate, a blood gas was obtained 7 minutes after the end of CPR: pH 7.14, pCO_2 27, pO_2 116, and BE −17. The child was then paralyzed pharmacologically…" Scallion, M.D.
	Code Sheet	RR — bagging; HR 117, BP 113/63, mean 84 Dr. Wilson here
	MD Notes	ENT (written at 1940) Called stat because of an arrest earlier. Many MDs in attendance and things stabilized when I arrived. Etiology of loss of airway unclear but subcutaneous emphysema suggests the trach was in a "false passage" at some point. Trach stoma was easily visualized with tension on stay sutures… Wilson, M.D.
1843	Code Sheet	Pulse strength 0/4; BP — unable to get Dopamine increase to 1.2 cc/hr
18__	Code Sheet	HR 133, BP 111/79, mean 107, RR — bagging
184_	Code Sheet	10 mEq $NaHCO_3$
18__	Code Sheet	Pulse strength 1+/4; HR 129, BP 118/92, mean 66, RR — bagging
1950	ICU Flow Sht	BP 114/80 and 133/84 Fentanyl 8 mcg/ml @ 0.5 cc/hr Norcuron 1 mg/ml — OFF
	ICU Notes	Patient received in regular ICU-A. Patient on code cart monitor with alarms set. Patient on pulse oximeter with alarms set. Patient being bagged per respiratory therapist. Ambu, suction O_2 at bedside. Code sheet at bedside. Pt BP 141/80 with mean 101. Sats 100% on 100% FIO_2. Chest tube being place by Dr. Sink. Dopamine decreased to 7 for BP >100 systolic. L. Metziger, RN

1910	ICU Notes	CXR done for chest tube placement and NG tube placement. L. Metziger, RN

1915	ICU Notes	Vital signs done — HR 135, BP 133/84, mean 111; RR 28. Patient gray yellow in color. Skin cool to touch. L. Metziger, RN

2015	ICU Notes	Dr. Jenkins remains at bedside; Overall generalized ed-ema. Pt has 3.0-cm OETT. See flow sheet for vent sett-ings. Alarms on __ set. Pulse oximeter with alarms set. Patient placed on ICU cardio and apnea with alarms set. L. Metziger, RN

1913	X-ray	**Portable Chest and Abdomen:** Portable film sequence suggests pneumomediastinum with air dissecting into the retroperitoneum and flank. There is no definite pneumothorax. Right thoracostomy tube is in place.

1920	MD Notes	**Pediatric Surgery:** Procedure note: Bilateral 2nd intercostal space 14-gauge angiocatheters were placed during a full arrest for suspected bilateral tension pneumothoraces by chest wall percussion and initial lack of improvement with oxygenation after tracheostomy tube replacement and endotracheal tube replacement by Dr. James Peters anesthesiologist. Marked social facial and trunkal subcutaneous emphysema was noted which was associated with a pneumomediastinum by chest x-ray. Air dissection along the right abdominal wall to the scrotum and back within the right abdominal wall musculature was also present on chest abdominal film with possible free intraperitoneal dissection of air. Impression: Oxygenation perfusion was observed promptly after intercostal needle placement without obvious rush of air suggesting that a pneumothorax may have been present and decompressed. Small ongoing air leakage from the right angiocath prompted placement of a right chest tube in the 4th intercostal space in MCL after betadine prep and infiltration with 2 cc 10% lidocaine with epi. A #12 French argyle chest tube was placed with small air leak documented and full lung expansion bilaterally on follow-up chest film. Note dictated. Sink, M.D.

1940	MD Notes	ENT:

Called stat because of an arrest earlier. Many MDs in attendance and things stabilized when I arrived. Etiology of loss of airway unclear but subcutaneous emphysema suggests the trach was in a "false passage" at some point. Trach stoma was easily visualized with tension on stay sutures. Chest tube placed by Dr. Sink with improvement.

Plan to keep sedated and attempt to replace trach tube tomorrow at same time. Will discuss with Dr. Sedgewick tomorrow. Discussed with Dr. Coates, Dr. Jenkins and Dr. Sink.

Wilson, M.D.

1940	MD Notes	Pulmonary:

Was called to see patient this evening because of acute O_2 desaturation. This occurred _____ with awakening from paralysis/sedation. Within 30 seconds, patient clearly had no airway (i.e., breath sounds absent, cyanosis) and then we attempted to replace tracheostomy tube. This did not improve ventilation — was then intubated with #2.5 ETT which passed with difficulty; however, this did not restore breath sounds, improve chest rise, or O_2 level. Drs. Jenkins, Sink, and Peters arrived. The tracheostomy tube was preplaced with an attempt at hand-ventilation. This led to manual dissection of air into the sub-cutaneous space and abdominal distention. We then inserted a #3.0 ETT transorally. The breath sounds were tympanic over the right chest. Bilateral thoracostomy tubes were placed with probable drainage of some free air via the right hemithorax. Concurrent with intubation and the tubes, the chest started to rise and color improved.

Assessment:

1. SQ emphysema — probably secondary to dislodgement of the tracheostomy
2. Right pneumothorax (in film), exact timing uncertain
3. Diffuse bronchospasm

The relative contribution of these to the spells is uncertain. I discussed with the parents, and have asked Dr. Jenkins to take primary attending responsibility.

Coates, M.D.

MD Notes

Pediatric ICU Note:

Asked by Dr. Coates to assume care. Joined in code which occurred while I was in ICU at 2–3 minutes into CPR. Child reportedly became cyanotic/agitated after Norcuron d/c'ed today. No chest movement with bagging. 2.5 ET placed by Dr. Coates with no improvement, trach replaced by Dr. Sink with pult (??) strings (??) _____, clean visualization of tracheal resp — no improvement, simultaneous placement of new ET 3.0 by Dr. Peters and chest tap by Dr. Sink resulted in restored chest expansion, return of pink color, BP, spint (??) heart rate. Heart rate returned after 15 minutes CPR. Resumed multiple doses of epinephrine and bicarbonate, 2 of $CaCl_2$. Child started moving again shortly after code. Norcuron given. Arterial line, 3 French arrow placed right several sterile conditions by Seldinger technique.

Child well perfused but had not radial pulse, good brachial pulse. Chest tube placed by Dr. Sink after persistent leak through tap catheter (14-gauge angio). CXR showed mediastinal emphysema and probable pneumoperitoneum. Child had air in scrotum and scalp after code. No infiltrate, good ET position.

ABG 7 minutes after CPR 7.14/27/116/–17. Other labs _____ 32, WBC 14,100, 2B, 83S, platelets 410,000, PT 13.5, PTT 21.4, Na 140, K2.3, BUN 10, Cr 0.4, Glucose 303, Ca 10.6, PO4 2.9.

History: Child has long-standing history of wheezing which has been poorly responsive to bronchodilators with four SRH admissions. Child taken to OR on day of admission by Dr. Sedgewick where bronchoscopy _____ done to bronchospasm — cords nodular. On 11/16, child experienced acute obstructive symptoms thought to be upper airway. Intubated with some difficulty per pulmonary and anesthesia staff with 2.5 ETT. Trach placed 11/17. Laryngoscopy at that time showed moderate _____ edema and possible subglottic stenosis.

Impression:

1. Reactive airway disease
2. History of upper airway obstruction
3. This episode: ? Acute trach dislodgment followed by false passage; ? Bronchospasm followed by pneumothorax
4. Rule out sepsis

Plan:

1. Norcuron/sedation
2. Ventilation
3. Weaned off low-dose pressors
4. Antibiotics for now (Vanco/Claforan)
5. Ativan as sedation, anticonvulsant
6. Chest tube to suction
7. Broncho/replace trach in am
8. Continue bronchodilators
9. D/C HAL, decrease glucose, increase K

Jenkins, M.D.

Oper Note   "A chest x-ray with the bilateral angiocaths placed demonstrated bilateral expanded lung fields without evidence of pneumothorax and in obvious pneumomediastinum with dissection onto the neck, face, right lateral chest wall to the scrotum dissection in the layers of the right abdominal wall musculature extended up to the level of the right hemidiaphragm. There was no clinical evidence of a perforated abdominal viscus but rather subcutaneous dissection to account for the demonstrated air. Following placement of the right chest tube, small ongoing air leakage was noted with full bilateral lung expansion by follow-up chest x-ray. Satisfactory oxygenation perfusion and blood pressure were noted at the completion of this with return of spontaneous movement and eye opening. Normal swallowing effort was present and normal response to needle stick at the time of the local anesthetic infiltration for the chest tube placement."

Sink, M.D. (dictated 11/19/95)

11/20/95
0000   ICU Notes   ...Ambu , suction, O$_2$ at bedside; 3 cm. pediatric ETT,
                                 Kelley forceps and scissors at bedside, code sheet at
                                 bedside...
                                 L. Metziger, RN

                Oper Note   Preop Diagnosis: Airway distress
                                 Procedure: Replacement of trach tube with
                                   bronchoscopy
                                 Findings. "...a #1 Shiley pediatric tube was easily
                                 placed through the trach stoma. Good breath sounds
                                 were heard and the patient stabilized...The 2.5 mm
                                 bronchoscope was introduced through the vocal
                                 cords. Some granulation tissue was seen on the left
                                 true cord. There was moderate edema of the
                                 subglottis. Some granulation tissue was seen in the
                                 left subglottic area causing moderate obstruction and
                                 there was the thought that this could be a
                                 hemangioma. The scope was passed into the trach
                                 stomas and beyond down to the carina and both
                                 mainstem bronchi were visualized. No evidence of
                                 disease was noted. The 3.0 and then the 3.5
                                 bronchoscope were passed and the subglottic
                                 granulations appeared to be less and less of a
                                 problem as dilatation occurred. The impression was
                                 that most of the glottic problem was edematous
                                 reversbile disease along with a small amount of
                                 granulation. The trach tube was then tied into
                                 position and the patient sent back to the ICU having
                                 tolerated the procedure well."
                                 Wilson, M.D. (dictated 11/21/95)

1315   MD Notes   ENT Op Note

Respiratory distress

Reinsertion of trach with bronchoscopy by Wilson.
General anesthesia; #1 Shiley pediatric tube

Findings — small amount of granulstroma (??) left post
true vocal cord; small left _____ subglottic mass
granulation VS hem___doma moderate edema of
subglottic. Stable to ICU.

Wilson, M.D.

1315	MD Orders	

1. CXR to check tube tip
2. Betadine ointment to trach site tid
3. #1 and #0 pediatric trach at bedside
4. Call Dr. Sedgewick/Jenkins for IV, meds, and resp
   orders
5. Chest tube to suction.

Wilson, M.D.

Appendix 17.5
Sample Review 1

MEMORANDUM

TO: Joseph Black, Esq.

FROM: Susan D. Johnston, RN, BSN
                 Legal Nurse Consultant

DATE: June 13, 1996

RE: CHRIS SMITH, deceased
                 Review of the medical records from Wender County Hospital
                 and Northside Medical Center
                 Confidential work product specifically requested by
                 Ms. Johnston

The ER Triage Assessment (6:10 p.m. on 2/18/96) reflects the abdomen to be tender, soft, and non-distended. Chris was noted to be diaphoretic and complaining of chest and abdominal pain and was "using a lot of profanity." The pain was described as sharp and constant and nonradiating.

Dr. Sigelman (ER physician) notes that the abdomen was "extremely tender" but with no rebound or actual guarding yet he found voluntary guarding upon deep palpation over the bladder. The bowel sounds were minimally diminished. There were two areas of induration on the lower abdomen (probably where Chris gave himself insulin shots). Sigelman felt that something had given Chris a "real bash" on the abdomen. Despite these observations, no abdominal flat plate x-ray was ordered nor was any further investigation of the abdominal pain done even though Dr. Sigelman decided to admit Chris "because of the amount of pain" that he was in. Chris requested morphine sulfate but Sigelman would only give him Toradol so that Dr. Collins would "be able to follow the abdomen without masking." (In other words — all his thoughts were on acute abdomen, though he really didn't try very hard to make the diagnosis himself.)

Sigelman ordered that Collins be notified of the admission because Chris "will need to have abdomen rechecked fairly often." (This sentence may have been added by Sigelman at a later time. It would appear that Collins was notified of the admission by the nurses sometime prior to 7:30 p.m. because he gave the orders for morphine and the first dose was given at 7:30 p.m. The question is: what was he told?)

Orders by Sigelman on admission are for "routine vitals including O_2 sat q1h × 8, then q4h × 2, then q shift." There is no indication in the records that this was done by the nurses as ordered. Chris was transferred to the floor at 6:55 p.m. The "admission" BP on the floor was 124/70. The BP was not taken again until 12:00 a.m. when it had dropped to 88/70 and then not again until 4:00 a.m. when it was 82/50. There is no indication that the 88/70 was called to

Sigelman or Collins. The respiratory rate was 20/min at 4 p.m., 24 at 8 p.m., 28 at 12 a.m., and 48 at 4 a.m. The rise in respiratory rate was also not called to any physician.

Collins ordered morphine sulfate 10 mg IVP q3h. (This is a *huge* dose especially to someone who is being "observed" — what can one possibly observe if you knock the patient out??)

The nurses noted the laceration to the left chest/abdomen on their initial assessment sheet. Nurse Mary Jones, RN (7a–7p) found the abdomen to be tender, firm, and rounded with positive bowel sounds in all four quadrants. She notes in the narrative notes "patient guards entire abdomen and screams with pain upon palpation." Neither Collins nor Sigelman were notified of these findings even though they· are different from the ER assessment.

Nurse Belinda Winston, RN (11–7) found the abdomen to be tender, firm, and *distended* with positive bowel sounds in all but the LLQ (questionable if you look at markings on page). She also notes in the narrative notes that Chris was complaining of pain in chest and knees and difficult respiration at 12:10 a.m. Neither Sigelman nor Collins was notified of this change in condition and, furthermore, nurse Jenkins gave Chris an additional 10 mg of morphine IVP at 12:10 a.m. (*after* the documented hypotension).

The graphics for the 3–11 shift show that Chris voided 725 cc of urine but was incontinent of urine and bowel movement (very unusual in a patient who does not have something extremely wrong with him) one time apiece (no note as to whether this occurred simultaneously). Neither Sigelman nor Collins was notified of this event. The 11–7 "checklist" filled out by nurse Winston reflects O2 saturation levels of 80% down to 60%. (This is hard to believe!)

Nurse Jenkins, RN recorded all the notes between 12:30 a.m. and 3:30 a.m. They all appear to have been written at the same time — or at least the notes from 2:15 to 3:30 a.m. The notes do not address abdominal pain specifically at all, i.e., no follow-up assessment by the nurses.

The patient was found by nurse Winston at 4:05 a.m. to be diaphoretic with no palpable pulses and no recordable blood pressure. Sigelman was notified at 4:10 a.m. and arrived on the scene and then Dr. Collins was notified at 4:30 a.m. Sigelman thought that the abdominal exam had changed "markedly" from the time of admission. There was marked involuntary guarding, guarding in the upper part of the abdomen, as well as lower and absent bowel sounds. Chris could not respond satisfactorily in order to assess for rebound tenderness.

ABG on admission to Northside Medical Center at 0635 was pH 7.09, pCO_2 40, pO_2 80, and B.E. −17.6 on 100% O_2. This shows severe metabolic acidosis (must have been present for quite some time — probably began when the respiratory rate was increasing as a compensatory mechanism). The admission PT and PTT were 14.1 and 34.4 indicating that a clotting disorder was present (probably early DIC). The admission CBC shows 23% bands (immature neutrophils) and 22% segmented neutrophils. (This is highly abnormal and indicative of bacterial infection which had been present for quite some time.) The hemoglobin and hematocrit on admission were 8.5 and 26.0 (one would expect them to be lower, but the hypovolemia, hypotension, and shock were probably sepsis related and not entirely from loss of blood).

The operative report by Robert D. Vasco, M.D., notes gross contamination of the peritoneal cavity with gastric contents from the laceration of the stomach and only mild active bleeding from the upper left quadrant. The actual repair of the stomach laceration and spleen removal appears to have been relatively easy to accomplish. Chris died at 4:15 p.m. on 2/19/96, approximately 24 hours after the accident.

As you requested, I will obtain a certified copy of the Wender County Hospital and Northside Medical Center records as soon as the client returns the medical authorizations (not in the file as of 6/13/95.) You indicated that you already have the X-rays from Wender County. It would appear that there is a good chance of proving negligence in this case. I will be happy to assist you in having this case reviewed by a medical surgical nurse as well as an emergency physician for standard of care issues and by a general surgeon for causation. We also need to look at the issue of Chris's severe brittle diabetes on his life expectancy in order to make an accurate assessment of damages.

Appendix 17.6
Sample Review 2

MEMORANDUM

TO: Martha Ann Bulow, Esq.

FROM: Lauren H. Griffin, RN, MSN
           Legal Nurse Consultant

DATE: February 22, 1996

RE: BISSON v. SOUTHERN MEDICAL CENTER
           Suzie Bisson, deceased
           Review of the medical records from Southern Medical Center
           Confidential work product specifically requested by Ms. Griffin

---

Facts of the Case:

Mrs. Suzie Bisson was 66 years old when she was admitted to Southern Medical Center (SMC) by Dr. John Tucker on 8/11/95 for an anemia workup. It was determined that the most probable cause for her anemia was gastrointestinal (GI) loss of blood since Ms. Bisson had a positive hemoccult test. A series of GI tests were ordered including an esophagogastroduodenoscopy (EGD) and a colonoscopy.

Initial laboratory tests showed abnormalities of the prothrombin time (but not the PTT) as well as the hemoglobin and hematocrit and Dr. C. Suarez (presumably a gastroenterologist) was called to consult with Ms. Bisson. He wanted to do an EGD but thought he would wait until Vitamin K had been given for several days because of the coagulopathy that was evident. Additionally, several units of packed red blood cells were transfused to treat the anemia.

On 8/12/95, a potassium (K+) level was noted to be low at 3.2 mEq/L (normal 3.5–5.3 mEq/L). The IV fluids were changed from D5 1/2 NS to D5 1/2 NS with 20 mEq KCl/liter by Dr. Tucker. The IV was to infuse at "KVO" or at a minimal rate to keep the vein open. A second IV was started for the purpose of delivering Zantac (to decrease gastric acid secretion) at 10 cc/hr. The first low K+ level was treated with an order by Dr. Tucker for three separate doses of 20 mEq KCl to be given 1 hour apart. This was done during the early hours of 8/13/95 and a follow-up K+ level at 0630 was 4.0. A CT scan of the abdomen later that day showed a 6 cm abdominal aortic aneurysm (AAA) with no signs of leaking or rupture.

On 8/14/95 (Saturday), the K+ level was 3.4 (low again) but no attempt was made to increase the level by medications. On 8/15/95, an order for two doses of K-Lor 20 mEq to be given 1 hour apart was given by Dr. Suarez (?? can't read writing) at 1900. The K+ level was to be checked again the next morning.

At 0552 on 8/16/95 (Monday), the K+ level was still low at 3.2 despite the supplementation the previous day. An order was written at 0925 for an additional 20 mEq of KCl to be given *IV over 2 hours "stat"* (which indicates concern) by Dr. Suarez (??can't read writing). The EGD was performed by Dr. Suarez that morning and showed no active bleeding from the stomach — only distended veins in the esophageal and cardia areas. The diet order by Dr. Suarez after the EGD was for "clear liquids" only. At this time he scheduled a colonoscopy to be done the following day on 8/17/95. An order was written for Ms. Bisson to receive nothing by mouth after midnight in anticipation of this. At 1700, a Go-Lytely gastrointestinal prep was started (this involves drinking a powder which is mixed with 4 liters of fluid which is intended to clear out the GI tract) for the colonoscopy. The last order for a K+ level was ordered by Dr. Tucker as a "stat" SMA-7 on 8/16/95 at approximately 2030. He ordered that K-rider 20 mEq be given over 1 hour if the K+ was <3.5. The result, reported at 2045 was 3.6 (low normal) which did not prompt additional K+ administration according to the orders by Dr. Tucker.

At 0830 on 8/17/95 (Tuesday), the PT results were again abnormal and called by the nurse to Dr. Suarez. As a consequence, he canceled the colonoscopy (presumably he was worried about bleeding as a complication due to the coagulopathy) and returned Ms. Bisson to a clear liquid diet. Two Dulcolax suppositories were ordered for later that day in anticipation of the rescheduled colonoscopy to be performed on 8/18/95. Another order was written for Ms. Bisson to receive nothing by mouth after midnight. Additionally, 3 units of fresh frozen plasma (FFP) were ordered (presumably due to the continued abnormal clotting factors). The infusion was stopped after the second unit because of sudden abdominal pain and worries about possible leaking from the AAA. The IV fluids of D5 1/2 NS were continued at KVO.

At 0430 on 8/18/95 (Wednesday), one of the nurses called Dr. Suarez regarding continuing abnormal PT results. No mention is made of anything relating to the K+ level from 8/16/95 even though the nurse was anticipating giving Ms. Bisson a tap water enema at 0600 that morning. The IV fluids of D5 1/2 NS were continued at KVO. At 0930, Dr. Suarez canceled the colonoscopy for the second time. A CT scan was done to reevaluate the AAA but no changes were found. An EKG, which appears to have been performed sometime that morning (there is no date and time on any of the EKGs), shows ST depression. Orders were written by Dr. Suarez for Ms. Bisson to receive another two Dulcolax tablets that evening and another tap water enema on the morning of 8/19/95 in anticipation of the re-rescheduled colonoscopy. An additional 5 units of FFP were to be given and an additional order was written by Dr. Suarez for 20 mg Lasix (powerful diuretic) to be given IV before the first unit and after the third unit. The first dose of Lasix was given at 2220 on 8/18/95 by Baldwin, LPN (?spelling).

At 0030 on 8/19/95 (Thursday), the nurse's notes written by Y. Pillets, LPN (the initial assessment sheet was either not done or is missing from the record) reflects that Ms. Bisson's heart rate was 120/minute (normally it was 70–84/minute) and that she was restless and trying to sit up in the bed. There is also a note to the effect that she was in a posey and some other kind of restraint device which leads me to believe that she was disoriented and possibly agitated. The second dose of Lasix was given by Nurse Pillets at 0050 on 8/19/95.

At 0205, Nurse Pillets notes that Ms. Bisson went into ventricular tachycardia but at 0212 the patient was defibrillated for the first of four times (indicating that there must have been ventricular fibrillation). CPR was begun immediately and a sinus tachycardia rhythm returned at 0220. Initial ABGs at 0223 reflect a pH of 7.293, pCO_2 of 34, and pO_2 of 196 on 100% oxygen and a base excess of –9.5. An SMA-7 was done at 0345 and showed a K+ level of 2.3 (drastically low). At 0615, an order was written by Dr. C. Lee for K-rider 40 mEq to be given IV in 100 cc of normal saline IV over 3 hours and 20 mEq KCl to be added to the regular IV fluids of normal saline infusing at 100 cc/hour. A repeat K+ at 1635 was 4.5.

Pillets' notes appear to have been written in retrospect because of their neatness and the fact that no assessment was done (the notes and the assessment are usually, or should be, started together soon after the beginning of the shift). Additionally, since there are no rhythm strips in the medical records documenting the arrhythmia causing the code, I suspect that the ventricular tachycardia actually occurred prior to 0205 and/or not very effective or timely CPR was employed because the patient sustained hypoxic encephalopathy. It may be, however, that the patient's emphysematous disease prevented effective oxygenation in a CPR situation.

Dr. Mission, a cardiologist, was consulted and concluded that the low K+ level probably caused Ms. Bisson to go into ventricular tachycardia. As a result of the cardiac arrest and code, Ms. Bisson's clinical condition deteriorated. She developed hypertension which was treated in the ICU with Nipride. It soon became evident that she had suffered hypoxic encephalopathy during the arrest. Ms. Bisson had a second cardiac arrest in the early hours of 8/21/95 and was noted to have blood in her endotracheal tube and a "rock hard abdomen" during the code. She was not successfully resuscitated. There is no autopsy contained in these records, but it would appear that Dr. Tucker felt as though she died due to a ruptured AAA.

Analysis of the Issues of the Case:

This is not an uncomplicated case in terms of the medical issues involved. Ms. Bisson was obviously a sick woman with a variety of medical illnesses which had to be addressed and evaluated at the same time. She obviously had a large AAA which needed repair, but the vascular surgeon felt that this was stable and that it was more important to determine the cause of her underlying medical problems causing the anemia, elevated PTs, etc. prior to operating. There was some question whether or not Ms. Bisson had multiple myeloma but this was never proved. The underlying medical problem (whatever it is determined or guessed to be) will be used as the defense in this case to question causation and to minimize life expectancy.

It is clear from the beginning of the hospitalization that Ms. Bisson was having problems maintaining a normal K+ level. She had been on Vasoretic (Vasotec and hydrochlorothiazide, a diuretic) prior to hospitalization, but once she was hospitalized, she was not given much in the way of food (most of the time she was on a clear liquid diet or NPO) or regular substantial potassium supplementation in her IV fluids. Obviously 20 mEq KCl/liter of IV fluids was not enough to maintain Ms. Bisson's K+ level given that she was only receiving her IVs at a KVO rate. KVO rates are left to the discretion of the nurses and it would appear that she did not receive any more than 50 cc/hour (and most times less) while she was hospitalized. It is difficult to tell how much IV and oral fluids she was receiving because the intake and output records are not complete. At the same time, from 8/16/95 through the time of the arrest on 8/19/95, Ms. Bisson was being prepared for, or undergoing, GI evaluation. In addition to limited fluids by mouth, she was given two Dulcolax tablets on 8/17/95, a tap water enema, two more Dulcolax tablets, and 20 mg of IV Lasix on 8/18/95, and shortly before the arrest on 8/19/95, was given an additional 20 mg IV Lasix. The reason for the Lasix was to minimize fluid overload in the face of receiving 5 units of FFP (about 1000 cc of fluid) to correct abnormal clotting factors.

The problem here is that no one, physicians and nurses alike, bothered to remember or check the laboratory studies regarding the previous K+ problems. As a result, Ms. Bisson was allowed to go for nearly 3 days *after* a borderline low normal K+ level on the evening of 8/16/95 without an additional K+ level being checked in the face of minimal K+ supplementation and numerous medications and procedures which are known to decrease K+ levels. As an additional physician concern, it would appear that the last EKG taken before the arrest showed ST depression which is typical for hypokalemia. The nurses notes also show tachycardia and restlessness and possible confusion which are also signs of hypokalemia. It is not reasonable for the nurses to have determined that Ms. Bisson was indeed hypokalemic, but it is reasonable for them to have suspected that may be a problem and communicated all abnormal findings to a physician.

Finally, the cardiologist, Dr. Macheski, concluded that the cause of the arrest (which subsequently caused the hypoxic encephalopathy, hypertensive events, and apparent AAA rupture) was a low potassium level (and he would be considered an expert regarding this) probably because there was minimal evidence for another cardiovascular or pulmonary cause. The only downside to this is the fact that the patient converted to a sinus rhythm rather easily after CPR was started and the potassium was not supplemented after the arrest until approximately 5 hours later, during which time there appears to be minimal problems with the cardiac rhythm. This may be explained by the use of IV Lidocaine during the arrest which "numbs" the heart and increases the threshold for arrhythmias. Additionally, often during CPR, K+ will be released from the cells into the plasma due to the inherent injury caused by the act of performing CPR.

Deviations from the Standard of Nursing Care:

It is my opinion that the nurses employed by Southern Medical Center were negligent in the following actions or omissions to act in the nursing care and treatment of Suzie Bisson:

    a. In administering medications including Dulcolax and Lasix and a tap water enema to Suzie Bisson on 8/17/95, 8/18/95, and 8/19/95. The nurses employed at Southern Medical Center administered two Dulcolax tablets on 8/17/95, two Dulcolax tablets, a tap water enema, and 20 mg. Lasix IV on 8/18/95 and an additional 20 mg of IV Lasix on 8/19/95 to Ms. Bisson without ever questioning her potassium level. They knew or should have known that such medications and a tap water enema can cause a decrease in the potassium level; that Ms. Bisson had had minimal amounts of potassium administered in her IV fluids during the previous 48 hours and the last measured potassium level on 8/16/95 was 3.6 mEq/liter. They also knew or should have known that Ms. Bisson had had nothing more than a clear liquid diet during this same period of time.

b. In failing to report changes in Ms. Bisson's clinical condition to a physician during the early morning hours of 8/19/95. The nurses employed at Southern Medical Center failed to report changes in Ms. Bisson's clinical condition, including sinus tachycardia, restlessness, probably confusion and the need for restraints, to a physician during the early morning hours of 8/19/95 when they knew or should have known that Ms. Bisson had a history of hypokalemia, had received a number of medications and a tap water enema which could potentially lower her potassium level to a dangerous level, had only minimal amounts of potassium administered in her IV fluids, and that the last measured potassium level on 8/16/95 was 3.6 mEq/liter.

It is my opinion, to a reasonable degree of nursing certainty, that had the nurses employed by The Medical Center appropriately evaluated and provided nursing care for Suzie Bisson, she would not have developed a dangerously low potassium level.

Chapter 18

Health Care Bill Analysis and Audit

Agnes Grogan

Contents

1-57444-123-X/98
© 1998 by American Association of Legal Nurse Consultants

Objectives

Upon completion of this chapter, the reader will be able to

- Describe the differences between hospital and non-hospital bill review processes
- Define the clinical and educational qualifiications necessary to perform bill audits
- List the essential tools to properly conduct bill review
- Discuss the value of bill review in litigation

Introduction

Bill auditing is an area relatively unexplored by the majority of legal nurse consultants (LNCs), yet there is a definite need and broad application for this expertise. Through this activity, the LNC's value to attorney clients is increased, whether in the plaintiff or defense milieu. This chapter discusses the auditing process and how it applies to the legal arena, the educational preparation, necessary tools for the task, benefits of bill review, and opportunities for the application of this skill. LNCs use bill-auditing skills to review claims submitted for inpatient hospital care and outpatient medical care as professional auditors employed by insurance companies under an umbrella of titles ranging from claims analyst to case manager, in the hospital setting as defense and/or revenue auditors, and for attorneys as part of the routine liability and damages evaluation in a wide variety of cases. Medical bills are an often overlooked rich source of evidence that can serve to support, mitigate, or even dismiss medical costs.

Bill Auditing Defined

Medical bill auditing cannot be defined simply as the verification of services billed or determining that the total charges are accurate. The process involves several other components that apply either to hospital bills or to bills from various medical providers, such as physical therapists, chiropractors, physicians, laboratory and radiology facilities. The method by which the audit process is performed also depends on where, why, and when the audit is performed.

Hospital Bill Review

Hospital bills are reviewed and adjusted by the insurance auditor by comparing the itemized bill to the complete medical record. Hospitals generally have specific audit policies relating to bill audits. The audit usually must be performed on-site and findings must then be reviewed by qualified hospital personnel before an adjusted total is accepted as payment in full. Some negotiation may take place between auditor and hospital personnel. However, audits can be performed off-site and this procedure is fittingly called a "desk audit." The hospital's objection to performing an audit away from the facility is that the insurance auditor does not have knowledgeable hospital resource personnel available to explain or discuss questionable items on the bill. Lacking proper explanation, the reviewer may make unacceptable reductions on the bill, but with experience the task can be accomplished without undue difficulty.

Briefly, the services or items listed on a medical bill must be (1) ordered by a physician or provided during a procedure ordered or performed by a physician; (2) performed in the operating room if no specific written order is located in the chart (usually drugs, laboratory, X-ray); (3) in accordance with a patient care policy/procedure, in which case a written policy/procedure must be available for examination if requested; and (4) received by the patient.

In addition to identifying and disallowing charges as described above, the LNC auditor in personal injury cases must be cognizant of charges on the hospital bill that are related to preexisting medical conditions and are the responsibility of the group health insurer. That auditor must also identify charges that would not have been incurred had not a particular incident occurred, such as alleged negligence on the part of medical personnel.

Detailed analysis of hospital bills can help support or refute claims of negligence. A simple example is a case in which a central line became infected leading to sepsis and death. Dressing, tubing, and filter changes were an issue. Hospital policy and procedures and medical records were carefully scrutinized, and charts were constructed demonstrating that documented care met standards. However, careful examination and comparison of hospital bills (more charts) showed discrepancies. Necessary supplies for dressing and tubing changes obtainable only through a controlled delivery system were not removed on days when medical records showed they were used.

At the present time there is no published database of charges relating to the usual cost of items for which hospitals charge. However, it is anticipated there may be such a reference available in the future. Information relative to this issue may be obtained from state medical auditor associations.

Another facet of hospital bill review that relates to insurance coverage contracts applied incorrectly by the facility and is primarily concerned with PPO (preferred provider organization) and HMO (health maintenance organization) criteria for payment determination. In this context, the auditor must be able to interpret what should be paid by the insurance organization and compare this amount to the charges billed by the hospital.

Non-Hospital Bill Review

Review of billings from providers other than hospitals requires additional expertise and familiarity with current procedural terminology (CPT) codes (described in detail later) and protocols for their application. Additionally, the reviewer should be knowledgeable of "usual and customary" fees, also referred to as "U & C" in the insurance adjuster world.

In this type of review, the medical records are reviewed (if available) and compared with submitted charges to determine if the services provided were in accordance with the specific medical description or CPT code listed. If not, the charges are adjusted by the reviewer to reflect the actual service provided. Often, recommendations will be made to disallow charges associated with excessive duration of care, excessive frequency of treatment, and lack of documentation. Additionally, the auditor must also distinguish charges associated with treatment of preexisting medical conditions that should be disallowed when determining an insurer's responsibilities.

Qualifications

The LNC who embarks on medical bill auditing in a variety of contexts should possess certain clinical and educational qualifications to perform the task in a competent and efficient manner.

Clinical Experience

First and foremost, the LNC auditor should be an experienced nurse with recent clinical experience. Clinical experience provides the hands-on knowledge of equipment and medical procedures necessary to evaluate the appropriateness of items listed on a bill related to a wide variety of procedures. The nursing background most helpful for hospital bill audits is in critical care or the operating room because these areas usually generate the most costly and therefore most-questioned charges. However, lack of such experience does not disqualify the LNC from auditing. A willingness to ask questions about unfamiliar items and to critically analyze the information to determine the appropriateness of the billing is more important. In contrast to the seasoned auditor, the inexperienced auditor will ask many more questions and therefore take longer to complete an audit, but the results should be comparable.

Knowledge of current treatment, the expected outcomes of care, and the rehabilitative process is extremely beneficial when reviewing orthopedic and/or neurological injury claims. These areas are frequently subject to close scrutiny by the insurance industry because of the increasing incidence of inflated, questionable, and/or fraudulent claims.

Auditing Experience

Nurses new to auditing are often amazed to discover the quantity of items listed on an itemized bill for a single procedure, such as an angiogram. Familiarity with the usual billing protocols of hospitals and other healthcare providers (chiropractors, physical therapist, acupuncturists, etc.) will assist the nurse in determining whether or not particular charges are unusual or excessive. For the uninitiated, billing protocols or procedures direct the acceptable or usual format in which services are billed. Hospitals that bill for daily setup of overhead trapeze equipment or bill for individual items from an OR pack are clearly unconventional. Another illustration of improper billing is when a surgeon bills for both a diagnostic and surgical procedure since a surgical arthroscopy always includes a diagnostic arthroscopy. In other words, the physician is billing twice for the same procedure.

It is important for the auditor to have a working knowledge of CPT Coding. Compiled and published by the AMA, the *Physicians Current Procedural Terminology* assigns a five-digit code to procedures and services performed by physicians, physical therapists, chiropractors, etc. The book is used by providers to bill for services. Each code is accompanied by a specific definition/description. The codes are usually required on bills submitted to insurance carriers by medical care providers, and are often used to determine the amount of reimbursement based on allowable charges for specific CPT codes. For codes to be considered valid, the medical record documentation of services provided must support the definition of the code used. In many instances, when there are discrepancies, the auditor adjusts the code to reflect the actual services provided. The experienced auditor develops an intimate familiarity with CPT coding and definitions.

Acquiring Bill Auditing Knowledge and Experience

How does one become experienced in bill auditing? There are several possible avenues.

- Inquire of medical bill auditors where they obtained their training.
- Inquire of local (and respected) physician's office personnel as to the availability of coding classes they attended.
- Purchase coding instruction books and begin a self-taught course of study.
- Volunteer to assist a local hospital's bill auditor (if there is one).
- Consider employment in a cost-containment, auditing, or insurance firm.

The LNC is advised to refrain from bill review in a formalized setting until comfortable with the process and possessing the necessary knowledge related to charges, regulatory guidelines, insurance coverage issues, and care guidelines.

Essential Tools

There are certain tools and resources that make the medical bill-auditing task much easier as well as provide credibility and validity to the audit. The resources most essential are briefly described below.

Coding References

- *Physicians Current Procedural Terminology*

As mentioned earlier, the CPT Code book is an essential reference for billing and audit purposes. It is published and updated yearly. Medical care providers are supposed to bill insurers using current codes, but often become complacent and use outdated codes. It is helpful and recommended to keep at least 3 years of CPT books on hand: current year and 2 previous years.

■ *ICD-9 CM*

The *International Classification of Diseases — Clinical Modification* is a book that lists diagnoses equated with a three-digit number that may or may not be modified further for accuracy and specificity. Many times charges are disallowed on a HCFA (Healthcare Financing Administration) form because the ICD-9 code refers to a diagnosis that is not applicable and for which there should be no financial obligation.

The HCFA form is used to submit charges for payment to carriers. It has become the "industry standard" among carriers for claims submission. Medicare mandates its use. It is clear, concise, and easy to follow. Everyone completes it in the same way, and it contains all the information necessary for most carriers to enter and process claims. ICD-9 diagnosis codes are entered along with the CPT codes and charges for procedures.

■ *Code It Right* and *Coders' Desk Reference*

Coding guidelines such as these books are helpful to coders. They provide definitions, guidelines, coding examples, and various terminology.

Pharmacy References

■ *Physician's Desk Reference*

This familiar "PDR" reference, published yearly, provides information relative to a drug's indications for use, the forms in which it is supplied, but does not provide any pricing information.

■ *Drug Topics Red Book*

Better known as the "Red Book," this text is relatively inexpensive and updated yearly. It lists medications by manufacturer, the forms/quantities supplied, and the average wholesale pricing, etc. This can be helpful in determining the extent of markup on a particular pharmaceutical.

■ *Physician GenRX*

This book is a combination PDR and Red Book and is published yearly as well. Unlike the PDR and Red Book, it is not available at most medical book stores, but is ordered by mail (see References). In addition to all the necessary medical data, it contains essential pricing information and those conditions for which FDA approves use of drugs, when approval was granted, and other bits of useful information. It is available in book form, on CD-ROM, and disk format which increases its usefulness.

Medical/Nursing/Procedure Texts

These books are helpful in acquainting the LNC auditor with unfamiliar procedures and assists in defining the equipment and supplies generated when such procedures are ordered and performed. Particularly helpful for bill review are texts devoted to radiology and surgical procedures.

Chiropractic and Physical Therapy Texts/Manuals

Publications in this area are especially useful to the LNC auditor who reviews billings for orthopedic and soft-tissue injuries. The reviewer should seek references that discuss indications for procedures, duration of treatment, and standards of care.

State Regulations

Many states have regulations pertinent to care delivered by medical providers, such as physical therapy and chiropractic treatment, that affect reimbursement. If care was not provided in accordance with these regulations, then such charges may be legally disallowed. To obtain these regulations, contact the state agency responsible for licensing the particular provider and request a copy. Research in a law library is another source for the regulations. It is suggested that the regulations be checked yearly as new laws may make certain sections obsolete.

Fee Schedules

Excessive charges can be identified and decreased through application of fee and coding reference books or software. The product used should provide a geographic-specific index for pricing of healthcare services in a specific geographic area relative to national average prices. Books are relatively inexpensive, but statistically reliable computer database software is beyond the budget of most auditors with costs ranging from $2,500 to $25,000 yearly for a national database. Both books and software are updated yearly.

Computers, Software, and Forms

The auditor who attempts to perform bill reviews without a computer will add unnecessary time to the task. With the proper software, work sheets can be devised with built-in formulas for calculations to replace the error-prone manual calculator. Not only will mathematical functions be accomplished with ease, but a professional-looking report easily generated for the client. Attempting a bill review without a methodical approach through use of a work sheet will not only prolong the task, but increase the risk of errors (Figures 18.1 and 18.2).

Calendars can be generated showing frequency and duration as well as patterns of care (Figure 18.3). Such a visual aid depicts visits to various medical providers much better than words. A user-friendly word-processor program will help the reviewer prepare explanatory narrative reports which describe in detail the rationale for decisions made in the bill review process. A printer with adequate memory is needed to print the audit results. A laserjet or deskjet printer is preferable to a letter-quality dot matrix type. A simple calculator with the basic arithmetic functions plus memory features is useful for the small tasks.

Date	Description	CPT Billed	$ Amount Billed	CPT Adjusted	U & C 80th Per-centile	Total $ Reduction	Total $ Amount Allowed	Rationale
1/23/96	O.V. New patient	99203	$200.00		$121.48	$78.52	$121.48	
1/23/96	Hot/cold packs	97010	$200.00		$29.27	$170.73	$29.27	CPT 96 states hot packs to one or more areas. MD charging for 5.
1/23/96	Elect. Stimulation	97032	$150.00		$22.05	$127.95	$22.05	CPT 96 states hot packs to one or more areas. MD charging for 3
1/23/96	Ultrasound-15 min.	97035	$250.00		$15.35	$234.65	$15.35	CPT 96 states hot packs to one or more areas. MD charging for 5.
1/26/96	Hot/cold packs	97010	$200.00		$29.27	$170.73	$29.27	
1/26/96	Elect. Stimulation	97032	$150.00		$22.05	$127.95	$22.05	
1/26/96	Ultrasound-15 min.	97035	$250.00		$15.35	$234.65	$15.35	
1/28/96	Hot/cold packs	97010	$200.00		$29.27	$170.73	$29.27	Sunday: Not open per MD's office
1/28/96	Elect. Stimulation	97032	$150.00		$22.05	$127.95	$22.05	Sunday: Not open per MD's office
1/28/96	Ultrasound-15 min.	97035	$250.00		$15.35	$234.65	$15.35	Sunday: Not open per MD's office
1/29/96		99211	$80.00		$27.66	$52.34	$27.66	
1/29/96	Hot/cold packs	97010	$200.00		$29.27	$170.73	$29.27	
1/29/96	Elect. Stimulation	97032	$150.00		$22.05	$127.95	$22.05	
1/29/96	Ultrasound-15 min.	97035	$250.00		$15.35	$234.65	$15.35	
1/31/96	Hot/cold packs	97010	$200.00		$29.27	$170.73	$29.27	
1/31/96	Elect. Stimulation	97032	$150.00		$22.05	$127.95	$22.05	
1/31/96	Ultrasound-15 min.	97035	$250.00		$15.35	$234.65	$15.35	
2/2/96	Hot/cold packs	97010	$200.00		$29.27	$170.73	$29.27	Saturday: Not open per MD's office
2/2/96	Elect. Stimulation	97032	$150.00		$22.05	$127.95	$22.05	Saturday: Not open per MD's office
2/2/96	Ultrasound-15 min.	97035	$250.00		$15.35	$234.65	$15.35	Saturday: Not open per MD's office
2/3/96	Hot/cold packs	97010	$200.00		$29.27	$170.73	$29.27	
2/3/96	Elect. Stimulation	97032	$150.00		$22.05	$127.95	$22.05	
2/3/96	Ultrasound-15 min.	97035	$250.00		$15.35	$234.65	$15.35	
2/5/96	Hot/cold packs	97010	$200.00		$29.27	$170.73	$29.27	
2/5/96	Elect. Stimulation	97032	$150.00		$22.05	$127.95	$22.05	
2/5/96	Ultrasound-15 min.	97035	$250.00		$15.35	$234.65	$15.35	
2/7/96	Hot/cold packs	97010	$200.00		$29.27	$170.73	$29.27	
2/7/96	Elect. Stimulation	97032	$150.00		$22.05	$127.95	$22.05	
2/7/96	Ultrasound-15 min.	97035	$250.00		$15.35	$234.65	$15.35	
2/9/96	Hot/cold packs	97010	$200.00		$29.27	$170.73	$29.27	
2/9/96	Elect. Stimulation	97032	$150.00		$22.05	$127.95	$22.05	
2/9/96	Ultrasound-15 min.	97035	$250.00		$15.35	$234.65	$15.35	
2/12/96	Hot/cold packs	97010	$200.00		$29.27	$170.73	$29.27	
2/12/96	Elect. Stimulation	97032	$150.00		$22.05	$127.95	$22.05	
2/12/96	Ultrasound-15 min.	97035	$250.00		$15.35	$234.65	$15.35	
2/14/96	Hot/cold packs	97010	$200.00		$29.27	$170.73	$29.27	
2/14/96	Elect. Stimulation	97032	$150.00		$22.05	$127.95	$22.05	
2/14/96	Ultrasound-15 min.	97035	$250.00		$15.35	$234.65	$15.35	
2/15/96	Hot/cold packs	97010	$200.00		$29.27	$170.73	$29.27	
2/15/96	Elect. Stimulation	97032	$150.00		$22.05	$127.95	$22.05	
2/15/96	Ultrasound-15 min.	97035	$250.00		$15.35	$234.65	$15.35	
2/16/96	Hot/cold packs	97010	$200.00		$29.27	$170.73	$29.27	
2/16/96	Elect. Stimulation	97032	$150.00		$22.05	$127.95	$22.05	
2/16/96	Ultrasound-15 min.	97035	$250.00		$15.35	$234.65	$15.35	
2/19/96	Hot/cold packs	97010	$200.00		$29.27	$170.73	$29.27	
2/19/96	Elect. Stimulation	97032	$150.00		$22.05	$127.95	$22.05	
2/19/96	Ultrasound-15 min.	97035	$250.00		$15.35	$234.65	$15.35	
2/21/96	Hot/cold packs	97010	$200.00		$29.27	$170.73	$29.27	
2/21/96	Elect. Stimulation	97032	$150.00		$22.05	$127.95	$22.05	
2/21/96	Ultrasound-15 min.	97035	$250.00		$15.35	$234.65	$15.35	

Figure 18.1 Bill review, patient John Smith.

Value of Bill Review

The LNC brings analytical skills and the ability to perceive and communicate the legal implications of the information gleaned from the billings and medical records. This information may be viewed differently depending on the purpose of the audit since results may validate, increase, or mitigate economic damages in a lawsuit. A brief list of the benefits that bill review offers for different employers of the LNC auditor are listed below.

Dept.	Item Description	Price Ea.	Qty. Billed	Qty. Doc.	Qty. Allowed	Plus or Minus	Overcharge	Undercharge	Rationale
						0	$0.00	$0.00	
						0	$0.00	$0.00	
						0	$0.00	$0.00	
						0	$0.00	$0.00	
						0	$0.00	$0.00	
						0	$0.00	$0.00	
						0	$0.00	$0.00	
						0	$0.00	$0.00	
						0	$0.00	$0.00	
						0	$0.00	$0.00	
						0	$0.00	$0.00	
						0	$0.00	$0.00	
						0	$0.00	$0.00	
						0	$0.00	$0.00	
						0	$0.00	$0.00	
						0	$0.00	$0.00	
						0	$0.00	$0.00	
						0	$0.00	$0.00	
						0	$0.00	$0.00	
						0	$0.00	$0.00	
						0	$0.00	$0.00	
						0	$0.00	$0.00	
						0	$0.00	$0.00	
						0	$0.00	$0.00	
						0	$0.00	$0.00	
						0	$0.00	$0.00	
						0	$0.00	$0.00	
						0	$0.00	$0.00	

Figure 18.2 Hospital bill review.

Calendar of Treatments, Procedures and Office Visits
John Smith   File No. xxxxx

	Evaluations by Baraque, and PT.
	Received PT, reevaluated by Baraque, then seen by Cabrera.
	ROM, Nerve, and Lift testing with Cabrera.
	Neurological consultation with Martinez.
	Received PT and went for EEG and Neurological follow-up

Figure 18.3 Calendar of treatments, procedures, and office visits for patient John Smith.

For the Plaintiff

- Verify bills for damages.
- Establish medical damages when care was provided by nonbilling institutions, such as Veteran's hospitals, National Institutes of Health, or managed care organizations.
- Determine if all provider records are present.
- Identify the billing issues upon which defense may focus, such as lengthy and/or excessive treatment, excessively high fees charged by physicians, etc.
- Identify the impact of preexisting conditions on billings.
- Corroborate plaintiff's allegations of malpractice.
- Provide basis for lien and/or settlement negotiation.

For the Defendant

- Verify medical damages.
- Decrease damages by disallowing charges
    Relating to preexisting conditions
    For services not provided to patient

> For services provided, but not in accordance with regulations
> For services provided, but not medically appropriate nor necessary

- Decrease damages by
  > Adjustment of CPT coding to reflect actual provided services
  > Utilization of U & C database
  > Application of U & C treatment schedule in absence of substantiating medical records from provider
- Dispute plaintiff's allegations of medical malpractice.
- Determine if all provider records are present.
- Point out "red flags" indicating possible fraud.
- Provide a basis for settlement negotiation.

In conjunction with the bill review, the LNC prepares an understandable and defensible report for the client, whether attorney, insurance adjuster, investigator, or other person. Clear explanations for decisions made during the audit process relative to charges, various legal issues, missing records, and possible suspicious activity should be presented. Regulatory citations and other references should be included when applicable.

Bill Review Testimony

There may be occasions when the client wishes testimony concerning the bill review report or when opposing counsel wishes to depose the auditor. In these instances, the LNC functions as a testifying expert and is expected to have the necessary credentials to perform in this role: credible experience, ability to present the issues in easy and understandable language, and proper courtroom demeanor. Prior to accepting an audit assignment, the LNC should inquire about the likelihood that testimony will be involved. Regardless, the auditor should always be prepared and willing to explain and defend the audit report at deposition or trial if necessary.

Opportunities for Health Care Bill Auditing for the Legal Nurse Consultant

Numerous opportunities exist for the LNC who desires to either augment services offered to clients or employers or to seek new arenas of practice. Examples of those areas in which the LNC's bill review experience can be exercised include

- Case management organizations
- Insurance firms
- Hospitals: risk management, defense and revenue auditing
- Law offices, plaintiff and defense
- Private investigative agencies performing medical investigations (fraud)
- Independent LNC practice

The addition of bill review to the LNC's practice can be rewarding, not only from the financial aspect, but in terms of task satisfaction as well. Although the initial investment in time and the proper tools may be costly, the end results will more than compensate. For those entrepreneurial LNCs who do not have the time, the budget, or the inclination to perform bill review, it is suggested that they affiliate with an accomplished LNC auditor. An experienced and sage LNC once said, "Never turn down a job. Find someone to do it for you."

References

Code It Right, Salt Lake City, Medicode, 1996 (1-800-999-4600).

Coders' Desk Reference, Salt Lake City, Medicode (1-800-999-4600).

CP "Teach", Dallas, MedBooks, 1994 (1-800-443-7397).

Drug Topics Red Book, Montvale: Medical Economics Data, updated yearly.

Fee & Coding Strategies, Salt Lake City, Medicode, updated yearly (1-800-999-4600).

Fee Facts, Woodstock, GA, Data Management Ventures, Inc., updated yearly.

Guidelines for Chiropractic Quality Assurance and Practice Parameters, Gaithersburg, MD, Aspen Publishers, 1993.

International Classification of Diseases—Clinical Modification, Salt Lake City, Medicode, updated yearly.

Physician Fees, Los Angeles, PMIC, updated yearly (1-800-MEDSHOP).

Physicians GenRX, Mosby-Year Book, St. Louis, MO, updated yearly (1-800-426-4545).

Physicians Current Procedural Terminology, Chicago, American Medical Association, updated yearly.

Procedural/Utilization Facts, 4th ed., Woodstock, GA, Data Management Ventures, Inc., 1992.

Chapter 19

Case Analysis: Evaluating Professional Negligence Cases

Doreen James Wise, Julie Bogart, and Sue Mahley

Contents

1-57444-123-X/98
© 1998 by American Association of Legal Nurse Consultants

Objectives

- To identify the key elements of professional negligence suits
- To describe and perform the steps in critically evaluating professional negligence cases for liability, causation, and damages
- To delineate the unique contribution of LNCs to professional negligence litigation, including developing case strategies
- To differentiate the unique properties of the selection/qualification process of expert witnesses for professional negligence litigation
- To address "other" issues which can impact the pursuit and outcome of professional negligence litigation

Introduction

Perhaps the most poignant litigation in which legal nurse consultants (LNCs) are involved, and that for which they are most specially qualified, is professional, i.e., medical or nursing, negligence. When a plaintiff believes that there has been an injury as a direct result of negligent healthcare, one avenue of recourse provided by law is the pursuit of litigation.

LNCs offer valuable informed assistance in the development of either the plaintiff's or defense case, and may be found serving as law firm employees, independent consultants, and testifying expert witnesses. The extensive education, analytical skills, and clinical experience of the seasoned LNC can contribute to the business-like evaluation and informed assistance with professional negligence litigation. However, such litigation is fraught with challenge: the LNC must perform a critical job in the face of powerful forces inherent in medical negligence work. The plaintiff may be profoundly injured, the family overwhelmed, and the amount of money at stake, staggering. Also at work is the still-prevailing societal view attributing almost godlike properties to healthcare professionals. Correspondingly, healthcare professionals remain reluctant to participate in candid clinical peer evaluation, and juries can seem hesitant to penalize even disturbingly negligent care. Complicating matters further, some attorneys accept cases based solely on the "jury appeal" driven by the potential financial value of the plaintiff's injuries, even when there may have been no professional negligence. Unhappily, in such cases even an innocent defendant is forced to prepare and mount a costly defense. In other cases in which there has been negligent care proven, some defense attorneys needlessly prolong litigation in order to maximize their hourly billing to the insurer client, or to exhaust the plaintiff's resources before the case is completed. These forces and others serve to make professional negligence a tumultuous, demanding arena of LNC practice.

The Key Elements

As always, the burden of proof is on the plaintiff. Thus, the LNC evaluating a plaintiff's action in consult to either plaintiff or defense attorney must appraise the case for four key attributes. If these particular qualities are not present, the plaintiff's attorney cannot "get to the jury," i.e., meet the requirements specified by law to bring or "prove" a plaintiff's action. Not uncommonly, the LNC's greatest contribution from either plaintiff or defense perspective is the sophisticated, dispassionate analysis of the events and outcomes in a medical misadventure for worthiness as a malpractice case.

Any professional negligence action must meet four demands, commonly known as the Four D's. The LNC can play a role in determining whether or not they are met; the criteria to be determined are

1. Was there a **D**uty for the defendant to provide care to the plaintiff?
2. Was there a **D**ereliction of that duty (negligence)?
3. Are there **D**amages?
4. Are they **D**ue to, or a **D**irect result of, the negligence (is there proximate cause)?

Is There a Duty?

Ordinarily, this consideration will be performed by the attorney, and is a matter of law. Although infrequently involved in this appraisal, the LNC may be asked to research the nature of the relationship between plaintiff and possible defendant. Was there a duty on the part of the healthcare provider to perform certain functions for the patient? A case in point is *Lunsford v. Board of Nurse Examiners of the State of Texas*. In this matter a supplemental staffing nurse followed hospital policy and the staff doctor's input by referring an emergent patient with a myocardial infarct in progress to a public hospital some miles distant, rather than assessing and initiating treatment herself. The patient arrested and died en route. In its findings, the Board of Nurse Examiners opined that because she was practicing under an RN license, issued at the pleasure of the state's citizenry, Nurse Lunsford held a duty to serve the patient that transcended doctor's orders and hospital policy! Nurse Lunsford lost her license and the right to practice, although the physician did not. A civil appellate court upheld the finding on appeal; as of this writing, the opinion stands.

Was There Negligence?

Negligence is the failure to meet the standard of care, i.e., failing to do what the reasonably prudent healthcare provider would do in similar circumstances. It must be differentiated from a mistake, an error in judgment, or a bad outcome resulting from acceptable care. Malpractice "refers to any professional misconduct that encompasses an unreasonable lack of skill or unfaithfulness in carrying out professional or fiduciary duties," (Flamm, 1995, p. 118). Because professional negligence litigation is more technical than the scope of common knowledge, the law requires in most circumstances that expert witnesses with special medical qualifications provide guidance to the judge or jury. The determination of standards of care ordinarily must be made through the articulation of published and practice standards through the informed opinion of a qualified testifying expert witness. In this manner, the jury is provided access to enough technical information to render a more-informed judgment.

The standard of care must be articulated through testimony of a properly qualified expert witness. Although rules of procedure vary by state, in general the best expert witness for either plaintiff or defense will have comparable education and experience to that of the defendant, will have been practicing in a similar setting at the time of the incident in question, and also will be in current active practice. Having been duly qualified, the expert may articulate the standard of care relevant to the matter in question, based on that professional's education and clinical experience. After independent review of all facts, and critique of care actually given and documented, the expert may then offer an opinion about whether the care in question met the standard or was indeed negligent.

To further the effort, the LNC reviews the healthcare literature to determine standards of care published by professional organizations and certifying bodies. The American Medical Association (AMA) prints and distributes a compendium of sources of professional practice standards across many health disciplines (AMA, 1997). The LNC studies the medical records, comparing and contrasting care documented with published standards, determining whether or not there was a breach of the standard of care in a given matter. This appraisal will help to educate the attorney and to determine the case issues and worthiness; it will also facilitate exacting selection of properly qualified experts. Based on federal or the individual state's rules for civil procedure, the LNC may search for and recommend appropriately qualified experts to the attorney (see Chapter 32). The LNC may coordinate the dispatch of records to the selected expert, then follow up to determine opinions and needs for additional materials. In matters concerning nursing care, the independent, clinically active LNC may be approached to serve as the reviewing and, later, testifying expert.

In rare instances, the issue in question in a professional negligence suit is deemed to be within the arena of common knowledge, or common sense for the jury. Known as *res ipse loquitur,* literally the thing speaks for itself, in most states these cases require no expert testimony for proof of the liability issues. In fact, all the plaintiff must prove is that the instrument or object causing the damages was "in the exclusive control of the defendant; that the plaintiff did not voluntarily contribute to the result; and that the injury was the type not normally occurring in the absence of negligence" (Hoffman, 1995, p. 134). Once the plaintiff has so proved, the burden falls to the defendant to disprove any such responsibility.

Example 19.1: After surgery, and a period of unexplained complications, a patient is determined to have a surgical instrument present in the operative site. Such a case can be litigated successfully without the testimony of a surgeon or nurse since it is evident that a foreign body left inadvertently is by definition negligent. Expert testimony might be helpful, however, in determining the mechanism of injury, i.e., exactly what the object left behind has done to harm the patient.

Example 19.2: In *Beverly Enterprises-Virginia v. Nichols* 441 S. E. 2d 1-VA(1994), the decedent was an elderly patient with Alzheimer's prone to choke if not spoon-fed as ordered. In fact, when left to feed herself unattended, despite orders to the contrary, she choked and died. Her family successfully brought a wrongful death suit against the nursing home. When the nursing home appealed the case because the plaintiff had failed to provide expert witness testimony, the appellate court upheld the lower court's ruling. "The nursing home and its staff were aware of the patient's mental and physical condition ... the fact that she was unable to feed herself and that she had had two prior choking incidents. In spite of this knowledge, the nursing home's employee left a tray of food with the patient and failed to provide assistance to her. Certainly, a jury does not need expert testimony to ascertain whether the defendant was negligent because its personnel failed to assist the patient under these circumstances" (*The Regan Report: Nursing Law*, 1994.)

Are There Damages?

To meet the requirements for proof in potential malpractice cases, there must be evidence of injury sustained as a result of the negligence alleged. Medical damages, i.e., "actual loss or damage to the interests of the patient" (Sanbar et al. 1995, p. 120) can be financial, physical, or mental in nature. As a general rule, the more observable, extensive, and comprehensible any damages are to a jury, the more "desirable" they are found by the plaintiff's attorney. For the same reasons, they seem more ominous to the defense attorney. Given the monetary costs of extensive care projected across a lifetime, and the value traditionally placed on youth in our culture, cases involving injury to an infant, child, or young person are also seen as greater financial threats to the defense, and potentially more rewarding to the plaintiff.

Documentation of damages is most often found in the medical records; for this reason collection, organization, and detailed assessment of complete medical records is critical to support or dispute damage claims. Another significant source of information about damages is the plaintiff and family themselves. Collection of data regarding damages also may be accomplished in a variety of ways allowed for under rules of discovery, including preliminary interview by the plaintiff's attorney considering taking the case; answers to requests for production and interrogatories from both sides; depositions of plaintiff, family, and treating health care professionals; private investigation; and independent examination of the plaintiff and family, augmented by assessment of their living conditions. The product of such inquiry is documentation and detailed understanding of the nature and extent of damages alleged.

Assessment of damages is one of the strongest arenas for positive LNC contribution. The painstaking review, summary, and evaluation of all medical information is best accomplished by an LNC, usually in two phases. For the LNC assisting a plaintiff's attorney, a preliminary review of the records for evidence of damages can be undertaken early in the case. Having already ascertained particular acts of negligence, the LNC entertains theories of damages for which to search the records, thereby focusing review efforts in an informed manner. This early review for damages by LNCs assisting plaintiff's attorneys can support responsible determination of whether suit should even be filed.

The business reality of medical malpractice litigation may mean that if there are no damages resulting from even grave acts of negligence, the plaintiff's attorney will not undertake the case. Plaintiff's attorneys may use the following four questions to gauge whether or not to accept a case:

- Does the damage justify contingency fee representation?
- Can the damages be readily proved to be due to negligent conduct?

- Can a board-certified, reputable physician provide clear and convincing evidence that the defendant breached the standard of care?
- Is the claim credible?

These are questions the LNC must also consider and address. There may be irrefutable negligence, but damages too small to warrant recommending that the attorney proceed with the case. Sometimes there is evidence of damages in the medical record of which the attorney is unaware.

Example 19.3: One LNC tells of reviewing a record involving a 33-year-old male alleging unnecessary GI surgery, who had been too embarrassed to reveal the resulting sexual dysfunction to his attorney. In the medical records reviewed by the LNC there was an almost illegible reference made by the treating urologist to "problems with erections." The LNC obtained and summarized a complete copy of that doctor's records and found documentation of permanent sexual dysfunction with plans made for future penal implant. This revelation of the extent of damages helped the attorney decide to commit to the case.

Once suit has been filed, and discovery is underway, the LNC working either side will want to perform a more extensive damage assessment. As seen in the example above, detailed documentation found in the records of medical providers' offers clues to the veracity and extent of the plaintiff's suffering. Typically, nursing notes are replete with such entries. Consistency is a crucial entity to assess — does the plaintiff complaining of unremitting pain have a correspondingly curtailed lifestyle? If at all questionable, the attorney may even go so far as to hire an investigator to videotape secretly the plaintiff in his normal daily routine. In one instance, an attorney taped his own would-be client, who was claiming unremitting back pain, as the "injured" man loaded a friend's furniture into a moving van! In another true story, a nursing note stated, "… patient shuffles and stumbles when around staff, but was observed walking normally when she thought no one was watching!" Comparison and contrast of current level of function with the plaintiff's premalpractice activity also help to document the extent of change resulting from the negligence. All such damages must be directly caused by the acts of negligence.

Is There Proximate Cause?

In order to proceed successfully with professional negligence cases, the plaintiff must show that any damages claimed were caused directly by the act(s) of negligence of the defendant(s). Correspondingly, the defense challenge is to dispute and disprove such a proximately causal relationship. Legal causation varies from medical causation in that it "refers to a single cause and not necessarily the only cause or even the most immediate cause of the injury, as is the case in medical causation…. [L]egal causation is sometimes the most complex and elusive concept in a professional negligence case" (Flamm, 1995, p. 119).

Legal causation involves *causation in fact* and *foreseeability*. The plaintiff must prove that defendant's negligence was the cause in fact of injuries and that those damages were reasonably foreseeable. Causation in fact can be tested with the so-called "but for" test, in which a certain event, in this case an injury, is caused by, or happens only because of the occurrence of another event, the negligence.

The damage in question would not have taken place *but for* the negligent acts of the health care provider.

> Example 19.4: Five hours following esophageal dilatation, a patient was found to have a gastric perforation. *But for* the negligently performed dilatation, there would have been no medical misadventure, i.e., the subsequent perforation. This meets the test for causation in fact.

Foreseeability implies that the damages must be "the foreseeable result of a defendant health care provider's substandard practice" (Flamm, 1995, p. 120). In the example above, perforation is a foreseeable and known risk of dilatation when the procedure is not properly performed. Delay in diagnosis and treatment is a common precipitant for professional negligence actions. The key issue is determining whether or not an obvious delay makes a difference in the occurrence of a negative outcome. The LNC would review and carefully evaluate related literature for the necessary information. Perhaps best of all failure to diagnose cancer cases exemplify this issue.

> Example 19.5: A patient experienced a 15-month delay between the onset of symptoms and diagnosis of small bowel malignancy. The attorney dismissed the case after learning that this patient's prognosis more than likely was *not* improved by earlier diagnosis, i.e., there was no causation between the failure to diagnose in a timely manner and the patient's condition (Fink and Chaudhuri, 1995, 1014).

In the above example the plaintiff's damages would have occurred even without the delay in treatment. "Many jurisdictions hold that in such a situation, a plaintiff cannot recover any damages unless she/he can prove that there was a greater than 50% chance of survival if the diagnosis would have been made earlier and treatment more timely" (Flamm, 1995, p. 126).

Proximate cause is so essential to the outcome of any case that legal professionals may seek the independent review and opinion of a qualified causation expert even prior to that of a liability expert. Expert opinions regarding causation are required under any circumstances, and often necessitate retaining additional, more-specialized health care professionals for the role. This is especially true in cases with extensive injury and/or in which the plaintiff is deemed to have very strong "jury appeal." To identify strong experts on causation, the LNC first will analyze the medical literature in refereed journals. By seeking medical experts in literature written and critiqued by credentialed medical professionals, one is more likely assured higher-quality opinion and compliance with the demands exerted by the *Daubert* decision. (The reader is advised to review Chapter 32.) No doubt the single most frustrating situation for a plaintiff's attorney is to be told by the consulting LNC or causation expert that while compelling evidence of negligence and tragic damage exist, there is no support for a causal relationship between the two because of an intervening cause. Perhaps no greater defense challenge exists than defending a professional who implemented the best care possible with an unavoidable tragic patient outcome. Starting case review with opinion from a strong causation expert can anticipate and resolve either dilemma.

Exception to the Rule: Loss of Chance

Generally, proof of causation requires expert testimony stating that to a reasonable degree of medical certainty the healthcare provider's failure to meet standard of care proximately caused the injuries alleged. The burden of proof is *more likely than not* said negligence caused the injury. There must be a probability of greater than 50% that the injury occurred as a result of the defendant's negligent care. If this burden of proof is met, the plaintiff can recover monetary compensation for 100% of the injury even if there is as much as a 49% chance that the injury would have occurred anyway. This is the *all-or-nothing* concept of determining damages once the burden of proof for causation is met.

There are cases in which proof of causation falls below this greater than 50% benchmark. If the plaintiff is shown, for example, to have a 30% or 40% chance of survival (or of avoiding injury) absent the negligent acts, shouldn't that plaintiff be compensated for the *loss of chance* to survive, or to be healthy? In the classic example of the patient with undetected cancer above, the decedent's chances of survival might have been markedly reduced by the defendant's negligent oversight. The plaintiff alleged that although a cure was not probable even when symptoms first appeared, the doctor failed to detect, diagnose, and treat in a timely manner. The cancerous tumor was discovered too late to cure and the patient's chances of survival were drastically reduced. Under the all-or-nothing rule, the patient would recover nothing unless earlier detection would have assured a greater than 50% chance of 5-year survival.

In some courts however, recovery can be made for a *50% or less* chance of survival. This has been done through relaxation of the standard of proof of causation or by allowing a new cause of action for loss of chance. Plaintiffs before these courts can recover for damages based on the percentage of harm actually caused by the defendant(s), reflecting an actual value of the chance that was lost. If the negligence is shown, for example, to have reduced a patient's survival from 45% to 25%, the negligent defendant is liable for 25% of the damages. Judge William Adkins' comment in *Fennell v. Maryland Hospital Center,* 580 A.2d 206,216(Md.1990) expresses the reasoning on which loss of chance theory is based:

> Tort law is not about mathematical niceties; it has to do with fairness to fault free victims who have suffered harm by reason of the tortuous acts or omission of others. It is a basic principle of our tort system that those who can prove they have been so harmed should be compensated. Why should we reject that principle when the harm is a loss of chance of survival that is less than 51 percent? Is it fair that one who can show that the doctor's negligence had a 51 percent possibility of producing harm complained of can recover full damages whereas if the proof is only a 50 percent possibility, there can be no recovery whatsoever? Obviously not.

In such cases, the plaintiff still must prove that there was a deviation from standard of care, and that negligence caused the patient to lose substantial possibility of survival or of avoiding injury.

Example 19.6: A patient with history of myocardial infarction, stroke, and unstable angina was admitted for a five-vessel coronary bypass. During the postoperative days he had several occasions of respiratory problems, was transferred to a critical care unit for a bronchoscopy and treatment, then returned to the nursing unit. The patient's wife testified that her calls for nursing assistance on the first day there went unheeded for 1 hour and 15 minutes, during which the patient stopped breathing. Her husband suffered a respiratory arrest from which he died 2 days later. Nurse expert Celia Krebs (an AALNC member) testified that the nurses fell below standard of appropriate care in many ways, including failing to note that the patient was at high risk for respiratory arrest and taking responsive precautions. Testimony by a physician panel member stated that the patient should have been cared for in the critical care unit, and that because of the negligent care rendered by the floor nurses, the patient's chances of survival were lessened. "Accordingly, the Court adopted a 'loss of chance' doctrine," *Ard v. East Jefferson General Hospital,* 636 So. 2d 1042 LA (1994).

The LNC is advised to determine state law regarding loss of chance proof of causation. If the damages failed to be more likely than not attributable to the negligence, were they nonetheless related, but to a lesser degree? Did the negligence substantially increase the risk of harm or, alternatively, eliminate a substantial possibility to survive, to recover, or to avoid injury? The LNC must answer these questions by reviewing the medical literature to determine:

1. That the suggested intervention is generally accepted by the medical community, and
2. That reliable medical studies or treatises confirm the likelihood of successful treatment.

One may then reason that by failing to institute proven treatment, the defendant was negligent, increasing harm to the patient and/or causing the patient to lose a reasonable opportunity to recover (Apfel, 1993; Hoffman, 1995).

Another key role for the LNC is to comb carefully the medical records and other discovery for signs of preexisting or intervening causes for the plaintiff's alleged damages.

Example 19.7: A plaintiff alleging "unable to walk" as a result of back surgery had engaged the plaintiff attorney's interest in taking his case. On review of the medical records, the plaintiff was found by the LNC to have had spina bifida, a congenital defect, confining him to a wheelchair from birth! The limitations associated with this preexisting condition must be differentiated from any changes resulting from the alleged negligence.

Example 19.8: A plaintiff alleging AIDS by an HIV-infected transfusion was found to have been subsequently exposed to an HIV-positive sexual partner. This was an intervening, and mitigating, factor in the case.

Example 19.9: A plaintiff alleged that her deceased husband contracted and succumbed to hepatitis C from an infected blood product given for emergent cranial hemorrhage. Initially doubtful about the case because hepatitis is a known risk of transfusion, the plaintiff's attorney only became enthused about the case through investigatory efforts of a local LNC engaged to review the case. Thorough review of prior medical records yielded evidence of an earlier malpractice. Some months before the hemorrhage, the patient had received several anticoagulant drugs but was never evaluated or followed for bleeding potential. The emergent hemorrhage was more likely than not the subsequent result. But for that earlier malpractice, there would have been no hemorrhage nor the need for blood products. Legal causation, though not proximate in time, was convincingly demonstrated nonetheless, and the case resolved for the plaintiff.

Once the LNC has reviewed the case for liability and causation, the next step in a plaintiff's practice is to prepare to file suit.

Filing a Professional Negligence Claim

If review of medical records and contrast with published standards and those articulated by expert witnesses reveal evidence of negligence and resulting damages, the plaintiff's attorney likely will "give notice" and file suit. The suit must be filed within the period of time allowed for such claims, the *statute of limitations*. Pleadings will be filed detailing the events, alleging negligence, and claiming damages suffered as a direct result of said breach of the standard of care. The defendant must "answer," usually through counsel. The defense attorney faced with a bona fide negligent defendant may advise the client to offer insurance policy limits to settle the matter early in the suit. This, of course, is the most elegant scenario when there has been negligence. Although money is at best an incomplete solace to any injured plaintiff, when offered in a timely manner and in keeping with the seriousness of injury, it can make the plaintiff's life more tolerable. However, this quiet acknowledgment of negligence and dignified resolution of the matter is a rare occurrence. There also may be some reluctance to settle prematurely since all settlements are noted in a national database.

The LNC may be a participant in the drafting of medically related portions of the pleadings, or reviewing and evaluating them for the attorney. Correspondingly, the LNC working with defense attorneys may advise about the veracity and significance of the allegations, medically speaking. LNCs may be participant-advisors in negotiation and settlement proceedings, providing medical information and support to the attorney (see Chapter 27).

Once suit has been filed, a growing number of states require that a written report or affidavit attesting to the merit of each plaintiff's malpractice action be submitted to the court within a specified short time after filing. Varying with the laws of individual states, there are some commonalties. Ordinarily, such affidavits confirm that the filing attorney has obtained a written opinion by a legally qualified healthcare professional outlining each named defendant's professional negligence. The written opinion must state that the defendant failed to use such care as a reasonably prudent and careful healthcare provider would have done under similar circumstances and that such failure to use reasonable care directly caused the damages claimed in the petition. The affidavit must cite the qualifications of the expert offering the opinion. In some states, such as Texas, the identity of the expert is revealed *in camera* (to the judge only); in others it is never revealed, and the "affiant," or author, of the affidavit never needs to testify. However, in ideal circumstances, the attorney seeks expert review and affidavits prior to filing suit. In the best possible case the expert writing the report or affidavit also testifies as an expert witness.

In cases with nurse defendants, or defendants who employ nurses and cover them under *respondat superiore*, the LNC may be qualified to prepare and submit such affidavits, later testifying as an expert. In those states in which the author of the affidavit must have special knowledge but is not necessarily required to testify, there is an even greater possible role for LNCs. It is incumbent on the LNC pursuing this role to research and comply with all state regulations; LNCs must be sure of their eligibility to qualify in this role before signing an affidavit.

Selecting the Best Experts

Appraisal of medical experts for malpractice cases demands particular attention to detail. In addition to those qualities highlighted in Chapter 32, there are several additional considerations in this particular arena of medical litigation. Although specific traits are valued depending on the locale, the following qualities, while sometimes appearing mutually exclusive, are *all* of value in a testifying medical expert.

Qualities desirable in an expert:

1. Well educated, clinically experienced, board-certified in at least one field; if not certified, then board-eligible (Check to see if there are any abnormalities, i.e., multiple attempts to pass the certifying exams.)
2. Current active clinical practice and practice at the time of the incident
3. No record of ever having testified before (If prior testimony, a balance between plaintiff and defense is preferred.)
4. Despite #3, above, sophisticated presentation as an expert witness
5. Alternatively to #4, an experienced, unflappable teacher (An outstanding expert remembers that the jury often approach their service with the respect they accord church attendance, and expect that level of mutual respect of attorneys and experts. The most appreciated expert establishes rapport with the jury and testifies steadfastly, respectfully, and in an unruffled manner even in the face of harrowing cross-examination.)
6. No prior malpractice suits against the expert, or more realistically, if sued, suits in which the expert clinician prevailed
7. No "skeletons" in one's personal closet (Some attorneys would include divorce, psychotherapy, traffic violations, prior professional negligence lawsuits, bankruptcy, discharge from employment, unflattering news coverage (even if inaccurate), having been retained through an LNC or other "service," or truly serious occurrences. In fact, most such "skeletons" do not necessarily rule out expert service. However, it is in the best interest of the case if such items are revealed proactively to the attorney so any "damage control" can be undertaken.)
8. Consistent opinions in public writings and testimony (Nothing is more embarrassing to the expert, nor more damaging to a case, than prior writings which contradict the expert's opinions in the case. The LNC is forewarned to review in detail all public utterances of any expert.)

9. Expert testimony as a minimal portion of total income (The strength of any clinical expert's opinion is drawn from clinical expertise. While an expert in another field may be able to make a career as an expert, the minute a medical professional leaves or dramatically reduces active practice, usefulness as an expert on medical negligence matters diminishes. A variation of this caution is an expert who demands an extraordinarily high hourly fee. Attorneys gravitate to the expert who has the same modest hourly fee for review and testimony or who donates fees to charity! It is advisable to avoid any expert who hints that the fee is based on the opinion, or opens by saying to the attorney, "What is it you want me to say?"!!)

While evaluation of the expert's credibility always is important, it is imperative when the case relies substantially on that expert's testimony.

Example 19.10: Beware the case that is not substantially proven by the written record, but must rely heavily on testimony from plaintiff, defendant, or other fact witnesses. The opposition will offer contradicting testimony from their witnesses in rebuttal. In such a "swearing match" the believability of the witness becomes the key to success rather than only hard evidence.

LNCs closely resemble and are knowledgeable about jurors. It is of considerable help for the experienced LNC to meet with critical witnesses in addition to the usual screening. To establish and cement credibility, the LNC can anticipate and ask, in a pretestimony setting, the same questions a juror would ask if allowed to do so. By listening and observing, making note of what is believable and what might be distrusted or discarded as false, the LNC can help to maximally qualify the expert for such cases. The LNC should also secure the expert's references, talking directly with any other attorney with whom the expert has worked.

Other Issues

Defense Issues

LNCs play a key role in both plaintiff's and defense cases. Those assisting defense attorneys can provide support to defendants in the form of updates on litigation progress and events, "reality testing" information (e.g., language used in documents stating allegations of negligence are routinely "boilerplated" on the plaintiff attorney's computer, and are not personal), and encouragement for the confused and baffled defendant. The LNC can also provide accurate information to the attorney about the defendant's capacity to testify in his or her own behalf and pinpoint any inaccuracy to the plaintiff's allegations. It is also extremely helpful to teach the defendant how to present well in deposition and trial; as in any other arena for practice, there are skills and approaches that work best in those settings. Defensiveness or arrogance can be masks for the fear and anxiety any defendant may feel; however, emphasizing the defendant's more humane traits can bring greater empathy and understanding from the jury.

Accusations of professional negligence can be devastating to healthcare providers. Such accusations often become turning points in their lives; some settle their cases prematurely or even leave practice rather than run the risk of future long and grueling litigation experiences. Most healthcare providers are sincere, caring professionals who do not intentionally err. They may be disappointed or disillusioned by allegations of negligence from patients they sought to cure. They can be stunned to find that medical colleagues will testify against them, sometimes even when no negligence has taken place. Inevitably, they are shocked when treated callously or worse by the plaintiff's, or their own insurer's, attorneys. Valuable practitioners can be lost to medicine following vigorous pursuit of an invalid lawsuit.

Plaintiff Issues

Life as a litigant is usually a lonely and a miserable one; this author actively discourages undertaking it in all but the most evident cases of medical negligence. As noted elsewhere (Wise and Green, 1996), the plaintiff in professional negligence cases becomes "fair game" for the defense attorney. By the time a negligence case is filed, then litigated to resolution, any number of years may have passed. Frequently, plaintiffs in catastrophic cases are financially, physically, and emotionally drained of all resources long before the process ends in some manner. Even plaintiffs whose previous lives had been balanced and joyful are usually enervated when it is finally time to go to trial. Their lives are routinely combed by the defense attorney seeking details which could potentially influence the case. A successful plaintiff's attorney will have conducted close inquiry before agreeing to represent them — are they who and how they claim to be? Did they contribute themselves in any way to the negligence? Are there skeletons in their own closets that will emerge under close inspection–history of drug abuse, psychiatric problems, etc.? As with experts, such skeletons rarely undo the plaintiff's day in court; they do need to be identified and proactively revealed by the plaintiff's attorney, however. Failing to do this homework can be disastrous during discovery; the diligent defense attorney surely will have done that same homework, revealing the findings as if the plaintiff had intended to deceive by withholding it.

Strategies need to be planned for coping with any unsavory qualities, or those with the potential to aggravate the anticipated prejudices of the jury. As part of the due diligence conducted for the would-be plaintiff, it is also important to point out the rigors of litigation; in high-stakes claims, any and all skeletons will be brought out with the worst possible spin placed on them. It is ethical to anticipate for the already stressed claimant that life is about to get much worse, at least for the duration of litigation, the outcome of which is uncertain at best. It is critical that the plaintiff understand the contract with the attorney, and the fee arrangements; this is not only the ethical thing to do, but may help to prevent later lawsuits by claimants unhappy with the terms of settlement.

Once the decision is made to proceed despite the risks, the LNC can help evaluate the plaintiff and family's potential impact on the jury, and "teach" them how to best present their view of the case. As described above for defendants, there are skills associated with being a successful plaintiff; the attorney who works well with the client has a better chance to win the case. Not having one's client working in concert with the attorney's strategy has lost more than one otherwise strong malpractice case.

LNCs working with plaintiff's attorneys can provide accurate information about medical precedent without being biased by the tragedy of the plaintiff's conditions. In this way, more responsible lawsuits are pursued; in addition, the strengths of the case can be emphasized and the lesser aspects of the case minimized.

In conclusion, LNCs play a responsible, informative role in plaintiff or defense preparation of professional negligence cases. It may be helpful for the LNC assisting with the development or defense of a professional negligence action to consult the following checklist.

Legal Nurse Consultant Professional Negligence Checklist

1. Are medical records complete? If not, create a list of others needed and see that they are obtained.
2. Has any conflict of interest been ruled out? Law firm and LNC must be certain there is neither an outright conflict, or even the appearance of a conflict. *Example:* Independent LNC working with both plaintiff and defense on same case is a conflict of interest.
3. Have all records been reviewed entirely? Has chronological summary of critical medical events been prepared?
4. Have medical-legal issues been identified? Has dispassionate assessment been made of both strengths and weaknesses of the case?
5. Has a list of all of the plaintiff's medical providers been prepared, with address, phone, and practice license number included? From this listing, have potentially culpable parties been identified with listing of negligent offenses (for plaintiff's case), or has each alleged act of negligence been independently assessed?
6. Are all "four Ds" met? Is there negligence? Are there damages? Is the negligence causally related to the damages?
7. Has glossary of medical terms relative to the case been prepared? Appropriate anatomic drawings? Has medical literature been reviewed and "learned treatises" prepared? Learned treatises consist of annotated review and critique of related professional literature, highlighted for support or possible disagreement with the medical-legal issues of the case. Be sure it includes, among others, publications written and cited as excellent by one's own and the opposition's expert witnesses.
8. Have all medical aspects of pleadings been prepared (plaintiff's) or answered (defense)? Have all medically related interrogatories been prepared and answered? During this phase, be certain to obtain all relevant internal policies and procedures from the defendant institution.
9. Have potential expert witnesses been identified, conflicts ruled out, curriculum vitae (CV) and current fee schedules obtained? Have background information, copies of relevant publications been critiqued? Are potentially applicable experts available during the time needed for review, deposition,

trial? Are they willing to go to trial? Has LNC and/or attorney interviewed expert by phone or face-to-face?

10. Have expert reports been solicited in a timely fashion? Do they contain the proper elements, i.e., citation/refutation of all acts of negligence, causal relationship to damages? Are reports complete enough to qualify the experts' testimony without being overfilled with information?

11. Have the opposition's experts been thoroughly investigated? Have sample questions been prepared for attorney's use in taking opposition's witnesses' depositions? The LNC should comb through opposition's expert's CV and publications for hints of inconsistency, unexplained breaks in service. Search *Science Citation Index* for other, possibly contradictory publications. Verify employment and references.

12. Have one's own experts been prepared for "worst-case scenario" questions they could be asked in deposition? Has background and *all prior testimony* of one's own experts been examined for possible vulnerabilities? If one's expert has testified numerous times, it is critical to be sure that testimony in similar cases is consistent. Beware of experts "for hire" who contradict themselves!

13. Have medically related trial exhibits been proposed and critiqued by experts? Has all testimony by medical experts been carefully reviewed; is testimony of own experts consistent and on point? Is there helpful/truly hurtful testimony from opposition's experts?

14. Has frank discussion been held with attorney: is this a case that should quietly settle, or is there true reason to try? What are the attorney's client's preferences?

Additional Case Examples for Discussion

Example 19.11: *Failure to Document* — An infant was born uneventfully to a mother with a history of herpes infection; although the mother's history was noted on the prenatal record, the newborn nursery RN failed to document same in her notes. The on-call pediatrician paged to the delivery looked no farther in the chart than the nurse's note, left the hospital after examining the baby, and mother and baby left the hospital 16 hours later. The baby developed neurological symptoms 12 days later, and was diagnosed with herpes encephalitis after the parents were finally asked about history of herpes; acyclovir was begun. The baby has spastic quadraparesis, developmental delays, and microcephaly. After trial, the jury was out for 2 days. They voted 9 to 3 exonerating the obstetrician and, surprisingly, the on-call pediatrician; they voted 12 to 0 to lay the entire blame on the hospital for the nurse's failure to make the proper entry into the record. There was a $3.6 million dollar award. "Perhaps ... [an] understandable error, but ... [an] expensive [one], was the failure of the nursery RN to note the history of herpes on the record. Why did the jury not fault the on-call pediatrician for failing to look beyond the top page (of the records)? Perhaps the jury's decision illustrates the vulnerability of an institution and the reluctance of a jury to hold a doctor liable" (Riverside County Superior Court No. 266494).

Example 19.12: *Failure to Assess, Intervene, Document* — T.B. was a 23-year-old gravida 1, para 0 admitted to labor and delivery (L&D) at 37-weeks gestation. A sonogram at 27 weeks had revealed "diminished" amniotic fluid volume, documented as well in subsequent sonograms. Nonstress tests (NSTs) scheduled weekly were consistently reported as "reactive." A persistent size–date discrepancy of approximately 2 weeks was evident at the office visits and confirmed by sonogram.

T.B. was scheduled for an NST the day before hospitalization; the one done 4 days prior was reportedly "reactive." Early the morning of the scheduled test T.B. had called her obstetrician's office complaining of decreased fetal movement beginning the day prior. The nurse advised her to come to the office as soon as possible. Arriving at 10:00 am, T.B. was seen by a nurse midwife; fetal heart rate was auscultated "with accelerations." T.B. was instructed to report for her NST as scheduled; at 1:15 the NST was documented as indicated for "decreased fluid volume and decreased fetal movement as reported by the patient," and interpreted as "not reactive with desired accelerations." Fetal heart rate was 150 to 160 beats per minute.

Reviewing the strip, the obstetrician noted "NST not strictly reactive but good beat-to-beat variability." The patient was released to go home, and scheduled for a biophysical profile with NST following the next afternoon. Although the nurse had assessed the patient with a nonreactive NST and a fetal heart pattern calling for further investigation (see Figure 19.1), she complied with the obstetrician's orders to release the patient.

The biophysical profile conducted the following afternoon was scored with 4 of a possible 10 points; the sonographer noted "fetus did not move or breathe during the 30 minute evaluation, nor did the fetus respond to larynx stimulation (Figure 19.2)." The sonographer went on to note that report had been called to the L&D nurse. The NST was interpreted as "questionable sinusoidal pattern" and the obstetrician had been notified of these results and those of the biophysical profile. Orders were then given for an oxytocin challenge test. This was initiated 2 hours later, although the obstetrician had been present on the unit, had examined the patient, and reviewed the fetal-monitoring strip (Figure 19.3).

Sterile vaginal exam revealed cervical dilatation of 1 cm. and thick. Oxytocin was begun and steadily increased. At 5:00 pm "subtle late decelerations; fetal heart rate pattern appears sinusoidal-like" was noted, and the obstetrician was called; fetal heart tones were 130 to 140 per minute, with contractions 2 minutes apart and 50 seconds in duration. A phone order from the obstetrician at 5:06 read "keep pitocin infusing." The nurse failed to object despite the nonreassuring FHT pattern.

At 5:40 spontaneous rupture of the membranes was recorded with concomitant decrease in long term variability and drop in baseline heart rate to 120 bpm. The nurse continued to administer oxytocin (Figure 19.4). At 6:00 the nurse noted that the obstetrician had called the unit and was advised of "questionable late decelerations"; by 6:05 he was on the unit turning off the oxytocin. There is no documentation of the nurse having begun intrauterine resuscitative efforts. Preparations for a cesarean section were begun.

Despite the fact that the delivery record indicated an emergency cesarean section was done for fetal distress, the 6-pound infant was not born until 7:03; Apgar scores were 2 at 1 minute and 3 at 5 minutes, the baby notably limp and pale. Cord blood was 7.15 with a base excess of −11.2. Initial hemoglobin was 2.8. The infant was judged to have suffered an acute intrapartum maternal-fetal bleed. Postdischarge the infant has experienced progressive developmental delays, definite left hemispheric insult with right-sided hypertonicity; she has spasticity and ophthalmologic involvement.

Comment: The reviewing nurse, an AALNC member, found three areas of nursing negligence

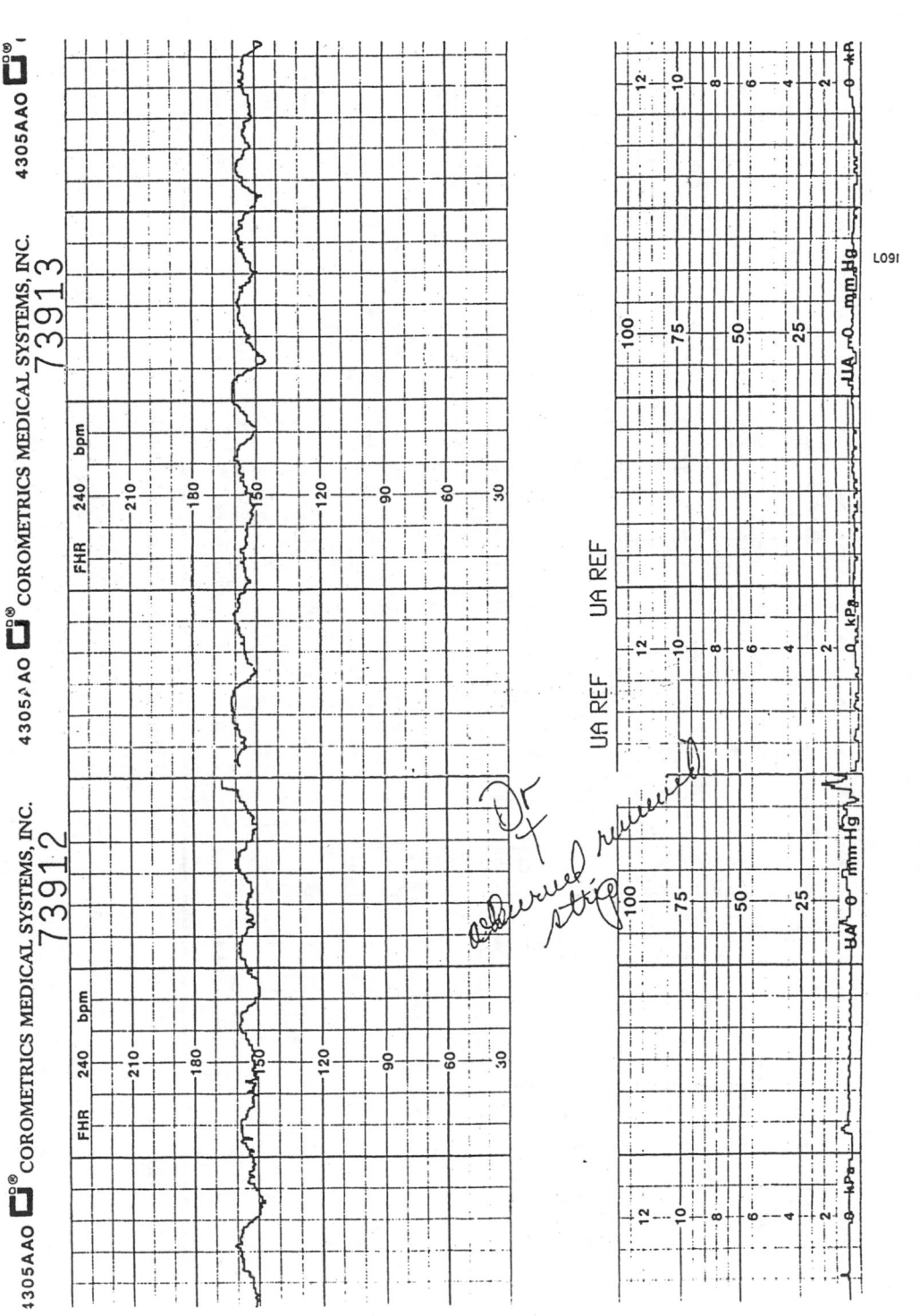

Figure 19.1   The sinusoidal pattern the nurse observed for 30 minutes during the NST on the day prior to admission. The nurse notes: "T. T. observed/reviewed strip."

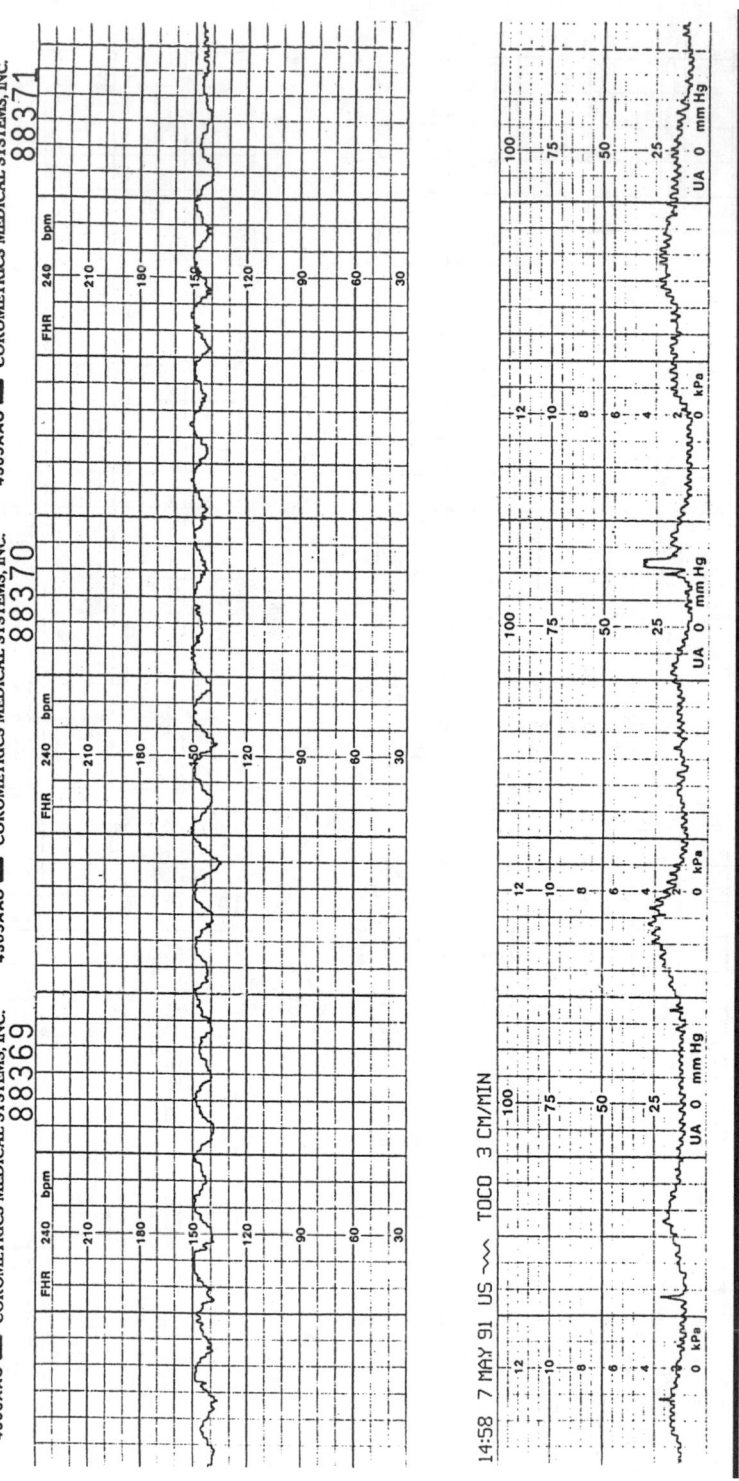

Figure 19.2 The NST of the day of T.B.'s hospital admission. The sinusoidal pattern continues.

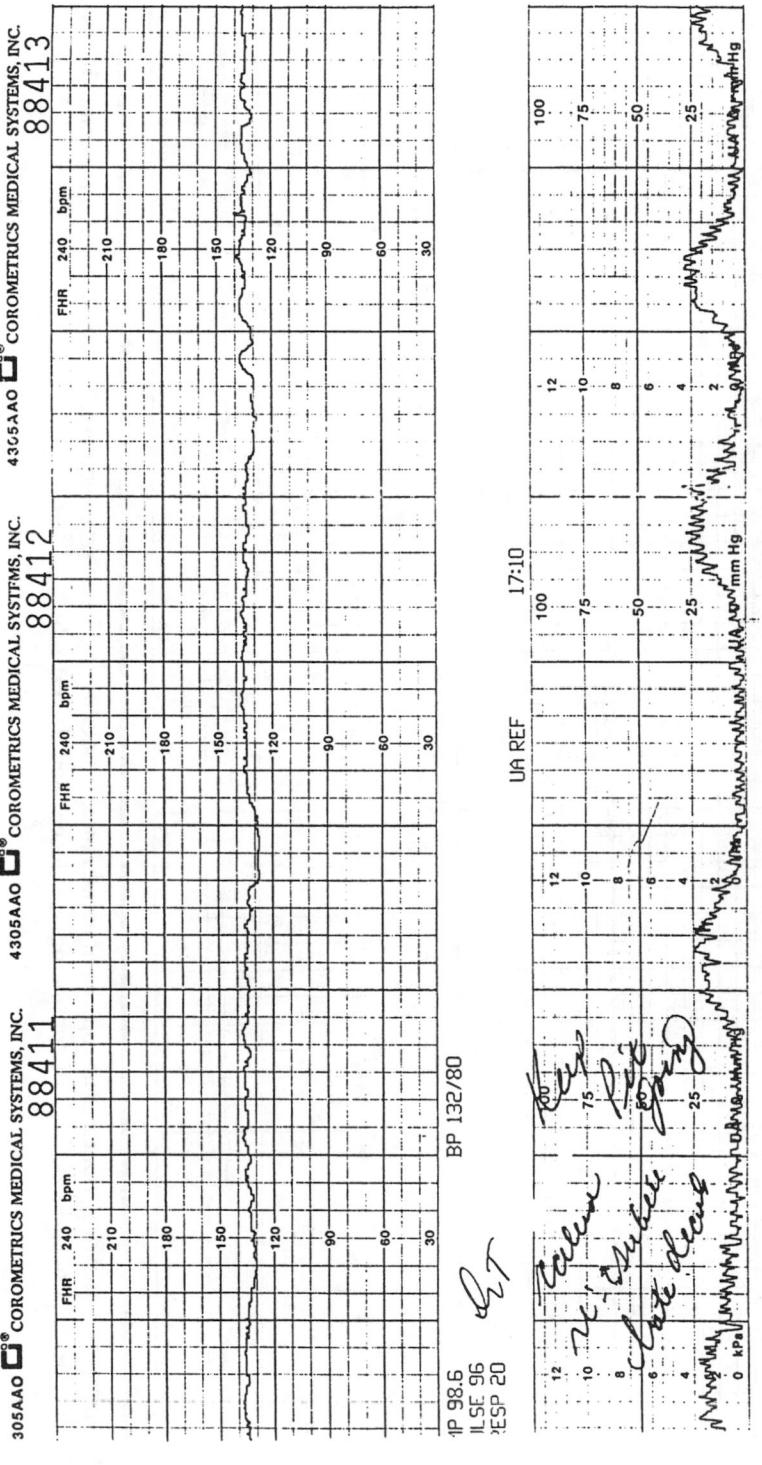

Figure 19.3 Pitocin was at 8 mu/min during this period of the oxytocinu-challenge test. The nurse notes: "Dr. T. called re: subtle late decels. Keep Pit going."

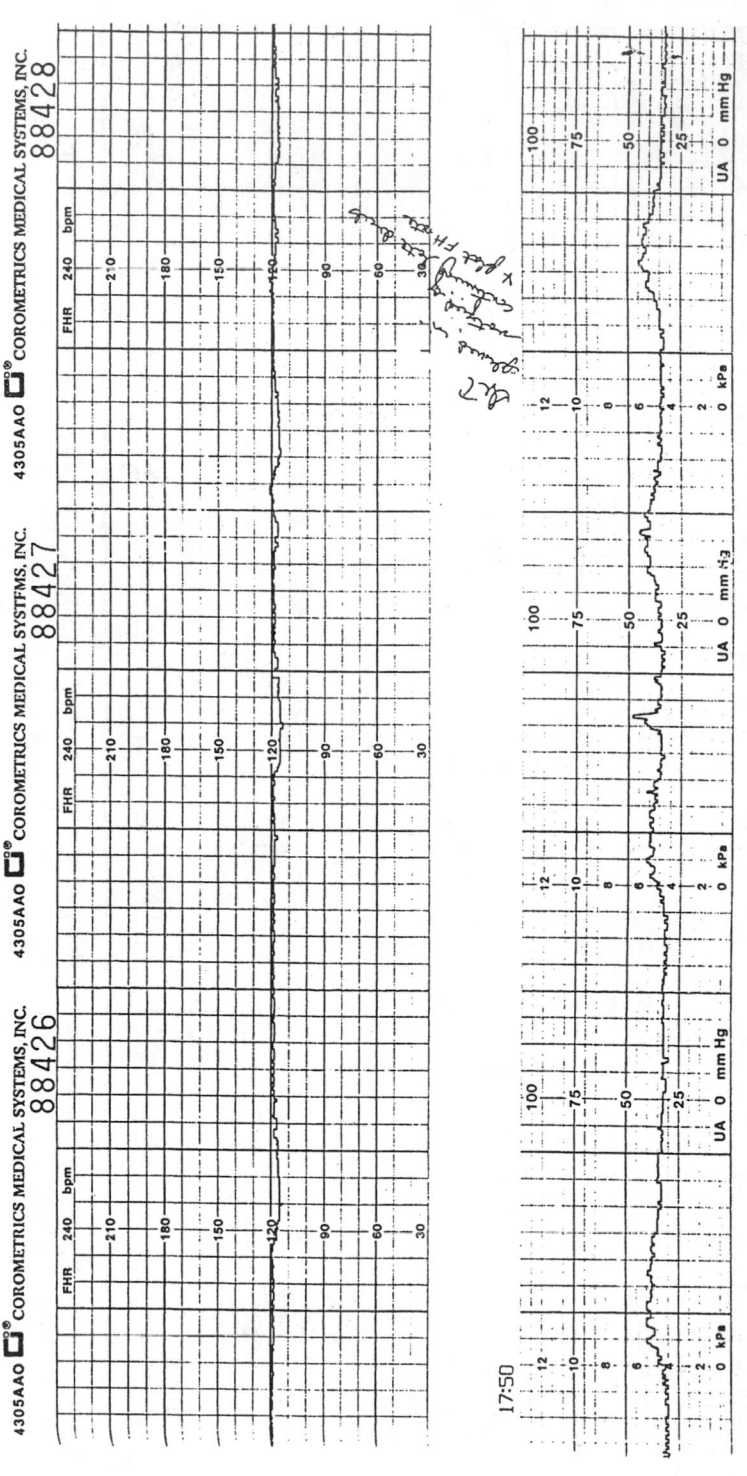

Figure 19.4 Following spontaneous rupture of membranes, variability and heart rate decrease. Pitocin is still at 8 mu/min. The nurse notes: "Dr. T. phoned in, notified of continuing late decels, and flat FH rate."

1. *Failure to assess, interpret, and document* adequately with the use of electronic fetal monitoring. The nurse was responsible for assessing and identifying fetal heart rate characteristic of true or pathological sinusoidal pattern. This pattern had been evident on both NSTs. The nurse also failed to interpret this pattern as nonreassuring and to so document.

2. *Failure to intervene* with intrauterine resuscitative measures to enhance blood flow and blood oxygen content to an oxygen-deprived fetus. During the oxytocin-challenge test, the heart rate revealed a progressively deteriorating fetus status. The nurse failed to initiate well-recognized measures — discontinuing the oxytocic agent, changing to a lateral maternal position, increasing fluid infusions, giving oxygen by mask, and notifying a physician. She also failed to document these.

3. *Failure to escalate concern* over the medical management notifying her immediate nursing supervisor, invoking the "chain of command." The nurse failed to question the injudicious use of oxytocin and to challenge medical management which fell below standard of care. This included allowing the patient to leave after the nonreactive NST. It was the nurse's responsibility to recognize that the patient was being medically neglected and was therefore in jeopardy.

The nurse expert for the case opined that the nursing care, more likely than not, contributed to the baby's tragic outcome. The hospital settled out of the case.

(Example courtesy of Sue Mahley, RNC, MN, Kansas City, MO.)

References

A Delay in Treatment of Herpes Encephalitis. Riverside County Superior Court No. 266494.

American Medical Association, *Guide to Professional Standards,* Chicago, 1997.

Apfel, D., Loss of chance in obstetrical cases, *Trial,* May, 48–55, 1993.

Failure to "spoon feed" patient: No expert needed, *Regan Report: Nursing Law,* 34(12), 1994.

Fink, S. and Chaudhuri, T K., Medical characteristics of 61 unwarranted malpractice claims, *Southern Medical Journal,* 88(10), 1011–1019, 1995.

Flamm, M. B., Healthcare provider as a defendant, in Sanbar, S. S. et al., Eds., *Legal Medicine,* St. Louis, Mosby, 1995.

Hoffman, A. C., Professional negligence, in Sanbar, S. S. et al., Eds., *Legal Medicine,* St. Louis, Mosby, 1995, 129–140.

Lunsford v. The Board of Nurse Examiners for the State of Texas, 648 S.W. 2d 391 (Tex. Civ. App. Austin, 1983).

Nurses fail to respond: "Loss of chance"-death, *The Regan Report on Nursing Law,* 35(3), 1994.

Sanbar, S. S. et al., Eds., *Legal Medicine,* St. Louis, Mosby, 1995.

Shrager, D., Trial, May 1993.

Wise, D. J. and Green, S. E., Psychiatric nursing malpractice, in Iyer, P., Ed., *Nursing Malpractice,* Tucson, AZ, Lawyers and Judges Publishing Company, 1996.

Chapter 20

Case Analysis: Drugs and Devices Product Liability

Shirley Cantwell Davis and Patricia L. Pippen

Contents

1-57444-123-X/98
© 1998 by American Association of Legal Nurse Consultants

Objectives

- To state the difference between the legal theories of strict liability and negligence in a product liability case
- To describe hypothetical instances of defective design and defective manufacturing of a medical product
- To discuss three criteria used to determine the adequacy of manufacturer warnings
- To formulate a request for an Adverse Drug Reaction Report or Medical Device Report under the Freedom of Information Act
- To knowledgeably rule out professional medical negligence and establish clear causation in a medical product liability case

Introduction

Few areas of litigation are as fascinating and complex for the lawyer and the legal nurse consultant (LNC) alike as pharmaceutical and medical devices product liability litigation. In order for an LNC to successfully work in product liability litigation involving drugs and devices, he or she must have a basic understanding of legal theories regarding strict liability and negligence as well as design defects, manufacturing defects, and failure to warn. The LNC must also be cognizant of the steps involved in Food and Drug Administration (FDA) approval of a new drug or device and the postmarketing processes. A good working knowledge of the standard of care practiced by health care practitioners who use prescription drugs and medical products is essential so that a differentiation can be made between a medical malpractice and a product liability matter. Additionally, the causal relationship between drugs and disease provides one of the most difficult challenges for the nurse consultant working on pharmaceutical litigation, as drug-induced damage may be highly obscure.

Theories of Liability

Product liability is a concept in the law holding a manufacturer strictly liable or responsible for the article placed on the market. Although the underlying legal theories of product liability stem from the common law, which is based on old English law and essentially "handed down" from generation to generation, common law comprises the principles of law which are generally recognized in the U.S. The definition of product liability can be found in the *Restatement (Second) of Torts*, Sec. 402A (1965) which states:

> One who sells any product in a defective condition, unreasonably dangerous to the user or consumer or to his property, is subject to liability for physical harm thereby caused to the ultimate user or consumer, or his property, if:
>
> a. the seller is engaged in the business of selling such a product, and
> b. the product is expected to and does reach the user or consumer without substantial change in the condition in which it is sold.

In other words, a manufacturer owes a duty to the public for the injuries caused by the product upon which the manufacturer made a profit. Within the realm of product liability law, three causes of action dominate: strict liability, negligence, and breach of contract. In practice, a plaintiff can allege negligence, strict liability, or both when failure to warn is alleged.

Strict Liability

Strict liability will almost always be a part of the plaintiff's cause of action. In strict liability, the plaintiff must prove

1. The defendant sold the product (this is especially true when there are several manufacturers of a generic drug or multiple retailers of a device as in breast implants).
2. The product was defective.
3. The defect was the proximate cause of plaintiff's injuries.
4. Plaintiff has damages.

Strict liability is responsibility without a showing of fault or the need to show fault. The emphasis is product oriented, focusing on the safety of the drug or device rather than on the reasonableness of the manufacturer's conduct. This places the responsibility for the drug or device on the pharmaceutical or medical device company. Thus, if the manufacturer produces a drug that harms a person, the manufacturer may be held strictly liable for the injury regardless of the fact that the medication may have been taken improperly or for an indication other than that for which the drug is approved.

Fundamental to a strict liability argument is proof by the plaintiff that the product was defective, that the defect existed when the product left the manufacturer's control, and that the defect caused the plaintiff's injury. In a strict liability analysis, it is assumed that the defendant knows the dangerous propensity of the product, whereas under negligence theory, the plaintiff must prove that the defendant knew or should have known of the danger. As such, the plaintiff's burden is less onerous under a strict liability theory than under negligence. However, under strict liability the plaintiff must still establish proximate cause between the product defect and the harm suffered by the plaintiff.

> Case Example 20.1: The Bjork–Shiley 60° C-C Heart Valve, once implanted, is not supposed to break, and if it does, it may be considered unreasonably dangerous or defective and the manufacturer may be found strictly liable for the damage caused by the broken valve.

When trying to prove that a product is defective or unreasonably dangerous, the LNC must remember that drugs and medical devices are designed and created with the inherent nature of causing side effects. In every case, drugs and devices used for medical purposes must be examined and analyzed from a risk/benefit ratio in order to assess whether or not they are unreasonably dangerous in the first place. It is important to examine the question of whether or not the desired and foreseeable actions of the drug or device are sufficiently beneficial to justify the risks of adverse reactions.

> Case Example 20.2: One of the known risks of artificial heart valves is thrombogenicity or the risk of clot formation. Because the artificial heart valve is a foreign object and does not have the hemodynamics of a natural heart valve, thrombus formation will occur in a certain number of patients. Thus, thrombosis is considered a reasonable risk for an artificial heart valve and, if thrombosis does occur, in most cases, the valve would not be considered unreasonably dangerous or defective.

Another issue in drug and device product liability involves the *Restatement (Second) of Torts* Section 402A, comment k, which deems some drugs as "incapable of being made safe." Comment k does not seek to prevent all suits against drug manufacturers, but rather seeks to protect the manufacturer against liability for design defects. (MacNeill, 1995, p. 170.) As such, comment k provides a special defense for what are termed unavoidably unsafe products. These products cannot be redesigned or otherwise changed to remove some inherent danger, but the substantial benefits of the product justify the risks created by its unsafe features. Pharmaceuticals are considered a classic example of such products. Because their formulas are a fixed, scientific constant, they cannot be redesigned to eliminate the risks that must necessarily accompany their use. As such, some drugs and devices are neither defective nor unreasonably dangerous when properly designed and accompanied by proper directions and warnings. If the manufacturer has met these obligations, then strict liability cannot be imposed. However, if the warning accompanying the prescription drug or device is deemed inadequate, protection by comment k is forfeited.

> Case Example 20.3: A good example of an unavoidably unsafe drug is the broad-spectrum antibiotic, chloramphenicol, which is of great value in the treatment of certain systemic infections but which has been linked to aplastic anemia in a small percentage of users. The manufacturer clearly denotes this association in all product labeling in order to provide adequate warning of this potentially fatal adverse reaction to the drug.

Vaccine Liability

In 1986, Congress passed the National Vaccine Injury Act (NVIA) partly in response to the overwhelming number of lawsuits claiming strict liability on the part of vaccine manufacturers for vaccine-related injuries. Parties seeking compensation for injuries from vaccines must do so now under the National Vaccine Injury Act. The act created a "no-fault" compensation program which provides vaccine manufacturers liability protection in order to let them continue to make their product without undue economic pressure from the threat of litigation. The act also enables children who have suffered vaccine hypersensitivity reactions easier access to compensation than going through the courts. Since 1986, the courts have ruled that the plaintiff must not only prove that he or she experienced symptoms of an injury after receiving a vaccination, but they had no symptoms of that injury prior to the vaccination (*Shalala v. Whitecotton*, 1995). Claimants who do not prove actual causation must show that the first symptoms or significant aggravation of the condition occurred within 3 days of the vaccination. Adverse effects are succinctly defined in the NVIA Act. For instance, encephalopathy is specified as significant acquired abnormality, injury, or impairment of brain function.

> Case Example 20.4: The parents of a 4-month old infant filed a compensation claim under the NVIA for brain injuries allegedly occurring following a vaccination for diphtheria, pertussis, and tetanus (DPT). A pediatric neurologist found that the infant had seizures within 3 days of the vaccine. However, the neurologist also found that the infant had significant preexisting microcephaly and concluded that the seizures were not the first symptoms of brain injury. As such, the claim was rejected under the rules of the NVIA.

Negligence

Negligence is the failure to use due care. This term refers to conduct that falls below the standard established by law for the protection of others against unreasonable risk of harm. When negligence is alleged, the defendant's conduct is central to the liability question. To succeed, the plaintiff must establish the following:

1. *Duty*. The manufacturer must exercise the ordinary care, diligence, and prudence of a reasonable manufacturer under like and similar circumstances when manufacturing and distributing the product.
2. *Breach of that duty*. One must prove that the manufacturer did not exercise ordinary care, diligence, and prudence that a reasonable manufacturer would have used in like or similar circumstances when manufacturing and distributing the product.
3. *Damages*. Plaintiff has to have suffered actual physical harm. In some jurisdictions, the harm may encompass emotional injuries for a perceived or future physical harm.
4. *Proximate cause*. The harm must be proximately caused by or have flowed directly from the breach of the manufacturer's duty.

A drug company has a duty to act prudently, and a breach of this duty would include, for example, not performing a product recall after several unexplained deaths in the first 3 months after FDA approval of a new drug. FDA approval does not in and of itself provide an adequate defense for a manufacturer when negligence is alleged. Alternatively, a product manufacturer may have breached its duty to act prudently by employing someone who is not qualified to run the product clinical trials. Both of these are examples of a pharmaceutical or medical device manufacturer not exercising ordinary care, diligence, or prudence, thus breaching its duty to the consumer or user of the product.

> Case Example 20.5: In 1982, Eli Lilly Pharmaceutical Corporation manufactured an antiarthritic drug, Oraflex, which was subsequently found to have significant hepatotoxicity. Later, it was determined that Eli Lilly did not fully research, follow up, or delineate to the FDA or the public the details regarding hepatotoxicity which was found during the clinical trials of this drug. Eli Lilly had a duty to reveal the results of its research and breached that duty by not revealing that information. As a result, numerous persons who were taking Oraflex suffered severe hepatic damage, among other injuries, and multiple deaths were reported in the first few months following FDA approval. The injuries or damages occurred as a proximate result of Eli Lilly's failure to disclose the full extent of the dangerousness of Oraflex; therefore, the company was considered negligent by many juries. Many plaintiffs also claimed strict liability because the benefit of relieving arthritic pain in taking Oraflex was not worth the risk of hepatotoxicity, and, in many cases, death, making it an unreasonably dangerous drug.

Warranty

Warranty is an assurance by the manufacturer, either express, which is an overt assurance, or implied, that the goods shall be merchantable and of average quality. A manufacturer implies a warranty of fitness by selling a product which the manufacturer contends is merchantable and reasonably fit for a particular purpose. For example, a heart valve should not fracture after implantation. If it does fracture, a breach of warranty may exist because the heart valve is not, by definition, merchantable or fit for the purpose for which it was sold. Warranty and breach of warranty are concepts used in both strict liability and negligence.

Important Concepts Used to Prove Liability in Product Liability Litigation

There are three theories of recovery used in product liability litigation, regardless of whether negligence or strict liability is alleged, and these theories include defective design, defective manufacture, and failure to warn.

Defective Design

Defective design exists when a drug or device is not reasonably safe for its intended use or a use that can be reasonably anticipated. This may occur when a drug or device is formulated to specifications but is not efficacious for the intended purpose or is a product with massive side effects. If the product's design is found to be defective, all the products manufactured using that same design are considered to be defective.

> Case Example 20.6: In the silicone breast implant litigation, the plaintiffs have alleged defective design of silicone-gel breast implants, claiming increased risk for connective tissue disorders, immune system illnesses, and implant rupture due to the faculty design of the implants. The plaintiffs claim that the manufacturers knew or should have known that the defective design of the implants would cause them to leak or rupture, with consequent migration of silicone, and ultimately result in systemic effects. However, to date, the immune system link is only alleged and not supported by epidemiological data or any pathophysiological theory.

Defective Manufacture

Defective manufacture can be alleged if the product is defective as a result of the manner in which it is manufactured and the defect existed when the product left the manufacturer's control. Defective manufacture is usually alleged when there is a one-time mistake, e.g., when one batch of a drug is tainted such that the flawed product differs from the manufacturer's intended design and manufacturing.

> Case Example 20.7: In August 1989, L-tryptophan, an essential amino acid defined by the FDA as a food supplement and popularly used as a natural sedative, was associated with an epidemic of eosinophilia myalgia syndrome (EMS). Over 1500 people were diagnosed with EMS and 38 deaths were reported as being associated with use of L-tryptophan. Studies proved the disease was caused by ingestion of contaminated L-tryptophan manufactured by a Japanese company, Showa Denko K.K. (SDK). The United States is the only country which allows L-tryptophan to be defined as a food supplement; all other countries categorize it as a drug and thus regulate it with the more stringent restrictions placed on drugs.

Failure to Warn

The duty of the manufacturer to warn of the dangers associated with the use of a product is crucial in any drug or device case whether the case encompasses strict liability, negligence, or both. The key issue when failure to warn is alleged is the adequacy of the product label. It is assumed that where a warning is given, the manufacturer may reasonably expect that it will be read and heeded. While that presumption operates to the benefit of the manufacturer, when there is judged to be an inadequate warning, the presumption operates to the benefit of the plaintiff as if there were no warning and the product can be presumed to be defective.

Drug and device companies routinely warn of adverse reactions in the labeling and package inserts which accompany each bottle or single package of the product or device, or in the case of drugs, the *Physician's Desk Reference*. The FDA requires a labeling revision, supplementation to the package insert, and in some cases direct notification of the physicians prescribing the product as soon as there is reasonable evidence of an association between a newly recognized serious hazard and a drug or device. A causal relationship does not need to be proven. Thus, the argument by a defendant drug company that it was not bound to provide a warning until the occurrence of the side effect was frequent and clearcut will often be rejected by the courts.

Learned Intermediary

In the case of prescription drugs and medical devices, the manufacturer's duty to warn goes to the physician rather than the patient, since the patient can only obtain the product through the physician. The learned intermediary stands between the manufacturer of a medical device or product and the person who uses the product. The physician acts as the "learned intermediary" with regard to the drug and is expected to convey to the patient the labeling information provided by the manufacturer. The plaintiff, as the patient and consumer, has to rely on the health care expertise of the physician to read and be cognizant of the warnings.

> Case Example 20.8: Schering Corporation, which manufacturers Garamycin (gentamycin) cannot be expected to warn patients directly concerning the potential for this drug to cause nephrotoxicity and neurotoxicity. The burden falls on the "learned intermediary," the person with knowledge who prescribes the drug, to be informed and to monitor the patient for these potential problems because Schering Corporation has warned of these adverse reactions through such sources as the package insert and the *Physicians' Desk Reference.*

By providing adequate information to the physician, the manufacturer in effect erects a barrier to liability. To the extent that the labeling information is inadequate, that barrier is weakened, and the manufacturer becomes more vulnerable.

Over-the-Counter Products

Conversely, a number of health care products are not dispensed by prescription. FDA Class II devices, such as tampons, which are available for purchase over-the-counter, must carry adequate warnings of potential hazards written in language that consumers can understand since there is no learned intermediary when using these products.

> Case Example 20.9: The adequacy of the tampon warnings were central to many lawsuits regarding toxic shock syndrome in the 1980s. As a result of litigation involving toxic shock syndrome associated with tampons, the warnings are now typically printed on the top of the box in simple language, or prominently located in the package insert placed on the top of the product, so that the consumer will be more likely to read and understand them.

Conduct of the Manufacturer

Whether the cause of action is negligence or strict liability, there are criteria regarding warnings against which the conduct of a manufacturer will be judged. These criteria focus primarily on three factors:

Knowledge of the Risk. The drug company may not be held liable for failure to warn of adverse effects unless the adverse effects were known or reasonably scientifically knowable at the time the product was distributed by the manufacturer. The manufacturer is held to the standard of an expert in the field and is charged with actual knowledge of adverse drug reactions arising from both its own research and knowledge of reported reactions from outside sources, such as the scientific literature.

> Case Example 20.10: In 1990, Eli Lilly, the manufacturer of the antidepressant, Prozac, should have been placed on notice when a letter to the editor appeared in the British journal *Lancet* regarding Prozac. The letter reported on five patients who became suicidal after initiation of Prozac in their therapy for depression. The case report was unsubstantiated, lacking in detail, and not a scientific study; however, the article itself, despite being in a foreign journal constituted a report of reactions associated with Eli Lilly's product. The company therefore had knowledge or should have had knowledge of these adverse effects.

The Nature and Timing of the Duty to Warn. The determination of whether or not the manufacturer acted reasonably regarding warnings depends on the company's knowledge of the risks associated with the product at the time the product was distributed to the plaintiff. The duty to warn does not expire when the product is placed on the market but, rather, is continuous. This imposes an obligation on the manufacturer to seek out information regarding its product. Thus, if information becomes available indicating that a certain danger is associated with the use of the drug, then the manufacturer cannot disregard the information in drafting or altering its warning simply because the manufacturer feels the evidence is unconvincing. The onus is on the company to communicate and warn physicians regarding a new risk as soon as it is reasonably practical. The drug or device manufacturer is not allowed to wait until a statistically significant number of people have been injured or until a causal relationship has been established by epidemiological studies. In previous cases, the courts have rejected the defendant manufacturer's argument that it was not bound to provide warnings until the occurrence of side effects was so frequent and the evidence of causation was so clear-cut that the manufacturer itself was convinced that the drug caused or contributed to such problems (*Wooderson v. Ortho Pharmaceutical Corp.*). On this issue, the court's view agrees with the FDA regulations which require a labeling revision as soon as there is reasonable evidence of an association of a serious hazard with a drug. A causal relationship need not have been proved.

> Case Example 20.11: A case in point was a problematic defibrillator manufactured by Marquette Electronics, Inc. The defibrillators used a special battery pack which was found to wear out prematurely, manifesting as a rapid loss of charge capacity after being removed from the battery charger. The FDA eventually initiated a Class I recall (complete recall) of the battery charger. However, FDA Medical Device Reports reveal that Marquette was on notice of this problem for a significant period of time prior to recall. A Freedom of Information Act (FOIA) request revealed a number of reports of the defibrillator failing to work due to rapid loss of charge capacity in the batteries, causing death in some instances, for a substantial period of time prior to Marquette warning users of this association.

Language Used to Convey the Warning. The FDA regulates all prescription drug and medical device promotional activities that fall within the definition of labeling and advertising. Once a determination has been made to include a warning in the drug or device labeling, it is incumbent upon the manufacturer to convey the warning to the doctor adequately. Product labeling includes written material both physically on the product and accompanying the product. Labeling has been widely interpreted to include the package insert, exhibits, brochures, product-detailing pieces, press releases, speeches by company officials, and other promotional materials such as "Dear Doctor letters."

The format and content of drug labeling is rigidly controlled by the federal regulations. Labeling must include indications, precautions, warnings, contraindications, and dosage, among other information. The product label is approved by the FDA during the drug-approval process; therefore, the label is not a document arbitrarily designed by the drug manufacturer. All subsequent promotional materials must conform to the language in the approved labeling. However, the FDA labeling regulations impose a continuing obligation on the manufacturer and new data must be incorporated in the label as it becomes available. Not only do regulations permit the manufacturer in specified instances to change its labeling without prior authorization of the FDA, but a failure to share new information could result in the drug being improperly labeled or misbranded which would constitute evidence for the plaintiffs in a product liability action.

The adequacy of the warning included in the labeling is not only measured by what is stated, but also the manner in which it is stated.

> Case Example 20.12: If Stevens-Johnson Syndrome has been reported on multiple occasions with the use of a drug, then the manufacturer must warn not only of a cutaneous reaction, but use terminology to indicate the seriousness of the side effect, such as severe exfoliative dermatitis or toxic epidermal necrolysis.

A warning can be found inadequate if the facts are insufficient, the response unduly delayed, or the manner of the words reluctant or lacking in intensity. The warning must be expressed in a tone congruent with the nature of the risk.

> Case Example 20.13: The court ruled against Ortho Pharmaceutical Corporation in a case involving birth control pills declaring a warning of abnormal blood clotting inadequate. The court ruled that the absence of the word "stroke" unduly minimized the warning's impact (*MacDonald v. Ortho Pharmaceutical Corp.*).

The following are important considerations in the review of warnings:

1. Warnings must be conspicuous and prominent. Warnings can be considered ineffective and insufficient if they are printed in a body of other information of the same size and color as other information. This means that it is incumbent upon the manufacturer to make the warnings conspicuous and prominent. As the result of litigation involving toxic shock syndrome associated with tampon use, the warnings are now usually printed on the top of the box or prominently located in a package insert placed on top of the product. In the *Physicians' Desk Reference*, drugs with particularly dangerous side effects, such as agranulocytosis or teratogenesis, have special warnings, sometimes referred to as "black box warnings," with bold print and placement at the beginning of the labeling.

2. To be adequate, warnings must convey the risk of the danger associated with the use of the product. The question of adequacy therefore depends upon the language used and the impression that such language might reasonably be calculated to make upon the physician or consumer. If a warning with reference to a particular side effect is labeled rare, the physician might be more inclined to use the product than if the side effect were labeled as "common" or "occasional."

3. Warnings must also be unambiguous. The warnings can be inadequate because of the lack of clarity or narrowness. The risks and types of possible adverse reactions must be clear and straightforward.

Overpromotion and such activities as direct consumer advertising may dilute the warnings or even render them insufficient.

Case Example 20.14: Excessive promotion of a certain aspect of a product occurred in the marketing of tampons in the early 1980s. Manufacturers were advertising "super absorbency" as the foremost marketing pitch without adequately warning about the association between super absorbency of these tampons and toxic shock syndrome. Consequently, the zealous advertisements of super absorbency were judged in many instances to render the warnings about toxic shock syndrome insufficient.

Furthermore, advertising claims can create such a high expectation of benefit in the consumer, that any warnings of risks may be disregarded by the consumer.

Case Example 20.15: In the case of Oraflex, an antiarthritic drug marketed by Eli Lilly in 1982, the word "cure" actually appeared in some of the direct advertising to the public. This led some people to believe that the risk of taking the drug was outweighed by the fact that the drug would "cure" their arthritis symptoms.

A manufacturer has a duty to keep abreast of the current state of knowledge regarding their products as gained through research, medical literature, and adverse reaction reports. The subsequently acquired knowledge may necessitate a further duty to notify both physicians, and potentially, consumers of this new information. Manufacturers have a duty to warn of all potential dangers either known or which should have been known in the exercise of reasonable care.

Case Example 20.16: A large verdict was returned in Georgia regarding the failure of Ortho Pharmaceutical to warn about the potential for teratogenicity of Ortho-Gynol Contraceptive Jelly (*Wells v. Ortho Pharmaceutical Corp.*). The plaintiff showed that substantial research proved a connection between spermicidal jelly and birth defects and that the manufacturer had failed to include this information in the warnings. The failure to change the warnings to reflect this knowledge meant that the warnings were inadequate and, therefore, the product was deemed defective.

FDA Regulatory Process for Product Approval

The FDA was formulated under the auspices of the Food, Drug, and Cosmetic Act of 1938. This act was aimed at strengthening government regulation of medications and required that there be evidence of safety prior to the marketing of a new drug. This act introduced the use of prescriptions for the majority of drugs and established a regulatory agency, the FDA, to oversee the market and set the policies for the sale of new drugs. Due to the grave adverse reactions associated with thalidomide, the Kefauver-Harris Amendments of 1962 to the Food, Drug and Cosmetic Act imposed strict guidelines regarding drug safety and labeling and resulted in 7000 drugs being removed from the market. Since that time, the FDA's role has been centered on identifying and communicating adverse reactions associated with pharmaceuticals and medical devices.

Clinical Trials of Pharmaceuticals

The FDA controls the regulation of medical and pharmaceutical products in the U.S. Before approving a new drug for marketing, the FDA must ascertain the drug's safety and efficacy. This verification process requires the drug manufacturer to put the drug through a lengthy experimental protocol. The FDA approves a drug based on these premarketing evaluations, or clinical trials, performed by the drug company to determine the safety and effectiveness of the drug. Clinical trials are considered the gold standard of pharmaceutical research, but the results only apply to a small range of questions and cannot be applied to the general population. Clinical trials compare outcomes among two or more groups — one which is deliberately exposed to the new therapy, while the others receive standard or alternative treatment or a placebo. These trials are used to test the efficacy of new treatments.

Prior to the submission of a New Drug Application (NDA) to the FDA, drug manufacturers undertake three phases of testing to demonstrate the safety and efficacy of a new drug. In Phase 1 trials, the drug is tested for the maximum tolerated dose. This research is typically carried out in a small number of healthy subjects using dose escalations and watching for side effects. Phase 2 trials evaluate the drug's safety and efficacy in the target population. This phase is typically done in small samples of 50 to 100. Phase 3 studies are randomized, blind, and, many times, placebo controlled. Randomization is a mechanism of assigning the study patients to treatment arms, like tossing a coin or throwing dice. The chance of being put on the study drug is usually 50%. The study researcher is not allowed to choose who receives the study drug and who receives the comparison study therapies. Blinding the studies means that both the study participants and the investigators who carry out the protocol and collect the data do not know which study subjects are receiving the study drug. Both of these elements are used to prevent researcher bias when treating and evaluating the study patients.

The FDA closely regulates all three phases of the clinical trial process in cooperation with the drug manufacturer. Safety is maintained by giving the drug under controlled circumstances with careful monitoring by physician experts in the treatment of the particular disease under consideration, with meticulous attention to reporting of adverse consequences of all types.

The results of all the clinical studies are submitted to the FDA for review. After sufficient research and review have been completed, the FDA grants an NDA and the drug can be manufactured.

As a result of the FDA's regulatory process, when the average drug is marketed, consumers have a reasonable expectation that serious adverse effects are unlikely to occur when the drug is used: (1) for its approved indication; (2) at its recommended dose; (3) for limited periods; and (4) in medically uncomplicated, nonpregnant young or middle-aged adults who are medically compliant. Because of limited sample sizes and duration of clinical trials, these studies often cannot detect or measure serious adverse effects that are infrequent or related to long-term use. Additionally, the effects of a new drug on a frail elderly patient with multiple illnesses may be difficult to predict even after the completion of the clinical trials.

> Case Example 20.17: Oraflex, the antiarthritic manufactured by Eli Lily, had serious hepatotoxicity associated with its use, especially in the elderly. Since the clinical trials did not typically include persons over 65, the adverse reaction was not detected in the original studies and only became apparent after widespread use in elderly persons.

At present, the FDA has no authority to require clinical studies after a drug has been approved. Most postmarketing studies are voluntary on the part of the manufacturer. This may involve studies on special populations, such as the elderly or young children. In drug development, it is logistically impractical, prohibitively expensive, and ethically questionable to delay the marketing of an effective drug until every potential risk associated with its use is known. Therefore, it is imperative for postmarketing surveillance to be done to learn additional information about the side effects and dangers of drugs which sometimes only become known when the drug is given to larger numbers of people.

> Case Example 20.18: A good example involves the drug, Zomax, a nonsteroidal anti-inflammatory drug, which was also used as an analgesic. McNeil Pharmaceuticals warned in their package insert that "as with other nonsteroidal anti-inflammatory drugs, anaphylactoid reactions have been reported..." but it was not until the drug had been marketed for quite a period of time that it became apparent that there were many anaphylactoid reactions occurring and the drug was finally recalled by the manufacturer. This is a classic case of postmarketing surveillance identifying the true incidence of a dangerous side effect.

Another reason for postmarketing surveillance is that clinical trials, while adequate for regulatory purposes, may not be adequately designed to detect an adverse reaction in certain patient populations.

Medical Devices

Medical devices were not subject to extensive FDA regulation until 1976, when the Medical Device Amendments to the Food, Drug and Cosmetic Act were passed. Before 1976, medical devices could be marketed without review by the FDA. Under the Medical Device Amendments, medical devices have been subject to the regulatory scheme that is similar to that utilized for pharmaceuticals. There are, however, important differences.

The statutory definition of a "medical device" is all-encompassing. Essentially, any item promoted for a medical purpose that does not rely on chemical action to achieve its intended effect is considered to be a medical device. *In vitro* diagnostic tests are also regulated as medical devices. Unlike the regulation of new drugs, in which standards of safety and effectiveness are applied uniformly, the regulation of medical devices is based on risk. Securing FDA approval of a new medical device before marketing requires that the manufacturer provide reasonable assurance that the device is safe and effective when used for the purpose for which the approval is sought. Safety and effectiveness are assessed with specific reference to the uses for which the device is intended, as set forth in the labeling on the device. Safety is evaluated by weighing the probable benefits to health against the probable risks of injury. The risk/benefit ratio must be acceptable, but proof that the product will never cause harm or will always be effective is not required.

There are three different regulatory classes for medical devices. Only devices classified as "Class III" undergo the strict scrutiny of a premarketing approval (PMA) process. This class is reserved for devices deemed "critical," such as heart valves, that are implanted within the body or whose failure would be life threatening. Class II devices do not undergo the PMA process but are subject to special controls, which usually take the form of additional quality control requirements imposed during the manufacturing process. Manufacturers of devices classified as "Class I" need only comply with good manufacturing practices (GMPs) in the manufacture of such products. Thus, most medical devices are not subject to FDA scrutiny, in sharp contrast to pharmaceuticals, all of which pass through the detailed approval process.

FDA's Spontaneous Reporting System

In order to document adverse effects not readily or reliably uncovered by clinical trials, federal regulations require adverse drug reaction reporting to the FDA. The central focus of the regulations, which are directed to drug manufacturers, is the timely collection, analysis, and reporting of the adverse drug reaction data to the FDA. An adverse drug reaction is defined in the regulations as any adverse event associated with the use of a drug whether or not it is considered drug related. Regulations require that a manufacturer submit a report to the FDA within 15 days of learning of any serious event, death, or hospitalization. Compliance with these regulations will constitute important evidence for a manufacturer in the course of a product liability suit and may be a key element in avoiding liability.

Once adverse events are known to occur in association with specific products, combination of products, or in association with specific diseases, the drug may be taken off the market or recalled either at the request of the FDA or voluntarily by the pharmaceutical manufacturer. Drugs have been taken off the market by a manufacturer after intense media attention based on anecdotal reporting. Examples of complete product recalls include Oraflex, a drug for rheumatoid arthritis, which was taken off the market in 1982 after it caused deaths in Britain, and the Bjork-Shiley 60° CC heart valve in the U.S.

The FDA's Spontaneous Reporting System of adverse drug reactions (ADRs) plays an important role in the litigation process. Physician reports, which are the mainstay of the system, are voluntarily made mainly to manufacturers, who are required by regultion to summarize and forward the data to the FDA in a timely manner. Some physicians report ADRs directly to the FDA, as do some pharmacists, patients, nurses, and others. Any death or hospitalization associated with the use of a vaccine must be reported directly to the FDA by a physician. This is the only type of product for which physicians are legally responsible to report an ADR. The burden of reporting ADRs for nonprescription drugs falls on the patients.

Meeting the standard of the reasonably prudent manufacturer with respect to ADR reporting requires a considerably greater allocation of resources today than it did in the past. The obligation to analyze and categorize each ADR report to ensure timely and appropriate reporting falls, for the most part, on the manufacturer. The manufacturer is responsible for analyzing adverse reaction reports from multiple sources, including foreign and domestic reports, from commercial marketing experiences, postmarketing clinical evaluations, postmarketing epidemiological surveillance studies, scientific and medical literature, and unpublished manuscripts.

While an efficient compilation of ADR reports is necessary to meet the regulatory requirements, these same documents may provide the plaintiff with important evidence regarding when the manufacturer became aware of the risk in question. A crucial element in the drug manufacturer's litigation control program is the establishment of procedures for timely internal investigations of ADR reports from the moment the data is first received. The drug company that is compliant with the regulations and has excellent documentation will inherently have a better defense in a product liability suit.

Since the manufacturer is responsible for keeping abreast of all written articles or letters to the editor reporting observed adverse effects of their product, the plaintiff should certainly address the issue regarding the length of time between the first reports in the medical literature and when the product label was changed to include an adverse reaction. The plaintiff can then follow the paper trail from the manufacturer including, for example, the date a "Dear Doctor" letter was sent to notify prescribing physicians of reported serious side effects, as well as when the product-detailing literature changed to reflect the inclusion of the side effect. The Spontaneous Reporting System of the FDA is no guarantee of drug safety; rather it serves public health as an early warning system to monitor possible drug risk. It may, in fact, be the most efficient and the only affordable method of detecting serious clinical events that occur less frequently than 1 in 10,000 drug exposures.

There are contributions and limitations to the adverse drug event reporting system. The contribution is that a "signal" is generated from the field of clinical use as to unacceptable, even rare, drug toxicities. The limitations are many, including reports laden with opinion, overreporting, misinterpretation, and underreporting. The most serious drawback to the system is the rate of underreporting. In several studies, a physician's perceived legal liability correlated with his or her unwillingness to report adverse reactions. Furthermore, the reporting may be biased and cluttered with events that are not attributable to the drug causing false negatives and false positives in the system. As such, the system must not be used for calculation of specific rates of adverse reactions. Only with proper epidemiological studies, where biases can be detected, can the true rates of adverse reactions and the nature of the causation of those reactions be determined appropriately.

In June 1993, the FDA instituted a new adverse event reporting system called MEDWatch, the FDA Medical Products Reporting Program, to ensure that health providers identify and report adverse events. (See Appendix 20.1 and 20.2.) The premise for emphasizing the health care provider's responsibility in reporting is that only by the reporting of events to the FDA or drug manufacturer can the FDA ensure the safety of drugs, biological, and medical devices. Even the large clinical trials of a new drug may only study several thousand persons. If an adverse event occurs for 1 in 1000 users, these trials may miss identifying a potentially harmful side effect. Only when the drug is released to the mass market and hundreds of thousands are utilizing the product, will a large number of incidences of the potentially harmful side effect be detected. Additionally, when the drug is taken with other medications or over-the-counter products, interactions may occur which were not previously identified in the limited study populations of the clinical trials.

The MEDWatch system was developed to make it easier for the health care provider, including doctors, nurses, and pharmacists, to report to the FDA serious events which are defined as death, risk of death, hospitalization, significant disability, congenital anomaly, or an event requiring intervention to prevent impairment or damage. Under this system the FDA should also be notified about medical device problems, such as defects, inaccurate or illegible product labels, package or product mix-ups, drug contamination, or drug stability problems. In the past, the notification of adverse reactions has resulted in critical FDA action on several occasions. MEDWatch will hopefully increase the ease of reporting resulting in higher numbers of reports for the FDA to analyze.

> Case Example 20.19: FDA examination of accumulated adverse drug reports from physicians led to the determination that *torsade de pointes* ventricular arrhythmias could occur when terfenadine (Seldane) was concomitantly taken with ketoconazole, an antifungal agent, or erythromycin, an antibiotic. Also, in 1992, a box warning was added to all angiotensin-converting enzyme inhibitor labels as a result of accumulated adverse drug reports to alert physicians to use caution with these drugs in patients in their second and third trimester of pregnancy.

The LNC's Role in Case Analysis

Rule Out Medical Negligence

The LNC has a large role in working on the pharmaceutical and medical device litigation team. The first and foremost responsibility of the nurse consultant when evaluating a medical product liability claim is to examine the standard of care practiced by the medical practitioner who prescribed the drug or medical device. If the health care practitioner has not prescribed the drug or used the device in accordance with the manufacturer's recommendations, common sense would dictate that the manufacturer might not be held liable for any injury that occurred as a result of the use. Findings of medical malpractice may shift liability in part or completely to the health care practitioner. Review of the plaintiff's medical records will be helpful in establishing clear causation and should be examined to confirm if there is misdiagnosis, below-standard medical treatment, or inadequate follow-up by any of the health care providers.

Develop Plaintiff's Medical History

The LNC must also obtain and thoroughly review all the records pertaining to the plaintiff. This includes medical, mental health, employment, education, criminal, and military records. The LNC should be aware that it is sometimes difficult to recognize drug-induced illness in a person who has multiple coexisting illnesses, such that the appearance of a drug-induced symptom may be difficult to distinguish from the plaintiff's preexisting problems or conditions.

> Case Example 20.20: For many years, Parlodel, manufactured by Bristol Meyers Squibb, was prescribed for lactation suppression in the postpartum period. Plaintiffs in recent litigation have alleged an unacceptably high incidence of hypertensive crises and cerebrovascular accidents (CVA) in women who take this drug in the first 7 to 10 days postpartum. (In 1994, the FDA required Bristol Meyers to withdraw its labeling regarding use of lactation suppression.) It is essential that the LNC working on such a case elicit all information regarding risk for stroke. The patient may have a strong family history for hypertension, she may have had pregnancy-induced hypertension or preeclampsia in the prenatal or postpartum period. Alternatively, she may be a smoker, have had a postpartum clotting disorder, or a preexisting aneurysm. Additionally, the LNC must be able to document the purchase and ingestion of the drug during the postpartum period and the medical history leading to the CVA.

It is imperative that the LNC fully delineate the plaintiff's pharmaceutical history. The history will identify possible drug–drug interactions, contraindications for prescribing the drug in question, prior use of the alleged drug or a drug in the same family without injury, or physician "hopping" and obtaining multiple prescriptions resulting in overusage. Also, the LNC should not overlook references to alcohol in the review, as alcohol can potentiate or interact with some drugs.

In alleged negligence matters, the plaintiff is bound to the statute of limitations or the period of time within which the plaintiff must initiate an action against the defendant. First, the LNC must know the statute of limitations for the product liability cases in the state in which the matter has been filed. Second, the LNC must review the medical records cross-checking the dates of the prescriptions, product use, or device implantation and failure against the date the suit was filed to ensure it falls within the statute of limitations.

Identify Possible Third-Party Counterclaims

A counterclaim is a separate cause of action which a defendant asserts against a third person or party. In the answer of the plaintiff's petition, defendants may allege a separate claim against the third party they believe is at fault in the matter. If an orthopedic surgeon purposefully bends a metallic plate to make it conform with the patient's spine and the plate subsequently fractures, the plate manufacturer may counterclaim against the orthopedic surgeon, if he or she is not already a defendant in the case, for improper use of the device. Cross-claims typically state that if the court or jury finds negligence did occur, then it was the negligence of the other defendant(s), and not the cross-claiming defendant, that resulted in the plaintiff's injury. In the previous example, the plate manufacturer would state in its claim that any negligence found occurred as a result of the orthopedic surgeon's actions.

Establish Clear Causation

Importantly, the LNC needs to make the causal link between the injury and the drug or device therapy. The medication in question must be shown to be the active cause that sets in motion a chain of events that brings about a result without the intervention of any other source. The plaintiff's LNC should utilize the medical records to show that the drug given or device used caused the ensuing injury and should exclude other contributing events or conditions. Causation can be formulated by the "but for" rule, which states that one event is a cause of another when the second event would not have occurred *but for* the first event.

> Case Example 20.21: A patient dies suddenly of an apparent anaphylactic reaction while taking Zomax. If the plaintiff can prove the decedent was taking no drugs but Zomax (McNeil Pharmaceuticals), and had no other history of bee stings or exposure to agents which could be inhaled or absorbed through the skin, the plaintiff could easily prove that *but for* the consumption of Zomax, no anaphylactic reaction would have occurred and the patient would not have died. Alternatively, if a patient had an imminent fracture in one of the struts of his heart valve and suffered a stroke as a result of clotting complications following the removal of the Bjork-Shiley valve, then one could argue that *but for* the presence of the defective valve which had to be removed, the patient would not have had the thrombotic stroke.

For the LNC consulting for the plaintiff, it may be difficult to prove clearly that one drug caused the symptoms/illness alleged in the suit. This is even more challenging when the drug-induced illness mimics the very condition for which the medication is prescribed.

> Case Example 20.22: Many antiarrhythmics, such as quinidine or Procainamide, have the well-known property of generating arrhythmias in certain doses in some patients. Thus, instead of decreasing the frequency of cardiac irregularities, the drugs may actually make them worse. Another paradoxical side effect is akathisia, or restlessness and an inability to sit down or be still, associated with many antipsychotic drugs. As restless behavior is often a clinical symptom of psychoses, there may be a failure to recognize this adverse reaction as a drug event associated with antipsychotic medication.

Research for Discovery

The LNC must perform thorough medical literature searches concerning the product prior to and during discovery. However, before beginning this task, the LNC must be knowledgeable regarding the complete circumstances of the use of the drug or device, including the indications for the product, as well as the patient outcome.

The LNC involved in pharmaceutical litigation will find that the drug or device label in the case will be the most-referred-to exhibit during the discovery and trial process. The LNC should be intimately familiar with this document, and any changes made in it from year to year. Importantly, the LNC should review the warnings for the year or time period that the medication or device was prescribed. The LNC should review not only the package insert, but the language and content of the advertisements published by the drug company.

Since the early 1970s, the National Library of Medicine (NLM) has made searching the biomedical literature faster and easier by providing on-line information retrieval on the MEDLARS (*MEDical Literature Analysis and Retrieval System*) family of databases. MEDLINE is the NLM premier database, having over 7 million citations of biomedical articles. The LNC should execute a computer on-line search, such as MEDLINE, ensuring that the drug and similar drugs are cross-searched with the resultant injury and similar injuries. For instance, instead of checking if a particular suspect drug causes cardiomyopathy, one should research the entire family of drugs and their association with cardiac effects, not just cardiomyopathy. Thorough research of the scientific literature has tremendous benefit both to case development and case strategy. The LNC must discover everything, both positive and negative, for a full understanding of the plaintiff's theories and defense positions in the case.

Research material can be crucial in establishing exactly what the manufacturer knew or should have known and when that knowledge was or should have been acquired. Additionally, this information can be essential in determining when certain information was known by medical researchers and experts in the field. The literature can be used to establish "duty," as the manufacturer has a duty to keep up with current information in the medical literature about the product. All information should be indexed and cataloged for use during discovery.

Obtain Adverse Reaction and Medical Device Reports

As mentioned previously, adverse effects of drugs and devices are reported properly in the postmarketing surveillance period of a particular product or device. The Medical Device Reports or Adverse Drug Reaction Reports (MDRs and ADRs as they are known in the industry) are requested by the FDA when an injury is linked to a medical product, drug, or device. Under the FOIA, every citizen is entitled to request this information from the FDA. The LNC may want to exercise her or his right under the FOIA and write to the FDA requesting information regarding ADRs or MDRs for a particular drug or device. To make an FOIA request, write: Freedom of Information Staff, HFI-35, FDA, Room 12A-16, 5600 Fishers Lane, Rockville, MD 20857. FOIA searches can be fruitful, although it often takes a long time to receive a response. If the drug has not been approved and is still investigational, the FDA will not give out information regarding the drug and the LNC will have to rely on medical literature and computer databases.

In response to an FOIA request, the LNC will receive a literal copy of the FDA's computerized tabulations of the various adverse reports for the requested drug or device. Specific requests can be made for edited (confidential patient information removed) copies of the actual reports themselves. These reports are often impossible to validate and the adverse effects can be a result of excessive doses or too frequent use of the drug. Yet, through FOIA responses, some plaintiffs have identified extremely compelling reports of a drug being associated with similar symptoms as those alleged in their claims. The LNC ought to remember these reports do not represent cause and effect, and the plaintiff cannot prove his or her case with adverse reaction reports.

Identify Epidemiological Studies and Epidemiologists

The final outcome of a pharmaceutical product liability case can depend on the court's acceptance or rejection of epidemiology evidence. Epidemiology is the study of disease in people, and epidemiologists are educated specialists in the science of defining and explaining the various factors that determine the frequency and distribution of disease. For instance, epidemiological studies have been pivotal in identifying the causal relationship between smoking and lung cancer. To provide meaningful conclusions, the epidemiology study must meet certain criteria of scientific method to avoid bias and error. The epidemiologist expert can speak to the reliability of these studies and validate whether or not the study can demonstrate cause and effect. The data considered by the epidemiologist in a product liability lawsuit includes epidemiology studies that show statistically significant evidence that the plaintiff is a member of the group that has been exposed to a drug or toxin at the required level and duration to cause an adverse effect. The epidemiology expert is able to show the interrelationship between scientific information, including laboratory, clinical, and experimental studies, and the plaintiff's alleged injuries. In any drug or device product liability case, the plaintiff has to prove that the product could cause the alleged injury and did cause the injury in the particular matter. Since the courts have recognized that epidemiology studies provide evidence on both sides of these issues, the LNC should ensure that the enlisted experts have knowledge of the strengths and weaknesses of the epidemiology data pertinent to the case.

Evaluate All the Evidence to Prove or Disprove the Legal Basis for the Plaintiff's Case

The LNC should review all the available data including medical and other records concerning the plaintiff, medical literature, drug and device labeling, and adverse reaction and medical device reports for clues as to the feasibility of the legal basis for the plaintiff's and the defendant's case. The LNC, in conjunction with the attorney, should analyze all the evidence which does or does not support a strict liability or negligence claim against the manufacturer. A checklist might include asking the following questions:

- Did the defendant sell the product?
- When and where was the product manufactured?
- Did the product reach the user or consumer without substantial change from the condition in which it was sold?
- When and where was the product consumed or used and for how long?
- Was the device unreasonably dangerous at the time it was manufactured?
- Is the product unreasonably unsafe based on the type of warnings given by the manufacturer?
- Did the manufacturer exercise ordinary care in manufacturing and distributing the product?
- Does the product have a design or manufacturing defect?
- Did the defendant know of the danger of the defect in the product at the time it was manufactured or sold?

- Was there a learned intermediary?
- Did the learned intermediary use the product correctly?
- Did the manufacturer adequately warn of the dangers associated with the use of the product in its labeling, package insert, and advertising?
- When should the manufacturer reasonably have known of the risk of danger and warned of it?
- Did the manufacturer act reasonably regarding the manner in which the warnings were formulated?
- Did the manufacturer change its product warnings without undue delay when the information of new risks became available?
- Is the language used to express the warnings adequate to convey the risk of danger associated with the use of the product?
- Are the warnings conspicuous and prominent?
- Are the warnings ambiguous?
- Was the product excessively promoted?
- Did the advertising falsely create high expectations on the part of the consumer such that the warnings were disregarded?
- Have the warnings been changed since the time of the events alleged in the case?
- What was the basis for the change in the warnings?
- Have there been any FDA enforcement actions regarding the product? If so, did the manufacturer comply with the FDA enforcement rulings?

The answers to the above questions may not be readily apparent, especially to the plaintiff LNC prior to filing a lawsuit, but the LNC should keep all of these questions in mind as the lawsuit proceeds since the answers will form the basis for the outcome of the litigation.

Obtain Medical Experts

An additional critical task for the LNC is obtaining qualified medical and technical experts who can explain to the jury, not only the medical issues of the case, but also the issues surrounding design and manufacture of a product, development of warnings, epidemiological studies, and perhaps marketing. An attempt should be made to utilize experts who have done research, performed clinical trials, or written medical articles regarding the medication or device in question. A review of all generally available scientific literature may assist both in determining the elements of causation and in the identification of potential expert witnesses. The enlisted experts should be extremely familiar with the drug or device and its indications, adverse reactions, metabolism, and method of action.

Case Example 20.23: The defense enlists one of the plaintiff's treating physicians as a defense expert to provide testimony that the plaintiff was diagnosed with the alleged symptoms before the drug in question was ever prescribed. However, on cross-examination by plaintiff's counsel regarding whether or not he or she utilizes or prescribes the suspect drug, the physician responds negatively. The fact that the "expert" does not use or prescribe the drug may have a devastating effect to the defense of the case.

The U.S. Supreme Court has ruled that judges are advised to take into account whether or not expert testimony is based on published data contained in peer-reviewed journals (*Daubert v. Merrell Dow Pharmaceuticals*). Thus, either side has the option to challenge whether the named experts are qualified to testify and whether their opinions are based on published scientific data.

It is imperative for the LNC to locate medical experts who can substantiate and support the legal theories of the case. The medical expert's role is primarily that of educating the jury, rather than acting as an advocate for the client. The LNC has a pivotal role in assuring that prospective experts have completely reviewed the entire records, medical and otherwise, in the matter prior to being designated, that they understand all of the issues, and they feel strongly about their opinions in the case.

> Case Example 20.24: At trial, plaintiff's counsel enters into evidence multiple ADR reports received in response to an FOIA request regarding a toxic side effect not mentioned in the product labeling. The plaintiff would benefit substantially from placing and FDA regulatory expert on the witness stand who could testify that spontaneous reports of adverse experiences in association with pharmaceutical use represents the most potentially powerful signal for early detection of rare but unacceptable drug toxicities.

Conclusion

Because of the complexity of the present-day world, especially in advanced medical science, much of the current theories driving drug and device suits are based on case law. Although many lawsuits are unique and applying legal theories can be difficult, case law is increasingly important with precedent-setting cases occurring on a daily basis. When consulting on drug and device product liability matters, the LNC will be challenged to utilize both legal knowledge and medical expertise. A complete understanding of manufacturers' responsibilities and regulatory processes is integral to a thorough review of the case. The LNC has the opportunity to be a valuable asset to the litigation team once these are learned and employed in the consulting process.

References

American Association of Legal Nurse Consultants (1995). *AALNC Standards of Practice*, Glenview, IL, American Association of Legal Nurse Consultants.

American Association of Legal Nurse Consultants (1995). *AALNC Scope of Practice for the Legal Nurse Consultants*, Glenview, IL, American Association of Legal Nurse Consultants.

Annas, G. (1994), Scientific evidence in the courtroom: the death of the *Frye* rule, *New England Journal of Medicine*, 330, 1018–1021.

Avorn, J. (1989). Detection and prevention of drug-induced illness, *Journal of Clinical Research and Drug Development*, 3(1), 5–13.

Daubert v. Merrell Dow Pharmaceuticals, Inc. (1993), 113 C. Ct. 2786.

Dukes, M. and Swartz, G. (1988). *Responsibility for Drug Induced Injury*, Amsterdam, Elsevier Science Publishers.

Everitt, D. (1989). Adverse drug effects as manifested by psychological symptoms, *Journal of Clinical Research and Drug Development*, 3(1), 15–27.

Food, Drug and Cosmetic Act of 1938, Ch. 675, Pub. L. 75-717, 52 Stat. 1040. Drug Amendments of 1962, 102, Pub. L 87-871, 76 Stat. 781.

Hallberg, M. (1995). The use of epidemiological studies and epidemiologists in proving or disproving causation, *Network*, 5(1), 19.

Health Devices Sourcebook (1996). Plymouth Meeting, PA: ECRI.

Inman, W. H. W. (1980). *Monitoring Drug Safety*, Philadelphia, PA: J. B. Lippincott.

Kessler, D. (1993). Introducing MEDWatch: a new approach to reporting medication and device adverse effects and product problems, *Journal of the American Medical Association*, 269, 2765–2768.

Kuc, J. (1995). A progress report on the FDA's MEDWatch, *Journal of Legal Nurse Consulting*, 6(3), 5–8.

MacDonald v. Ortho Pharmaceutical Corp. (1975). 475 N.E. 2d 65 71 (Mass.).

MacNeill, M. (1995). Pharmaceutical product liability, in Sanbar, S., Gibofsky, A., Firestone, M., and LeBlang, T., Ed., *Legal Medicine*, 3rd ed., St. Louis, MO, Mosby-Year Book, 168–179.

National Childhood Vaccine Injury Act, Pub. L. 99-660, 100 Stat. 3755.

Physicians' Desk Reference (1996). 50th ed., Montvale, NJ, Medical Economics Company, Inc.

Restatement (Second) of Torts (1965). Section 402A.

Ray, W., Griffin, M., and Avorn, J. (1993). Evaluating drugs after their approval for clinical use, *New England Journal of Medicine*, 329(27), 2029–2032.

Shalala v. Whitecotton (1995). U.S. Sup. Ct., No. 94-372.

Shulman, S. and Ulcickas, B. (1989). Update on ADR reporting regulations: products liability implications, *Journal of Clinical Research and Drug Development*, 3(2), 91–103.

Sloan, M. (1994). *DiRosa v. Showa Denko, Network*, 5(2), 6–7.

21 USC Section 321 (h) (1982).

21 USC Section 360c, d, e, & i (1982).

Wells v. Ortho Pharmaceutical Corp., 615 F. Supp 262 (N.D. Ga. 1985).

Wooderson v. Ortho Pharmaceutical Corp., 681 P.2d 1038, 1051 (Kan 1984).

Additional sources of information for research on drug reactions or device complications include

- *Pharmaceutical News Index:* Current news about drugs and medical devices.
- *Health Devices Sourcebook:* Current information regarding diagnostics and therapeutic medical devices.
- *Health Devices Alert:* Reports problems with diagnostic and therapeutic medical and implanted equipment.
- *F-D-C Reports:* Current information on the worldwide health care industry.
- *Federal Register and Federal Register Abstracts:* Daily publication of the U.S. government providing notification of official agency actions, regulations, proposed rules, and legal notices, such as when the FDA requests that a drug company change its warning.

Additionally, the following recommended traded journals may provide beneficial information:

Pharmaceutical Litigation Reporter (monthly): summaries of the latest verdicts in pharmaceutical litigation.

Devices and Diagnostics Letter (weekly) and *Clinica: World Medical Device & Diagnostic News* (weekly): updates on what is new in research and development, legislation, and recalls of drugs and devices.

Appendix 20.1:
FDA MEDWatch Form for Voluntary Reporting of Adverse Events and Product Problems by Health Professionals

MEDWATCH
THE FDA MEDICAL PRODUCTS REPORTING PROGRAM

For **VOLUNTARY** reporting
by health professionals of adverse
events and product problems

Form Approved: OMB No. 0910-0291 Expires:12/31/94
See OMB statement on reverse

FDA Use Only

Triage unit
sequence #

Page _____ of _____

A. Patient information

1. Patient identifier	2. Age at time of event: or Date of birth:	3. Sex	4. Weight
In confidence		☐ female ☐ male	_____ lbs or _____ kgs

B. Adverse event or product problem

1. ☐ Adverse event and/or ☐ Product problem (e.g., defects/malfunctions)

2. Outcomes attributed to adverse event (check all that apply)
- ☐ death _____ (mo/day/yr)
- ☐ life-threatening
- ☐ hospitalization – initial or prolonged
- ☐ disability
- ☐ congenital anomaly
- ☐ required intervention to prevent permanent impairment/damage
- ☐ other:

3. Date of event (mo/day/yr)	4. Date of this report (mo/day/yr)

5. Describe event or problem

6. Relevant tests/laboratory data, including dates

7. Other relevant history, including preexisting medical conditions (e.g., allergies, race, pregnancy, smoking and alcohol use, hepatic/renal dysfunction, etc.)

C. Suspect medication(s)

1. Name (give labeled strength & mfr/labeler, if known)
#1
#2

2. Dose, frequency & route used	3. Therapy dates (if unknown, give duration) from/to (or best estimate)
#1	#1
#2	#2

4. Diagnosis for use (indication)
#1
#2

6. Lot # (if known)	7. Exp. date (if known)
#1	#1
#2	#2

5. Event abated after use stopped or dose reduced
- #1 ☐ yes ☐ no ☐ doesn't apply
- #2 ☐ yes ☐ no ☐ doesn't apply

8. Event reappeared after reintroduction
- #1 ☐ yes ☐ no ☐ doesn't apply
- #2 ☐ yes ☐ no ☐ doesn't apply

9. NDC # (for product problems only)

10. Concomitant medical products and therapy dates (exclude treatment of event)

Suspect medical device

1. Brand name

2. Type of device

3. Manufacturer name & address	4. Operator of device
	☐ health professional ☐ lay user/patient ☐ other:

5. Expiration date (mo/day/yr)

6.
model # _____
catalog # _____
serial # _____
lot # _____
other # _____

7. If implanted, give date (mo/day/yr)

8. If explanted, give date (mo/day/yr)

9. Device available for evaluation? (Do not send to FDA)
☐ yes ☐ no ☐ returned to manufacturer on _____ (mo/day/yr)

10. Concomitant medical products and therapy dates (exclude treatment of event)

E. Reporter (see confidentiality section on back)

1. Name, address & phone #

2. Health professional?	3. Occupation	4. Also reported to
☐ yes ☐ no		☐ manufacturer ☐ user facility ☐ distributor

5. If you do NOT want your identity disclosed to the manufacturer, place an " X " in this box. ☐

FDA
Mail to: MEDWATCH
5600 Fishers Lane
Rockville, MD 20852-9787
or FAX to: 1-800-FDA-0178

FDA Form 3500 (6/93)   Submission of a report does not constitute an admission that medical personnel or the product caused or contributed to the event.

ADVICE ABOUT VOLUNTARY REPORTING

Report experiences with:
- medications (drugs or biologics)
- medical devices (including in-vitro diagnostics)
- special nutritional products (dietary supplements, medical foods, infant formulas)
- other products regulated by FDA

Report SERIOUS adverse events. An event is serious when the patient outcome is:
- death
- life-threatening (real risk of dying)
- hospitalization (initial or prolonged)
- disability (significant, persistent or permanent)
- congenital anomaly
- required intervention to prevent permanent impairment or damage

Report even if:
- you're not certain the product caused the event
- you don't have all the details

Report product problems – quality, performance or safety concerns such as:
- suspected contamination
- questionable stability
- defective component
- poor packaging or labeling

How to report:
- just fill in the sections that apply to your report
- use section C for all products except medical devices
- attach additional blank pages if needed
- use a separate form for each patient
- report either to FDA or the manufacturer (or both)

Important numbers:
- 1-800-FDA-0178 to FAX report
- 1-800-FDA-7737 to report by modem
- 1-800-FDA-1088 for more information or to report quality problems
- 1-800-822-7967 for a VAERS form for vaccines

If your report involves a serious adverse event with a device and it occurred in a facility outside a doctor's office, that facility may be legally required to report to FDA and/or the manufacturer. Please notify the person in that facility who would handle such reporting.

Confidentiality: The patient's identity is held in strict confidence by FDA and protected to the fullest extent of the law. The reporter's identity may be shared with the manufacturer unless requested otherwise. However, FDA will not disclose the reporter's identity in response to a request from the public, pursuant to the Freedom of Information Act.

The public reporting burden for this collection of information has been estimated to average 30 minutes per response, including the time for reviewing instructions, searching existing data sources, gathering and maintaining the data needed, and completing and reviewing the collection of information. Send your comments regarding this burden estimate or any other aspect of this collection of information, including suggestions for reducing this burden to:

Reports Clearance Officer, PHS
Hubert H. Humphrey Building,
Room 721-B
200 Independence Avenue, S.W.
Washington, DC 20201
ATTN: PRA

and to:
Office of Management and Budget
Paperwork Reduction Project (0910-0230)
Washington, DC 20503

Please do NOT return this form to either of these addresses.

FDA Form 3500-back   **Please Use Address Provided Below – Just Fold In Thirds, Tape and Mail**

Department of
Health and Human Services
Public Health Service
Food and Drug Administration
Rockville, MD 20857

Official Business
Penalty for Private Use $300

NO POSTAGE
NECESSARY
IF MAILED
IN THE
UNITED STATES
OR APO/FPO

BUSINESS REPLY MAIL
FIRST CLASS MAIL. PERMIT NO. 946 ROCKVILLE, MD

POSTAGE WILL BE PAID BY FOOD AND DRUG ADMINISTRATION

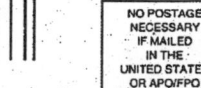

MED**W**ATCH
The FDA Medical Products Reporting Program
Food and Drug Administration
5600 Fishers Lane
Rockville, MD 20852-9787

Appendix 20.2:
FDA MEDWatch Form for Mandatory Reporting of Adverse Events and Product Problems by User-Facilities, Distributors, and Manufacturers

FDA Form 3500A (6/93)

Medication and Device Experience Report
(continued)
Refer to guidelines for specific instructions

Submission of a report does not constitute an admission that medical personnel, user facility, distributor, manufacturer or product caused or contributed to the event.

Page ____ of ____

U.S. DEPARTMENT OF HEALTH AND HUMAN SERVICES
Public Health Service • Food and Drug Administration

FDA Use Only

F. For use by user facility/distributor–devices only

1. Check one
   ☐ user facility ☐ distributor

2. UF/Dist report number

3. User facility or distributor name/address

4. Contact person

5. Phone Number

6. Date user facility or distributor became aware of event (mo/day/yr)

7. Type of report
   ☐ initial
   ☐ follow-up #

8. Date of this report (mo/day/yr)

9. Approximate age of device

10. Event problem codes (refer to coding manual)
   patient code ___ – ___ – ___
   device code ___ – ___ – ___

11. Report sent to FDA?
   ☐ yes ____ (mo/day/yr)
   ☐ no

12. Location where event occurred
   ☐ hospital
   ☐ home
   ☐ nursing home
   ☐ outpatient treatment facility
   ☐ outpatient diagnostic facility
   ☐ ambulatory surgical facility
   ☐ other: ____ specify

13. Report sent to manufacturer?
   ☐ yes ____ (mo/day/yr)
   ☐ no

14. Manufacturer name/address

G. All manufacturers

1. Contact office – name/address (& mfring site for devices)

2. Phone number

3. Report source (check all that apply)
   ☐ foreign
   ☐ study
   ☐ literature
   ☐ consumer
   ☐ health professional
   ☐ user facility
   ☐ company representative
   ☐ distributor
   ☐ other: ____

4. Date received by manufacturer (mo/day/yr)

5. (A)NDA # ____
   IND # ____
   PLA # ____
   pre-1938 ☐ yes
   OTC product ☐ yes

6. If IND, protocol #

7. Type of report (check all that apply)
   ☐ 5-day ☐ 15-day
   ☐ 10-day ☐ periodic
   ☐ Initial ☐ follow-up # ____

8. Adverse event term(s)

9. Mfr. report number

H. Device manufacturers only

1. Type of reportable event
   ☐ death
   ☐ serious injury
   ☐ malfunction (see guidelines)
   ☐ other: ____

2. If follow-up, what type?
   ☐ correction
   ☐ additional information
   ☐ response to FDA request
   ☐ device evaluation

3. Device evaluated by mfr?
   ☐ not returned to mfr.
   ☐ yes ☐ evaluation summary attached
   ☐ no (attach page to explain why not) or provide code:

4. Device manufacture date (mo/yr)

5. Labeled for single use?
   ☐ yes ☐ no

6. Evaluation codes (refer to coding manual)
   method ___ – ___ – ___
   results ___ – ___ – ___
   conclusions ___ – ___ – ___

7. If remedial action initiated,
   ☐ recall
   ☐ notification
   ☐ inspection
   ☐ replace
   ☐ patient monitoring
   ☐ relabeling
   ☐ modification/adjustment
   ☐ other:

8. Use of device
   ☐ initial use of device
   ☐ reuse
   ☐ unknown

9. If action reported to FDA under 21 USC 360i(f), list correction/removal reporting number:

10. ☐ Additional manufacturer narrative   and/or   11. ☐ Corrected data

SAMPLE

The public reporting burden for this collection of information has been estimated to average one-hour per response, including the time for reviewing instructions, searching existing data sources, gathering and maintaining the data needed, and completing and reviewing the collection of information. Send your comments regarding this burden estimate or any other aspect of this collection of information, including suggestions for reducing this burden to:

Reports Clearance Officer, PHS
Hubert H. Humphrey Building, Room 721-B
200 Independence Avenue, S.W.
Washington, DC 20201
ATTN: PRA

and to:
Office of Management and Budget
Paperwork Reduction Project (0910-0291)
Washington, DC 20503

Please do NOT return this form to either of these addresses.

FDA Form 3500A - back

Chapter 21

Case Analysis: Evaluating Toxic Torts Cases

Marva J. Petty, April Clemens, and Kathy Araiza

Contents

1-57444-123-X/98
© 1998 by American Association of Legal Nurse Consultants

Objectives

- To define the concept of a toxic tort
- To describe the relationship between a claimant's risk factors and exposure history
- To identify information resources for researching chemical substances
- To describe the importance of a complete review of medical, educational, social, and occupational records in the preparation of a toxic torts case
- To identify the types of experts that may be required in preparing the toxic torts case

Introduction

During the last two decades, the world news has been full of stories of toxic torts cases involving thousands of plaintiffs, many of whom allege repeated exposures to one or more toxic substances. Even the casual newswatcher is aware of the Chernobyl radiation leak; complaints of groundwater contamination resulting in spontaneous abortion and birth defects; and the years-long asbestos litigation which has raised public awareness of individual and collective vulnerability to exposures to toxic substances in the home, work, and global environment.

Toxic torts cases have their origins in product liability litigation and much of the case law is still found there. A toxic torts case shares many of the properties of other tort cases: negligence theories; causation issues; insurance coverage issues; and the determination of fraudulent, possibly even criminal behavior of involved parties.

A toxic torts case requires both sides to prove that an injury occurred as the result of exposure to a product. Therefore, discovery involves the need to develop both medical causation issues as well as scientific proof that the alleged injury occurred as the result of exposure to the product and proving or disproving the relative safety of one or more chemical products. Consequently, these types of cases tend to produce staggering numbers of documents.

The LNC assisting in a toxic torts case may find him or herself experiencing significant anxiety when confronted with voluminous medical records to review and summarize, the need for extensive literature searches, mile-high stacks of scientific papers and abstracts to be analyzed, and a maze of federal regulations to be deciphered. The key to preparing the case lies in careful strategic planning and in maintaining the information in an organized fashion as it is received.

Generally, toxic torts cases center around efforts to prove or disprove the relative safety of one or more chemical products. The toxic torts case offers the LNC an exciting opportunity to combine his or her nursing and medical knowledge with research, pure science, and regulatory law. During the preparation of such a case, the LNC will also have the chance to work with experts in toxicology, industrial hygiene, and occupational health and with other medical specialists.

This chapter is not meant to be an exhaustive work regarding toxic tort litigation, but rather is meant as a general framework for the LNC preparing a toxic torts case for the plaintiff or defendant.

Toxic Torts Cases: A "Complex" Subject

Whether the LNC is working from a plaintiff or defense standpoint, he or she will likely follow similar procedures in developing the case. The first step involves the identification of the type of case involved. It is not uncommon for a toxic torts case to involve multiple plaintiffs and multiple defendants, each with their attendant attorneys experts and consultants. The plaintiffs may also allege single or multiple exposure events to multiple toxic substances.

These types of cases are usually extremely complex and, where possible, the LNC should participate in the early planning processes for managing the case. Without adequate planning and budgeting for file management, data acquisition, and document storage, it becomes nearly impossible to manage the thousands, and even millions, of pages of depositions, opinions, scholarly papers, and medical records that will accrue throughout the life of the case. Not all toxic torts cases are, however, complex. A single claimant case may involve an individual exposed to one or more substances in a single exposure or over the course of a lifetime. Multilitigant cases typically involve many individuals with similar exposure, but with medical claims differing in type and severity. In some cases involving multiple litigants, attempts may be made for the court to certify a "class action" suit. Class action suits involve multiplaintiff litigation and may have benefits for both attorneys and litigants, but certain standards established by the court must be met in order for the class to be certified.

Learning the "Language" of the Toxic Torts Case

Before the LNC can tackle a toxic torts case, he or she must first learn the basic language of this specialized area of litigation. This language deals with how the exposure occurred, how it is measured, the acronyms of measurement, and even the acronyms by which the regulatory agencies are most commonly identified. Appendix 21.1 lists and defines the basic terms used in describing how exposure dosing is measured (Gots, 1991).

Often, in the early stages of a case, only a portion of the chemicals or compounds is identified. The discovery process will reveal whether the injured party was exposed to a single chemical, a chemical compound, or numerous chemicals and/or compounds. Recalling any college chemistry lecture will remind the LNC that there is an important distinction between a single chemical and a combination of chemicals to create a compound.

The plaintiffs may allege that injury occurred as the result of synergistic effect between two chemicals in a compound. Such an effect can render two relatively "harmless" chemicals more potent and able to cause dramatic afflictions that the individual chemicals are not known to produce by themselves. The LNC should work with designated consultants to determine the validity of any such assertion; in chemistry, true synergistic effects are rare despite what an ardent attorney may assert.

Measuring Exposure

The most important determination to be made during the preparation of the case is confirmation that an exposure occurred. Exposure is measured in terms of the *route* or means of exposure. Discovery will reveal facts about whether the plaintiff sustained an exposure by inhalation, oral ingestion, or cutaneous absorption, including ophthalmic exposure.

Once the type of exposure is known, one must look carefully at the *duration* of the exposure. How long was the injured party a victim of exposure? Various advisory panels and regulatory agencies set forth guidelines for safe exposure time to many chemicals and compounds (see Appendix 21.2). The LNC will find that most of the experts in the toxic torts cases will have a connection to one or more of these advisory bodies.

Not only must one know the duration of the exposure in understanding the event and alleged injuries, one must also know the *frequency* of the exposure. Did the individual experience a single sustained exposure, also known as an acute exposure, or was it an exposure that occurred repeatedly during the day, over the course of weeks or years, or intermittently over a period of time, producing a condition called chronic exposure?

When the information regarding the route, the frequency, and duration of exposure has been obtained, the LNC can work with toxicologists and industrial hygienists to estimate the *dose* of the exposure. It is important to determine whether the plaintiff experienced a sustained or repeated exposure and whether the amount ingested, inhaled, or absorbed was at a minimum or maximum dose.

Product Labeling Information

Strict interpretation of the aforementioned exposure guidelines presents other challenges for both the plaintiff and the defendant(s). Issues of accurate labeling, storage, proper use of protective equipment and clothing, and the proper disposal of the chemical substance must be examined.

Proper labeling and safe use guidelines are important in cases of chemical exposure. The manufacturer's safety data sheet, or MSDS, describes what is in a compound and how best to use, store, and dispose of it. MSDS forms are found in the home and workplace. Anyone changing a toner cartridge in a printer or copier will find an MSDS in the box. In the workplace, MSDS forms may be found in or on the packaging container. Because the MSDS of a product may change over the years, all of the MSDS forms for the relevant time periods are likely to become exhibits in the litigation.

The MSDS can also provide a quick reference for delineating changes in exposure guidelines over a period of time. In 1989, the Occupational Safety and Health Administration (OSHA) set permissible exposure limits (PEL) for nearly 500 hazardous chemicals. The American Conference of Governmental Industrial Hygienists (ACGIH) has developed hundreds of exposure limits which in some cases are lower than the OSHA PELs. These limits are reviewed and published annually by the ACGIH. ACGIH values have been adopted by many countries and administrative agencies throughout the world (Lewis, 1993). In a case involving workplace exposure, it is important to determine which exposure limits the workplace relied on at the time of the alleged exposure.

The Mechanics of Chemical Exposure

In preparing toxic torts cases, consideration must be given to how the exposure actually occurred. The vast majority of toxic torts cases involve inhalation exposure. Many chemicals are absorbed through the lungs. Inhalation exposures are not limited to gaseous chemicals such as chlorine, solvents, and isocyanates, but also include particulate matter such as fiberglass, asbestos, animal dander, silica dust, and bacterial and viral pathogens. Inhalation exposures can occur in the home, workplace, or in the environment. Environmental exposures cases include "sick-building" syndrome, tobacco cases, surface and groundwater contamination. Noxious fumes from carpets, glues, paints, and fiberglass are typically found in the home.

In many instances, inhalation exposure cases involve damage to other parts of the body in addition to the respiratory system because when chemicals are inhaled, they are also absorbed into the organ system (Hathaway et al., 1991). Inhaled chemical substances may be causally related to an increased risk of some types of cancers. As an example, the solvent benzene is easily inhaled but causes little damage to the respiratory system when inhaled at low doses, even over a long period of time. However, over time, low doses can cause leukemia (Zenz, 1994).

Inhalation exposures are also alleged to be associated with changes to the immune and nervous systems. It is important to realize that the practice of immunology is relatively new. Many diagnostic immunology tests which determine "dysfunction" of the immune system are experimental and may be performed in nonstandard laboratories. Such tests may be considered outside the mainstream of general medical practice, and the LNC should seek reputable professionals as experts and information sources concerning these tests.

Toxic torts cases involving immune system dysfunction typically include complaints of allergies, hayfever, hives, and asthma. Autoimmune disease has been alleged as a response to a variety of drugs, vaccines, and bacterial toxins. These disorders must be looked at carefully for determination of idiopathic autoimmune disease such as lupus or scleroderma. While certain immunodeficiencies are congenital, others are acquired, such as radiation sickness and radiation-related cancers. Others occur as the result of exposure to environmental toxins such as pesticides, nuclear waste, and groundwater contaminants.

Ingestion exposures may occur anywhere. The plaintiff may have accidentally swallowed solvents or other substances in the workplace or at home, or may have ingested unwashed fruits or vegetables contaminated with pesticides or fertilizers. Even handling food or other items with unwashed hands may transmit undesirable substances via ingestion. Measuring the dose of an ingested substance may be difficult to quantify. A toxicologist or pharmacologist may be required to use simulation to calculate how much chemical was ingested and metabolized, or excreted unchanged. Some compounds may be rendered harmless by the liver and not affect any organ systems while others may be destroyed in the digestive process.

Cutaneous exposure results from direct skin contact with a substance. Because of the protective function of the skin, cutaneous exposures may often be limited to local reactions such as irritation, pruritus, and urticaria. The popular press has recently carried stories relating to the purported increase in generalized reactions to dermal exposure to substances such as newsprint, latex, detergents, and other substances commonly found in the home and work environments. Since a chemical may enter the body via skin, hair follicles, sweat glands, and sebaceous glands, particular attention should be paid to determining the preexposure condition of the skin. Was more chemical absorbed because of rashes, cuts, or other skin breaks?

The Legal Nurse Consultant's Role in Establishing and Evaluating Causation

Legal causation is defined differently from scientific causation. Like other tort cases, legal causation theories must meet a legal standard of preponderance of evidence. However, toxic torts cases center around establishing that exposure caused injury. This requires establishing scientific causation. Scientific causation is established using statistical methods to determine a high-confidence or statistically significant relationship between exposure and illness.

A key element in establishing causation is the basic concept of cause and effect. A causal relationship must exist between the exposure event and the adverse outcome alleged. The illness or injury must be substantiated in the medical and social records and the substance at issue must be proved to cause the alleged injury. Other causes for the illness must be ruled out and a temporal relationship must exist between the exposure and the onset of illness (Gots, 1991).

This temporal relationship may include a latency period between exposure and the onset of symptoms. The LNC assists in evaluating whether or not the onset of illness and clinical patterns associated with the substance are consistent with what is known about the product and the disease process. The clinical picture must be carefully evaluated for the presence of unrelated disease or other pathological processes.

If the chemical substance at issue is known to cause a particular illness or disease at a known dose, the diagnosis of that illness must be confirmed in the medical record. At toxic levels all chemicals attack a target organ or organ system. For example, benzene, a well-known solvent, is known to cause a specific type of leukemia; it is not known to cause bowel cancer. Through the use of the time lines and comparative charts, the defense team could easily demonstrate the lack of causal link between the alleged exposure, e.g., benzene, and the symptom cluster, e.g., bowel cancer symptomatology.

The LNC must be mindful of the alleged specifics of the exposure when he or she initially reviews the medical records. LNCs working for the plaintiff or the defendant(s) are likely to follow the same process in their goal of advancing the client's case. Both will be establishing the extent of the injury and trying to prove or disprove the causal link between exposure and injury.

The LNC working for the defense team may or may not be able to visit the worksite or other location where the alleged exposure occurred. If such a site visit is not possible, the LNC reviews the materials produced during discovery for references to the presence or absence of the client's product at the site. If it can be established that the product was available in the workplace at the time of the exposure, the LNC will try to prove whether or not the product was actually in use in an area where the plaintiff could experience an exposure, whether the substance was properly stored and maintained, and whether or not it was used in accordance with suggested and/or required guidelines.

The defense team may try to prove that their client's product was not present, or, if present, that it was improperly stored and/or was improperly used by the plaintiff. They may try to show that claimed injuries were not caused by the client's product, or that any alleged injuries are not consistent with those known to be caused by the subject product. Finally, the defense team may also try to prove that the plaintiff failed to seek timely or appropriate treatment for the injury, and this failure affected his or her recovery and/or prognosis.

The LNC working with the plaintiff's team may have unlimited access to the injured party if the plaintiff, for instance, is the owner of a contaminated property. The plaintiff's team will try to prove that their client used the defendant's product and sustained a measurable exposure to that product, that the product was properly stored, and that the product was used appropriately, or that despite care in the use of the substance, compensable injury to person and/or property occurred.

> Case Example 21.1: As an example, a young insulation worker presents with a history of shortness of breath documented by pulmonary function testing. A chest X-ray shows a mass that upon further evaluation proves to be malignant mesothelioma, a type of cancer often associated with asbestos exposure. Knowing that the young man works with insulation, a diagnosis of asbestos-related exposure is made and he files suit. The literature reveals that there may be a 20-year latency period between exposure to asbestos fibers and the development of cancer, and there is a directly proportional relationship between the length (or chronicity) of exposure to asbestos and the risk of developing disease (Miller and Miller, 1991). The LNC advises the attorney that in the absence of the temporal relationship described in the literature, it would be unlikely for a young worker with a single exposure to a small amount of asbestos to develop cancer.

Evaluating the Plaintiff's Medical History

The importance of obtaining a complete set of medical records, along with other information about the plaintiff, cannot be overemphasized. Detailed information about the plaintiff is the crux of establishing the validity of the injury.

All parties must obtain the medical records from as many of the plaintiff's health care providers as soon as possible. Individuals are often unprepared for the degree of personal invasion of their privacy when they enter litigation. Many are embarrassed about certain medical treatments, including treatment for sexually transmitted disease, plastic surgery, chemical dependence, or psychiatric treatment, and may conveniently "forget" or even refuse to identify the relevant providers. Other plaintiffs may be too old, too ill, or genuinely cannot remember all of their health care providers.

Plaintiffs often allege neurological or central nervous system (CNS) injury in toxic torts cases. In no other area of the case preparation is the LNC likely to face more challenge than in the evaluation of the medical and social records for prexisting and concurrent psychoemotional disorders. Neurological or CNS complaints are often subjective, vague, and difficult to measure. Some neuropsychological testing is poorly standardized and results are directly related to the effort put forth by the test subject. Some tests are sensitive to the subject's efforts to present their physical and mental condition falsely.

The LNC should work with expert neurologists, neuropsychologists, and neuropsychiatrists, and others skilled in measuring cognitive function when evaluating claims of toxic encephalopathy, organic brain syndrome, and convulsions. Claimed injuries to the peripheral nervous system may include allegations of neuropathy and sensorimotor dysfunction, including memory loss, diminished IQ, and psychoemotional illness.

The medical record establishes the plaintiff's preexisting health status; defines the existence and extent of the injury; describes the treatment rendered; and often gives a prognosis for recovery. This information not only provides an outline, but a focus to the case as it develops.

When the financial, personnel, and equipment resources are available, computerized databases are recommended for cataloging specific information about the plaintiff's symptom history, such as when each symptom appeared, what events were related to the symptom, what precipitants were identified, and what treatment was given. This information can be used to create a sophisticated time line to show the presence or absence of causal links between exposure and injury.

With or without such high-tech support available, it is recommended that the LNC prepare a chronological summary of all medical records (Orr, 1994). These summaries should document the date of each contact with health care providers, laboratory and other test results, anecdotal information entered by the health care provider, and, of course, details about the treatment regimen.

A time line of symptoms, perhaps broken down by organ systems, may also be useful. It is suggested that both objective data and the plaintiff's subjective statements and complaints be entered in these tables. When the dates of exposure are superimposed on these summaries and time lines, the existence of preexposure illnesses becomes readily apparent. The course of the illness may not correlate with what is known in the accepted medical literature.

Preparing time lines and summaries in complex cases can pose a daunting task. Collecting, summarizing, organizing, and storing information for such cases is most easily done with a computer database. This format allows the attorney to examine the data quickly and accurately to evaluate information about symptom clusters within the population of plaintiffs. There are commercially available products that many LNCs use successfully, while others may work with a database programmer to develop a specific format for each case. Care must be taken in collecting data; analysis of nonrelevant information can yield nonrelevant or misleading information.

Evaluating the Plaintiff's Social History

The plaintiff's social history may yield valuable information about other sources of exposure and other risk factors for disease. The LNC working with the plaintiff will have opportunities to obtain this information directly from the client. The defense LNC will have to assist the attorney in obtaining this information through discovery. Well-crafted interrogatory and deposition questions, as well as requests for production, can elicit this information. Both sides will want to add the information to their time lines, summaries, and databases.

Vital information may be found in an individual's school records. Other records from childhood may describe debilitating childhood illnesses, or traumatic events that affected the plaintiff. Neurological or IQ testing may confirm that the plaintiff has a limited earning capacity based on limited intellectual and learning abilities.

Workplace exposure cases depend heavily on a thorough employment history. For example, did the plaintiff spend the summers pumping gas and sustain exposure to benzene? Did he or she ever work in a shipyard or in an environment where there was asbestos? Does the plaintiff currently work in an environment where there are other substances or conditions that might adversely affect him? A former mechanic may have been exposed to airborne concentrations of chlorinated fluorocarbons, have cleaned parts in other solvents, and have inhaled endless amounts of lead and benzene-laden exhaust, yet his claim may arise out of his current employment in a film laboratory. Which chemical or compound caused his illness?

Obviously, exhaustive deposition questioning must be used to obtain a complete history of chemical exposures sustained over a plaintiff's lifetime. Occupational health records may contain some of this information. These same records are likely to include preemployment physical examinations, regular medical screenings, laboratory results, and attendance records. In evaluating the work history, efforts should be made to determine whether or not in each place of employment, the workplace was in compliance with federal "right-to-know" laws regarding the health and safety hazards of workplace hazardous chemicals (Code of Federal Regulations, 1995).

Lifestyle habits of the plaintiff and others who live with him or her are also important. Is the claimant living with a smoker or doing laundry for someone whose clothing may be contaminated with pathogens or carcinogenic chemicals? Does the plaintiff pursue hobbies that involve exposure to chemicals? Avid gardeners may be exposed to pesticides, fungicides, rodenticides, and organic and inorganic fertilizers. Crafters may be exposed to paints and glues full of solvents, phenols, ketones, and other dangerous substances. Does the plaintiff spend large amounts of time in a manicure salon inhaling noxious amounts of the chemicals used in preparing and painting fingernails? Does the plaintiff use "harmless" household chemicals to keep the bathroom sparkling clean? Furniture polish, bleach, ammonia, spot removers, and pine cleaners are solvents that are known to produce a variety of transient symptoms.

Case Example 21.2: A 58-year-old man presents to an attorney inquiring about filing suit against his employer. He points to a rash around his face, neck, and chest and says that he works in a warehouse "around a lot of chemicals." He believes that as the result of his exposure, he has become sensitive to the sun and burns easily. The LNC is asked to review the medical aspects of the case.

The LNC takes an extensive history from the client, attempting to obtain a complete list of exposures that might have been sustained at the workplace and at home. Eventually, the claimant brings in a list of the chemicals and a notebook full of MSDS forms from his workplace. Upon research, it is learned that most of the chemicals are inert liquids and not in use by the plaintiff.

The potential plaintiff's doctor has confirmed a diagnosis of contact dermatitis and attributes the cause to the chemicals in the work environment. Since a workplace exposure has been ruled out, the LNC must look to the social history. She visits the claimant's home, making an extensive list of products in use there. The client shows her his bathroom and she sees many bottles of aftershave cologne. When she begins to make a list of the product names, the claimant tells her that he no longer uses those products as they irritate the pruritic areas on his face and neck.

Research reveals that a number of the claimant's aftershave products contain musk ambrette and two preservatives, methylparaben and Quaternium-15. The literature reports that musk ambrette is known to cause not only contact dermatitis, but photosensitivity, as well. The LNC also learns that members of the paraben family are the most commonly used preservatives in cosmetics and generally considered to be among the safest. Quaternium-15 has been identified as an antibacterial preservative belonging to a family of formaldehyde-releasing chemicals. Further research reveals that combining preservatives can cause sensitivity characterized by localized dermatitis to develop.

The would-be plaintiff is advised that he does not have a good exposure case against his employer and/or any product manufacturer of the workplace chemicals.

It is easy and dangerous to overlook other sources of exposure. Because everyone is exposed to chemicals and other substances every day, most individuals do not consciously consider the variety of exposures that they sustain daily. Both the defense and plaintiff teams must construct questions via written and deposition outlines that will prompt the individual to confront these alternative exposures.

"Environmental" exposures are also important and may require the LNC to visit the plaintiff's home and neighborhood, possibly even requiring interviewing the neighbors. Recently, efforts have been made to bring a new category of environmental exposure cases. These involve exposure to microwave and electromagnetic radiation fields (EMF). Cases involving environmental exposures can be problematic for both sides — particularly with regard to EMF.

Over the past few years, more and more claims have been made based on exposure to EMF. While it is true that personal electrical appliances such as electric blankets, clock radios, hair dryers, and cellular phones exert a weak EMF field, most individuals living in civilized countries are exposed to EMF sources at home and at work, these cases have been difficult for plaintiffs to develop, as Earth exerts its own, constant electromagnetic field and all beings are constantly exposed. Experts have a difficult time isolating which exposures caused their clients' injuries.

Case Example 21.3: A plaintiff claims that she developed leukemia as the result of her exposure to EMF. She and her husband live near power lines; he has lived in the house for the past 18 years, she and her 5-year-old twins for 7 years. She also alleges that her children have severe allergic problems as the direct result of EMF exposure.

The plaintiff is undergoing experimental chemotherapy for her leukemia, but her life expectation is shortened. The children have brought suit for their allergies and are also alleging loss of consortium as the result of their mother's illness. The husband is well, but is also alleging loss of consortium. The case against the power company is valued by the plaintiffs as being worth many millions of dollars.

Upon researching the world literature base, the LNC is unable to find a connection between the type of leukemia afflicting the plaintiff and exposure to EMF. The LNC's work with an expert oncologist and an epidemiologist confirms this lack of causal link.

The case against the defendant power company is eventually dismissed when it is learned via the plaintiff's occupational work history that as a teen, she spent 5 years working part-time in a tire-manufacturing plant, sustaining regular exposures to benzene. The literature search confirms that since the plaintiff's years in the tire plant, the TWA of benzene was lowered because of its association with a high incidence of blood dyscrasias, including leukemia.

Evaluating the Corporate Defendant's History

Plaintiffs aren't alone in having to reveal personal information about themselves during the course of discovery. When the defendant is a corporate entity, it will have to reveal corporate practices and how those practices may or may not relate to the allegations made against it. The LNC may be asked to evaluate "in-house working papers" or other documents prepared by the client during the research, development, manufacturing, and marketing of the product in question. These papers are likely to include both *in vivo* and *in vitro* studies conducted with cellular, animal, and human subjects. These internal documents are generally considered to be proprietary and should be handled as confidential material.

Since the relative safety of the subject product is important to the case, the defense must demonstrate that it was properly labeled and packaged with instructions for safe use. The LNC may be asked to compare MSDS inserts with their contemporaneous package labeling and any other packaging information in an effort to evaluate claims of proper labeling. Over the last several years, litigants in breast implant and cigarette cases have tried to prove that internal studies were flawed, fraudulent, and resulted in mislabeling and misrepresentations to the FDA and the public (Bolton, 1991).

Despite organization, diligence, and persistence, it may be difficult for the plaintiff to prevail in attempts to prove that a corporate defendant showed reckless disregard and conspired to defraud the public regarding the safety of the product. This is not to say that litigants *are not* successful in proving these claims. In many instances, when it can be demonstrated that a corporate entity has committed a civil wrong, executive and supervisory staff may be found not only civilly liable, but may face criminal charges as well.

Evaluating Causation — Examining Preexisting Conditions

Like other areas of civil litigation, when there is no causal link, there is no case. Therefore, the LNC will need to examine closely the relationship among the exposure, the claimed injury, and the plaintiff's preexisting medical condition. Medical and social records should provide detailed information about many preexposure conditions.

The LNC compares postexposure complaints against preexisting problems to determine whether or not there is a relationship between the two. Pathological processes are dynamic in nature, sometimes resulting in a "natural" and progressive decline in health. Such declines may be completely unrelated to the exposure, although the plaintiff may allege that his or her condition developed or worsened as the result of the exposure. Such allegations require the defense to prove that the underlying disease either did not worsen, or that the plaintiff sought medical care because he thought he or she was affected, or that he or she was anticipating litigation. If it is determined that an exposure caused an exacerbation of a preexisting condition, such injury is usually compensable.

As the LNC develops chronologies, summaries, and time lines concerning the facts of the case, he or she will add information from the literature that describes symptoms known to be associated with a particular substance. With those additions made, one can readily compare the plaintiff's symptoms against those known to be associated with exposure. Further comparison can be made between the preexisting ailments and the postexposure complaints.

Chronologies such as these make excellent teaching tools for the LNC who must digest and explain the medical and scientific elements of the case for the trial attorney. These tools serve as a quick reference for all members of the trial team and may ultimately be used as trial exhibits to aid the jury in understanding the relationships, or lack of relationships, between exposure and injury (Lobb et al., 1994). Charts, and all demonstrative evidence presented, should be user-friendly so that nonmedical professionals such as attorneys, insurance adjusters, workers' compensation panels, and judges may be able to identify causal links easily.

Evaluating Causation — The Literature Review

Along with data collection about the plaintiff and the defendants, both sides will do literature searches. Factual data to back up all toxicological and medical findings and conclusions are required to substantiate or refute claims. In some instances, the LNC will perform this task for the experts; others may prefer to have the experts perform their own searches for purposes of strategy. When experts perform their own search, they will be free of any accusation that conclusions were drawn and opinions formed on the basis of another's bias in how the literature search was conducted.

Ideally, the LNC will have access to a library with such basics as references on occupational health, toxicology, chemistry, and medicine. The Internet is a valuable tool for locating specialized on-line databases, providing access to the various regulatory and advisory agencies, as well as to extensive medical information.

The world literature discusses and describes the illnesses and symptoms known to be caused by the product at issue. Detailed information may be found about signs and symptoms of illness as the result of acute and chronic exposures in humans and animals. In the area of solvent toxicity, for example, Sweden has conducted long-term studies of individuals with exposures to various solvents. These studies address findings ranging from serious illness to subtle changes seen only at the cellular level.

As in other areas of legal nurse consulting, attention must be paid to gathering data relevant to the time frame of the case, but to be complete, the literature search should also contain the most current information. Where possible, it is suggested that research specialists and librarians familiar with scientific databases be consulted in conducting literature searches.

Often, the toxic torts case requires a jury to sit through tedious testimony regarding biochemistry, pharmacology, toxicology, and physics, subjects they may be unable to understand. As a result, attorneys may present as evidence "studies" with jury appeal that were not conducted by proper scientific method. These "studies" may have had inadequate numbers in their study population, were not subject to peer review, or may have been published in the popular literature rather than in scholarly journals. In some venues, courts have been very generous in allowing spurious findings to be accepted into evidence in the toxic torts case, believing that because the subject matter is complex, it is better to allow all literature and expert testimony. Poor epidemiological studies and their attendant "findings" may be properly relegated to the "junk science" category. New case law severely limits the ability to include such material as evidence.

The literature search may include obtaining journal articles and abstracts published in foreign journals. The LNC who overlooks or disregards materials simply because they are in another language may be missing articles published by distinguished researchers from well-respected institutions. Articles published in a foreign language may have English-language abstracts that will provide a clue to the usefulness of the article.

Ultimately, the literature search will yield such diverse items as doctoral dissertations, medical journal articles, textbook reference materials, regulatory position papers, and even "letters to the editor" making anecdotal reports of findings. From this eclectic assembly, each side will find relevant materials to prove its own and dispel the opposition's causation theories.

Identifying and Working with the Experts

The LNC may participate in the selection of experts for preparation of the case. It is worth noting that while the LNC may have the skills and credentials to participate in a toxic torts case as a testifying expert, these cases tend to be advanced through the use of specialized experts such as toxicologists, epidemiologists, industrial hygienists, safety engineers, and physicians practicing in such specialty areas as occupational medicine, neurology, oncology, immunology, and pulmonology.

The literature review may be augmented and/or evaluated by a consulting epidemiologist. Epidemiologists evaluate causal links based on observations of the relationships between a disease entity and its presence in the general population. According to Hallberg (1994), epidemiologists use the scientific method to evaluate whether or not a substance can cause the claimed injury and whether or not, in the subject case, it did. Like other scientists and researchers, epidemiologists must have a well-defined research hypothesis, a well-defined and adequate cohort, high-quality data, analysis of attributable actions, and minimal bias or skew in the data.

Like the epidemiologist, the toxicologist also contributes significantly to the case. The toxicologist may be the best expert to describe or refute the soundness of methods used in evaluating or testing a chemical substance. The toxicologist evaluates "poisonous" materials and their effects on living organisms. This is known as the "dose–response effect." To a toxicologist, even a chemical considered "harmless," "safe," or "nontoxic" in small doses can be toxic at very high levels. For example, two aspirin can relieve pain, but a full bottle is lethal.

Because the toxicologist must evaluate dose–response when assessing any chemical substance at issue in a case, the discovery process must obtain the most-accurate-possible data regarding the exposure and the environment in which the exposure occurred.

Various medical experts may be called on to evaluate the medical and psychosocial data in a toxic torts case. Neuropsychologists and other cognitive experts may offer testimony about any changes or lack of changes in cognition or perception in the postexposure plaintiff. Early school records may become important in these cases as the only objective baseline data available that delineate the subject's ability to process cognitive and sensory information.

The search for the experts may be pursued through the writings found in the literature search and through various professional organizations, such as the ACGIH, the American Institute of Chemists, and other organizations, such as the National Environmental Law Center. Appropriate experts may include practitioners, researchers, and academicians from universities, the National Institutes of Health, the EPA, the FDA, and other research facilities. The appropriate experts must be identified for trial testimony, but, in researching possible experts, consideration must be given to whether or not any of the candidates could be considered biased if any of their research was funded by a defendant company.

The LNC is often the person on the litigation team best suited to working with the experts on a day-to-day basis as the case develops. The attorney must be able to rely on the LNC to summarize the findings of the various experts, his or her assessment of the expert's suitability as a witness, and the relevance of the expert's testimony. Moreover, as the liaison between the experts and the attorney, the LNC is in the best position to coordinate the efforts of the various experts, often preventing costly overlap of research and testimony.

Summary

It is insufficient for a litigant to profess that he or she is ill as the result of working with chemicals. The plaintiff's trial team must prove that their client sustained a sufficient period of exposure to a substance at a dose high enough for harm to have occurred. The defense team will work hard to prove otherwise. Common defense strategies include showing

1. The claimed illness resulted from another, unrelated exposure
2. Any alleged injury was wrongly diagnosed and is inconsistent with what is known about related disease processes
3. The illness is related to a preexisting condition or other risk factor

Undoubtedly, work experience in specialty areas of nursing may assist the LNC in preparing the toxic torts case. Experience in occupational health or in pulmonology or respiratory therapy may be helpful. For other types of cases, the nurse who is knowledgeable regarding immunology, neurology, or oncology may find it easier to master the reading material. There is no requirement that the LNC be an expert in occupational medicine or other specialty areas in order to assist ably in preparing these cases. The real requirements include a willingness to use one's nursing and general science backgrounds in preparing cases with objectivity and careful analysis. Whether the LNC is working for an attorney or a consulting firm, he or she must possess the ability to review and analyze information from a variety of sources; to work with experts; and to act as a liaison between the experts and the attorney, to bring a powerful, proficient multidisciplinary team approach to this novel area of litigation.

Discussion Questions

1. Select three agencies or advisory bodies that would have informational resources on chemical exposures:
   a. The Environmental Policy Consortium, the Food and Drug Administration, and the Occupational Safety and Health Administration
   b. The National Institute for Occupational Safety and Health, Society of Inhalation Therapy, and the Environmental Protection Agency
   c. The Society of Toxicology, the National Institute for Occupational Safety and Health, and the American Conference of Governmental Industrial Hygienists
   (Answer: b)
2. You are working for the plaintiff's attorney in an environmental exposure case and are asked to obtain information about the health of the plaintiff's neighbors. Why?
   a. The plaintiff and his attorney care about those around the plaintiff and want to be assured that they are healthy.
   b. If the neighbors are sick all of the time, the plaintiff's case will look better to the jury. If many of the neighbors have a variety of symptoms, it will prove that the chemical in the groundwater has made everyone sick.
   c. The attorney wants to prove that his client's illness is part of a cohort of individuals who have been made ill by exposure. Similar symptoms in the neighbors may strengthen the claim.
   (Answer: c)
3. Mrs. Jones has alleged that since she had breast implants, she has developed a tendency to develop rashes and rhinitis. You review the medical and social records. Identify items of importance in your review.
   a. Mrs. Jones has had saline implants for 10 years. She has her hair colored every 4 weeks at the same salon where she has her nails done.
   b. Mrs. Jones has eight children, six of whom are being treated for eczema and multiple food allergies.
   c. Mrs. Jones had silicone implants until one of them broke and was replaced with saline.
   d. Only c.
   e. a, b, and c.
   (Answer: e)

4. A worker had a single, acute exposure to formaldehyde and claims that as a result he has elevated liver enzymes. He has approached a plaintiff attorney regarding the merits of his claim. You are asked to do a literature search and compare it against the medical record. You find that the worker has had intermittent elevations over the last few years. The employer's occupational health clinic notes make a reference to his being referred to a chemical dependence treatment program.
   a. You have discovered evidence that the plaintiff is an alcoholic and advise the plaintiff attorney not to accept the case.
   b. You consult the databases for information on liver injury as the result of exposure to formaldehyde.
   c. You ask what the route of exposure was before starting the reviews.
   (Answer: c)
5. The plaintiff has claimed that as the result of life-long exposure to EMF radiation, he has developed non-Hodgkin's lymphoma. The defense attorney has asked to you to participate in preparing the case. You will anticipate being asked to do the following:
   a. Go to the plaintiff's home with an industrial hygienist while air samples are taken.
   b. Review and summarize extensive medical records from various providers.
   c. Review position papers from the National Cancer Institute regarding risk factors for non-Hodgkins lymphoma.
   d. Both b and c.
   e. Both a and b.
   (Answer: d)

References

Bolton, D. (1991). How to build a breast implant suit, *Leader's Product Liability Law and Strategy*, July, 1991, 3–5.

Code of Federal Regulations (29 CFR 1910 1200); OSHA Hazard Communication Standard (Worker "Right-to-Know Rule"), July 1, 1995 edition.

Gots, R. E. (1991). *Seven Steps to Toxic Tort Analysis and Defense*, Chicago, The Defense Research Institute.

Hallberg, M. (1994). The use of epidemiological studies and epidemiologists in proving or disproving causation, *Network: News for the Legal Nurse Consultant*, (5)1, 19.

Hathaway, G. J., Proctor, N. H., Hughes, J. P., and Fischman, M. L. (1991). *Proctor and Hughes' Chemical Hazards of the Workplace*, 3rd ed., New York, Van Nostrand Reinhold.

Lewis, R. J. (1993). *Hazardous Chemicals Desk Reference*, 3rd ed., New York, Van Nostrand Reinhold.

Lobb, M., Riley, G. C., and Clemens, A. (1994). The LNC's role on the defense team in a medical malpractice suit, *Network: News for the Legal Nurse Consultant*, 5(4), 3–7.

Miller, E. W. and Miller, R. M. (1991). *Environmental Hazards. Toxic Waste and Hazardous Material. A Reference Handbook*. Santa Barbara, CA, ABC-CLIO.

Occupational Safety and Health Administration, (1996). *Mission*, Http:/www.osha.gov/oshinfo/mission.html (October 4).

Orr, M. (1994). The role of the legal nurse consultant in assisting with a toxic tort case, *Network: News for the Legal Nurse Consultant,* 5(2), 9–10.

Zenz, C. (1994). *Occupational Medicine: Principles and Practical Applications,* 3rd ed., Chicago, Mosby-Year Book.

Suggested Reading

Adams, R. M. (1990). *Occupational Skin Disease,* 2nd ed., Philadelphia, W. B. Saunders.

The American Conference of Governmental Industrial Hygienists (1994). *Threshold Limit Values for Chemical Substances and Physical Agents and Biological Exposure Indices* (1994–1995), Cincinnati, The Conference.

Ballantyne, B., Marrs, T., and Turner, T. (1993). *General and Applied Toxicology,* New York, Stockton Press.

Baselt, R. C. and Cravey, R. H. (1989). *Disposition of Toxic Drugs and Chemicals in Man.,* 3rd ed, Chicago, Year-Book Medical Publishers.

Consumer Product Safety Commission (1996). *Guide to Information Services.* Http://www. parentsplace.com./readroom/cpsc/infoser2.html (October 4, 1996).

Food and Drug Administration (1996). *Overview,* April 19, 1995. Http://www.fda.gov/opa-com/hpview.html (October 4, 1996).

Gosselin, R. E., Smith, R. S., and Hodge, H. C. (1984). *Clinical Toxicology of Commercial Products,* 5th ed., Baltimore, Williams and Wilkins.

Hodgson, E. and Levi, P. (1987). *A Textbook of Modern Toxicology,* New York, Elsevier.

Lewis, R. J. (1996). *Sax's Dangerous Properties of Industrial Materials,* 9th ed., New York, Van Nostrand Reinhold.

Mudge-Grout, C. (1992). *Immunologic Disorders — Mosby's Clinical Nursing Series,* St. Louis, Mosby-Year Book.

Nothstein, G. Z. (1984). *Toxic Torts: Litigation of Hazardous Substance Cases,* Colorado Springs, Shepard's/McGraw Hill.

Patnaik, P. (1992). *A Comprehensive Guide to the Hazardous Properties if Chemical Substances,* New York, Van Nostrand Reinhold.

U.S. Department of Labor (1996). *OSHA. PELS Update.* Http://spider.osha.gov.oshinfo/priorities/pel.html (October 4).

Appendix 21.1
Measuring Exposure

TLV	Threshold limit value — Also known as TWA or time weighted average. The daily exposure that a worker can sustain to airborne concentrations 8 hours per day × 40 hours per week without adverse effect. These exposures may be described in parts per million (ppm) or billion (ppb), or in the case of dermal exposure, in milligrams per cubic meter (mg/m^3).
PEL	Permissible exposure limit — Similar to TLV/TWA.
STEL	Short-term exposure limit — A short exposure added to the TLV/TWA. STEL exposures may not exceed 15 minutes, more than four times daily and with each exposure separated by at least 60 minutes. Workers must not suffer irritation, chronic tissue damage, or inability for self-rescue.
IDLH	Immediately dangerous to life and health — The maximum concentration from which one could escape within 30 minutes without experiencing irreversible health effect or impairing self-rescue.
MSDS	Material safety data sheet — Form included with shipment of products containing chemical substances. The MSDS lists the chemical ingredients, their CAS registry identification information, and information related to exposure and handling. Manufacturers and/or vendors are legally required to include this with each shipment of product.
PPE	Personal protective equipment — Includes protective garments, masks, goggles, and respirators worn to protect the individual from exposure to chemicals and pathogens.

Appendix 21.2
Advisory and Regulatory Agencies

ACGIH	American Conference of Governmental Industrial Hygienists
AIHA	American Industrial Hygiene Association
EPA	Environmental Protection Agency
OSHA	Occupational Safety and Health Administration
NAS	National Academy of Sciences
NRC	National Research Council, not to be confused with the Nuclear Regulatory Council
NIOSH	National Institute for Occupational Safety and Health
SOT	Society of Toxicology

Chapter 22

Case Analysis: Evaluating Criminal Cases

Patricia Ann Steed

Contents

Objectives

- To discuss how the burden of proof for a criminal case differs from a civil case

1-57444-123-X/98

- To describe the roles and responsibilities of law enforcement, the prosecuting attorney's office, and the medical examiner or coroner in the investigation of a criminal case
- To identify three ways in which the LNC can assist the attorney in the prosecution or defense of a criminal case
- To describe how the processes of evaluation, assessment, and implementation are ongoing in a criminal case and why this is important

Introduction

The purpose of this chapter is to provide the legal nurse consultant (LNC) with basic concepts of the criminal justice system as they relate to the analysis of criminal cases. The information presented is intended to offer insight into the analysis of criminal cases. It is not intended to be a comprehensive study of criminal law, nor does it attempt to address every aspect of a criminal case.

There are inherent differences between civil and criminal cases. Civil cases involve wrongs which are personal in nature such as property, contracts, and torts. Civil actions are considered private matters between individual parties (Neubauer, 1996). Criminal cases involve wrongs against society. A crime is defined as any act which is forbidden by law or as the omission of an act required by law. Criminal law is statutory and will vary from municipality to municipality. Crimes are generally divided into misdemeanors and felonies. Legislatures enact criminal codes that distinguish between the two basic types of crimes (Swanson et al., 1996). Generally, a misdemeanor is a crime punishable by imprisonment of up to 1 year, and a felony is a crime punishable by imprisonment of more than 1 year or death. The same act may give rise to both civil and criminal causes of action. The reader is referred to Chapter 5 for a more in-depth look at criminal law.

Although the law applying to criminal and civil cases is different, the basic concept of determining the truth based on evidence is common to both. For purposes of discussion, this section will address crimes against persons which include assault and battery, child abuse, sex-related offenses, and murder.

Investigation

The initial investigation in a criminal case is conducted by law enforcement, and perhaps by representatives of the prosecutor's office, the medical examiner's office, county coroners, or other interested parties. The investigation of a crime by law enforcement is critical. There is only one opportunity to process a crime scene. Processing a crime scene includes identifying, collecting, marking, measuring, photographing, documenting, and preserving evidence (Swanson et al., 1996). The initial investigation also includes interviewing victims and/or witnesses. In suspicious deaths or homicides, the medical examiner or coroner will also be called to the scene to process the scene and the body (or bodies) to assist in determining the cause and manner of death.

All physical evidence collected at the crime scene will be carefully processed, documented, and placed in the proper custody until such time as it is utilized in the legal process. Any physical evidence that may be introduced in court must be identified, described, and maintained in proper custody. In handling evidentiary material, care must be taken not to disturb the viability of the material for later examination (Swanson et al., 1996). From the time it is collected and identified until it is presented at trial, physical evidence must at all times be accounted for and secured. This is accomplished by having anyone who handles the evidence providing the date, time, purpose of handling, and their signature. Anyone who handles the evidence may be called to testify at trial to verify this information and again identify the evidence. This meticulous process ensures that the evidence has been maintained properly. It also ensures that only authorized personnel come in contact with the evidence and that the evidence has not been subject to tampering. This process is commonly referred to as the chain of custody. Any variance in the above can result in physical evidence being inadmissible in court. This is an especially important consideration when reviewing a criminal case.

Forensic science is that which is applied to answering legal questions by examining, evaluating, and explaining evidence. It encompasses pathology, toxicology, biology, serology, chemistry, anthropology, odontology, and psychiatry among other fields. One branch of forensic science is criminalistics which deals with the study of physical evidence related to a crime. It encompasses firearms, questioned documents, toolmark comparison, fingerprints, photography, and trace elements among other fields (Swanson et al., 1996). The reports generated by experts in the various forensic fields may play important roles in the presentation of evidence during a trial. The LNC interacts with many of these experts in understanding and applying the specific field of science. This represents one aspect of his or her involvement in a criminal case.

Preliminary Hearing, Arraignment, Indictment

Once a suspect has been arrested and accused of a crime, the accused is entitled to a timely hearing to determine whether probable cause exists that a crime was committed and whether the accused committed it. The accused cannot be detained prior to trial unless this has occurred. The exact process will be determined by the seriousness of the crime and the jurisdiction in which the matter is pending. The accused is brought before a judge for an initial appearance at which time he or she is told what charges are pending, advised of his or her rights, and given the date for a preliminary hearing. The information gathered during the initial investigation is presented to a judge in the form of a preliminary hearing or to a grand jury for review. In some jurisdictions and in some instances, preliminary hearings are not held.

If a grand jury determines enough evidence exists to hold a defendant for trial, an indictment is returned charging the defendant with a crime or crimes. At the time of arraignment, the accused is given a copy of formal charges, is once again informed of his or her rights, and is asked to enter a plea. As opposed to civil cases in which several years may pass before a case reaches a trial calendar, criminal trials are usually held within a year of the indictment. This is because the defendant may be incarcerated during this period of time, depending on the seriousness of the crime, and has the constitutional right of an accused to a speedy trial.

Prosecution

The job of prosecuting criminals is within the purview of the prosecuting attorney's office. The prosecutor attempts to determine that the right person (the accused) has been identified, located, and apprehended and that there is evidence sufficient to indict. If an indictment is not possible, then neither is a conviction. The burden of proof in a criminal case rests solely on the prosecution and is proof "beyond a reasonable doubt." The verdict must be unanimous and is returned as guilty or not guilty. Since a crime by definition is against the state, the prosecution has the state's resources at its disposal in investigating and developing cases. This includes law enforcement agencies, the office of the medical examiner, the coroner, the state crime laboratory, and other state agencies, such as family and children services, mental health, etc.

Defense

The job of the criminal defense attorney is to be an advocate for the client. This gives the attorney the responsibility of ensuring that the client's civil rights are respected. The Constitution guarantees everyone the right to a fair and speedy trial regardless of the evidence concerning guilt or innocence. The criminal defense attorney does not enjoy the same readily available access to the state's resources (such as those discussed in conjunction with the prosecution) and therefore, at times, must utilize private laboratories and forensic scientists in private practice for testing and consulting. The conclusions or test results provided by these private entities may challenge or refute conclusions or tests provided by the state. The conclusions or test results may also provide a sufficient basis on which to create a reasonable doubt for a jury concerning the state's case.

Civil proceedings have rules governing the disclosure of information (discovery) prior to trial which are broad and entitle every party to relevant information. The same rules do not apply in criminal proceedings. The type and amount of information that is discoverable in a criminal case will vary from state to state. Therefore, the criminal defense attorney may or may not be privy to the state's case theory depending upon the working relationship between the criminal defense attorney and the District Attorney's office or the usual practices of the municipality. The criminal defense attorney will therefore need to become an expert on any anticipated theory which the state may utilize. The LNC can assist the defense attorney in developing case theories and strategies. For example, if the state is pursuing DNA evidence, it would behoove defense counsel to know as much as possible about DNA in order to present testimony or additional evidence which could create reasonable doubt about the evidence. The LNC can produce medical literature on the topic. The LNC can also locate, identify, retain, and work with experts in the field as part of case development.

Legal Nurse Consultant's Role

The LNC's analysis of the facts of the case will be the same regardless of which side of a criminal case one might be working. The scope of the LNC's duties may include one or more of the following. (*Note:* The following list is not intended to be all-inclusive as the actions of the LNC will be determined by the type of case and the LNC's work environment.)

1. Reviewing and analyzing medical records to assess the extent of injuries to determine if injuries match history given, to determine if sex was forced or consensual, to determine if previous injuries exist (especially in domestic violence cases), or to determine if a medical condition existed which could contribute to defendant's actions.

2. Reviewing and analyzing autopsy reports to assess the extent of injuries, to determine if injuries match history (victim strangled, then house set on fire to make the death appear accidental); to determine if previous injuries exist which were untreated (especially in domestic violence cases); to determine if gunshot wounds are entrance or exit wounds (claims of self-defense when victim is shot at a distance from behind) and to determine the range of the gunshot; to determine the type of weapon used (blunt instrument, tire iron, rock, knife, electrical cord) from wounds in, on, and through the body, the cause and manner of death, and if the body had been moved, mutilated, or further injured postmortem, the approximate time of death; to determine if the death was an accident, a suicide, or a homicide; to determine how much time elapsed between the fatal injury and the time of death, etc.

3. Reviewing and analyzing police reports to assess the initial crime scene (from measurements, photographs, drawings, and descriptions contained in the report), to identify witnesses, to determine who and what was removed from the scene and the destination of same (by the police, hospital, morgue), to determine the investigating officer and who made the initial call to police.

4. Reviewing and analyzing other investigative reports which might include reports of police detectives or investigations from the prosecuting attorney's office or private investigators working for the criminal defense attorney. These reports may provide additional information concerning witnesses and witness statements and the additional gathering of evidence by the investigator(s) involved in the case.

5. Reviewing and analyzing psychological testing/reports to assess the competency of the accused to stand trial, to assess the state of mind of both the perpetrator and the victim at the time of the crime, to assess the effect of the crime on the victim, to determine if the accused had a history of mental illness (diagnosis, treatment, medications, compliance), to assess recommendations made by health care professionals, and to assess psychological profiles in the case of serial offenders.

6. Reviewing and analyzing forensic science reports to assess if accused can be linked to the scene by trace evidence, fingerprints, blood, semen, DNA; to determine if illicit or prescription drugs or alcohol were involved; to determine if bite marks on victim match the bite of the accused; to determine the sex and race of skeletal remains; to assess the evidence gathered during a sexual assault exam (semen in body orifice or on the body, pubic hair not belonging to the victim); to determine if the weapon

(if located) is consistent with the type of weapon used in the commission of the crime.

7. Interviewing clients, witnesses, and potential experts to gather information about the crime from clients and witnesses and to determine if the information supports or refutes physical evidence, and, if differences exist, to determine how to reconcile the differences and to provide information to experts regarding the case.

8. Assisting in obtaining experts and acting as liaison between expert and attorney which may involve research of the literature to determine experts in a given science and then contacting the experts to determine if they are willing to review the case; to provide information to experts regarding the case, to determine if their conclusions or findings support or refute issues of the case; and to learn as much as possible about a particular issue from the expert(s).

9. Performing medical research as indicated which could involve searches through medical literature, forensic science literature, and law enforcement literature. Research could also include interviews, telephone calls, or correspondence.

10. Providing input into the case development based on the above to assess and evaluate the ongoing development of issues of the case.

Examples of Types of Criminal Case Analyses Performed by the Legal Nurse Consultant

Child Abuse

In a case of alleged child abuse, it is important to consider the concept of the differential diagnosis to assure that premature decisions about a diagnosis are avoided (Reece, 1994). What is the medical history of the child? What was the psychological condition of the child before and after the alleged incident? Do the injuries match the history given? Are there signs of previous injuries (e.g., scars, untreated fractures, enlarged rectum)? Are there patterns of inflicted bruising? Patterns of inflicted burns? Bite marks? Does the child test positive for any sexually transmitted disease? Does the child act out sexually? Is there a history of recurrent urinary tract infections? Were drugs or alcohol involved? Has the child previously been removed from the home? If so, why?

If the child was examined by a medical professional, was physical evidence collected? If so, where is the evidence? Were laboratory and/or radiographic studies performed? If so, what were the findings? Was proper documentation made? Who performed the exam? Is that person available to discuss his or her findings? Will that person be available to testify at the time of trial, if applicable?

If the child is school aged, are school records available? Has the child demonstrated any changes in behavior at school? What is the school history?

Domestic Violence

In a case of alleged domestic violence, is this the first such incident? If not, are there previous police reports? Arrests? Convictions? If this was not the first incident of abuse, what steps had been taken (if any) by the victim to remove him- or herself from the perpetrator or have the perpetrator removed? Had any previous protective orders or warrants been served on the perpetrator? If so, what was the response of the perpetrator? Had previous charges been dropped by the victim? If so, why? Had the victim ever sought refuge in a shelter? If so, what happened? Had the couple undergone any type of counseling or therapy? If so, what were the conclusions? What was the victim's account of the incident(s)?

What is the medical history of the victim? What is the medical history of the perpetrator? Are there children involved? If so, what is the medical history of the children? Have the children been removed from the home? If so, how many times? Are the children in foster care or in the care of other family members? If the children have been removed from the home, who is the caseworker? Was there any evidence or indication of physical or sexual abuse of the children?

If the victim was examined by a medical professional, what were the findings? Were physical injuries photographed? Was evidence obtained? If so, where is the evidence? What diagnostic tests were performed and what were the results? Were statements made to medical professionals documented? Were drugs or alcohol involved? What was the psychological/emotional state of the victim at the time of exam? How much time elapsed from the time of the physical abuse to the time treatment was sought? If rape occurred, was a sexual assault examination performed? If so, what were the findings?

Does the perpetrator have a previous history of violence, rage, or uncontrollable anger? Does the perpetrator have a criminal record? Do previous police reports exist concerning the perpetrator? Who was the officer(s) involved and what do the reports reveal? Is the officer(s) available to discuss the report(s)? Does the perpetrator have a history of drug or alcohol abuse? If so, have they sought treatment? Does the perpetrator have a history of psychological or mental disorders? Has the perpetrator ever been evaluated by a mental health professional? If so, what were the findings? If not, would the perpetrator agree to undergo such an evaluation? What was the perpetrator's account of the incident(s)?

DUI

In the case of someone driving under the influence and causing a motor vehicle accident, does the driver have a previous history of DUI? Has the driver's license ever been revoked or suspended? If so, why? What is the driving history of the driver? What facts are documented on the police report concerning driving conditions, road conditions, speed at the time of impact, skid marks, time of day, appearance and behavior of driver, etc.? If injuries occurred, how serious were the injuries? Was emergency assistance required? Was anyone removed from the scene by ambulance? If so, to which facility? What were their conditions at the scene and what were their conditions at the time of arrival at the emergency room? What treatment was required? What were the findings? If drug or alcohol tests were performed, were they blood or urine or both? What were the results? How much time had elapsed since the time of ingestion of drug and/or alcohol and the time of the accident and also the time that the drug or alcohol test(s) was performed?

Murder

Case Example 22.1: A female body is reported in a shallow riverbed. The story given to police investigators is that the victim fell off an overpass and into the river. Attempts to rescue the victim by a male friend were in vain. There are noticeable cuts and bruises on the body which would corroborate the story. However, on autopsy, it is determined that many of the injuries do not match the description of the incident. Upon further investigation, it is determined that an insurance policy had recently been taken out on the victim by the person who attempted the rescue.

Was there a history of domestic violence with this couple? What interpersonal characteristics did this couple display prior to this event? What were the toxicology findings of the autopsy? Was anything found at the scene that would be consistent with the types of blunt injury wounds to the victim's head? Were there any findings at the time of autopsy to indicate if the head trauma were the fatal injury? Were there any findings consistent with drowning? What was the affect and/or response of the rescuer at the time police arrived on the scene? Who reported the incident? What was the financial situation of the couple? What was the work history of the rescuer? Was anyone else with the couple? If so, what was their relationship to the victim, etc.?

Summary

As is true in any case analysis, the processes of evaluation, assessment, implementation, and planning are ongoing as new information becomes available. The LNC who pursues this area of practice will benefit from objectivity, thoroughness, and inductive and deductive reasoning. The pursuit of a career within the criminal justice system requires patience and persistence but can be extremely rewarding.

Glossary

Arraignment: The stage of the criminal process in which the defendant is formally informed of the charges and is allowed to enter a plea.

Assault: Unlawful, intentional inflicting, or attempted inflicting, of injury upon another.

Battery: The unlawful use of violence against another.

Beyond a reasonable doubt: The degree of certainty required for a juror to legally find a criminal defendant guilty. It means that the proof must be so conclusive and complete that all reasonable doubts of the fact are removed from the mind of the ordinary person.

Burden of proof: The need to prove a fact or facts in dispute.

Crime: Performance of an act which is forbidden by law or the omission of an act required by law.

Forensic science: Science applied to answering legal questions by the examination, evaluation, and exploration of evidence.

Grand Jury: A body of people randomly selected in a manner similar to trial jurors whose purpose is to investigate and inform on crimes committed within its jurisdiction and to accuse (indict) persons of crimes when it has discovered sufficient evidence to warrant holding a person for trial.

Indictment: A formal accusation from a grand jury of a criminal offense made against a person.

Probable cause: Standard used to determine if a crime has been committed and if there is sufficient evidence to believe a specific individual committed it.

Acknowledgments

The author wishes to thank the following individuals for their time and contributions:

Bruckner, W. D., Chief Investigator, Office of the District Attorney, DeKalb County, GA.
Gowitt, G., Medical Examiner, DeKalb County, GA.
Harvey, B., Criminal defense attorney.
Roberts, S., Special Agent, Georgia Bureau of Investigation.
Shockley, J. M., Director, Office of the Medical Examination, DeKalb County, GA.

References

Gifis, S. H., *Law Dictionary,* 2nd ed., New York, Barroni's Educational Series, Inc., 1984.
Knight, B., *Forensic Pathology,* 2nd ed., New York, Oxford University Press, 1996.
Neubauer, D. W., *America's Courts and the Criminal Justice System,* 5th ed., Belmont, Wadsworth Publishing, 1996.
Reece, R. M., *Child Abuse: Medical Diagnosis and Management,* Philadelphia, Lea & Febiger, 1994.
Swanson, C. R., Chamelin, N. C., and Territo, L., *Criminal Investigation,* 6th ed., New York, McGraw-Hill, 1996.

Chapter 23

Case Analysis: Evaluating Damages

Mary Baldwin, Joan E. Miller, and Nathan Dean

Contents

1-57444-123-X/98
© 1998 by American Association of Legal Nurse Consultants

Evaluating Damages in Personal Injury Litigation by Mary Baldwin

The four critical elements a plaintiff must prove to be successful in a personal injury lawsuit are

1. A duty must have existed
2. Negligence must have occurred
3. Damages must have been sustained
4. There must be a causal relationship between the defendant's breach of duty and the injury

Many personal injury cases are expensive to litigate. Medical malpractice cases traditionally require a variety of professional experts as well as hours of research and preparation by all members of the legal team. Plaintiff attorneys frequently express regret that they cannot afford to litigate a medical malpractice case unless the damages are worth at least $100,000.00. Early case screening, therefore, includes concurrent and thorough analysis of damages as well as evaluation of liability.

When no injuries or losses can be demonstrated to have resulted from an alleged negligence, the case cannot go forward. Likewise, the case cannot go forward when the anticipated award or compensation for damages is calculated to be below that which would be required to compensate the attorney and legal team members for time and expenses during the proposed litigation.

The legal nurse consultant (LNC) plays a key role in damages assessment. Whether in-house or independent, assisting plaintiff or defense counsel, the LNC may provide any of the following services related to development and management of the damages aspect of a case.

- Identify evidentiary proof of damages in medical records to help establish the damage profile with the attorney, or help mitigate damages.
- Prepare detailed analysis and costs of care and services report for either limited or lifetime injuries, or critique the report of the opposition.
- Identify and consult with appropriate damages experts.

- Help to coordinate and integrate reports and testimony of a variety of damages experts into an organized, comprehensive damages package.
- Help prepare expert damages witnesses for deposition and trial so that complicated testimony is clear, concise, easily understood by the trier of fact, and not redundant.
- Assist in preparation of audiovisual aids and exhibits for trial.

The purpose of any award granted in any personal injury case is to compensate the plaintiff for injury, loss, or harm caused by the defendant. Damage awards in any type of personal injury case are determined at the time of settlement or at trial by the judge or jury. Damage awards can be compensatory and/or punitive.

Compensatory damages include all losses and expenses incurred as a result of an injury, economic as well as general damages. Economic or special damages include the cost of past and future medical care, lost wages, and funeral expenses. The majority of states allow for compensation for pain and suffering, loss of consortium, and mental anguish or emotional distress. Some states also allow compensation for hedonic damages for loss of enjoyment of life. These damages are called general damages or noneconomic damages. In some jurisdictions, for example, California, a cap has been set on the general damages for pain and suffering in medical malpractice cases. California, however, has set no limits on special damages. For example, a jury may find for the plaintiff and award $1,000,000; however, a statutory cap may limit payment by the defendant to a specific dollar amount such as $500,000.

The plaintiff (if alive) and/or family members can usually best testify regarding the noneconomic damages. This is frequently reflected in the amount of pain or suffering the plaintiff has endured. Testimony may include limitations on their enjoyment of life. An expert witness, frequently a treating psychiatrist or physician, is able to testify regarding the amount of pain medication the person requires or the changes in lifestyle. Emotional distress damages frequently require testimony from a treating psychologist or therapist.

A trial lawyer will frequently present a "Day in the Life" video to the jury to exhibit the amount of pain and difficulty caused by the injury. The video can visually demonstrate facial expressions as the person attempts to walk, the amount of time required to feed a severely injured child, details of long, frequent, and grueling physical therapy sessions, as well as obstacles to performing previously routine activities of daily living.

In a wrongful death claim, the general damages are the loss of comfort, companionship, and society. For example, when a mother dies, the plaintiff's attorney will often ask in their closing argument, "Who will read to this young child and tuck him into bed?" "Who will help to prepare for the daughter's wedding day or first prom?" In a wrongful death claim the deceased's family can also make a claim for loss of earnings or loss of earning potential.

Life expectancy and working-life expectancy are issues that must be addressed in testimony by economist and/or vocational experts. Projecting life expectancy is usually an important issue in personal injury cases. It is important for both general and special damages. Experts for both plaintiff and defense opine about the life expectancy had negligence not caused a premature death. The total amount of money requested to pay the cost of lifetime care for a catastrophically injured infant or adult is dependent on how long that individual is projected to live and require the care.

Claims for special damages also require expert testimony by economists, accountants, and, when there are future medical needs, a life-care planner, other rehabilitation experts, and/or current or past treating physicians in addition to the retained experts.

Punitive or exemplary *damages* (noneconomic damage) are intended to punish the defendant and to serve as a deterrent to others. The negligent act precipitating a punitive award usually is described as "despicable" conduct, or conduct that constitutes wanton, willful, malicious, or reckless misconduct or disregard for human life. These situations would include a surgeon who is impaired by alcohol or drugs while performing surgery or a caregiver who sodomizes an unconscious patient. Punitive damages may also be granted in a medical malpractice case when fraud is involved. In seeking a just punitive award, the plaintiff endeavors to establish the defendant's net worth so the jury can determine a monetary amount that is sufficient to punish the defendant. Permission from the court is usually required before the plaintiff can bring a claim to the jury for punitive damages against a health care provider.

Calculating Noneconomic Damages

I. Investigate and tabulate restrictions and/or dollar amount limits *ordered* by state or local statutes
   A. Dollar amount limitations
   B. Types of cases affected
   C. Types of cases exempted
II. Determine nature of losses
   A. Physical pain
      1. Length of hospitalization
         a. Typical of similar injuries
         b. Number, frequency, and severity of surgeries
         c. Frequency and duration of therapies
      2. Strength and frequency of pain medication administered
      3. Nursing, medical, and other documentation containing comments regarding plaintiff's complaints of pain
   B. Emotional pain
      1. Nature and extent of disfigurement
      2. Required plastic surgery
      3. Nature and extent of disability
         a. Physical disability limiting movement (use of one or more extremity), loss of sight or hearing
         b. Mental disability limiting interpersonal relationships, enjoyment of vocational and/or recreational activities
      4. Activities prohibited or limited
         a. Extent of involvement in those activities prior to injury
         b. Importance of those activities to plaintiff, family, community
      5. Risks of treatment or surgery

III. Determine value of similar cases in the same and/or similar geographic settings
    A. Research the community
        1. How does the community and, therefore, the jury pool view the type of injury and/or disability incurred by the plaintiff?
        2. Would the jury pool typically include persons of similar occupation, interests and hobbies, employment, or disability?
    B. Research jury and arbitration results in the geographic area in similar cases

Role of the LNC in Assessing Noneconomic Pain and Suffering Damages

I. Research the medical records
    A. List, define, and describe
        1. Nature of each injury
        2. Pain caused by such injury
        3. Pain caused by surgery(s)
        4. Pain caused by treatment, therapies
        5. Pain caused by complications and sequela
    B. Document use of pain medications and correlate to above
        1. Note date, time, amount, relative strength, results of dosages
        2. Note circumstances surrounding increased amount or frequency of dosages
II. Research literature regarding pain medications and injury
    A. Anticipate assertions of overuse of narcotics and/or analgesics
    B. Consider possibility of enhancement of symptoms or fraud by plaintiff
III. Determine extent or impact of preexisting conditions
    A. Compare pre- and postinjury medical records
    B. Compare pre- and postinjury lifestyles, work and/or school participation, vocational and avocational activities

Life-Care Planning
by Joan E. Miller

Introduction

A life-care plan is developed to document the projected future medical costs of a catastrophically ill or injured individual. The costs reflected in the life-care plan are in addition to those medical costs which have previously been incurred as well as other types of compensatory damages in the case, such as lost wages and others.

Definition

The life-care plan is a comprehensive summary of future health and medical needs and services, and their associated costs.

Life-care plans provide the information necessary to fund adequately the short- and long-term needs of individuals involved in catastrophic injury or illness claims. They are utilized by attorneys, insurance companies, case managers, and others involved in the long-term care of the catastrophically ill or injured. The life-care plan can also serve as a guide for families and an education tool for anyone involved with the individual for whom the plan was developed. Life-care plans are of benefit for any diagnostic group requiring extensive service. However, in the legal arena, they typically involve those who have experienced traumatic or anoxic brain injury, injuries at birth, spinal cord injury, amputations, burns, cancer, musculoskeletal trauma, physiological insults which will result in the need for transplantation, and chronic pain syndromes.

Life-care plans are frequently utilized in personal injury, product liability, and medical malpractice cases. They are requested by both plaintiff as well as defense attorneys.

The life-care plan costs are based on current-year dollars. Although there are some instances when the computation of present value is not required, life-care plans are often referred to an economist to compute the present value of the future medical and care costs. The economist takes into consideration the fact that the costs of the various items included in the plan will not remain static over an individual's lifetime.

Because damages are frequently funded through the use of structured settlements, financial planners may be called upon to develop funding options. The goal is to assure monies are available to purchase products and services when they are needed over the lifetime of the injured person.

Qualifications of Life-Care Planners

It is critical that the individual retained to develop a life-care plan (whether plaintiff or defense) is a well-qualified, knowledgeable habilitation or rehabilitation expert. The life-care planner must have knowledge of the principles of rehabilitation as well as a thorough knowledge of the medical aspects of the disability. Depending upon the purpose of the plan, this individual should be certified in rehabilitation, habilitation, rehabilitation counseling, workers' compensation, or some other form of counseling. The individual preparing the vocational portion of the plan should be a vocational counselor.

Certification in life-care planning is currently available from several groups, and is likely to be offered by many more in the future. Caution should be exercised, however, in selecting a life-care planner based solely on certification. Certification merely testifies to the fact that the individual has attended some type of educational offerings, or has passed an examination. Certification does not necessarily mean the individual has the clinical experience or expertise to develop and defend a life-care plan.

Most frequently, life-care plans are developed by RNs, medical case managers, or certified rehabilitation consultants. Psychologists, MDs, and social workers also offer these services. The life-care planner must be actively practicing as a coordinator of health services for injured persons. The expert who is not is vulnerable to questions from the opposing attorney which can result in jeopardizing the expert's credibility before a judge or jury. Professional activities, such as publications, presentations, and professional memberships, all serve to increase the credibility of the life-care-planning expert. These can create some problems, however, in that, some opposing attorneys will request copies of all publications or texts from all presentations in order to identify any discrepancies between what the life-care planner has included in the plan and what he or she has stated in other forums.

Life-care plans are most commonly developed by a single individual. However, in some instances a team approach is utilized whereby the plaintiff is evaluated by a number of professionals and their recommendations are incorporated into the life-care plan. When this is the case, the choice, typically, is to use one individual as the testifying expert for the team. However, opposing counsel may insist on deposing each team member individually.

If the life-care planner is limited in expertise to one area, e.g., vocational rehabilitation, it is imperative that input from other professionals be incorporated into the plan. If the life-care planner has no vocational expertise, that portion of the plan should be developed by another individual qualified to address vocational issues.

When to Retain the Life-Care Planner

It is advisable to retain the life-care planner early in the case. One potential role of this expert is to educate the attorney and LNC for the firm on the nuances of the damages sustained. In addition, early assistance in identifying records to be obtained, individuals to be deposed, and experts to be retained can be invaluable.

Although there are times when life-care planners are retained as purely consulting experts, more often, the individual developing a life-care plan will be expected to function as an expert witness.

Whether to use the life-care plan expert as a testifying witness must also be decided early. If the consultant retained is to testify, it is vital that the attorney and LNC are aware of the rules of discovery and evidence of the jurisdiction which would affect the discoverability of work product. Any notes, research, and written documents generated by the consulting expert could become discoverable if the decision is later made to use that individual as an expert witness.

When the life-care plan is developed early in the case, care must be taken to update the services, information sources, and other details of the plan. In some instances, the life-care plan must be developed in order to meet the requirements of the legal process, and extended periods of time may elapse from the date the life-care plan was developed to the actual date of trial. The litigant may have gained in functional capabilities, have experienced several complications, or otherwise changed in needs. There are times, when a complete reassessment of the litigant and modification of the life-care plan must be performed, in order to assure a meaningful and accurate plan.

The Life-Care Planning Process

Record Review

The initial step in developing a life-care plan is a thorough review of all records. These should include

- All treating physician medical records from the date of onset of the injury
- All medical records prior to the date of injury, if applicable
- All psychological and neuropsychological records
- All hospital records
- All records from acute and postacute rehabilitation providers
- All records required by the vocational expert such as employment history and educational records

It is helpful for the life-care planner to have access to bills for services to date.

The initial medical records not only provide invaluable information for identifying the most obvious injury, but also those conditions that might present complications and/or medical needs in the future. Obviously, in the case of the traumatically brain-injured person, the initial Glasgow coma score, length of coma, and length of postraumatic amnesia provide clues concerning the projected life-long needs of that individual.

The existence of previous rehabilitation efforts, and the injured person's responses to those efforts, may directly influence what is included in the life services plan. Medical complications and their frequency must also be taken into consideration.

Previous medical records may reveal diagnoses which could influence future needs. However, only those which impact (or are impacted by) the injury should be included in the life-care plan.

As the case evolves, it is important to remember to provide the life-care planner with updated records, depositions, and disclosure statements (in some states) as they become available.

Assessment

If possible, a thorough assessment of the client should be conducted by the life-care planner. Frequently, the defense life-care planner is denied access to the plaintiff and the treatment team. In that event, the court should be requested to allow the assessment in order to assure an accurate plan as well as avoid plaintiff's argument that the defense expert has never seen his client.

Some jurisdictions have patient/physician, or other privileges, whereby the defense-retained experts are not allowed to interview the treatment team. In that event, a defense team, similar to the treatment team, must be utilized.

If the defense life-care planner is allowed to meet with and assess the plaintiff, the plaintiff attorney may wish to have a representative in attendance.

The assessment by the life-care planner ideally should take place in the client's home, and should include the family, significant other, and caregivers. If the individual is institutionalized, a separate evaluation of the home environment might be indicated. It is also helpful to evaluate a child in the school environment in order to address educational issues fully.

The assessment process should be tailored to the individual. During the initial assessment, information should be elicited concerning the current costs of equipment, services, and supplies, as well as the vendors being utilized.

In general, during the assessment phase of life-care planning, information concerning the following should be obtained and documented:

- General data
    - Date and location of the interview
    - Other parties present at the time
- Family and support information
    - Spouse's name, age, and general health
    - Names, ages, and health of children
    - Names, ages, and health of others living in the home
- The plaintiff's age
- The plaintiff's hand dominance
- Information regarding the injury or onset of illnesses
    - Date of the injury
    - Data concerning the primary and any secondary injuries
    - Subjective description of residual impairment by the injured party, family, or significant other
- A description of a typical day
    - Activities
    - Time required for activities of daily living and assistance needed
- Current treating physicians
    - Specialty
    - Frequency of visits
- Current medications
    - Dosage
    - Frequency
- Medical history
    - Dates
    - Sequelae of previous injuries or illnesses
- Nutritional status
    - Height
    - Normal weight
    - Current weight
    - Special diets
- Integumentary system
    - History of decubiti
    - Location of decubiti
    - Dates, and treatment
    - Pressure relief techniques and products utilized
    - Skin tolerance
    - Turning schedule
    - Ability to prone
    - Wheelchair cushion type
    - Skin care products used

- Respiratory system
    Frequency and treatment of infections
    Need for assisted coughing or suctioning
    Tracheotomy or ventilator dependency
    Use of respiratory aids, i.e., inhalers, oxygen, etc.
- Gastrointestinal system
    Type and frequency of bowel program, who performs the bowel care
      and supplies needed
    Amount of time required
    Need for enemas
    Frequency of incontinencies
    Presence of hemorrhoids
- Cardiovascular system
    History of deep vein thrombosis
    Postural hypotension
    Hypertension
    Anemia
- Any hematologic system pathology
- Genitourinary system
    Current bladder program
    Types of catheters or condoms
    Types of bags and tubings (for day and night use)
    Use of sterile or nonsterile gloves
    Bed liners
    Frequency of accidents
    Frequency of urinary tract infections
    Frequency of urinalyses or cultures, and laboratories used
    The need for routine urologic studies
    The need for assistive devices for sexual functioning
    Reproductive issues
- Musculoskeletal systems
    Presence or absence of spasms, what precipitates and relieves them
    Pain syndromes including precipitating factors and treatment
    Any weakness, paralysis, or other physical limitations
- Neurological system
    Seizures: frequency, symptoms, treatment, and diagnostic studies
    Presence, frequency, and management of dysreflexia
- Cognitive functioning status (Due to the propensity for brain-injured individuals to deny or to be unaware of their cognitive deficits, information should be gathered from both the injured individuals as well as from others who are familiar with that individual. Often perceptions of cognitive ability are very different.)
- Sensory system
    Taste
    Smell
    Vision
    Hearing
- Endocrine system

- Language or communication issues
  Use of a telephone
  Writing abilities
  Verbal communication abilities (receptive and expressive)
  Assistive devices
- Psychological status
  Treatment since the injury or onset of illness
  Whether the individual and family are amenable to treatment
  Sleep disorders
  Drug or alcohol use
  How he or she copes with anger and frustration
  Parenting skills
  The need for sexuality counseling
- Behavioral issues
  Directly related as a consequence of the brain injury or illness
  In response to the injury or illness
- Safety issues
  Ability to exit in case of fire or natural disaster
  Presence or absence of smoke detectors
  Ability to summon assistance in case of an emergency
  Ability to be left unattended for any period of time
  Safety issues impacted by cognitive or behavioral aberrancies
- Quality of life issues
  Description of self prior to the injury and at the present time
  Recreational activities prior to the injury and currently
- Functional status
  Dressing
  Grooming
  Feeding
  Bathing
  Meal preparation
  Shopping
  Cleaning
  Laundry
  Yard work
  Home maintenance
- Mobility status
  Ability to stand, kneel, bend, stoop, sit, climb stairs or ladders
  Ability to transfer on and off all surfaces, and assistance or equipment needed
  Ability to manipulate ramps and curbs
  Ability to self-propel wheelchair
  Type of wheelchair and cushion used including year purchased and replacement schedule
  Ability to recover from falls
- Transportation issues
  Ability to drive or potential for driving with education
  Current vehicle, model, year, and state of repair
  Need for hand controls, other adaptive equipment or van

- Current equipment and aids to independent function
    Year purchased
    Replacement schedule
- The home environment
    Size and accessibility of rooms
    Presence of stairs
    Bathrooms
    Heating/cooling systems
    Number and accessibility of exits
    Presence and accessibility of garage or covered parking
    Type of yard and maintenance required
    Presence of a pool and maintenance required
- Leisure and recreational activities
    Prior to the injury or illness
    Since the injury or illness
    Equipment required
- Vocational issues

Consultation and Interviews

In addition to the plaintiff assessment, those familiar with the medical and psychological status, as well as anyone who can contribute to the projected needs, should be interviewed.

Often, in the case of brain injury the spouse, family, significant others, and caregivers can contribute valuable information, especially as relates to behavioral issues, true functional abilities, and psychosocial problems. Even highly functioning survivors of brain injury may be unaware of, or in denial of, some of the residual deficits related to the injury.

Family and significant-other interviews provide information concerning support systems available to the injured party as well as clues regarding the likelihood of follow-through with the specifics of the plan. Family member's or significant other's age, psychological status, and health will impact the services included in the plan. Treating physicians and other involved professionals are frequently invaluable in contributing to the items included in the plan.

Development of Life-Care Plan

The Plan Format

The actual format of the life-care plan varies depending upon the individual developing the plan, the needs of the injured individual, and the requests of the attorney or LNC. It is critical that the plan, whatever the format, be completely objective and provide all the information necessary in an understandable format. In general most detailed life-care plans include the following sections:

- Introduction or medical record summary
- Information sources
    Records reviewed
    Interviews, conferences, and assessments
- Equipment/service sources

- Cost summaries
- Detailed description of future needs and costs

Some life-care plans also include the cost of potential complications. In some jurisdictions, however, if there is not a 50% probability of those complications, the entire plan can be jeopardized. These issues should be clarified with the attorney prior to development of the plan.

If the plan is being developed for the setting of reserves by an insurance company or as a guideline for the case manager, trust attorney, or family, the costs for complications should almost certainly be included.

If an economist will be computing the present value of the costs outlined in the plan, he or she will usually place items into the broad classifications of medical services, nonmedical services, medical commodities, and nonmedical commodities. The age at which a service commences and/or ends is also of value to the economist in certain cases. The life-care plan format should take these issues into consideration.

Introduction. Most life-care plans include some type of introduction, as well as rationalization, for the items included in the plan. Some are very long and detailed, while others are extremely short. In general, the introduction should include at least a brief synopsis of the patient's medical and functional status since the date of injury. Any information which is pertinent to the plan itself should be included somewhere in the document.

Some life-care planners prefer to include the history and rationalization in the introduction, while others prefer to place that information directly on the pages outlining the costs. The decision is, to some degree, a personal one. The advantage of placing the rationalization for costs on the same page as the specifics concerning the costs is that it makes the document clearer and easier to understand. However, in some jurisdictions, if the opposing attorney is able to discredit the rationalization, the entire page of the document is not admissible. As a consequence, the services and costs found on that page will be deemed inadmissible as well. These issues should be addressed with the attorney prior to actual development of the life-care plan.

Information Sources. These typically include all records reviewed, as well as interviews and conferences. Most life-care planners are fairly specific as to the records which were utilized in the development of the plan. Dates and document sources are cited in addition to general information concerning the records reviewed. If records were in the possession of the life-care planner, but either not reviewed or not considered important to the development of the plan, they may be omitted from the life-care plan document. The attorney should provide input as to whether or not this is recommended or allowed, dependent upon the case and jurisdiction.

The dates of any on-site assessments, meetings, or communication with the litigant or family should be cited, as well as any communication with other health care providers and professionals.

Equipment/Service Sources. In this section, the life-care planner enumerates any sources used to identify the costs reflected in the life-care plan. In addition to specific vendors, other resources are sometimes used such as catalogs and various types of publications.

Cost Summaries. In this section, the life-care planner summarizes the costs over a lifetime. The format is dependent upon the details of the plan itself. The actual format may be based on age grouping, annual vs. one-time costs, or by specific items. The goal is to provide a brief, clearly understandable synopsis of costs in conjunction with when those costs are likely to occur.

Detailed Description of Future Needs and Costs. This section provides the specific information concerning services needed and includes the original cost, duration of use, frequency of services, and replacement timetable. Some costs may be incurred one time only while most will be annual costs. Life-care planners differ in the actual inclusions in the detailed cost section of the plan. Some representative examples are

Example 23.1:

Service or Item	Age Beginning and Age Ending	Frequency of Replacement	Purpose	Cost	Comment	Recommended by	Vendor

Example 23.2:

Service or Item Including Age Beginning and Ending	Cost	Frequency of Replacement	One-Time Costs	Annual Costs

Topics

Topics that might be included are determined by the injury and are then included in the plan. Typically, topics include the following:

- Hospitalizations
- Surgical intervention or aggressive treatment
- Medical care
- Therapeutic interventions/professional services (including evaluations, counseling, and educational needs)
- Diagnostic tests and procedures
- Medical supplies
- Medications
- Durable medical equipment
- Aids for independent function
- Leisure/exercise equipment and services
- Orthotics or prosthetics
- Nursing care/home care
- Institutional care
- Home modifications
- Home furnishings and accessories

- Transportation
- Potential medical complications

Some plans include vocational retraining, loss of earning capacity, and related topics. More often, the life-care plan is strictly limited to medical and health care products and services and a separate document is developed by the vocational expert.

Determination of Services Required

It is recommended that a plan of care be the basic premise for the life-care plan. It should include preventative measures as well as treatment of specific problems. The plan should reflect an assumption that the therapeutic interventions will be successful. This frequently results in a reduction of services at a later time.

There are situations, however, where the success of therapeutic strategies is questionable. In those instances, it may be more appropriate to develop alternative costs reflecting those which would be incurred if the plan were successful and those which would be incurred if the plan were unsuccessful.

In some instances the potential complications and their associated costs are included in the life-care plan. If so, validation of the percentage of chance for experiencing the complication should be assured by the testifying medical expert. Certain circumstances, depending on the jurisdiction under which the case is tried, may allow the costs of potential complications even if the chance for experiencing those complications is remote.

Cultural issues must also be considered when developing a life-care plan. However, the plan must always be objective and reflect no bias or prejudice.

Determination of Costs

After the specific topics and services required have been identified, the life-care planner then determines the cost of each item at the time the plan was developed. In most instances, the costs cited reflect those which would be incurred at the individual's location. If the plan includes transferring to another locale, then costs in that area would be most appropriate.

If the actual cost of the item is known from recent billing records, those may be used. An exception would be if a different vendor was to be recommended. The majority of life-care planners use an average of prevailing costs in the area. Some will obtain three quotes to average, while others may put a range of costs in the plan. If an economist must calculate the present value of the costs reflected in the life-care plan, however, most would prefer one number with which to work.

Some litigants, at the time of the life-care plan development, are receiving services through city, county, state, or federal programs, i.e., Medicaid, etc. In many instances, if the individual receives monies from the litigation, he or she would no longer be eligible for funding through those sources. As a consequence, most life-care planners utilize retail costs in their plans without consideration for alternative funding.

Depending upon the nature of the litigation, alternative funding sources may or may not be allowed in evidence. If they are allowed, the defense attorney may question the life-care planning expert on the availability of these collateral sources. The life-care planner must be prepared to respond to these types of questions.

Validation of the Plan

In order for the life-care plan to stand up under scrutiny, it is important that the need for the items included be valid. Whenever possible, the plan should be discussed with the identified testifying medical expert to assure agreement with the inclusions.

Further validation of the plan is accomplished by obtaining the agreement of the other testifying physician experts, by the personal expertise of the life-care planner, or by inclusion in the medical records.

In order to eliminate any uncertainty and chance for challenges by the opposing attorney, some life-care planners prefer to include the "source" of the information determining the need for the service or equipment in the detailed portion of the plan.

Testimony

The life-care planner must be able to withstand, and appropriately respond to, challenges by the opposing attorney. The strategies used by attorneys and specifics related to expert testimony itself are elaborated upon elsewhere.

In attempts to discredit a life-care planner, subjects frequently raised by opposing attorneys include

- Percentage of income generated from litigation services
- Percentage of income generated from clinical practice
- Prior retention by the same law firm
- Percentage of plaintiff vs. defense life-care plans developed
- Whether the expert is a patient advocate (this is further addressed in the Ethics subsection of this chapter)
- Financial affiliation with any of the services reflected in the life-care plan
- Whether the need for modalities included in the life-care plan, which require a physician prescription, have been verified by a qualified physician
- The area of expertise of the life-care planner

Implementation of the Plan

Frequently, life-care plans are developed by highly qualified individuals; cases are concluded with the client receiving funds; and no one is retained to assist in implementing the plan. As a consequence, the client does not receive appropriate services; often those which are received are at highly inflated prices; or the funds available are not spent in a cost-effective manner.

The same professionals who develop life-care plans are the most qualified to assist the client in implementing the plan. It is incumbent upon the attorney and the LNC for the firm to recommend strongly that their client retain the services of a professional to assist in utilizing the funds to obtain appropriate services and equipment in a timely and cost-effective manner.

Ethical Considerations

Frequently, the professionals preparing the life-care plan have other aspects of their practice whereby they provide case management services, counseling to the catastrophically ill or injured, or provide some other services which might be included in the plan. Prior to accepting an assignment to develop a life-care plan, the life-care planner must ask appropriate questions concerning the case to assure no conflict of interest. The life-care planner must make the attorney and the firm LNC aware of any potential problems.

The role of the life-care planner is that of educator of the attorney and all persons involved in the litigation process. The life-care planner *is not* a patient advocate. His or her responsibility is to determine objectively the necessary services required as a consequence of the illness or injury, and present the costs of those services.

The attorney and the LNC for the firm, whether plaintiff or defense, frequently have in mind what they would like to see in terms of the life-care plan. Some are more vocal than others in attempting to direct the life-care planner in inclusions or exclusions in the plan itself. It can be very tempting to include a multitude of services or high-tech equipment in a life-services plan. Those costs related to recreation and quality of life issues are frequently the most challenged by defense attorneys. On the other hand, many plaintiff attorneys will request a "conservative" estimate of costs, rather than risk having the entire plan discredited because of "frivolous" inclusions by the life-care planner.

Each life-care plan must be approached with the attitude that it is unimportant whether it is being prepared for a plaintiff or defense law firm. The items included must be completely objective and tailored to meet the needs of the individual.

In reality, when both plaintiff and defense life-care planners develop their plans in an honest and ethical manner, basic formats and some specific services may differ. However, there will be minimal differences between the two plans.

Summary

Life-care plans are an integral part of the litigation process where residual damages will result in a lifetime of needs. They should be developed by professionals familiar with the future needs of individuals who have experienced catastrophic illness or injury. The life-care planner must be accomplished at providing testimony and educating the public regarding the services and equipment outlined in the life-care plan.

Life-care plans must be individualized, thoroughly researched, objective, comprehensive, detailed, and easily understood by a judge, jury, or others who have the ultimate decision-making authority in determining damage awards for the litigants involved.

The life-care plan should not be an isolated portion of a lawsuit, but should be considered a process which must be continued after the litigation has been completed. It is incumbent upon the attorney, and the LNC for the firm, to assist the client and family in identifying qualified individuals to assist, advise, educate, and collaborate with them, to assure maximum functional independence and quality of life for the injured or ill individual.

Glossary

Cognition: The process of knowing or perceiving.

Cognitive deficit: Difficulty with one or more of the basic functions of the brain: perception, memory, attentional abilities, and reasoning skills.

Dysreflexia: Abnormal or faulty physiological reflexes due to spinal cord injury at or above the T-6 level. Occurs as a crisis in response to some noxious stimulus such as distended bladder or bowel, etc. May be fatal.

Glasgow coma scale: A standardized system used to assess the degree of brain impairment and to identify the seriousness of injury in relation to outcome.

Habilitation: The process of providing specific learning experiences for persons with disabilities.

Litigant: The person filing suit.

Posttraumatic amnesia: A period of time after a brain injury when the individual exhibits a loss of day-to-day memory. The individual is unable to store new information and therefore has a decreased ability to learn.

References

Deutsch, P. M. (1990). Presentation of life-care plan: Who is qualified? *Life Care Facts,* Winter, 1990.

Deutsch, P. and Sawyer, H. (1985). *Guide to Rehabilitation,* New York, Matthew Bender.

Dillman, E., Economic perspectives of life-care plans; *NARPPS Journal,* 9(2 and 3).

Gunn, L. life-care planning — a defense perspective, *NARPPS Journal,* 9(2 and 3).

Patterson, T. S. (1992). Role of the life-care planner on legal consultation, *Viewpoints,* 21, Summer, 1992.

Weed, R. O. and Riddick, S. N. (1992). Life-care plans as a case management tool, *The Case Manager,* Jan./Feb./Mar.

Whitmore, M. (1996). Life-care plan and economic data: evaluating and funding the catastrophic needs case, *The Neurolaw Letter,* 5(12).

Assessing Vocational Damages
by Nathan Dean

As an LNC you will be involved in injury cases which require an objective evaluation of vocational damages. The LNC must know how to select and manage a vocational expert. Your role requires an understanding of the methods utilized in the evaluation of vocational damages and the limitations of vocational experts. What constitutes vocational damages? How are these losses measured? The following section will assist the LNC in understanding these issues. This chapter is not intended to be a step-by-step guide but rather an overview of current practice in disability litigation.

Individuals who sustain an injury resulting in temporary or permanent impairment often seek financial remuneration for their loss. When the injured party seeks recovery, he or she becomes a plaintiff. Legal actions to recover financial losses include workers' compensation claims, personal injury, toxic tort, product liability, and medical malpractice civil suits. In most states, workers' compensation laws limit the injured worker's right to recover losses. Each state has enacted specific workers' compensation statutes. Federal employees and longshore or harbor workers are covered under laws established by federal jurisdiction. Individuals who are injured while performing their job may elect to file under the applicable workers' compensation law. If a third party contributed to the injury through negligent or wrongful action, then the injured worker may seek legal remedy through civil litigation. Workers' compensation carriers may file a lien against a potential third-party litigation award to recover expenses. Vocational damages are of paramount importance in such litigation.

When to Refer to a Vocational Expert

Refer to a vocational expert when the injured party is not working, is underemployed, may lose his or her job, has never worked, loses current job, or when the need arises to evaluate the individual's employment capacity.

How to Select a Vocational Expert

Selecting a vocational expert who can provide sound, objective evidence in a specific injury case may require research. If you have worked with a vocational expert in the past, you may want to discuss the case prior to assignment. If the nature of the injury (i.e., spinal cord injury, brain injury, severe burn injury) demands specific experience, then you may want to examine the vocational expert's past experience in providing rehabilitation services to individuals with similar injuries. You will want to avoid the risk and delay of employing an inexperienced vocational expert.

Rehabilitation counselors represent the largest professional group available to fulfill the role of vocational expert in litigation. Rehabilitation counselors are employed in a variety of settings including state-operated agencies such as the Rehabilitation Service Administration of each state, rehabilitation hospitals or clinics, nonprofit rehabilitation centers, large nationwide private for-profit rehabilitation companies, insurance companies, small private for-profit rehabilitation companies, and independent practitioners.

Some states require licensure of rehabilitation counselors; however, most states have not legislated licensure requirements. Nationally recognized certifications include Certified Rehabilitation Counselor (CRC), Certified Disability Management Specialist (CDMS), and Certified Vocational Evaluator (CVE).

The requirements for these certifications include educational (a masters degree in Rehabilitation Counseling or a closely related field), supervised experience in vocational rehabilitation, and demonstrated skill competency. The certification examination for CRC is an intense, 8-hour-long competency-based test. Certification maintenance requires 30 continuing education credits each year. The Commission on Rehabilitation Counselor Certification (CRCC) is located in Rolling Hills, Illinois. Vocational experts should provide a copy of their current certification.

Attorneys, physicians, rehabilitation service providers, workers' compensation claims representatives, and other practicing LNCs are sources of informtion about vocational counselors in any metropolitan area. The National Association of Rehabilitation Professionals in the Private Sector (NARPPS) publishes an annual directory of members. This directory is available at a cost of $50.00. Reduced costs are available for multiple purchases. To order, contact:

> NARPPS
> 313 Washington Street, Suite 302
> Newton, MA 02158
> Phone (617) 692-2035
> Fax (617) 692-2040

The *NARPPS Directory* lists rehabilitation professionals by geographic area served and provides detailed information regarding education, certification, years of experience, and areas of specialty.

Most rehabilitation practitioners do not advertise as vocational experts. Professionals with extensive experience often find themselves in the role of expert witness as a result of their casework. As a general rule, select a vocational expert with at least 5 years experience (Vanderkok, 1993). To further qualify a rehabilitation practitioners, you may want to ask the following questions:

1. Have you provided expert testimony in the past?
2. In what type of injury cases have you provided testimony?
3. What is the extent of your professional experience in providing rehabilitation services to individuals who have sustained this type of injury?
4. How many similar injury cases have you provided rehabilitation services for during the past 5 years?
5. What was the nature of your testimony in past injury cases?
6. Who retained your services in those cases wherein you provided expert testimony?

The rigorous demands of deposition, hearing, and trial examination require an individual who can think and speak clearly under pressure. An expert witness must be well prepared and confident in his or her opinions and able to withstand the challenge presented by the opposing legal counsel. The emotional response of the rehabilitation practitioners to anger feigned by the opposing attorney must be managed without negatively affecting his or her professional role. The expert witness must be able to remain focused when his or her qualifications and competence are challenged by the opposing legal counsel. The typical rehabilitation practitioner has no training or experience that prepares him or her for the experience of courtroom testimony. The effectiveness of any given rehabilitation professional as an expert witness will depend in great measure upon your preparation of the individual.

Preparing the Rehabilitation Expert

When you engage the services of a vocational expert, clearly define the reason for the referral. Follow up verbal directions in writing to avoid any misunderstandings. Request that the vocational expert provide you with a copy of his or her *curriculum vitae* (CV), certifications, licenses, professional liability insurance, and rate schedule. Ask the vocational expert to provide an estimate of costs for services; then hold him or her to it.

Remember that the costs for services will vary depending upon the complexity of each case. It is difficult to estimate cost accurately because one attorney may request moe or less than another attorney. The cost of the expert witness will also increase if there are delays or postponements in trial dates.

Provide the consultant with copies of all medical records, psychological and psychiatric evaluations, therapy progress reports, functional capacity evaluations, vocational testing, depositions, and, if available, a job description of the plaintiff's job, school records, the plaintiff's tax returns for the past 5 years, and employment records including performance reviews (Wright, 1980). The vocational expert should review any written reports and testimony of the opposing vocational expert in order to identify any weaknesses or discrepancies in the conclusions. The attorney should prepare the vocational expert for trial through rehearsal and a discussion of anticipated issues and questions from the opposing lawyer.

What to Expect from the Vocational Expert

Expect the vocational consultant to request authorization for vocational testing if such an evaluation has not been furnished. Vocational testing consists of an aptitude test, temperament surveys, interest inventories, academic/achievement tests, intelligence tests, specialized work samples, and observations regarding the plaintiff's tolerance for work activities, social skills, cooperation, and work habits.

A thorough vocational assessment by the vocational expert will include a summary of the plaintiff's education, military experience, vocational history, school records, employment records, social history, relevant medical history, long-term goals, financial status, hobbies, areas of interest, volunteer activities, perceived physical limitations, level of support, independence, self-esteem, readiness to reenter the workforce, and job-seeking skills.

An analysis of the plaintiff's knowledge, academic skills, and past employment will identify transferable skills. Transferable skills are skills that can be used in jobs other than the job held at the time of injury. Examples of transferable skills are public speaking, keyboarding, problem solving, supervising others, and assembly. Most individuals possess transferable skills; however, eight out of ten job seekers cannot adequately describe their skills (Farr et al., 1992). The vocational consultant uses a variety of resource publications and knowledge of jobs to identify occupations that are within an individual's physical ability and that utilize the transferable skills possessed by the individual. A list of resource publications is available in the *Guide to Rehabilitation,* Tables 8-1 and 802, section 8, pp. 8–16 (Deutsch and Sawyer, 1985).

The rehabilitation consultant can provide specific information, such as

1. The plaintiff's loss of earning capacity without rehabilitation
2. The nature, length, and cost of a rehabilitation plan
3. The plaintiff's loss of earning capacity (if any), once the rehabilitation is provided
4. Alternative sources of funding for vocational rehabilitation services
5. An accurate picture of how the plaintiff is limited by the results of an injury
6. The plaintiff's ability to access the local labor market
7. Qualification of actual loss of earnings including benefits

Expect that the vocational evaluation report will include the following data:

1. A determination of the plaintiff's ability to return to former employment with or without job modifications
2. An identification of transferable skills that would allow the plaintiff to perform other jobs
3. An evaluation of the plaintiff's physical, intellectual, and psychological capacities, and an opinion regarding the plaintiff's ability to perform specific jobs utilizing transferable skills
4. An assessment of the plaintiff's ability to find suitable employment in the local labor market
5. An evaluation of the plaintiff's earning capacity both before and after the injury (Vanderkok, 1993)

What Are Vocational Damages?

Vocational damages consist of a variety of specific kinds of losses: lost wages, diminished future earning capacity, loss of benefits, and the cost of vocational rehabilitation. The cost to purchase services formerly performed by the plaintiff is an additional damage or loss that the vocational expert may address. These losses are not vocational in nature, but are closely related.

Lost wages are the dollars not earned by the plaintiff during a period of time beginning on the date of injury or onset of disability and ending when the injured party reaches maximum medical improvement (Vanderkok, 1993). Lost wages are usually simple to establish.

Loss of future earning capacity is generally the most critical issue in personal injury cases. To accurately define an individual's loss of earning capacity, the vocational expert must first establish the plaintiff's preinjury earning capacity and then his or her postinjury earning capacity (Vanderkok, 1993). Earning capacity is a dynamic construct. The factors affecting earning capacity include education, age, transferable skills, ability to learn new skills, physical and mental stamina, psychological status, local labor market trends, wage growth trends, hiring practices of local employers, the individual's ability to access employment, transportation and work life expectancy. An accurate assessment of earning capacity must address all of these variables.

Preinjury earning capacity is not necessarily represented by the wage or employment at the time of injury. A child or young adult who has not established a career possesses an earning capacity that cannot be demonstrated by actual earnings. An individual may be underemployed at the time of injury for a variety of reasons. Some examples might be an individual who recently relocated and accepted an entry-level job while seeking employment in his or her usual field, or a recent college graduate who is attending graduate school supporting himself or herself in a menial job. The role of the expert witness is to define accurately the individual's employability and earning capacity prior to injury. An examination of school records, aptitude tests, achievement tests, interest inventory, temperament survey, vocational plans, parental or family education level, and attained employment goals may provide a range of education and employment expectations (Wright, 1980; Vanderkok, 1993).

Individuals with established careers and vocational history provide demonstrable earning capacity and future earning capacity. The vocational expert should examine income tax records of the plaintiff for at least the prior 5 years to establish actual earnings. Future earning capacity must consider wage growth trends for the occupation or industry. Data regarding 10 to 15 year wage growth trends are the most reliable (Vanderkok, 1993). Wage data and trends are available from a variety of sources including Job Service, the Department of Labor publications, the *Occupational Outlook Handbook,* and labor market survey.

An individual's earning capacity increases as he or she gains experience, knowledge, and skills, and as a result of increases in the cost of living. Promotional opportunities and the rate of wage increase vary from one occupation or industry to another. A case study will illustrate the relationship between pre- and postinjury earning capacity.

Case Study

Mark, G. is a 42-year-old, married man who sustained a herniated disk at the L4–5 level in an automobile accident. He underwent surgical repair including discectomy and fusion. He was rated (following the AMA guidelines) with a 5% permanent impairment of the whole person. His physical restrictions included no lifting over 40 pounds on an occasional basis and no continuous lifting of more than 20 pounds. He can bend, twist, and stoop on an occasional basis, but not continuously. These restrictions represent Mark's physical impairment.

Mark graduated from high school in 1971 where he earned average grades. He has worked in the construction field since leaving high school. For the past 15 years, Mark has worked as a block layer. This job requires lifting of up to 100 pounds, frequent stooping, bending, and a full range of motion. Mark is disabled because he cannot return to his usual work. His job cannot be modified to accommodate his physical impairment. His employer does not have any other jobs available.

After vocational testing, counseling, and vocational exploration, an employment goal was identified. Mark expressed interest in fiber optics. A labor market survey indicated that fiber-optic connector and installation jobs were within Mark's physical ability. His transferable skills include the ability to read and interpret blueprints and schematics. He possessed a good work ethic. Mark completed a short-term certification class in fiber optics. He was instructed in job-seeking skills including a model employment application, résumé, and interviewing skills. He was placed within 2 weeks with a local communications installation contractor.

Mark earned approximately $24.00 per hour as a block layer. After 15 years experience, his rate of pay was based on a price per linear or square foot. Mark's experience as a block layer and his speed and accuracy allowed him to earn above the average income for this occupation. He worked substantially more than 40 hours per week. Occasionally he could not work because of rain or weather conditions. A review of his tax records revealed that he had earned in excess of $50,000 in each of the past 5 years. An average earning increases of 2% per year was demonstrated over the past 5 years. Mark's expertise and skill allowed him to work even during periods of economic recession. His employment provided full health and dental insurance coverage and a 401K retirement plan with matching contributions from his employer. Mark was fully vested in the retirement plan and invested 3% of his annual income within this 401K plan.

In his new job, Mark negotiated a starting wage of $9.00 per hour. After 90 days, he was provided with health insurance benefits. His new employer does not offer a retirement plan at this time. The wage growth in the communications industry is 5% annually. The employer provides no overtime. A calculation of Mark's loss of earning capacity is represented in Table 23.1.

Mark G's vocational damages are

Lost Wages	
10 months from date of injury until return to work	
calculated at $4,279.16 per month =	$42,791.66
Loss of Earning Capacity	
Not including interest lost on 401k from employer	
contributions after date of injury and not reduced to	
present value =	$741,055.55
Cost of Rehabilitation	
Rehabilitation counseling/testing — $1650.00	
Cost of tuition/certification in fiber optics — $1295.00	
Tools — $500.00 =	$3,445.00
Total Vocational Damages	**$787,292.21**

A vocational expert is not qualified to compute present value of future loss of earning capacity. An economist should be consulted or retained as an expert witness to explain the current value of future dollars.

Additional economic damages include the costs to purchase services previously performed by the plaintiff. Examples of such services are home and auto maintenance. A plaintiff who owns rental property may incur additional damages if repairs and maintenance services previously performed by the plaintiff must be purchased. These losses are not accepted as vocational damages but are closely related.

Insurability is another area of vocational damages. If an individual is not insurable by a health insurance carrier as a result of injuries sustained, then future medical care costs must be included in an assessment of damages. The loss of additional employment benefits such as company vehicle, bonus programs, dental benefits, eye wear insurance, and provided housing are included in calculating

Table 23.1   Calculation of Mark G's Loss of Earning Capacity

Year	Preinjury[a] Wage Capacity	+	3% Employer[c] Contribution =	Total Preinjury Earning Capacity	−	Postinjury Earning Capacity =	Loss of Earning Capacity
1	$51,350.00		$1,540.50	$52,890.50		$18,720.00	$34,170.50
2	52,377.00		1,571.31	53,948.31		19,656.00	34,292,31
3	53,424.54		1,602.73	55,027.27		20,638.80	34,388.47
4	54,493.03		1,634.79	56,127.82		21,670.74	34,457.08
5	55,582.89		1667.48	57,250.37		22,764.27	34,498.10
6	56,694.54		1,700.83	68,395.37		23,891.98	34,503.39
7	57,828.43		1,734.85	59,563.28		25,086.57	34,476.71
8	58,984.99		1,799.54	60,784.53		26,340.89	34,443.64
9	60,164.68		1,804.94	61,969.62		27,657.93	34,311.39
10	61,367.97		1,841.03	63,209.00		29,040.82	34,168.18
11	62,595.32		1,877.85	64,473.17		30,492.86	33,980.31
12	63,847.22		1,915.41	65,762.63		32,017.50	33,745.13
13	65,124.16		1,953.72	67,077.88		33,618.37	33,459.51
14	66,426.64		1,992.79	68,419.43		35,299.28	33,120.15
15	67,755.17		2,032.65	59,787.82		37,064.24	32,723.58
16	69,110.27		2,073.30	71,183.57		38,917.45	32,266.12
17	70,492.47		2,114.77	72,607.24		40,863.32	31,743.92
18	71,902.31		2,157.06	74,059.37		42,906.48	31,152.89
19	73,340.35		2,200.21	75,540.56		45,051.80	30,488.76
20	74,807.15		2,244.21	77,051.36		47,304.59	29,746.97
21	76,303.29		2,289.09	78,592.38		49,669.60	28,922.78
22	77,829.35		2,334.88	80,164.23		52,153.08	28,011.15
22.8[b]	52,871.02		1,586.13	54,457.15		36,470.64	17,986.51

Total $741,055.55

[a] Benefits not included.

[b] 22.8 is the work life expectancy from Standard Actuary.

[c] Retirement contribution from preinjury employer.

preinjury earning capacity and must be compared with the postinjury earning capacity.

Review

Readers should now have a clear concept of when to use a vocational expert, how to find the right expert, what he or she can provide, and what to expect in the vocational expert's report and opinion. Take time to research when making the selection. Keep the vocational expert informed of any changes in medical status, and copy him or her with all reports on an ongoing basis. Assure that the vocational expert is well prepared by the attorney before the case goes to trial. Following these practices will enhance the effectiveness of the expert, and the outcome in litigation.

Glossary

Disability: The vocational impact of the specific impairment. An impairment does not necessarily result in a disability. A disability exists when the individual is unable to perform work tasks as a result of the impairment.

Earning capacity: The amount of income an individual is capable of earning in a defined labor market at a specific point in time.

Essential functions: A term used in the Americans with Disability Act enacted in 1992. Essential function describes the most important aspects of a given job. When asked, "Why does the job exist?" the answer defines the essential function of the job. Nonessential functions which exceed the capability of an otherwise qualified candidate may be assigned to another worker.

Functional capacity evaluation: A comprehensive objective evaluation of the individual's capacity to perform work-related tasks.

Impairment: The actual physical or metal deficit.

Impairment rating: The percentage of impairment rating provided by a qualified physician following AMA or another established guideline. For example, 20% permanent impairment of the dominant hand or 8% of the whole person.

Job modification: Alterations in how tasks are performed, reassignment of tasks to accommodate an individual who can perform the "essential functions" of the job, or physical adaptations to a work site to accommodate the individual with an impairment.

Job-seeking skills: A set of abilities utilized in finding and obtaining employment including understanding and describing skills, completing an employment application, and interviewing.

Labor market survey: A survey of local employers conducted by the vocational expert to gather data regarding wages, benefits, promotional opportunities, physical and cognitive tasks, and the availability of employment opportunities.

Lost wages: The income lost from the onset of vocational disability (usually the date of injury) until the individual reaches maximum medical improvement.

Physical capacity: The functional limitations and abilities demonstrated by an individual after reaching maximum medical improvement.

Transferable skills: Skills that can be utilized in other jobs.

References

Deutsch, P. M. and Sawyer, H. W. (1985). *Guide to Rehabilitation,* New York, Matthew Bender.

Farr, J. M., Gaither, R., and Pickrell, R. M. (1992). *Getting the Job You Want: The Work Book,* Indianapolis, Jist Works, Inc.

U.S. Department of Labor, Bureau of Labor Statistics (1994). Occupational Outlook Handbook, 1994–1995 ed., Indianapolis, Jist Works.

U.S. Equal Employment Opportunity Commission. (1993). *Americans with Disability Act: A Technical Assistance Manual on the Employment Provisions,* Indianapolis, Jist Works, Inc.

Vanderkok, C. J. (1993). *Litigated Disability Cases. A Guide for Utilizing the Vocational Expert,* Athens, Elliot and Fitzpatrick.

Wright, G. (1980). *Total Rehabilitation,* Boston, Little, Brown.

Chapter 24

Literature Research

Karen L. Wetther

Contents

1-57444-123-X/98
© 1998 by American Association of Legal Nurse Consultants

Objectives

- To identify the steps in a database search
- To list three ways to access information from the National Library of Medicine (NLM)
- To list five NLM databases other than MEDLINE which may be helpful in accessing information on specific medical diseases or topics
- To describe the difference between MEDLINE and MEDLARS
- To identify the NLM retrieval system associated with Grateful Med
- To state one advantage of searching via the Internet
- To identify two sites on the Internet which might be beneficial in researching information for a case relating to AIDS
- To list two directories which may be used to research a physician's credentials
- To state two ways to determine the validity of published information
- To list two sources for locating practice parameters and guidelines

Introduction

One of the valuable services a legal nurse consultant (LNC) can offer to her clients is the ability to identify and locate biomedical information specific to issues in their cases. Most nurses are relatively comfortable doing research in health sciences libraries and have had considerable experience in retrieving information from medical and scientific textbooks and journals. However, they may not perform on-line literature searches with the same amount of ease.

We live in an information society and much of the information is not available in textbooks. Textbooks, due to the time constraints in the publication process, cannot have the most recent information, although textbooks remain useful in many situations and are a good source of detailed and in-depth material. Because the LNC often researches information concerning conditions, procedures, standards, and practice guidelines which were relevant at the time of the subject incident or accident, textbooks are often very relevant and helpful.

The most current information can be accessed by computer on the Internet through networks which link minds worldwide. Information on certain topics and at different sites may still be somewhat limited but the body of information is rapidly growing. The information explosion is exciting but can be daunting to the LNC who may not yet have ventured into cyberspace.

This chapter will help the LNC develop the art of identifying and locating information appropriate to the clients' needs, to increase awareness of the many resources available and, perhaps most importantly, to analyze the information obtained for its validity and credibility in the medical and scientific community.

Research Methods

There are a variety of sources one may consult to identify the best available evidence on a medical topic or to research a medical professional's credentials:

1. Consultation with a professional in the appropriate specialty
2. Textbook research
3. Professional specialty organizations [e.g., American Association of Critical Care Nurses (AACN) and American College of Obstetrics and Gynecology (ACOG)]
4. Governmental agencies (e.g., FDA, CDC, NIH)
5. Nonprofit organizations (e.g., American Cancer Society and National Kidney Foundation)
6. Directories (e.g., the *Official ABMS Directory of Board Certified Medical Specialists and the Directory of Physicians in the U.S.*)
7. Computerized literature searches using a bibliographic database such as MEDLINE
8. The Internet (which can provide access to all of the above-listed resources)

Overview of the Research Process

The nursing process serves one well when conducting research because each element of that process is critical to developing and implementing a research strategy which will deliver the best results.

Assessment

This initial step in the process involves assessing what information is needed from the client in order to conduct a valid search. Failure to collect the important data at the outset may result in delays and may not provide complete information specific to the client's case. In addition to knowing the topic which should be researched, the LNC should know the issues involved in the case; the date of loss (e.g., the date when the incident or accident occurred); the age and gender of the plaintiff; ethnicity; concurrent medical conditions; medications taken; whether the client has a preference for textbook information or medical or nursing journals; how far back in years the search should extend; and the date of the subject incident. An easily retrievable form is helpful in prompting the LNC to solicit the necessary information (see Figure 24.1).

Client _____ Date _____

Firm _____ Due date _____

Address_____ Date of loss_____

_____ _____

_____ _____

Phone _____ Fax_____

Case Name _____ File # _____

Client represents _____Plaintiff _____Defendant

Type of case _____Med Mal _____PI _____Products Liability

      Other _____

Issue(s): _____

_____

_____

Topic(s)/Author(s) to be searched (be specific): _____

_____

_____

Gender: _____Female _____Male   Age:_____

Ethnicity _____

Diagnoses (primary and secondary) _____

_____

How far back should search extend? _____

Limit search to (circle letters): a b c d e f

a Medical journals   b Nursing journals   c English language

d Medical text books   e Nursing textbooks   f Other_____

Figure 24.1   Literature search or medical research request. (From Wetther, K., *The Nuts and Bolts of Legal Nurse Consulting*, Carlsbad, CA, Medical Legal Resources, 1994. With permission.)

Analysis and Issue Identification

The LNC must use analytical and critical thinking skills to sort out the primary issues to be addressed. Clients may have identified one issue which they consider to be the key issue, whereas the LNC may have a different opinion once the initial data is solicited and the situation is analyzed.

Example 24.1: A client reports to the LNC that his client is a woman who has asked him to file a wrongful death suit against a hospital due to the death of her husband. Her husband, subsequent to undergoing coronary bypass surgery, became increasingly depressed and agitated. He presented to the Emergency Department (ED), accompanied by his wife, and she told the triage nurse that she felt he needed medication to treat the worsening depression and agitation as he no longer had any interest in anything and refused to eat. His primary physician was paged but was on vacation, the house MD was paged but said he could not authorize treatment because he was not one of the patient's HMO providers, and a third physician was paged who was an HMO provider. After waiting in the ED for 4 hours, the patient left and, later that afternoon, committed suicide by shooting himself in the head.

The attorney tells the LNC that he needs to know what the Standard of Care is for a triage nurse in the ED when a patient offers complaints of depression and agitation. The LNC agrees that this is a key issue but also feels that, since the nurse did follow through initially to reach three physicians and was unable to obtain authorization for treatment, perhaps the larger issue is the protocol the HMO has in place for authorizing treatment when psychological complaints are offered and observed and for obtaining treatment for a patient whose primary physician is unavailable (i.e., on vacation).

Outcome Identification

Having collected the initial data from the client, analyzed it, and identified the primary issues, the LNC must identify the desired outcome of the literature search. What does the client need to prove? Is there controversy relating to the key issues? Does the client want the actual articles or are article abstracts or synopses sufficient? How soon are they needed?

Planning

For purposes of this chapter, planning would involve determining which type of textbooks to research (if textbook research is required), researching standards of practice or a physician's credentials, or, in the case of performing a computerized search for journal articles, selecting the most relevant Medical Subject Heading(s) [MeSH] for the search, deciding on appropriate subheadings, and/or limiting the search to certain age groups, English-language articles only, specific years, etc.

Planning is an essential part of performing a computerized search in order to expedite the process and to insure that the most relevant articles are retrieved.

> Example 24.2: An LNC is asked by an attorney to research abdominal rhabdomyo-sarcoma because she has a potential client who thinks a delay in diagnosis of her 14-year-old daughter's condition resulted in her death in September of 1994. The LNC may decide to look for information in pediatric oncology textbooks and to perform a computerized literature search. By choosing the MeSH term "Rhabdomy-osarcoma" for the MEDLINE search, 187 citations are identified. By limiting the search to the subheadings of "Classification," "Diagnosis," "Mortality," and "Pathology," the number of citations decreases to 110. By further limiting the search to human studies/cases (rather than animal studies), age (adolescence, i.e., 13–18 years old), female, English-language articles, and those which have abstracts available, the result is 32 citations of articles published in 1993 and 1994.

Implementation

The previous example using the MeSH term "Rhabdomyosarcoma" actually leads right into implementation, i.e., following through with the established plan. The

LNC chose the appropriate MeSH term, identified 4 subheadings out of a list of 14, and further limited the search to fit the parameters of her client's case. This decreased the number of citations from 187 to 32, a reasonable number to search.

To actually implement the plan, the LNC viewed the 32 citations and their abstracts and selected 8 of those which were appropriate to her client's case. (Some of the 32 citations related to rhabdomyosarcoma in adolescents but involved sites such as the head and neck, which did not relate to the site she was researching.) The next step in implementing the plan is to print out the citations and abstracts selected. In some cases, these may be forwarded to the client by fax or mail and in other cases, depending on the client's preference, the LNC may retrieve the 8 journal articles from the library shelves or via the Internet.

"Loansome Doc" is the document-retrieval system provided by the NLM. In order to retrieve the articles via Loansome Doc, health care professionals must establish an account with a library for articles that can be held for them in the library or faxed or mailed to them. If this library does not have the articles requested, they can obtain them from outside sources. The cost varies by library so the LNC should clarify this when establishing an account.

Evaluation

Prior to copying textbook information and/or articles for the client, the LNC should review them to evaluate whether or not the information is relevant to the client's case and needs. The attorney client may need broad information on a medical topic or issue for his or her own education prior to accepting a case or deposing medical professionals or may need very specific information to support his or her position. This, of course, should have been determined early in the process and can at this point be evaluated.

The LNC must be able to answer the question "Will this information meet my client's needs for this particular case?" If not, "Plan B" must be formulated, followed by implementation of the plan and subsequent evaluation. If the first four steps of the process are thoughtfully completed initially, implementation and evaluation should prove to be successful.

Textbook Research

The LNC should not find this type of research particularly challenging as long as she has access to a health science library. One's personal library is helpful for immediate access to information but may not be extensive enough to rely on for many research projects.

The following pointers will help to safeguard the LNC who relies on printed information to support a position relating to a medical issue or topic:

1. Use grandfather texts, i.e., authoritative textbooks which are widely accepted in the general medical and scientific community. Grandfather texts are generally those used as textbooks in medical and nursing schools. (*Examples: Harrison's Principles of Internal Medicine, Williams Obstetrics, Swenson's Pediatric Surgery, Nelson Textbook of Pediatrics.*) A good source

of authoritative textbooks is the Brandon-Hill list, which is published annually in the *Bulletin of the Medical Library Association.*

2. Make sure the book is time-appropriate to the case. If the LNC is researching an issue related to a 1995 incident which is the subject of a medical malpractice lawsuit, the books consulted should have been published in, or prior to, 1995. Any information relating to standards or guidelines would have to have been available to the treating health care practitioners at the time of the subject incident.

3. It is a safe practice to refer to a minimum of three authoritative sources to confirm that there is general agreement or controversy among the experts regarding the issue in question.

The LNC should keep in mind that references and bibliographies at the end of textbook chapters may direct the reader to additional information on the subject. Also, editors and authors may be considered as potential expert witnesses since they have published in an authoritative text and are therefore often considered experts in their specialties or specific aspects of their specialties.

Professional Specialty Organizations, Governmental Agencies, and Nonprofit Organizations

The *Encyclopedia of Medical Organizations and Agencies* (Gale Research, Inc.) provides a subject guide to over 11,000 associations, foundations, federal and state government agencies, research centers, and medical and allied health schools. The table of contents lists medical organizations and agencies by subject, e.g., Birth Defects, Child Abuse and Family Violence, Emergency Medicine, Chiropractic, and Nursing. The reader is then directed to the pages which include listings and a brief description about the organizations which relate to the topic being researched.

For example, the section on Obstetrics and Gynecology lists 61 national and international associations, including the American College of Obstetricians and Gynecologists (ACOG), the American College of Nurse-Midwives (ACNM), the American Society for Colposcopy and Cervical Pathology (ASCCP), the International Society for Twin Studies (ISTS), the National Perinatal Association (NPA), and the Society for the Study of Breast Disease.

An LNC who has difficulty reading chiropractic records and understanding chiropractic records or who needs to locate recognized standards for chiropractics might benefit from consulting the section in that encyclopedia on chiropractics. The Commission on Accreditation of the Council of Chiropractic Education is listed with address and phone number as well as the chiropractic schools, listed by state, which are approved by this commission.

Another source of valuable information for the LNC are nonprofit organizations such as the American Cancer Society, the Arthritis Foundation, and the National Kidney Foundation, to name a few. They can often provide statistics, other resources relating to the condition being researched, prospective medical experts, and other valuable information. Governmental agencies such as the Centers for Disease Control (CDC), the Food and Drug Administration (FDA), and the National Institutes of Health (NIH) are also invaluable resources. These may all be located through the *Encyclopedia of Medical Organizations and Agencies* or through the Internet (see Table 24.3, below).

The *Health Care Standards Directory* (published by ECRI) can help direct the LNC to health care standards, guidelines, and recommended practices which are often difficult to locate. It includes listings for standards issued by medical societies, professional associations, government agencies, and other health-related organizations. The directory includes the following:

- Complete citations to standards, legislation, and referenced articles
- An alphabetical listing of organizations that have issued standards related to health care. Listings include the full name, address, and telephone numbers of each organization as well as the title of each standard issued by the organization and information relating to price or how to order the standards
- An alphabetical listing of federal and state agencies which have issued health-related regulations or guidelines; it includes the name, address, and phone number of each agency
- A quality-of-care bibliography which lists significant articles relating to assessing and providing quality health care

Computerized (On-Line) Searches

In this information society, numerous sources of information are available via computer and awareness of and access to that information can significantly enhance the LNC's value to his or her clients. On-line information retrieval is the process of identifying desired information by direct interactive communication with a computer (Bunting, 1994, p. 34).

If the reader needs specific instruction about getting on-line, there are various local resources which often offer instruction, such as community colleges, adult education centers, and public libraries. There are a number of books available to help also, such as Shortliffe and Perreault (1990), Comer and Angell (1994), Rosenfeld et al. (1995), Hancock (1996), and Hogarth and Hutchinson (1996). Software is also available at stores or through catalogs that is designed to instruct one how to access the Internet.

Several software programs are available allow one to access MEDLINE, such as Grateful Med (the NLM program), Bibliomed, Ovid, Dialog and Westlaw (see Resources near end of chapter).

The National Network of Libraries of Medicine

It is helpful to understand the nationwide network of libraries which comprise the National Network of Libraries of Medicine (NN/LM), as it provides the nation with access to biomedical information.

The NN/LM is based in Bethesda, Maryland. The NLM serves as the overall coordinator and acts as a backup resource for all other libraries in the network. The NLM is the largest and most prestigious medical library in the world and is part of the NIH. The NLM computer files contain approximately 15 million records covering its holding of books, journal articles, and other literature. The library provides direct access to these holdings via their Grateful Med software program.

The NN/LM is made up of the Library of Medicine and the following:

- 3600 Primary Access Libraries — These libraries are the local connection to the vast amount of biomedical information in the NLM. They are usually housed in community hospitals.
- 146 Resource Libraries — These are larger libraries, usually located in medical schools, which offer a wider scope of resources than community hospital libraries, i.e., more extensive collections of books and journals and more library staff.
- 8 Regional Medical Libraries — These institutions across the country are under contract to the NLM. They coordinate health sciences information services within a particular region. Three of the libraries are on-line training centers. Anyone calling the 800 number for information or assistance is automatically connected with the Regional Medical Library in his or her region (see Resources).

Services Provided by the NN/LM

- Outreach, which provides access to health professionals in any location who desire biomedical information.
- Grateful Med demonstrations and training to simplify MEDLINE searches with demo disks. Will present brief demonstrations or in-depth workshops. (An annual listing of MEDLINE training and updates is included in the *NLM Technical Bulletin* and is also accessible on-line in the NLM news file or obtainable from MEDLARS management at 1-800-638-8480.) Searchers who use a system other then NLM should contact the vendor for training information (Bunting, 1994, p. 59).
- Document delivery via Loansome Doc, the electronic document retrieval feature of Grateful Med.
- Reference services, which will obtain access to information that is difficult to find or will refer the caller to a source that has that information.
- Education through on-line centers that provide training and technical support to individuals who desire more information about searching NLM databases.
- Exhibits and training at professional meetings across the country.

On-Line Access to the NLM

The Medical Literature Analysis and Retrieval System (MEDLARS) includes numerous databases and MEDLINE is "MEDlars on-LINE." MEDLINE is a database of over 7 million references and abstracts of articles contained in more than 4000 journals published since 1966 (Blonde et al., 1995, p. 38). It includes three printed indexes:

- *Index Medicus*
- *International Nursing Index*
- *Index to Dental Literature*

Other NLM databases which, with MEDLINE, make up MEDLARS include information such as citations or factual information about specific diseases or medical
conditions such as AIDS, cancer, chemical compounds, health planning and
administration, ethics, toxicology, as well as a listing of books (CATLINE) and
audiovisual materials (AVLINE) (Blonde et al., 1995, p. 38) (refer to Table 24.1).
Further information on these databases is available from the NLM (see Resources).
Charges for searching various databases vary and the LNC should be aware that
some may be costly. These costs should be factored in with the consultant's fees
and costs submitted to the client, but it is important to be as cost- and time-
efficient as possible and to get authorization if a search is anticipated to be costly.

Grateful Med Software

Grateful Med is the NLM user-friendly, menu-driven interface to the MEDLARS
databases of the NLM. It is one of the most widely used and fully developed of
the searching products. It is easy to learn and use, even for novices.

Some of the major benefits are its cost-effectiveness, it entitles the user to
unlimited annual complimentary updates (provided the user's current address is
on file), a tutorial program is included, and it is available for both for Apple
Macintosh and DOS-based computers, including Windows. The menus are clearly
organized and the MeSH dictionary helps the searcher to organize the search
before actually connecting to the NLM computer, thereby decreasing on-line
charges. Grateful Med "calls" the NLM computer, quickly and efficiently conducts
the search, disconnects from the NLM computer, and analyzes, stores, or prints
the search results for review at no additional cost. Searching may be done by
MeSH terms, authors, title words, text (abstract) words, date or type of publication,
language (may limit to English only), and other criteria alone or in combination
(Blonde et al., 1995, p. 41).

Grateful Med may be ordered from the National Technical Information Service
(NTIS) at a very reasonable cost or it may be accessed through commercial on-
line vendors or at health sciences libraries. It requires a computer, a modem, a
user ID, and a password.

Steps to Performing an On-Line Search

There are many types of software which may be used for on-line searching. The
following steps should apply to all, although each software program has a slightly
different way of formulating and performing a search.

1. Collect adequate information from the client to formulate a focused search
   strategy.
2. Formulate the overall search strategy.
3. Input the MeSH term(s), author, or journal which is the focus of your search.
4. Limit or explode your search, if desired (the program will allow you these
   options).
5. View the citations (and abstracts as desired).
6. Select (mark) citations which appear to be relevant.
7. Print out search results.
8. Locate/order articles.

Table 24.1   Selected Databases for the Health Sciences

Database/Producer	Description
AIDSDRUGS/NLM	Dictionary of chemical and biological agents being evaluated in the AIDS clinical trials
AIDSLINE/NLM	AIDS information hotline
AIDSTRIALS/NLM	AIDS clinical trials
Birth Defects Information (BDIS)/Center for Birth Defects Information Services	Full-text of articles and monographs, differential diagnosis system for birth defects
CANCERLIT/U.S. National Cancer Institute	Cancer literature contained in journals, monographs, reports, dissertations, and meeting papers
CATLINE/NLM (CATalog onLINE)	Cataloged titles (books) in the NLM
CHEMLINE/NLM	Factual information on chemical substances and properties
DIOGENES: Washington News Document Retrieval Network/FOI Services	Full-text *Federal Register* notices and reports, FDA approvals, Washington Business Information publications, and Medical Device Reports
DIRLINE (DIRectory of Information Resources onLINE/NLM)	Directory of organizations providing information services
DRUG INFO/University of Minnesota	Drug information published in journals, books, and other print formats
Hazardous Substances Data Bank (HSDB)/NLM Toxicology Information Program (TIP)	Full-text information on potentially hazardous chemicals
Health Device Alerts/Emergency Care Research Institute (ECRI)	Full-text problem-reporting network for medical equipment and supplies industry
MEDLINE/NLM (MEDlars onLINE)	Journals contained in the NLM
MeSH Vocabulary File/NLM	Dictionary of current biomedical subject headings for MEDLINE and other NLM databases
NIOSH/U.S. National Institute for Occupational Safety and Health	Published and unpublished technical material, NIOSH reports, and conference proceedings
Nursing and Allied Health Database (CINAHL)/CINAHL Informations Systems	Journals, ANA and NLM publications, dissertations, books, and popular literature
PsychINFO/American Psychological Association (APA)	Periodicals, reports, and dissertations on psychology topics
TOXLINE/NLM	Journals, monographs, reports, theses, meetings, papers, and abstracts

MeSH Term Searches

This is the most common type of search and it should be noted that searching for text words (such as "rhabdomyosarcoma" in the earlier example) in titles and abstracts may miss many important and relevant citations. A searcher using Grateful

Med might input "rhabdomyosarcoma" on the Subject Line of the "Input Your Search" screen.

One benefit of searching MEDLINE is that it allows the searcher to utilize the Boolean operators "AND" and "OR" to combine search terms. This will result in a more-focused search.

> Example 24.3: To search for citations using the MeSH term "rhabdomyosarcoma" for the case referred to previously, adding the search term "abdominal" with the Boolean operator "AND" (i.e., rhabdomyosarcoma AND abdominal) will shorten the search because it will exclude citations relating to rhabdomyosarcoma of sites other than abdominal.

Limiting Your Search

Some programs allow the searches to limit the search to citations for which the MeSH term is the main focus of the article by placing an asterisk (*) before the MeSH term. Searches may also be limited to human studies, a specific age group, clinical trials (such as randomized control trials), review articles, English-language articles.

Author Searches

This type of search is often used when an attorney needs to review published works of an opposing expert. The search is usually simple and straightforward, as no search strategy or analysis is required initially. The searcher needs only to input the author's last name and two initials (of first and middle names). If the author's middle initial is not known, it is sufficient to enter the last name and first initial. This will call up all authors with that name and initial. Entering the middle initial is helpful in that it will narrow the search, especially if the last name is common, such as SMITH J. There may be many authors with this name, whereas there will be fewer by the name of SMITH JS.

The LNC may be asked to analyze or prepare a synopsis of the author's articles once they have been located and retrieved.

Journal Searches

Limiting a search to one particular journal is time-efficient in certain situations. For instance, an attorney may be told by an opposing expert at his deposition that an article was recently published in *JAMA* which related to a particular issue in the case. However, he is unsure of the date of publication of the issue or of the title of the article. The attorney will probably relay this to the LNC so the article can be retrieved. To perform this type of search, the name of the desired journal or the abbreviated title would be typed in instead of or in combination with a MeSH term or author's name. A health sciences reference librarian can refer you to a list of accepted journal abbreviations.

Printing the Abstracts

As the searcher views the citations and abstracts (when the latter is available) to see if the citation is relevant to the case, the relevant citations can be "selected" by using the correct command (such as "shift" and the "+"). After selecting all the relevant citations, the computer can then be told to print them. The searcher will be asked to choose from a menu of "Citations only," "Citations and abstracts," or "Citations and abstracts and MeSH headings."

Internet Access to Biomedical Information

The amount of information available on the information superhighway is staggering. In fact, the Internet is doubling in size and traffic every 2 months (Hancock, 1996, p. 23). The Internet may be described as a vast conglomeration of computers which are connected in a variety of ways to form a worldwide network (Hogarth and Hutchinson, 1996, p. 7).

To access the Internet as an independent consultant, one needs to have a computer, a modem, and an account with a commercial Internet provider such as America On Line, CompuServe, or Prodigy or local on-line vendors. In most cases, it is simply a matter of obtaining the provider's diskette, loading it into one's computer and dialing the number. While commercial providers are easy to use, subscribers are sometimes limited to their software. An LNC who is thinking of subscribing to a service should inquire as to whether subscribers are limited to using that provider's software.

Another option is to subscribe to an Internet Service Provider (ISP), although some provide only Internet connections and do not offer services such as forums, chat rooms, or proprietary libraries. Some have only local numbers while others have national access numbers. One advantage of using a national Internet service provider as opposed to a commercial on-line provider is the pricing structure. ISPs usually have flat rate pricing rather than charging by the hour. Examples of ISPs are Netcom, Internet MCI, InterRamp, and IBM Internet.

Benefits of Accessing Information via the Internet

The primary benefits of using the Internet to access information of any type are speed and volume. Communication can be processed and sent via the Internet at speeds 10 to 100 times faster than those sent over telephone lines with the use of a modem. This enables one to transmit large files, including those with color images, sound, and even motion pictures. With regard to volume, vast numbers of computer users can simultaneously send mail and take part in electronic bulletin board discussions (Kleeberg and Masys, 1995, p. 133).

Authenticity of Information

Before discussing the types of biomedical information available on the Internet which can greatly enhance an LNC's practice, it is important to caution users regarding two potential problems to be aware of: authenticity of information and confidentiality (discussed below).

Anyone who uses information obtained via the Internet should be cautious about the source of the information. Anyone who is on-line can publish information on the Internet, resulting in a wealth of unsupported as well as supported on-line information. The user must determine what information can be relied on.

The Internet has no single owner and is not subject to the laws of any one nation. The Internet Society develops protocols used to transmit information, but many aspects have developed by consensus, adaptation, and the free exchange of information and programs (Hogarth and Hutchinson, 1995, p. 12).

There are still no standards, review committees, or authorizing organizations to monitor or control new information which has made its way onto the Internet, so there is nothing to assure authenticity of the information. Even sites which may seem to be credible, such as the College of _____ or the "XYZ" Institute, may be created by anyone who may have simply copied information and/or graphics from some other site.

The LNC may find an article which seems very relevant to a case, but it is important to know if it is a peer-reviewed article. Many medical sites do have articles from peer-reviewed journals so it may be prudent to confine journal article searches to those. The guidelines are much the same as those used when retrieving articles from a health sciences library (see "Assessing the Validity of Medical Literature" later in this chapter, also).

The user who submits a question to a bulletin board or subscribes to a mailing list (LISTSERV) to gain some feedback must be very careful if the information obtained is to be used for a case. However, it can be a helpful source for locating professionals who may have expertise on a particular subject. Responders should be questioned about their credentials and these should be verified in some way. A physician's credentials are not difficult to research by finding the physician's listing in the *Official ABMS Directory of Board Certified Medical Specialists* if the physician is indeed board certified, by calling (800) ASK-MEDI (which runs searches on physicians for a nominal fee), or calling the institution where the physician claims to be on staff. (See Table 24.2 for a sampling of medical mailing lists.)

Confidentiality

The guidelines for maintaining confidentiality on the Internet are much the same as those which should be followed by any clinical nurse or LNC. A patient or the details of a case should never be discussed in public. The Internet is the epitome of "public" as anyone may be on-line. The LNC must use utmost caution when discussing anything relating to a case on the Internet. All comments should be confined to general statements which cannot be specifically related to the case.

Assessing the Validity of Medical Literature

It is often said that "You can prove anything you really want to prove." All published information is not valid and the LNC should be mindful of this when selecting journal articles for clients or for using information to support a position while fulfilling the role of a nurse expert.

Table 24.2   A Sampling of Medical Mailing Lists Available on the Internet

List Name	Topic	Address
ACCRI-L	Anesthesia and critical care	listserv@uabdpo.dpo.uab.edu
AIDS	AIDS issues	listserv@rutvm1
ALTMED-RES	Alternative medicine	majordomo@virginia.edu
AT-HMS	Health and medical sciences	listserv@vm.its.rpi.edu
bcmgradfac	Baylor Graduate School of Biomedical Sciences information distribution list	listserv@listserv.bcm.tmc.edu
BIO-HLTH	Biomedical research/health care	listserv@asuvm.inre.asu.edu
biomed	Biomedical Engineering Departtment	majordomo@acpub.duke.edu
CANCER-L	Cancer	listserv@wvnvm.wvnet.edu
CLINALRT	Clinical alerts from NIH	listserv@umab.umd.edu
DRUGABUS	Drug abuse	listserv@umab.umd.edu
EMFLDS-L	Electromagnet fields related to medicine	listserv@ubvm.cc.buffalo.edu
FAMILY-L	Family practice medicine	listserv@mizzou1.missouri.edu
GERINET	Geriatrics	listserv@ubvm.cc.buffalo.edu
HMATRIX-L	Online health resources	listserv@ukanaix.cc.ukans.edu
HOMEHLTH	Home health	listserv@usa.net
HYPBAR-L	Hyperbaric medicine	listserv@technion.ac.il
HYPERMED	Hypertext and medical applications	listserv@umab.umd.edu
I-SPRT	Traumatic brain injury	listserv@sjuvm.stjohns.edu
NEUROL-L	Neuroscience	listserv@uicvm.uic.edu
OB-GYN-L	OB/GYN	listserv@bcm.tmc.edu
REPRENDO	Reproductive endocrinology	listserv@umab.umd.edu
Rheum-L	Rheumatology	listserv@mizzou1.missouri.edu

LNCs learn to develop critical thinking skills to analyze critically the facts of their cases. This skill should extend into the area of analyzing medical literature also, whether it is obtained in the library or from an on-line source.

As mentioned previously, textbook research should be confined primarily to grandfather texts. Clues to their validity may be found by looking at the publishers, editors, and contributors. If the texts are published by well-known publishers of medical textbooks (examples would include but are not limited to Mosby, W. B. Saunders, Lippincott, Appleton & Lange) and if the editors and contributors are from reputable and well-known medical centers, one can generally feel safe using those texts. However, it is always a good practice to use at least three texts to be sure whether there is general agreement or controversy regarding the issues being researched.

Having said this, it should be emphasized that there may be many texts that contain valid information which are published by publishers who are not as well known.

To help physicians critically review journal articles and to determine whether or not results of published clinical studies are valid, the Evidence-Based Medicine Working Group was developed and has published a series of articles on the subject entitled "Users' Guides to the Medical Literature" (Guyatt and Rennie, 1993,

p. 2096). LNCs may find this resource helpful. They suggest that the following questions be answered:

- Are the results of the study valid?
- Primary guides
    Was the assignment of patients to treatments randomized?
    Were all patients who entered the trial properly accounted for and attributed at its conclusion?
    Was follow-up complete?
    Were patients analyzed in the groups to which they were randomized?
- Secondary guides
    Were patients, health workers, and study personnel "blind" to treatment?
    Were the groups similar at the start of the trial?
    Aside from the experimental intervention, were the groups treated equally?
    What were the results?
    How large was the treatment effect?
    How precise was the estimate of the treatment effect?
    Will the results help me in caring for my patients (or, in the case of LNCs, will the results help me with my case)?
    Can the results be applied to my patient care (i.e., the LNC's case)?
    Were all clinically important outcomes considered?
    Are the likely treatment benefits worth the potential harms and costs?

(Guyatt et al., 1993, p. 2599; may not be applicable to the LNC depending on the issues of the case.)

It is a good practice to use information primarily from refereed (i.e., peer-reviewed) journals. This can be determined by looking for a statement identifying it as such within the first few pages of the journal. These are generally viewed in the medical and scientific community as being more credible and authoritative than those which have not been peer-reviewed. Throwaway journals may publish some interesting articles which may relate to cases in litigation but should not be relied on solely. Likewise, there is much controversy over "junk science" and its place, if any, in the courtroom. Junk science is a term which has been used to refer to information presented by a person or persons as being scientific but which is not widely accepted in the medical and scientific community. Since every article an LNC presents to an attorney may potentially be relied on in a court of law, this must be taken into serious consideration.

To sum up much of the information above, the researcher should ask the following questions to help evaluate the validity of the information found in journal articles and books:

- What qualifies the author to publish on this topic?
- What is his or her reputation?
- Did the author refer to other relevant literature on this topic?
- What is the reputation of the journal (if it is an article in a medical or scientific journal)?

- Is the article in a refereed (peer-reviewed) journal?
- Who is the book publisher (if referring to a book)?

Biomedical Resources Available via the Internet

The specific resources which an LNC might wish to access on the Internet are too numerous to list or discuss in this chapter. However, some of the most frequently accessed databases are listed in Table 24.1; a few of the important Internet Web Guides (Medical sites) are listed in Table 24.3; Medical Specialty sites (many of which link to other sites relating to that specialty) are listed in Table 24.4; Nursing and other health-related fields (such as chiropractics and alternative medicine) are listed in Table 24.5; and a few medical journals and publications are listed in Table 24.6. A number of the medical specialty sites also provide access to many of the mainstream peer-reviewed medical journals.

Table 24.3   Internet Web Guides (Medical Sites)

Web Site	Description	Address
Martindale's Health	Links to other sites Provides annotated descriptions Goal is to be *the* multi-media and medical education center on the Internet	http://www-sci.lib.uci.edu
MedWeb: Biomedical Internet Resources	Good starting point to search medical topics Sites listed by medical specialty	http://www.cc.emory.edu/WHSCL/ medweb.html
The Medical List	A central resource for medical and health information Maintained by the Internet Group of the American Medical Informatics Association	http://www.kumc.edu:80/mmatrix
Virtual Medical Center	Medical sites are listed by subject Specializes in sites with multimedia offerings	http://www-sci.lib.uci.edu/ ~martindale/Medical.html
WWW Clinical Information	Lists main web sites including CancerNet, MMWR, Oncolink, the Visible Human, etc.	http://gimserver.intmed.mcw.edu/ MedInfo.html

Table 24.4   Medical Specialty Sites on the Internet

Specialty	List/Site	Description	Address
AIDS	AIDS information	Maintained by National Institute of Allergy and Infectious Diseases (NIAID)	gopher://odie.niaid.nih. gov/11/aids
		Information on guidelines for treatment, treatment complications, and current clinical trials	
		Links to the CDC, MMWR, National Commission on AIDS	
	AIDS resource list	Briefly annotated list of AIDS resources on the Internet	http://www.teleport.com/ ~celinec/aids.shtml
	CDC AIDS clearing-house	CDC reference, referral, and distribution service for AIDS-related information	gopher://cdcnac.aspensys. com
		Provides guidelines, brochures, videos, and reprints from MMWR	
		Free online service to qualified organizations	
	MedWeb AIDS page	Links to sites with AIDS resources and information	http://www.cc.emory.edu/ WHSCL/medweb.aids. html
Anesthesiology	Anesthesia clinical manuals	Good information on handling the latex-allergic patient during anesthesia	http://www.anes.ccf.org: 8080/lab2.htm
	GASNet; Global Anesthesia Network	Excellent anesthesiology resource from Yale University	http://gasnet.med.nyu. edu
		Multi-media textbook	
		Journal abstracts	
		Links to other Internet resources	
Cardiology	Cardiology compass	Helpful index to sites and professional organizations	http://osler.wustl.edu/ ~murphy/cardiology/ compass.html
		Clinical data and trials, e-mail lists, etc.	
	Cardiovascular pathology	Designed for interns	http://synapse.uah.ualberta. ca/synapse/000p0057.htm
		Pathological cardiac conditions covered	

Table 24.4   Medical Specialty Sites on the Internet (continued)

Specialty	List/Site	Description	Address
	Heart Surgery Forum	Links to other sites Includes information on legal, economic, and research issues Message board	http://www.hsforum.com/ heartsurgery/homehsf.html
Critical Care	Archives of the Critical Care mailing list	Full text of articles related to critical care medicine Information on code status, drug therapy, medical and nursing management, resource management	http://www.pitt.edu/ ~crippen/index.html
	Pediatric Critical Care	Links to a few other resources	http://amber.medlib.arizona. edu/ped-crit/ pcc.html
Dentistry	Implantological Web Site	Information relating to dental implants	http://www.dru.nl/onderwijs/ implants/ english/ implant.htm
	Internet Dentistry Resources	Links to dentistry sites	http://galaxy.einet.net/galaxy/ Medicine/Dentistry/janice-quinn/dentist r.html
	TMJ Foundation	Excellent site on TMJ syndrome Articles and explanations for the public and professionals	http://www.tmjfound.com/ ~sbroock/index.html
Emergency Medicine	MedWeb: Emergency Medicine	Links to sites relating to this specialty	http://www.cc.emory.edu/ WHSCL/medweb. emergency.html
	UTHSCSA Trauma	Annotated index to critical care, emergency medicine, and trauma WWW sites	http://rmstewart.uthscsa. html
Endocrinology/ Diabetes	American Diabetes Association	Detailed information on diabetes	http://www.diabetes.org
	Children with Diabetes	Commercial site for general information on juvenile diabetes Links to other commercial companies with diabetes-related products	http://www.castleweb. com/diabetes/d_01_000. htm
	Diabetes on the Web	Links to other sites with information on diabetes	http://www.tyrell.net/ ~diabetes/other-ds.html

Table 24.4   Medical Specialty Sites on the Internet (continued)

Specialty	List/Site	Description	Address
	National Institute of Diabetes and Digestive and Kidney Disease	A part of the NIH	http://www.niddk.nih.gov
	On-Line Resources for Diabetics	A good starting point for searching the Internet for diabetes-related information Has an annotated list of Web sites, Gopher sites, Usenet groups, and LISTSERV discussion groups	http://www.cruzio.com/ ~mendosa/faq.html
Family Medicine	Family Medicine Resources	Links to other sites which relate to this specialty	http://www.uwo.ca/fammed/ resource.html
	Family Practice Handbook	A handbook for interns and residents from the Virtual Hospital Covers all major areas	http://indy.radiology.uiowa. edu/Providers/ClinRef/FP Handbook/FPContents.html
Forensics	Forensic Information Services	Links to other sites relating to this specialty	http://www.bart.nl:80/ ~geradts/forensic.html
Gastroenter- ology	Gastroenterology Web	Links to other sites relating to this specialty Extensive information on liver disease	http://cpmcnet.columbia. edu/dept/gi/
Genetics	Institute for Medical Genetics	Links to web sites in genetics	http://medgen.rz.charite. hu-berlin.de:80/~pnh/
Geriatrics	Alzheimer's Web	Links to the Alzheimer Foundation Articles, books, conferences, research sites, mailing lists	http://werple.mira.net.au/ ~dhs/ad.html
	Gerontology Resources	Does not link to other sites but provides an extensive guide to resources	gopher://gopher.os.dhhs. gov:70/00/dhhs/aoa/ aoa/jpostlst.txt
Immunology	American Academy of Allergy, Asthma and Immunology	Links to medical sites related to these specialties	http://glamdring.ucsd.edu/ others/aai/

Table 24.4   Medical Specialty Sites on the Internet (continued)

Specialty	List/Site	Description	Address
	Ask an Immu-nologist	Provides a forum for general discussions relating to immunology for laypersons or professionals	http://glamdring.ucsd.edu/others/aai/askAAI.html
Infectious Disease	Emerging Infectious Diseases	A peer-reviewed journal published by the National Center for Infectious Diseases and CDC	http://www.cdc.gov/ncidod/EID/eid.htm
	MMWR (*Morbidity and Mortality Weekly Report*)	Published by the CDC Full text of the reports with searchable index The Adobe software may be downloaded to get charts and tables	http:/www.crawford.com/cdc/mmwr/mmwr.html
		Text of the journal Good for simple online reading of the text Readable without the Adobe software	gopher://cwis.usc.edu/11/The_Health_Sciences_Campus/Periodicals/mmwr
Internal Medicine	Yahoo: Internal Medicine	Links to sites relating to relevant topics	http://www.yahoo.com/Health/Medicine/Internal_Medicine/
Medicine	American Medical Association	Links to peer-reviewed journals on the Internet Full text of JAMA Archived abstracts of back issues of JAMA Directory of medical societies, all states	http://www.ama-assn.org/
Microbiology	Food-Borne Pathogenic Micro-organisms	FDA handbook Excellent site Provides a glossary which includes organism, name of disease, nature of disease, diagnosis, relative frequency, complications, target population, major outbreaks, FDA regulations, etc.	http://vm.cfsan.fda.gov/~mow/intro.html
	MedWeb: Microbiology and Virology	Links to sites relating to microbiology and virology	http://www.cc.emory.edu/WHSCL/medweb.microbiology.html

Table 24.4   Medical Specialty Sites on the Internet (continued)

Specialty	List/Site	Description	Address
Nephrology	National Institute of Diabetes and Digestive and Kidney Disease	Information on diabetes and kidney, urologic and endocrine diseases	http://www.niddk.nih.gov/
	Renal Parameter Database	Database of articles from the NIH Medline format	gopher://gopher.nih.gov/11/res/renal
	RenalNet	Provides clinical information, publications, government and education organizations, ESRD centers, and more Information regarding sites on the Internet about nephrology and kidney transplantation Discussions in clinical nephrology, hemodialysis, peritoneal dialysis, nursing and patient forum	http://ns.gamewood.net/renalnet.html
Neurology	Neurology	Links to other pages Information presented at the medical student, intern level Includes neuropsychological information also	http://www.neuro.mcg. edu/
	Neuro-sciences on the Internet	Links to sites with information on neurology and neuroscience	http://www.lm.com/~nab
Obstetrics and Gynecology	Breast Cancer Information Center	Extensive index Medical information, 800 numbers, LISTSERVs, and regional groups	http://nysernet.org/bcic
	Gynecologic Oncology Handbook	Good source of information on patient care, radiation, and chemotherapy, and administrative matters House staff level	http://gynoncology.obgyn. washington.edu/ Documentation/ GYN%20Onc%20 Handbook.html
	Gynecology Handbook	Designed for house staff Short, practical	http://indy.radiology.uiowa. edu/Providers/ClinRef/FP Handbook/07.html

Table 24.4 Medical Specialty Sites on the Internet (continued)

Specialty	List/Site	Description	Address
Occupational Health	Index of Occupational Safety and Health	Good listing of sites with relevant topics	http://turva.me.tut.fi/ ~tuusital/oshlinks.html
Oncology	CancerNet	NIH site Major source of cancer information Full-text documents available by e-mail	gopher.nih.gov/11/clin/ cancernet
	Michigan Cancer Center	List of active protocols	http://www.cancer.med. umich.edu
	OncoLink, University of Pennsylvania Cancer Resource	Excellent site for the layperson or professional for cancer information	http://cancer.med.upenn. edu
	Pediatric Oncology Group	This group is an umbrella organization for pediatric cancer studies involving over 100 institutions and over 2000 patients Research protocols	http://pog.ufl.edu/
	Sloan-Kettering Institute	Searchable article database Enter a word/topic for a hyperlinked list of related articles and abstracts	http://www.ski.mskcc.org/
Ophthalmology	Vision Science: The Virtual Library	Links to sites with ophthalmology information Orientation: research as opposed to clinical data	http://vision.arc.nasa.gov/ Vision Science.html
Orthopedics	Biomechanics World Wide	Links to sites relating to orthopedics Information about orthopedics, prosthetics, sports, ergonomics, gait and locomotion, and biomedical engineering	http://dragon.acadiau.ca/ ~pbaudin/biomch.html
	Musculoskeletal Research Center	Abstracts of articles relating to orthopedics	http://motion2.ortho.pitt. edu/msrchome.html
	Southern California Orthopedic Institute	Good site for reviewing information on anatomy, basic orthopedics, arthroscopies, etc.	http://www.scoi.com

Table 24.4   Medical Specialty Sites on the Internet (continued)

Specialty	List/Site	Description	Address
		High-quality education page	
		Excellent graphics	
Pathology	PathPics	Links to other pathology sites	http://amber.medlib.arizona.edu/pathpics.html
	WebPath	Archived images of pathology	http://www-medlib.med.utah.edu/WebPath/webpath.html
		Indexed by body system or disease	
		Mini-tutorials on many diseases	
Pediatrics	Global ChildNet	Not-for-profit organization (organizes the Child Health 2000 World Congress)	http://www.gcnet.org/gcnet/
		Links to many sites	
		On-line journal	
		Searchable database of organizations relating to child health	
	Pediatric Cancers	Information about childhood cancer, various conditions, trials, etc.	http://oncolink.upenn.edu/disease/pediatric.html
		A part of Oncolink	
	Pediatric Interest Group	Links to other sites related to pediatrics	http://www.kumc.edu/student/PIG/pig.htm
		Site for medical students	
	Pediatric Neuro-surgery	Information on a number of pediatric conditions requiring neurosurgical intervention or expertise	http://cpmcnet.columbia.edu/dept/nsg/PNS
Pharmocology	PharmWeb	Annotated listing of publications, electronic products, journals related to pharmacology	http://www.mcc.ac.uk/pharmacy
		Links to pharmacy-related sites, including pharmaceutical companies	
Primary Care	Primary Care Informatics	Links to primary care sites and resources	http://sl.cxwms.ac.uk/Academic/AGPU/staffpag/robinson/interest/medcomp/homepage.html

Table 24.4 Medical Specialty Sites on the Internet (continued)

Specialty	List/Site	Description	Address
	Primary Care Handbook	Primarily for primary care physicians ACLS algorithms, diagnostic tests, organisms, diseases, drugs Drug and disease interactions	http://www.med.ufl.edu/ medinfo/baseline/ hnl.html
Psychiatry	Forensic Psychiatry Resources	Law relating to the field of psychiatry Additional sites Landmark court cases Legal databases	http://ualvm.ua.edu/ ~jhooper/tableofc.html
	Grohol's Mental Health Page	Good index site for mental health, psychiatry, and psychology information Good place to start a search relating to these areas Mailing lists, Web sites, and direct links to Usenet groups	http://csbh.mhv.net/ ~grohol/
	National Institute of Mental Health	Governmental agency which conducts and supports research on mental illness and mental health Information regarding their programs, grants and documents	gopher://gopher.nimh.nih. gov
Radiology	Brigham and Women's/ Harvard Medical School	Database of teaching files on diagnostic radiology Used for teaching house staff	http://www.med.harvard. edu/BWH
	Collaborative Hypertext of Radiology	Hypertext links within the listings Over 1000 documents designed specifically for health care professionals	http://chorus.rad.mcw. edu/chorus.html

Table 24.4 Medical Specialty Sites on the Internet (continued)

Specialty	List/Site	Description	Address
		Diseases, differential diagnoses and radiology findings indexed by organ system and condition	
	Penn State Radiology	Practice guidelines Digital Imaging and Communications in Medicine (DICOM) standards Links to a few other sites	http://www.Xray.hmc.psu. edu/home.html
Rehabilitation	American Paralysis Association	This not-for-profit organization provides education on spinal cord injury Well-linked hypertext teaching site Well organized Excellent graphics	http://teri.bio.uci.edu:80/ paralysis
	Association of Academic Physiatrists	Index to sites related to this specialty	http://al.com/aap/index. html
Rheumatology	Criteria for Classification of Rheumatic Diseases	Criteria from the American College of Rheumatology	http://biomed.nus.sg/ MedClass
	Pediatric Rheuma-tology	Covers the major syndromes, drugs, guidelines for referrals, alternative therapies For patients and health care professionals	http://www.wp.com/ pedsrheum/
	The Rheumatology Page	Good index to sites Foundations, societies and organizations relating to rheumatic diseases	http://www.crl.com/ ~fredt/rheum.html
Sports Medicine	Sport Management homepage	Covers research on sport management from 1990 to the present	http://137.142.20.1/ ~mirandma/sportmgt.html
Surgery	American Share Foundation	Patient-oriented site Information regarding transplants List of organ transplant centers	http://www.asf.org

Table 24.4   Medical Specialty Sites on the Internet (continued)

Specialty	List/Site	Description	Address
	TransWeb	Organ transplant information for patients and health care professionals	http://www.med.umich.edu:80/trans/transweb
Surgery (Plastic)	Plink, the Plastic Surgery Link	Links to sites relating to plastic surgery	http://www.IAEhv.nl/users/ivheij/plink.html
Toxicology	National Library of Medicine Tox Page	Links to various government toxicology resources	http://tamas.nlm.nih.gov/~boyda/htdocs/

The LNC should view a computer as a window to the world, through which he or she can explore the world from thousands of miles away in a matter of minutes. While it may take some time to learn to navigate the information superhighway initially, experience and patience will lead to more expedient searches and will also uncover new resources.

The LNC should be aware of the types of information available on the Internet which may enhance his or her practice. The following are a few of the possibilities:

- Search the medical and scientific literature and other databases from the NLM and other information providers
- Receive concise, current synopses of diseases and treatment
- Send and receive medical images (still or animated)
- Obtain standards of care from professional medical/nursing/dental/scientific organizations
- Obtain pharmaceutical databases
- Receive detailed information on medical devices and products
- Send and receive electronic mail (e-mail) with colleagues anywhere in the world in a matter of seconds
- Read and post notes to electronic bulletin boards which are accessed by thousands of people with similar interests
- Stay abreast of current medical news which appears in newspapers and from news services
- Access regulations and other information from governmental agencies such as the CDC, FDA, NIH, and the Occupational Safety and Health Administration (OSHA)
- Obtain research reports, practice guidelines, medical protocols, and digests of conferences and meetings
- Locate experts

Web Sites

One of the benefits of accessing web sites is that most of them have links to other related sites. In addition, some are referred to as value-added sites because

Table 24.5   Nursing and Other Health-Related Fields

Subject	Site	Address	Description
Alternative Medicine	Alternative Medicine Home Page	http://www.pitt.edu/ ~cbw/altm.html	Links to other sites related to this topic (annotated)
Child Abuse	National Data Archive on Child Abuse and Neglect	gopher://gopher.ndac an.cornell.edu	Disseminates information on child abuse/neglect
			Provides training and technical support for analysis of the data
Chiropractics	Chiropractic Page	http://www.mbnet. mb.ca/~jwiens/ chiro.html#soft	Links to other chiropractic and alternative medicine sites
Home Health	Belson/Hanwright Video, Inc.	http://www.earthlink. net/~bhv/	Links to home health equipment vendors
			Home health videos
Nursing	American Journal of Nursing Company	http://www.ajn.org	Selected articles from *American Journal of Nursing* (AJN) and *Maternal Child Nursing* (MCN)
			AJN Network in progress provides instruction, databases, news, access to consultants, bulletin board
			ANA annual conference information, CEUs, career guide
	Chronic Wound Healing	http://coninfo.nursing. UIOWA.EDU/www/ nursing/virtnurs/chr onwnd/!int.htm	Extensive graphics
			Instruction in proper wound care
			Good teaching tool for students (or attorneys!)
	NURSE	gopher://nurse.csv. warwick.ac.uk: 70/11/	British site (University of Warwick, England)
			Attempts to organize all nursing-related sites on the Internet
	NurseNet	gopher://vm.utcc. utoronto.ca:70/11/ LISTSERV/nursenet	Forum for discussion of nursing issues
			Archive of the NurseNet LISTSERV group
	NurseWeb at UCSF	http://nurseweb.ucsf. edu/www/ ucsfson.htm	From the University of California, San Francisco

Table 24.5 Nursing and Other Health-Related Fields (continued)

Subject	Site	Address	Description
			Links to other nursing Web pages
	Nursing Index	http://www.lib.umich.edu/tml/nursing.html	Well-annotated links to sites
			Information regarding clinical topics, educational programs, research, organizations, and more
Nursing AIDS	National Institute of Allergy and Infectious Diseases	gopher:odie.niaid.nih.gov/11/aids/nursing	From the National Institute of Allergy and Infectious Diseases (part of the NIH)
			Information, including teaching handouts, regarding nursing practice related to AIDS patients, assessment, alternative treatments, etc.
Nutrition and Wellness	Electronic Sources of Food and Nutrition Information	gopher://una.hh.lib.umich.edu/00/inetdirsstacks/foodnut% 3abussmann	Good source for descriptions and guide to nutrition databases from a number of organizations and agencies
	The Internet Doctor	http://www.montrealnet.ca/netdoctor/index.html	You send your questions and physicians who operate the service answer them
			There is a moderate charge for their services
Osteopathic Medicine	Osteopathic Medicine	http:/www.demon.co.uk/osteopath/index.html	An introduction to this field
			Some abstracts and bibliographies from the online journal (The Osteopath)
Physician Assistants	Physician Assistant training	http://dmi-www.mc.duke.edu/cfm/pap/	Information about P.A. training at Duke University
Public Health	Hazardous Substances & Public Health	http://atsdrl.atsdr.cdc.gov:8080/HEC/hsphhome.html	An on-line journal from the CDC

Table 24.5   Nursing and Other Health-Related Fields (continued)

Subject	Site	Address	Description
	Health Services and Public Health Sites on the Internet	http://weber.u.washin gton.edu/~larsson/ hsic94/resource/ hsr-ph.html	Annotated index of sites, primarily governmental
	National Center for Health Statistics (CDC)	http://www.cdc. gov/nchswww/ nchshome.htm	Publications may be down-loaded or are available on CD-ROM, diskette, or paper
	National Health Information Center	http://nhic-nt. health.org/ odphp.htm	Has extensive listings and links
			Provides referrals to appropriate organizations

they also provide information, such as full-text books, journal abstracts, and graphics (See Tables 24.3, 24.4, and 24.5).

Due to the amount of traffic on the Internet, it is sometimes difficult to connect to a site. If this occurs, the following strategies may help:

- Attempt to connect at a later time or even on another day, as sites may be busy or may even go down completely at times.
- Try to connect directly to the site computer, rather than to the actual document. For example, on Table 24.5, the Medical Specialty Sites, the Heart Surgery Forum (under "Cardiology") address is: http://www.hsforum.com/heartsurgery/homehsf.html. You might try connecting to "http://www.hsforum.com/" rather than using the entire address, which includes a subdirectory and the type of document. To put it simply, omit everything other than the part of the address between http:// and the next slash (/). This will connect you to the host computer for the organization and you can search the listings for the specific document you want.
- Try one of the index sites for the specialty.
- Try a general subject listing.

Ethics

The Medical Library Assocation (MLA) Code of Ethics offers several guidelines which are applicable to any researcher who acts as an intermediary between a client and the information, whether the information is obtained manually or by computer. The following guidelines which directly apply to LNCs have been adapted from the MLA Code of Ethics (Bunting, 1994, pp. 64, 65):

- Use interview techniques to clarify the client's needs prior to doing research on any case

Table 24.6 Medical Journals and Publications on the Interne: A Sampling

Journal/Publication	Address	Description
CNN Food and Health News	http://www.cnn.com/HEALTH/ index.html	Source for locating media coverage of health and medicine
		Provides short abstracts on current stories, with links to full text
Essential Medical Resources	http://www.aladdin.co.uk/ biopages	Links to a list of peer-reviewed journals
		Compiled by the AMA
International Health News	http://www.perspective. com/ health/index.html	Abstracts and articles from mainstream medical journals (*JAMA, Lancet,* etc.)
		Monthly on-line newsletter
Journal of the American Medical Association (JAMA)	http://www.ama-assn.org	Full text of *JAMA* and archived abstracts (back issues)
Journal of NIH Research	gopher.enews.com/11/ magazines/alphabetic/ all/nih	News, research, NIH resources, funding, clinical trials, legal and ethical issues
		Some articles available online from each issue
		Information about research and science policy in the biomedical field
MedWeb: Electronic Newsletters and Journals	http://www.cc.emory.edu/WHS CL/medweb.ejs. html	Provides a comprehensive listing of medical and nursing journals, news-letters, and tables of contents which are available on-line
		Publications are primarily mainstream medical and nursing journals
MMWR	gopher://cwis.usc.edu/11/ The_Health_Sciences_ Campus/Periodicals/ mmwr	Text of the *Morbidity and Mortality Weekly Report*
		Free reader software available to print the publication verbatim

- Maintain awareness of the range of information resources so as to fairly and impartially advise the client
- Maintain a reasonable skill level in the systems available if performing on-line searches
- Avoid bias in the selection of appropriate databases and systems when performing on-line searches

- Maintain alertness with regard to information which might be detrimental to the client's case
- Maintain confidentiality

Conclusion

Searching the literature is a challenging adventure which will expand and enhance the LNC's knowledge base and practice. The sooner skills are developed, the easier it will be to add to one's repertoire of services as the information super-highway expands.

Discussion Questions

1. The first three steps to performing an on-line database search are (in order)
   a. Inputting the MeSH term(s), author, or journal which is the focus of your search
   b. Collecting adequate information from the client to formulate a focused search strategy
   c. Formulating the overall search strategy
   d. Marking the citations which appear to be relevant
   e. a, c, and d
   f. b, c, and a
   g. none of the above
   (Answer: f)
2. Information may be accessed from the NLM via
   a. Grateful Med
   b. Loansome Doc
   c. Commercial vendor
   d. Telephone
   e. a and c
   f. All of the above
   (Answer: f)
3. Databases produced by the National Library of Medicine include
   a. CHEMLINE
   b. CANCERLIT
   c. CATLINE
   d. AIDSTRIALS
   e. a, b, and d
   f. b and d
   g. a, c, and d
   h. all of the above
   (Answer: h)
4. Two benefits of using the Internet to access information are
   a. Cost
   b. Volume
   c. Speed

d. a and b
e. b and c
f. all of the above
(Answer: f)
5. The NLM document retrieval system is called
a. PaperChase
b. DialogLink
c. Loansome Doc
d. SilverPlatter
(Answer: c)

Glossary

Access: Approach to electronic information through any storage medium. When used in relation to the term *on-line*, it implies the availability of suitable telecommunications, plus user IDs and passwords for the on-line host system.

Address: (1) A label or number which identifies a database disk location where information is stored in the computer. (2) May also refer to the location of a host computer on an on-line network.

Backfile: A portion of a database or directory that is separate from the original file. Used as a backup for information which may somehow become lost or deleted.

Bit: A binary digit, i.e., either 0 or 1. The smallest storage unit for data in a computer.

Boolean logic: Consists of logical "operators," also referred to as Boolean operators (AND, OR, and NOT), which allow a searcher to create logical search statements or sets that show relationships. (Example: Meperidine OR Demerol.)

Byte: A group of bits sufficient to define a character. Usually represents eight bits but ten bits are used per character for on-line transmission.

Citation: The bibliographic information (author, title, publication, volume, date, pages) in a complete reference. Often used synonymously with the term *reference.*

Command language: Instructions entered by the searcher which tell the computer retrieval program to perform specific tasks or operations. The command languages vary by vendor system, and symbols may be utilized.

Connect time: The time between log-on to a database and/or termination. It is one of the primary components of on-line searching costs.

Controlled vocabulary: An authorized listing of subject heading or descriptor strings used by indexers to assign subject terminology to items described in records in a database or in files. May also be referred to as a *thesaurus.* (An example is the extensive list of MeSH for MEDLINE.)

Database: An organized collection of data in electronic form, generally related by subject, concept or idea. (*Examples*: MEDLINE, TOXLINE, CHEMLINE.)

Descriptor: A word or phrase used to describe a subject, concept, or idea.

Disk: A circular plate coated with magnetic material used to store digital or machine-readable data. May be "hard" or "floppy."

Downloading: The practice of copying data in electronic form on a computer which may then be manipulated or stored permanently on a personal computer.

Field: An area of a unit record used to store a defined category of data.

File: A collection of related records. The term is often used as a synonym for *database*. Sometimes used to refer to part of a database structure.

Floppy disk: A thin, flexible disk with magnetic surfaces which is used to store computer programs and data. Available in two sizes: 3.5 or 5.0 in.

Free text: A method by which a searcher may select the terms on which searching will be performed without the requirement of matching them to a controlled vocabulary list or thesaurus. Also referred to as text words, *which see.*

Gigabyte: The largest unit of mass storage used in common parlance. One gigabyte is equal to 1000 megabytes, 1 billion bytes, or 500,000 pages of information. Used in huge computer storage depots by major vendors of on-line databases.

Gopher: A service which provides a menulike interface to voluminous amounts of information available on the Internet. The data in "Gopherspace" may be efficiently browsed using a Gopher client.

Hard disk: A rigid storage device coated with a magnetic surface on which computer programs and data may be stored. Typical capacities for personal computers range from five megabytes to 120 megabytes.

Hardware: The equipment and computers used in data storage and processing systems.

Hits: *See* Postings.

Hypermedia: Similar in concept to hypertext (*which see*) except that it also includes multimedia capabilities such as sounds and graphics related to the subject.

Hypertext: A hypertext document contains live links to related pieces of information. (*Example:* In a hypertext document about photography there may be a link or button from the word *camera* which, when pressed, sends the reader to another document which includes both terms or concepts.)

ID code: A code issued by a vendor to individual users for identification.

(the) Internet: The name given to the worldwide collection of data networks (an internet or internetwork) which all speak the TCP/IP network protocol, or "language."

Internetwork: A collection of two or more distinct networks joined together typically using a router to form a larger "network of networks."

Key words: Single words or terms of importance in an article drawn from titles, abstracts, subject headings, or any part of a record which is used for indexing.

Kilobyte: The most common memory storage unit quoted. It is 1000 bytes, or approximately one half page of single-spaced, printed material.

Logical operators: Also called Boolean operators (*see* Boolean logic).

Mainframe: A very large computer which has many megabytes in the central processing unit, or CPU. Because it can store many gigabytes of disk memory, it may act as a host computer which controls searches from instructions or commands from many remote terminals.

Megabyte: One million bytes, 1000 kilobytes, or 500 pages of data.

Modem: Acronym for Modulator-Demodulator. It is a device which allows a terminal to interface with the telecommunications network and converts the electrical or digital signals of a terminal.

Natural language: A language which uses natural speech (words) rather than symbols.

Nettiquette: Ettiquette (manners) on the "net."

Network: A collection of computers linked together by a physical medium (wires, microwaves, etc.) for transmission of data between computers or "nodes" on the network.

Network protocol: The set of rules or "language" used by computers on a network to communicate. (*Examples*: Novell IPX, Appletalk, and TCP/IP.)

Off-line printing: Printed records generated at the mainframe after the user has logged off the computer system. They are usually mailed or faxed to the user.

Off-line searching: Computer processing of a search after the user has entered the appropriate strategy and has logged off the system.

On-line: The term describes the status of a searcher conversing with the host computer in the interactive mode.

Password: A unique set of characters assigned to a user for security purposes to grant access to specific databases.

Postings: The number of citations or references retrieved as a result of a search. Synonymous with *hits*.

Records: Groups of related elements which, when handled as units, make up files.

Reference: *See* Citation.

Search statement: A user-entered instruction that combines key terms and Boolean operators (*which see*) to retrieve a set of citations or records.

Search strategy: The selection of an essential set of planned search statements.

Software: Computer program or sets of computer-readable messages/language which instructs a computer to perform specified tasks.

Stopword list: A list of terms which are ignored for on-line searching, such as articles and prepositions.

Telecommunications: Transmission of voice or data by means of telephone networks or carriers.

Terminal: An electronic device for transmitting to and receiving signals from a computer.

Text word: A single word which appears in the title or abstract of a citation which may be used as a search tool rather than, or in addition to, the subject terms (such as MeSH terms) assigned by an indexer. *Also see* Free text.

Truncation: (1) A means of retrieving words which share a common root or stem. (*Example:* Various kidney conditions truncating as "nephr" would retrieve all terms which use "nephr" as the root, such as nephritis, nephrology, nephropathy, etc.) (2) A means of limiting a lengthy abstract. (The phrase "Abstract truncated at 250 words" may appear at the end of an abstract.)

Update service: A periodic on-line search of a previously selected topic. The search strategy is stored and activated periodically (i.e., monthly or quarterly) to provide new citations. Also known as "Selective Dissemination of Information" or "SDI."

Vendor: A service company which stores databases electronically and makes them available, via telecommunications, to clients for a fee.

World Wide Web (WWW): A collection of hypermedia documents which reside on computers (Web servers) located all over the Internet which are linked together in a "worldwide web" of information. A Web browser (such as Mosaic or Lynx) is needed to gain access to the World Wide Web.

References

Anderson, P. (1994). How to get started with computer literature searches, *American Journal of Hospital Pharmacy,* 51(18), 2303–2304, 2307.

Begg, C. and Berlin, J. (1988). Publication bias: a problem in interpreting medical data, *J. Royal Statistical Society,* 151; 445–463.

Blonde, L., McKibbon, K. A., Zaroukian, M., and Guthrie, R., Jr. (1995). Medical literature management, in Osheroff, J., Ed., *Computers in Clinical Practice: Managing Patients, Information, and Communication,* Philadelphia, American College of Physicians, 37–57.

Bunting, A. (1994). *Current Practice in Health Sciences Librarianship,* Vol 1: *Reference and Information Services in Health Sciences Libraries,* Metuchen, NJ, Medical Library Association and The Scarecrow Press.

Comer, D. and Angell, D. (1994). *The Internet Book,* Prentice-Hall, Englewood Cliffs, NJ.

Department of Clinical Epidemiology and Biostatistics, McMaster University (1982). How to read clinical journals, I. Why to read them and how to start reading them critically, *Canadian Medical Association Journal,* 124, 555–558.

Easterbrook, P., Berlin, J., Gopalin, R., and Matthews, D. (1991). Publication bias in clinical research, *Lancet,* 337, 864–872.

Free Access to Electronic AIDS Information (News). (1995), *MCN-American Journal of Maternal Child Nursing,* 20(2), 118.

Guyatt, G., Sackett, D., and Cook, D. (1993). Users' guide to the medical literature: II. How to use an article about therapy or prevention. A. Are the results of the study valid? *JAMA,* 270(21), 2598–2601.

Hancock, L. (1996). *Physicians' Guide to the Internet,* Philadelphia, Lippincott-Raven Publishers.

Haynes, R., McKibbon, K., Fitzgerald, D., Guyatt, G., Walker, C., and Sackett, D. (1986). How to keep up with the medical literature. V: Access by personal computer to the medical literature, *Annals of Internal Medicine,* 105, 810–814.

Hogarth, M. and Hutchinson, D. (1996). *An Internet Guide for the Health Professional,* 2nd ed., Sacramento, CA, New Wind Publishing.

Jaeschke, R., Guyatt, G., and Sackett, D. (1994). Users' guide to the medical literature: III. How to use an article about a diagnostic test. A. Are the results of the study valid? *JAMA,* 271(5), 389–391.

Kilby, S. (1991). Database searching made easy, *Nursing Education Microworld,* 5(3), 18.

Kleeberg, P. and Masys, D. (1995). Telecommunications, in Osheroff, J., ed., *Computers in Clinical Practice: Managing Patients, Information and Communication,* Philadelphia, American College of Physicians, 127–148.

Nicoll, L. (1993). The practical computer: keeping abreast of the literature electronically, *Nursing Research,* 42(5), 315–317.

Oxman A., Cook, D., and Guyatt, G. (1994). Users' guide to the medical literature: VI. How to use an overview, *JAMA,* 272(17), 1367–1371.

Oxman, A. and Guyatt, G. (1988). Guidelines for reading literature reviews. *Canadian Medical Association Journal,* 138, 697–703.

Oxman, A., Sackett, D., and Guyatt, G. for the Evidence-Based Medicine Working Group (1993). Users' guides to the medical literature: I. How to get started, *JAMA,* 270(17), 2093–2095.

Rogers, G. (1995). Innovative informatics: nurses and the Internet, *Journal of Emergency Nursing,* 21(2), 160–162.

Rosenfeld, L., Janes, J., and Vander Kolk, M. (1995). *The Internet Compendium: Subject Guides to Health and Science Resources,* New York, Neal-Schuman Publishers.

Rowlands, J., Morrow T., Lee N., and Millman, A. (1995). ABC of medical computing: on-line searching, *British Medical Journal,* 311(7003), 500–504.

Shortliffe, E. H. and Perreault, L. E. (1990). *Medical Informatics: Computer Applications in Health Care,* Reading, MA, Addison-Wesley.

Simpson, A. (1990). Grateful Med, a software review, *JAMA,* 263(9), 1293.

Tomaiuolo, N. G. (1995). Accessing nursing resources on the Internet, *Computers in Nursing,* 13(4), 159–164.

Ventura, M. R. (1994). Finding the facts on computer software. *Nursing Dynamics,* 3(3), 19.

Wetther, K. (1994). *The Nuts and Bolts of Legal Nurse Consulting,* Carlsbad, CA, Medical Legal Resources.

Resources

National Network of Libraries of Medicine (NN/LM)
National Library of Medicine (NLM)
8600 Rockville Pike
Bldg. 38, Room B1-E03
Bethesda, MD 20894
(301) 496-4777

For regional services and information, call (800) 338-7657

National Technical Information Service
5285 Port Royal Road
Springfield, VA 22161
(800)-423-9255
Distributor for Grateful Med software

On-line Database Services

The following services provide a number of databases, including MEDLINE. They are quite costly and may be cost-prohibitive for the independent consultant. Law firms or other corporate offices often subscribe to these services, however, providing access for in-house consultants.

- Dialog Information Services, Inc.
  http://www.dialog.com/ (URL, e.g., World Wide Web addresses)
  (415)858-3785 or (800)334-2564

- Mead Data Central, Inc.
  Lexis-Nexis
  http://www.lexis-nexis.com/lncc/
  (513)865-6800 or (800)543-6862

- OVID On-line (formerly CD Plus Technologies)
  http://www.ovid.com/ (URL, e.g., World Wide Web address)
  (212)563-3006 or (800)950-2035

- Westlaw
  http://www.westpub.com/WLAWInfo/
  (612)687-7000 or (800)328-9352

Chapter 25

Discovery and Disclosure

Julianne Hernandez, Barbara Noble, Barbara Stilwell, and Mary Lanz

Contents

Objectives

Upon completion of this chapter, the reader will be able to:

- List five discovery tools used in litigation
- Give one example of non-discoverable, i.e., privileged information
- List two advantages and two disadvantages of interrogatories

- List three purposes of depositions
- Identify three specific ways in which the LNC may assist in deposition preparation

Introduction

The legal nurse consultant (LNC) makes a strong contribution to the litigation process by identifying and refining the medical issues and theoretical underpinnings of the case. While this remains the focus of LNC work, frequently LNCs find themselves in unfamiliar territory during the legal process. The meshing of medicine and law requires some basic understanding of legal terminology and processes. In the same way that neophyte nurses once painstakingly gained familiarity with anatomy, physiology, and pharmacology, new familiarity with "legal anatomy" is essential to cross over to the legal arena. Though not lawyers, LNCs are dealing with the law, which is organized very differently from medicine. A basic knowledge of the legal process will build the LNC's confidence in the role and delineate the boundaries of the medical/legal process.

Rules of Civil Procedure

The entire litigation process is regulated by detailed instructions known as the rules of civil procedure. These rules are an invaluable resource to the LNC, describing exactly how to get around the game board of litigation, from serving the initial complaint to final determination of the matter. Although this chapter will refer to the Federal Rules of Civil Procedure (FRCP), the rules have been adapted either totally or in part by most states. In addition, states have their own rules which are not directly derived from the federal rules. The rules are the LNC's new tool box. It is best to assume nothing, referring to the rules of civil procedure of the state as needed.

Discovery

The purpose of this chapter is to provide general background and insight into the discovery portion of litigation. The courts and legislatures have created various pre-trial tools allowing each adversary to "discover" certain nonprivileged information about the other party's position in the dispute.

Civil action commences with the filing of a complaint with the court, the plaintiff's initial pleading. Under the FRCP, the complaint need only contain a short, plain statement of the claim upon which relief is sought, indication of the type of relief requested, and justification that the court has jurisdiction to hear the case. A complaint's purpose is to inform the defendant and the court of the basis for the plaintiff's claim.

After the complaint has been served and the defendant has responded, each side may still have only a very sketchy view of its adversary's position. *The goal of discovery is to narrow the issues in the case, both legal and factual; to ascertain the opposing party's allegations; to obtain relevant information at the least cost to the clients; to preserve testimony of witnesses unable to testify at trial; and to eliminate the element of surprise in litigation.* This process facilitates and encourages settlements of litigation prior to trial. Thus, during the discovery process, each party learns the strengths and weaknesses of the other's position.

The LNC must be aware that if communication is privileged, the subject matter may not be learned through the discovery process. The most common form of privilege is attorney/client privilege, preventing any third party from obtaining information about the subject matters discussed by attorney and client. Documents containing privileged information should be clearly identified as "attorney work product," thereby making such documents exempt from discovery. FRCP 26(b)1 establishes the guidelines for discovery within the federal court system:

> Parties may obtain discovery regarding any matter not privileged, which is relevant to the subject matter involved in the pending action whether it relates to the claim or defense of the party seeking discovery, or to the claim or defense of any other party, including the existence, description, nature, custody, condition and location of any books, documents or other tangible things and the identity and location of persons having knowledge of any discoverable matter. It is not grounds for objection that the information sought will be inadmissible at the trial if the information sought appears reasonably calculated to lead to the discovery of admissible evidence.

Generally, there are five discovery tools: written interrogatories; requests for production of documents, things, and inspections; requests for admission; physical and mental examinations; and depositions.

Written Interrogatories

Interrogatories are sets of written questions that one party submits to another and which must be answered in writing and under oath; see Appendices 25.1 through 25.4 for an example. FRCP 33(a) provides that: "Any party may serve upon another party written interrogatories to be answered by the party served," meaning that only a plaintiff, defendant, or additional party is required to answer interrogatories. Interrogatories may relate to any matter not privileged that is relevant to the subject matter of the litigation. In practicality, they are a relatively inexpensive discovery tool, but the answers are only as good as the questions asked. Answers to interrogatories are not spontaneous responses and thus do not provide the examining party with the same flexibility as a deposition might. In a deposition, the questioner has the capacity to ask follow-up questions and to probe the witness further for response. Also, as mentioned above, interrogatories may only be directed to the parties in the case and not third persons, and therefore are more limited than depositions.

It is important to review carefully the original complaint for the allegations made. Then, the LNC prepares a list of further information needed to determine the liability aspects of the case, the damages, and an evaluation of the opponent's position. The LNC must know all pertinent medical facts. Often the LNC working in a law firm also assists in preparing and/or answering interrogatories. There are resources available to assist in this process. For example, the state rules of civil procedure offers a *forms* section, setting forth standard questions for medical malpractice and other areas of litigation. If the case involves a unique situation, for example, a nuclear spill, it may be more difficult to determine specific questions which should be asked in interrogatories. An excellent resource is *American Jurisprudence Proof of Facts* (AmJurPOF). This publication describes in detail each aspect of any legal topic and provides background information. One example is the section on hospital-acquired infections, which includes causes, complications, treatment, control measures, accreditation standards, specific liabilities, collateral references, sample testimony of plaintiff and plaintiff's expert, and case illustrations.

Both parties can learn from preliminary information gathered by interrogatories about the opponent's position and expert witnesses to be called at trial. The LNC will learn from additional sources which records still need to be requested. The LNC working with the plaintiff's attorney, will look for information supportive of the plaintiff's case. Working on the defendant's case involves seeking weak areas in the plaintiff's case, including facts that will limit damages.

Each state has laws regarding the length of time parties have to answer the opposing party's discovery request. Answers must be produced within a strict time frame. FRCP 33 states that answers must be served to opposing counsel within 30 days after service of interrogatories, 45 days if the interrogatories are served along with the original complaint. Some states include an additional 5 days for mailing. Toward this end, it is important for the LNC to develop good rapport with the client and to stress the need for timeliness in response. The LNC reviews questions and requests with the client and assists in drafting answers. The completed draft is then submitted to the attorney for final review. Importantly, the client will need to execute the jurat sheet (see Appendix 25.4), a notarized signature sheet attached to the interrogatory answers whereby the client swears that the answers are true and correct. When the final draft responses are complete, the client will receive them for review well before the date for submission to opposing counsel.

Requests for Production

The request for production is a formal written request for copies of relevant, nonprivileged documents, including medical records, personnel records, income tax returns, medical bills, treating physician reports, copies of nonprivileged correspondence, photographs, any and all documents that the opposing party intends to introduce into evidence or use at time of trial, copies of bills, contracts and/or special medical equipment, plane fares related to treatment, and any other documentation of damages claimed in the lawsuit. The LNC then examines the responses to interrogatories to discover additional documents that should be requested. A request to produce can be sent with the initial complaint or at any time during the litigation. The 30 or 45 day period provided for answers to interrogatories also applies to requests for production. Requests for production are governed by FRCP 34. These requests are limited to documents and things that are in the possession, custody, or control of the party upon whom the request is served. Anything not within the party's control or possession need not be produced.

If the LNC needs to examine an original medical record, the request for production should specify "a reasonable time, place, or manner for doing this and the opposing party should reply that the review will be permitted, and when, or state a basis for the objection to this request." (See Appendix 25.5, Defendant's Request for Production.)

Review of Interrogatories and Request for Production

Litigation can grow complicated with the exchange of requests for documents, X-rays, and medical records. Therefore, it is essential for the LNC to develop a method of tracking both what is being produced and what is being received. Checklists serve this purpose. When producing records, the wise LNC counts the number of pages being sent and tracks who is getting a copy and when. Later, when another party, or the same party, requests the materials, there will be a simple record in place to show who got what and when. If the requesting party asks for documents a second time, documentation will verify the previous request and date of mailing.

The LNC must carefully review the opposing party's answers and summarize those answers. Then the medical records are analyzed and information placed into a concise format, easy for the attorney to understand. Usually a narrative of medical issues and facts is valuable for the attorney's use and for potential experts to review. These summaries will be discoverable. The LNC should provide a chronology of all that happened to the plaintiff, identified by date and time. One way to summarize the data and to present it is in a flow sheet format as shown in Table 25.1 or in a summary as shown in Appendix 25.6. It is helpful to include the specialty of all treating physicians, to offer normal ranges for any laboratory testing done and described, and to define and give rationale for prescribing all medications. Another approach is to calendarize medical treatment as in Figure 25.1. In this example, calendarizing is useful in that it reveals to the attorney the number and frequency of prescriptions issued to the plaintiff, by whom, and where they were filled. The LNC's job is to relate the facts of the case in a format easily understandable by the attorney.

Request for Admissions

Requests for admissions are written requests by one party asking another party to acknowledge the truth of certain facts or the authenticity of certain materials. The party served must file a written answer or objection within 30 days, or such time as the individual state allows. The answer must admit parts that are true, deny any other parts specifically, or detail a reason why the party can neither truthfully admit or deny the matter. If the party upon whom the admissions are served fails to respond, the requests are admitted as written. Requests for admission are used most often to narrow issues of fact or law that are essential to one's case. They also provide one way to establish the authenticity of documents provided during discovery.

Table 25.1 Medical History Chronology
Mary Owens — Re: Owens vs. Smith et al.

Date	Physician/Place	Diagnosis	Diagnostic Exams	Observations/Procedures	Treatment
6/19/31				Date of birth in Choctaw, Oklahoma	
6/13–19/76	George Gaynor The Oaks Hospital	1. Rule out cardiac disease or coronary insufficiency 2. Possible degenerative disk disease with radicular pain to the left upper extremity 3. Rule out polycythemia	STRESS TEST: Abnormal findings GALLBLADDER X-RAYS: normal except for a small sliding hiatus hernia CHEST X-RAY: showed interstitial fibrosis and some degenerative changes to C5–6 of the cervical spine	She had a high blood count and a complaint of chest pain. She also complained of neck pain and numbness to the left upper arm along with some radicular paid down the left trapezius. Bone marrow studies showed the borderline polycythemia to be due to pulmonary fibrosis. She was seen by a cardiologist.	℞: Persantine (vasodilator) Aspirin Physical therapy to include cervical traction and hot packs Inderal (antiarrhythmics) Valium Febridyne #3 (analgesic with codeine)
6/20–22/76	D.G. Richards City Hospital		CORONARY ANGIOGRAM: exam was essentially normal with no mitral valve prolapse or undue thickening of the left ventricle	45-year-old female with a 1.5 year history of intermittent discomfort in the left inframammary area radiating to the left arm. A recent treadmill test at The Oaks was positive. Blood pressure 130/60, pulse 100. Exam revealed a positive left thoracic outlet syndrome with minimal costochondral tenderness on the left. Based on testing, it was felt that her discomfort was due to left thoracic outlet syndrome.	℞: Low fat diet Ascriptin (Maalox-coated aspirin) Persantine

Date	Location	Diagnosis	Findings / Test	Clinical Notes	Treatment
6/24/76	George Gaynor Office			Weight: 142.5 lbs. Patient had a negative coronary arteriogram, but does have thoracic outlet syndrome. Has numbness of the left hand. Also has diminished sensation to pain in L4–5.	℞: Motrin, Robaxin
8/11/76	George Gaynor Office			Still has burning of the left scapular area between the medial border and spine.	Injection of Aristocort into two trigger points. Injection into right mid thoracic/paraspinal region
8/18/87	George Gaynor Office			Weight: 144 lbs. Patient in constant pain.	
8/27/76	George Gaynor Office	Possible cervical disk rupture		Weight: 142 lbs. She may be a little bit improved, but she still has pain. There was no improvement from the injection. Will admit into the hospital.	
8/31/76–9/2/76	George Gaynor Medical Plaza Hospital	Herniated nucleus pulposus at C6–7 of the cervical spine	CERVICAL MYELOGRAM: showed an extradural defect at C6–7 with bilateral widening of the nerve root	Chief Complaint: neck pain radiating down the left upper extremity into the left upper chest area. Exam showed tenderness and limitation of range of neck motion due to pain. Deep tendon reflexes are normal. Her blood chemistry did show an elevated blood sugar, but this was not felt to be significant.	℞: Motrin (mild analgesic), Robaxin (musculo-skelatal relaxant)
9/17/76	George Gaynor Office			Weight: 144 lbs. Patient still having trouble. Return as needed.	

Table 25.1 Medical History Chronology (continued)
Mary Owens — Re: Owens vs. Smith et al.

Date	Physician/Place	Diagnosis	Diagnostic Exams	Observations/Procedures	Treatment
9/13/90–10/12/90	George Gaynor Medical Plaza Hospital	Recurrent herniated lumbar disk, L4–5 with degenerative disk	MRI OF LUMBAR SPINE: large herniated pulposus at L4–5 which is centered slightly to the left of midline; post-op changes at this level from prior laminectomy LUMBAR SPINE X-RAY: status post laminectomy at L5–S1 and interbody fusion at L4–5; no spondylolysis or spondylolisthesis is noted CT SCAN OF LUMBAR SPINE: status post inner body fusion at L4–5 with minimal protrusion of the bone plug into the spinal canal; massive epidural fibrosis surrounding the thecal sac and nerve roots at L4–5 BLOOD CHEMISTRY: Glucose 165 (66–110) Sodium 130 (135–145) Potassium 3.0 (3.5–5.0) LDH 350 (83–200)	SURGERY: Assisted by Dr. Ralph Dodge, Drs. Miller and Christensen performed a posterior L4–5 re-exploration with L4 & L5 nerve root decompression, with reexploration, removal of large central recurrent L4–5 disk, with discectomy and posterior lumbar interbody fusion. Prognosis is guarded due to the discovery of a great deal of scar tissue at the L4–5 nerve root and surrounding epidural sac. HOSPITAL COURSE: Post-operatively, she had weakness of the left leg and weakness of dorsiflexion of the left foot.	℞: Baclofen Flexeril Anaprox

10/24/90 Thomas Miller Office

CURRENT MEDS:
Baclofen (skeletal muscle relaxant)
Anaprox (non steroidal, anti-inflammatory agent)
Vicodin (analgesic)

She is improving. A good majority of her left leg pain is resolving and her foot strength is improving. She still does not have much dorsiflexion of her toes, but her anterior tibialis muscle group is better. She is wearing a back brace. Overall, things seem to be improving. To return in 2 weeks

11/15/90 Thomas Miller Office

She has had more back pain. This may be related to her activities. She has some slight residual discomfort in the lateral calf, but most of her pain is in the back and right hip. This should resolve with time. She continues to cut down on the Vicodin. To return in 2 weeks when she sees Dr. Christensen.

11/26/90 Thomas Miller Office

CURRENT MEDS:
Flexeril (musculoskeletal relaxant)
Anaprox
Vicodin
Baclofen

She still has "a great deal" of back pain along with pain in the right hip and groin. However, she has been increasing her activities and she is finding things somewhat easier to do. She was on Percodan before her surgery and now she is down to 3 Vicodin a day. She reports that upon rising in the morning she has bilateral leg cramping and numbness which improves during the day. He wants her to get down from 2 pills to 1 a day. She can dorsiflex her foot. Discussed with the patient and her daughter the need for surgery and her overall limitations. She has a good disposition and seems to be accepting things in stride. To return in January.

**Table 25.1 Medical History Chronology (continued)
Mary Owens — Re: Owens vs. Smith et al.**

Date	Physician/Place	Diagnosis	Diagnostic Exams	Observations/Procedures	Treatment
1/7/91	Thomas Miller Office			She seems to be doing well. Her leg and foot weakness have improved almost back to normal and she has been having less leg pain — the pain is tolerable. She still takes Vicodin 3–4 tablets/day. Told to stop taking the Baclofen.	CURRENT MEDS: Vicodin Flexeril Baclofen Anaprox

Physical and Mental Examinations

An adverse party may require a physical or mental examination of a person by a "impartial" doctor when that physical or mental condition is at issue in a lawsuit. In practice, physical and mental examination usually is limited to personal injury or paternity suits. If there is no agreement between the parties as to medical examinations, a compulsory exam is available when (1) the mental or physical condition, including the blood group of a person, is "in controversy"; and (2) the requesting party demonstrates there is "good cause" for ordering such an examination. The party requesting the exam can select the doctor to conduct it. The role of the LNC in this case can be to assist the attorney in selecting said physician, make arrangements for the actual examination, and attend the exam as an observer.

Depositions

A deposition is the oral examination of any person a party believes has relevant information. Deposition testimony is like trial testimony in that the entire process is conducted under oath and recorded by a court reporter. The deposition is an opportunity to question the party and further assess the strength of the case. It is the opportunity to evaluate the impression a witness will make on a jury. The principal purposes of deposition are

- Identify the opposition's issues and opinions
- Explore issues likely to arise at trial
- Preserve testimony if the witness is unavailable at the time of trial
- Identify other sources of relevant evidence
- Provide material for summary judgment motion and impeachment of witnesses at trial
- Identify and explain documentary and physical evidence
- Identify what witnesses *do not* know
- Obtain admissions

The LNC has a strong role before the actual deposition of witnesses. Before any oral deposition, the attorney and LNC should review answers to previous interrogatories, all documents produced, and any other information obtained relating to the lawsuit. This review makes it possible to identify persons whose oral depositions should be taken, and areas and wording of questions to be pursued at deposition.

To prepare the attorney for the medical malpractice deposition, the LNC must identify the applicable standards of care and the failure of each deponent to meet the standard. It will simplify the task to list specifically each standard and how it was breached, indicating what supportive documentation appears in the medical records. The attorney needs to quickly access this information with page numbers from that medical record.

The LNC should also prepare deposition questions for the attorney in all areas relating to medical issues. A review of interrogatories and medical records, identifies areas that need clarification. For example, if a nurse deponent documented in the

Sun	Mon	Tues	Wed
		1	2
6	7 • Vicodin #50 ^^^^^^^^^^^^^^^^^^ Vicodin #50 filled at City Pharmacy in Austin	8	9
13	14	15	16
20	21 • Vicodin #50 ^^^^^^^^^^^^^^^^^^^^^ Vicodin #50 filled at City Pharmacy in Austin	22	23
27	28 • Xanax 0.5 mg #42 ^^^^^^^^^^^^^^^^^^^^ Xanax 0.5mg #42 filled at City Pharmacy in Austin	29	30

Figure 25.1   June 1993 Office Records from Dr. Sam Smith on John Jones

nurses' notes that the patient was "uncooperative" but did not relate the behavior to its apparent cause, for example, poor oxygenation, the attorney would need to explore this area further. The LNC could educate the attorney regarding types of safety features of relevant monitoring equipment, etc.

Preparation is key to winning lawsuits, and the LNC soon realizes that oral depositions are extremely important in evaluating the strength or weakness of the opponent's position. Prior to each, the LNC must gather as much information about the deponent as possible. If the deposition of a medical expert will be taken, the attorney needs all related information. A review of a copy of that expert's *curriculum vitae*, determines board certification in the appropriate areas and prior practice experience. One would contact the relevant medical board to determine if the deponent has been subject to formal disciplinary action against his or her license. Competency is at issue and should the individual deponent have had problems in the past, it will strengthen the opposition's case. It is wise to request copies of all such investigative files for use during deposition.

Thurs	Fri	Sat
3	4	5
10	11	12
17	18	19
24	25	26 • Vicodin #30 as needed 4 times daily for severe headaches

Figure 25.1 (continued)

In addition, it is important to determine if the testifying expert had ever been a defendant in a medical malpractice case. Requesting searches of the applicable civil trial record in the state in which the individual practices medicine and a copy of the complaint and docket sheet to determine any relevant allegations is appropriate. If the expert has also testified in other cases, requesting copies of previous depositions is useful. Contradicting testimony in the current deposition will lessen the credibility of that witness.

The LNC must perform an exhaustive literature search to find everything the expert has written in regard to the specific issue in contest. Computerized medical literature searches help to do this quickly. It is also important to get hard copies of relevant journal articles, book chapters, and textbooks. The LNC should summarize each article, pointing out areas of inconsistency with the opposition's point of view in the particular case. An expert testifying in contrast to written articles may lessen the expert's credibility. Intense preparation for deposition prevents surprises.

One must not overlook the importance of a deposition. It is the one time it is possible to require a nonparty to appear for questioning or to produce documents. The LNC needs to understand the purpose and use of subpoenas toward that end. A subpoena is a tool requiring a witness or a non-party to appear, or to produce documents. Subpoenas preserve one's rights at the time of trial by preserving the ability to assess cost to anyone not complying. More importantly, subpoenas have the force and effect of a court order and are strictly interpreted in accordance with the language written therein. Therefore, accuracy is crucial. If the individual is not named correctly, the person does not need to comply with the subpoena. During the trial phase of litigation, a subpoena to appear is a command from the court and ought not to be ignored. Without a subpoena, there is no recourse if the witness fails to show. During the discovery phase, the subpoena makes it possible to retrieve documents from third parties. One caveat: a subpoena *duces tecum* (to appear accompanied by certain documents or things), and subpoenas for deposition *are not* required for a party to the lawsuit, but are for nonparties.

In summary, the discovery phase of litigation is key to the outcome of any case. LNCs are unique members of the law team because of their superior knowledge about the medical aspects of complex litigation. Therefore, the LNC contributes greatly to each phase of discovery and assists in defining and redefining the issues of the case.

Appendix 25.1
Defendant's First Set of Interrogatories to Plaintiff

NO. 96-1234-Z

JOHN PLAINTIFF	§	IN THE DISTRICT COURT OF
	§	
VS.	§	HARRIS COUNTY, TEXAS
	§	
DAVID DEFENDANT, M.D.	§	007th JUDICIAL DISTRICT

TO: Plaintiff, John Plaintiff, by and through his attorney of record, W. E. Cheatum, DEWEY, CHEATUM & HOWELL, P.C., 555 N. 23rd, Houston Texas 77001

Pursuant to Rule 168 of the Texas Rules of Civil Procedure, the Defendant, , serves the attached Interrogatories upon you, the answers to which shall be made under oath separately and fully in writing within thirty (30) days after the service of such interrogatories and shall be given to the undersigned counsel of record. To the extent possible, each interrogatory should be answered in the spaces following each interrogatory. The answers should be signed under oath in the space following the last interrogatory. The Defendant also requests that the Plaintiff continue to supplement the answers to the interrogatories as provided by Rule 168. The original of the Interrogatories is being forwarded to the above attorney as required by the Texas Rules of Civil Procedure.

Respectfully submitted,

GOOD DEFENSE FIRM

By: _____
   Ima Good
   SBN 01010101

Address
Houston, Texas 77001
(713) 555-5555
(713) 555-5555 FAX
Attorneys for Defendant
David Defendant, M.D.

Appendix 25.2
Certificate of Service

I hereby certify that I have caused a true and correct copy of the foregoing instrument to be served upon opposing counsel of record herein, by certified mail, return receipt requested, or by hand delivery, and upon all other counsel of record herein, by regular mail, on this _____ day of _____, 19___.

_____
Ima Good

Appendix 25.3
Defendant's First Set of Interrogatories to Plaintiff

1. Please state your name, date of birth, place of birth, current address, social security number, driver's license number, date of each marriage, and the name and age of each dependent child.
2. State what education you have had, including the names and addresses of the schools you have attended and list all diplomas and degrees you have received.
3. Please state specifically the nature of any damage and/or injuries suffered by you which you allege to have been caused by this Defendant.
4. Have you recovered from the damages and/or injuries you allege to have been caused by this Defendant in this lawsuit? If not, what complaints do you still have?

5. If you have been hospitalized since the date of the incident made the basis of this suit for any reason, please state:
    a) the name and address of the hospital;
    b) the date of admission and date of discharge; and
    c) the total hospital charges.

6. For all of the doctors you have seen for any reason related to the incident made the basis of this suit, please give:
    a) the names and addresses of said doctors;
    b) the date you saw each doctor;
    c) what each doctor charged you; and
    d) the diagnosis as related to you by each doctor of your injuries, damages, or complaints.

7. If any doctor has told you that you will need to undergo a surgical procedure or other treatment as a result of the injuries and damages which you allege were caused by this Defendant, please state:
    a) the name and address of each doctor;
    b) the date such doctor(s) told you that you needed surgery or other treatment;
    c) the type of surgical procedure or other treatment such doctor(s) said you would need to undergo; and
    d) the approximate cost of such surgery or other treatment.

8. Has any doctor been critical of the care given to you by this Defendant? (This excludes consulting experts whose opinions are privileged by the Texas Rules of Civil Procedure or are protected by the attorney client privilege.) If so, please state:
    a) the name and address of said doctor(s);
    b) the date and place such statements were made;
    c) the names and addresses of all persons who heard said statements;
    d) the substance of such statements.

9. Has anyone every told you that this Defendant or anyone else caused the injuries or complaints made the basis of this suit? If so, please state:
    a) Specifically, what was said about who caused said injuries;
    b) The date these statements were made;
    c) The names and current addresses of all witnesses who heard such statements; and
    d) The names and current addresses of all persons making such statements.

10. Please state the following information regarding your employment history for ten (10) years prior to the date of the incident made the basis of this suit:
    a) the name and address of each employer for whom you worked, and the name of your immediate supervisor;
    b) the period of time you worked for each employer and the reason each employment terminated;
    c) what you earned per hour in each employment and your average weekly wage in each employment; and
    d) the nature of your duties in each employment.

11. Please furnish the following information with respect to your work history since the date of the incident made the basis of this suit.
    a) the name and address of each employer or whom you have worked and the name of your immediate supervisor;

b) the approximate period of time that you worked for each employer and details concerning the reason that such employment was terminated;

c) your average weekly wage for each employment period;

d) the nature of your employment for each employer and the duties that you performed; and

e) whether any complaints have been made to you by any employer regarding the manner in which you performed your job. If so, please describe these complaints.

12. Have you missed any time from work as a result of any injuries or damage allegedly caused by this Defendant? If so, please state how much time you have lost from work and how much in wages. If any, you have lost as a result of the incident made the basis of this suit.

13. Provide a complete chronological medical history for the last ten years listing all hospital admissions (include name and address of hospital or medical care facility), physicians who have treated you (include names, addresses, and telephone numbers for each), medications prescribed to you, the conditions you were treated for, and the treatment you received.

14. State whether you have ever had or now have any unusual physical or mental condition or ailment such as diabetes, a heart condition, arthritis, etc., and if so, describe them in detail and state whether you have ever received medical treatment for these conditions.

15. State whether you have ever been convicted of or plead guilty to any felony offense or misdemeanor involving moral turpitude, and whether you have ever been confined in any jail or prison. State whether you are presently on probation in connection with any conviction and, if so, state the name and location of your probation officer.

16. State the amount of taxable income that you reported for the preceding five (5) years. If you will do so without a Motion to Produce, attach your answers to these interrogatories a copy of your income tax return for each of the aforesaid years.

17. State whether you have ever had a claim for workmen's compensation or any other type claim and/or lawsuit for personal injury against any person, firm, corporation or such claims or lawsuits and the details surrounding such claims or lawsuits, including the part of your body alleged to have been injured.

18. Please state the name, current business address and business telephone number, and area of specialty of any expert witness which you may call to testify at the time of trial of this cause. Also, please state each expert's mental impressions and opinions.

19. Please state the specific text of each report, factual observation and opinion that each expert identified in response to the preceding Interrogatory has made regarding this lawsuit. In the alternative, please attach true and complete copies of each expert's report(s).

20. State in detail the treatment, alleged complications arising from the treatment, lack of treatment, omissions, and/or all negligent acts you contend were committed or omitted during this Defendant's course of treatment which contributed to any injuries or damages claimed by you. Include the date and time of treatment when describing acts or omissions and include *which* agent or representative who committed such act or omission.

21. What expenses or monetary losses, other than lost wages and medical expenses, do you attribute to injuries and/or damage which you allege to have been caused by this Defendant?

22. Please state the names, addresses, and telephone numbers of all persons with knowledge of relevant facts concerning Plaintiff's claim(s) against this Defendant, the treatment in question, Plaintiff's alleged damages, or any other aspect of this suit.

23. Please list the name, address, and telephone number of any pharmacy where you obtained medications for two (2) years prior to the incident giving rise to this lawsuit and to the present. Please include your prescription number(s) and medication(s) obtained.

24. Please state the name, current and/or last known address, current and/or last known employer, home and telephone number of all eyewitnesses to the treatment made the basis of this lawsuit.

25. Please state whether there exist any Medicate/Medicaid liens, or whether any Plaintiff herein receives Medicare/Medicaid benefits related to the care and treatment made the subject of this lawsuit.

Appendix 25.4
Jurat Sheet

THE STATE OF TEXAS	§
	§
COUNTY OF HARRIS	§

BEFORE ME, the undersigned authority, on this day personally appeared JOHN PLAINTIFF, known to me to be the person whose name is subscribed to the above and foregoing instrement, who, after being by me duly sworn, upon oath stated that he has read the foregoing instrument and knows the contents thereof, and states that the answers are true and correct.

_____

JOHN PLAINTIFF

SUBSCRIBED AND SWORN TO BEFORE ME, the undersigned authority, on this the _____ day of _____, 1996, to certify which witnss my hand and seal of office.

_____

Notary Public in and for
The State of Texas

My Commission Expires:

_____

Appendix 25.5
Request for Production

CAUSE NO. 96-1234-Z

JOHN PLAINTIFF	§	IN THE DISTRICT COURT
	§	
VS.	§	007TH JUDICIAL DISTRICT
	§	
DAVID DEFENDANT, M.D.	§	HARRIS COUNTY, TEXAS

REQUEST FOR PRODUCTION

TO: Plaintiff, JOHN PLAINTIFF, by and through his attorney of record, W. E. Cheatum, DEWEY, CHEATUM & HOWELL, P. C., 5555 N 23rd, Houston Texas 77001

Pursuant to T.R.C.P. 167, Defendant DAVID DEFENDANT, M.D. requests that the following documents and/or tangible things be produced for inspection and copying at the offices of the undersigned within thirty three (33) days from receipt of this request.

1. Plaintiff's federal income tax returns for the past five years, including W-2 forms, if any lost wages or diminished earnings capacity is claimed in this suit;
2. All doctor, hospital, medication and all other medical bills and expenses that are claimed in this suit;
3. The names, addresses, and phone numbers of all expert witnesses whom Plaintiff may call to testify in this case;
4. All reports, correspondence or writing of any kind from all expert witnesses whom Plaintiff may call to testify in this case;
5. All statements, as defined by T.R.C.P. 166b(2)(g), made by this Defendant or any of his agents or employees;
6. All recordings of any expert witness in this case whom Plaintiff may call to testify in this case;
7. All correspondence or writings from Defendant to Plaintiff or members of Plaintiff's family;
8. All medical, doctor, or hospital records related to Plaintiff's alleged injuries in Plaintiff's possession or constructive possession (please sign and return with your responses to these Requests the attached medical authorization);
9. Any and all documentation of any damages claimed in this lawsuit;
10. Any and all documents or written materials which you contend were authored by, published by, produced by, manufactured by, or made by this Defendant that is in any way relevant to the above-styled lawsuit, including but not limited to documents the Plaintiff intends to introduce into evidence at the time of trial;
11. Any and all photographs taken of the Plaintiff's alleged damages or injuries;
12. Any and all documents which the Plaintiff intends to introduce into evidence or use at the time of trial for any purpose. This is an ongoing request requiring supplementation pursuant to the Texas Rules of Civil Procedure;
13. All statements, as defined by T.R.C.P. 166b(2)(g), made by any witness with knowledge of relevant facts concerning the incident or treatment made the basis of this suit;
14. Any and all pharmacy records on Plaintiff regarding medications obtained in the five (5) years prior to the incident made the basis of this lawsuit and to the present time, including but not limited to, records indicating the name of the medication, the name and location of the pharmacy filling each prescription, the date each prescription or medication was received, and the name of the physician prescribing such medication;
15. All documents and other tangible items provided to any expert witness whom Plaintiff may call to testify at the trial of this cause or whose work product forms a basis, in whole or in part, of the mental impressions and opinions of a testifying expert.

WHEREFORE, PREMISES CONSIDERED, Defendant, DAVID DEFENDANT, M.D., prays that the above items be produced at the time and place as requested.

Respectfully submitted,

GOOD DEFENSE FIRM

By:_____
Ima Good
SBN: 01010101

address
Houston, Texas 77001
(713) 555-5555
FAX: (713) 555-5555
ATTORNEYS FOR DEFENDANT
DAVID DEFENDANT, M.D.

CERTIFICATE OF SERVICE

I hereby certify that a true and correct copy of the above and foregoing dociment has been forwarded to Plaintiff's counsel of record by certified mail, return receot requested, on this _____ day of _____, 1996.

_____
Ima Good

MEDICAL AUTHORIZATION

TO WHOM IT MAY CONCERN:

This will authorize you to allow Ima Good, or her agents or representatives, to inspect the originals of any and all medical records on JOHN PLAINTIFF which are in your possession or subject to your control, to allow copies to be made of such records, and to discuss JOHN PLAINTIFF'S medical care and treatment with you, PROVIDED:

1. Information obtained by this authorization is for use in the pending litigation, and shall not be disseminated for any other purpose;
2. You are specifically and expressly authorized to accept a copy of this authorization as though it were an original; and
3. You are specifically and expressly released from any liability which would otherwise arise from the release of this information.

Also, a copy of this release may be used as an original.

_____
JOHN PLAINTIFF

S.S. No._____

GIVEN UNDER MY HAND AND SEAL OF OFFICE, this _____ day of _____, 1996.

_____
NOTARY PUBLIC IN AND FOR THE
STATE OF TEXAS

_____
Printed name of notary and expiration
date of commission

Appendix 25.6
Medical Record Summary

JANE JONES
RE: JONES VS. SMITH, ET AL

REGIONAL MEDICAL CENTER
JUNE 22 - 28, 1993

ADMITTING DIAGNOSIS:
Severe dysmenorrhea, rule out endometriosis

ATTENDING PHYSICIAN:
Dr. Ken Smith

JUNE 22, 1993

TIME	CARE PROVIDER	DOCUMENTATION*
6:30 am	Nurse's Notes	44-year-old obese Caucasian female ambulatory to room 13 with male friend. States allergy to sulfa, Demerol, and synthetic plastics.
6:50 am	Nurse's Notes	EKG done. To X-ray via wheelchair. Error. States she had X-ray on 6/21/93.
7:00 am	Nurse's Notes	To OR via stretcher with OR staff.
7:45 am	Anesthesia Record	Height: 5'6", Weight: 270 lbs.
7:50 am	Operating Room Record	Arrival in OR
8:10 am	Operating Room Record	Incision
	Operative Report	Pre-Op Diagnosis: Severe dysmenorrhea, rule out endometriosis. During the laparoscopy, dense adhesions were noted between the rectosigmoid and the posterior uterus. The uterus was densely adherent to the bladder. There was no readily discernible plane of dissection between the left ovary and the rectosigmoid and the pelvic side wall. There was brisk bleeding noted and it was decided at this point that exploratory laparotomy was indicated.

---

* Although not showing in this Appendix, it is always a good practice to reference statements to a page number in the record.

The patient's significant other was notified of the findings and the need to proceed with an exploratory laparotomy.

There was a very hard mass at the rectosigmoid which was densely adherent to the pelvic side wall and posterior lateral aspect of the uterus on the left. Dr. Smith performed a total abdominal hysterectomy and he removed the fallopian tubes and ovaries. Dr. Al Miller performed a resection of the rectosigmoid colon followed by reanastomosis.

Post-Op Diagnosis (per Dr. Smith): Severe pelvic adhesive disease, diverticulitis and pending pathology. (per Dr. Miller): Mass in pelvic colon, probably inflammatory, but cannot exclude malignancy.

11:10 am	Progress Note Dr. Smith	Admitted to diagnostic laparoscope this morning to rule out endometriosis. The patient has severe dysmenorrhea that is progressive and becoming quite incapacitating. The patient requested surgical intervention. She underwent a diagnostic laparoscopy; however, because of severe adhesions surrounding rectosigmoid and left ovary, pelvic side wall and posterior-lateral aspect of uterus, the ---- ---- was not possible and an adequate plane of dissection was not obtained. There was brisk bleeding noted, as such then it was decided to proceed into an exploratory laparotomy. The patient's significant other was apprised of the findings and then of management. In light of patient's symptoms and the severity of the adhesions and a palpable mass in colon, it was decided to proceed with total abdominal hysterectomy and bilateral salpingo-oophorectomy and intraoperative surgery consult. Dr. Miller consented and proceeded with bowel resection and secondary reanastomosis. The patient tolerated this procedure well. Estimated blood loss 600 cc's.
11:15 am	Operating Room Record	Closure
11:30 am	Operating Room Record	To the Recovery Room
11:30 am - 1:10 pm	Recovery Room	[uneventful period]

| 8:00 pm | Progress Note
Dr. Smith | Patient resting well. Vital signs stable. Afebrile. Abdominal incision dressing in place. No vaginal bleeding. ---- draining adequately. Continue present therapy. |
| Untimed | Progress Note
Dr. Miller | Resection of pelvic colon with end-to-end anastomosis. Probable diverticulitis. |

JUNE 23, 1993

| 7:18 pm | Progress Note
Dr. Smith | Complains of being thirsty, No flatus, no bowel movement. Vital signs: Blood Pressure 118/70. Afebrile. Chest — clear. Heart — regular rhythm & rate. Abdomen — obese, soft, appropriately tender. No bowel sounds. Abdomen binder in place. Scant vaginal discharge. Extremities — nontender and negative Homan's sign. Pathology: endometriosis, adenomyosis, diverticulitis. Labs: white blood cell count 10.2, hemoglobin 12.2, hematocrit 34.7, sodium 139, potassium 3.9, chloride 99, carbon dioxide 27, glucose 133, BUN 7.0, creatinine 0.8. Assessment: status post total abdominal hysterectomy and bilateral salpingo-oophorectomy. Stable today. Awaiting return of bowel functions. Plan: continue present management. (2) ambulate. (3) continue nothing by mouth. (4) pathology discussed with patient. |
| 7:40 pm | Progress Note
Dr. Miller | Doing well. ---- explained the colon pathology. Patient states was diagnosed to have diverticulitis some years ago in Austin, Texas. |

Chapter 26

Independent Defense Medical Examinations

Karen L. Wetther

Contents

Objectives

- To state the purpose of a defense medical examination (DME)
- To realize the importance of clarifying with the client the stipulations relating to DMEs which apply to the state in which the client's case was filed
- To list two reasons why a plaintiff's attorney might request the presence of an LNC at the client's DME
- To describe two services an LNC may be asked to provide during a DME
- To state two documents which should accompany the legal nurse examination who attends a DME
- To list two things the LNC should do to prepare for the exam

Introduction

During the discovery phase of litigation, the opposing parties may reach a stalemate regarding physical or mental health issues. The plaintiff is unwilling to accept the settlement offered by the defense, yet the defense is unwilling to offer a greater amount, often based on the belief that the claims of the plaintiff or the medical opinions of the plaintiff's treating physicians or experts are exaggerated. The law allows the defense to have the plaintiff undergo a medical, and under certain circumstances a mental, examination by a health care practitioner of their choice, generally referred to as a defense medical examination (DME) or independant medical examination (IME).

The term *Independent Medical Examination* is rarely used by plaintiff attorneys, who often feel the term is a misnomer since the examination is not really independent or necessarily unbiased as it is performed by a health care practitioner who is selected and paid by the defense. Plaintiff attorneys therefore generally refer to such examinations as DMEs. However, the term *independent* actually means that it is an examination independent of the plaintiff's case.[1]

A similar type of examination, most commonly used in the context of workers' compensation claims, is an agreed medical examination. The plaintiff and defense counsel in those cases generally "agree" on an examiner to examine the injured worker. Workers' compensation cases are governed by different, though similar rules and vary from state to state. Examinations may also be done in the context of Social Security Disability claims and these are governed by federal rules. This chapter, however, is limited to a discussion of DMEs.

Legal nurse consultants (LNCs) may be asked by plaintiff counsel, primarily in personal injury cases, to attend and observe the DME as his or her representative.

This chapter will discuss some of the legal requirements relating to these examinations and the role of the LNC who attends DMEs/IMEs (hereafter referred to as DMEs).

Rule 35 in the Federal Rules of Civil Procedure governs the use of DMEs in federal cases so they will be consistent from state to state. However, the reader should be mindful of the fact that statutes vary by state. There are many similarities from state to state but it is the LNC's responsibility to become familiar with the statute in the Code of Civil Procedure for the state in which the exam he or she is asked to observe is performed. In the statute, there may not be a reference to independent or defense examinations but they may instead be referenced under "Physical and Mental Examinations."

Since every state's statute concerning DMEs cannot be referenced here, the California statute (CCP Section 2032 — Physical and Mental Examinations) is used as an example throughout this chapter.

Purpose of a DME

A physical or mental exam of an opposing party is the best method of evaluating claims of injury, illness, or incapacity by that party. It provides the defendants in personal injury cases the opportunity to select a physician or physicians to examine the plaintiff and to evaluate the injury(s) claimed.

Major Advantages and Disadvantages from the Defense Perspective

Advantages

- May have the opposing party examined by a physician of their choosing
- May provide defense counsel access to reports which might otherwise be protected from discovery (*Note:* discovery rules vary from state to state)
- May provide an opportunity for the defense to initiate surveillance of a plaintiff who has been difficult to locate

Disadvantages

- Costs, such as the examiner's fees for reviewing medical records, performing the exam, and preparing a report
- Necessity to obtain cooperation from plaintiff's counsel with regards to obtaining medical records and X-rays prior to exam
- Necessary reliance on examiner to review medical records and X-rays prior to the exam
- Examination may backfire, e.g., there is the risk that the examiner's findings and report may support or even amplify the examinee's claims. The examiner's testimony in court may therefore weaken the defendant's case

Legal Requirements

A defense medical exam may be ordered or initiated in one of the following ways:

- Stipulation or consent
- Demand
- Court order

Examinations by Stipulation

Most DMEs are arranged by a written stipulation between counsel. The stipulation should clearly define the conditions of the examination (date, time, location, examiner, who may be present, etc.) and should identify the scope of the examination as well as each test and/or procedure that may be performed.

Examination by Demand

A defendant or cross-defendant (e.g., a party who is brought into the case by a defendant who feels that party shares some or all liability and therefore files a cross-complaint against that party) in a personal injury case is allowed one physical examination of the plaintiff by simply serving a written demand on the plaintiff or cross-complainants.[2]

Limitations

- Only a physical examination of a personal injury plaintiff is allowed by demand,[3] even if the plaintiff claims psychological damages, a mental examination may not be obtained by demand, although it may be ordered by the court unless the plaintiff limits the specific claims and evidence of mental suffering which will be made.
- The physical exam is limited to the specific injury or condition which is in controversy, e.g., that which is the subject of litigation.[4]
- The defense is limited to one examination only, even if multiple injuries are claimed. Should the defendant feel additional examinations are necessary, he or she may seek a court order.
- The examination of the plaintiff is not to include any diagnostic test or procedure that is painful, protracted, or intrusive.[5] A court order may authorize such tests or procedures, although this rarely happens because few physicians will perform them without the patient's express consent.
- The demand in most cases must specify the date, time, and place of examination, the identity and specialty of the examiner, and the manner, conditions, scope, and nature of the examination.[6]
- The California statute requires that the examination must be conducted within 75 miles of the plaintiff's residence.[7]
- In most states, the examination must be conducted by a licensed physician "or other appropriate licensed health care practitioner."[8]

Unclarified Information

Although it may not be expressly stated in the statute, it may be permissible for the examination to be performed by persons working under the general direction of a licensed physician or other health care practitioner. (This would apply particularly in cases where the examination is actually performed by the retained examiner but X-rays and laboratory tests, if allowed, are done by someone under the examiner's direction.)[9]

Even though the statute may not specifically stipulate the conditions of the examination, the demand should be as specific as possible to avoid unpleasant surprises or refusals by the plaintiff, e.g., observers who will be present (such as LNCs), the examiner's intent to photograph or audiotape the exam, and the types of tests and procedures which may be utilized during the exam.[10]

Objections by the Plaintiff

The plaintiff may state any objections to the demand in writing and may refuse to be examined, forcing defendants to obtain a court order if they wish to proceed.

Examination upon Court Order

Requirement of "Good Cause"

A court order for physical or mental examination must be based on a showing of "good cause,"[11] which in most cases requires that the examination has relevancy to the subject matter and that specific facts are presented which justify discovery, such as a need for information sought and lack of means for otherwise obtaining it.[12]

Good cause may be found in the event that the plaintiff claims additional injuries, that his or her injuries have worsened, if tests or procedures are requested, or because there has been a lapse of time since the initial exam. If the plaintiff's injuries are complex, several exams with various specialists may be necessary and may be allowed by the court if the defense is successful in showing good cause.[13]

Purpose

The purpose of requiring a court order in specific situations relating to IMEs is to protect the privacy of the examinee by preventing "fishing expeditions" by the opposing party who speculates that something of interest might surface.[14]

Medical Examinations

If there is a showing of good cause, a mental examination may be performed by either a licensed physician or a licensed clinical psychologist with a doctoral degree and at least 5 years of experience diagnosing mental and emotional disorders.[15]

Site of Medical or Mental Examination

When the examination is pursuant to court order, the person to be examined may be required to travel to wherever the examiner is located.[16] However, if an examinee is required to travel more than 75 miles from his or her place of residence, the court's order must be based on a finding of good cause for the travel involved and be conditioned on the moving party paying the examinee's reasonable travel costs.[17]

Limit on X-Rays

Due to public concern regarding excessive exposure to X-rays, the Discovery Act allows an examinee to avoid submitting to X-ray examinations for purposes of an IME but provides the examiner access to the plaintiff's existing X-rays of the same site to be examined. No additional X-rays may be taken without the consent of the plaintiff or on court order for good cause shown.[18]

Who May Attend?

State courts generally permit certain other persons to attend a physical examination conducted for discovery purposes, but not a mental examination. The examinee's attorney may observe and record a physical examination in person or through a representative designated in writing.[19] The attorney or representative is permitted to observe every phase of the examination to assure that the examination is restricted to the scope ordered by the court and to prevent improper questioning by the examining physician.[20] An LNC often attends as an attorney's designated representative.

The examinee's attorney is entitled to record stenographically or by audiotape any words spoken to or by the examinee during any phase of the examination to assure an objective record, thereby avoiding disputes between the attorney and the examiner. Videotaping of the examination is not permitted. Any additional person's presence is at the discretion of the court.

Some examiners have the examinee's history taken by a staff member and may also have a staff member record the findings of his examination according to his instruction during the examination. The examiner may also choose to have a female staff member from his office present during the examination of a female as a matter of practice. In this situation, the LNC should obtain the name of that staff member and include in the report the time when the staff member entered and exited the exam room and how attentive he or she was during the exam. In some states, the staff members who assist the examiner are not allowed to take notes and the defense is not entitled to have an observer present.

Use of an Interpreter

According to the California statute, an interpreter is required in any medical examination requested by the defendant or by an insurance company if the examinee does not proficiently speak or understand English.[21]

Controls on Abuse

If the examination is disrupted by the attorney or designated representative, such as by instructing the examinee how to answer questions, the examiner may suspend the exam. The party who ordered the examination may move for a protective order and for a monetary sanction.[22]

Conversely, if the examiner becomes abusive to the examinee or attempts to perform unauthorized tests or procedures, plaintiff's counsel or designated representative may also suspend the examination and move for a protective order and monetary sanctions against the party who ordered the examination.[23]

Deposition of the Examiner

In the event that the examinee's counsel is concerned about the accuracy of the examiner's report or conclusions, he may depose the examiner, inspect the notes and records from the examination, and introduce contradictory evidence at trial.[24]

Exchange of Medical Reports

Whether the DME in a personal injury case is obtained by stipulation, demand, or court order, the plaintiff may demand in writing that the defendant provide the examiner's report and a copy of all earlier examinations of the same condition of the examinee made by the DME examiner or any other examiner.[25] Earlier examinations may include candid reports of examiners which may have been generated when the claim was being investigated by the insurance carrier, some of which may be devastating to the defense and may provide information about the weaknesses of their case. Consideration must be given to this possibility by defense counsel prior to ordering a DME.

The California statute (and those in many states) only requires that reports of actual examiners be exchanged so presumably the requirement does not apply to reports of medical consultants who have not personally examined the plaintiff, although this is not clearly stated in the California code. It appears that those consultants' reports are still protected as work product.[26] However, if they are designated as experts at a later time, this protection no longer applies.

The Role of the Legal Nurse Consultant

Once the LNC understands the legal requirements relating to DMEs in their state, the role of the LNC as "designated observer" should become clear. However, clients may not always be specific as to what they expect of the LNC so it is his or her responsibility to determine the expectations for each examination observed.

The following suggestions may help to prepare the LNC who is asked to attend and observe a DME:

- The details of the case should be discussed with the client so the LNC is familiar with the site of the body to be examined, the date of loss, prior treatment, etc. A copy of the response to the stipulation, demand, or court order should be requested and should be reviewed and taken to the DME. It is also helpful to have in one's possession a copy of the rules from the Code of Civil Procedure which apply to the exam.

- Clarify with the client prior to the exam what the LNC is expected to do at that particular DME, since clients' expectations may differ.

- Research, if necessary, the type of examination that is appropriate for the site of the body to be examined.

- Arrive at the examiner's office well ahead of the examinee, who should be instructed to arrive a few minutes before the scheduled examination time. This way the LNC can be assured that the examinee will not be taken directly into an examination room and can also prevent the examinee from completing any forms or questionnaires at the request of the physician's office staff if the examinee's attorney has prohibited this (this should be stated in the response to the stipulation, demand, or court order).

- If the plaintiff is unknown to the LNC, the two should converse briefly and make introductions. The examinee's case should not be discussed. The attorney in almost all cases will have told the examinee that a registered nurse will attend and observe the examination as their representative.

- The LNC and examinee should be aware that the office receptionist may have been asked by the physician to observe the examinee's actions and behavior in the reception area to determine whether they are different than those observed in the examining room.

- In most cases, the LNC will be asked to keep a detailed written account or time log of what occurs from the time the plaintiff arrives until they exit the office. This should include time spent filling out forms in the waiting room prior to the examination (in the rare situation in which this may be allowed), sitting in the waiting room, having X-rays taken or blood drawn (if authorized), being escorted to the examining room, waiting in the examining room, time that the examiner or any staff members enter or exit the room, a detailed account of what transpires in the examining room, or anything that happens once the examination is completed prior to leaving the office. If the examiner exits the room for phone calls or for any other reason, this should also be recorded. The times of commencement and completion of the examination are of specific importance to the attorney. In case of a dispute regarding the examination, the written notes and audiotape can be consulted and compared for clarification.

- The LNC should politely introduce himself or herself as a representative of the attorney who retained the LNC when the examiner enters the room. Plaintiff's counsel may want the LNC to conceal the fact that he or she is a nurse, preferring that the examiner assume the LNC is an attorney or paralegal (i.e., nonmedical). While the LNC should not lie if asked his or her title specifically, this information does not need to be offered unsolicited.

- The attorney who has retained the LNC may not want the LNC to provide the examiner with a business card, as the attorney does not want the examiner or opposing counsel to be able to contact the LNC directly. If the LNC has been advised not to give the examiner a business card, the LNC can simply state that he or she can be reached through the attorney (in most states, they would be prohibited from contacting the LNC directly). Often the examiner asks for the business card so that the persons present at the examination can be noted in the examiner's report. The LNC can simply spell his or her name if the examiner requests the LNC's card for this purpose.

■ While audiotaping is allowed in most states, the examiner may not have been informed of this by his or her client so it is imperative for the LNC to know what the law allows in order to confidently inform the examiner if a dispute arises. Having a copy of the response to the stipulation, demand, or court order in hand should quickly resolve this problem.

■ If the examiner has any dispute concerning the LNC's presence during the examination, what is disallowed in that particular case (such as intrusive tests or X-rays), or audiotaping and the legal nurse consultant does not have a copy of the response to the stipulation, demand, or court order, the prudent way to handle such a situation is to suggest that the examiner contact the defense counsel who retained the examiner's services. In most cases, it is simply a lack of communication and knowledge of the law and can be clarified with a telephone call, if necessary.

■ The LNC should maintain a low profile during the exam. The observer is generally not permitted to interfere with the examination unless the examiner is abusive to the examinee, examines sites which are not a subject of the litigation, causes the examinee pain, or follows a line of questioning not permitted. If any of these occur, the LNC may bring this to the examiner's attention and may be permitted to suspend the examination and leave with the plaintiff. The client should be notified expediently.

■ Observations may include (depending on the type of exam):
  1. The examinee
     a. Use of any assistive devices (crutches, cane, walker)
     b. Gait
     c. Limitation of movements
     d. Ability to tolerate sitting
     e. Position changes
     f. Grimacing or verbal responses during exam (examiner is not allowed to hurt the patient)
     g. Degree of effort expended during active range of motion, resistance testing, push/pulls, and other participative portions of the exam
     h. Clothing worn
     i. Visible scars in area of injury
  2. The examiner
     a. Interaction with examinee
     b. Examination technique (gentle, moderate, or forceful palpation; thorough or cursory exam)
     c. Use of examination tools (reflex hammer, pinwheel, etc.)
     d. Presence of medical records and/or X-rays in the exam room (does the examiner indicate whether they were reviewed prior to the exam?)

■ The examiner is generally limited to the injury in question and prior medical history is usually off-limits. The examinee should be made aware of this so prior medical history is not offered inadvertently.

■ Clarify with the client whether an additional report is required in addition to the detailed account of events and the audiotape. If so, submit all requested work product with the billing statement.

Billing Considerations

The LNC may charge her hourly fee for services rendered or may charge a flat fee. Occasionally an attorney will inform the consultant that the attorney pays a flat fee for attending DMEs and the amount of that fee will then have to be evaluated by the consultant to make sure it is sufficient remuneration for the LNC's time and expertise.

Any fee should allow for travel time, waiting time, observing the examination, and report and/or time log preparation. The method of payment should be clarified with the client prior to the exam. This would not be an area of concern for the in-house consultant who is a salaried employee.

Benefits of Using an LNC

A nurse is considerably more comfortable in a medical environment than a nonmedical observer, and often creates rapport that may not occur between medical and legal professionals. More importantly, a nurse is knowledgeable about what should be included in the examination of various body parts and may therefore be able to alert plaintiff's counsel to important omissions in the examination. The nurse may also be able to detect whether or not a particular part of the examination is performed correctly. A prior review of the type of examination to be performed at the DME will enhance the LNC's awareness and confidence.

An example of an important observation by a nurse which may not have been noticed by a nonmedical person is a case in which a female plaintiff presented to the IME for an examination of her right knee following a slip and fall injury. She was wearing long leggings and was never asked to remove any of her clothing for the examination. The entire knee examination was therefore performed with the leggings covering her entire leg. The physician, rather than viewing the knee directly, simply asked the plaintiff how many holes there were (apparently referring to an arthroscopy which had been performed) and she responded with "three." This was not verified visually by the examiner, an orthopedic surgeon. He also asked his medical assistant whether they had received any of the plaintiff's medical records, indicating to the nurse observer that he had not reviewed them previously.

In this case, if the examiner's report included specific information about skin temperature, swelling (or lack of swelling) of the knee, a description of arthroscopy scars, or similar findings, the LNC would be able to point out to her attorney client that the examiner could not have made these observations.

The LNC should be cognizant of the fact that, should there be discrepancies or a dispute between the examiner's report and that of the LNC, testimony at trial may be needed to verify the information presented by both under oath.

Conclusion

The object of a DME should be to obtain objective, accurate information about the examinee's physical or mental status relating to the subject injury(s) which can be used to effect a fair settlement or verdict. Regrettably, some examiners' reports do reflect some bias. For this reason, many attorneys retain the services of LNCs to objectively assess, observe, monitor, and report detailed objective information to facilitate the disposition of a case.

Discussion Questions

1. The purpose of a DME is:
   a. To give the defense an opportunity to evaluate the plaintiff's claims of injury, illness, or incapacity
   b. To determine the impact of preexisting illnesses or injuries on the subject complaints/claims
   c. a and c
   (Answer: a)
2. The plaintiff attorney may request the presence of an LNC at the client's DME to
   a. Determine whether an adequate exam is performed
   b. To ensure that the examiner does not abuse the client
   c. To ensure that no X-rays or diagnostic tests are performed unless they have previously been agreed to
   d. a and b
   e. a and c
   f. All of the above
   (Answer: f)
4. Services an LNC may provide at a DME include
   a. Audiotaping the exam
   b. Providing the examiner with the plaintiff's past medical history
   c. Videotaping the exam
   d. Questioning the examiner about omissions in the exam performed
   e. a, b, and d
   f. All of the above
   (Answer: a)
5. Two potential disadvantages to the defense attorney who orders a DME are
   a. Examiner's fees
   b. Examination may be videotaped by the opposing party
   c. The examiner's findings and report may be detrimental to the case
   d. a and c
   e. All of the above
   (Answer: d)

References

1. *Mercury Cas. Co. v. Sup. Ct.* (Garcia), supra, 179 CA3d at 1033, 225 CR at 103.

2. CCP Section 2032(c)(1)(2).
3. CCP Section 2032(c)(2).
4. CCP Section 2032(a).
5. CCP Section 2032(c)(2).
6. CCP Section 2032(c)(2).
7. CCP Section 2032(c)(2).
8. CCP Section 2032(b).
9. See *Reuter v. Sup. Ct.* (1979)98 CA3d 610, 615, 159 CR 669, 672.
10. CCP Section 2032(c)(2).
11. CCP Section 2032(d).
12. *Vinson v. Sup. Ct.* (Peralta Comm. College Dist.)(1987)43 C3d 833, 840, 239, CR 292, 297.
13. *Shapira v. Sup. Ct.* (Sylvestri)(1990)224 CA3d 1249, 1255, 274 CR 516, 5169.
14. *Vinson v. Sup. Ct.* (Peralta Comm. College Dist.), supra, 43 C3d at 840, 239 CR at 298.
15. CCP Section 2032(b).
16. CCP Section 2032(d).
17. CCP Section 2032(d).
18. CCO Section 2032(g)(1).
19. CCP Section 2032(g)(1).
20. *Sharff v. Sup. Ct.* (1955)44 C2d 508, 510, 282 P2d 896, 897.
21. Ev. C. Section 755.5(a).
22. CCP Section 2032(g)(1).
23. CCP Section 2032(g)(1).
24. *Edwards v. Sup. Ct.,* supra.
25. CCP Section 2032(h).
26. See *Queen of Angels Hosp. v. Sup. Ct.* (Jones)(1976) 57 CA3d 370, 374, 129 CR 282, 284.

Chapter 27

Alternative Dispute Resolution — Settlement, Arbitration, Mediation

Tracye Chovanec, Barbara Levin, and Janet Kremser

Contents

1-57444-123-X/98
© 1998 by American Association of Legal Nurse Consultants

Objectives

- To define alternative dispute resolution
- To define arbitration and compare and contrast the process of binding arbitration and nonbinding arbitration
- To define mediation
- To discuss the role of the LNC in the mediation process
- To review the steps used in the preparation of a settlement brochure to be used at mediation
- To discuss other settlement methods

Introduction

Alternative dispute resolution is a method used to aid in resolving lawsuits outside of the courtroom. *United States Code Services* defines alternative dispute resolution as "any procedure that is used, in lieu of adjudication, to resolve issues in controversy, including but not limited to settlement negotiations, conciliation, facilitation, mediation, fact finding, minitrials, and arbitration, or any combination thereof." While alternative dispute resolution may be used in cases involving many types of issues, it is perhaps most useful in those cases involving personal injuries, medical malpractice, employment issues, and contract disputes. With court dockets becoming more and more overcrowded, judges are ordering for lawsuits to attempt to resolve the dispute through alternative dispute resolution.

The advantage to alternative dispute resolution is both sides avoid the cost of continuing litigation and it allows a claim or dispute to be resolved in a timely fashion and without the necessity of a lengthy and expensive trial. This chapter focuses on two types of alternative dispute resolution that have gained the most in popularity nationwide, arbitration and mediation, and the legal nurse consultant's (LNC's) role in the process.

The Arbitration Process

Arbitration is an arrangement for abiding by the judgment of selected persons in some disputed matter, instead of carrying the dispute to established tribunals of justice. The intention is to avoid the formalities, the delay, expense, and vexation of ordinary litigation (*Black's*, 1979, p. 96). There are two categories of arbitration: binding arbitration and non-binding arbitration.

Binding Arbitration

Binding arbitration is an agreement between the parties in advance to abide by an arbitrator's decision. The process usually takes place when a contractual agreement states the conflicts will be resolved by binding arbitration.

Because there is a finality to decisions under binding arbitration, the process is generally covered by state statutes that outline specific guidelines and require explicit warnings to the participants about the consequences of entering into arbitration. In Texas, for example, the statute, *Vernon's Annotated Statutes,* Article 4590i, Sec. 15.01(a) states:

> No physician, professional association, or health care provider shall request or require a patient or prospective patient to execute an agreement to arbitrate health care liability claim unless the form of agreement delivered to the patient contains a written notice in 10-point bold-face type clearly and conspicuously stating:
>
> UNDER TEXAS LAW, THIS AGREEMENT IS INVALID AND OF NO LEGAL EFFECT UNLESS IT IS ALSO SIGNED BY AN ATTORNEY OF YOUR OWN CHOOSING. THIS AGREEMENT CONTAINS A WAIVER OF IMPORTANT LEGAL RIGHTS, INCLUDING YOUR RIGHT TO A JURY. YOU SHOULD NOT SIGN THIS AGREEMENT WITHOUT FIRST CON-SULTING WITH AN ATTORNEY.

The Texas statute also states that violations of the above section by a physician or professional association of physicians constitutes a violation of the Medical Malpractice Act. This action would be subject to enforcement provisions and sanctions.

Some states allow hospitals to place arbitration clauses in hospital admission agreements. A prudent LNC should inspect all hospital admission agreements signed by any patient to determine if the patient has agreed to arbitrate any conflict.

The binding arbitration process usually involves submitting a contested matter to a three-member panel. Appeals to the binding arbitration decision are very limited. As a result, this process is the least desirable in personal injury or medical malpractice cases. Binding arbitration is more commonly used in contract disputes.

Non-Binding Arbitration

Non-binding arbitration usually involves one arbitrator, and the decision is not final. If either the plaintiff or defendant is dissatisfied with the arbitrator's decision, the case remains on the court's docket. The non-binding arbitration process is often preferred over the binding arbitration process because the non-binding type is less final. An individual can still have his or her day in court if arbitration did not produce any resolution.

The Mediation Process

By far, the preferred process for most litigants considering alternative dispute resolution is the mediation process. Mediation is defined as "...the act of a third person in inter-mediating between two contending parties with a view to per-suading them to adjust or settle their dispute...." (*Black's,* 1979, p. 885). In this forum, the plaintiff and defendant agree for an impartial third party known as a mediator to conduct a settlement conference. The case needs to have reached a mature status to be ready for mediation. That is, exhibits have been collected and discovery has been near completion.

Retired judges and/or lawyers with special expertise and training offer services as mediators. The mediator's fee is agreed upon in advance by all parties. Average daily mediation fees vary, ranging from approximately $600 to $1,500 per party. Sometimes mediators charge fees on an hourly basis.

Mediations occur when courts order parties to mediate or when either side informally approaches the other to inquire if mediation is desirable. Both sides must agree upon the selection of a mediator and the date the settlement conference will be held.

Although the mediator is an impartial third party, it is important to educate and inform him or her about the issues of the case prior to the settlement conference. One tool frequently used by the plaintiff is a settlement brochure, which is discussed in depth later in this chapter. The mediator can study the brochure and then develop an opinion, which would most likely reflect the potential outcome in the courtroom. The plaintiff, of course, hopes to convince the mediator of the possibility of a large jury verdict. On the other hand, the defense wishes to convince the mediator of the opposite. The ideal result of mediation is for the mediator to persuade both sides to meet somewhere on middle ground and resolve the claim without a jury trial.

During mediation, the settlement conference itself is often a friendly atmosphere. At the beginning of the settlement conference, all parties meet together with the mediator, and counsel for each side presents an oral, brief synopsis of the case. The parties then proceed to separate conference rooms. Privately with each party, the mediator strives to influence each party to adjust expectations. During these private conferences, the mediator points out strengths and weaknesses of each side's case. The ultimate goal is to resolve the differences between the parties and reach a settlement that is satisfactory to both sides. The mediation process requires that all parties have representatives present who have the authority to finalize settlement agreements.

In a successful mediation, the plaintiffs probably feel they settled for too little and the defense feels they paid too much. The successful mediation, however, results in resolution of the lawsuit and removes the gamble of a jury trial.

The LNC's Role in Mediation

LNCs often play a very visible role in mediation, both before and during the settlement conference itself. Using a medical malpractice case to illustrate, the LNC could be employed by either plaintiff or defense side to audit the presentation during mediation with the aim of detecting discrepancies or inaccurate information. The LNC would, of course, privately relay such information to the employing attorney. The LNC can also serve as an informed educator at the mediation forum. When complex medical issues are introduced, the mediator sometimes needs more information on the standard of care, on the medical issues in dispute, or to explain medical terminology. The LNC can be a resource liaison to the mediator.

An LNC can offer valuable assistance in mediations as educator of the medical aspects of a medical malpractice or personal injury case. The following is a mediation presentation outline of the medical aspects of a case:

1. Overview of the case
2. Health history of the plaintiff
3. Injuries sustained and definitions
4. Long term/short term rehabilitation goals
5. Questions and clarifications

In the following example, the LNC played a vital role in the successful outcome of a mediation in a personal injury case. The mediator and parties were able to gain a comprehensive understanding of the medical issues and damages which helped move the case to settlement. (Example submitted by Barbara Levin, RN.)

> Example 27.1: Mrs. Smith, a 41-year-old married woman with two children, was in a motor vehicle accident on a snowy February 1, 1995 at 2:30 p.m. While Mrs. Smith was driving north, Mr. Jones' car was driving south and crossed over the median strip and hit Mrs. Smith's car head-on at 30 mph.
>
> Mrs. Smith's injuries included a left open grade 3B tibia fracture, left shoulder dislocation, and a 4-in. laceration to the parietal area of the head. She required emergent open reduction internal fixation (ORIF) surgery to stabilize the tibia fracture, and 20 sutures to the left parietal area. A week later, she underwent a Bankart procedure to stabilize the left shoulder.
>
> Approximately 8 months after the surgery, a nonunion of the tibia was diagnosed on X-ray. A second ORIF with right iliac crest bone graft was performed. A month later, the hardware in the tibia fractured due to the nonunion of bone. Another surgical procedure was required to replace it.
>
> Mrs. Smith's health history included a history of smoking 2 packs per day for 20 years and adult-onset diabetes mellitus treated with insulin, both of which contributed to ineffective healing. At approximately 7 months after the accident, Mrs. Smith showed signs of osteomyelitis. Intravenous and oral antibiotics were administered. Within 5 months and following multiple irrigation and debridements, she required a left below-the-knee amputation.
>
> Three long-term goals for Mrs. Smith were identified and presented:
>
> 1. Return to previous level of function
> 2. Bipedal ambulation utilizing a prosthesis
> 3. Return to her job as a corporate secretary
>
> During the presentation, the LNC provided detailed information regarding the grade of the fracture, the surgeries, the effects of diabetes and smoking on the healing process, and definitions of medical terminology, such as osteomyelitis and the Bankart procedure.

Production of a Settlement Brochure

Prior to the settlement conference, the LNC is a major contributor to the production of a settlement brochure. The term brochure is somewhat of a misnomer. In reality, the term *brochure* is often a simple trifold document. When used as a settlement tool it is several inches thick and is bound with dividers. The settlement brochure can vary in size depending on the issues and evidence to be presented. Both plaintiff and defense sides prepare brochures although the plaintiff's is usually the more extensive. Three purposes are served by a settlement brochure.

- It aids the trial team in focusing on specific medical issues that may later be used for trial of the case in the courtroom.
- It educates the mediator as to the strengths and weaknesses of the medical aspects of the case.
- It presents evidence that the parties are prepared for trial.

The Plaintiff's Brochure

There are a number of formats used in preparing an effective brochure from the plaintiff's perspective. The guidelines below can be incorporated in the brochure format. Begin by dividing the document into six sections titled Table of Contents, Brief Statement of the Case, Detailed Discussion of Medical Management Issues, Damages and Injuries, Negligence, and Exhibits.

- The table of contents refers the reader to the pages where specified information is located.
- The brief statement of the case is a precise statement of position. An example is: John Doe collapsed and died from cardiac arrest while waiting to be attended to at ABC Hospital. Avoid conveying a description of the case in the statement. The theme of the case can sometimes be used in the brief statement.
- The detailed statement of medical management issues should be prepared by the LNC in consultation with the attorney. An in-depth study of medical records and medical references enable the LNC to prepare a detailed synopsis of the medical issues.
- The LNC may also have input in the section for damages and injuries. The one purpose of this section is to humanize the plaintiff, to show the impact of the injuries to the plaintiff and his or her family. What can they do or not do anymore? An example would be John Doe whose left leg was amputated. An avid skier, he and his two daughters used to take yearly vacations to Colorado at Christmastime to ski, snowboard, and cross-country ski. The reader is referred to photographs of last year's vacation in Tahoe. Poetic license is often used to dramatize the plaintiff's injuries and damages. The damage section should include an itemized accounting of the economic losses (i.e., medical expenses, lost earnings, property damage, etc.). An offer of settlement is also noted.
- Negligence and/or gross negligence can also be addressed by the LNC. Violations of standards of care or deviations from policies and procedures falls within the area of the LNC's expertise. Expert reports and expert's *curriculum vitae* are also presented in this section. Also include authoritative papers, guidelines, and standards written by specialty or other organizations that receive attention in this section.
- The section for exhibits consists of pertinent medical records (appropriately highlighted), medical expense invoices, funeral and burial expense

invoices, photographs, greeting cards, letters, school records, employment records, certificates, graphs, charts, etc. This section contains references to supporting data for the brochure. These exhibits are numbered and may be referred to in the narrative of the brochure by number.

The Defendant's Brochure

For the defense, the brochure could be divided into five similar sections:

- The brief statement of the case from the defendant's viewpoint
- The detailed statement of medical management issues may or may not be addressed by the defense; in its place, the defense may wish to insert the defendant doctor's qualifications, experience, and a listing of professional and community services
- The section for damages and injuries could be used by the defense to address any mitigating factors
- The negligence and/or gross negligence issue may be addressed by the defense by discussing defense experts' opinions about the standard of care or any contributing negligence of the plaintiff(s)
- The exhibits section may or may not be applicable for defense

In general, a settlement brochure may present any factor or aspect of a case on which either side wishes to focus. There are no rules or requirements. This is a place for the evidence to be presented creatively for effect.

Other Settlement Modalities

Minitrials

Continuing a step beyond alternative dispute resolution, other settlement tactics have been created. For example, minitrials have been used in injury or medical malpractice cases. The plaintiff's attorney(s) invite the defense attorney(s), insurance representatives, risk mangers, and all pertinent parties to attend a formal preview of their version of how the trial will proceed. They present an introduction, summary of the issues, and theories of liability. They anticipate the defense theories and offer rebuttals. A verdict form detailing monetary amounts being requested for damages is presented. There may be a discussion of punitive damages, if applicable, with supporting case law. Audiovisuals and exhibits are effectively displayed. The goal is to entice an otherwise reticent defendant to settlement. Minitrials usually contain only the plaintiff's presentations with a set time limit after presentation for a defense response to plaintiff's settlement offer.

Trial Consultants

There are a variety of consultants who aid trial attorneys in developing themes of a case, sometimes using mock jury presentations or focus groups before entering into settlement discussions or going to trial. These mock juries and focus groups can give the trial team valuable information as to what an uninterested third party feels about the facts of a case, the plaintiffs, the defendants, and the experts. This information can be crucial to the strategic planning and development of the case. Such sources of information can help to determine the overall chances of obtaining a satisfactory verdict or judgment. This impartial information can assist the LNC in evaluating complex medical issues in the case to see if additional explanations or evidence is necessary.

Jury Research

It is extremely important for a legal team member to research adequately jury verdicts on similar case scenarios prior to the offer of settlement. Reference sources would be databases kept by insurance companies, the American Trial Lawyers Association, and special reports that are usually compiled by private sources working through the local courthouse records of verdicts rendered.

The Medical Review Panel

Many states have adopted variations on the medical review panel to provide for resolution of medical malpractice cases outside of a formal trial. Goals of such panels are to reduce the courts' caseload, the costs of medical malpractice litigation, and to provide a better means of resolving cases. The panel's evaluation of the case provides an objective expert view for both plaintiff and defense counsel. The panel's decision may induce a settlement or convince a plaintiff to reconsider filing a lawsuit. Expensive litigation in court is thus avoided. Louisiana's medical review panel system is but one example. A description of Louisiana's panel system follows (submitted by Janet Kremser, RN).

> Example 27.2: Louisiana permits its health care providers to become "qualified." The advantage of being a qualified health care provider is that all medical malpractice claims must go through a medical review panel prior to filing suit. To become qualified, the participant health care provider must pay an annual premium that supplements the malpractice insurance premium paid to the patient's compensation fund.
>
> Once qualified, there is a cap on the amount awarded in a malpractice claim. The health care provider, or its insurer, is responsible for the first $100,000. The maximum amount awarded by the patient's compensation fund will be $400,000 for a total award of $500,000 plus medical costs.
>
> Prior to filing a lawsuit, a case will be reviewed by a medical review panel. This panel consists of an attorney chairman and three health care providers, usually physicians; one chosen by the plaintiff, one chosen by the defendant(s), and one chosen by the two selected health care providers.
>
> All parties involved submit evidence to support their positions for the members of the medical review panel. After reviewing the information, the medical review panel attorney chairman convenes a meeting to discuss the information. The panel delivers one of three decisions:

1. The evidence supports the conclusion that the defendant or defendants failed to comply with the appropriate standard of care as charged in the complaint.
2. The evidence does not support the conclusion that the defendant or defendants failed to meet the applicable standard of care as charged in the complaint.
3. That there is a material issue of fact, not requiring expert opinion, bearing on liability for consideration by the court.

In rendering an opinion, the panel provides typed reasons to support its decision. The plaintiff(s) has a specified period of time following the panel decision in which to file a lawsuit.

The LNC contributes to preparation of the case for presentation to the panel in the same way as for mediated settlement conferences or for trial. Attending the panel presentation, the LNC plays a vital support role for the attorney to detect errors in the opposition's case presentation and to analyze the strengths and weaknesses of the case. The LNC may also serve as a panel member in nursing malpractice cases.

Glossary

Conciliation: Adjustment and settlement of a dispute in a friendly, unantagonistic manner.

References

Black's Law Dictionary, 5th ed., St. Paul, West Publishing, 1979.

Cravez, G. E., Eight mediation myths: comments from the not-so-frozen North. *Trial,* June, 24–26, 1996.

Danner, D., *Medical Malpractice: Checklist and Discovery*, New York, Clark, Boardman, Callahan, 1994.

Fitzpatrick, R. B., Common non-binding mediation of employment disputes, *Trial Magazine,* June, 40–43, 1994.

5 U.S.C.S. Sec. 571(3) (Supp.1993).

Levy, D., Alternative dispute resolution: take the decision out of the courtroom, *Network,* 5.3, 6–7, 1994.

Ritter, R. F., Lecture: Alternative to ADR: the Mini Trial, Missouri Association of Trial Attorneys, 30th Annual Convention, Continuing Legal Education, Lake Ozark, Missouri, June 21, 1996.

Tex. Rev. Civ. Stat. Ann. art. 4590i, Sec. 15.01.

Weinstein, J. L. and Song, T., Advocacy in Mediation, *Trial,* June, 29–33, 1996.

Chapter 28

Trial Preparation

Judy Ringholz

Contents

1-57444-123-X/98
© 1998 by American Association of Legal Nurse Consultants

Objectives

Upon reading this chapter, the legal nurse consultant (LNC) will be able to:

- Describe the purpose of having well-organized trial and witness notebooks and identify 8 to 10 items to include in each
- Explain the difference between "admissible" and "inadmissible" medical records
- State one issue to be considered when preparing each type of evidence for trial, specifically, deposition testimony, documents, and physical evidence
- List three examples of demonstrative evidence
- Identify three points to keep in mind with regard to how a witness may feel about testifying, the purpose of preparing for trial testimony, and one way to put a witness more at ease

Introduction

There are significant variations in the role of the LNC during trial preparation, as well as during the actual trial. Variations occur, not only between different areas of the country, but even within the same law firm, depending on the attorney with whom the LNC is working. A LNC who combines nursing expertise with creative, independent thinking soon becomes an essential member of the litigation team. It is important to keep in mind that the attorney's role is different from that of the LNC. Therefore, the LNC should not expect the attorney to be able to teach what the LNC needs to know or to show the LNC how to accomplish a particular task in order to be able to perform the job well. An experienced LNC will be the new LNC's best resource. Oftentimes, the LNC will be expected to assume the responsibility for tasks that are routinely performed by a paralegal. In this type of situation, an experienced litigation paralegal will also be an invaluable resource. If the LNC is working on a litigation team that is composed of both paralegals/legal assistants and LNCs, a clear division of responsibilities must be established. All members of the team must be aware of which person is responsible for which task. This will eliminate duplication of efforts, as well as prevent an important task being overlooked. On the other hand, the trial "team" must display the true meaning of the word. A cooperative effort is necessary in order for things to run as smoothly as possible during trial.

Trial is the culmination of all of the efforts put forth in developing a case. Depending on the nature of the case, as well as the jurisdiction, the LNC and the team may well have spent years working up to this point. Thorough preparation is the key to a successful outcome. The attorney must be able to rely on the LNC to assist him or her in presenting the case in an organized fashion. The jury becomes a watchful panel of spectators during the trial. The team that is organized is considered to be competent by the jury. The ultimate outcome of the case will be influenced by how well, and in what manner, each side makes its presentation before the jury.

Trial Notebooks

It is recommended that the LNC begin to prepare the trial notebook during the initial phases of developing the case and update it as necessary. Organize the trial notebook in a three-ring binder with tabs to include the necessary documents pertaining to each section of the trial. Color coding various sections may prove to be helpful. Prepare a concise index and organize the notebook with enough detail to allow the attorney or anyone working at his or her side instant access to pertinent documents by simply turning to the appropriately tabbed section at any time throughout the trial. Trial notebooks commonly contain pleadings and discovery for both plaintiff and defense.

You may also wish to incorporate all or some of the following elements into the trial notebook:

1. Motion in Limine
2. Proposed Jury Instructions
3. Notes on Voir Dire Examinations
4. Notes on Opening Statement
5. Notes on Final Argument
6. Pre-Trial Order
7. Court's Docket Control Order
8. Designation of Witnesses by Plaintiff
9. Designation of Witnesses by Defendant
10. Order of Proof (order in which witnesses will be called)
11. Plaintiff's List of Exhibits to Be Admitted at Trial
12. Defendant's List of Exhibits to Be Admitted at Trial
13. Relevant Portions of Medical Records at Issue
14. Summaries of Medical Records/Medical Chronologies
15. Pertinent Medical Literature
16. Definitions of Pertinent Medical Terminology
17. Relevant Portions of Other Significant Records (Educational, Employment, etc.)
18. Expert Reports
19. Expert *curriculum vitae*

Witness Notebooks

In addition to preparing a well-organized trial notebook, it is also important to prepare a separate notebook for each individual witness. Some attorneys prefer that a file folder be created for each witness. These notebooks or folders should include:

1. Contact information
2. Copies of correspondence sent to or pertaining to the witness
3. Notes taken during meetings with witness
4. Any written item or statement prepared by witness
5. Compressed transcript (miniscript) of deposition with concordance

6. Errata sheet with revisions to deposition testimony and signature page
7. Summary of deposition
8. Outline of direct or cross-examination
9. Copy of report (for experts)
10. Copy of *curriculum vitae* (for experts)
11. Other pertinent documents (i.e., medical literature authored, notes regarding significant entries made by witness in medical records, etc.)
12. Pertinent investigative reports

There are computer programs available that will store the transcripts of all depositions taken pertaining to the case being tried. This allows the attorney to have deposition testimony easily accessible during trial by way of a laptop computer. Actual testimony is displayed on the screen at the touch of a button, thereby allowing the attorney to refer to previous testimony and make certain that it is not being mischaracterized.

Burden of Proof

The concept of negligence was discussed in Chapter 4. Recall that the burden is on the plaintiff to prove each (and every) one of the four elements of negligence. Both sides prove their respective case through the evidence that they present at trial.

Evidence

Status of Admissibility of Records

Evidence comes in many forms, including testimony of parties and witnesses, as well as various types of records. LNCs are often involved with preparing parties and witnesses for trial, which will be discussed later in this chapter. The LNC also plays a crucial role in obtaining, reviewing, and summarizing records, especially medical records. This was discussed in detail in Chapter 17. However, it is important when considering trial preparation to reinforce the fact that medical records must be in admissible form in order to be introduced into evidence at trial. It is necessary for the LNC to understand what makes medical records admissible. This is determined by the method through which the records are obtained (refer to Chapter 9). In Texas, for example, medical records can be obtained in admissible form by subpoena or with an affidavit that is accompanied by a current medical authorization that has been executed by the patient. However, if records are obtained with affidavits, they are not admissible unless the affidavits are filed with the court at least 14 days before the trial begins. When records are obtained by subpoena, the ordering party receives the "original" or "court" copy of the record. Therefore, if a codefendant who ordered records settles or is nonsuited before trial, you must remember to obtain the "court" copies from that party. If the codefendant obtained the records by affidavits with an authorization, be certain to obtain proof that the affidavits were filed in a timely fashion. Procedures for obtaining records vary from state to state. A reputable records retrieval service in your area should be able to effectively explain the difference between admissible and inadmissible records. Imagine the potential result of not learning until after trial has begun that the most significant medical records are not admissible and, therefore, cannot be used as evidence or referred to during the course of trial. Needless to say, the effect on your case can be devastating. Appendix 28.1 suggests the information to be included in your list of medical records. This information should be easily accessible and updated as additional medical records are received. There are computer databases that are designed for this purpose. You may, however, wish to design one yourself, so that it best meets your needs. Appendix 28.2 displays another example of how the information can be recorded and stored on a computer database. This format would facilitate the process of updating your information, especially as trial approaches.

Deposition Testimony

For those witnesses who are not being called "live" to testify at trial, each side will identify the portions of the deposition testimony of the witness that they wish to offer into evidence and the portions to which they will object. These offers and objections will be exchanged with opposing counsel prior to trial. Particularly if the witness is a health care professional, the LNC may be asked to review the transcript or videotape of the witness' deposition and to draft proposed offers and objections. In order to do this, the LNC must be aware of and note any revisions made by the witness to the deposition testimony by way of the amendment page or errata sheet. Indicate the page number and line number in the transcript where each section that is being offered or excluded by objection begins and ends. The reason for any objection must be indicated. Of course, the reason must be supported by the rules (i.e., form, hearsay, privilege, etc.). Once the offers and objections have been exchanged and, if necessary, ruled on by the court, the videotape can be edited to include only the testimony that will actually be offered. If a video is not available, the portions to be offered will be read from the transcript at trial. The LNC may be asked to role-play the witness and read the responses contained in the deposition transcript of the witness from the witness stand.

Preparing Exhibits

The attorney must determine, in advance, which documents he or she intends to use as trial exhibits. The LNC must establish the order in which the attorney plans to use the exhibits. Upon doing so, organize the documents in the order in which they will be used at trial. Create a separate folder for each exhibit. Mark the document as Plaintiff or Defense Exhibit ____ (the blank will be filled in by a letter or number according to your local court rules), and prepare a corresponding "exhibit list." Once again, it is necessary to be familiar with the local procedural rules in order to mark the exhibits properly for identification during trial. Whenever possible, you will want to have the original document, as well as a copy, available in the exhibit folder. Never mark, staple, or alter the original in any way. If the original document is not available, insert a note in the folder regarding where it is kept and how it can be obtained if necessary.

In some jurisdictions, the actual exhibits are exchanged between the parties before trial begins. Some court clerks prefer that exhibit lists be submitted on computer disks, so that they can input the data into their files. During the pre-trial conference, as well as during the trial, it will be necessary to keep your exhibit list, as well as the opposing party's exhibit list, available at all times. Note directly on the list when each exhibit is offered into evidence, objected to, admitted, or withdrawn. The attorney must be able to know "at a glance" which exhibits have been properly introduced into evidence and which have not. The LNC must also be aware of whether or not the attorney intends to introduce specific documents, records, or other exhibits into evidence through a particular witness by having that person "prove them up" or authenticate them while under oath. If so, be certain that the documents are organized before the witness takes the stand. In addition, if the LNC is coordinating the offering of exhibits with a codefendant, be certain to determine ahead of time which party will be responsible for which exhibit. This will prevent the submission of duplicate exhibits.

Physical Evidence

Physical evidence refers to any tangible item that may be used or displayed as an exhibit during trial, such as a medical device (i.e., intravenous infusion pump or fetal monitor) that has been positively identified as the one used or is representative of the one used during a procedure at issue. The item must be appropriately marked and identified on the exhibit list.

Demonstrative Evidence

Demonstrative evidence allows the attorney to "demonstrate" certain issues to the jury in a way that will assist in their achieving an understanding of the concepts being presented. The LNC, as the person on the litigation team who is most familiar with the often voluminous medical records, can be particularly helpful in identifying issues that can best be presented through demonstrative evidence. Be creative. Issues can be demonstrated in the form of a chart, table, diagram, illustration, or animation. You can blow up a document contained in the medical records that illustrates a specific point. Medical illustrations are often helpful in explaining an anatomic matter, while computer-generated animations can be used to reconstruct an accident. Consider what it is that the attorney is trying to prove or disprove and how that information can best be presented. Then make certain to have the necessary equipment available in the courtroom for the presentation. Call the clerk ahead of time to determine what audiovisual equipment is on hand and what will need to be brought. There are many companies that will create medical illustrations, courtroom graphics, animations, etc. to be used as demon-strative exhibits. Some will even provide the necessary equipment and assist with the actual presentation. Be aware that it may take an outside vendor more time than anticipated to create a desired exhibit, so plan accordingly. It stands to reason that elaborate exhibits can be quite costly. It may be necessary, however, to weigh the cost against the benefit of successfully communicating your position to the jury so that they clearly understand the concepts.

The following case, in which the names have been changed, provides two examples of actual demonstrative evidence that were used at trial. In this case, Emily Smith, an elderly woman, aspirated a piece of solid food while eating lunch at home with her husband. As a result, her lower airway was partially obstructed. She was brought to Lakeside Hospital for treatment to remove the obstruction. Ms. Smith had been diagnosed with Parkinson's disease more than 10 years prior to the time of this incident. Her family members alleged that her deteriorating condition was caused by delays in the treatment that was rendered by the defendants. The hospital, the emergency room physician, and the pulmonologist were sued. Our firm represented the defendant hospital. Defendants claimed that Ms. Smith's condition was a result of the progression of her Parkinson's disease. Appendix 28.3 quotes excerpts from multiple medical records in an effort to establish the progression of her disease prior to the time of the incident in question. Appendix 28.4 displays the chronology of events that took place at the defendant hospital on the day that the incident occurred in an effort to controvert the plaintiff's claims that there were extended periods of time during which Ms. Smith was not attended to by the hospital staff. Appendices 28.5 and 28.4 were enlarged to 30 × 40 in. for display at trial.

Medical Literature

Medical literature research was discussed in Chapter 24. Once again, for purposes of trial preparation our focus is on organization. A medical literature notebook, organized in a three-ring binder, is recommended. The LNC should begin to collect and organize medical literature during the early phases of case development. The literature may assist in the development of defense theories. Beginning early also makes the task more manageable. The LNC should include pertinent journal articles, articles from newspapers or periodicals, and chapters or excerpts from medical textbooks that support the theory of the case. The items can be organized chronologically, by topic, or by author. Each item should be tabbed to correspond with a concise index. The LNC should always be sure to include identifying information, such as a copy of the title page with the date of publication.

Once the LNC has obtained and organized pertinent medical literature, it is just as important to review it thoroughly. The LNC should keep in mind that the same article that includes the statement that says exactly what the LNC needs to support the case may also say something that is quite damaging to the case. For that reason, the LNC may wish to consider the color-coded method for literature review. The LNC should use three different colored highlighters — pink, yellow, and green — as the LNC carefully reviews the item. Associate the highlighters with a traffic signal. Information highlighted in pink (stop) signals the attorney that it may be damaging to the case. That which is highlighted in yellow (make note) is significant to the case in some way, but neutral in nature. Portions that are highlighted in green (go) are supportive of the theory of the case and potentially damaging to the other side. If the LNC chooses not to use this method, but instead to highlight with only one color, he or she should be certain to bring potentially damaging information to the attention of the attorney in some way. Insert the highlighted copy in the notebook in order to help the attorney find the information that the attorney needs more easily, and be certain to insert an unmarked copy of the article as well. Always be sure that a "clean" copy is submitted to the court when applicable. The attorney will also find it helpful to have a concise summary of the article to use as an easy reference before and during trial.

When preparing medical literature to be used at trial, it is important for the LNC to be aware of the rules that speak to what is and is not admissible. For example, in some jurisdictions it is permissible to refer to literature that speaks to issues pertaining to standard of care only if it was published prior to the date of the alleged incident. However, articles that speak to causation issues, and were published subsequent to the occurrence, may be allowed. It is also important that the LNC be aware of major court decisions that will have an effect on what may be submitted, such as *Daubert v. Merrill Dow* (U.S.), which limits what is referred to as "junk science."

Witness Preparation

Effective preparation of a witness prior to giving testimony at trial is absolutely necessary. This requires both time and patience. Keep in mind that, in most cases, the witness has never seen the inside of a courtroom. The witness will be anxious and perhaps even frightened. The LNC should explain that he or she will attempt to relieve the witness' anxiety by helping him or her understand what will take place at trial. The LNC may be asked to assist the lawyer or to actually be responsible for preliminary preparation.

The first step is to establish a rapport with the witness and to put the witness at ease. The LNC should not make the mistake of role-playing the attorney for the opposite side and asking the "tough" questions a short time into the meeting with the witness in the interest of saving time. It is likely that that would only increase the witness' anxiety and make the preparation more difficult. The purpose of preparation is to make certain that the witness can anticipate the questions or type of questions that he or she will be asked on the witness stand, as well as how the witness will answer those questions. The LNC should explain what is meant by direct-, cross-, redirect-, and re-cross-examination. Make certain that the witness clearly understands the theory of the case.

The following suggests important points to address when preparing the witness. Tell the witness,

- Maintain a demeanor that is polite and sincere. On cross-examination, the attorney may make an effort to make you "lose your cool" by making you angry or defensive. Do not lose your composure or be condescending.
- Be aware of body language. Maintain eye contact with the attorney when he or she is asking you a question. Shift your glance between the attorney and the jury when responding. Do not cross your arms. Do not put your hands over your mouth or near your face.
- Dress appropriately for the courtroom and make sure that any family members or friends who may accompany you dress appropriately as well.
- Be aware of the techniques that attorneys use in an effort to get you to answer the question in a certain way, such as hook, compound, and hypothetical questions. (A hook question is one that incorporates or implies

facts which, if not corrected by the witness prior to the time that he or she responds, will be assumed to be true by virtue of the witness' silence regarding the issue. A compound question is one that incorporates two or three questions into one. If the witness responds, the same answer may be assumed to apply to each component of the question. A hypothetical question usually begins with, "Assume with me....")

- It is most important to listen very carefully to the question and answer only what is directly being asked. Do not offer additional information.
- Never answer a question that you do not understand. Ask the attorney to repeat it or rephrase it. Do this as many times as necessary until you understand the question.
- If you perceive that the attorney is asking a question that you have answered previously, but he or she is wording it differently, give the same answer that you did before.
- Always be certain that the attorney has finished asking the question before you begin to answer. Pause for a moment. This allows you time to reflect on your response. It also allows the opposing attorneys time to object if they choose to do so. Do not attempt to answer if an objection is made. Wait for the judge's ruling and respond accordingly.
- Speak clearly and slowly. Also, speak loudly enough so that each juror can hear your answers without straining.
- Use your own words. Do not adopt the attorney's language. If there is a portion of the question that you disagree with or would phrase differently, do so before you answer.
- If the attorney references a specific document in the question (i.e., medical record or journal article), request a copy of the document and read it carefully before responding.
- If you do not know the answer to the question being asked or you do not recall, say so. Never guess or speculate.
- Always tell the truth based on your personal knowledge. Give brief and concise answers.
- After practicing repeatedly, you will begin to memorize the answers to anticipated questions. Do not let your responses sound as though they were rehearsed.

The LNC should be sure to review adequately with the witness any materials that could be used for impeachment purposes. These would include prior deposition testimony, answers to interrogatories, answers to requests for admission, and any oral or written statements that were made previously. Explain the process of impeachment and provide examples.

Discuss the probable testimony of other witnesses in order to ascertain whether or not the witness has strong feelings regarding issues that may be raised and whether or not there may be a potential for inconsistencies in testimony at trial. If so, the LNC should advise the attorney as soon as possible. Review and discuss any exhibits that the attorney has determined he or she will "prove up" or authenticate through the witness.

Even if all parties are in agreement as to who will appear at trial, it may be necessary in the jurisdiction, or the attorney may prefer, that all witnesses and parties be served with a subpoena or notice to appear at trial. Determine what is required by local rules and discuss with the attorney what his or her wishes are (Mauet and Maerowitz, 1996). If the attorney plans to serve a subpoena on a "friendly" witness (one who agrees to testify and is supportive of the theory of the case), be certain to discuss the matter with the witness ahead of time. Explain the rationale for issuing a subpoena even though the witness has agreed to testify at trial. Also remember to alert the witness's office staff, if applicable, so that they are not surprised when the process server arrives.

Supply Box

Maternal–child health nurses and those who have children may relate to the analogy of the new parents who were preparing to take their infant on their first family outing. They created a list of every item that they might possibly need while away from home. Then they carefully packed the supply bag. Unfortunately, when the time came to leave, they were so excited and concerned about whether or not the baby was dressed appropriately for the weather and secured properly in her safety seat that they left the supply bag behind. After an LNC has spent years assisting with the development of a case, it is likely that he or she will feel as though it is the LNC's "baby." The LNC will organize it, box it securely, and see that it is safely transported to the courthouse. However, this will serve as a reminder not to leave the supply box behind. Suggested items to be included:

> Various types of pens and pencils
> Easel
> Colored markers (for easel)
> Thick black permanent marker
> Highlighters
> Legal pads
> Extra folders
> Two-hole and three-hole punch
> Post-it notes® and tabs in various sizes
> White-Out® and correction tape
> Scotch tape or transparent tape
> Stapler and staples
> Paper clips and binder clips
> Ruler
> Pointer
> Exhibit stickers
> Envelopes
> Business cards (attorney's and the LNC's)
> Rolls of quarters (for pay phones)
> List of phone numbers for those whom the LNC will need to contact
> Medical dictionary and relevant medical textbooks
> Copy of the Rules of Civil Procedure and Rules of Evidence that apply in
>   your jurisdiction

Acetominophen, ibuprofen, and aspirin
Antacids
Facial tissues
Energy snacks in the event of missed lunches
Extension cords
Luggage cart

"Special Items"

The attorney will expect the LNC to have available all of the items that are routinely packed in a supply box. However, if the LNC knows that the attorney has a passion for a particular brand of bottled water, and the LNC sets a bottle at the attorney's place at the beginning of each day, the attorney will be appreciative. By the same token, if in the middle of the afternoon, after the attorney has talked for most of the day, the LNC hands the attorney a roll of his or her favorite throat lozenges or hard candy, the attorney will make note of the extra efforts. It often is the little things that matter most.

Packing Up and Heading Out

There is one task that will benefit the LNC greatly while in trial if he or she takes the time to do it with precision while packing. Number each box (i.e., 1 of 25, 2 of 25...). Then, list the contents of each box. This will prevent the LNC from having to "rummage" and appear disorganized during trial. The LNC should remember that he or she will be observed and monitored from the moment that the LNC first walks into the courtroom until the time that the trial ends.

Conclusion

Assisting at trial can be challenging and stressful, but it can also be exciting and rewarding. Ascertaining that the LNC has done everything possible to help the attorney present the case effectively will not only enable the LNC to have a feeling of "ownership" in the outcome of the trial, but it will also give the LNC a feeling of personal satisfaction (not to mention job security).

Reference

Mauet, T. and Maerowitz, M. (1996). *Fundamentals of Litigation for Paralegals,* 2nd ed., Boston, Little, Brown.

Appendix 28.1— Medical Records Pertaining to Emily Smith

Records from	Obtained by	Date Obtained	Dates of Service	Care and Treatment
Diagnostic Neurology Center	Ellen Roark (Admissible)	03/02/95	11/80–07/91	Drs. Brown and White: Treating neurologists until 07/86 (when care assumed by Dr. Feldman) Dr. Geiger: Provided treatment during hospitalization at Lakeside in June of 1991
Peter Benton, M.D.	Jake Brigance (Admissible)	02/28/94	08/81–10/93	Primary physician
Ben Stevenson, M.D.	Jake Brigance (Admissible)	06/30/94	01/18/83–06/09/89	Rheumatologist — Treated arthritis
Aaron Feldman, M.D.	Rufus Buckley (Inadmissible)	10/07/93	07/31/86–01/31/94	Neurologist — Treating Parkinson's disease
General Hospital (Vol. I & II)	Jake Brigance (Admissible)	05/13/94	04/89; 05/89; 12/90	4/89 — Admission for "drug holiday" 5/89 — (Home care) for Parkinson's/anemia/arthritis 12/90 — Right subcortical infarct
John Davis, M.D.	Jake Brigance (Admissible)	02/08/94	04/89–05/89	Gastroenterologist — GI workup for anemia
Phillip Watters, M.D.	Jake Brigance (Admissible)	02/22/94	04/90–04/91	Ophthalmologist — Treated cataracts
Gastroenterology Associates	Jake Brigance (Admissible)	03/14/95	06/91–08/91	Esophagogastroduodenoscopy by Drs. Casey and Welby
Rockview Medical Center Rehabilitation Center — (Volume I and II)	Jake Brigance (Admissible)	02/08/94	07/91	Rehabilitation (subsequent to discharge from Lakeside Hospital)
Monica Helmsley, Ph.D.	Ellen Roark (Admissible)	08/25/94	05/02/94	Neuropsychological evaluation

Appendix 28.2
Sample Database for Medical Records Log

<u>BLACK V. SMITH</u>

<u>MEDICAL RECORDS LIST</u>

Agency/Physician	Date Ordered/Initials	Date Received/Initials	Record Service/Name
Dr. Ruth Westheimer	1/1/97 bbb	2/1/97 bbb	Rapid Records Service/Mary
	Date summarized	2/3/97 bbb	
Patient	Date summary to client	2/4/97 bbb	
Doug Black	Custodian Original	Clark Kent (attorney's name)	

Comments	non-admissable with affidavit
Confirm of order rcvd.	1/4/97
Authorization	not needed

Appendix 28.3
Excerpts from Medical Records Pertaining to Emily Smith

Date	Doctor	Page(s)	Entry
11/14/80	Brown	17	(History and Physical from Lakeside Hospital) ... Hospitalized in January of 1980 with arthritis.
11/17/80	Brown	14	(Discharge summary from Lakeside Hospital) Ms. Smith is a 63-year-old lady who has a history of arthritis, but over the past year has had difficulty with her mobility and noticed that she has had some tremor in her right hand. She has difficulty initiating movement, but denies any specific paralysis. Her neurological exam was suggestive of probable Parkinson's disease. She was admitted to work up other possible problems... Final Diagnosis: Probable Parkinson's disease The patient will be discharged on Sinemet 10/100 mg ...
01/18/83	Stevenson	1	... Has had arthritis of the back for the past 3 years... She complains of low back pain, upper back pain, and neck pain, some decreased strength in her hands, but no real peripheral arthritis.
02/18/85	Brown	9	... Complains of slowness of movement
02/10/86	Brown	10	Very upset ... depressed
05/28/86	Brown	11	Exam: Speech much slower; slurs; shuffles more

Appendix 28.3 (continued)
Excerpts from Medical Records Pertaining to Emily Smith

Date	Doctor	Page(s)	Entry
07/16/86	White	41	(History and Physical from Lakeside Hospital) ... The patient has become very stiff, immobile like there is a heavy weight pulling her down to the ground. She has Parkinson's disease.... This morning she had an unusually severe episode of this, associated with severe, excruciating, unbearable back pain.... The patient is stiff and rigid, almost statue-like, very immobile, has to be helped to do anything ... Impression: 1. Parkinson's disease with "off-on" phenomenon 2. Severe back pain
07/16/86	White	36	(EEG Report) Interpretation: Abnormal EEG indicating diffuse cerebral dysfunction. The record is abnormal by virtue of increased amounts of slow activity consistent with a mild diffuse encephalopathy.
07/31/86	Feldman	50–52	(Initial Neurological Evaluation) ... She has noted increas-ing difficulties with her gait, which has become slow and shuffling, and she has difficulties turning.... She has diff-iculties arising from a chair and, in fact, occasionally has to get down on her fours in order to get up from a chair.... She occasionally spills liquids when she brings them to her mouth.... She had noted some insomnia, which she attributes to generalized body discomfort during the night. In fact, she sleeps on the floor.... Has a 7-year history of slowly progressive Parkinson's disease.... Amitriptyline will be substituted.... This latter medication should improve her insomnia as well as mild depression.
09/23/87	Feldman	46	... She also occasionally "stammers" and has increased forgetfulness. According to her husband she is "less alert" and has occasional visual hallucinations. Most recently, a month ago, she saw "mice" in her bed....
07/27/88	Feldman	43	There has been some deterioration in her symptoms since her last visit. She seems to "stutter" more and is frequently "mixed up" occasionally having hallucinations. Her balance also has deteriorated and she has fallen on two occasions ... possibly developing into PSP (progressive supranuclear palsy).
04/24/89	(General)	10–12	Intermittent bouts of confusion and irrational pain for approximately 6 months. These spells are described as forgetting her surroundings, believes she is in different places with different people. These spells have been increasing in intensity and duration, occasionally lasting an entire day.... There is question of a "stroke" 8 years ago, although husband refuses this....
04/25/89	(General)	63	(EEG Report) Impression: This is an abnormal record, characterized by the following: (1) Diffuse slowing of the background activity, indicating a diffuse disturbance in brain function. (2) A focus of very slow (Delta) activity in the left temporal region, indicating the presence of a lesion involving that region.

Appendix 28.3 (continued)
Excerpts from Medical Records Pertaining to Emily Smith

Date	Doctor	Page(s)	Entry
04/27/89	(General)	57	Magnetic Resonance Images (MRI) of the brain — Impression: Mild to moderate age-related and/or atrophic changes as described with periventricular white matter ischemic change.
08/15/89	Benton	21	(History and Physical from Lakeside Hospital) ... Initially had a little tightness in the chest.... Then later on she began to notice a fluttering in the chest.... Impression: Ventricular tachycardia; parkinsonism; degenerative arthritis.
08/18/89	Stevenson	5	... Her arthritis is stable.... Her parkinsonism is progressing...
09/27/89	Feldman	32	During the last month her condition clearly has deteriorated. She has developed more dyskinesias, particularly after 11 a.m., and this interferes with her eating. She also has become more "nervous" and depressed and has had periods of palpitations lasting 5–10 minutes, associated with "a smothering" feeling.... She continues to have some anxiety and phobias, particularly phobias of crowds....
08/14/90	Benton	6	... 47-pound weight loss over 2 years. Now 100 pounds. Parkinson's...
12/17/90	(General)	256	(EEG Report) Impression: As compared to the previous EEG of 4/25/89, there continues to be diffuse slowing of background activity, indicative of a diffuse disturbance in cerebral function...
12/18/90	(General)	255	(MRI of the brain) Impression: (1) Small focal ischemic insults ... (3) The ischemic changes have appeared since the last study dated 4/27/89.
12/20/90	Feldman (General)	23–26 (235– 238)	(Discharge Summary from General Hospital) Discharge Diagnosis: 1. Right subcortical stroke. 2. Parkinson's disease ... evidence of a left nasolabial droop with drooling from the left corner of the mouth, wide-eyed stare with decreased blinking and hypermetric. The patient's stance was stooped ... EEG was done on the patient and compared to the previous EEG done in April of 1989. There continued to be diffuse slowing in the background and activity indicative of a diffuse disturbance in cerebral function.... The patient also had an MRI scan done that showed small focal ischemic insults.... The ischemic changes were not seen on the last MRI done in April of 1989....
12/26/90	Feldman	27	Ms. Smith has recently been discharged from the hospital after suffering a mild stroke that gave her swallowing difficulties.... At this time, she is very frozen and has difficulty moving about. This improves after taking Sinemet, but she becomes quite confused and begins hallucinating....
04/12/91	Feldman	21	According to the patient and her husband, she is clearly worse. She has more fluctuations...

Appendix 28.4
Demonstrative Exhibit

JUNE 17, 1991

3:00 p.m.	Ms. Smith arrives in emergency room and is assessed by Carol Jones, RN. Cardiac monitor applied. Dynamap applied and oxygen begun by Ms. Jones.
3:05 p.m.	Examination by Dr. Green. Order received by Ms. Jones. IV started, arterial blood gases obtained and pulse oximeter applied by Ms. Jones.
3:08 p.m.	Dr. Benton notified. Portable chest X-ray obtained. Dr. Ross notified by Dr. Green.
3:30 p.m.	Arterial blood gases redrawn and oxygen changed to 100% per face mask.
3:45 p.m.	Ms. Smith continuously monitored by Nurse Jones who describes respirations as easy and nonlabored. Dr. Green speaks with Dr. Ross.
4:05 p.m.	Nurse Jones speaks with Dr. Ross. Orders received. Consent signed for bronchoscopy.
4:25 p.m.	EKG obtained.
4:30 p.m.	Ms. Smith is transferred to pre-op holding area on continuous monitors accompanied by orderly and Carol Jones, RN, and received by Susan Lewis, RN — Report given and continuous monitors exchanged.
4:40 p.m.	History and assessment by John Carter, CRNA Preoperative assessment by Nurse Lewis.
5:00 p.m.	Ms. Smith is continuously monitored by Nurse Lewis who notifies Dr. Ross that she is ready for bronchoscopy.
5:45 p.m.	Dr. Ross arrives to OR holding area. Receives report from Susan Lewis.
6:00 p.m.	Ms. Smith is transferred to MICU. Continuous monitors are exchanged. Report received by head nurse who admits Ms. Smith to unit.
6:30 p.m.	Amanda Parker, RN. receives report from head nurse and assumes care of Ms. Smith. Dr. Ross and respiratory therapist at bedside upon her arrival. Assessment performed by Nurse Parker. Flexible bronchoscopy initiated.

Chapter 29

The Trial Process

Barbara Loecker

Contents

1-57444-123-X/98
© 1998 by American Association of Legal Nurse Consultants

Objectives

- To name and describe the major portions of a civil trial
- To identify the role of the LNC during jury selection and presentation of testimony
- To discuss jury awards including comparative and contributory negligence and punitive damages
- To demonstrate proper courtroom etiquette during a trial

Introduction

The role of the legal nurse consultant (LNC) in trial is as varied as the practice settings and specializations of nurses in the field. The common theme is anticipation — anticipation of the testimony from witnesses of both the plaintiff and the defense. The LNC must be familiar with trial procedure and be comfortable in the courtroom. This applies to all LNCs who have a role in the courtroom — whether as expert witness or as a member of the trial team.

Preparation for the LNC's role in the courtroom begins well before trial during the discovery phase of the case. Trial strategy, testimony, and exhibits are developed during discovery in anticipation of trial. The trial is the showcase for the case and, barring appeals, is the culmination of years of work for all parties. Meticulous preparation and presentation are vital for success in the courtroom. Juries do not decide cases based on the merit of the claim alone. Cases often are won or lost by the presentation by the attorney, not by the merits. An attorney who fumbles for exhibits, forgets key information, and backtracks when presenting testimony is not viewed as a winner and is not successful in the courtroom.

The LNC is a key member of the trial team for a medical case. He or she participates in the development of trial strategy and the testimony and exhibits to present the case. Organization of testimony and exhibits is crucial to a smooth, professional presentation of the case. The trial is the opportunity for the plaintiff and defense to tell a story, and the party who convinces the jury will prevail. The LNC's role is to develop the medical side of the story while the attorney concentrates on the legal side with constant communication between the two. Neither develops one part of the case in isolation from the other.

The LNC may share many responsibilities with a legal assistant or paralegal in preparing and taking a case to trial. Although a legal assistant/paralegal frequently attends trial and takes notes during voir dire and testimony, the LNC is uniquely qualified to appraise the medical testimony. In this respect, the LNC becomes the ideal nonlawyer member of the team to attend the trial because he or she can perform the routine duties necessary during trial, as well as the analysis of the medical testimony, the role for which his or her attendance is essential. The LNC at trial therefore must be prepared to perform a wide variety of tasks if the lone assistant to the attorney.

The key elements of a trial include motions in limine, voir dire, opening statements, presentation of testimony by witnesses through direct examination, cross-examination and rebuttal, closing arguments, and the verdict. Exhibits are used to enhance testimony from witnesses. Jury instructions are given to the jury to outline the law and usually are prepared by the attorney and approved by the trial judge.

This chapter will outline the key elements of a trial, the preparation for the trial for each of the key elements, and the conduct of the trial.

Initial Trial Proceedings

Courtroom Etiquette

The LNC is an integral member of the trial team for a medical case. Some jurisdictions allow the LNC to sit at the counsel table at the discretion of the attorney. Others require the LNC and all other nonattorney members of the trial team to sit in the spectator area. The LNC should sit in the first row of these seats in order to be easily available for courtroom conferences with the attorney. Courtroom etiquette requires all people in the courtroom to stand when the judge and jury enter the courtroom and to remain standing until they are told to be seated. The same is required when the judge and jury leave the courtroom. The LNC should avoid entering or leaving the courtroom during examination of a witness as it is disruptive to the jury, the witness, and the attorney. Of course, there are circumstances when the LNC is required to leave the courtroom to make phone calls or to otherwise obtain critical information for the attorney.

The LNC's courtroom attire should be conservative and professional with a minimum amount of jewelry and subdued makeup.

Major trial segments:

- Motions in limine
- Voir dire and jury selection
- Opening statements
- Presentation of testimony
- Closing arguments

- Deliberations and verdict
- Post-trial activities

Motions in Limine

A motion in limine is a written motion which is usually made before or after the beginning of a jury trial for a protective order against prejudicial questions and statements. The purpose of such motion is to avoid injection into trial of matters which are irrelevant, inadmissible, and prejudicial. In the case of a defendant doctor, a motion in limine may involve the physician's failure to pass a specialty board examination or other cases in which he has been a defendant. A plaintiff may file a motion in limine seeking to exclude testimony regarding previous psychiatric or chemical dependency treatment on the grounds that this treatment is irrelevant to the issues of the case.

LNC Role

The LNC's role during trial for motions in limine begins after the judge has ruled on the motion. Records may need to be removed from exhibits if the judge rules that certain records are not admissible. Failure to do so may result in sanctions or a mistrial. Outlines of witness testimony may need to be revised to reflect the judge's decision. Exhibits may need to be altered or information removed from the records if they have been the subject of the motion in limine. In some cases, it may be advisable for the LNC to prepare a second set of exhibits or records with the information in question removed prior to trial if it is anticipated that the judge's ruling on a motion in limine may require the removal. This will eliminate the need for hasty changes during trial after a ruling.

Voir Dire

Voir dire means to speak the truth. The voir dire process in trial denotes the preliminary examination which the court may make of one presented as a witness or juror, where competency, interest, etc. is objected to. Voir dire and jury selection is perhaps the most important phase of the trial. Jurors are chosen from a panel of citizens who bring their values, opinions, and prejudices to the courtroom. The jury selection process affords the parties the opportunity to impanel a group of jurors whose values and opinions mirror theirs.

The jury selection process has become a science with a host of trial and jury consultants available to the trial team. Studies show that jurors are most influenced by personal bias, second, by legally inadmissible information acquired during trial, and only third, by legally admissible evidence (Singer, 1996). Jury consultants use jury focus groups and trial simulations to identify jurors' attitudes toward trial issues.

Most attorneys combine their personal experience with demographic statistics of the jury pool to determine the characteristics of the "ideal" juror for the trial and to develop a jury profile. Preparation for jury selection begins in the pre-trial phase and concludes with the actual voir dire of the prospective jurors.

LNC Role

Throughout voir dire and jury selection, the attorney concentrates on the interview of each juror. Although the attorney makes notes as the process continues, it is the responsibility of the LNC to take detailed notes of the process. It is critical that the notes be accurate and reflect the potential juror's responses to the key items identified in the juror profile. Other characteristics such as juror behavior during questioning of fellow panelists should also be noted. A panelist who evidences no interest in the process will probably not listen to the trial testimony but will have an equal vote in the deliberation process.

At the conclusion of voir dire, the panel consists of potential jurors with some characteristics more compatible with the "ideal" jury profile than others. In most trials, the attorneys request a recess after the completion of voir dire to review the responses of the panelists before the selection of the jury begins. Some panelists will have been stricken for cause by the judge or dismissed for other reasons. Panelists may be stricken for cause if the judge or attorneys show a specific reason why the individual should not be seated on the jury. This reason may be for bias, knowledge of the case, or personal hardship. Individuals from the remaining members of the panel will sit on the jury and determine the fate of plaintiff and defendant. The trial team (including the LNC) may have only a short recess to review the responses of the panelists and determine which individuals they will select and which they will strike. Each party is allowed a set number of preemptory challenges which allows them to dismiss a juror without cause or a stated reason. In most jurisdictions, each party is allowed a set number of preemptory challenges in addition to challenges for cause.

The trial team reviews the notes of voir dire and ranks the jurors in order of compatibility with the juror profile. Those panelists who do not fit the profile are identified for preemptory challenge. Others who fit the profile of the "ideal juror" are placed at the top of the list. Generally, if one were able to compare the lists of the plaintiff with the lists of the defendants, the lists would be inverted; i.e., those jurors most wanted by the plaintiff are those least wanted by the defendant. Few panelists will have all of the characteristics of the "ideal juror." The trial team will rely on the notes and impressions formed during voir dire to select the jury. Detailed notes are crucial to this process.

Each LNC develops his or her own method of note taking during voir dire. Any method is acceptable as long as the notes are accurate and detailed. The outline and form should be determined prior to the trial as the actual process of voir dire leaves little time for experimentation and development as the questioning proceeds. Many courts will make a list of jurors available to the parties prior to the trial. These lists may contain demographic information about the potential juror and are usually numbered or in alphabetical order. The LNC should use these lists and the jury profile to develop a system for note taking. A preprinted form with the questions the attorney will ask each panelist can be prepared for each potential juror. In addition, such demographic information as gender, age, occupation, marital status, religion, and experience with legal matters should be noted. It may be helpful to note a brief description of the juror such as hair color and clothing in order to trigger the memories of the trial team during the discussion of voir dire responses. The note-taking system should allow space for identification and separation of responses which fit the jury profile and those that do not fit the profile. One system that has been used effectively lists demographic information followed by the attorney questions with sections for responses perceived as positive or negative (Table 29.1).

Table 29.1   Sample Jury Voir Dire

NAME _____

ADDRESS_____

AGE_____ OCCUPATION_____

MARITAL STATUS_____ CHILDREN_____

GENDER_____ DESCRIPTION_____

PREVIOUS EXPERIENCE WITH LAW_____

	Questions	Positive	Negative
1.	Education		Engineer degree
2.	Belief in lawsuits for injury		NO
3.	Negative experience with medical treatment	NO	

The LNC should be prepared to present her impressions of the potential jurors in a clear and concise manner when the trial team discusses the voir dire. Detailed notes will clarify impressions and trigger memory of responses by the panelists.

Opening Statements

An opening statement is an outline or summary of the nature of the case and of anticipated proof presented by counsel at the start of a trial. Its purpose is to advise the jury of facts relied upon and of issues involved, and to give the jury a general picture of the facts and the situations so that the jury will be able to understand the evidence. Opening statements are made by the plaintiff's attorney at the beginning of the trial just prior to presentation of the first witness. The defense counsel may give his or her opening statement following the plaintiff's statement or may elect to wait until the opening of the defense case.

LNC Role

The LNC should listen closely to the opening statements of both parties. He or she should note specific promises made to the jury regarding proof of the claim and remind the attorney for his or her party of such promises throughout the trial. Juries remember the promises of proof made in opening statements and question why such testimony and evidence is lacking if it is not presented. The LNC analyzes the opposing party's statements for any new theories which may require a change in trial strategy or emphasis and additional follow-up. The LNC should take detailed and accurate notes of opening statements and be prepared to discuss them with the attorney.

Presentation of the Case

Witnesses

Witnesses take center stage in a trial; through their testimony, the story is told to the jury. Two types of witnesses testify in a civil trial: expert and fact or lay witnesses. An expert witness is one who by reason of education or specialized experience possesses superior knowledge about a subject, about which jurors have no particular training and would be incapable of forming an accurate opinion or deducing correct conclusions without their testimony. An expert witness is a witness who has been qualified as an expert and who thereby will be allowed (through his or her answers to questions posed) to assist the jury in understanding complicated and technical subjects not within the understanding of the average lay juror.

In a professional negligence trial, the role of expert witnesses is to explain the medical facts of the case to the jury. Plaintiff experts describe deviations from accepted standards of care and the care that should have been provided to the plaintiff. Plaintiff damage experts describe the injuries to the plaintiff and project the impact on his or her life in the future. These witnesses describe the financial, emotional, and physiological changes the plaintiff can expect. Defense witnesses testify in the same areas but are supportive of the care provided by the defendant physician. Defense damage experts present a different evaluation or refute the testimony regarding financial, emotional, and physiological impact on the plaintiff.

Medical expert witnesses also testify in other types of personal injury cases not involving professional negligence as cause for the injury. These experts do not testify about standard of care issues, but do explain the plaintiff's injuries, treatment, and projected impact in the future. Defense expert witnesses present another view of the impact of plaintiff's injuries, and highlight other possible causes for the plaintiff's injuries.

Fact witnesses may present testimony about the mechanism and impact of the injury. In a professional negligence case, these witnesses often are family members or close friends who have observed the care provided to the plaintiff and witnessed the impact of his or her injuries on the plaintiff's lifestyle. They may also include employers or co-workers, ministers, etc. Fact witnesses in other personal injury cases may also be witnesses to the event which caused the injury.

LNC Role

The LNC generally has the responsibility to ensure the witness is available when called for testimony. This may mean meeting an expert at the airport and transporting him or her to the hotel or courtroom. The attorney may ask the LNC to summarize previous testimony and review anticipated testimony with the witness (see Table 29.2). This transportation time is an opportunity to discuss testimony and consult with the expert about issues which have arisen in the course of the trial. The LNC may have to coordinate local transportation for fact witnesses or simply greet the witness as he or she arrives outside the courtroom. Many witnesses are nervous about testifying before a jury and are not familiar with courtroom etiquette or appropriate attire. It is the responsibility of the LNC to explain courtroom procedures, etiquette, and provide reassurance and information to the witness. The witness should always be reminded not to discuss any aspect of the trial while in the halls or restrooms of the courthouse. The witness should also be reminded never to speak to the jurors.

Table 29.2   Sample Notes for Witness Testimony

	Examination	*Follow-Up*
1.	Board Certification	How many times taken?
2.	Hospital Privileges	Any revoked?
3.	Informed Consent	Plaintiff given any narcotics before discussion of risks?

At the conclusion of the testimony, the LNC may be responsible for transporting the expert witness to the hotel or airport or coordinating transportation for local witnesses. She or he may be asked to correspond with expert witnesses regarding their testimony or the outcome of the trial. If the case settles prior to the witness' testimony, it may be the responsibility of the LNC to notify the witness of this and to provide other information as allowed in the settlement agreement.

Examination of Witnesses

Following opening statements, the judge will instruct the plaintiff's attorney to begin the presentation of his case. It is the responsibility of the plaintiff to prove his or her case to the jury. The case is proved by examination of expert and fact witnesses and the introduction of exhibits which assist the witnesses in telling the story to the judge or jury.

After the plaintiff has presented his or her case to the jury, the defense has the opportunity to present a case to disprove the plaintiff's case. The defense does not have to disprove the plaintiff's case but generally presents witnesses to do so.

Although the plaintiff's case and the defendant's case are presented separately, examination of each witness is performed by both parties. Examination of witnesses has three primary phases, direct examination, cross-examination, and rebuttal. Redirect and re-cross-examination may also be warranted.

Presentation of Testimony

- Direct Examination
- Cross-Examination
- Redirect Examination
- Re-cross-Examination
- Rebuttal

Direct Examination

Direct examination is conducted by the party who calls the witness. Leading questions generally are not allowed. A leading question gives the witness clues about the response expected by the attorney. An example would be: "Tell the jury what you did when you approached the intersection and saw the red light?" Direct questions may be open-ended to allow the party's witness to elaborate on an answer or may be closed-ended and require a brief response. A direct examination question may ask "What happened when you approached the intersection?" Close-ended questions are used often for adverse or hostile witnesses for which a simple answer without elaboration or explanation is desired. A direct closed-ended question may be: "Did you step on the brake when you saw the red light?"

Cross-Examination

Cross-examination is conducted by the adverse party at the conclusion of direct testimony. Examination is limited to the subject matter of the direct examination and to matters which affect the credibility of the witness. Questions may be leading, such as "You then stepped on the brake, correct?"

Redirect and Re-Cross-Examination

Cross-examination may be followed by redirect examination. The attorney uses this examination to clarify or reinforce previous testimony. This questioning may be followed by re-cross-examination. Again, this testimony is used to clarify or emphasize specific testimony. New subjects cannot be introduced during redirect or re-cross-examination.

Rebuttal Testimony

Rebuttal testimony is offered after the close of the defendant's case. The plaintiff may wish to call additional witnesses to contradict or dispute testimony given by a defense expert witness. The same rules for direct and cross-examination of witnesses are in effect for rebuttal witnesses. Rebuttal testimony provides an opportunity to respond to testimony of the defendant's witnesses other than through cross-examination.

LNC Role

The LNC follows the planned testimony as the attorney questions each witness making detailed notes of the responses by the witness, and noting additional areas for examination by the attorney. Detailed and accurate notes are imperative. Trial transcripts generally are not available on a daily basis so the trial team must rely on memory and notes for their review of testimony and planning for additional witnesses. The attorney often will consult with the LNC in the courtroom before concluding his or her examination of the witness. At that time, the LNC must be prepared to suggest specific questions, further areas of questioning, or point out inconsistencies in previous testimony. If an expert has quoted from an article or textbook, the LNC must be prepared to advise the attorney if the testimony is incorrect or incomplete. The LNC will also be very familiar with the relevant medical records and can point out inaccuracies in testimony regarding the records. The LNC may need to provide this information in written form if the court discourages verbal conferences in the courtroom.

Throughout the trial, the LNC should listen to the testimony of each individual witness to analyze the impact of the testimony on the case as a whole. Trial strategy is dynamic and may change during the trial. The LNC must observe the jurors as the case is presented and note their response to witnesses and exhibits. These observations and the notes of the testimony will assist the trial team in evaluating the progress and potential for success of their case. Alterations in demeanor, emphasis on a particular point of testimony, or presentation of an exhibit can be made during the presentation of the case. The LNC as a member of the trial team must always be cognizant of the fact that this is a one-time opportunity for the plaintiff or defendant to tell the story. Critique and discussion of the testimony and exhibits *following* the trial does not help win the case. Inconsistencies in testimony must be noted immediately for effective impeachment. If jurors do not appear to be listening to specific testimony or do not appear to understand testimony, alterations in questions or demeanor of the attorney or witness must be made immediately.

Each LNC will develop his or her own method of note taking. A legal pad with a vertical line dividing the page in half will allow notes for testimony on one side and areas for follow-up on the other side. Notes to be handed to the attorney in the courtroom should be made on a small note card and written legibly. The cards should be unobtrusive and written clearly to avoid lengthy discussions in the courtroom while the jury is present.

Trial testimony can be frustrating for the LNC who primarily is an observer to the process. Witnesses may not respond as planned and new theories may be propounded by the opposing party. The LNC may need to conduct additional literature searches on specific topics during the trial to develop new theories or expand on earlier ones. New theories need to be communicated by the attorney witnesses in preparation for their testimony.

Trials can be exhausting and invigorating at the same time. Long hours may be necessary to ensure the client's case is presented as clearly and convincingly as possible. It is rewarding to see the years of work by the trial team and the client come together to tell the complete story to the jury.

Exhibits

Exhibits are used to help tell the story to the jury. An exhibit is a paper or document produced and exhibited to a court during a trial or hearing in proof of facts. After being accepted and marked for identification, the exhibit is made a part of the case. Exhibits may be admitted as evidence and sent with the jury for deliberation. Exhibits may also be used for demonstrative purposes only. In this case, witnesses use the exhibits to demonstrate a point of their testimony.

Medical records generally are admitted as evidence, but enlargements of specific portions of the records may be used as demonstrative evidence. Anatomic models, drawings, or scaled replicas of equipment may be used as demonstrative evidence to assist the jury to understand the technical testimony of an expert. Scaled drawings of an accident site or photographs of the site or equipment help the jury "see" the event.

Exhibits help the jury understand and retain key elements of the testimony. Jurors become tired and distracted when technical testimony is presented without the visual relief of exhibits. Exhibits are also used to enhance the memory of witnesses for details of complex records.

LNC Role

During trial, the LNC may be responsible for transporting the exhibits to the courtroom and securing them at the close of each trial day. He or she may need to coordinate audiovisual equipment and technicians for the presentation of video- or audiotapes, arrange for overhead or slide projectors or easels for presentation of charts or enlargements of records. Most courts require exhibits to be marked prior to trial. The LNC should keep a list of each exhibit and its exact location for quick retrieval by the attorney. It is critical that the LNC note each exhibit as it is admitted (see Table 29.3). Exhibits which are not admitted are used for demonstrative purposes only and are not viewed by the jury during deliberations.

It is imperative that the LNC make a check of all exhibits and presentation equipment before the start of trial each day. It is frustrating for participants to wait during trial for an exhibit to be assembled or a bulb replaced on a piece of equipment. Be sure extension cords are adequate and operational.

Table 29.3 Sample List of Exhibits

No.	Exhibit	Date	Introduced	Offered	Accepted
1.	ER report	1/1/96	11/4/96	11/4/96	11/4/96
5.	Consent	1/2/96	11/4/96	11/5/96	11/5/96
8.	Consent	1/10/96	11/5/96	11/5/96	11/5/96
15.	Death certificate	2/1/96	11/4/96	...	...
18.	...	...	...	...	...
55.	...	...	...	...	...

Conclusion of the Case

Closing Arguments

Closing arguments are the summation of the testimony by the attorneys for each party. These final statements are made by the attorneys to the jury or court to summarize the evidence they think they have established and the evidence they think the other side has failed to establish. These statements are the final words from the attorneys before the judge's charge to the jury. The arguments by the attorney do not constitute evidence and may be limited in time by the court.

LNC Role

The LNC assists the trial team in development of the closing argument by providing his or her notes and impressions to the attorney as the summary of the case for final presentation to the judge or jury is drafted. During the summation of the opposing counsel, the LNC should note any areas for rebuttal or areas which require further clarification by his or her party. Generally, a brief time may be allotted for rebuttal by each party.

Jury Instructions and Deliberations

Jury instructions are written explanations of the law which jury members must follow when determining the outcome of the case. Proposed jury instructions are presented to the judge by each party prior to the start of the trial. At some point before or during the trial, the attorneys and the judge discuss the proposed instructions. The judge determines which instructions will ultimately be presented to the jury. At the conclusion of closing arguments, the judge will read the instructions to the jury and provide any necessary explanations or clarifications.

In most civil trials, the jury is not sequestered; that is, they are allowed to go home each evening during the presentation of evidence and during deliberations. The jury will be escorted to the jury room by the bailiff and will deliberate during hours established by the judge. During deliberations, the jury may request clarification of the jury instructions by the judge or may request that portions of the transcript be read to them.

Burden of Proof

The burden of proof is different for civil trials than it is for criminal trials. In civil trials, the plaintiff must prove his or her case by a preponderance of the evidence. Some states now use "clear and convincing evidence" as the standard for civil trials. That is, the scales must tip only slightly toward one party or the other for the jury to find in favor of that party. In many jurisdictions, the jury may find the defendant negligent but also find the plaintiff to have been negligent.

Plaintiff's Negligence

Under comparative negligent statutes or doctrines, negligence is measured in terms of percentage, and any damages allowed shall be diminished in proportion to the amount of negligence attributable to the person for whose injury, damage, or death recovery is sought. Many states have replaced contributory negligence acts or doctrines with comparative negligence. Where negligence by both parties is concurrent and contributes to injury, recovery is not barred under such doctrine, but plaintiff's damages are diminished proportionately, provided plaintiff's fault is less than the defendant's and that, by exercise of normal care, plaintiff could not have avoided consequences of the defendant's negligence after it was or should have been apparent.

Contributory negligence is the act or omission by the plaintiff which, along with the defendant's negligence, was the proximate cause of the plaintiff's injury. Most jurisdictions allow the jury to find either comparative or contributory negligence by the plaintiff.

Jury Ballot

A ballot is prepared by the plaintiff's attorney and submitted to the jury. The ballot requires several questions to be answered by the jury before deliberations are completed. The first question requires the jury to determine if the plaintiff has proved negligence by one or more of the defendants. The next question asks the jury to determine the percent of negligence attributed to each defendant. In jurisdictions with comparative or contributory negligence, the jury must then determine what percent, if any, the plaintiff was negligent.

Damages

If negligence has been found, the jury must determine the monetary award to the plaintiff. The award may be divided into past damages for actual expenses, past wage loss, and future damages for expenses and wage loss. The jury may also award damages for pain and suffering, although these awards may have statutory limits in some jurisdictions.

Punitive Damages

The jury may also award punitive damages if plaintiff has demanded such damages in the complaint. Punitive damages are awarded to punish the defendant and deter others from similar behavior. Punitive damages are requested most often in product liability cases. This penalty may be applied in cases of outrageous conduct.

When punitive damages are demanded, the trial may be bifurcated, that is, divided into two separate phases of liability and damages. The jury will hear testimony on liability and causation, then deliberate on these issues. If they find negligence by the defendants and that the negligence caused the plaintiff's injuries, the damages phase of the trial begins. Evidence is presented to prove damages as well as the economic worth of the defendant. The jury deliberates and establishes an award for the plaintiff in an amount intended to substantially penalize the defendant.

Verdict

When the jury has concluded deliberations, the foreperson will notify the judge through the bailiff. The verdict may be read in open court after the parties have been summoned or may be given telephonically to the parties by the judge or his representative.

Posttrial Activities

Jury Interviews

The LNC may be assigned the task of interviewing the jurors after the trial is concluded. The jurors are under no obligation to talk to any party but are free to do so. Valuable information for future trials may be gained from juror interviews. Questions regarding the presentation by the attorney including demeanor, the exhibits, or the witnesses may yield areas for change or improvement in the attorney's next trial. The jurors should be questioned about the presentation by the opposing party's attorney and experts as well.

Bill of Costs

Most jurisdictions allow the prevailing party to recover the costs of the trial from the opposing party. The LNC may be asked to calculate the amounts of the medically related costs such as expert witness fees, medical exhibit fees, and time spent on case presentation by the LNC.

Motion for a New Trial or Appeal

The attorney is responsible for meeting deadlines for filing motions for a new trial or for an appeal. The LNC may be asked to contribute information for the motion. The LNC should be aware of the strict time limits set by the rules for filing such motions.

Discussion Questions

1. Motions in limine are used to
   a. Highlight the key points of the trial strategy
   b. Prohibit introduction of certain testimony into trial
   c. Determine the order of witnesses
   d. Object to the other party's witnesses
2. An attorney may use a preemptory challenge to
   a. Dismiss a potential juror without specific cause
   b. Object to a question by the opposing attorney
   c. Question the qualifications of an expert witness
   d. Attempt to remove a judge from the case
3. Demonstrative evidence is
   a. Evidence used by the jury to show how they reached a verdict
   b. Evidence used to assist a witness in explaining his or her testimony
   c. Sent to the jury room with the jurors for deliberation
   d. Evidence used only in opening statements or closing arguments
4. The types of examination of witnesses and the sequence of their presentation are
   a. Direct examination, indirect examination, and rebuttal

    b. Direct examination, cross-examination, redirect examination, re-cross-examination and rebuttal

    c. Cross-examination, rebuttal, and direct examination

    d. Direct examination, rebuttal, and cross-examination

5. When a plaintiff is assessed with comparative negligence it means his or her

    a. Award is compared with other awards for similar injuries

    b. Negligence is compared with the defendant's and his or her award reduced proportionately

    c. Injuries are compared to those of individuals in similar cases

    d. Negligence is compared to the defendant's but his or her award is not changed

6. Punitive damages

    a. Are jail terms determined by the judge

    b. Monetary damages awarded to the plaintiff to discourage similar behavior by others

    c. Monetary damages awarded by all juries in all negligence cases

    d. Punishment for the plaintiff's negligence

Glossary

Burden of proof: Obligation to provide evidence necessary to establish a disputed fact or a degree of belief in the mind of the court.

Comparative negligence: A proportional division of the damages between the plaintiff and the defendant in a tort action according to their respective shares of fault contributing to the injury.

Contributory negligence: Negligence of the injured person which contributes to the injury and precludes his or her recovery in a tort action.

Cross-examination: The questioning of the opposition's witness in order to test the truth and accuracy of that witness's testimony given on direct examination.

Direct examination: The examination in chief of a witness by the party who called him to testify.

Exhibit: (Noun) An object displayed in court as evidence, such as a document, photograph, or gun. A paper attached to a document. (Verb) To display or show.

Expert witness: One whose special knowledge of a subject enables him or her to express opinions and draw conclusions in testimony at trial. Persons without such knowledge are not allowed to do so and are restricted to testifying only to the facts.

Negligence: The inadvertent or unintentional failure to exercise that care which a reasonable, prudent, and careful person would exercise.

Opening statement: Presentation made by attorneys at beginning of trial in which they summarize their client's case and the evidence which they will present on the client's behalf.

Punitive damages: Award of damages not related to actual harm caused to plaintiff, but instead intended to punish the defendant and deter future wrongdoing.

Rebuttal, rebutting evidence: Evidence which defeats, refutes, or proves the contrary of facts or presumptions offered in evidence by the opposing party. Rebuttal evidence may be offered at the close of the opponent's case.

Voir dire: Latin for "to speak the truth." An examination of a person as a prospective juror to test his competency and prejudice. Preliminary examination of a witness in order to determine his or her competency to speak the truth. Examination is conducted under oath by judge or attorneys.

Reference

Singer, A. (1996). Trial consulting: a much-in-demand, highly effective, and nicely profitable professional subspecialty for legal nurse consultants, *Journal of Legal Nurse Consulting*, 7(2), 2.

Suggested Readings

Branson, F. and Branson, D. (1992). Successful voir dire, *Trial*, 28(2), 21–24.

Carpenter, W. (1995). Low-cost exhibits: more than making do, *Trial*, 31(9), 43–44.

Fargo, M. (1993). Juror questionnaires can supplement voir dire, *Trial*, 29(10), 23–27.

Gibbins, B. (1990). Closing argument: consolidating your theme, *Trial*, 26(1), 83–88.

Haydock, R. and Sonsteng, J. (1994). *Planning to Win: Effective Preparation*, St. Paul, MN, West Publishing.

Haydock, R. and Sonsteng, J. (1994). *Jury Trials*, St. Paul, MN, West Publishing.

Haydock, R. and Sonsteng, J. (1994). *Opening and Closing: How to Present a Case*, St. Paul, MN, West Publishing.

Haydock, R. and Sonsteng, J. (1994). *Examining Witnesses: Direct, Cross, and Expert Examination*, St. Paul, MN, West Publishing.

Haydock, R. and Sonsteng, J. (1994). *Evidence, Objections and Exhibits*, St. Paul, MN, West Publishing.

Herman, R. (1989). Jury selection in civil litigation: using voir dire as a foundation to win your case, *Trial*, 25(1), 71.

Herman, G. (1995). How to master direct examination: practical perspectives, *Trial*, 31(4), 70–72.

Lubet, S. (1993). Eight techniques for direct examination of experts, *Trial*, 29(12), 16–18.

Pyle, R. (1992). *Foundations of Law for Paralegals: Cases, Commentary, and Ethics*, Albany, NY, Delmar Publishers, Inc. and Lawyers Cooperative Publishing.

Ring, L. (1993). Effective closing arguments in civil trials, *Trial*, 29(10), 61–64.

Siemer, D. (1992). The heart of a trial: direct examination, *Trial*, 28(2), 48–53.

Section VIII
Business Principles for the Legal Nurse Consultant

Chapter 30

Starting a Business: Legal and Business Principles

Doreen James Wise and Adrienne Bond

Contents

1-57444-123-X/98
© 1998 by American Association of Legal Nurse Consultants

Introduction

Service businesses are more likely to fail than to succeed. With nursing's roots originating in the tradition of the church and the military, successful nurse-owned consulting business practices do not happen "naturally." For most nurses, the skills must be learned. Nonetheless, many nurses are quite successful at the business of legal nurse consulting. Those surviving, and indeed *thriving*, reduce their success to several core elements and a few basic rules. Minding the store includes taking care of legal, business planning, financial, and marketing issues. The basic rules are (1) keep it simple, (2) protect the business owner's personal assets, (3) do it right the first time, (4) intend to be successful, and (5) remember what you already know.

Legal Principles

Choosing the Right Legal Professional

In starting a business, the first function of an attorney is to separate personal and business matters, legally and financially protecting the business and the individual client. Given the high failure rate of new businesses, the right attorney can assist in protecting personal assets from creditors of the (potentially failed) business. Despite one's optimism (and maybe in support of it!), finding appropriate legal counsel early is essential. Experienced legal counsel can offer *prevention of*, and *protection from* problems. As nurses often tell patients, preventive maintenance is far less expensive than treating a serious problem; of course, the same advice is true for preventing legal problems. In addition, the right attorney can help to solve those inevitable business legal problems while the problems are still manageable. This does not necessarily mean that once engaged, the attorney will begin to charge fees or work full-time. What it *does* mean is that the correct professional is in place, and in the entrepreneur's corner when it is time to work.

The Search Process

The process of seeking counsel for one's new business requires careful research and interviewing, as would undertaking any other major financial commitment. Seeking and engaging a specialist in corporate law, with a subspecialty in business start-ups is ideal. Avoiding the attorney friend or relative whose specialty is in an unrelated area of the law is advised. Despite fear that a subspecialist might charge more per hour, in the long run fees generally will end up the same if not lower. Engaging a seasoned practitioner ordinarily results in fewer hours being spent by the more knowledgeable professional and in business legal disasters being prevented or well managed. It is true that larger firms will have senior practitioners, with proportionately "senior" fees. These same firms also may have less-experienced attorneys working under close supervision, who can carry out more routine portions of the work at a lower billable rate. For some legal nurse consultants (LNCs) these "younger" attorneys mature with the business owner, making for a successful career-long affiliation! The smaller specialty or "boutique" firms concentrating their work in the business start-up arena are an attractive alternative. One may find quite competent and experienced attorneys seeking a more client-centered approach than the "bill, bill, bill" mentality of some larger firms.

Although costs for services do vary from one area to another, looking beyond the billable hourly rates is advised, as indicated above. A $250/hour specialist may spend half the time and do a better job than a $175/hour general practice attorney. Asking potential lawyers for a fee schedule and for an estimate of billable hours and fees for each job requested is advised. Then, it is wise to pursue references for clients' actual experiences with the attorney's time and billing.

To research and find the proper professional, it makes sense to consult a legal directory, such as Martindale-Hubbell; this and similar directories are found at any public or law library and most business libraries. Legal directories include biographic information about attorneys and a brief description of legal practice and experience. Frequently, the attorney's representative clients are listed; the LNC entrepreneur should look for other professional service companies as examples of clientele served.

Generally, there are two basic divisions in corporate/securities practice. They are specialists in (1) office and (2) trial practice. Although the trial attorney may be familiar to most LNCs, the office practitioner is more likely the desired professional for structuring the business start-up.

It is advisable to consult with LNC colleagues and friends, asking who they have retained and whether they could recommend that attorney or another. One can call the state bar for a list of expert speakers at continuing legal education offerings on emerging business seminars. The bar may also send membership rosters for business law or related committees within its ranks. Finally, having identified some practitioners in this area, it might be smart to secure names of their most serious competitors as well. Eventually, the same names and firms will be recommended repeatedly.

The next step is examination of credentials. Not all law schools are created equal, nor are all law students; both are regularly ranked from the outside and from within. Individual attorneys may have earned such badges of merit as law review or had similar publication experience, won "Order of the Coif" or other honors, and/or been inducted into honor societies. One should examine the attorney's work record once in practice: has there been a logical progression from large, well-established firm with business specialty departments to partnership therein? Alternatively, has the attorney ventured from the larger firm into a private practice specializing in business law? In addition, there are many opportunities to review, write, teach, and speak within the legal profession; participation in these activities heralds acknowledged expertise in a given area of practice, and savvy attorneys will have reported same in legal directory publications.

Once the realm of possibilities is narrowed to a short list, perhaps three to six, the next logical step is arranging for personal interviews. Once there, inquire what the attorney provides for and needs from new clients, and what fee arrangements are to be made. It is smart to ask how services are delivered, and in what ways that particular lawyer differs from the others on one's short list. The wise LNC next asks for personal references, calling each and discussing the attorney's strengths and weaknesses. Some LNCs then call attorney friends and clients to ask about the targeted professionals.

The final appraisal calls for some personal inquiry beyond professional qualifications of competency. The LNC must ask: Is this a person I trust? Will this attorney give truthful advice, even if painful? Will this lawyer litigate aggressively when called for, but not recommend that course unless absolutely necessary? Each LNC has questions of this nature which must be satisfactorily answered for a successful long-term relationship.

Choosing the Right Legal Entity

Once counsel is selected, it is imperative to educate oneself about the tasks to be undertaken, for several critical decisions must be made. *The single most important function for an attorney at this stage is to separate personal from business assets of the client*. This is accomplished by establishing a legal entity, such as a corporation, separate from the individual LNC starting the business. The basic tasks to be accomplished with one's attorney are to (1) set up a separate legal entity that minimizes the owner's personal liability; (2) ensure that the new entity has the legal rights necessary to conduct its proposed business; and (3) make certain that the new business entity pays its federal, state, and local taxes as required by law.

Establish a Clean Legal Structure

The business needs to be established from inception with a clean legal structure. This results in an entity that has (1) absolute clarity about its ownership and (2) limits the owner's liability to the fullest legal extent possible. The choices include incorporation, limited partnership, and a limited liability corporation (LLC). Selecting from among these is effected depending on

1. The number of owners, in that partnerships and LLCs require two or more persons
2. The tax effects of formation
3. Choices about day-to-day management
4. The type of assets placed in the entity
5. Pension and insurance concerns
6. Exit strategies
7. State regulation and taxation

One's attorney will need to provide concise analyses for each relevant issue and to identify the choices appropriate to the LNC's personal situation and state laws. Any will work, but there are best choices for each LNC, dependent on the unique situation and preferences.

Most independent LNCs start as *sole proprietors*. This simply means that the individual LNC personally is in business and has no separate legal identity. The LNC is the only owner and may be the only employee. To undertake this approach, the LNC visits the county courthouse, filing a "DBA" (for "doing business as...") or assumed name certificate. The name is then registered within that county, assuring the LNC of being the only business entity with that name. For example, one would then be Florence N. Gale, *doing business as* "LNC Enterprises" or the like. For legal purposes, the LNC is the responsible individual whose personal assets are unprotected legally as separate from the business. Personal tax returns report the LNC owner's income generated from all professional activities including the sole proprietorship.

Other LNCs have begun to incorporate their business endeavors. *Corporations* are relatively easy to form and operate, and are generally taxed separately from the individual owner. This means that the owner faces double taxation on income earned in the corporation, once on the corporate level and again as an individual "shareholder." It is possible to avoid such double taxation through a federal tax election as a subchapter S corporation. An "S corp" is a regular corporation under state law that qualifies and affirmatively files a written election to be taxed similarly to a partnership. There are strict qualifying requirements for an S corp about which the attorney will advise.

Some LNCs prefer to venture with a friend or colleague, forming partnerships. *Partnerships*, and close cousin, *the LLC*, are more difficult to form. Regular general partnerships do not shield the owners (partners) from personal liability, although some limited liability exposure is offered through a limited partnership or an LLC. Day-to-day business affairs in a limited partnership or an LLC also require some forethought and training. With these drawbacks, however, there is the benefit of "pass-through" taxation; properly formed and operated, neither entity pays federal income tax. Other crucial considerations include state tax, the number of owners, and how the assets of the new business, if any, are to be contributed to the new entity.

Comment: Many new business corporations may qualify for the S election with the Internal Revenue Service, allowing taxation similar to that of the partnership and avoiding double taxation. Corporations generally are more cost-effective because the (1) cost of filing fees is lower, (2) standardization of forms for incorporation lowers the setup costs, and (3) again because of standardization, business owners ordinarily are more familiar with standard day-to-day operations which lowers costs. *The S election, if available, offers the benefit of partnership or pass-through taxation, with the cost-effectiveness of the corporate form.*

> Example 30.1: (While each business situation must be individually assessed, the following is representative of standard formation of an S corp.) The entire start-up budget for Florence N. Gale, an LNC, is $2000, so cost considerations are important. Although the LLC is an option, this LNC opts for an S corp as the best type of entity for her planned operations and also the best bargain. Our budding LNC entrepreneur lives and works in Texas, where corporate filing fees are $300. The attorney's time in document creation for Ms. Gale's practice is one quarter of that required to prepare a limited partnership agreement! (This is because corporate forms are fixed by the state, and can be "boilerplated," while partnership forms require more extensive, individualized drafting.) Because of service in her AALNC chapter, Ms. Gale has working knowledge of such corporate terms as "president," bylaws, and "Board of Directors." The attorney had advised against a partnership, partly because of costs but also because the education necessary to conduct business is more time-consuming.
>
> Florence N. Gale's attorney did warn that there are certain disadvantages to the S corp. There are tax limitations on the type and number of shareholders; S corps are limited to one class of stock, and therefore, it is almost impossible to separate ownership control from profit sharing, perhaps necessary to raise outside capital. An S corp may not be able to take advantage of deductions available to regular corporations for many employee benefit programs. Finally, assets placed into the corporation may not be taken out without incurring tax at both the corporate and shareholder level (70%), requiring careful consideration before placing hard assets into corporate solution.

Checklist of Required Documents

If one *incorporates* a new business, the first document required to form the entity is the Articles, or Certificate of Incorporation; the document's contents are dictated by state law. The Articles of Incorporation are filed, as a matter of public record, with the secretary of state in the same state in which the entity is formed. Bylaws, usually relatively standardized, and minutes of an "organizational meeting" of the board of directors are created next. The minutes should record election of officers, the issuing of shares, and any other business matters related to the corporation's forming. If there is more than one shareholder, it is advisable to commit, in writing, agreement about *voting* the shares and *selling* the shares. It is imperative that this shareholders' agreement clearly delineate what will happen upon the divorce or death of the shareholders, and whether or not a shareholder may use shares as loan collateral. Because of community property laws in many states, and the rights of spouses to equity interests in the business, the death or divorce of an owner can cause problems in any business. In community property states a simple shareholders agreement concerning rights upon death and divorce is advisable. Once again, lack of clear equity ownership can create havoc in times of life change, so *good records are essential.* It is recommended that the issue of transfer of shares to spouse or children as a means of estate planning be addressed directly. In small entities, where the same people who manage the business also share ownership, it is advisable to set and keep strict boundaries on what is permitted under law. Many prosperous businesses (and long-term friendships) were demolished because decisions regarding the business were not made in advance of crisis. Further, *the most frequent cause for failure of an existing business is the death or divorce of an owner. Forethought about such matters can make all the difference.*

For an *LLC*, the documents are substantially the same, but bear different names and serve slightly different functions. Although the forms are similar, they are *not* dictated by state statute, so they require careful drafting.

If the entity selected is a *limited partnership,* there will be two documents. The first will be a Certificate of Limited Partnership, in many states a one-page notice of filing of the name and address of the partnership. The second document will be an Agreement of Limited Partnership, a document containing all features of organizational content, bylaws, and shareholders agreement.

Whatever form is undertaken, the LNC should clarify ahead with the attorney what documentation is recommended, how long the work will take, what the work itself will cost, and what alternative approaches there might be.

If the endeavor is creating start-up "jitters" for the LNC business owner, and it is the attorney who is causing the jitters, a second opinion is recommended! Starting a business is difficult work, and working with an attorney with confidence can make a significant and positive difference.

Keep Clean Legal Records

Once the business entity is formed, using it correctly is the next critical step. Bearing in mind the purpose of the entity, i.e., separating personal from business assets, one must be scrupulous about making proper use of its advantages. At a minimum this implies the creation and preservation of careful legal records. Two critical tasks flow from this commitment. The first task is making sure that the ownership is absolutely clear, and the second is making sure that technology or other intellectual property rights used by the business are properly owned by it. Although there are other tasks of importance in forming a business, these two tend to be the ones commonly creating trouble if not handled correctly. One's attorney can advise about other issues that may arise in the unique contractual situation.

Clarity of "Technology" Rights

The other early, potentially fatal problem involves whether employees of the new company contractually are free (1) to work in the job for which they are being hired and (2) to bring processes and devices, i.e., the technology, they developed in other employ. Both must be explored on start-up, and prior to hiring. It is well advised to consider carefully any legal obligations to current or former employers. One's business attorney should review and analyze any preexisting agreements held by intended employees or associates. The existence of an employment agreement probably implies a noncompete, nonpiracy, and/or a confidentiality agreement. If any of these are in existence they must be honored; it is extremely risky to ignore them. Many companies seriously enforce such agreements for reasons of principle, pursuing violators on an individual basis at great expense so that a point is made. *It falls to the business attorney to ensure that all owners and personnel of the start-up business have the right to engage in the new occupation, and under what limitations.*

   The new business also must have the right to use its "technology." Those technologies, devices, or processes developed while in the employ of another may belong exclusively to the former employer. Any technology rights must be properly assigned to the new entity, through direct ownership or license. Because that technology can be key to the new business, the attorney must be sure the rights are properly held.

> Example 30.2: An LNC seeking to work with Florence N. Gale was interviewed, in part, because she had created innovative software for a chronological medical records summary. On review of the LNC's employment agreement with her former company, Ms. Gale's attorney found that all devices and technology the LNC had developed while in their employ remained their property. The LNC was not free to use the summary format once she had left their employ to join Ms. Gale's company.

Avoid Devastating Personal Liability

It is a difficult, but unavoidable, fact that a majority of new businesses fail. As a result, from inception the attorney for a business start-up will be focused on minimizing the LNC's personal risk.

Use the Limited Liability Vehicle Properly

The S Corp, or other limited liability entity holding the business, offers important protection for the individual LNC owner. However, once incorporated, or having instituted any other entity, the LNC owner must properly operate the legal entity to maintain its protective effect. The attorney should provide clear written instructions for operating the entity. This will allow the LNC to avoid errors defeating the protective liability limitations afforded. For example, an LNC choosing incorporation should be counseled to establish separate personal and business bank accounts. All "communication" from and about the incorporated company should indicate the legal designation. This would include answering the phone, preparing wording for signs in an exhibit booth, printing letterhead, etc. Each and every use of the company name should include the assignation "Inc."

   There should be a separate corporate telephone line and listing, office space delineated as such even if working in one's home, and if the LNC owns several businesses, there should even be separate office areas marked as such. Personnel must be paid and accounted for through the new entity, and items such as leases, equipment contracts, and other operational agreements need to be in the name of the new entity, not the owner's name. Instead, the owner executes such documents as an officer of the company, in a "representative capacity" on behalf of the company. As such, all signatures must contain a designation for the office held on behalf of the entity, lest the individual signing be considered executing individually and thus be personally liable.

It is smart to attempt to negotiate any and all business agreements in this manner. One must bear in mind, however, that new business owners almost always are forced to give a personal guarantee for business obligations such as equipment or office leases, at least at first. Practically speaking, most landlords and equipment lessors usually look to the business for repayment rather than to the individual owner, or accept a limited guarantee from the individual owners. For example, limits for personal guarantees, even if required, can be in *time* (the first 2 years of operation) or *amount* (fixed number or percentage). Even bankers will consider guarantees that are limited to the percentage of the business that the individual owns. So, it may be worth fighting to limit personal guarantees, and to renegotiate as soon as possible any that are demanded.

In summary, the best advice for the LNC entrepreneur intending to limit liability is (1) plaster the legal designation for the entity, such as "Inc.," everywhere, (2) sign all documents as an officer of the company not as an individual, and (3) never accept contractual personal liability without a good fight!

> Example 30.3: Florence N. Gale will serve as President of the new entity, an S corp to be called LNC, Inc. She has leased office space in her capacity as President, signing the lease as such. Newly designed letterhead reads LNC, Inc., as do the business cards. The new receptionist is trained to answer the telephone, "Good morning. Thank you for calling LNC, Inc. How can I help you?"

Buy Insurance

One is wise to arrange for casualty, property, and umbrella liability insurance, in an amount sufficient to settle a serious lawsuit. It is smart to shop around for insurance carriers, investigating and comparing coverage, exclusions, and claims payment history of the companies. A cheaper quote on insurance may be false economy if the carrier runs up legal bills fighting all claims. For some partnerships or associations, so called "Key Man" insurance might be considered. If the business plan is critically dependent on one entrepreneur, then for the cost, key-man life insurance can prevent costly liabilities for the other players if one has an untimely exit. The attorney author of this chapter (A.B.) advises avoiding exotic insurance products such as product liability or officer and director insurance for the LNC entity. The insurance professional can assist in setting up safety procedures and answering questions about premises liability; client education materials are usually available from the carriers on this, as well as about any type of liability coverage. However, *there is no substitute for careful reading of the policy and thoughtful inquiry about items not understood*. As always, time spent preventively helps avoid the worst disasters from occurring. Prevention strategies can be set in place from the outset to avoid large claims later.

Note: One solid source may be insurance carriers for professional organizations who often offer member business owners policies including necessary elements at a competitive cost.

Pay Unto Caesar

It is essential to file and pay all federal, state, and local taxes in a timely fashion. For many years the federal government has had the right to assess personal liability for officers of entities that did not file and pay taxes on time for that entity. This includes income and payroll taxes; not paying is said to be the most expensive money anyone can "borrow" because there are not only subsequent interest payments, but also significant penalties. The penalties are significant enough that it is advisable to borrow money from a bank or use a credit card to pay federal taxes than to delay filing and paying the federal government. Most states have enacted personal liability provisions so that individual executives are also personally liable for payment of state taxes, including income, franchise, and employment. There are in many jurisdictions requirements for "licenses" to operate businesses, which serve as another source of revenue for those jurisdictions. Therefore, part of one's start-up strategy should include determining if local licenses are required to commence business, and budgeting for them. *It is important to understand that entities of government have almost limitless powers to pursue collection of deficient tax and licensing fees. Compliance is absolutely mandatory.*

Business Principles

For many individuals, starting a business is the culmination of a life's dream. Years of education and experience are brought to bear on what many regard as the ultimate financial freedom — the right to plan, pursue, and benefit from the direct results of one's own hard work. Nurses, predominately female and traditionally employees of large corporations, have flocked to the concept, and many have succeeded. For some, it has meant the long-awaited opportunity to apply highest standards of patient care in a private clinical practice, unhampered by the political realities of today's corporate health systems. For others, starting and running a business mean hope for financial independence. Still others start businesses in order to evolve from nursing to other professional interests. No matter their individual choices and circumstances, all entrepreneurs imprint their businesses with their talents, life experiences, and personal values. Each business absolutely is reflective of all that the unique entrepreneur has been, has achieved, and has dreamed of becoming.

Although nursing curricula traditionally have scant inclusion of business topics, *per se*, much about nursing resonates happily with the conduct of business. The systematic planning and decision-making process, the emphasis on "customer service," the creative utilization of limited resources, and the ideology of commitment to what is highest and best, all translate from successful nursing practice to thriving business!

The Business Plan

Sound business practice flows from the same *systematic approach* as does the nursing process. A business plan, not unlike a nursing care plan, essentially drives the business decision-making process and orchestrates a systematic, goal-oriented approach. Successful businesses uniformly have a plan, usually committed to writing. Keeping goals clearly in mind and view can make a significant difference in the outcome of business efforts.

The Purpose

In essence, the business plan helps the would-be entrepreneur to create and commit to a plan of action. It demands that outcomes be related to time and resources and literally provides the structure by which the new (or growing) business proceeds. Failing to commit to the concept of deliberate planning leads to disaster. Few successful business owners prosper without at least an informal plan of action from inception. The discipline of going through the steps of writing a plan, referring to it regularly through the year, and making responsive course corrections virtually assures progress toward goals and efficient use of resources.

One traditional use for the business plan is to obtain financing; however, the true function is directing the business decision-making process. The main purpose of the business plan is to crystallize the year's goals. Greenbaum (1990) says the "formal business plan forces you to think through the key elements necessary to start and run a business, financial aspects, sales requirements, etc. and to build and service a client base, i.e., manpower needs, systems, etc.," (p. 21). Those goals are accomplished through: (1) a marketing and sales activities plan and (2) a financial management plan consisting of cash-flow and profit plans. "In effect, this process is a feasibility study of the owner's goals and objectives for the year," (Torrence, 1992, p. 182). Does the marketing plan make sense? Is the sales plan attainable? Does the company have the right employees to accomplish the planned tasks? Does the profit plan indicate that the effort is worth the outcome? What will the cash requirements be, and can enough cash be generated to meet the need?

Components of the Business Plan

The following describe some main components of a business plan. The components include: company background; key personnel; marketing concept and analysis; and financial components, which includes profit plan, cash-flow plan and financial request for funding. Examples, though not exhaustive, demonstrate information that might be included in each component. The examples provided were prepared for the purpose of obtaining outside funding from an LNC's bank.

Company background describes the nature and history of the business; it may give its location, facilities, and details of operation. It presents the essence of the business understandable in layperson's terms, and should directly reflect the mission statement of the business.

> Example 30.4: LNC, Inc., is a nurse-owned medical information service, established during the owner's graduate studies. LNC, Inc. provides medical/legal consultative services and products to clients involved in the litigation process. Clients traditionally served are defense attorneys in the medical malpractice arena and professional liability insurance carriers. Services include medical record and case analyses, medical literature research, and preparation for litigation.

Key personnel gives a resume of the owner's education and experience, emphasizing those aspects relevant to success in this particular enterprise. Other managers are featured, as are outside consultants with critical roles in the company.

Example 30.5: The owner of LNC, Inc., Florence N. Gale, has master's degrees in nursing and business, as well as 30 years of critical care and trauma clinical nursing experience prior to founding LNC, Inc., in 1990. Company staff includes equally skilled clinicians, with bedside and management expertise in obstetric and medical/surgical areas. A full-time office manager and secretary support these professionals. Established relationships with a CPA and business attorney augment the corporate structure and personnel.

Marketing concept describes special factors making the company effective in the marketplace. The purpose is to define how the company has succeeded thus far, and the plan for continued future growth.

Example 30.6: The owner of LNC, Inc., in addition to active participation in nursing professional organizations, participates in the planning committee for continuing legal education programs for the Defense Research Institute. Through that affiliation the company maintains cordial collegial relations with its target clientele. In addition, because LNC, Inc., was the first such service in this community, because it provides quality service and keeps pricing competitive, LNC, Inc., enjoys an established practice and continuing confidence of the defense bar. During the upcoming fiscal year, plans include expanding the client base to provide consultation and expert testimony to selected, credible plaintiff's attorneys in neighboring states.

Marketing analysis presents information in more detail about clientele and prospects for sales. It provides detailed analyses of projected sales volume, growth trends, competitors and other market factors.

Example 30.7: Current clientele includes defense attorneys representing professional liability insurance carriers. In the coming fiscal year, an advertising campaign will tap the identified need for medical/legal services among plaintiff's attorney members of the Trial Lawyer's Association. By the end of the fiscal year, it is projected that income from services can be increased by 25% while maintaining fixed costs of doing business. A local medical student has initiated a medical/legal consulting business, and offers the possible threat of competition. Her fees are lower, but her time is constrained by studies. This potential competitor has limited clinical experience which is dwarfed by the cumulative experience of nurses at LNC, Inc.

Sales plan is the logical outcome of the preceding sections, projecting the monthly income from services for the upcoming year. Such projections are to be solidly based on past performance and current market conditions. Specific selling strategies are included. These will be evaluated at the close of the upcoming year.

Example 30.8: The company plans to continue its practice of careful selection of marketing and sales venues, in keeping with the values of the health professions. The bulk of new clients has always come from word-of-mouth reference by satisfied clients, and quality work. However, for the first time, a low-keyed display booth will be arranged at Trial Lawyer's Association meetings in five nearby states. A professional staff member will attend each meeting, and marketing materials will be sent by direct mail to targeted groups of attorneys in each of the five states. Customary marketing to local clients will continue, and, in addition, staff members will attend all bar association meetings. Each current staff member will increase annual billable hours by 500 for a total of 1500 hours, and a new staff member to be hired will produce an additional 500 hours, as well.

Financial components of the plan: financial background lays the foundation for financial projections and requests for outside funding. (For those LNCs wishing more information, see section on Financial Issues, below.) Financial statements and tax returns from the prior 3 years, and personal financial statements for the company's principals are generally required in requests for funding.

Profit plan is the first portion of the financial plan and demonstrates the projected profitability of the planned enterprise. Critical assumptions on which the profit plan are based should be emphasized including percent of revenues for service over prior year, ratio of gross profit to revenue, level of expenses contrasted to prior years, and comparisons to competitors revenues if known,

Example 30.9: (narrative attached to financial statements) Current revenues are $255,000, or 1000 hours billed at $85 for each of three nurses. Projected revenues of $340,000 are based on an increase in business through marketing and the addition of one nurse working 500 hours @ $85/hour ($42,500) and an additional 500 hours to be accomplished by existing staff. In addition, selected expenses are planned for reduction: transfer to a lower-cost long-distance carrier, ending monthly payments on copier by using cash to pay it off, and replacing departing secretary with less costly staff will save 2000 hours @ $5/hour ($10,000). Costs will also be reduced by selling LNC, Inc.'s medical records collection service, the Company's least-profitable current activity, to a thriving competitor in the medical records business.

A cash-flow plan is done informally by all business owners to predict the money needed to pay upcoming obligations. In this day-to-day operations approach, and in the more formal business plan, it is wise to address how and when money owed to the company or accounts receivable are to be collected. Cash-flow planning addresses work and invoicing schedules, scheduling of major purchases, and routine operating expenses paid on a regular basis, such as rent, telephone, and payroll. Addressing plans for collection of past-due accounts is advised, including reports of progress made. It is best to include information about seasonal fluctuations, if any. Torrence (1992) states that this phase of the business plan is "the best tool available … for assessing cash requirements … (and) great care should be taken in working out the critical assumptions underlying the analysis."

Example 30.10: Accounts receivable report reveals ten accounts seriously delinquent. Personal calls and letters will be generated in an attempt to obtain or negotiate payment. Delinquent collection alternatives include small claims court for smaller amounts, and initiating litigation for larger accounts. Revisions will be undertaken for more proactive collection strategies to reduce future delinquencies. A new policy will be instituted to collect a $500 retainer for each new case to generate cash with which to pay employees while work is in progress, and before invoices can be sent for completed projects. This will help to offset the need for additional operating capital for predictable first- and third-quarter rushes.

The financing request formally addresses moneys requested from the bank or nonbank funding source. It should include amount desired, plans for how it will be used, and repayment schedule. More detail is provided in the following section on Financial Issues.

> Example 30.11: Based on the information herein, LNC, Inc., requests a loan of $10,000 to create a local area network computer system, to add one faster computer for a new person, and to update existing machines with additional memory, fax modems, and electronic mail. Staff will be able to prepare, fax, or e-mail reports directly to clients, saving personnel costs, staying in better communication with clients and each other while making more productive use of their time. LNC, Inc. proposes to finance the loan over a 3-year period to reduce drain on current monthly cash flow, while utilizing the new equipment to generate income from new clients.

No matter the ultimate use for business planning, be it orchestrating day-to-day operations or securing outside funding, the outcome is a goal-oriented, systematic enterprise. It is a process which is critical both for start-up and mature businesses. "The [best-run] consulting organizations will make a commitment to the planning process which will continue…[updating] the plan annually to review where the business has gone in the previous year and to ensure that the goals and objectives established … are realistic" (Greenbaum, 1990, p. 22). Conducting business without a plan is like driving at night in strange terrain without a map, and therefore unthinkable. In summary, Torrence (1992) correctly claims that "the chief beneficiary of this hard-nosed planning is the business owner…. [P]reparing a sound business plan is the biggest bargain in management," (p. 187). Amen.

Establishing the Business

Once legally in place, the business must be housed, staffed, equipped, and grown, or alternatively, maintained purposefully as a one-person enterprise.

Choosing the Site

Selection of the site for one's offices reflects individual preferences, business goals, and unique circumstances. Some LNCs prefer establishing offices at home; others lease or purchase property in an office complex or freestanding building. In general, several considerations usually are at work in this decision making and will be specific to each individual LNC business owner. Some considerations common to most are the image desired, initial costs one is willing to invest, one's individual strengths and weaknesses, and preferences based on personnel issues. Some benefits and detriments for each approach to housing one's office are discussed. However, each LNC must carefully and candidly reflect on personal work strengths, experience, and unique lifestyle situation as each of the decisions is made in keeping with the unique qualities of that individual.

The Home-Based Office. Independent consulting particularly lends itself to the home-based office model. Available technology affords an entirely professional operation with the convenience of a home-based location. Since the legal nurse consulting process can be conducted largely through receipt, review, and evaluation of medical records and other written materials, it may be accomplished largely out of sight of the client. Face-to-face meetings are usually scheduled in the client's office or a public building. Work product can be delivered, mailed, or faxed to one's client, all readily initiated from the home office. In many instances, the client may wish only verbal reports, which can be executed by telephone, teleconference, or in person. Vast resources finally are available to support the home-based enterprise. Entire publications are devoted to setting up and operating successful home office endeavors (see References at end of chapter).

Benefits are reduced start-up and maintenance costs, and no daily commute. There are specific tax benefit considerations, best made in consultation with a tax specialist CPA during start-up. In this way solid business practices are established early. Another benefit includes the possibility of achieving better balance between family/personal and business life. Those with young families (or aging parents) at home may wish to be available while working. Physical safety may be better assured, and outside distraction by co-workers is reduced.

Those who prefer an outside office say that working at home can be lonely, and they miss the informal exchange of ideas "over the watercooler." Others find the management and distraction of one's home even more frustrating than the presence and interruption of co-workers. One needs to think through any desired separation of home duties from those related to work, and to plan a work space reflecting it. Some home-based LNCs retain housekeepers and babysitters to provide services during business hours as they would do in leaving home to work. Others find that at home they lack the same discipline imposed by outside office expectations for a dress code and work ethic. For these individuals, consciously planning and establishing business-like routines and practices for the home office may be advised. Many home-based LNCs dress in business attire, mentally leaving home behind each day before walking into the office in the next room to go to work! They return "home" again at the end of each day.

Outside Office. Many LNCs begin their careers as employees of law firms and develop a preference for the office routines and setting. Some set up office space physically close to major clients, even leasing space from them. Others prefer to find and set up an entirely separate office space. There are tax benefits associated with leasing or purchase of an office. All rent or mortgage payments are deductible, as are many of the related expenses. The lease or purchase of space depends on a favorable credit history. Committing to the first lease or making the first purchase, and doing it responsibly, sets a positive foundation for all like transactions to follow. As mentioned above, the first-time lessee likely will have to guarantee financially at least a portion of the lease as an individual, as well as an agent of the business entity.

Advantages cited to going out to work include mental and physical separation of work and home for those desiring it. Establishing credit through leasing in one's own right can be seen as an advantage, even though typically it is considerably more expensive than maintaining a home office. If one's goal is to grow a business to substantial size, an outside office is almost required. Some business owners wish to purchase an office property, viewing it as an investment, and a way of arranging the integrity of the office space to their preferences.

Choosing the Size

Although some may think that size just happens, it can be planned as surely as any other business aspect. Proponents of small and larger businesses advocate for the advantages of their own preference and are articulate about the disadvantages of the other model. For any business person, thinking through one's preferences and perhaps tolerances early on is essential. Taking a thoughtful, deliberate approach sponsors the intention to grow, or conversely to remain small, and the decision is reflected automatically in all business planning (Wise, 1993). In addition, this intentionality allows for change in the plan as one's business evolves over time, reflecting uniquely changing needs and preferences across a career.

Proponents of the *keep it small* approach state their preference for working alone, or in concert with a very few chosen co-workers. These entrepreneurs equate higher-quality work and better-managed work flow with limited size and volume. One way to accomplish this is to narrow efforts by serving a select group of desirable clients to a higher level of quality. Keeping things small is a way to limit expenses, especially fixed financial commitments. Everything from office space to payroll is likely to cost less.

One downside of small is less revenue. For most solo practitioners, revenue is limited to the number of billable hours they themselves can produce in a given time frame. It may leave one overdependent on a few significant clients; if even one client moves on, it can create significant problems. A more numerous and diverse client mix is desirable for any business. For the LNC exquisitely aware of individual limits to knowledge and resources, narrowing of focus and client base may seem too confining. On the other hand, it may represent hands-on casework and rewarding collegial relationships with a few valued clients. Nurses preferring one-to-one bedside care see this latter as the legal nurse consulting equivalent.

For those individuals wanting to nurture a *growing business*, the challenge of locating, training, and encouraging other professionals along the business plan is attractive. The advantages are the possibility for more revenue, a more diverse client and product mix, the excitement of interprofessional synergy, and a chance to build an entity that will live beyond the founding individual, which ultimately could be sold. For the LNC with desire for revenues beyond one person's billable hours, there are also the headaches associated with managing staff and a larger business. There is the whole topic of dependence on co-workers with which to contend. For the LNC who swore on leaving the frustration of his or her last hospital management position that the largest organization she or he would ever manage again was a household, working as a solo act may seem like heaven! The less-attractive elements could be viewed as the hassle of making and enforcing policies and procedures, dealing with complex governmental employment and interpersonal issues, finding ways to convince other people to work in the planned manner, and praying that expenses do not always outgrow revenue! Growth is expensive, and must be closely orchestrated to result in profit. More than one owner of a growing business has been stunned that, at the very same time that more money than imaginable is rolling in the door, there can be significant cash-flow crises (Torrence, 1992)!

There may be a midpoint compromise with one's business between keeping it small and allowing it to grow. The trends of recent workforce reductions or "rightsizing" in industry, and refocus on working "smarter, not harder" offer provocative alternatives to the traditional small vs. large arguments. By carefully planning the work, selecting and directing employees/consultants wisely, and making maximal use of technology, even the solo practitioner has the option to attract more clients, produce more work product, and generate more profit. A variety of resources address this concept, and some are referenced below.

Choosing the "Stuff"

Equipping the office depends on the individual's planned work, intention for growth, space, and budget. In general, most LNCs select a computer with fax modem, printer, telephone arrangement, office supplies, and furniture. For start-up businesses, financial caution is advised. It is incredibly easy to overbuy, committing the fledgling business to fixed expenses beyond ready ability to pay. There are classy alternatives for creating workable attractive space without undoing financial stability. In most communities, office furniture and equipment are available in a recycled state. Shopping the used-furniture stores can be helpful, and many companies rework computers offering them "loaded" and with warranties for truly bargain prices. Some entrepreneurs shop through catalogs with satisfactory results. Multiple resources are available with product information, finance advice, and lists of minimum requirements. See below for ideas, and consult with other business owners for best buys in one's home community.

Hint: Your friendly (but slightly tightfisted) banker may be more comfortable loaning money for "capital" expenditures such as computers, furniture, etc. than working capital for start-up expenses. Since there is tangible property to be repossessed if the loan fails, banks may be more willing to make a loan. Financing such selected purchases through the bank, even those one could easily finance with a credit card or cash, might be in the business' best interest. Longer payout periods may augment much-needed cash flow for day-to-day use and help build credit for future loans.

Choosing the Staff

Much has been written and said about hiring, firing, and managing employees (see References). Perhaps not surprisingly, in general, it makes the most sense to follow the golden rule. If the business owner meets and treats employees in a way that appealed to the owner while still an employee, it minimizes problems and moves the workplace closer to what is humane, yet business-like. Moreover, our government has set some standards for this aspect of business; it is essential to know about these requirements (see References) and to act in accordance with advice from one's attorney.

For those LNCs with administrative experience, the issue of employee selection and retention may seem a "no-brainer." This essay assumes the reader would fall on a continuum somewhere between having minimal knowledge or experience with management theory or techniques and having continuing questions and curiosity about this significant and fast-evolving subject. Key questions include

1. How do I know when to hire, and under what guidelines?
2. How do I know who to hire? How do I keep the employee for the long term?
3. How much do I pay? How else do I compensate, and for what?
4. How do I know if it is working out?
5. What if it doesn't?
6. What do I owe the people who work for me?

A good time to hire is shortly before one is shorthanded and the current staff is overworked; knowing when that time is may seem a mystery! The answer lies in setting objectives for company and individual employee productivity. One should set goals for the amount of work expected in a reasonable period of time. Clearly, for a new business such an appraisal will be an informed guess refined by experience over time. If there are goals for revenue, one calculates how many billable hours it would take to generate that amount of money at the hourly fees to be charged. If the owner cannot accomplish the task of meeting revenue goals alone, it is time to seek help. Help can come in two forms: employee or contract worker. There are Internal Revenue Service guidelines to differentiate between the two.

Employees are paid hourly for their time, or a salary with associated time and productivity expectations. They work in a place set, and do tasks designated, by the employer, using equipment and other resources the employer provides. This provides their primary source of revenue from work. Even if there is a slowdown in work for the company, the employee is to be paid an agreed-upon wage. In addition, the employer is responsible for a set portion of state and federal withholding, unemployment, and social security taxes. For employers of more than 15 employees, there are strict hiring, compensation, and firing guidelines.

Contract workers create their own offices and are dependent on more than one source of income. They set and schedule their work, provide their own supplies and equipment, and are responsible for all taxes. The employer is in actuality the "contractor," requesting services (and only held responsible for wages) when work is needed. The employer determines whether or not the worker will be requested to work. There is continuing challenge to employers by the Internal Revenue Service about who qualifies as contract workers. There seemingly is eternal fear that the government will be cheated of taxes by contract workers (a myth not upheld by industry statistics). Accountants and nurses working for temporary placement services frequently qualify as contract workers. In general, employees must have W-2 forms submitted annually reporting all compensation. Contract workers paid more than $600 annually must have 1099 forms reporting income submitted in a timely manner on their behalf by the contracting company. The contract worker attaches a copy to the individual tax return as well.

For the beginning business, it may make the most sense to retain help through contract workers. The variability of volume of work at first (and, frequently, on a continuing basis!) makes committing to employees a daunting thought, whereas simply arranging for outside workers to do the "overflow" makes more sense to many. Advantages of using contract help therefore include avoiding financial and managerial commitments when the amount of work (and income) is unpredictable. Another advantage is a more-extensive array of talent and expertise (such as diverse clinical specialties) without having to pay for additional work space, equipment, and supplies. Disadvantages to reliance on contract workers may be less "control" over workers' time, their availability on short notice, and variable work quality. It is important to protect one's proprietary client base by insisting that all workers sign noncompete or nonpiracy agreements. These constrain the worker from marketing to the employer's client base in a delineated geographic area for a reasonable period of time, usually 1 to 2 years. Sample documents appear in Appendix.

Selecting staff is an art, but can be approached systematically even by the novice. Starting with a job description, a list of tasks to be accomplished by the new staff member, one then develops a statement of attributes and experience necessary to achieve the tasks. Some small business employers announce to friends and colleagues that hiring is in progress. Others prefer to call employment services specializing in professional staff placement. The agencies research each applicant's job history and references and conduct personal screening interviews before recommending applicants for placement. In addition, most agencies offer a guarantee if the employee does not work out well. One shortcoming is the agency fee, often a relatively large portion of the new employee's annual compensation. Other employers run advertisements in professional newsletters and hold group "auditions." And then, many make the possible mistake of hiring friends or family (see more on this below).

Experienced employers consult and follow government policies and guidelines before *hiring*. Potential applicants need to submit a summary of past education and job experience, with references included. It is essential that the potential employer verify any licensee with state authorities and pursue each reference, no matter how frustrating the task. In this day of restrained communication, it may be all but impossible to determine accurately what the applicant's status was on leaving the last employment. Some references actually read, "due to corporate policy, only dates of employment can be verified." One excellent approach is giving the potential LNC employee a "test case" to work, including medical records and other discovery. The would-be employee then prepares a written report as directed, accounting for time spent in preparation. This allows not only for viewing the LNC's analytic and writing abilities, but also for noting how long it takes to accomplish the project.

Compensation is another issue warranting volumes of space and attention. In summary, experts advise planning compensation prior to hiring, based on the pay scale in the hiring community for the caliber of employee and experience. Insuring that the company makes money enough to cover the cost of the employee's total compensation package (moneys, all taxes, vacation, insurance, etc.) and some profit is rudimentary to successful enterprise. One approach to paying hourly service employees is the so-called rule of three's. By this formula the company pays one third of what ultimately will be charged for the employee's time. For example, if the employee is paid $25 per hour, following the rule of three's implies charging at least $75 for each hour of service provided. Most seasoned employers urge hiring for lower wages during a probationary period. Once the stability and viability of the employee as a positive contributor to the company's efforts is assessed, compensation can be increased accordingly. Compensation in its ideal state is a dynamic combination of components, including salary or hourly wages, bonus for productivity toward the individual and/or the company goals, and other benefits, such as vacation, insurance, retirement moneys, etc. In general, nurses and other employees tend to be most drawn by flexibility of scheduling and a sense of making a positive contribution to the company, given roughly equivalent dollar amounts of salary. Devanna (1994) states that businesses are being more creative with compensation, and employees value, in addition to those components cited above, career opportunities such as new job challenges, responsibility for meaningful work contributing to the success of the business, autonomy in decision making, meaningful praise and recognition, a workplace marked by mutual respect, and job security (pp. 189–190).

Employee evaluation is another topic about which volumes are written. A behavioral job description coupled with an ongoing dialogue between supervisor and employee allows for objective and constructive evaluation of performance. *The focus of evaluation is ongoing employee learning.* At its best, the evaluation should be mutually instructive, lead to a clearly stated plan for improvement based on both employee and company objectives, and leave both participants with a sense of understanding and even satisfaction. Goal-based employee evaluation makes it possible to set performance outcomes and to determine how closely they are being met. Ordinarily, employee goals should include statements of what is to be done, to what degree of excellence, and in what time frame.

The intention of employee evaluation is development of a mutually satisfying relationship between a thriving business and productive, adaptive employee. In situations where the company goals and those of the employee do not mesh, it may become necessary to release the worker from service. Ideally, the termination will be a mutual decision, crafted over time and with the input of both parties. The evaluative process will have laid out, over time, problems and recommendations for improvement in the employee's performance. It should be apparent when progress is not made, and the employee counseled to begin seeking work elsewhere. Once again, governmental rules may apply and the LNC is advised to know and comply with them. In addition, it is humane to allow time and resources for the severed employee to identify other opportunities.

The workers of any business are its most valuable asset. This is especially true of professional service businesses, such as LNC practices. Careful thought and planning for successful identification, selection, and reward of one's employee/colleagues can pay off in financial rewards for owner and worker alike. This humane, "21st century" approach also builds a stable work group of professionals willing to try new jobs, work in unique ways, and take the risks necessary to empower the thriving company of the future.

Financial Issues

Selecting the Financial Consultant/Employee

As with selecting an attorney, choosing the right financial consultant takes thought and planning. For most initial business efforts, the owner may do all of the financial planning, implement day-to-day financial operations, and prepare the tax return for filing. However, even if one has extensive prior financial management experience in a successful business, it is wise to select a consultant to look in on the business periodically from a financial perspective. In essence, *one is choosing a financial partner who will have intimate knowledge about the business, so care and caution are of absolutely critical importance.* The techniques described above for selecting an attorney are also applicable in the selection of an accountant as a member of the business team.

Accountants receive extensive basic and continuing professional education and have one of the most formidable professional licensing examinations in existence. In addition to preparation in accounting principles, they receive special instruction on client relations and are often skilled educators. As with selected attorneys, some accountants may have special interest and skill in small business start-up and growth. It is wise to inquire regarding each of these qualities when searching for the accounting consultant. In addition, the integrity of the accounting professional is of special significance. This aspect must be closely investigated before one can feel totally safe in hiring the financial consultant. Careful scrutiny of references, inquiry to licensing boards and such community resources as the better business bureau, and recommendations from trusted friends and colleagues all are essential to selection of the financial consultant. Careful monitoring as the collaboration begins and proceeds remains important as well.

Once the business is underway, the owner's attention becomes focused on strategic planning, managing growth, and getting the work done. When the daily operations require more than one person to do the work, the accounting professional can take on a greater role. If an employee is hired to perform the financial functions of invoicing, collections, payments, and preparing financial statements, the accountant should consult in setting the financial system up. In addition, the accountant will provide education to that employee and can monitor performance of the company *and* the employee. The accountant will advise a system of "internal controls," routine procedures for the office which add a layer of protection against theft. Ideally, the accounting professional will continue to consult as the business matures toward predictable developmental milestones and encounters the inevitable financial crises.

Financial Records and Reporting

Internal Reporting. Clear, accurate, and timely financial information is essential to the success of any business. It is the single source of data about how the business is actually doing. "The foundation of ... financial management is good bookkeeping. The failure to set up good bookkeeping lies at the heart of ... financial failure," (Torrence, 1992, p. 72). Knowledge of critical elements for even start-up businesses include money owed to the business (accounts *receivable*), money owed to others (accounts *payable*), and the view of general financial health of the business found in *profit and loss reports* and the company *balance sheet.*

External Reporting. The same data useful to the internal running of the business can serve as foundation for reporting to outside authorities. As mentioned above, our government has set regulations for reporting and payment of workers' income and taxes, and those for the business entity. Accurate and timely reporting and payment *must* be done or business, by law, can be brought to a halt. Other external reporting can include updated financial information required when funding is requested or received. Ordinarily, quarterly financial statements for the company are submitted to the loan source as a measure of progress and as a way to monitor appropriate use of loan money.

Financial Statements

Financial statements are the financial map by which the business is run. Torrence (1992) says that one of the true predictors of the successful entrepreneur is learning how to read and make use of financial statements (p. 13). *Profit and loss* reports lay out major sources of revenue and expenses. One's accountant can help determine exact categories to list in the "chart of accounts," but typically they include the various sources of income to the business balanced with typical expenses, such as cost of outside consultants, salaries, rent, supplies and equipment, advertising, etc. The so-called bottom line of the business is revealed here. This cites whether there is more income than expense; i.e., the business is profitable, or not profitable, i.e., more expenditures than income. *The balance sheet* lays out the exact financial status of the business, both assets and liabilities, and yields a statement of what exactly the owner has to show for all the work and risk taken, i.e., the owner's *equity*.

Start-up businesses tend to employ *cash basis accounting* which reports money received by the business vs. money actually paid out; this is a good tool for day-to-day cash management. The difference between moneys collected vs. moneys paid out is the number used to report earnings to the Internal Revenue Service for income tax purposes. Cash basis accounting has one serious flaw—it neglects to take into account moneys owed by the business but not yet disbursed. Cash in the bank has given false comfort to more than one unsophisticated business owner. What lurks in the accounts payable report can quickly undo that sense of comfort when the bills come due and available cash is not enough to pay them. Therefore, some entrepreneurs convert to *accrual accounting* for a more complete picture of exactly how profitable the business has become. The accrual statement includes additional information on revenues billed but not yet collected, as well as moneys owed and not yet paid out. Income tax reporting is based on the difference between all the money paid and owed to the company and all the money the company paid or owed others, i.e., the net profit. Consulting with one's business accountant will result in the best approach for any individual business.

Financing a Business

As a first step to running a financially sound business, the LNC owner must plan and budget the movement of money through the business. Anticipating how much money will be needed, and having tight control over its movement in and out of the business, makes it possible to start and conservatively run a business. Continuing to employ the same responsible practices builds the good habits essential to every successful business. Even one-person, part-time businesses require a budget and cash management plan. Business consultants recommend that the budgeting should flow logically from the business plan. The plan should include projected work, the money needed to complete the work, and built-in evaluative measures to monitor and control for success.

Planning and Budgeting

As one might expect, the accountant will be a key resource prior to undertaking the budget plan, but a simple approach can be worked out by even a beginner. First, plan the work to be accomplished; how many clients are in place, and how much work will each require? How many hours will be billed as a result? This tells expected or desired *revenue*. Then, calculate how many hours the owner has available to work during a certain time period, and what hourly billing rate will be desirable and realistic for the community? If there is more work than can be done by the owner, how many additional hours will need to be done by outside help, and for what cost? This information yields the costs of doing business, also known as *direct expenses*. Then, one determines what materials, supplies, and equipment are needed to accomplish the work and to get the money in the door. Answers to these and similar questions lead to the budget.

Cash-Flow Issues

It is obvious that the business owner's responsibility includes seeing that there is enough money to pay the obligations of the company in a timely way. The budget lays out the plan, but the owner must make the plan happen. A process must be set in place for seeing that one's time spent and amount of work done are recorded, and bills sent in a timely manner. Of critical importance, provision must be made for qualifying the clients' ability and intention to pay, and there must be a way to see that money is collected. Knowing what money is owed and making sure it comes in time to be useful are part and parcel of the business owner's responsibility. And, of course, all of this must be accomplished with a strict eye to the bottom line, as the owner manages for profit.

Some owners establish a paper-and-pencil ledger system in which they record all time spent by case and send bills either monthly or at completion of the work. Business owners need be aware of the mistaken temptation to send bills only when cash is needed to pay bills! Instead, establishing and maintaining invoicing as an orderly and predictable routine reduces the chance of "cash crunch" crises. The other critical part of this process is getting the money in the door. *It is highly recommended that LNC business owners require a retainer to begin each new project.* Retainers are familiar to attorneys as they often collect them as part of their own office procedures. Smart business owners set collection procedures in place and adhere to them. One method which works well includes these steps:

1. Clearly state, and repeat in writing, the exact payment procedures the client is to follow. If the policy includes remitting a $500 retainer with the records, so state verbally and again in written correspondence. Some LNCs go so far as to have clients sign a contract indicating that they understand and commit to honoring the policies. See sample fee statement.
2. Always collect a retainer from every client for every matter. For established clients who may pay more slowly than 30 days, it is acceptable to require a larger retainer and to bill against it, replenishing it often.

3. Bill frequently, at the conclusion of each phase of work or monthly at the longest interval.

4. Make a point to inquire about, and then follow, the exact payment process followed in the client's office. Determine responsible employees, make note of their names, and stay in close touch with them. This can also make a significant difference in feeling reassured that someone will see that payment is made and/or in working out an amicable payment plan. Attorneys sometimes have their own cash-flow problems. Defense attorneys may be paid slowly by their insurance company clients. Plaintiff's attorneys have to win the case to collect any money. Obviously, there may be times when working with a client over a longer payment cycle makes sense. However, more than one small entrepreneur's business has failed through slow pay practices by even well-meaning clients.

5. At 30 to 45 days after the bills go out, a call can be made to each client from whom payment has not been received in full. Politely inquire whether or not the bill was received, were there any questions or concerns to be answered, and when can payment be expected. Surprisingly, attorneys may not even know the bill has been received or may have placed it out of the pay process to get questions answered, but were too busy to call. This simple call by the business owner or clerk can prevent many slow payment problems by staying in communication. *Almost always this step prevents having to take any of the following actions which may seem harsh to some LNCs.*

6. At 45 to 60 days *fax* a reminder letter with copy of the bill, stamped "PAYMENT OVERDUE." Some LNCs begin at this point to add 18% annual interest to the bill. *Note:* This practice should be included in all contracts, fee statements, etc. so clients are forewarned.

7. At 60 to 75 days, send a letter on pink paper with a windowed envelope for all to see that the bill is overdue. The letter should state that all work on the matter will cease in 2 weeks until payment in full is received. If the LNC is serving as, or is providing an expert witness for the case, it is acceptable to indicate in the letter that if payment is not received immediately the expert will be notified in writing to cease all work. Remember that all correspondence in the testifying expert's file is discoverable, so attorneys will pay to avoid the letters being sent.

8. If payment is still not received shortly thereafter, send letters to all experts contracted through the LNC service and have the business attorney take over the collections. It may also help to write to the state bar association complaining about the attorney's payment practices.

Taking a business-like and proactive approach to billing and collections prevents or resolves many cash-flow issues and can make the difference in whether the business succeeds or fails.

Cash-Flow Management

Torrence (1992) states that "cash flow is a complex process" (p. 101), but it need not baffle the LNC business owner if procedures are worked out with one's accountant and religiously followed. Hours billed to the client create an account receivable, which becomes cash when payment is made. In the interim, the owner and other workers must be paid and any rent, routine payments, bills for supplies, etc. must be paid. It makes sense to plan ahead.

To control and manage cash, some LNCs create cash-flow projections to calculate need for money on a scheduled basis. Torrence suggests looking ahead for the next 12 months, which essentially is long-range forecasting. Then one would look at the next 3 of those months, and finally at the current week and the one following. For each time period one anticipates bills which must be made and what money is expected to come in and when. Plans for bill paying are made accordingly with contingency plans created for any shortfalls. Although sometimes tedious, cash-flow planning is essential for small struggling businesses and, perhaps surprisingly, for thriving, growing profitable enterprises as well. "Cash flow planning is an orderly analysis of the uncertainties of the future, and as such, lies at the heart of good financial management" (Torrence, 1992, p. 103).

Funding Sources and Issues

One key reason that even apparently thriving businesses sometimes fail is too little money when it is needed. Understandably, some LNC business owners take pride in paying cash for all purchases and relying totally on the business' own revenues to finance growth. However, there are times when it might make better business sense to borrow money in a responsible way. Building credit and allocating smaller routine payments during times that cash is needed elsewhere in the business can foster growth or, in more trying times, make the difference whether or not the business survives. The management of money absolutely remains the prerogative of the LNC business owner. This section is for those undertaking thought about alternative funding sources.

Banks. Every business owner has a bank account and the potential for a mutually satisfying business relationship with that bank. The smart entrepreneur recognizes that the bank's only true business is to make money by loaning it out to its customers, including small business owners. It is smart to select a bank that specializes in small business operations resembling one's own business. Each LNC owner should request a meeting with the officer assigned to one's business account, to introduce the business and the owner's professional experience and plans. Taking written information about the business and even recent financial reports can help impress the banker. Taking the time to know one's bank, the services offered, and the officers working with small business accounts is in the owner's best interest. It is widely believed that "bankers are heavily influenced by the past," (Torrence, 1992, p. 187). There also may be some truth to the stereotype that bankers only loan to business owners who do not "need" the money. This may discourage the LNC venturing into a first business, even one who has sought a working relationship with the bank.

However, there are steps to take to build that "past" that bankers seek. In addition to getting to know one's banker, taking an unemotional look at one's past personal financial asset management is an essential first step. Remedying any unpaid loans, overdrawn accounts, and the like is best done prior to starting the business. Requests for start-up or later financing will be met with demands to take these same steps, and bankers will be impressed if time has elapsed since any curative action took place. As indicated above, there will likely be insistence on personal guarantee by the individual owner for all debt incurred, even that secured with equipment or property. If so, asking the banker for a date when all personal guarantee restrictions can be lifted is smart, as is determining all requirements needed to accomplish that goal.

As indicated above, the bank makes money when its customers borrow and repay loans. Rather than being shy about requesting loan money, it makes sense to discuss frankly under what circumstances one's business is "bankable" and then taking steps in that direction. What types of loans does the bank make? Is it a certified lender with the federally funded Small Business Administration (SBA)? In keeping with other such government programs, the SBA gives special consideration to "minority" business owners, including persons of color, females, disabled individuals, native Americans, and Vietnam veterans. Most LNCs qualify under one or more of these considerations. At the time of this writing, it appears that the SBA is especially interested in funding the purchase of business real estate, but priorities shift and current information should be sought. Will the bank loan money secured by the LNC business accounts receivable rather than property? Will they extend a line of credit, a loan of sorts, that is activated by drawing down on one's business account during times of need and paying interest on any moneys taken over one's actual balance? Will they consider a first-time loan to a new business owner if it is personally guaranteed by an already established "bankable" individual or business?

Other Funding Sources. Because bank loans may be scarce, some start-up businesses turn to family sources for the funds. Still others "bootstrap" by working at a job and using paychecks to finance a business initially run part-time. Starting an LNC practice is ideal for such an approach, as the work often can be accomplished on one's own time at reasonable expense. While not always advisable for a long-term financial approach, borrowing from family and/or bootstrapping are the most often cited funding sources of start-up businesses. These strategies may be the way to start and run the business until there is history enough to build the bank's confidence and to become bankable.

Some entrepreneurs make a point of borrowing a small amount from a bank and then religiously repaying the loan to build a track record of borrowing and timely repaying. A related strategy is to place an amount of money in savings at the desired bank, then borrowing that amount as a business loan, using the savings account as collateral. The cost of the interest in either approach is a legitimate business expense, and the confidence of the loan officer definitely worth the price to enable future loan opportunities. Although the concept seems counterintuitive, the more a business grows, the greater the possibility that a loan of some sort will be essential to survive and thrive in the growth. *It is a lifeblood function for successful businesspeople to make and cultivate cordial, effective relationships with their bankers.*

Comment: Bankers look for the qualities implied in the truism "doing business on a handshake," i.e., the portrayal of confidence and integrity. They seek evidence that the business owner is competent to run that business, a "satisfactory" financial condition based on the banker's review of financial information provided, and the inclusion of a "realistic" set of goals. Setting out to accomplish this will speed the process of becoming bankable.

Marketing and Sales Issues

Marketing is the process of "defining, developing and delivering value," to clients (Webster, 1994, p. 130). Traditionally, marketing was regarded as an extension of selling. One simply took an existent product and sold it to all available customers. Current thinking in marketing strategy refines the focus to three C's — analysis of *client needs* and satisfaction, company *capabilities* and positioning relative to one's *competitors*. For the LNC entrepreneur, this might be translated as finding out what attorneys want and still need most in their practices *vis-à-vis* the LNC's special clinical and/or consulting expertise. One then fashions the best possible fit of the two and positions the service appropriately. *The purpose of this particular marketing approach is to establish and maintain enduring "business partner" relationships with clients to profit both parties for years.* The best-case scenario is the LNC having the opportunity to offer a uniquely valued and specialized service to clients who are satisfied and want more!

Choosing the Client

In the current thinking about marketing, the customer's interests are at the forefront of every business consideration, certainly a value resonant with the patient-centered tradition of nursing. Through marketing, one strives to have "the best possible understanding of the customer's needs, wants, preferences and buying patterns" (Webster, 1994, p.132). As Torrence (1992) says "to be an effective marketer you must be able to put yourself in the minds of your customers" (p. 22). The first step is finding out exactly *who* this might be. *Determining the "right" customers, or clients, is at the heart of marketing strategy.*

Webster opines that there are right, or good client-customers and bad ones, too. "Good customers ask the company to do things it can do well and challenge it to continue to develop knowledge, skills and resources that are at the heart of its distinctive competence. Good customers value the things ... done for them and are willing to pay for the resources the company commits to those tasks ... they will take the company in directions consistent with its business ... strategies" (Webster, 1994, p. 137). "Bad" customers do the opposite, asking for things one cannot provide well or efficiently, complaining about or avoiding payment, and taking the company in other directions than its intended one. Such customers will remain dissatisfied, tempting the business owner to focus, and waste, resources attempting to accomplish the impossible, and leaving the company worse off than it had been. *One will thrive by identifying those clients with the best chance of being well and satisfactorily served by the core competence one's efforts will provide.* "The objective of business is to satisfy customer needs, but that only becomes a meaningful objective after it has identified target customers.... [Q]uality only has meaning as a concept in terms of meeting customer expectations" (Webster, 1994, p. 141).

An LNC in independent practice likely will wish to attract attorney clients involved in medically related litigation. It makes sense that a medical malpractice attorney has greater potential as a "good" client than one specializing in probate or business office practice. Obviously, these latter might make perfectly fine customers for consultants with other expertise, but not usually for an LNC. One can, however, identify potential clients using similar sources to those used in selecting one's business attorney. Searching *Martindale-Hubbell* in a preferred geographic area for attorneys specializing in medical litigation is an excellent start. Reading topical legal publications, e.g., *Trial* published by ATLA, *For the Defense* published by the Defense Research Institute, and reviewing local court reports for attorneys litigating medical malpractice and personal injury cases may provide leads to future satisfied customers. In particular, depending on one's core competence, it makes sense to seek out the attorneys specializing in a medically related practice. For example, if one's core competence is obstetrical nursing, perhaps the best potential client is the nearby attorney representing a group practice of midwives or a mother-and-children's hospital.

An additional qualifying step of potential attorney clients needs to include payment practices. Too many expert witnesses and small business owners tell horror stories about "being stiffed" to ignore this important evaluation for inclusion in one's "good" customer base. Appraisal of attorney willingness to meet financial commitments can be found in Dunn & Bradstreet ratings of the law firm, and the local credit bureau may offer interesting information as well. Arrangements can be made to join either for access to information about potential clients' financial standing and payment practices. Another good source of payment information is talking with attorneys and other LNCs about the potential client's reputation among colleagues. Most communities are "small" in the sense that word of unprofessional business practices seems to get out and becomes accessible to even the beginning business owner. Coupled with smart business practices employed by the LNC, information of good financial standing in the community, and a law practice specializing in medical litigation herald the potential of a worthwhile client. Strategies successfully employed by LNCs for locating and engaging attorney clients are described in more detail below under Successful LNC Strategies.

Choosing the Product

An LNC's "product" *per se* is usually a service. It should be based on that LNC's unique attributes and talents. What skills and resources are particular strengths of the business owner? What does the individual LNC do or know better than others in the marketplace? It is on these special skills and knowledge, or what Webster (1994) calls *core competence* that a successful business should be founded. Ideally, the core competence should be (1) valued by clients, (2) relevant to several types of clients, (3) knowledge based, and (4) neither geographically limited nor readily duplicated by the competition.

New business owners are tempted to accept whatever business they can get and feel grateful for it! However, Greenbaum (1990) warns that this is a short-term strategy, insisting to would-be entrepreneurs to "develop a strategy relative to what you want to be, and importantly, what you are not, [and] the chances of achieving your objectives for the [consulting] practice are dramatically greater than if you pursue a strategy of accepting any work you can get" (p. 29). Selecting and defining one's *core competence* is the logical next step in the marketing process.

The LNC might start this introspective process by dissecting his or her own résumé or *curriculum vitae* as if reading it for the first time. If the professional life of the LNC were analyzed from the outside, what signs of expertise are most notable? In what specialty has the most clinical education and experience taken place? In what arena have there been publications, speeches, or teaching assignments, i.e., indicators of special expertise? Has the LNC created a particular clinical innovation for which there has been collegial recognition, an award, or financial royalties? Answers to these questions will offer direction for choosing an area of excellence, or core competence, to highlight in the LNC independent practice. This might be especially true if one's core competence fits with a highly litigated clinical specialty in medical malpractice, e.g., obstetrics, plastic surgery, or neurology, and/or one's expertise is focused in the so-called damages aspect of injuries, e.g., care of patients in rehabilitation, the neurologically affected, and/or orthopedic patient populations.

Another area of self-inquiry would be exploring one's preferences, talents, or skills. A nurse with many years of graduate education or clinical research experience likely has special expertise in reviewing, critiquing, and translating the medical literature into lay language, words a jury would understand. This may be a highly valued core competence to clients of an LNC practice. Another LNC may have spent years working in a respected law firm learning skills and making contacts which will serve uniquely well in independent practice. Teaching and speaking experience will enhance the marketing of core competence as an expert witness, as will many of the other skills identified above.

One is well advised to note what is professionally *enjoyable*. In keeping with the truism "be careful of what you ask because you *will* get it," successful marketing should bring the chance to perform the core competence over and over again! Best that it be something in which the LNC takes pride and finds considerable pleasure. Then, having identified that core competence, the next step is to practice *describing* it accurately, quickly, and easily to others not familiar with legal nurse consulting. Greenbaum (1990) states that "this is probably the single most important consideration in defining a business. If you have thought through what business you are really in, you should be able to tell someone about it in a very brief period of time" (pp. 32–33).

It is wise to consider strengths and weaknesses in the individual LNC, and in resources available to his or her business. Perhaps one's expertise is pediatric neurology; the likelihood of being consulted on obstetrical misadventure is strong. If one has an obstetrical nurse colleague on whom to call for consult, and to make available as another resource of the business, the business will be strengthened by being better able to serve the client. If one specializes in brain-damaged baby cases, but has no neuroradiologist colleagues on whom to call for assistance, it might be viewed as a possible weakness and an area to be addressed for improvement in services offered.

Choosing the Marketing Approach

Positioning the Business

Having defined the potential client base, as above, and the core competency one wishes to feature, it pays to explore and fashion the best fit between the two. One might practice describing the "ideal" consulting assignment. Include the desired type of attorney practice to be served, the specific work that would be contracted, the most attractive geographic area, and the possible revenue to be generated. Another related preparatory exercise is defining the types of assignments one can complete effectively, specifying the tasks, the times they would take, revenues for services that could be generated, and the type(s) of client(s) who would pay for that work. This process is *positioning*.

The developers of the concept of positioning say:

> Positioning starts with a product. A piece of merchandise, a service, a company, or even a person. Perhaps yourself.

> But positioning is not what you *do to a product*. Positioning is what you *do to the mind* of the prospect[ive client.] That is, you position the product in the mind of the [client.] (Al Ries and Jack Trout, quoted by Webster, 1994, p. 142).

The next critical step, then, is to offer and place the LNC "product" or services with the clients identified as having the best chance of valuing it, i.e., "good" customers. Positioning is a systematic process starting with the two steps above. The first, choosing one's product or service, and then identifying any weaknesses and all strengths, is also to be performed regarding one's competitors. Who else is out there? What are their strengths and vulnerabilities?

How real of a threat are they to the same business for which one is positioning one's own business? The other step above, identifying a best-case scenario client prospect to be served well by one's core competence, can be reviewed regarding competitors as well. Are competitors positioning themselves to serve the identical market? Can they, or are they now, serving as well or better in the same market niche?

Next, one is to develop what Greenbaum (1990) calls a matrix of the prospective client's needs and one's own core competence. On one axis of a simple graph *client needs* are listed, with *LNC core competencies* listed along the other. Lines are drawn to intersect points in which key client needs and services to be offered meet. These are potential points of positioning strength. This process needs to be worked for competitors as well.

Finally, one selects a point of strategic interface between client need and core competencies to focus on those services with which to be identified, i.e., positioned. In essence, all information about the company and its services will reflect this interface, or this positioning. Before making the final commitment ask these questions: (1) Can I deliver this service as described? Is this, in fact, our expertise, and to the depth required? Can we respond in a timely way and with a consistently high level of quality? (2) Is the message I am putting out about my services meaningful to the client? Is positioning in this way responsive to what the client perceives is the need? Is the message expressed in an appealing way? and (3) Does this particular positioning feel comfortable? Can I live with this for a long time? The product of the positioning process is "a meaningful statement about the services of the organization … [which] is appealing to the customer" (Greenbaum, 1990, p. 54).

As described above, the effective marketing plan identifies the LNC entrepreneur's core competencies, targets would-be satisfied clients, and recognizes the synergistic interface between them. Experienced LNCs have employed a wide variety of creative approaches to each of these elements. Description of some ideas follows for the reader's consideration.

Successful LNC Strategies

Where LNCs Can Find Attorneys

1. Attend and network at attorney seminars on medical malpractice, personal injury, product liability law
2. Exhibit at Bar Association meetings, or ATLA, DRI, etc. seminars; consider offering free consults on actual cases as part of the exhibit
3. Attend charity functions and "work the crowd"
4. Consult directories such as *Martindale-Hubbell, Texas Legal Directory,* or the yellow pages under "attorneys," and trial reports in *Medical Malpractice Verdicts, Settlements and Experts,* or *The Blue Sheet* or its equivalent in the target venue
5. Actively participate in AALNC or legal assistant professional organizations — many attorneys rely heavily on recommendations of their LNC employees about which outside services to employ
6. Ask college and church friends for referrals to attorneys they know, even if they do not practice in a medical litigation specialty — they all know attorneys who do, or wish they could practice there but think they lack clinical expert witnesses
7. Purchase member lists from legal professional organizations and mail an introductory letter with brochure and business card, and/or a newsletter periodically

Where Attorneys Find LNCs

1. Advertisements in legal publications, AALNCs directory, *Texas Lawyer's* expert directory
2. Published learned articles in legal publications
3. Speeches at legal seminars and meetings
4. Court reports citing cases in which LNC has worked as an expert witness
5. Former LNC employees of their, a competitor's, or an adversary's law firm
6. Social functions to which attorneys are also invited
7. LNCs who have worked as experts in adversary's cases
8. Clinical certification listings
9. Medical or nursing publications on topics within the LNCs core competence

10. Letters of congratulation from an LNC on an important court victory or settlement
11. Letters of introduction and referral from attorney colleagues
12. Mass mailings of LNC brochure and card, with inventive letter
13. Business yellow pages under "attorney service bureaus"
14. Excellent nursing care of attorney, friends, and family when they are in the hospital

Creative Sales Approaches

1. Write and distribute an informative, but brief newsletter on litigated medical topics
2. "Invite" selected attorneys to lunch, to AALNC functions, or provide lunch for their staffs
3. Arrange to Christmas carol at the law firm, leaving your card and samples of your work wrapped as gifts
4. Offer to teach CPR at law firms or teach CPR at bar association meetings
5. Publicize and give an annual award for the attorney doing the most to improve health care in your community
6. Sound well informed on attorney chat lines on the Internet
7. Give a donation to charity or benefit sponsored by an attorney organization in your community
8. Send e-mail to attorneys on-line
9. Appear on health topic radio or TV shows as an expert in clinical area
10. Do good work as an LNC — word gets around!

Choosing the Sales Approach

The sales effort flows directly from the marketing premise and positioning. While marketing is "the development of a context or structure with which the company will attack the marketplace ... sales effort is the actual dealing with the customer to get the sale" (Torrence, 1992, p. 32). In order to be successful, the LNC owner or designated sales professional must understand the market position, focusing sales efforts on the market segments with the highest potential for buying the product or service. Sales success varies widely by industry. "The *nature* of the sales effort depends on how the marketplace for that industry works, and it will depend on the style of the owner and the strengths and weaknesses of the company" (Torrence, 1992, p. 33).

The Sales Plan

As in all other aspects of nursing, the LNC entrepreneur will start with a sales plan to set the tone for the operation. Every business owner has expectations, whether formally stated or not. A portion of one's resources, money, and/or time, is committed to pursuit of clientele. Having a formal plan for this endeavor allows for evaluation of results, periodic adaptation of the plan, and subsequent appropriate reallocation of resources. It is the responsibility of the owner to direct and monitor the plan closely, as it can make or break a business. "Knowing where your sales should be during the year, and then comparing that to where you actually are on a timely basis, is the first crucial step of management control" (Torrence, 1992, p. 51). LNCs may feel that sales is beneath or beyond them and that they should not have to "sell" to make a living. However, no matter how excellent one's core competence, if the concept does not get sold to the potential satisfied client, the LNC will not be making a living! Ironically, there are more similarities between traditional nursing activities and selling than one might initially recognize. All nurses educate patients and families; selling can be viewed as an extension of the teaching–learning process in that one informs the potential client about services offered, perhaps demonstrating how well they solve the would-be client's need. Or, convincing the nursing administrator of need for additional staff on a hospital unit requires the very same skills employed in selling one's services!

The Sales Process

The sales process, focusing on a potential client, includes five steps. These include

1. Initial contact with the prospective client
2. Screening of the prospective client
3. First meeting with the prospective client
4. Development of a proposal
5. Follow-up with the client

Initial Contact. The best-case scenario is if the client contacts the LNC first; the chance of undertaking quality business is better than if the reverse is true. This means that the prospective client already has realized the need for such a service and has some information about the LNC business. In addition, this prospect may have a specific project and deadline in mind. The question is not whether the LNC gets the work as much as it is whether the LNC is available to do it! The best of all marketing conditions is when the *LNC's excellent work is known by reputation and brings in new clients on its own merits.*

There are things that can be done to make best use of the first encounter. *Expressing interest, enthusiasm, and concern* for the prospect's needs is of paramount importance, as is *taking action* during the first encounter. Even if the LNC is not the best person to perform the work and referral to a colleague results, the prospect will recall the LNC's interest and concern favorably. As mentioned above, it is critical to prepare a *concise description* of the business and scope of operations. This will be what the prospect wants to know, and it needs to be effectively conveyed in the first few minutes of contact. Remembering that the LNC only gets to make one first impression helps to concentrate on making it as positive and productive an event as possible.

As mentioned above, the best chance for a great new client may come from the unsolicited call on referral from a happy customer. Even that has a downside, however, against which one wants to guard. Despite the flattering experience of being sought out to do work, Greenbaum (1990) indicates that there are some negative features to being approached first by the prospect — the LNC may have no information about whether that prospect will make a suitable client nor does the LNC have knowledge of or control over scheduling and work practices. Every business person can tell at least one horror story of a last-minute rush project for a new prospect which disrupts good paying work, is characterized by hassle, and for which one is never paid! Each one can also tell tales of the apparent would-be client who calls only to secure free advice, rather than to become an enduring, paying, and satisfied customer.

Qualifying the Client. For this and other reasons, it becomes important during the first encounter to "qualify" the prospect, identifying whether it is a suitable match with the LNC's core services. Inquire how the caller got the name and number of the LNC business; this provides feedback about how one's marketing is going and likely how well informed the caller is about the services offered. A call from the yellow pages will be very less informed than one from a speech given or an article written by the LNC. Of course, the best call is one referred from a satisfied client; another is from the attorney who won a case the caller lost! In general, calls about specific case-related problems usually auger better for solid business than nonspecific inquiries for general information about services offered.

   During the first contact it helps to gather as much information as possible about the prospect and the need. Ask questions about the firm, the type of cases it takes, and whether or not there is an LNC on staff. *Determine the reason for the call*, whether or not there is a specific case on the caller's mind and the *most pressing need* the caller has then; is there something the LNC can accomplish in the caller's behalf while on the phone? Experienced LNCs note that meeting the need uppermost on the caller's mind first, even if it is not the most-pressing need in the LNC's opinion, builds trust and rapport with the client. (Educators will recognize this phenomenon as meeting the client's "felt" need first, then, later, meeting the "observed" need. Solving the problem uppermost on the client's mind first by answering a case-related clinical question with ease and grace could "sell" the LNC's services more strongly than a battalion of sales people and allow a future working relationship to help solve many other such problems.)

Initial Meeting. If the caller seems a likely prospect, it helps to offer to visit the firm for an introduction. This will allow for some interim discrete investigation about the firm's reputation and the preparation time on the case or question precipitating the call. If the caller's purpose is to secure the LNC's services as an expert witness, the attorney may encourage such a visit. The expert's appearance and presentation are two factors which can be best assessed in person. However, if the purpose is to secure a confidential review of medical records, a visit may be discouraged as too time-consuming and the entire transaction conducted by telephone, delivery service, and fax. Most independent LNCs wouldn't recognize some of their best clients in person as they have never met, and may never meet! For most, this is an acceptable alternative contemporary professional model for service.

   If there is to be a meeting during which an appraisal of the LNC will be made, clarify who will be there, be punctual, and dress professionally. "The primary objective during the initial meeting is to sell yourself and your company ... so that [the prospect law firm] ... will want to hire you as a consultant" (Greenbaum, 1990, p. 149). Select carefully what is to be presented, calling on that concisely worded description of services, and offering anecdotes of case examples resonant with the potential client's caseload. A cautionary note is appropriate at this juncture, however — every LNC must maintain all clients' confidentiality unless specifically released to divulge their identities, as references, and the details of their caseloads. Some attorney clients would rather their employment of consulting services not be known, perhaps viewing any such revelation as giving away secrets to their success! More seriously, even a major city is a small town when it comes to courthouse gossip. *It is absolutely imperative to honor the very same confidentiality rules of clinical practice in one's LNC practice.* As the World War II admonition warns, "loose lips sink ships!" When millions of dollars and injured people's lives are at stake, the slightest impropriety can undermine a case and destroy an LNC's career.

Successful consultants utilize first meetings to appraise the prospective client law firm, noting information about numbers of attorneys, types of practice, the presence of any medically related staff, and research facilities available to them. Introductions must be made, shaking hands and making eye contact with each person present, while determining who the decision makers are in the firm. Exchanging business cards with all present is important toward this end. A formal presentation may be requested; others may request an informal "chat," wishing to appraise intelligence and integrity the old-fashioned way, that "doing business on a handshake" mentality mentioned above. It helps to clarify exactly what is expected prior to arrival so appropriate preparations can be made. Time likely will be limited, so planning to make the most-efficient and most-effective use of the time is advised. Discussion of formal presentations for consulting services can be found in Greenbaum, 1990, pp. 154 ff.

Proposal Development. The "proposal" may be a brief letter introducing the LNC and services, or it could be an extensive, specifically targeted document created on request. In either case, the purpose is to delineate exactly what can be done in the client's behalf, how and when it will be done, and what it will cost. In essence, the proposal is both a sales method and a confirmation or contract of services to be rendered.

In circumstances where an inquiry has been made by a potential client, but no work yet requested, the LNC's brochure, card, and other written sales materials can be submitted with a personal letter to the attorney acknowledging the first contact introduction. A sample of one's work and writing may be included with a recent résumé or *curriculum vitae*. In general, less is more, as most firms are inundated by job applicants' and vendors' materials. *Even the LNC on a budget might consider retaining a consultant for the development of these essentials, striving to present unique, professional-quality materials that stand out from the blizzard of paper found in most law firms.* It could be money well spent if it obtains the business opportunity sought.

If a proposal or work is requested, then the following guidelines should be considered. Include an *opening* indicating the purpose for the correspondence. Next, *background* outlining the project or case follows; this communicates associated facts, states assumptions, and reassures the prospective client one is knowledgeable enough to undertake the work.

Example 30.12: (On invitation of a law firm, Florence N. Gale is sent a medical record to review for indication of medical malpractice. Her proposal is sent to clarify the work and fees.) "I appreciate the opportunity to work with your firm. I am in receipt of the medical records for Jane Doe and her infant, Baby Doe. It is my understanding that you would like the records reviewed, summarized, and analyzed for evidence of nursing negligence. I have enclosed my *curriculum vitae* outlining in more detail clinical experiences in the care of laboring mothers and their newborns. Fees will be as in the enclosed fee schedule. Please note that the usual retainer has been waived since it is your firm's practice to pay on receipt of work product. The report will be submitted prior to the upcoming statute of limitations on December 5."

The example also includes brief rendering of other key components of proposals, which may be further elaborated in more-detailed versions if required. These include *objectives of the assignment, scope of the engagement, planned approach to the assignment, timing, staffing, qualifications, fees,* and *summary.* Such a proposal helps eliminate the chance for misunderstanding about the work to be done, conditions, and fees.

Conclusion

In summary, all LNC entrepreneurs can benefit from a well-thought-out view of the needs in the marketplace *vis-à-vis* their special talents. Creating a market niche and positioning it deftly can be the beginning of a successful practice. Legal nurse consulting is a relatively new subspecialty of nursing; also novel is the concept of nurse entrepreneuring. However, the same foundations on which one bases an effective nursing career will also serve the founding and growth of a successful LNC independent practice. To reiterate: (1) keep it simple, (2) protect the business owner's personal assets, (3) do it right the first time, (4) intend to be successful, and (5) remember what you already know.

References

Devanna, (1994).
Greenbaum, (1990).
Torrence, (1992).
Webster, (1994).
Wise, (1993).

Chapter 31

Legal Nurse Consultant Practice within a Law Firm

Phyllis Miller

Contents

1-57444-123-X/98
© 1998 by American Association of Legal Nurse Consultants

Introduction

Law firms are very different environments in which to work compared with a hospital, a corporation, or even an independent practice. They are different in structure, function, economics, measures of productivity, and almost every other way as well. It is for this reason that many nurses making the transition from a medical environment or independent practice to the law firm feel a bit at sea. It is the intent of this chapter to discuss these differences and provide an orientation to the law firm environment.

Structure of the Law Firm

Personnel

From the traditional perspective of an attorney, there are two categories of personnel working in any law firm; attorneys and support staff. This latter category includes legal assistants (LAs), paralegals, secretaries, messengers, and any other nonlawyer employee of the firm, including legal nurse consultants (LNCs). In the culture of many law firms, the distinction between attorneys and support staff is so sharp as to make even lunching together akin to being a "private in the officer's club." It is to be understood that in most firms, a new associate is considered to rank above even the most tenured and experienced LA or LNC by the lawyers of that firm. In general, the larger the firm, the greater the distinctions made between support staff and attorneys. In many firms, large and small, however, LNCs are treated with more respect than they have ever experienced in traditional nursing roles. In a well-functioning law firm, all personnel understand the importance of teamwork and have a common goal of representing their clients well.

Among the lawyers there are a number of distinctions in rank depending on the size and economics of the firm. Generally speaking the lawyers are divided into partners and associates.

Partners are more experienced in the practice of law, may have voting rights in the running of the firm depending on how the partnership is structured, and have a monetary compensation formula different from associates. Partners generally have worked for the firm for a number of years, usually at least 6, and proved their worth to the firm in terms of bringing in business or skill as an attorney before being invited to become a partner. In large firms there may be varying degrees of partnership, such as senior and junior partners or voting and nonvoting partners. The higher up on the partnership ladder, the more power wielded.

Associates are nonpartner attorneys. They may range from recent graduates of law school with no experience to attorneys with 6 or more years of experience on the verge of becoming partners. It is useful to compare associates to medical school graduates. A first-year associate is much like a new intern. They are rarely in a position to bring in new business, have virtually no experience, and have the distinction of working long hours doing legal research. However, with time and experience, associates move up the ladder toward partnership, just as the intern moves eventually to senior resident or fellow. Associates are generally assigned to work for a partner in the area of practice they wish to pursue.

Support staff includes LAs, LNCs, secretaries, receptionists, messengers, librarians, and other personnel who function in a support capacity to billable members of the team. Generally speaking, the larger the firm, the more support persons. Many other services necessary to the LNC either on a daily basis or from time to time may not be available in-house, but can be contracted through outside vendors. These services include: messengers, large volume or color reproduction/copying, audio/video technicians, computer support, process servers, and document coders/data entry. In a small firm with fewer personnel and a less formal structure, there are fewer divisions of rank among support staff. However, the larger the firm, the more layers of command. An example would be a division between senior and junior LAs, or between LNCs and LAs. All support staff are directly responsible to the attorney(s) to whom they are assigned. They may also be responsible to a legal assistant manager or coordinator.

Delegation

The ability to delegate is in direct proportion to power. Generally speaking, all partners are delegators. An effective partner delegates what he or she needs done to associates, LAs, LNCs, and secretaries, as appropriate, keeping only the bottom-line decision making and other pieces as required.

The associate's power of delegation is in direct proportion to seniority and the culture of the firm. As an example, in a large firm, it might be unseemly for a new associate to attempt to delegate to an LNC or LA. In contrast, a more senior associate may have powers of delegation approaching a partner. Usually, a senior associate can delegate to junior associates, LAs, and LNCs much like a partner.

The LNC's ability to delegate extends to her secretary, if he or she has one, and may extend to an assigned LA or project clerk.

Management of a Law Firm

The management of a law firm has traditionally been a function of the partnership, with the partners being responsible for personnel decisions and decisions on the day-to-day nuts-and-bolts operation of the firm. In more recent times, some larger firms have begun hiring nonlawyer administrators and office managers, the theory being that people trained to manage a business should do so, freeing the attorneys to attend to their clients and the practice of law.

Mission of the Law Firm

The law firm's mission is tightly tied to the type of cases and clients represented. On the most elemental level, clients fall into two categories: (1) individuals or (2) corporations and businesses. The later category could include interests as diverse as a product manufacturer, insurance company, hospital, or municipality.

The next consideration is the type of claims handled. Areas of representation in which in-house LNCs work include medical malpractice, workers' compensation, personal injury, product liability, and toxic torts.

Last is the question of whether the firm is representing the plaintiff or the defense. In medical malpractice cases, working for the plaintiff involves representing the injured party in a claim against physicians, nurses, dentists, and health care facilities. Working for the defense means representing the interests of a malpractice insurance company and a physician, nurse, or health care facility. In personal injury plaintiff claims, one also works for the injured party. On the defense side, the client is usually an insurance carrier and its client which may be an individual, corporation, or manufacturer.

Diversity of Roles by Setting

The roles played by the LNC in each of these settings are very diverse. The LNC working on the plaintiff's side of malpractice or personal injury claims usually has quite a bit of client contact and is often called on to find experts and meet with them. He or she also may take an active role in deposition, trial preparation, and during trial. The LNC is often the case manager of the file as it moves through the system. There may be a great deal of research, writing, and teaching. In many plaintiff firms, the LNC actually performs much of the work traditionally delegated to an associate attorney.

Working for a firm specializing in mainly plaintiff's personal injury, the LNC may be assigned to photograph the accident scene, accompany a client to physical therapy sessions for filming or to an independent medical exam (IME), and provide summaries of injuries suffered and medical bills. Little research, writing, or teaching may be involved. In fact, when there is no medical issue at hand, many lawyers utilize LNCs as LAs.

Assisting with the preparation of a medical product claim with hundreds of claimants may mean literally years of summarizing medical records on the same topic. It could also mean months of sorting through and reading thousands of documents produced by the defendant.

In contrast, the LNC working in defense of a malpractice claim or personal injury action may play a role more behind the scenes. There is less client contact and often less in the way of clerical or secretarial support for the LNC. Since physicians are often much more desirous of working for the defense, experts are easier to find for the defense LNC. LNCs, however, do have similar responsibilities in finding and interviewing experts, reviewing medical records, researching medical issues, and preparing exhibits for mediation and trial. They also may meet with defendant doctor(s) or nurse(s) and help prepare them for deposition and trial testimony. Attendance at deposition or trial may or may not be a feature of the role for the in-house defense LNC to help with documents and witnesses.

Obviously, the differences in work performed in various settings can be tremendous, and, therefore, if one is considering a position as an in-house LNC, it would be wise to ask questions to determine exactly who the firm's clients are and whether the firm represents the plaintiff or defendant. If the firm represents both at various times, the LNC must be flexible and able to focus on the viewpoint of the client represented. (More on this topic in the section on Economics of the Law Firm.)

Culture and Politics of the Firm

Evaluation of the culture of the firm begins when the visitor or prospective employee walks through the door. The office may be sparsely furnished and nondescript in a suburban office complex or be marble floored and oak paneled with pictures of the founders on the wall. The receptionist may be casually dressed and typing away or be very conservatively dressed, formal in her greeting, with no typewriter in sight. It is best to begin to gauge your comfort level here.

A further survey of the office environs should include a tour if possible. Note the types of offices or cubicles assigned to support staff. If there are senior legal assistants or other LNCs employed by the firm, ask to see their offices or workstations. This office tour should give the prospective in-house LNC a basic impression of how support staff are valued in that particular firm. If the support staff, including LAs and LNCs, are dressed fairly casually in contrast to the attorneys in the office, it is possible they have little or no client contact. If the most senior of the support staff is at an open desk or cubicle and the newest associate is in a window office, that may indicate the division between attorneys and support staff.

Another element of law firm culture is power and status. In any working environment, it is important to know who has the power. Those who bring in the most business, consistently bigger verdicts, or most successfully defend their clients will have the most power in a law firm. They will also have a considerable amount of status. In many cases they are the lawyers after whom the firm is named. Senior partners have the most power. Other partners also wield a great deal of power, particularly over those associates and support staff assigned to work directly for them.

Economics of the Law Firm

For the in-house LNC, a reasonable understanding of the economics of the firm for which he or she works is vital to any understanding of productivity measures. Ignorance of the economic issues pertinent to the law firm will have an adverse impact on the career of an in-house LNC.

Above all else, a law firm is a for-profit enterprise. The share of profit each attorney receives is a decision made solely by the partnership. The lawyer who brings in new business and sees to it that it is successfully concluded will be rewarded with a share of the profits. An attorney with the ability to consistently bring in new business through effective marketing, networking, or personal charisma is highly regarded and referred to as a "rainmaker." This is a powerful person. Junior associates who have not yet built up networks for bringing in new business or learned to market generally are not part of the profit sharing, but work strictly on salary. Learning to market and having one's own clients is usually part of the equation when associates are considered for partnership.

The fact that marketing translates into income can affect the in-house LNC in a number of ways. First and foremost, the LNC needs to recognize how important bringing in new business is to attorneys and that attorneys must nurture and protect their sources of referral business and those relationships. Members of the support staff including the LNC must also take care to protect these relationships and take care not to cause a referring attorney or potential client to have doubts about the firm's ability to handle their litigation or make them unhappy or uncomfortable in any way.

Fees and Costs in Litigation and How They Impact In-House LNCs

At the most basic level, attorneys are paid a fee for their services in one of two ways: contingency, meaning a percentage of any recovery, or per diem, meaning by the hour. Plaintiff attorneys most often work on a contingency basis, and defense firms per diem. The fee is meant to cover the time and expertise of the lawyers and support staff involved in the case and the overhead of the firm. It does not cover costs. Cost is anything paid out of the firm's pocket as the case moves along. Examples of items of cost are experts, record service copy fees, court reporter charges, and travel expenses. Knowledge of these distinctions and how they apply to in-house work is essential.

All attorneys, LAs, paralegals, and LNCs working on a claim, with few exceptions, are considered "billable." Secretaries, copy clerks, and other support personnel are not. Each category of billable personnel has an assigned value for each single hour of time. A senior partner's time might be billed at $300/hour, a junior associate $125/hour, and the LNC $75/hour. These values are not arbitrary but arrived at through a general consensus of what the market will bear, the market being the client.

Timekeeping by all billable personnel, including LNCs, is customarily done in blocks of a tenth of an hour (0.1 or 6 min increments) or sometimes quarter of an hour (0.25 or 15 min increments). The strictness and accuracy of time-keeping records and the requirements for how much time is to be accounted for each day are somewhat variable from firm to firm and between large and small offices. When working on a per diem file, these time records are the basis for billing the client. Further, in most firms they provide the basis for measuring the productivity of the timekeeper. Nonbillable hours are to be accounted for each day. Nonbillable time might include time spent at educational seminars, department meetings, or even checking over the weekly time log. There may be a limit on the number of nonbillable hours allowed with the exception of vacation or sick time, and billable employees may be required to log at least 7 hours of billable time per day. The amount of description required on the time sheet varies with the requirements of the client, particularly when working in the per diem setting.

Sample Time Sheet

Client/Case Name	File Number	Billable Hours	Non-billable	Description
Johnson, Clyde	12345	0.4		Telephone w/client
General Office	00000		1.25	Label medical library shelves
Henderson, Charlene	67890	5.35		Research re: preeclampsia
Anderson, James	34567	0.1		Proof corresp. to client

Fees and Costs in the Contingency Claim

Contingency fees are well advertised in the popular media. The text goes something like, "We don't get paid unless you get paid." Most plaintiff attorneys representing individuals are paid on a contingency basis as injured individuals rarely have the assets to pay an experienced attorney by the hour. In a contingency case, the fee is an agreed-upon percentage of the recovery, either by settlement or verdict, if there is one.

Many attorneys take their fee "off the top" of any recovery followed by the reimbursement for costs paid out by the firm. Other firms take costs off first and then their fee. The client collects the remainder, assuming there are no health care insurers or others with liens on the recovery. As an example: A case settles prior to trial for the sum of $100,000. The plaintiff's lawyer has a contingency agreement with the client for 30% and has spent $15,000 in out-of-pocket costs. $100,000 minus $30,000 minus $15,000 leaves the client with $55,000. If costs are first deducted, $100,000 minus $15,000 leaves $85,000, minus 30% equals $25,500 for the attorney's fee, leaving the client with $59,500.

Contingency Work and the LNC — Measuring Productivity and Profitability

While the number of hours worked on a particular contingency case may not seem important, as the client is not actually billed for time, it is very important to the profitability of a case. Timekeeping records for the LNC working in-house on a contingency matter serve as an important measure of productivity and profitability.

In determining whether or not a particular claim was profitable, the value of the hours worked by all billable personnel involved on the file is calculated and compared with the amount of fees generated. For example, fees generated on the ABC case were one third of a $30,000 settlement ($10,000). Costs were $3,000. The client received $17,000. On the face of it, it would appear that the firm made $10,000 and had all cost covered. However, a closer look at the billing records indicates that the value of the time spent by the partner, associate, LA, and LNC on the file amounts to $16,250. In other words, there was $6,250 worth of time expended over what was recovered in the settlement. This file would *not* be considered profitable.

In determining productivity over a longer time period, hours worked are balanced against revenue generated on a particular file and on all files or over the course of the quarter or fiscal year. An example would be the LNC who has worked 20 hours researching issues of liability and only later stumbles onto the fact that the statute has obviously run. This would *not* have been productive time. Too much unproductive time such as this does not make for a good performance review. On the other hand, the LNC who spends 30 hours and little money for experts on a given case enabling a settlement in excess of a million dollars has been very productive indeed.

Economic Decision Making for the In-House Contingency LNC

From time to time, most firms will expend both time and money on cases that never result in revenue, or are deemed not profitable in the end. Thus, it falls to all the members of the team, including the LNC, to see to it that nonproductive time and wasteful spending are kept to a minimum.

Many plaintiff attorneys employing in-house LNCs rely on them almost exclusively to advise as to whether or not to accept, or even perform a preliminary investigation on, all potential claims involving medical issues. While ultimately it is the attorney's decision whether to accept or reject any case, the in-house LNC may be in the best position to help sort out those claims that are economically not viable, or prevent cost or fee overruns as the litigation moves forward.

In order to be of assistance in making case-specific economic decisions and to maintain efficient productivity, the LNC learns as much as possible about the claim from the beginning if possible. Succinctly conducted client interviews which are goal and information focused is the first step. These interviews should be directed toward obtaining information specific to seven areas: *liability, causation, damages, contributory negligence, statute of limitations, attorney conflict of interest,* and *economics.* Even if the in-house LNC is not responsible for obtaining the initial information from the client, assessment of the information gathered for appraisal of these areas is important. Discovering a major obstacle or a series of small ones at the outset will result in less time spent on unprofitable cases and, therefore, an increase in productivity for the LNC and profitability for the firm. The productive LNC in the contingency setting also recognizes when every stone should be overturned, and when just looking under the biggest rocks is sufficient.

One way in which the LNC can be of assistance from the outset of any claim is by making an informed assessment of the damages in terms of potential monetary recovery in light of projected expenses. One would not want to recommend to the attorney that money be spent on collecting X-rays and records, retaining multiple experts, and litigating a claim where the ultimate damages to the client may represent, in monetary terms, less than the cost of even one expert. The attorney finding himself or herself with a $20,000 settlement offer, $15,000 in costs, and a client retainer for 30% will not be very pleased. The attorney in such difficulty may well look to the LNC for an explanation of how such a situation could have occurred.

The LNC also needs to be mindful of the difference between reasonable and unreasonable cost. Ordering complete and certified hospital records to evaluate a potential emergency room claim sounds fine, but could result in a big problem when two boxes of records and a bill for $2,000 arrives. Since most attorneys do not bill their contingency fee clients for costs if the case either does not proceed or is lost, the attorney will never recoup this money.

The LNC who recommends sending a case out for expert physician review without first having considered the economics of the claim may be spending money needlessly. *An example:* While the negligence in a failure to diagnose a heart attack case initially appears clear, damages may be a problem, if the prospective plaintiff has essentially returned to his previous lifestyle and vocation. If the case is going to require the services of an emergency room expert, a nurse, and a cardiologist on causation as well, costs could mount quickly. Encouraging the attorney to press ahead because of obvious negligence may eventually result in an economic disaster. Careful evaluation is essential.

Fees and Costs in the Per Diem Claim

In the per diem claim, the firm bills the client by the hour for work, based on the hourly rates of the various timekeepers. The firm is paid whether it wins or loses. Given sufficient business and appropriate use of personnel, the fees generated should be sufficient to cover overhead of the firm, including all support staff salaries, rent, etc. Any moneys earned in excess of the overhead is profit for the partnership. It is therefore to the advantage of the per diem firm to use personnel with the highest billing rate on any given file, within a range acceptable to the client. Generally speaking, in the per diem setting, usually a defense firm, the clients are insurance companies and/or health care providers. They may work with one firm exclusively, or shop around for the lowest rates just like any other consumer. Because the hourly rates for LNCs are generally lower than that of an attorney, many clients see considerable value in having an LNC as part of the team. A firm that utilizes time efficiently will ensure profits, as well as future business from the client. The LNC can play an important role in this by performing the preliminary claim assessments and providing time lines and organized records to experts to enable them to review cases in fewer hours, thus holding down costs of case preparation. Costs on per diem files are billed separately.

When working in the per diem setting, the LNC must be aware of what he or she can and cannot bill to the file and how time is to be entered. If the client is adamant about not paying for work by persons above or below a certain title or billing rate, the LNC should make it a point to know this before embarking on work for that client. Since the in-house LNC likely will be doing work for many clients on many files at once, it is wise to discuss the peculiarities of billing with the attorney managing each file at the outset. Some clients have special fee arrangements and the LNC should be aware of these.

Per diem clients often scrutinize their bills carefully when it comes to time records and may dispute certain entries or refuse payment for others. *Example 1:* The LNC logs 2 hours and 12 minutes (2.2 hours) on file XYZ for punching holes in records in preparation for trial. The client refuses to pay for these services explaining that this type of work should have been done by nonbillable staff such as a secretary. *Example 2:* A carelessly entered time record reflecting a 24-min phone call, 0.4 hour, may also be disputed by the client saying it lasted no more that 6 min, 0.1 hour. This may seem insignificant, but if enough discrepancies are uncovered, at the LNC's billing rate, the amount of revenue lost to the firm could be significant. This also reflects sloppy record keeping by the LNC. If allowed, being more descriptive in time entries helps explain why a particular task took as long as it did.

Some Pitfalls of Timekeeping and Productivity Measures for the LNC

Another difficulty of timekeeping in relation to productivity is determining how best to log time spent on things that may or may not be directly related to any one file but are necessary just the same. Organizational tasks, waiting at the copier, looking for missing or misfiled documents are all part of everyday work but not considered billable. How and whether or not this type of time is billed and to what file in large measure depend on the billable hour requirements and the policies of the firm. One would not want to bill 2 or 3 hours of time to look for a missing document. The per diem client would likely not feel inclined to pay for the LNC's mistake in losing it. Logging it to a contingency file may cause the LNC to look unproductive. On the other hand, if required to bill at least 7 hours a day, the dilemma is how to account for this time. One answer may be to delegate the search to a secretary. Unfortunately, that may not be possible. Sometimes, all one can hope is that it "all comes out in the wash."

Large vs. Small Firms

Differences between small and large law firms can be quite dramatic. Law firms range in size from the sole practitioner to firms with hundreds of attorneys and satellite offices all across the country. The smaller firms may practice a variety of law including not only personal injury, but bankruptcy, divorce, probate, and any number of other nonmedically related types of cases. It is rather rare for an LNC to be employed in this type of setting as the volume of cases requiring medical expertise is low. The exception is the small firm specializing in personal injury or medical malpractice, where the contribution of one or more LNCs is significant.

Medium-size firms (25 to 75 attorneys) and large law firms usually have areas of specialty practice which may not be medically related. For instance, a law firm may have 125 lawyers but only two working in an area appropriate for the skills of the LNC. Size of the law firm alone should not be taken as an indicator of sufficient volume of work for the LNC. A small firm with six attorneys may need two LNCs because of a large volume of medical malpractice work.

The LNC looking for long-term employment should also be cautious of the attorney anxious to hire an LNC "to help me move these two big cases along." This attorney may not have another medically related case for years or may decide never to do another. On the other hand, the two cases may require 1 to 3 years to litigate, during which time the novice LNC may gain valuable experience.

Compensation

Hourly or Salary

Most in-house LNCs are paid hourly. The calculated amount in gross pay over a year of full-time work is often referred to as the annual salary. Employees paid by the hour are nonexempt meaning that all state and federal rules of overtime, maximum number of hours worked per day, etc. all apply. The nonexempt employee is paid for overtime and must account for hours off work with either personal or vacation time. In contrast, the LNC who is truly salaried, is paid a certain amount regardless of the number of hours worked. This LNC may be permitted to take off half a day to compensate for 4 hours of work the evening before. This is known as "comping back the time." In contrast, the nonexempt hourly LNC would be obliged to log in the overtime and would not be able to take the afternoon off unless vacation or personal time were used. If the prospective LNC has a choice, the frequency of overtime and flexibility of hours should be carefully considered.

Market Expectations for LNC Salaries and Benefits

No market salary survey has been published for LNCs. However, it is known that many attorneys feel completely justified in offering a potential LNC employee a wage less than he or she would make in a hospital setting because of the "trade-off of weekend and holiday work for a nine to five office job." It is also well known that many nurses find that offer sufficient, if not attractive. As long as this remains the case, in-house LNC salaries will rarely match those of the successful, full-time independent practitioner. There are variances between what large and small firms are willing to pay, between in-house plaintiff and defense firms, with defense generally paying less, and regional differences.

Many larger plaintiff's firms are beginning to realize that LNCs can do the work of an associate attorney and are more willing to pay salaries in the range of an associate, assuming the LNC is experienced and takes an active management role in each case. In many parts of the country in that context, the salary range may be roughly $45,000 to $60,000, with some variance at either end depending on benefits.

Bonus Programs

A bonus is a portion of the profits which the partners decide to share with employees. Very large firms with many partners among which to divide profits are not as likely to give bonuses. Smaller firms have more leeway to grant bonuses to reward employees for a job well done without regard for politics or precedent. Bonuses may or may not have anything to do with an individual's productivity or profitability, but may be calculated by seniority, a percentage of salary, or be equal for all support staff.

Benefits

As in any other position, the benefits menu may or may not include health and dental insurance, retirement or pension plans, paid vacation and sick time, and others. In addition, four specific firm-paid benefits are definitely worth inquiring about: cost of RN state licensure renewals, AALNC national and chapter dues, costs for required continuing nursing education fees, and paid membership in a specialty organization such as the American Association of Critical Care Nurses. It can be pointed out that well-credentialed LNCs are more respected by the physicians and nurses the LNC works with every day as either defendants or experts. Further, and perhaps more important to the attorney is the fact that continuing education is a must in order to evaluate claims appropriately based on current standards of practice and theories of disease. Out-of-date knowledge is not of much use and may in fact be quite detrimental.

Job Security

The only job security for the in-house LNC in most firms is profitability and performance. There are no unions or appeals boards. Most of the time the attorney who hired and supervises the LNC's work also has the power to decide that the LNC's services are no longer required. Doing one's utmost to ensure continued profitability of the firm contributes to job security. There are also certain personal and professional attributes and skills which engender job security for the in-house LNC.

Attributes of the Successful In-House Legal Nurse Consultant

Skills

The skills required of the successful in-house LNC vary somewhat depending on the type of practice and position description of the individual LNC. Applied in the broadest sense, the following discussion describes required skills.

Writing. The ability to produce final copy of daily business correspondence and memoranda on the first draft cannot be over emphasized. Much time can be squandered reworking a simple status letter to the client or summary memo of a short phone call. Having the skill to construct artfully crafted letters of persuasion, informative research summaries, forceful answers to expert interrogatories, succinct medical record summaries, and any number of other required documents efficiently on a daily basis is the bread and butter of most in-house LNCs. A good lawyer will recognize this talent and make the most of it. Learning and adopting the writing style of the attorney who will sign the ultimate product is also a plus. Careful proofreading is vital. The fewer revisions required of the attorney, the more valuable the LNC. Most attorneys are meticulous in perfecting the written document. Writings and documents are their work product. Like the pride of an auto worker in a car rolling off the assembly line, no attorney wants the final work product to be "dented or scratched." More importantly, a misplaced comma or missing word can change the entire meaning of a sentence and document and render an argument invalid. Retyping and printing because of careless proof-reading is a waste of everyone's time. A document filled with typos or grammatical errors can be just as tiresome as poor writing. (*Hint:* Do not depend on the spell checker in the word-processing program. It will not catch the difference between hear and here or on and of. To the spell checker, both words are spelled correctly.)

Teaching. In most in-house practices, particularly in plaintiff work, where the medical defendant and experts are not readily available or are very expensive to access, the all-important job of teaching the medicine to the attorney falls to the LNC. This could mean teaching a senior partner how to read 12-lead EKGs in preparation for a deposition, the how-to of intubating an infant, the technique for inserting a subclavian catheter, or any other topic. It means being able to explain clearly the underlying rationale for actions taken, how and why things occurred or could have occurred as they did in the case at hand, and why, what, and how things should have been done differently. These teaching sessions may take place many times over the life of a case and become more sophisticated as the case moves ahead. The LNC must be prepared to lead the session having determined the objectives for learning of the attorney. In order to be successful, the LNC must "do the homework" and prepare pictures, diagrams, demonstrations, or any other tool that will aid the attorney in processing and understanding very technical information. Keep in mind that the attorney must be on equal footing with the experts in discussions, must ask informed questions at depositions, and ultimately must be prepared to teach the medicine to a jury in opening statements. It is the LNC who enables the attorney to do so.

Prioritizing. The busy in-house LNC usually has dozens of competing concerns and multiple attorneys requesting attention all at once. Unlike a hospital setting, it usually is not possible to enlist the aid of co-workers. Further, unlike the independent consultant, the in-house LNC does not have the luxury of declining another assignment or new file. Therefore, the in-house LNC must prioritize work/tasks and perhaps more than once a day. There are some rules to follow in prioritizing. Some deadlines are hard and fast and must be met. Others are softer and can be manipulated. Last are self-imposed deadlines that can be changed as needed.

In the category of hard-and-fast deadlines are court-ordered or statute-required deadlines. *These must be met.* Other matters should be put on a back burner for these items. Examples are drafting and filing of a complaint to meet a statute of limitations date, filing of witness and exhibit lists as ordered by the court before trial, and statute-required disclosure of expert witnesses. Missing deadlines such as these can result in summary dismissal of the claim and a *potential lawsuit against the firm.*

The second category is the daily tasks required to move a case along. This might be a soft deadline set for completing a summary of records within 30 days of receipt, or having experts retained 60 days before required disclosure. Moving such deadlines a week or two will not result in any penalty or sanction. However, the LNC may need to inform the attorney that these items have been reprioritized and why. These deadlines may have been agreed upon with a client such as an insurance carrier.

The last category, of self-imposed deadlines, is obviously the most flexible. Preparing a daily To-Do list including items from each category, if possible, is very helpful. If a new case with a statute of limitations about to expire is assigned, there will always be something that can be temporarily shelved to get the complaint drafted and filed. Attorneys sometimes forget that the LNC has competing deadlines and delegate without regard to timeliness or workload. This results in a To-Do list that has no flexibility, not to mention a job that seems to consist of putting out one fire after another. It is the LNC's responsibility to anticipate upcoming deadlines if at all possible and take the initiative to complete the task before the due date becomes a crisis deadline.

Organizing. All LNCs can remember their days at the bedside and the nurse on the unit who never seemed to have the supplies needed, was disorganized, and always used overtime to complete charting, etc. A successful in-house LNC needs to be organized. Having an office with stacks of paper piled high on the floor, piles of phone messages, a tower of X-ray envelopes, and general clutter does not give the appearance of an organized professional. Such a work space also fails to inspire confidence and does not lend itself to the efficiency required of the position. Generally speaking, the higher the volume and responsibility, the more organization required.

Organization also means creating a pattern or work flow for daily production. For example, have a morning routine: open the mail first, then return phone calls, then address in-box paperwork. Time sheets should be completed every day before leaving for the day. For efficient case management, a system of file come-ups (calendar dates denoting upcoming important due dates and events) or a tickler system is helpful to remind one to draft regular client update letters or documents, or to check on the arrival of ordered records. Any system is fine; the point is to *have a system*.

Characteristics of the Successful In-House LNC

Clinical Background. The required clinical background depends on the type of work to be performed. However, most in-house LNCs will be most successful with a broad clinical background or critical care experience. The latter is important because the experience and education of the critical care nurse requires an in-depth working knowledge of all body systems and disease processes. This knowledge stands the nurse in good stead when trying to explain such things as the chemistry of diabetes, how pressure affects the brain, or how and why ventilator settings are adjusted. A nurse with many years as a clinician in a narrow specialty, such as adult psychiatric nursing or infection control, may not be able to assess adequately the merits of liability or causation arguments or teach effectively without first investing a great deal of time in research. This affects productivity.

Exceptions to the above would be LNCs working exclusively in personal injury or a specialty area of torts. In personal injury work, a background in orthopedics and surgery or trauma would be most helpful. An attorney specializing in obstetrical malpractice would be delighted with an LNC with a neonatal ICU and/or obstetrical background. In mass tort work in which all clients have the same injury caused by the same product, a more general background would be sufficient.

Personality Traits. Self-confidence is a key trait for the in-house LNC. The learning curve is measured most of the time in years. It may be 3 to 4 years before the LNC competently manages his or her first case through trial. It requires a great deal of self-confidence and courage to learn essentially a new language and way of thinking, to become a proficient writer and researcher, and to make effective decisions and recommendations on issues that may involve many thousands of dollars.

Confidence is also most necessary when teaching attorneys. As previously mentioned, attorneys rely on the LNC to make them as knowledgeable as the opposing physician expert. If the LNC does not feel and look and behave in a confident manner during these sessions, the attorney will not trust the LNC's information.

Assertiveness. In concert with self-confidence, assertiveness is an absolute requirement. The in-house LNC spends most of his or her time working with attorneys and physicians who can be intimidating. They have spent many years in school and practicing their profession. Some may not take kindly to even gentle criticism or challenge of their opinions or ideas. However, the LNC who is timid about challenging or redirecting opinions or strategies by either a physician or an attorney when appropriate may not be successful. If an expert telephones following review of a record and has obviously missed something in the records, or expresses an opinion that does not seem to be consistent with the facts, the LNC must tactfully question the opinion directing the expert's attention to the facts. Knowing the file and the medicine, the LNC may suggest, "Perhaps you didn't see the nurses entries for that date, Doctor," or "Doctor, recent literature would seem to show otherwise," and be fully prepared to continue the discussion. *Simply listening and recording what was reported by the expert is of little use. If that was the case, no special expertise would be required.*

The assertive, confident, and well-prepared LNC serves the case well and gains the respect of attorneys, experts, and clients.

Pros and Cons of In-House Practice

The reader will have doubtless noted a number of differences between in-house and independent practice, but some of these differences deserve particular mention. The first is the inability to have any input into the types of cases assigned or to decline any assignment. Personal and ethical conflicts may therefore be more frequent for the in-house practitioner and control of work flow a daily struggle. The in-house LNC needs to understand that each claim represents, in addition to the interests of the parties involved, potential income for the attorney and the firm. When one considers each claim from the perspective of the attorney, it can be quite a different view. The attorney has an incentive that the LNC does not, as the LNC's compensation is not case dependent as is the attorneys. This different perspective is perhaps best illustrated by example: A case involving a comatose young father has consumed a great deal of time and effort on the part of the firm representing him. Then, suddenly, he awakens from his coma and the event is hailed as a miracle. While, of course, the attorney is happy for the man and his family, it still means a loss of millions of dollars in the value of the claim and perhaps even a net loss to the firm if expenses are already high. A case with difficult liability issues but big damages may be pursued quite vigorously because of the potential income. In the converse, a case of clear negligence, but little in the way of damages, may not be pursued at all, as it would cost more than could ultimately be collected.

A lack of peers in the workplace can make both in-house and independent practice lonely occupations. Finding and developing relationships with other LNCs in the community is important.

Another drawback to in-house practice is the lack of a career ladder or upward mobility in a law firm for the LNC. This contrasts with the independent practitioner who has the ability to grow and expand the business and range of services offered. A sense of stagnation can, at times, lead to burnout. The in-house LNC, however, can continue to expand his or her expertise and importance in the firm, which is personally satisfying. The LNC's unique expertise brings a great deal of respect from employers and co-workers over time.

In-house practice does have some advantages over independent practice. The in-house LNC enjoys relative freedom from marketing pressures and decision making regarding office and business management. The in-house LNC does not have to worry about hiring and firing of employees and has the security of a regular, dependable paycheck. There is also no worry about collections or accounts receivable. No capital outlay is required. The extensive resources and expensive equipment of the firm are available to provide support for the LNC's work. For many, there is also the satisfaction of working on a case from beginning to end, rather than being involved with only isolated assignments.

In-house work can be very satisfying and rewarding. As more and more attorneys become aware of the service LNCs can perform for their clients and business, more will hire professional LNCs.

Appendix 31.1
Position Description*

Legal Nurse Consultant
Position Description

Position: Legal Nurse Consultant (LNC)   **Revised:**   July 1, 1996

Department: Mass Tort/Medical Malpractice/Personal Injury

Reports To: Supervising Attorney and Legal Assistant Manager

FLSA Status: Non-exempt

POSITION PURPOSE:

The role of the LNC is to provide the attorney with management of all assigned cases and substantive input on medical and legal issues of each case.

ESSENTIAL FUNCTIONS:

The Legal Nurse Consultant's responsibilities are to be carried out with minimal supervision by an attorney. Those <u>responsibilities include, but are not limited to the following, dependent upon the speciality of the department</u>:

- Triage: Make recommendations to the attorney regarding each potential claim's merit through an analysis of liability, causation, damage, economics, conflicts and applicable statute of limitations. Prepare appropriate correspondence after each such analysis and maintain records of each call through the firm's Litigation Support Department (LCS).

- Determine medical records, x-rays and other data necessary for each review and arrange for same, while being mindful of the economics of each case.

- Organize and then analyze medical records and other pertinent data to define issues of liability, causation, damages, conflicts, identification of parties, and advise responsible attorney of conclusions and recommendations

---

* Courtesy of Robins, Kaplan, Miller, Ciresi, LLP.

Appendix 31.1
Position Description (continued)

- Conduct medical research as deemed necessary based on the issues identified in the case analysis.

- Determine tentative statute of limitations for each case and present to attorney for approval.

- Determine type of experts testimony for aspects of liability, causation and damages. Locate necessary experts, prepare and send materials needed for expert's review, including a summary of records and facts and secure expert's opinion.

- Locate treating physicians and other fact witnesses and interview same.

- Maintain contact with all clients on a frequent basis.

- Perform client, witness and expert interviews.

- Maintain a written records of all file activity including; conversations, conclusions, recommendations, analyses, research and medical record summations.

- Assist with preparation for depositions of clients, medical experts, and medical defendants and attend those depositions.

- Identify, design and coordinate demonstrative evidence assuring relevance and accuracy.

- Educate members of the legal team on the substantive medical issues of each case.

- Prepare for and attend trial.

- Draft correspondence, pleadings and other documents.

- Utilize computerized information systems.

- Maintain monthly case status report.

- Organize, maintain and utilize a comprehensive medical library.

- Maintain medical expert/consultant databank.

- Attend and participate in departmental meetings.

- Prioritize workload daily based on applicable legal deadlines for each case and other factors.

- Maintain knowledge of current medicine and evolving standards of care, treatment and prognosis through regular review of medical and nursing journals.

Appendix 31.1
Position Description (continued)

TARGET BILLABLE HOURS ANNUALLY:

- 1700 (145 month)

EDUCATIONAL REQUIREMENTS:

- Four year B.A. or B.S. degree

- Current registered nursing license in the state of Minnesota

- Compliance with continuing education as required by the State of Minnesota to maintain nursing license.

PRIOR EXPERIENCE:

- Significant clinical nursing experience. Medical specialities may be relevant when hiring for specific matters of litigation.

SPECIAL KNOWLEDGE OR SKILLS:

- Working knowledge of the laws and rules applicable to medical malpractice, personal injury and/or product liability.

- Ability to apply medical knowledge to the legal process.

- Keen analytical, research and investigative ability.

- Ability to exercise accurate professional and legal judgment, and to understand and apply ethical standards required by the American Bar Association, the American Nurses Association and the American Association of Legal Nurse Consultants.

- Proficiency in computerized medical research.

- Strong oral, interpersonal and written communication skills.

- Strong problem solving skills and ability to exercise creativity in the process.

- Ability to work independently, with little supervision or direction.

Section IX

The Legal Nurse Consultant as Expert Witness

In medical litigation, one key component that makes or breaks a case is the medical expert witness. In candor, famous trial attorneys confide "the money in medical litigation is in who has the best experts!" Because legal nurse consultants are so instrumental in selecting, developing, and even serving as experts, they often make the critical difference in medical litigation outcomes. This section focuses on that critical difference, and how the successful LNC creates it.

Chapter 32

Introduction: The Legal Nurse Consultant and Expert Witnesses

Doreen James Wise

Contents

1-57444-123-X/98
© 1998 by American Association of Legal Nurse Consultants

Objectives

- To state the role and purpose of medical expert witnesses in civil litigation
- To describe three types of experts, identifying similarities and differences among them in approach to case review and testimony
- To indicate, when presented with a resume for a nurse, evidence for qualifying/disqualifying that individual for the role of testifying expert on case provided
- To draft a sample code of professional conduct for experts

Introduction

Virtually all legal nurse consultants (LNCs) work as consulting experts; many work with testifying expert witnesses in some capacity as well. The LNC employed by a law firm may be asked to locate suitable experts for medical malpractice, personal injury, toxic tort, or product liability cases. In addition, the LNC often determines whether or not a potential expert meets court qualifications, serves as the firm's primary link of communication with the expert, and prepares the expert for testimony. LNCs in independent practice may provide some or all of the same services as those employed by law firms.

Other LNCs' clinical and/or research credentials may qualify them to serve as testifying experts. This determination depends on the unique talents, qualifications, and preferences of the LNC, the area of litigation addressed, and the facts of a given case.

For this chapter, discussion is limited to cases involving the medical aspects of civil tort litigation, although the LNC may participate in any litigation with medical elements. Experts may consult confidentially with the attorney and/or also testify in court. Three types of experts are included in this chapter — liability, damages, and expert fact witnesses.

Purpose of Expert Witnesses in Medical Litigation

In most jurisdictions, the plaintiff's counsel must present qualified experts in order to pursue a case. Each expert must render an opinion verifying that the plaintiff's case has merit. In medical malpractice cases a suitable expert for the plaintiff must give evidence demonstrating that negligence has occurred and that the usual and customary standards for professional practice have been violated (i.e., there is liability on the part of the defendant). In addition, an expert is called upon to testify that the damages alleged by the plaintiff were caused directly by the negligence of the defendant (proximate cause). This latter is true in personal injury cases as well. In all but a few instances, if the expert does not qualify with the court and/or does not give testimony sufficiently convincing of negligence and proximate cause, the plaintiff's case does not prove meritorious enough to proceed with the litigation, i.e., "get to the jury." In these cases, the defendant's motion for summary judgment may well be granted. The consequences of poorly planned litigation vary from state to state, but generally involve risking disqualification of the expert, dismissal of the suit and subsequent legal malpractice claims. In the best of all worlds, the responsible plaintiff's attorney will have filed suit with a compelling case, and an equally compelling expert.

An exception to the expert requirement in medical malpractice litigation is that of *res ipsa loquitor* cases. Literally translated "the thing speaks for itself," these cases are thought to be so obvious that an expert testifying to the evident negligence is superfluous. An example is the case in which a surgical instrument is left in the patient after surgery. An expert is not required to testify that the standard of care calls for removal of all materials and instruments on closing. However, an expert might be required by practicality to testify to exactly what damages resulted.

Although attorneys may hold a differing view from medical professionals, the purpose of the medical expert witness is education of the attorneys and "triers of fact," i.e., juries and judges. Attorneys are taught that the average American juror has a sixth-grade education; yet, that same juror in a medical negligence or personal injury case may be called upon to make decisions about highly complex matters of fact, law, and medicine. Without benefit of instruction on the relevant medical issues by expert professionals, most jurors would find it all but impossible to render informed verdicts.

The role of the expert medical witness is one of the most critical in civil litigation.

Types of Expert Witnesses

Consulting Experts

Consulting experts are educated, trained, and experienced in at least one medical field. Their role is to educate the plaintiff's attorney seeking to pursue an action, or the defense attorney faced with defending one. In a confidential process protected by law, the consulting expert for either side may review and summarize the medical records, explore the relevant medical literature, and discuss the case with the attorney and knowledgeable clinical colleagues. The outcome is an informed and private evaluation of the worthiness of the case in review. The process, and its protective confidentiality, is analogous to the peer-review process in health care settings.

Consulting experts may, or may not, later testify. In actuality, all testifying experts are first consulting experts as they make their preliminary review of the case and form an opinion. If the consulting expert finds the case worthy, that individual may then agree to become a testifying expert. If the plaintiff's case is found nonmeritorious, the expert may decline the case and recommend it be dropped. If the matter is pursued nonetheless, the consultant may maintain a continuing assistive role in the matter from "behind the scenes." Another testifying expert may be sought. The attorney faced with defending a medical malpractice case may seek an ongoing independent, objective view of the case; this supplements information provided by the often emotionally charged viewpoint of the defendant client.

The opinions and work product of the consulting expert are nondiscoverable in most instances. This creates the opportunity for the attorney confidentially to explore the facts of the case independent of the recollections and biases of the client and to test a variety of legal theories before permanently committing to any. The work product (notes, files, reports, and opinions) of the consulting expert remains private and nondiscoverable. In most venues, however, if the subsequent testifying expert relies on that work product to formulate opinions later given in testimony, the consulting expert and the work product are then subject to discovery. If a consulting expert becomes a testifying expert, all materials reviewed and resources used to form the expert opinion can be compelled to be produced into discovery.

The LNC as Consulting Expert

Probably the foremost role in medical and injury cases for the LNC is that of consulting expert. Conversant on medical issues, and usually privy to a network of clinical colleagues, the LNC offers an informed, cost-effective view on even highly specialized and complex medical issues. Some law firms hire LNCs as employees to review all medical matters considered for litigation. Others prefer to retain independent LNCs as occasional consultants, seeking their services within certain clinical specialties and issues relevant to a given case. In either event, all work product remains confidential and is shielded from discovery, since it is considered attorney work product. The wise LNC prominently so marks correspondence and other writings.

Should the attorney opt to present the testifying expert with the LNC's work, however, the LNC and work product are subject to discovery. The LNC can be subpoenaed for testimony about the work product, and all that was relied upon to create it. The LNC wishing to remain totally "behind the scenes" should so inform the attorney employer/client. It is in the best interest of the attorney to oblige such requests; the LNC's opinion can, and often does, vary from that of the testifying expert. Protecting the LNC's work product from discovery prevents possible embarrassment from revealing legitimate differences of opinion among the litigation team members. It also allows the attorney an uncensored view of all medical strengths and any weaknesses in the case.

Testifying Expert Witnesses

Testifying experts in medical malpractice cases will have had equivalent or higher education, board certification, and experience to that of the defendant, and will have been practicing contemporaneously with the event in question in a similar clinical setting. They are considered knowledgeable of the circumstances, the "reality" faced by the defendant in a given clinical setting at a given time. Each potential testifying expert is asked to review the data then available to the defendant, to formulate a statement of what the reasonably prudent clinician would have done in the same or similar situation, then to compare and contrast this "standard" with the actual performance of the defendant. This expert is said to be addressing liability, i.e., negligence, or whether or not the standard of care has been met. The same or a different expert may be asked to opine regarding the causal relationship between negligence and damages suffered by the plaintiff; this expert will be addressing proximate cause. An expert may address the damages suffered as a result of the negligence as well. In personal injury cases the medical expert may be testifying about mechanisms of injury, causation, medical damages, and/or future medical care requirements.

The chief function of the testifying expert is to teach the trier of fact enough relevant medicine to enable an informed decision about the case in litigation. Thus, the successful testifying expert not only must qualify under the law as a suitable expert, but also must be skilled enough at establishing rapport and communicating with lay jurors to teach them about science and medicine. Inevitably, the jury will be comprised of nonmedical individuals. The testifying expert must teach the medical basics of the case, convey and interpret the events in question, then render a compelling and intelligible opinion based on the evidence. It is a significant accomplishment, one not easily achieved by every otherwise clinically competent medical professional.

The LNC and the Testifying Expert

In the early stages of any medical lawsuit, the LNC may be the person most intimately knowledgeable of the facts and issues inherent. It is therefore common for the LNC to lead the search for qualified testifying experts and to recommend the choice of relevant medical specialties. The LNC may then plan and initiate the search for just the right expert to evaluate the case more closely, refine the issues, and present the medical portions of the case in testimony.

In selecting an expert, the LNC will need to detect any potential conflicts of interest and eliminate those experts subject to it. The *curriculum vitae* of expert candidates must be closely reviewed for education, experience, certification, relevant publications, and teaching, and for even hints of impropriety. The wise LNC will closely check the expert's references from medical colleagues and will secure and evaluate transcripts of, and feedback about, any prior testimony. Investigation about one's own and/or the opposition's experts might include determining how balanced between plaintiff and defense the expert's reviews and testimony have been; a history of reviewing and rejecting cases from both sides is often regarded as evidence of cautious, objective review. It is also prudent to explore the expert's publications and transcripts of prior testimony for consistency of opinions on issues in question in the case to be reviewed. Determine the percentage of the expert's total income derived from forensic activity; especially in medical malpractice litigation the most desirable experts are those with a relatively modest percentage of total income coming from any but clinical or research activity. Although the above considerations or even "skeletons in the closet" of would-be experts do not automatically disqualify them, the vulnerabilities are best detected and proactively revealed prior to their becoming discovered independently by the opposition. Attorneys like surprises less than anyone, especially when they come in the form of bad news about one's own expert testifying from the stand!

It is often the LNC who shepherds the medical testimony in a case to successful conclusion. During initial discussions with the selected expert, the LNC may briefly describe the facts of the case, then provide available medical records and materials for expert review. Following the expert's preliminary review, the LNC discusses the case with the expert, noting opinions, theories, and recommendations for the attorney. The LNC may remain as the intermediary between the expert and attorney or may step aside as the attorney assumes a more active role in the process. Some LNCs review and critique expert reports and prepare the expert to give testimony. Caution about how directive a role an LNC takes with the expert is advised, compliant with a given state's rules of discovery; it is rarely in the best interest of the case for the consulting LNC to be subpoenaed for testimony with heretofore confidential files, correspondence, and opinions.

The LNC as Testifying Expert

Independent LNCs may serve as testifying experts for a variety of reasons. Skilled, active nurse clinicians may opt to review given cases and to testify on those found meritorious. The LNC will need to qualify as the nurse expert in the same ways as do other nurse experts. The LNC wishing to testify on liability issues will need to hold equivalent credentials and experience to those of the defendant nurse and to have been practicing in a similar setting contemporaneously with the event in question. For the full-time LNC this may be an unrealistic role — it is difficult to maintain both an active clinical role and a demanding LNC practice.

Nonetheless, there are a number of LNCs maintaining a substantial enough clinical commitment to qualify as testifying nurse experts on liability issues. This occurs despite the fact that some states narrowly define minimum qualifications for testifying experts. In Kansas, for example, the expert must have spent at least half of all professional time in the clinical specialty practice about which testimony is to be provided during the 2 years prior to the litigated incident. Even in states with less stringent practice requirements, almost certainly there will be additional questioning by the opposition's attorney into the detail of one's clinical commitments; for obscure reasons it seems that medical professionals working with attorneys on either side of the bar or attending law school are often treated as if suspect!

For LNCs addressing the damages aspect of injury litigation, prospects for review and testimony may be favorable. Life-care planning with attendant expert testimony is a growing specialty among LNCs. Experienced and knowledgeable in the planning and execution of long-term care for the injured, these LNCs often evolve from clinical careers in rehabilitation or vocational rehabilitation. The life-care planner meticulously assesses the plaintiff's injuries and care required, then plans, quantifies, and testifies to future care and costs.

The role of expert fact witness is one in which the nurse serves as an "interpreter" for the trier of fact about complex medical care in lay terms. The expert fact witness presents the relevant factual evidence contained in medical records and professional literature. Whether appointed by the court or retained by counsel, the expert fact witness epitomizes the teaching function of testifying experts. Because of specialized education in health care, clinical experience, and preparation as educators, nurses are uniquely qualified to testify in this capacity.

Ordinarily, the role of expert fact witness includes review and summary of the medical records, "translation" of that record into layperson's terms, then presentation of same for the trier of fact in a comprehensible and interesting way.

Description of human anatomy, definition of medical terminology, explanation of treatment procedures, and characterization of pain and suffering will likely be the stuff of the testimony. Ordinarily, the role does not include explicit rendering of an opinion on the quality of care provided or the causes of any injury, unless those are already detailed in the medical record. The role is strictly instructive.

Nurses have testified as expert fact witnesses in medical malpractice, personal injury, and product liability cases in the civil courts, and even in criminal cases. The role of expert fact witness is an innovative and new niche, perfect for the LNC.

Qualifications of Expert Witnesses

Legal Requirements

Although exact qualifications for suitable expert witnesses may vary on the state level, there is some general agreement. Most agree that an expert must be educated and experienced in the topic of testimony. A current, valid professional license to practice is an obvious requirement. Certification by a recognized specialty board is fast becoming a minimum requirement for expert witness acceptability (American College of Physicians, 1990). In addition, there should be evidence of a logical professional progression from the period following formal education to the present. Breaks in service, while sometimes unavoidable, must be documented.

More-specific requirements usually include, for professional liability litigation, evidence of like practice in a similar setting at the time of the incident under scrutiny. For example, in birth trauma liability cases with extended statutes of limitations, the expert is most certain to meet qualification requirements if practicing in a similar type of practice setting at the time of the misadventure which might well have been 18 to 20 years prior! One might also be expected to have published in refereed journals in which articles submitted were received by experts in the field prior to publication. In addition, considerable scrutiny is being placed on the validity of scientific premises for expert opinion.

In cases where experts have relied on less than worthy scientific theory, so-called junk science, the experts may be disqualified and their opinions disallowed. A recent Supreme Court decision, *Daubert v. Merrell Dow Pharmaceuticals, Inc.*, 113 S. Ct. 2786, 2795, 125 L.Ed.2d 469 (1993), specified that Rule 702 of the Federal Rules of Evidence requires expert testimony to be reliable and relevant. Federal court judges have the responsibility to ensure that experts base testimony on a "reliable foundation." This means that expert witnesses must prove that theories relied upon have been tested, subjected to peer review and publication, evaluated for error, and held generally acceptable by the relevant scientific community. The implication is that the testifying expert is in fact "expert" on the subject at hand and has provided evidence that all theories relied on for opinion meet these qualifications. As of this writing, there is at least one example that this federal opinion is also now applicable on the state level. *In E.I DuPont de Nemours and Company v. C. R. Robinson and Shirley Robinson*, (TX. No. 94-0843), the testimony of an expert was excluded. The Supreme Court of Texas upheld the lower court's decision (1995 WL 359024 Tex.) because the expert's testimony was "not based upon reliable scientific foundation" — the expert had employed problematic methodology, had tested his theories for the first time in preparation for testimony, and had utilized spurious reasoning. While the implications of *Daubert* are more immediately applicable on the federal level, and specifically to product liability and personal injury cases, there is every reason to believe that the state courts "will look to the high court for guidance" (Gold et al., 1993) and that medical malpractice experts will be held to this standard as well.

Professional Credibility

It is imperative that medical experts maintain the professional respect of their peers. In general, expert consultation and testimony is just another practice venue option for the skilled professional. Codes for professional behavior and ethics are as applicable as in any other setting. The National Forensic Center has published one such code of ethics for experts from all disciplines. It echoes those of most medical codes and anticipates the essence of *Daubert*, including honest representation of professional credentials; impartial and properly formulated opinions; remuneration within reason and independent of one's opinion; and strict confidentiality.

Beyond these basic ethical requirements, the conscientious medical professional makes additional commitments as a testifying expert. Despite the now-antiquated contingent of experts testifying exclusively for one side of an issue or another, practicality and integrity demand balance between plaintiff and defense cases. One must review cases from either side, weighing the evidence impartially and testifying only in cases that are, in truth, found meritorious. In addition, medical experts must continue professional practice in order to maintain credibility; the credibility of experts whose sole source of income is full-time testimony is suspect.

Remuneration is a complicated issue. Those medical professionals whose income is largely dependent on expert work are considered less than acceptable by attorneys and are confusing to jurors. Fee sharing with nonattorneys is in violation of attorney and expert witness professional codes, at the least, and may be in violation of the law. Determining the amount of compensation based on the opinion of the expert, and/or contingent on the outcome of the case, are beneath professionally correct conduct. In most cases, the same approach used for compensating any other professional activity away from the office or a simple fee for hourly work approach serves best (American College of Physicians, 1990).

Caveat to Would-Be Experts

Experts in medical cases may undergo grueling attempts by the opposition's attorneys to discredit, distract, or annoy them on points sometimes irrelevant to the facts of the case. For undetermined reasons, those medical professionals submitting themselves as expert witnesses also must prepare to subject themselves to occasionally aggressive lines of questioning about professional, economic, and even personal matters. The opposition's attorney may well have carefully researched the expert's *curriculum vitae* for any vulnerability. If there has been an unexplained break in service, it may be viewed as a detriment. If the expert has been less than scrupulously honest in reporting accomplishments and honors, it may be used to discredit. If research efforts and publications are infrequent, inconsistent with other activities cited, and rarely accepted in journals refereed by colleagues, an otherwise perfectly adequate clinician may prove vulnerable to legitimate criticism. In addition, the opposition's attorney may have researched thoroughly all prior testimony given by that expert. Any inconsistency can be brought out for discussion while the expert is under oath. The medical professional, accustomed to respect and even deference from patients and colleagues, may be surprised and horrified by the "hardball" inquiry tactics of attorneys in medical cases. The LNC may serve a useful purpose by carefully prescreening experts, helping the would-be expert anticipate such tactics, and preparing tactful, yet effective replies.

There is a tacit, sometimes double standard in the realm of medical testimony that deserves sober thought by any individual willing to entertain the role of testifying expert. This "running the gauntlet" practice may stem from the traditional code of protective silence among medical professionals that predates peer-review efforts of modern times; any who dare to step outside the code of silence to speak openly of a colleague's misadventures runs the risk of harassment. However, experts appearing for the defendant may also suffer aggressive treatment. The combined human misery inherent in medical litigation, injury, or malpractice and the huge dollar amounts at stake may tend to bring out more-aggressive, less-courtly behavior and strategies. Although addressed by codes of legal ethics or statutory law, testifying medical experts nonetheless occasionally are subjected to unfamiliar abuse which can serve to discourage their continued responsible and essential role in litigation. Careful attention to one's professional conduct, exacting formulation of one's opinions, and agreeing to testify only on meritorious matters not only is in the best interest of the case, but reduces wear and tear on the expert as well.

Summary

The LNC has numerous creative opportunities to serve in the litigation process. In addition to consulting confidentially with attorneys, the LNC may play a more assertive role in identifying, qualifying, and preparing testifying expert witnesses. Some LNCs venture into the role of testifying experts themselves, addressing liability issues and damages. Still others seek innovative and expanding testifying roles, exemplified by expert fact witnesses.

LNCs provide critical support in the lifeblood function of developing expert witness participation in medical litigation.

Glossary*

Affidavit: Sworn, voluntary statement of fact or declaration.
Attorney work product: Those notes, files, sources, ideas which are developed in confidence by the attorney, attorney staff, or consultants as they develop a case.

---

* MacHovec, 1987.

"But for" test: Used in malpractice and negligence cases to determine whether there would have been injury or damages except for ("but for") the defendant's actions.

Captain of the ship: Legal doctrine that, when applied to medical malpractice, holds doctor liable for the actions of others, such as nurses, attendants, and other staff.

Case: Cause, conflict situation, lawsuit.

Credibility: Worthy of belief; must be preceded by establishment of competency (legally qualified and fit to testify).

Damages: Loss or injury to a person, property, or rights expressed in monetary terms, caused by the negligence of another.

"Deep pockets": Refers to suing any and all parties involved directly, or not, to ensure sufficient assets or insurance coverage to pay damages.

Defendant: The person or party sued.

Deposition: A witness's sworn verbal or written pre-trial testimony to questions by opposing attorney who can cross-examine; part of discovery process not done in court.

Discoverable: That which can be brought into discovery, pre-trial acquisition of knowledge from the opposing side.

Due process: Legal procedures (process) protecting rights of both sides for a fair trial by impartial judge or jury due them by constitutional right.

Impeachment of witness: Attack on the credibility of the witness.

Liability: The defendant's adjudged responsibility on the issues in question.

Medical expert: For the sake of this text "medical" encompasses all health care professionals; an expert is qualified to speak authoritatively by reason of special knowledge, skill, training, or experience; experts are nominated by the litigant and qualified by the court.

Motions: Written or oral requests by attorneys to the court.

Negligence: Failure to do what a reasonable and prudent person with ordinary considerations in a similar situation would or would not do.

Pain and suffering: Physical discomfort and/or mental distress claimed as recoverable damages.

Plaintiff: The claimant, person who files suit.

Proximate cause: In negligence cases it must be proved that the plaintiff's injuries were directly caused by the action or inaction of the defendant.

Res ipsa loquitor,* or *res ipsa iquito: When damages or injury is an obvious result of negligence.

Respondeat superior: Legal doctrine whereby in certain cases an employer is responsible for wrongful acts of employees.

Statute of limitations: A legislatively enacted law governing time limits for filing negligence actions.

Summary judgment: Declaratory judgment.

Testimony: Spoken or written evidence by a competent witness under oath.

Tort: Wrongful act by direct violation of another's rights or neglect of duty which causes injury or damages. The three necessary elements for tort action are a legal *Duty* binding on the defendant to the plaintiff, a *Dereliction* of that duty, which then causes *Directly* the *Damages* (sometimes recalled more easily as the "four Ds).

Trier of fact: Judge or jury.

Wrongful death: Suit brought to recover monetary damages for the death of a person due to negligence.

References

American College of Physicians (1990). Guidelines for the physician expert witness, *Annals of Internal Medicine,* 113(10), 789.

Gold, J. A., Zaremski, M. J., Lev, E. R., and Shefrin, D. H. (1993). *Daubert v. Merrell Dow* — the Supreme Court tackles scientific evidence in the courtroom, *JAMA,* 270(24), 2964–2967.

MacHovec, F. J. (1987). *The Expert Witness Survival Manual,* Springfield, IL, Charles C. Thomas.

National Forensic Center. *Code of Professional and Ethical Conduct.*

Chapter 33

The Liability Nurse Expert Witness

Janet G. Foster

Contents

1-57444-123-X/98
© 1998 by American Association of Legal Nurse Consultants

Case Preparation

Introduction

In a medical malpractice lawsuit, there are four criteria the plaintiff attorney must establish, including duty, breach of duty or negligence, causation of injury, and damages (Feutz-Harter, 1993). In order to prove the four necessary elements in the case, a discovery process is undertaken, which commonly requires the services of expert witnesses. The expert witness provides testimony establishing the standard of care and identifies deviation from the standard of care. The expert witness is of the same discipline, qualified by experience, education, research, and publications, and articulates complex, technical information to lay juries, attorneys, and judges. The expert has no firsthand knowledge of circumstances in the case, but bases an opinion on review of relevant documents (Feutz-Harter, 1993).

Agreement to serve as an expert witness is a serious undertaking and may require a commitment lasting several years. Although most cases settle without necessitating a trial, the witness should accept the case with the assumption that it will culminate in a jury trial and be willing to accept the responsibilities accordingly. This may include such things as cumbersome record storage; flexibility in scheduling for meetings, deposition, and trial; and time allotment for literature and document review; and report preparation. More important, the expert must recognize the professional accountability in the entire process and in expressing opinions, which must be well founded, free of emotion, and expected to be heard by a jury.

The Standard of Care

One of the first activities undertaken by the expert witness is to establish the standard of care and determine if a breach in standard has occurred. The legal connotation of standard of care is the degree of competence and skill exercised by a reasonable and average practitioner in similar circumstances (Aiken and Catalano, 1994). The standard serves as a measuring stick by which to compare the actions of the practitioner to determine negligence. Formerly, the standard found in a particular geographic area or similar community formed the basis for experts to assess negligent practice. However, due to the growth in telecommunications, global transportation, standardization in education, professional publications, development of standards by national specialty organizations, and other networking opportunities, the courts no longer justify lower, local standards of care (Clark, 1990).

The standard of care on which liability experts determine negligence includes state statutes and regulations, national standards, academic curricula, certification criteria, and hospital policies and procedures. Statutes are laws sanctioned by state legislatures and include practice acts and recommendations from specialty organizations. Regulations are rules that govern practice, such as state board licensing agencies (Aiken and Catalano, 1994). National standards include those published by the Joint Commission on Accreditation of Health Care Organizations, organizations representing health care disciplines such as The American Nurses Association, and specialty organizations; for example, the use of published standards reduces subjectivity by the expert when judging negligence and enhances reliability and validity of evidence provided (Clark, 1990).

Case Analysis

A breach in the standard of care may constitute negligence and result in liability on the part of the health care professional. The expert serving in the capacity of liability expert witness analyzes the facts in the case, compares the actions and behaviors to the standard of care, determines if a breach in standard is evident, describes the precise nature of the violation, and relates the negligent acts to harm or damages that occurred. In order to ascertain negligent actions, the expert witness reviews all materials pertinent to the case, including the medical record, testimony by the defendants and fact witnesses, and any other documents relevant to the case. The expert should request any additional materials needed in order to conclude fully and accurately that alleged negligence did or did not occur. Additionally, the expert should try to rule out conflicts of interest prior to the review, as this could be a source of bias (Wilson, 1996). For example, one might have been employed by the agency, or involved parties may be friends or colleagues. Maintaining objectivity may be difficult and certainly credibility of the expert is threatened, risking impeachment later in the proceedings. It is important for the expert to (1) avoid an advocacy role for the attorney or attorney's client, (2) remain objective and unbiased, (3) provide truthful information, and (4) adhere to the strictest of ethical and professional standards when serving as an expert witness.

Record Review

Generally, a bulk of records is provided to the expert. During the initial review, the expert must delineate the significant portions of the documents, determining what is important to validate or dispute negligence. The expert should focus on the incident that triggered filing suit and look for events leading up to it, conflicting or supportive data, and patient outcomes. The witness looks for documentation of patient assessment findings, interventions by health care providers, and patient responses. *Narrative documentation, rather than check-marked flow sheets, is generally the best place to look for a comprehensive description of the events.* Additional records and graphs supplement narrative information and include items such as physician orders, medication administration records, vital sign graphs, monitoring strips, flow sheets, resuscitation records, checklists, care plans, clinical pathways, laboratory reports, and radiology reports. Often, obtaining a complete picture of the patient's status and respective care requires piecing together various segments of the record, and is particularly helpful for filling in gaps in the narrative documentation and detecting conflicting information. Additionally, appropriateness of care based on patient data can be gleaned from test results. For example, abnormal blood gases reported in the laboratory section correlating with a narrative description of respiratory distress elsewhere in the record more fully portrays a deterioration in status of the patient.

Although the expert centers on the incident triggering the lawsuit, all gross deficiencies or errors noted, even if not directly related, often heighten the expert's impression of the hospital's or practitioner's incompetence (Milazzo, 1993). There is a commonly held notion, "if it wasn't documented, it wasn't done." The seasoned expert also considers the activity level suggested by what is documented, is able to prioritize the events, determine critical elements in documentation, and knows alternative places in the record to search for information. This facilitates judgment of what is reasonable, average, "C" level rather than "A+" level practice.

In addition to medical records, the liability expert witness reviews deposition transcripts of individuals directly and indirectly involved with the case. These may include those of health care providers, family members, and other expert witnesses. The expert looks for contradictions and inaccuracies among deposition testimony from multiple individuals and documentation contained in the medical record. Also, depositions may elucidate information not explicit in the medical record. For example, the defendant in the case has the opportunity to provide firsthand interpretation and explanation of the events experienced. Content in the deposition transcript often provides insight into the knowledge level, attitude, and judgment exercised by the allegedly negligent practitioner. Additionally, the expert considers plausibility of the testimony according to his or her experience in similar circumstances.

Hint: Caution is advised in reading testimony by other experts, as the opinions expressed may bias one's own opinion. It is recommended that review of other expert testimony be done after one's opinion is tentatively formed, with review of other expert testimony undertaken for purposes of clarification, corroboration, or to seek convincing alternative explanations.

It is important to substantiate one's opinion with adequate data. Thus, the liability expert witness may require additional materials before rendering an opinion. Additionally, the expert may be asked during the deposition if materials were requested, and if not, why not. Examples include institutional policies and procedures, employee performance standards and job descriptions, staffing assignment records, census reports, and in-service and orientation educational records. Records such as these are especially useful when determining institutional negligence and establishing a relationship to a patient's detriment. Lack of policy, failure to provide necessary education for a worker's designated job performance, or failure to determine competency during employee orientation may be cause for negligence on the part of the institution. Furthermore, deviation from the institution's own policy by an employee can be a fairly straightforward approach to proving negligence, provided there is proximate cause or causal connection, i.e., damages resulted from the negligent acts (Aiken and Catalano, 1994). In addition to materials provided by the institution, the witness relies on journals, books, and other publications germane to the specialty to validate expert opinions. The references must have been published prior to the event designated in the lawsuit. The expert is required to provide a list and, in some cases, the actual references used in preparation for the case (Federal Rules of Civil Procedure, 1996).

It is beneficial for the expert to take notes during review of the records. Time lines, charts, and graphs depicting minute-to-minute patient events and actions of health care providers help clarify deviations from the standards of care. A chronology of data gathered from several sources enables the expert to view the full picture, test the logic in testimony concerning events and the relationship to time, and judge the appropriateness in care accordingly. It is important to realize, however, that *any materials reviewed or written are discoverable by the opposing attorney.* This includes any informal notes, formal reports, charts, and other written communication from the attorney or legal nurse consultant (LNC). Therefore, it is advisable to limit written documentation in order to avoid providing too much information to opposing attorneys.

Meeting with the Attorney

Following initial review of the documents, a meeting with the attorney is advised. During this meeting, both the expert and the attorney are looking for a "good fit." The attorney evaluates the expert to (1) determine if the expert's views complement the case theory, (2) discover biases and potential conflicts of interest, (3) identify personality compatibility, and (4) assess verbal communication skills for persuasiveness and articulation. A summary of the expert's analysis of the case is provided and the attorney and expert then determine whether or not the expert will be retained on the case. Also, at this time, the expert's fee is established if not done so previously (Wilson, 1996). A retainer may be paid to the expert to formalize the agreement, which serves as a tool for reinforcing the professional's commitment to the case.

If the expert disagrees with the attorney's case theories, all records are generally returned, and ordinarily the contract terminates at this time. If the expert's opinion supports the side of the attorney seeking one's services, the expert points out all additional key factors in the case, delineating all compliance with and any breach of standard, and all resulting harm. A thorough picture of the situation is essential in order for the defense attorney to determine if and how the case is defensible and for the plaintiff attorney to determine whether or not to file the lawsuit.

Opinions should be restricted to one's own discipline; to state an opinion of the standard of care for another discipline seriously damages credibility of the expert. Also, limitations to one's expertise within the discipline should be volunteered at this time along with recommendations for other types of experts, if possible.

Rule 26

A set of discovery rules has been established by the federal court system for use by all states to facilitate a systematic and uniform approach to establishing facts in civil lawsuits. "General Provisions Governing Discovery; Duty of Disclosure," which is Rule 26 (Federal Rules of Civil Procedure, 1996), addresses disclosure of expert testimony and specifies that a written report must be provided prior to deposition. Rule 26 delineates the content of the expert's written report: qualifications, including a list of publications authored by the witness in the past 10 years; compensation to be paid to the witness for work on the case; a list of other cases in which the witness testified as an expert within the past 4 years; a statement of the expert's opinions in the case, along with the rationale for those opinions; publications and other information used by the expert in forming the opinions; and any exhibits used to support the expert's opinions (*Federal Rules of Civil Procedure*, 1996). The essence of Rule 26 concerns the assertion and tenacity of expert opinion disclosed in the written report; once submitted in writing, the expert is held to that opinion. Even if opinions change as new evidence surfaces, the initial report serves as the foundation from which the expert must explain any future divergence, with corresponding rationale.

The Report

In general, the expert should submit written reports only when requested by the attorney. When requested, the expert provides a report in accordance with Rule 26. Although other information is required, the primary focus of the written report is a detailed account of relevant circumstances in the case (*Federal Rules of Civil Procedure*, 1996). Critical elements of the case analysis include a thorough description of salient actions of the health care professionals with the same specialty as the expert, comparison with the standard of care, detailed account of any breach in standard, and correlation of any breach in standard with resultant harm to the patient. It is important to use an explanatory tone, avoiding complex medical terminology whenever possible. However, the expert should use professional language appropriate to the discipline, as this enhances credibility of the expert, and fosters succinct wording of the report. One should avoid legal jargon, as it may sound unnatural, and detract from one's credibility. Furthermore, since the expert is retained to offer opinions and assist in educating legal professionals and lay individuals about health care issues, legal terminology is best left to those with legal expertise.

There is a potential for the expert's opinion to change as additional documents become available for review. It is vital that the expert communicate this immediately to the attorney so that different opinions do not arise for the first time during the deposition or at the time of trial. The attorney should have the opportunity to discuss new developments and opinions of the case so that fair representation of the client is possible.

Additional Materials

Written documents prepared by the expert will be labeled as exhibits at the time of the deposition and again at the time of trial. This involves consecutive numbering of each piece of supporting evidence throughout the process and filing with the court reporter's written records of testimony in order to provide a means of organizing cumbersome legal files. The expert may be asked to assist with the development of additional flowcharts, graphs, and other audiovisual materials developed specifically for their sensory appeal, ease in interpreting complex circumstances and events, and the correlation of multiple sources of data. These, too, will be marked as evidence for the court and will be available to both sides in the case.

Finally, the expert may be asked to advise the attorney on deposition and trial questions. The expert is restricted to advice on the content of the question, while the attorney devises the structure of the question (Milazzo, 1993). Advice concerning the content of questions is an important part of the expert role, which facilitates discovery of all pertinent facts. It is recommended that communication about the subject of questions be limited to verbal exchanges rather than written. Preparation of written questions can be construed as advocacy, which is the role of the attorney rather than the expert witness, and becomes apparent when the written documents are discovered.

The Deposition Process

Introduction

A deposition is a recording of sworn testimony which serves as a discovery tool for attorneys to learn as much as possible about the alleged malpractice (Sullivan, 1995). The attorneys use this opportunity to evaluate the strength of the case and the credibility of the witness. The deposition takes place out of court, however, the witness testifies under oath and is sworn to truthfulness and accuracy. If the case goes to trial, statements made during the deposition may be read to the jury and judge. Therefore, testimony given in the deposition must be given as if the jury and judge were listening, and must remain consistent throughout trial proceedings (Sullivan, 1995). Preparation for the deposition is vital to success as an expert witness.

Preparation

Preparation for deposition includes a reexamination of the records and a practice session of questions and answers with the attorney. Often the deposition takes place weeks or months after submitting the written report, necessitating additional review of the records. Marking portions of the medical record containing pertinent evidence enables the expert to locate important information quickly when under pressure during questioning, reduces frustration while searching for critical evidence, hastens the process, and increases the effectiveness and credibility of the expert. The expert should be prepared, however, to explain the significance of any markings in the records.

The expert should anticipate answers to proposed questions in order to better articulate responses during the deposition. It is important to consider alternative explanations and responses, in preparation for disagreement with your opinion by the opposing side's experts.

A meeting with the attorney by whom the expert has been retained generally takes place immediately prior to the deposition. Strategies and style of the opposing attorneys and areas of focus are addressed, which cues the expert about the general direction of the deposition. The meeting with the attorney is an opportunity to discuss the primary issues in the case and explain one's opinions in front of an audience. A practice session of questions and answers is advisable, though one should avoid sounding rehearsed when giving testimony. This is also an opportunity to reflect on circumstances for which uncertainty exists, which benefits preparation for hypothetical questions likely to be asked by opposing counsel during questioning.

The expert is required to bring all case-related materials to the deposition for opposing attorneys to examine, to mark as exhibits, and to copy as desired. A subpoena *duces tecum* to appear for testimony either may be delivered to the attorney with whom the expert is working or directly to the expert, accompanied by a specific list of items and documents the expert is instructed to bring to the deposition. The list generally includes requests for the expert's current *curriculum vitae*, a copy of all literature reflecting the basis of the expert's opinion, all correspondence between the attorney and consultants for the case, all records reviewed, and all reports and notes pertaining to the case written by the expert. The expert is cautioned to keep written reports and notes brief in order to limit information to be discovered by opposing counsel (Milazzo, 1993). Additionally, copies of all publications authored by the expert and copies of legal opinions and reports written for other medical malpractice cases may be requested. Inconsistency in opinion among cases, revealed through examination of filed records, discredits the witness. Even when the expert no longer possesses documents from other cases, it is important to realize that past testimony remains on file and is attainable through the courts.

The Deposition

Credibility

The deposition is conducted by opposing counsel to discover information and to develop the case for trial (Calkins, 1996). It takes place in the presence of a court reporter, who serves as an agent of the court, procures an oath of truthfulness by the witness, and transcribes a word-for-word account of the dialogue. The process begins with establishing a foundation. The opposing attorney will seek to challenge credibility of the expert, questioning the expert's education, experience, research efforts, and publications. It is important, therefore, to validate that the expert has firsthand knowledge and experience in situations similar to those in the case and can accurately and authentically testify to what a reasonable and prudent practitioner would do in comparable circumstances. Questions about other professional endeavors such as research participation and publications further define the qualifications of the expert, required by the legal system (Grant, 1995).

Common tactics used by attorneys in an effort to discredit opposing expert witnesses include attempts to illustrate dissimilar practice situations between the defendants and expert, insinuations that inadequate time is devoted to clinical practice, and implications that fees charged by the expert are paid in return for testimony, suggesting that the testimony has "been bought." The expert should provide direct and honest answers about his or her practice and avoid misrepresentation of any aspect of professional roles, including inflation of professional time commitments. Compensation for time and expenses incurred during work on the case is legitimate. The expert should charge the customary fee consistent with the expert's discipline and qualifications. If uncertain about appropriate fees, the expert should contact other experts or the professional association.

Opinions

Following interrogation about credibility issues, the adversarial attorney will seek to establish facts and circumstances germane to the case, asking for a detailed account of any alleged breach in standard of care. The deposition provides the opportunity for reiterating testimony previously stated in the written report. Statements and opinions must remain consistent with previous written testimony. If an opinion has changed since writing the report, the changes and the rationale must be described at this time.

During this period of questioning, it is vital that the witnesses limit their responses to the scope of their expertise and practice discipline. Despite attempts by the opposition to elicit a comment about another discipline, the expert must resist the temptation to respond by declaring that "I'm not qualified to answer that"; this focus prevents damage to the witness's credibility. The expert may be asked to render an opinion on the probability of outcome; the response should be based on the expert's own experience and knowledge only, and deferred to other experts if necessary.

It is imperative that the expert maintain objectivity and impartiality in all efforts related to the case, communicating that message during questioning at time of deposition. The *purpose of expert testimony is to provide information, to assist triers of fact in understanding complex situations, and to voice an opinion of care provided compared to professional practice standards* (Grant, 1995). To enhance truthfulness and accuracy in providing information, the expert should listen carefully to all questions and pause for approximately 2 seconds prior to answering. The expert should answer convincingly and confidently, paying attention to voice pitch, volume, and tone. Answers should be simple and complete, using "yes" and "no" whenever appropriate. Never volunteer information and do not explain your thought processes, as the purpose of the deposition is to discover information, not educate (Morrow, 1996). One should avoid sounding condescending or argumentative, even when provoked. Never use obscenity, slang, racial innuendos, or sarcasm.

The expert is cautioned to avoid absolutes such as "always" and "never"; to avoid guessing, speculating, or giving inaccurate information if unsure of an answer; and to resist anticipating or prematurely answering questions. Listen carefully during questioning by the attorney, and then correct factual errors or incorrect assumptions, particularly when the attorney restates your testimony (Sullivan, 1995). Never allow the attorney to lace your testimony with adjectives and adverbs; respond with facts. For example, "It took the nurse a long time to respond to the call light when the patient was lying on the floor, didn't it?"; respond with, "It took approximately 3 minutes." Whenever necessary, the expert may request the attorney or court reporter to repeat questions, often needed when questions are lengthy or compound. Always rely on documents when necessary to answer. Do not feel pressured to answer hurriedly or to guess; take the needed time to locate facts in the document (Morrow, 1996).

The attorney may ask hypothetical questions and these may be answered by the expert (Sullivan, 1995). Hypothetical questions are questions including situations similar to those in the case but not specifying names, places, and other information specific to the case. They are used to gain an understanding of "the norm" and to evaluate the case comparatively. The questions must contain all relevant facts in evidence in the case and cannot address issues not in evidence (Horsley, 1995). As is true in answering all questions, the expert should limit response to the expert's area of expertise, remaining objective and impartial (Horsley, 1995). One should listen carefully, clarify all points, compare the hypothetical situation to the case, explain how the hypothetical situation differs from the actual case, and be cautious not to include information in the response that has not yet been introduced by the attorney as evidence.

Reference to authoritative sources is appropriate during the interrogation. In fact, the attorney may ask for the basis of the expert's opinion. Authoritative sources include standards, practice acts and other legislation, publications, and academic curriculum. Also, records specific to the case serve as a source on which an opinion of negligence is formed. Copies of any referenced materials not already provided may be requested by the attorney.

Videotaping the Deposition

Sometimes attorneys choose to videotape deposition proceedings. Most often, videotaping is undertaken when there is a risk that the expert may be unable to appear in court, yet the outcome of the case hinges on the expert's testimony (Brown, P. M., 1996). Videotaping may also be used for the visual and auditory effect of presenting demonstrative evidence. For this reason, the expert may be videotaped in "the field," or demonstrate on tape with props, such as anatomic models, sketches, and X-rays. The tape is shown to the jury as a convincing means of coupling facts and opinions with impressive visual images. Another reason to videotape the deposition is to deter an opposing attorney reputed to be obnoxious and abusive (Brown, R. G., 1996). Knowing the attorney will appear before the judge and jury on videotape may subdue abhorrent behavior and promote a more cordial and productive discovery process.

When the deposition takes place before a video recorder, the methodology of the deposition may differ. Generally, it is faster paced, more orderly, and the questions are more straightforward (Brown, R. G., 1996). The goal is to limit the playback time to 30 minutes in order to hold the jury's interest. The expert must pay close attention to appearance, mannerisms, facial expressions, and posture in addition to verbal responses. One should always wear conservative business clothing that contrasts well with the backdrop, and minimize jewelry, being cautious not to wear earrings that move. Maintain good posture, avoid fidgeting, appear interested and alert, and look at the camera when responding to questions.

In addition to the videotape, testimony will be transcribed by a court reporter and a hard copy will be provided for audit, corrections, and notarized signature of the expert. Both copies will be retained as part of the permanent file for the case.

Lawyer Strategies

In addition to the plaintiff's counsel, multiple attorneys representing several named defendants may participate in each deposition. Each advocates for his or her client and therefore may attempt to place liability on another defendant. The expert should be aware of this during the deposition, and refrain from testifying about another discipline, neither criticizing nor commending their actions. The various attorneys present may object to questions asked by the interrogating attorney or to responses by the witness. Objections constitute a legal procedure for the record, are especially important should the case undergo appeal to a higher court, and are no substitute for a reply. However, they can be distracting, causing the witness to forget the question and disrupt the witness in forming a response. The witness should not be intimidated by this interruptive procedure but should listen carefully to the objection; the wording of the objection may well highlight a problem with the question (Morrow, 1996). If necessary, the witness should feel comfortable requesting the attorney or court reporter to repeat the question.

Generally, the attorney on the side for whom the witness testifies withholds questions until the time of trial, in order to prohibit opposing counsel from gaining any further information or knowledge of strategy to be used in the case. The deposition concludes when no further questions are raised by the attorneys. Alternatively, if the attorney intends to settle the case prior to trial or knows the expert is unavailable for court, full questioning may proceed.

Audit the Transcript

The court reporter prepares and distributes printed copies of the deposition. Changes or corrections may be necessary due to transcription errors, misspelled words, unclear or incomplete answers, misinformation, or responses resulting from misunderstanding the question during the deposition. The expert should carefully audit the testimony, document corrections and changes, provide the rationale for each alteration, and provide a signature witnessed by a notary public when required. The signed testimony becomes a permanent record that very possibly will be referenced in the future, especially if the case goes to trial, when portions are likely to be read, or replayed on video to the judge and jury. Accuracy and truthfulness are critical. The expert's signature indicates truthfulness in the testimony while under oath. Opposing counsel has the right to know of any variations in testimony, therefore a copy incorporating these changes will be provided by the transcription service.

Trial Testimony

Introduction

More often than not, the case reaches settlement by the attorneys outside the courtroom. However, in situations in which agreement is not reached, the case will be tried before a judge and jury. The expert is then required to testify on the witness stand.

The procedures during trial are quite different from those during deposition and other pretrial proceedings. A fundamental difference is that at trial there will be opportunity to answer questions from the attorney who requested the expert's appearance, in addition to questions from the adversarial attorney (Feutz-Harter, 1993). It is a time for broader, open-ended questions as well as greater depth in responses. The expert is asked to explain important aspects in the case including the standard of care, negligent acts, and resulting damages. Additionally, the expert should anticipate questions regarding complex phenomena, such as anatomy and physiology, clinical manifestations of illness, interpretation of physiological monitoring, and intricacies of health care technology (Feutz-Harter, 1993). *During trial, the expert serves as educator to the judge and jury.*

Preparation

Because several months may have passed since the deposition, the expert will need to review the materials again. The witness should carefully review opinions expressed in the written report and the deposition transcription; full knowledge of one's previous testimony guards against discrepancies during trial, reinforces one's credibility as an expert witness, and optimizes shaping of the case strategies. Other beneficial preparation includes preparing responses to probable questions, practicing breathing and voice exercises to enhance tone and volume, and employing any strategies the witness finds to build self-confidence. Whenever possible, a visit to the courtroom can aid visioning techniques that may reduce anxiety (Feutz-Harter, 1993). The expert should make every effort to project a powerful and convincing courtroom presentation.

On the Witness Stand

During the trial, direct examination, cross-examination, redirect, and re-cross by opposing attorneys are used to present facts in the case and opinions of the experts to the judge and jury. The witness begins by swearing an oath to tell the truth, requested by the court reporter. The attorney who commissioned the appearance begins direct examination by first establishing credibility of the expert. The attorney highlights every item on the *curriculum vitae* that strengthens the judge and jury's view of expert qualifications to render an opinion in this case and asks the witness to affirm each item. The attorney then raises questions specific to the case by asking the witness to explain the circumstances relevant to the alleged malpractice, provide a temporal sequence of events, and describe the actions of the defendant. The expert is asked to elucidate the standard of care and recount actions that represent or deny a breach in standard. Upon conclusion of questions by the initial attorney, the adversarial attorney then conducts a cross-examination of the witness. During cross-examination, the opposition attempts to discredit both the qualifications and testimony of the witness. The attorney may ask leading questions and attempt to demonstrate inconsistency among testimony documented during the trial, deposition, and written reports. The attorney may also try to show the judge and jury that the witness is biased, accusing the witness of rehearsed responses, claiming inordinate meetings with opposing counsel, and asserting that the opinions result from the attorney "putting words in your mouth" (Mandell, 1993). Next, in pendulum fashion, the initial attorney during redirect, has the opportunity to address issues raised during opposing counsel's cross-examination. Finally, during re-cross, the adversarial attorney further challenges testimony raised during redirect.

The witness should understand that these techniques are not a personal attack but strategies employed by the attorneys on behalf of the clients they represent. The attorney on whose behalf the expert testifies should protect the witness from unnecessarily destructive tactics such as badgering, maligning, or blatant discourtesy (Mandell, 1993). The witness should remain calm during responses, never defensive, sarcastic, condescending, or dogmatic. The witness should avoid medical jargon and simply explain the facts, using a presentation style similar to that used during patient education. The witness should look at the jury, not the attorney, during responses. Eye contact with the jury is important, as it establishes rapport, aids in holding the interest of the jurors, and portrays sincerity, competence, and confidence by the witness.

Additional recommendations for a court appearance include attention to presentation and demeanor. Always dress conservatively and professionally. Adhere to courtroom etiquette, which includes addressing the judge by "Your Honor" or "Judge _____"; standing when the judge or jury enters or exits the courtroom; extending courtesy to all witnesses, defendants, attorneys, jurors, judge, court reporter, and bailiff; and maintaining punctuality for all appearances (Feutz-Harter, 1993).

Summary

The expert is reminded to maintain objectivity, impartiality, and truthfulness, to maintain the highest level of integrity, and to conform to the principal functions of an expert witness. To summarize, the role of the expert is to educate the judge and jury about the standard of care, render an opinion about negligence, and dispute or explain any relationship between the negligent actions and damages that occurred. To withhold information, distort the facts in the case, misconstrue the standard of care, or exercise bias in opinion increases the risk of impeachment as an expert witness. This results in extreme disservice to the client and jeopardizes the reputation and effectiveness of both the health care professions and the legal system. Furthermore, the expert risks irreparable damage to his or her integrity that may pervade many aspects of professional life. Providing expert testimony is a challenging and rewarding experience permitting further professional growth and opportunity to positively impact outcomes for clients, health care professionals, and the health care system at large.

References

Aiken, T. D. and Catalano, J. T. (1994). *Legal, Ethical and Political Issues in Nursing,* Philadelphia: F. A. Davis Company.

Brown, P. M. (1996). Depositions of expert witnesses: the lawyer's perspective *Effective Deposition Techniques* (p. G-37–G-50), Kansas City, Missouri: Missouri Bar Association.

Brown, R. G. (1996). Taking depositions, *Effective Deposition Techniques* (p. B-1–D-12). March, 1996: Missouri Bar.

Calkins, J. W. (1996). Deposition practice, *Effective Deposition Techniques* (p. A-9–A-14), Kansas City, Missouri: Missouri Bar Association.

Clark, A. P. (1990). Legal implications of being an expert, *The Diabetes Educator, II* (Special Issue), 52–56.

Federal Rules of Civil Procedure (1996). Rule 26, General provisions governing discovery; duty of disclosure, 105–125.

Grant, A. (1995). Expert witness testimony, *Canadian Nurse,* 91(5), 51.

Harter-Feutz, S. (1993). *Nursing and the Law* (5th ed.). United States of America: Professional Education Systems, Inc.

Horsley, J. (1995). Serving as an expert witness, *RN*, 58(10), 61–65.

Mandell, M. S. (1993). Surviving destructive cross-examination, *American Journal of Nursing*, 93(6), 22–24.

Milazzo, V. L. (1993). Why would an attorney hire a nurse?, *American Journal of Nursing*, 93(22–26).

Morrow, J. C. (1996). Use of depositions in court, *Effective Deposition Techniques* (p. F-11–F-14), Kansas City, Missouri: Missouri Bar Association.

Sullivan, G. H. (1995). Giving a deposition, *RN*, 58(9), 57–62.

Wilson, M. E. (1996). Preparing your expert witness for deposition, *Effective Deposition Techniques* (p. F-15–F-25), Kansas City, Missouri: The Missouri Bar Association.

Chapter 34

The Life-Care Planning Expert

Mona Yudkoff

Contents

Objectives

- To utilize a life-care plan in the assessment of damages in a personal injury case
- To choose an appropriate and qualified life-care planner
- To state the steps required to complete a life-care plan
- To describe the legal/ethical principles critical to the effective use of life-care planning in the assessment of damages
- To understand the deposition process
- To prepare for testimony for deposition
- To better prepare the life-care planner for deposition
- To understand the trial testimony process
- To prepare for trial testimony on damages
- To assist the LNC preparing the life-care planner for trial testimony

Case Preparation

Introduction

The unspoken question foremost on the minds of anyone involved in litigation is: "How much is this case worth?" In personal injury cases, including medical malpractice and product liability, the damages are directly related to the injuries suffered by the plaintiff. These injuries may include bodily harm, psychological damage, loss of future earnings, and pain and suffering. A quantifiable estimate of the future costs to the plaintiff resulting from the injury is critical to the assessment of the value of the case.

The life-care plan is an extension over time of the traditional nursing-care plan. The primary purpose of the document is to allocate resources, both economic and noneconomic, over the injured person's lifetime. In the clinical setting, the completed plan is a comprehensive assessment of all of the patient's future needs over time. In litigation, a life-care plan relates specifically to disability consequent to the catastrophic illness or injury alleged to have been caused by the defendant. Costs of care that are related to the plaintiff's preexisting conditions are not included in future projections.

Insurance companies and medical case managers were the first professionals to use such a systematic projection of future costs, usually to set reserves for high-cost cases. Deutsch and Rafta (1981) first described the forensic use of the life-care plan in the early 1980s. Today, the use of life-care planners in personal injury litigation has become a standard procedure in presenting future medical damages in cases involving catastrophic injuries or illnesses.

The Use of the Life-Care Plan in the Assessment of Damages

The life-care planner's role is to educate the parties concerned about the impact of the disability on quality of life. The detailed analysis of the injured person's medical, paramedical, and psychosocial needs presents a clear picture of the dollar costs, as well as the cost in noneconomic resources, such as time, relationships, and self-esteem.

The life-care plan is "an indispensable tool of the plaintiff's attorney in catastrophic injury cases. A valid Life Care Plan based on quantifiable data adds credibility to the plaintiff's proposal for settlement by providing a realistic picture of the plaintiff's future needs" (Elliot, 1994, p. 69). *Money sought for settlement therefore is based on a factual description of need that is derived from firm and indisputable data.*

In those cases which go to trial, the life-care plan assists the jury in understanding the need for the plaintiff's monetary demands. During this process, the jury also learns of the physical and emotional resources which are required to care for the plaintiff.

Defense attorneys are responsible for mitigating damages if they fail to disprove liability. Life-care planners are frequently retained by the defense to evaluate the validity of the proposal for plaintiff's damages. The defense attorney must present "reasonable" damages without offending the jury or appearing insensitive to the plight of the injured party. The life-care planner may be retained by the defense counsel to develop strategies for cross-examination of the plaintiff's expert and/or to present an alternative strategy for meeting the injured party's needs in a more economic manner (Gunn, 1994).

Choosing an Appropriate and Qualified Life-Care Planner

Choosing a life-care plan expert is, in most ways, similar to choosing any medical expert. Credibility, the most important factor in an expert's success, is determined by a combination of appropriate education and relevant experience, recognized credentials, and, of course, communications skills and professional appearance.

A life-care planner should always be a rehabilitation professional. Significant hands-on experience in the provision of care to persons with chronic and catastrophic deficits is critical. In addition, the life-care planner should have case management experience, a role which includes the coordination of services to the catastrophically ill or injured. Familiarity with vendors and health care providers, and the ability to locate these sources in various geographic locales, is essential. The expert should have the professional background, certification, and/or experience that is relevant to the diagnosis, age, and medical needs of the plaintiff.

> Nurses are often uniquely qualified to prepare life-care plans. They have the medical training and experience to understand the needs of an injured person and to anticipate those needs or services which have not yet been addressed by health care providers. In addition, nurses traditionally have played a pivotal role in rehabilitation medicine as facilitators of the management of disabled patients. Nurses are well

experienced in organizing plans of care and coordinating the recommendations of team members (Yudkoff, 1996, pp. 829 ff).

The credibility of the witness is, in large part, dependent on credentials. Advanced academic preparation shows an enriched knowledge base and a commitment to professionalism. Attendance at professional meetings, conferences, and continuing education courses demonstrates ongoing acquisition of skills and knowledge current to the field.

Rehabilitation nurses can earn specialty certification, demonstrating peer recognition of experience and expertise. Valid certifications are offered by professional organizations that are independent of special interests. Certification may help the law firm to identify the rehabilitation nurse whose background best suits the individual case. Life-care planners will often have one or more of the following:

- CRRN (Certified Registered Rehabilitation Nurse) — demonstrates experience in rehabilitation nursing and the strong knowledge base required to understand, address, and explain complex medical needs resulting from severe injuries or illnesses. This medical background may be especially important when the damages represent only a part of the total impairment, e.g., a case with a preexisting medical condition.
- CCM (Certified Case Manager) — indicates multidisciplinary certification reflecting experience and expertise in coordinating and obtaining rehabilitation services.
- CRC (Certified Rehabilitation Counselor) and/or
- CIRS (Certified Insurance Rehabilitation Specialist) — may be the appropriate expert in a case where significant damages are related to the retooling of the plaintiff's vocational life.
- CLCP (Certified Life Care Planner) — a new credential, requiring continuing education in the preparation of life-care plans.

Note: Inclusion of the above certifications in this chapter does not imply validation by AALNC. It is the responsibility of the retaining attorney, or the firm's legal nurse consultant (LNC), to evaluate the validity of the certifications presented by an expert witness.

Steps Required to Complete a Life-Care Plan

Assessment

The life-care planning process begins with a complete assessment of the injured person and the medical history. All records relevant to damages should be reviewed. Record packets prepared for experts in liability and/or causation are often irrelevant and incomplete for the purpose of determining damages. It may be necessary to request ongoing treatment records and even additional assessments to provide an adequate foundation for the opinions set forth in the life-care plan. In some cases, a literature search may be needed to define the expected course and treatment of a particular diagnosis.

It is almost always beneficial to have a face-to-face meeting with the injured person. The injured person's home is usually the most productive environment for the gathering of information. A detailed description of the home is necessary when accessibility modifications are recommended. The primary caregiver should be included in the assessment interview. When the plaintiff has sustained cognitive injuries, is unable to communicate, or is a minor child, the caregiver will be the primary source of information regarding daily care.

The injured person's health care providers should be solicited for input into future care. When future care is not discussed in the records, it is usually appropriate to solicit information directly from the physician or other providers. It is always necessary to inform the plaintiff's attorney before contacting any parties regarding the plaintiff. In many cases, it is necessary to obtain release forms from the attorney's office. It is often more difficult to contact providers when working for the defense attorney. The defense attorney will need to provide assistance in obtaining necessary input.

Determining the Needs

Each recommendation in the life-care plan must be supported by the medical record and the input received from health care providers. Services and products must be available in reasonable proximity to the plaintiff's residence. The plan should provide the reader with a clear rationale for the relationship between the recommended service and the damages. It is critical to evaluate the duration and frequency of the recommended services and products, and to delineate changes in frequency which could be due to growth, disease process, complications, aging or other factors.

Cost of Services

The life-care plan is always costed in today's dollars, without regard to cost-of-living, inflation, or other economic factors. It is up to the economist to ensure that the final cost projection conforms with local jurisdiction rulings. Costs should reflect the usual and customary rates in the geographic area proximate to the injured person's home. Whenever possible, the plaintiff's own treatment providers should be used as a resource upon which to develop cost estimates. If the injured person is not currently receiving the recommended service, a representative sample of appropriate providers should be referenced. The life-care planner should either use the middle of the range of costs as a reasonable estimation of the cost of future care, or show the range and let the reader determine the appropriate allocation.

The Life-Care Plan

The life-care planner should always determine if a written report is desired. In some cases, the attorney may request a verbal report before a written — and discoverable — document is prepared. This occurs more often when the plan has been prepared for the defense.

Although life-care planners use a variety of formats, the basic principles of writing any expert report apply. *The ultimate goal is to present a clear picture of the injured person's needs, as well as the relationship of these requirements to the plaintiff's injury.* Clarity and brevity are essential. A well-prepared life-care plan projects damages in a defensible and organized report. Each plan is unique, reflecting the medical needs, family composition, values, cultural variants, and premorbid lifestyle of the plaintiff.

In most cases, the plan will begin with a brief summary of the plaintiff's medical history and current status and a description of the impact of the injury on his or her life. In addition to the presentation of the plaintiff's needs and the associated costs, the report should also identify documents which were reviewed and costing sources which were utilized.

The life-care plan should project a fair and comprehensive assessment of the needs of the plaintiff, relative to the damages in the case. All aspects of the plaintiff's care should be addressed, including medical care, therapeutic modalities, surveillance, preventative care, equipment, supplies, medications, diagnostic testing, hospital care, accessibility (housing), transportation, psychological support, case management, and attendant care. It is the goal of the life-care planner to include those services which will allow the injured party to approximate as closely as possible the levels of independent function and quality of life which could have reasonably been expected had the injury not occurred.

Medical care projections should incorporate costs of care by physicians, allied health professionals, and therapeutic modalities, as well as costs associated with diagnostic testing and anticipated hospitalizations and/or procedures. Surveillance or preventative care should be included to prevent or retard further complications. The costs of durable equipment should include the replacement costs, length of service, and annual maintenance charges. Both the unit cost and the frequency of use should be described when listing the costs for medications and supplies. When housing modifications are needed to improve accessibility, the life-care planner should provide a detailed assessment of the current home and the specific modifications recommended. In most life-care plans, the cost of attendant care or respite services is the most costly item. The level of home care personnel recommended must be carefully justified. The frequency of service should also be clearly explained. Services should not be duplicated. If services are provided to prevent complications, then the cost of those complications should not be included.

The cost of care in future years is predicted using the cost of the service at the time of the preparation of the plan. *In other words, the life-care plan is always costed in today's dollars.* An economist is usually retained by the attorney to interpret the numbers, incorporating inflation, interest rates, and other economic factors. These calculations are beyond the scope of expertise of most rehabilitation nurses.

The cost projections in the life-care plan should be organized by modality and by the years the service will be required. A summary table (see Table 34.1) can significantly facilitate the work of the economist and also allows the jury to understand clearly that the life-care plan is a fluid document. It will be apparent that the rehabilitation nurse has taken into account any changes that the plaintiff will undergo over the course of his or her lifetime. Appendix 34.1 shows a sample life-care plan.

Table 34.1 Summary of Annual Costs (by year of age)

	6 Yrs	7–16 Yrs	17–21 Yrs	22 Yrs–Life Home	22 Yrs–Life Facility
Medical care	$ 49,547	$ 49,547	$ 49,035	$ 49,035	$ 49,035
Equipment	$ 11,855	$ 11,855	$ 10,599	$ 10,599	$ 9,079
Rehabilitation	$ 1,184	$ 1,184	$ 1,184	$ 592	$ 0
Housing	$129,300	$ 1,500	$ 1,500	$ 1,500	$ 0
Transportation	$ 5,009	$ 5,009	$ 5,009	$ 5,009	$ 0
Supportive services	$ 6,200	$ 1,800	$ 1,800	$ 1,200	$ 0
Attendant care	$ 60,636	$ 60,636	$ 60,636	$271,560	$ 73,000
Total Annual Costs:	**$263,731**	**$131,531**	**$129,763**	**$339,495**	**$131,114**

Life-Care Plan Reviews

The rehabilitation nurse may be retained by the defense attorney to provide commentary on the life-care plan presented by the plaintiff. A life-care plan review addresses only those issues presented in the plaintiff's plan. Each issue should be evaluated for appropriateness to the injury, relevance to the litigated damage, reasonableness of the cost, and availability of the service in an area that is geographically proximate to the plaintiff. The defense attorney may request an oral report prior to the commitment of the rehabilitation nurse's opinions to writing. A face-to-face assessment of the plaintiff should always be requested, so that the plaintiff's attorney cannot utilize the absence of such a meeting to impeach credibility. In some cases, the defense attorney may request a complete life-care plan, independent of the plaintiff's submission.

The rehabilitation nurse can often assist the defense attorney in building the defense. The attorney may be particularly interested in potential sources of investigation to delineate the premorbid condition. For example, examining school records or work history may show premorbid cognitive deficits which mitigate some of the alleged damages.

Government or private agencies may provide necessary services and equipment at a reduced fee. The admissibility of such collateral sources depends upon the local rules of evidence. When admissible, collateral sources show that the plaintiff would not go untreated if the litigation favored the defendant. Appendix 34.2 shows a sample life-care plan review.

Legal/Ethical Principles Critical to the Effective Use of Life-Care Planning in the Assessment of Damages

The life-care plan should present a comprehensive and accurate representation of the plaintiff's needs. The life-care planner's role is to *educate* the attorneys and the jury about the disability sustained by the plaintiff. All services in the plan must be appropriate, reasonable, and necessary. The life-care planner is not an advocate for the injured person. *The opinions of the life-care planner should not be dependent on whether he or she is retained by the attorney for the defense or for the plaintiff.*

The quality of life is often an issue in determining needs. Proposed services should reflect an attempt to restore the plaintiff (or the plaintiff's family) to an approximation of the lifestyle that may have been realized if the disability had not occurred. This discussion is particularly relevant to aspects of the plan intended to increase the plaintiff's independent function and/or to provide respite for the primary caregiver.

The life-care plan should be a unique document, which has been individualized to the circumstances of the plaintiff's injury and premorbid lifestyle. It is usually appropriate to consider cultural and sociological factors in determining needs.

The costs included in the overall projections should be relevant to the damages, addressing only incremental costs specific to the litigated injury. Costs associated with preexisting conditions should be clearly identified. The use of collateral funding sources as an offset for projected costs is dependent on the local jurisdiction of the case. In some states, collateral sources are allowed as evidence. The distinction between those needs which will possibly occur and those which are *probable* within a reasonable degree of professional certainty must be clearly noted. The vendors, health care providers, and projected costs should be clearly annotated in the report. All sources should be local to the plaintiff.

The damages expert should not address liability, causation, or standard of care. It is critical that the life-care planning expert remain within that field of expertise. The report should provide an appropriate foundation for all opinions, especially those related to future care from physicians, therapists, and other nonnursing health care providers. Opinions on life expectancy or economic considerations related to the life-care plan, but not within the expert's scope of practice, should be clearly referenced. It is rarely appropriate for the life-care planner to serve also as a liability expert on the same case.

As is true with all expert witnesses, compensation should never be dependent on the outcome of the case.

The Deposition Process

(This discussion is specific to depositions on damages. General instructions regarding preparing for a deposition are included in Chapter 15, 16, 25, 32, and 33.)

File Review

In preparation for the deposition, the expert witness should carefully review the file. In many cases, the deposition request will include a call for the expert's entire file. The opposing attorney is entitled to review all notes, drafts, resources, and records in the file. Obviously, file maintenance should be a priority throughout all stages of consulting. The expert should bring an updated *curriculum vitae.* The opposing attorney will often want to explore the expert's background in great detail.

Prior to the deposition, the expert witness will need to review any current medical records that have been generated between the completion of the report and the date of the deposition. The plaintiff's expert will want to recontact the plaintiff or his caregiver if the deposition is several months (or more) after the completion of the report. The defense expert should request an update on the plaintiff's condition through the defending attorney's office.

Depositions and reports of other expert witnesses should also be reviewed.

Preparation with the Attorney

The deposition is essentially a "dress rehearsal" for trial testimony. The opposing attorney uses the deposition to evaluate the validity of the testimony and the quality of the presentation. "The expert can be challenged on each and every aspect of his review of the material, familiarity with it, the course and conduct of the examination and the opinions. The plaintiff attorney is there to test the knowledge of the witness and also to judge the relative effectiveness of the defense RHEs (Rehabilitation Expert) presentation versus his own" (Vandenberg, in Deutsch, 1990, p. 17).

Prior to the deposition, the attorney should review all areas of anticipated questioning with the expert witness.

Testimony

Deposition testimony differs from trial testimony in that the questioning begins with the opposing attorney. Most deposition time is allotted to the opposing attorney for cross-examination. The retaining attorney may elect to ask questions at the end of the deposition in order to get certain facts on the record before trial. Successful testimony in damages is dependent on consistency, credibility, and clarity, just as in all expert witness testimony.

In some cases, the deposition may be videotaped and used at trial in lieu of "live" testimony from the expert.

Trial Testimony

(This discussion is specific to trial testimony on damages. General instructions regarding preparing for trial are included in Chapter 15, 16, 28, 29, and 32.)

File Review

The first step in preparing for testimony is, of course, a careful review of the file. Because there may be many months or even years between the preparation of the report and the trial date, an update of the file may be required. The expert witness should have a comfortable grasp of the details of the case during testimony. It is much more convincing to demonstrate knowledge of the plaintiff's condition without constantly referring to the files.

It is essential to be well informed about any changes in the plaintiff's condition in the interval between the preparation of the report and the trial. Updated medical records must be obtained from appropriate health care providers and reviewed. It may be helpful to speak with physicians, therapists, home health nurses, and vendors. The plaintiff and/or his caregiver should be contacted. An assessment interview is often appropriate.

A careful review of deposition testimony of the plaintiff, caregivers, other damages experts, and defendants will provide critical information about the opposing attorney's theories in the case and also about the attorney's style of cross-examination.

It is also very helpful to review carefully one's own deposition testimony. The opposing lawyer may seek to elicit contradictions in prior testimony and is permitted to read sections of the deposition to the jury. It is helpful to have carefully considered explanations for any changes in opinions that have occurred between the deposition and the trial.

Preparation with the Attorney

The retaining attorney should carefully review all aspects of trial testimony with the life-care planner. Some attorneys prefer to practice direct examination, while others prefer a more general discussion of the points to be covered. Preparation is most critical in regard to anticipated areas of cross-examination. The attorney and expert witness must anticipate the strategy of the opposing attorney and prepare concise answers to expected areas of "attack."

Expert testimony involving damages is usually presented toward the end of the testimony. This affords an opportunity to discuss previous testimony. It is very helpful for the expert witness to know what the jury has already heard.

Testimony

Testimony is initially focused upon the qualification of the expert. The witness must be able to present background information and credentials in a clear, confident, and impressive manner. The jury must regard the witness's testimony as credible and important, in order for it to have the desired effect on the verdict. The opposing attorney may attempt to disqualify all or part of the life-care planner's opinions by arguing that a nurse may only testify with respect to nursing issues. It is critical that the rehabilitation nurse's role in recommending the participation of other health care disciplines be established during the presentation of the witness's credentials. It is often helpful to have the expert witness qualified as an expert in rehabilitation and/or case management and not solely as an expert in nursing.

The life-care planner will be asked about remuneration, in the attempt to assign "hired-gun" status to testimony. It must be clear that fees are not related to the outcome of the case. It is usually helpful if the expert has testified in prior cases on behalf of both plaintiffs and defendants.

During direct examination, the opinions expressed by the life-care planner will be presented. The attorney will usually lead up to the specifics of the plan with an introduction to the life-care planning process itself. The opposing attorney will attempt to prove that the life-care planner's opinions are invalid. A well-written, defensible life-care plan is the best preparation for cross-examination. Consistency and foundation make for a credible witness.

References

Deutsch, P. (1994). Life care planning: into the future. *NARPPS* Journal*, 9(2&3), April, 79–83.

Deutsch, P. (1990). *A Guide to Rehabilitation Testimony: The Expert's Role as an Educator*, Orlando, FL, PMD Press.

Deutsch, P. and Rafta, F. (1981). *Damages in Tort Action*, Vols. 8 & 9, New York, Matthew Bender.

Deutsch, P. and Sawyer, H. (1985). *Guide to Rehabilitation*, New York, Matthew Bender.

Weed, R. and Field, T. (1994). *The Rehabilitation Consultant's Handbook*, Athens, GA, Elliot and Fitzpatrick, Inc.

Elliot, T. (1994). The plaintiff's view of the life care plan for the catastrophic case, *NARPPS Journal*, 9(2&3), April, 69–72.

Gunn, L. D. IV, (1994). Life care planning — a defense perspective, *NARPPS Journal*, 9(2&3), April, 63–77.

Yudkoff, M. (1996). Working with nurse expert witnesses: life care planning, in *Nursing Malpractice*, Patricia Iyer, Ed., Tucson, Lawyers and Judges Publishing Company, 829–834.

Powers, A. S. (1994). Life care planning: the role of the legal nurse, *NARPPS Journal*, 9(2&3), April, 51–56.

*NARPPS National Association of Rehabilitation Professionals in the Private Sector.

Certifying Bodies

Rehabilitation Nursing Certification Board, Association of Rehabilitation Nurses, 4700 W. Lake Avenue, Glenview, IL 60025-1485; 800-229-7530 (CRRN)

Certification of Insurance Rehabilitation Specialists, 1835 Rohlwing Road, Suite D, Rolling Meadows, IL 60008; 708-818-0292 (CCM, CIRS, CRC)

Commission on Disability Examiner Certification, 13325 Queensgate Road, Midlithian, VA; 804-359-3563 (CLCP)

Appendix 34.1
Sample Life-Care Plan*

LIFE-CARE PLAN

Donald Jackson

Date of Birth 6/1/xx

Date of Report 12/24/xx

MONA GOLDMAN YUDKOFF, RN, MPH
CRRN, Certified Rehabilitation Nurse
P. O. Box 266
Bala Cynwyd, PA 19004 (610) 664-8760

Contents

Introduction to the Life-Care Plan for Donald Jackson

Donald Jackson is a 54-year-old male who, in 19xx, was injured in a motor vehicle accident that left him with a residual hemiparesis, aphasia, dyslexia, and cognitive deficits. Prior to the accident, Mr. Jackson led an active and independent lifestyle, including employment as an instructor of physical fitness. He enjoyed swimming and other sports, as well as a myriad of social activities. Mr. Jackson was also pursuing a master's degree in social work.

Today, he is unable to perform most physical activities of daily living without assistance. He is dependent on friends for the organization of his daily life, for help with bathing and personal hygiene, and for all executive functions, including financial management, planning for medical and social needs, and transportation to activities and appointments.

His neurological injury has compromised his independence, and he is unable to be alone for more than a short period of time. He cannot make decisions

---

* Mona Goldman Yudkoff, RN, MPH, CRRN, Sample Life-Care Plan, 1996
P.O. Box 266, Bala Cynwyd, Pa., 19004, 610-664-8760

about his daily routine and he has severe impairment of his short-term memory. He frequently loses his balance and falls. Prior to his accident, Mr. Jackson made a significant contribution to the community as an award-winning teacher. Today, he cannot manage a weekly budget or make plans for his own well-being. He now requires assistance from friends and neighbors to organize simple activities.

The purpose of this report is to outline those necessary services and devices which Mr. Jackson will require to promote independent function, maximize quality of life, and provide for his physical and emotional needs. Medical care is provided to ensure early detection of complications. Equipment is provided to maximize comfort, physiological function, and independence. Personal assistance, housing modifications, and transportation are planned to enable him to remain in his home and access community activities.

Mr. Jackson was evaluated on December 16, 19xx, for this report. His girlfriend, Susan Jones, was present for the assessment.

Life expectancy for Mr. Jackson is 22.9 additional years based on Table 6-3, "Expectation of Life at Single Years of Age, by Race and Sex: United States, 1987" from *Vital Statistics of the United States, 1987*, National Center for Health Statistics, Hyattsville, Maryland, Volume II-Mortality, Part A, Section 6, Page 11.

All costs are based on today's dollars without regard for inflation, cost-of-living increases, or other economic considerations.

Medical History

Donald Jackson is a 54-year-old white male who was in generally good health prior to a motor vehicle accident, on February 19, 19xx. Following the accident, Mr. Jackson was treated in the local emergency room and discharged. The next day, Mr. Jackson noticed difficulty with speaking for about 1 minute. The following morning he experienced difficulty with the use of his hand. He also noted slurred speech. These episodes lasted about a minute and were repeated twice over a 30-minute period. Mr. Jackson went to the emergency room at General Hospital. While waiting for the physician, he had four more transient periods of difficulty speaking, numbness, and decreased function in the right hand. The symptoms increased in severity and duration over the next 2 hours. Donald then was evaluated by a neurologist, who ordered CT scan and admission to the hospital for further diagnostic workup. He continued to experience episodic loss of speech and the use of his right hand and arm for several more hours. Heparin therapy was initiated and there were no more functional losses. However, there were some residual physical deficits, including foot drop on the right side and difficulty with using his right hand for writing. He noticed difficulty in chewing, characterized by frequent accidental biting of his tongue. Some deficits in memory also were noted. The CT scan showed blood pooled on the left side of the brain.

Mr. Jackson underwent a surgical evacuation of the hematoma. He was awake and alert for a short period of time following the procedure, but he soon became unresponsive and had to be returned to the operating room, where a blood clot at the surgical site was removed. Following this procedure, Mr. Jackson required mechanical ventilation. After he was weaned from the ventilator, he was alert, but he had an expressive aphasia and could not attend to his physical needs. He remained in the hospital about 3 more weeks. At the time of his discharge, Mr.

Jackson could speak only one word, i.e., "one" which he articulated with varying intonation in order to communicate. He had virtually no use of his right arm or hand. His upper and lower extremities on the right side frequently were in spasm. He had only minimal voluntary use of his right leg, and he could neither walk nor assist with his transfer from the bed to the wheelchair.

On 3/21/xx, Mr. Jackson was transferred from General Hospital to Belle Rehabilitation Hospital. After 2 months of rehabilitation therapy, Mr. Jackson was discharged home. He was ambulatory for short distances with a cane and an orthotic on his right foot. He could assist in his dressing and self-feeding. Speech had not improved significantly. He received outpatient speech therapy at the Easter Seal Society. He responded somewhat to this therapy, and after 18 months he could pronounce a few words, recognize letters, and speak some two- or three-word phrases.

Current Status

Donald Jackson is a 54-year old male who was injured in a motor vehicle accident in February, 19xx. Residual effects of the accident include right hemiparesis, aphasia, alexia, and cognitive deficits.

His right arm and leg are weakened and capable of minimal voluntary activity. They are subject to painful muscle spasms. Mr. Jackson is able to grasp some large objects, but he is unable to voluntarily let go. He can shrug his shoulder, but he cannot reach or carry. Donald can walk unassisted for short distances, but he easily tires. He propels his leg from the hip and he requires an orthotic device to keep his foot from dragging. He trips and loses his balance frequently. A slight lateral scoliosis has been noted.

Mr. Jackson requires some assistance with most activities of daily living. He can feed himself, but requires assistance in setting up the meal, since he cannot open jars, manipulate some objects, or lift pans from the stove or oven. He can put on most articles of clothing, but he has difficulty with many fasteners or tightly fitting garments. He requires assistance entering and leaving the tub. He can shower with a chair and bars for support.

He is generally continent of bowel and bladder and he is independent in toileting if he reaches the bathroom in time. Mr. Jackson frequently has stress-related urgency for bowel movements and he occasionally has embarrassing accidents because he cannot walk quickly enough to the bathroom. Sexual activity has been negatively affected by physical limitations and decreased stamina.

He complains of deficits in the upper left quadrants of his visual fields. Otherwise, vision is corrected with glasses. He reports a 10% hearing loss in his right ear.

Neuropsychologic testing indicates severe deficits, including postaccident intellectual function that borders on the mentally defective. He exhibits severe deficiencies in concentration and attention, difficulty with abstract thinking and concept formation, and impaired short-term memory. Mr. Jackson can no longer read books, magazines, or newspapers, although he does recognize a limited number of single words, symbols, and pictorial messages. He cannot plan or complete any executive functions. He cannot balance a checkbook, devise a shopping list, or revise his wardrobe to accommodate the changing seasons.

He is only able to say a small number of isolated words and occasionally he is able to combine two or three words. Expressive communication is somewhat enhanced by the drawing of small, primitive pictures to represent ideas. He is not able to write sentences in any meaningful way. Donald appears to understand much of what is said to him, but he must be reminded frequently to look at the speaker and attend to the conversation. He often does not understand simple queries and his answers may be irrelevant to the intent of the question. For example, when asked if he had skin irritation from his foot brace, he indicated (through drawings and the word "hot") that he gets a skin rash when it is hot outside.

Mr. Jackson can drive, but he cannot follow written or spoken directions. Nor can he ask for directions if he is lost, make adjustments for weather or traffic conditions, or identify detours in his route.

Needs
Total Life-Care Needs For Donald Jackson $ 1,735,243

Summary of Annualized Costs

	First Year	Subsequent Years
Medical Care/Rehabilitation	$ 28,381	$ 5,309
Equipment/Supplies/Medications	$ 5,810	$ 5,810
Transportation	$ 5,009	$ 5,009
Residential	$212,800	$51,600
Total Annual Costs	**$252,000**	**$67,728**

Explanation of Costs
Medical Care/Rehabilitation

Rehabilitation Therapy

Mr. Jackson should have annual evaluations by a physiatrist, and semiannual evaluations by professional physical and occupational therapists to monitor his functional capabilities and design a home program for maintenance therapy. Intermittent visits will allow for adjustments to the home program, timely use of assistive devices, and early detection of complications.

Cost:	$	249	physiatrist
	$	172	physical therapy evaluation
	$	197	occupational therapy evaluation
Annual Cost:	**$**	**987**	

Speech therapy is indicated to instruct Mr. Jackson in the use of communication devices and computer learning aides. Intensive therapy is recommended for 6 months, with weekly follow-up for 6 months. Ongoing maintenance therapy is needed to assist in fostering communication alternatives and to instruct the home health aide in the use of equipment and reinforcement techniques. Therapy is costed at three times per week for 6 months and then weekly for 6 months (200 sessions the first year). Maintenance therapy is costed at ten sessions per year.

Cost:	$ 100	session
Annual Cost	**$20,000**	**first year**
	$ 1,000	**subsequent years**

Neurologist

Mr. Jackson is followed by the neurologist annually.

Annual Cost: $ 200

Counseling

Neuropsychologic testing indicates that Mr. Jackson suffers from signs of depression that may influence his level of function. Counseling therapy to facilitate a positive adjustment to his limitations and altered body image is recommended. Mr. Jackson should have weekly counseling for 1 year and then 6 weeks of maintenance therapy in each subsequent year.

Cost:	$ 88	visit
Annual Cost:	**$4,400**	**first year**
	$ 528	**subsequent years**

Case Management

Mr. Jackson is followed by many different health care providers. Equipment and supplies come from various sources. A rehabilitation case manager will ensure communication among the various specialists, as well as follow-up on recommendations. Mr. Jackson needs professional assistance in the management of his daily routine. A rehabilitation professional will help him develop strategies to maximize independent function and maintain a safe environment. The case manager will make quarterly home visits (3 to 4 hours per visit) for 1 year and then semiannual visits, with telephone management as needed, for an annual average of 10 hours.

Cost:	$ 50	hour
Annual Cost:	**$ 700**	**first year**
	$ 500	**thereafter**

Future Surgical Procedures and Medical Complications

Decreased mobility puts Mr. Jackson at risk for pneumonia and other respiratory conditions, skin breakdown, muscle contractures, skeletal deformities, and urinary and bowel dysfunction. In addition, he is at risk for head injury, fractures, and other trauma as a result of instability. While it is impossible to predict actual costs for these problems, it is conservative to estimate that he will have, on average at least 7 days of acute hospitalization every 5 years.

> Cost: $ 1,460   day
> **Annual Cost: $ 2,044**

Note: These charges do not include surgical procedures, surgeon fees, and operating time.

Equipment/Medications

Equipment was selected to allow Donald Jackson to achieve his maximum level of independence. Emphasis is put on allowing him mobility and, at the same time, providing him with a safe environment.

Item	Cost	Replacement	Annual Maintenance	Annualized Cost
Wheelchair, Quickie 2, accessories (for distances and crowds)	$2,000	7 years	$100	$ 386
Electric wheelchair (for independence on unlevel ground, distances, crowds, shopping)	$7,000	5 years	$200	$1,600
Quad cane	$ 40	2 years	—	$ 20
Shower chair	$1,270	5 years	—	$ 254
Adaptive equipment for ADL (personal aids, extra telephones, hygiene, feeding, etc.)	$ 250	1 year	—	$ 250
Leg orthotic	$ 400	2 years	—	$ 200
Adaptive communication device (to allow increased expressive communication)	$8,000	5 years	$200	$1,800
Computer (for cognitive retraining, with educational software and capability for use of graphic representation)	$5,000	5 years	$300	$1,300
Total Annual Cost				**$5,810**

Transportation

Prior to the accident, Mr. Jackson drove a car. Although he can travel in a car, he requires a wheelchair for activities demanding more than a minimum of walking. He is unable to fold up the chair and place it in or out of the trunk of the car. A minivan with a semiautomatic lift and wheelchair tie-downs will allow him access to various activities.

Item	Cost	Maintenance	Replacement
Van, (e.g., Ford Aerostar)	$22,000	$500	7 years
Semiautomatic power lift, tie downs	$ 3,260	$300	with van
Raised roof, doors, etc.	$ 3,500	$100	with van
Annual Cost			**$5,009**

Residential

Mr. Jackson is not able to prepare meals, do his laundry, attend to his personal environment, or assist in maintaining his home and property. He cannot shop for food, clothing, and other personal effects. He requires assistance with dressing and hygiene. He cannot manage his money or budget. He is unable to plan activities. Mr. Jackson could not quickly remove himself from a potentially dangerous situation and therefore should not be left alone at night. He therefore requires supervision and housekeeping assistance around the clock because of his physical and cognitive deficits. A live-in attendant is a more economical alternative to using hourly personal care attendants. The attendant will assist with personal hygiene, shopping, daily physical and occupational therapy exercises, transportation, and socialization.

Mr. Jackson's home is a multilevel row house in an unstable neighborhood in Elm City. There are many levels and the steps are difficult for him to negotiate, and the house lacks sufficient emergency exits. In addition, his physical and cognitive weakness make him vulnerable to physical abuse in the neighborhood.

Mr. Jackson requires a one-story home in a safe neighborhood if he is to enjoy maximal functioning. A wheel-in shower and grab bars are needed in the bathroom. Closet storage needs to be modified, so that Mr. Jackson can access shelves, hangers, and drawers. Kitchen storage should be modified. An emergency exit from the bedroom area is recommended. As Mr. Jackson ages, ramps may be needed for the entryways. Flooring should be wheelchair friendly. Costs are estimated.

Ongoing Costs:	$	120	day, live-in attendant
	$	50	week, home health aide living expenses
	$	100	week, heavy cleaning and routine home maintenance
Annual Cost:	**$**	**51,600**	

One-Time Costs:	$ 125,000	purchase price of new home less value of current home
	$ 7,500	bathroom renovations
	$ 7,000	kitchen renovations
	$ 4,200	ramps, railings, landings
	$ 4,200	widen doorways
	$ 2,800	flooring
	$ 5,500	widen hallways, storage closet
	$ 5,000	misc. electrical, intercom, bedroom emergency exit, painting/patching, etc.

Total One-Time Cost: $161,200

Sources of Costing Estimates for this Life-Care Plan

(*)	Based on previously incurred expense
(**)	Based on local facilities, vendors
(***)	Based on national facilities, vendors

Medical Care

(*)	Alan Smith, MD, general practice, State
(*)	Thomas Fee, MD, neurology, State
(***)	Current Trends in Health Care Costs and Utilization, 1992, Mutual of Omaha Insurance Company, Omaha, NE.
(**)	General Rehabilitation Hospital, Washington, D.C.
(**)	Disability Associates, Silver Spring, State
(**)	Mary Plume, RN, Bethesda, State

Equipment

(**)	Fred Sammons, Inc., Catalogue, Brookfield, IL
(**)	JA Preston Corp., Catalogue, Jackson, MI
(***)	Invacare Corporation, Elyria, OH
(***)	Sears Health Care Catalogue

Transportation

(**)	John Kennedy Ford, Feasterville, PA
(**)	Bryner Chevrolet, Jenkintown, PA
(***)	Drivemaster Co., Inc., Fairfield, NJ
(***)	Independent Mobility System, Farmington, NM

Residential Services

(**)	Kimberly Quality Care, Tose, State
(**)	Medical Personnel Pool, Elm, State
(**)	Adaptive Design Associates, Pottstown, PA

Documents Reviewed for this Life-Care Plan

General Hospital	Admission	2/20/XX
Psych Associates	Evaluation	2/6/XX
Susan Jones	Deposition	4/9/XX
Donald Jackson	Deposition	3/24/XX

Appendix 34.2
Review of Plaintiff's Life-Care Plan

Tom Hammer

Date of Birth 6/12/88

Date of Report 7/5/94

MONA GOLDMAN YUDKOFF, RN, MPH
CRRN, Certified Rehabilitation Nurse
P. O. Box 266
Bala Cynwyd, PA 19004 (610) 664-8760

Response to the Life-Care Plan for Tom Hammer

This report has been prepared as a response to the Life-Care Plan for Tom Hammer, a 6-year old boy with cerebral palsy and mental retardation. To simplify comparison, the sections in this report follow the outline used in the Life-Care Plan presented by the plaintiff, prepared by Sara Nurse, RN, on March 17, 1993.

The following records were reviewed for the preparation of this report:

Life Care Plan for Tom Hammer, Sara Nurse, RN, March 17, 1993

Plaintiff's Complaint

University Hospital, admission 6/12/88 to 7/8/88, outpatient records, and clinic records

Pediatric Rehab Hospital, admission 7/8/93 to 9/2/93, outpatient records

United Cerebral Palsy records

Joan Sander, MD, 11/1/92

All costs are based on today's dollars, without regard for inflation, cost-of-living increases, or other economic considerations.

Summary of Costs

Table I: Annual Costs To Age 21

	Home Care SN RN	Home Care Yudkoff	Facility SN RN	Facility Yudkoff
Medical Care	$ 1,933	$ 1,520	$16,333	$ 1,520
Rehabilitation	$ 38,656	$ 4,403	$ 2,176	$ 0
Supplies and Equipment	$ 6,286	$ 4,847	$ 5,338	$ 1,000
Medications	$ 120	$ 0	$ 0	$ 0
Lab/Diagnostic	$ 333	$ 333	$ 333	$ 333
Attendant Care (one only)				
HHA	$ 40,880	$30,800	$ 0	$ 0
LPN	$ 87,600	—		
RN	$102,200	—		
Transportation	$ 4,950	$ 2,586	$ 4,800	$ 1,200
Home Modifications	$ 3,500	TBD	$ 300	TBD
Education	$ 30,000	$ 0	$ 0	$ 0
Facility	$ 0	$ 0	$36,500 to $87,000	$36,500

Once Only Costs	SN RN	Yudkoff
Behavioral Hospitalization	$ 42,000 to $56,000	$ 0
Environmental Control Unit	$ 11,000	$ 0

Table II   Annual Costs Age 22 to Life

	Home Care SN RN	Home Care Yudkoff	Facility SN RN	Facility Yudkoff
Medical Care	$ 1,253	$ 1,103	$ 1,253	$ 1,103
Rehabilitation	$ 1,352	$ 1,009	$ 1,112	$ 49
Supplies and Equipment	$ 5,386	$ 3,947	$ 4,438	$ 900
Medications	$ 120	$ 0	$ 0	$ 0
Lab/Diagnostic	$ 200	$ 200	$ 200	$ 200
Attendant Care (either/or)				
HHA	$122,640	$51,100	$ 0	$ 0
LPN	$262,800	—		
RN	$306,600	—		
Transportation	$ 4,950	$ 2,586	$ 4,800	$ 1,200
Home Modifications	$ 4,700	TBD	$ 300	TBD
Facility	$ 0	$ 0	$36,500 to $87,000	$36,500

Once Only Costs	SN RN	Yudkoff
Behavioral Hospitalization	$ 42,000 to $ 56,000	$ 0
Environmental Control Unit	$ 11,000	$ 0

I. Review of Costs Projected for Home-Based Care
Medical Care

Item	Discussion	SN RN's Projected Annual Cost	MGY's Projected Annual Cost
Pediatrician/ General Practitioner to age 21 ($40/visit) age 22 to life ($75/visit)	Semiannual visits to the Children's Health Center are for routine child care. These are not specific to the alleged damages. Medical care related to the anoxic encephalopathy is provided by the specialist listed below.	$ 80, to 21 $ 150, 22 to life	$ 0 $ 0
Neurologist ($200/visit)	OK	$ 200	$ 200
Physiatrist/Developmental Specialist, annual to age 21 — then every 5 yrs ($190/visit)	OK	$ 190, to 21 $ 38, 22 to life	$ 190, to 21 $ 38, 22 to life
Academic testing to age 21 every 2 yrs ($665/visit)	This service is provided by the school system under PL 94-142, as noted in SN RN's report, on page 19.	$ 333, to 21	$ 0

Ophthalmologist to age 21 — then every 2 yrs ($150/visit)	OK	$ 150, to 21 $ 75, 22 to life	$ 150, to 21 $ 75, 22 to life
Specialty consultations, annual to age 21, then every 2 yrs to life ($190/visit)	OK	$ 380, to 21 $ 190, 22 to life	$ 380, to 21 $ 190, 22 to life
Acute hospital, 35 days, $1,500/day	OK	$ 600	$ 600
Behavioral, hospitalization	The records do not reflect the need for this service.	$42,000 to 56,000, once	$ 0

Rehabilitation

Item	Discussion	SN RN's Projected Annual Cost	MGY's Projected Annual Cost
Physical therapy to age 21 ongoing ($80/visit)	Will be provided by the school system under PL-142. It is reasonable to allow for weekly therapy during vacations. The school year is 36 weeks. Costing for 16 sessions at $80/visit.	$12,480, to 21	$1,280, to 21
Physical therapy evaluation age 22 to life ($240/visit)	OK	$ 480, 22 to life	$ 480, 22 to life
Occupational therapy to age 21 ongoing ($80/visit)	Will be provided by the school system under PL-142. It is reasonable to allow for weekly therapy during vacations. The school year is 36 weeks. Costing for 16 sessions at $80/visit.	$12,480, to 21	$1,280, to 21
Occupational therapy evaluation age 22 to life ($240/visit)	OK	$ 240, 22 to life	$ 240, 22 to life
Speech therapy to age 21 ongoing ($80/visit)	Will be provided by the school system under PL-142. It is reasonable to allow for weekly therapy during vacations. The school year is 36 weeks. Costing for 16 sessions at $80/visit.	$12,480, to 21	$ 1,280, to 21
Speech therapy evaluation age 22 to life ($240/visit)	OK	$ 240, 22 to life	$ 240, 22 to life
Psychology:			
Family counseling ($125/visit);	OK	563, to 21	$ 653, to 21
Individual/ Behavioral ($145/visit)	It is not clear that Tom's cognitive level is high enough to benefit from individual neuropsychological intervention.	$ 563, to 21 653, to 21	$ 563 to 21

Periodic therapeutic service for life ($80/visit)	SN RN projects five occurrences of intensive therapy (six sessions/week, 6 months each) from age 22 to life. The life-care plan also recommends 24 hour coverage with a personal care aide. This aide will be able to perform a home therapy program supervised by professional therapists. Two therapy evaluations per occurrence (in addition to the four annual therapy evaluations already provided) will cover the need for periodic intervention. (10 times $240/evaluation, 22 to life)	$ 392, 22 to life	$ 49, 22 to life

Supplies and Equipment

Item	Discussion	SN RN's Projected Annual Cost	MGY's Projected Annual Cost
Personal care supplies	OK	$ 900	$ 900
Orthoses	OK	$ 200, to 21 $ 100, 22 to life	$ 200, to 21 $ 100, 22 to life
Self-care equipment	OK	$ 120	$ 120
Hospital bed, $2,500/ 10 years	OK	$ 250	$ 250
Postural wheelchair, $4,000, to age 21/ 5 yrs	OK	$ 800, to 21	$ 800, to 21
Electronic wheelchair, $7,000 to $15,000/ 5 yrs	An appropriate electric wheelchair should cost under $9,000. It is not clear to me that Tom has the cognitive skills to operate an electric wheelchair safely, but one is being utilized in the school program.	$ 2,200	$ 1,800
Annual maintenance	OK	$ 25	$ 25
Desk Chair, $385/3–5 yrs	What is the difference between a desk chair and an activity chair? Why are both pieces needed?	$ 96	$ 0
Pediatric/adult prone, stander $685 /3–5 yrs	OK	$ 171	$ 171
Activity chair, $550/3–5 yrs	OK	$ 138	$ 138
Mobile prone stander, $850, 1 every 3–5 yrs	Why is this needed in addition to the prone stander discussed above?	$ 213	$ 0
Lift, $2,200, 1 every 7 years	OK	$ 314	$ 314

Bathing System $3000–$3,900, 1 every 15 years	This will be built in and is included in the allowance for home modifications	$ 230	$ 0
Shower commode chair, $900, 1 every 7 years	OK	$ 129	$ 129
Environmental control/communication system, $11,000 once, then $500/yr for purchase, installation, and maintenance	Cognitive testing does not indicate that Tom will be able to use this kind of equipment. Tom will always have a caretaker in attendance to monitor his environment.	$11,000 once $ 500 per year	$ 0

Medications

Item	Discussion	SN RN's Projected Annual Cost	MGY's Projected Annual Cost
OTC medications, $120/yr	Not specific to the alleged damages.	$ 120	$ 0

Laboratory/Diagnostic Studies

Item	Discussion	SN RN's Projected Annual Cost	MGY's Projected Annual Cost
Laboratory/ diagnostic $1,000 to age 21 — every 3 yrs age 22 to life — every 5 yrs	OK	$ 333, to 21 $ 200, 22 to life	$ 333, to 21 $ 200, 22 to life

Attendant Care (one of the below)

Item	Discussion	SN RN's Projected Annual Cost	MGY's Projected Annual Cost
HHA 8 hour, $14/hr HHA 24 hour age 22 to life	Tom attends school 180 days per year. 5 hours/day on school days and 8 hours per day on other days would provide coverage until 9:00 pm during the week and for a large part of the day on weekends and holidays. Live-in care after age 21 for around-the-clock coverage.	$ 40,880, to 21 $122,640, 22 to life	$ 30,800, to 21 $ 51,100, 22 to life
LPN 8 hour LPN 24 hour (assumes change in status requiring LPN care)	Tom's injuries resulted in a static encephalopathy. Future medical instability would have to result from an unrelated process. There is no reason, given his current status, to assume medical instability.	$ 87,600, to 21 $262,800, 22 to life	$ 0

RN 8 hour	Tom's injuries resulted in a static	$102,200	$ 0
RN 24 hour (assumes change in status requiring RN care)	encephalopathy. Future medical instability would have to result from an unrelated process. There is no reason, given his current status, to assume medical instability.	$306,600	

Transportation

Item	Discussion	SN RN's Projected Annual Cost	MGY's Projected Annual Cost
New van, $20,000 – $25,000/5 years	This purchase price is reasonable, however the cost of a family car ($10,000) may be deducted from the cost of the van, to show the cost of transportation related directly to the alleged damages. The van should be amortized over 7 years.	$ 4,500	$ 1,786
Used van $11,000–$20,000/ 5 yrs	See above	$ 3,100	$ 0
Van rental per day	This is not a practical solution.	$ 300 – $ 400/day	$ 0
Van upkeep	Maintenance costs should run about $800/year. Insurance, gas, and other usual costs are not related specifically to Tom's impairments.	$ 1,850	$ 800

Home Modifications

Item	Discussion	SN RN's Projected Annual Cost	MGY's Projected Annual Cost
Complete wc mods, $40,000–$60,000, every 20 yrs	I cannot address this area without seeing the Hammer's current home.	$ 2,500	To be determined
Maintenance	See above	$ 1,000	To be determined
Household maintenance age 22 to life	The premise of Alternative I is that Tom will be living in his parents' home.	$ 1,200, 22 to life	$ 0

Education

Item	Discussion	SN RN's Projected Annual Cost	MGY's Projected Annual Cost
Academic placement	These costs must be covered by the school system under PL 94-142	$ 25,000– 35,000 to 21	$ 0

II. Projections of Costs Based on Facility Placement
Medical Care

Item	Discussion	SN RN's Projected Annual Cost	MGY's Projected Annual Cost
Pediatrician/ General Practitioner to age 21 ($40/visit) age 22 to life ($75/visit)	Semiannual visits to the Children's Health Center are for routine child care. These are not specific to the alleged damages. Medical care related to the anoxic encephalopathy is provided by the specialist listed below.	$ 80, to 21 $ 150, 22 to life	$ 0 $ 0
Neurologist ($200/visit)	OK	$ 200	$ 200
Physiatrist/Developmental Specialist, annual to age 21 — then every 5 yrs ($190/visit)	OK	$ 190, to 21 $ 38, 22 to life	$ 190, to 21 $ 38, 22 to life
Academic testing to age 21, every 2 yrs ($665/visit)	This service is provided by the school system under PL 94-142, as noted in SN RN's report, on page 19.	$ 333, to 21	$ 0
Ophthalmologist to age 21 — then every 2 yrs ($75/visit)	OK	$ 150, to 21 $ 75, 22 to life	$ 150, to 21 $ 75, 22 to life
Specialty consultations, annual to age 21, then every 2 yrs to life ($190/visit)	OK	$ 380, to 21 $ 190, 22 to life	$ 380, to 21 $ 190, 22 to life
Acute, 35 days, $1,500/day	OK	$ 600	$ 600
Behavioral, for life	These services could be provided by the residential facility, however, the records do not reflect the need for this service.	$42,000– 56,000, once	$ 0

Rehabilitation

Item	Discussion	SN RN's Projected Annual Cost	MGY's Projected Annual Cost
Physical therapy to age 21 ongoing ($80/visit)	This therapy will be provided by the school system under PL-142.	$ 480, to 21	$ 0
Physical therapy evaluation age 22 to life ($240/visit)	This service will be provided by the residential facility.	$ 240, 22 to life	$ 0
Occupational therapy to age 21 ongoing ($80/visit)	This therapy will be provided by the school system under PL-142.	$ 240, to 21	$ 0

Occupational therapy evaluation age 22 to life ($240/visit)	This service will be provided by the residential facility	$ 240, 22 to life	$ 0
Speech therapy to age 21 ongoing ($80/visit)	This therapy will be provided by the school system under PL-142.	$ 240, to 21	$ 0
Speech therapy evaluation age 22 to life ($240/visit)	This service will be provided by the residential facility	$ 240, 22 to life	$ 0
Psychology, family counseling for life ($125/visit)	Behavioral management is not needed if Tom is in a residential facility.	$ 563, to 21	$ 0
Individual/ Behavioral for life ($145/visit)	It is not clear that Tom's cognitive level is high enough to benefit from individual neuropsychological intervention.	$ 653, to 21	$ 0
Periodic therapeutic service for life ($80/visit)	SN RN projects five occurrences of intensive therapy (six sessions/week, 6 months each) from age 22 to life. The life-care plan also recommends 24-hour coverage with a personal care aide. This aide will be able to perform a home therapy program supervised by professional therapists. Two therapy evaluations per occurrence (in addition to the four annual therapy evaluations already provided) will cover the need for periodic intervention (10 times $240/ evaluation, 22 to life).	$ 392, 22 to life	$ 49, 22 to life

Supplies and Equipment

Item	Discussion	SN RN's Projected Annual Cost	MGY's Projected Annual Cost
Personal care supplies	Supplied by the facility.	$ 900	$ 0 to life
Orthoses	OK	$ 200, to 21 $ 100, 22 to life	$ 200, to 21 $ 100, 22 to life
Self-care equipment	Supplied by the facility.	$ 120	$ 0
Postural wheelchair, $4,000, to age 21 — 1 every 5 yrs	OK	$ 800, to 21	$ 800 to life
Electronic wheelchair, $7000–$15,000, 1 every 5 yrs	This client will not be able to use an electric wheelchair safely.	$ 2,200	$ 0
Desk chair, $385, 1 every 3–5 yrs	Supplied by the facility, if required.	$ 96	$ 0

		SN RN's Projected Annual Cost	MGY's Projected Annual Cost
Pediatric/adult prone stander, $685 — 1 every 3–5 yrs	Supplied by the facility.	$ 171	$ 0
Activity chair, $550, 1 every 3–5 yrs	Supplied by the facility.	$ 138	$ 0
Mobile prone stander, $850, 1 every 3–5 yrs	Supplied by the facility, if required.	$ 213	$ 0
Environmental control/ communication system, $11,000 once, then $500/yr for purchase, installation, and maintenance.	Cognitive testing does not indicate that Tom will be able to use this kind of equipment. Tom will always have a caretaker in attendance to monitor his environment.	$11,000 once $ 500 per year	$ 0

Laboratory/Diagnostic Studies

Item	Discussion	SN RN's Projected Annual Cost	MGY's Projected Annual Cost
Laboratory/diagnostic, $1,000 to age 21 — every 3 yrs age 22 to life — every 5 yrs	OK	$ 333, to 21 $ 200, 22 to life	$ 333, to 21 $ 200, 22 to life

Transportation

Item	Discussion	SN RN's Projected Annual Cost	MGY's Projected Annual Cost
Van rental	SN RN notes that there is specialized transportation and cab transportation available for intermittent use. Paratransit services are heavily subsidized. Allow $100 per month.	$ 4,800	$ 1,200

Home Modifications/Facility

Item	Discussion	SN RN's Projected Annual Cost	MGY's Projected Annual Cost
Minimal home modifications, $6,000 every 20 years	SN RN has projected that Tom will be incontinent (see supplies). Therefore, an accessible bathroom will not be necessary for intermittent visits home. Ramps to the entrances may be necessary, but I would need to see the home to make this evaluation.	$ 300	To be determined

| Residential Placement, $36,500–$87,000 | Which of these facilities are recommended? Why not the first suggestion? If all of these are equally appropriate, then choose the most cost-effective. | $ 36,500– $ 87,000 | $ 36,500 |

Chapter 35

The Expert Fact Witness: Noneconomic Damages Testimony

Jenny Beerman

Contents

1-57444-123-X/98
© 1998 by American Association of Legal Nurse Consultants

Objectives

- To describe the role and purpose of an expert fact witness in personal injury and product liability cases
- To discuss foundation issues for the role
- To describe the approach to organization and presentation of medical records to a jury
- To identify steps in preparing to testify as an expert fact witness

Introduction

Legal nurse consultants (LNCs) have recently developed new testifying roles as "expert fact witnesses" (Bogart and Beerman, 1995). In this role, an LNC evaluates, summarizes, and explains the contents of medical records to the jury at trial, thus aiding understanding of the extent of a plaintiff's injuries, pain, and suffering. This testimony is particularly useful in cases where the plaintiff eventually recovered or died from the injuries. A life-care plan is not necessary. Damages consist of the economic losses and the pain and suffering endured.

The expert fact witness is not engaged to express opinions about the quality of care and treatment rendered but to educate the judge or jury about that care and the plaintiff's response to it. Though treating physicians have customarily provided this information to the court, attorneys are recognizing the LNCs can effectively fulfill much of this function.

Historically, nurses have testified as experts about standards of nursing care in malpractice cases. Nurses also testify as life-care planners about projected costs and services of future care. The expertise of an LNC is also helpful to describe and explain in detail the events associated with initial hospitalization following an injury through discharge and rehabilitation. The injuries, care, and attendant pain and suffering often represent substantial damages. At trial, the LNC's presentation of the medical record evidence of these damages bridges the gap in testimony between the liability for the accident and the life-care plan. The jury needs a clear, concise, understandable accounting of the events of this period based on medical records.

Definition of the Role

A fact witness is a person not named as a party in a lawsuit. As a witness to events, however, the fact witness testifies about what he or she saw or heard. The expert witness possesses specialized knowledge and skills and offers opinion testimony and education to the jury. The expert fact witness is a combination role, using special knowledge necessary to interpret, describe, and explain the facts he or she has read and exerpted from the medical records to the court. Medical records are considered business records, recorded contemporaneously with events, and as such admissible as evidence of those events. Though not a witness to the actual events, the expert fact witness is allowed to act as a conduit of medical record information to the judge or jury. Expertise in health care and medical records is essential, but no opinions are provided about the facts. Frequently, this testimony concentrates on presenting the facts in the medical records that support the allegation of plaintiff's pain and suffering, a key component of the damages package, and important for the judge or jury to understand.

Foundation for This Role

As with other expert witnesses, the attorney must offer proof to the court that the nurse is qualified to testify in this role. The nurse and attorney must plan this issue far ahead of the trial. Judges may not understand that nurses are qualified to present medical record evidence by virtue of their specialized education and certification, their familiarity with hospital procedures and processes, medical records, medical terminology, and their clinical education and experience. Key members of the health care team, nurses spend more time with patients and medical records in the clinical setting than any other care provider. Nurses do not make medical diagnoses or prescribe medical treatment. However, they do teach patients about health and diseases, medical terminology, diagnostic tests, procedures, and a wide variety of treatment modalities. Nurses are qualified to provide this same information to educate jurors.

Qualification of the expert fact witness is at the judge's discretion. If qualified, the judge may restrict testimony to strict and narrow boundaries, or liberal and wide boundaries may be extended. It is important to understand and abide by any limits imposed by the court.

The goal is to present the facts of the medical record clearly and accurately.

Review and Chronological Summary of Medical Records

Summarizing often voluminous records is the first step for the LNC. Records may have been received from a variety of facilities and providers and may span a considerable amount of time. A computer program that sorts the information by date or provider is a necessity.

When condensing and summarizing the records, caution is necessary not to alter the facts. Testimony under oath requires accurate reporting without embellishment or deletion. Meticulous, accurate, and complete testimony is difficult for the defense to discredit.

The LNC's familiarity with medical records allows early recognition of records that are missing. Since records are often delivered in a disorganized state, assessment of completeness is essential. Missing records should be requested as soon as possible. The attorney may have unknowingly requested only the records that the client or family remembered. Careful reading of referral and discharge summaries often provides a directional map of care.

Malpractice identified in the record should be pointed out to the attorney as it may affect the damage issues. Malpractice may decrease the defense's responsibility for damages. For the plaintiff, another defendant may be identified to share responsibility for damages.

Other treating physicians and health care providers should also be identified during record review. The courtroom testimony may contribute to an understanding of the damages.

The LNC must differentiate preexisting conditions from those caused by the accident. At the same time, preexisting conditions exacerbated by the injuries should be noted. All damages or potential damages found by the nurse consultant in the medical records of which the attorney may be unaware should be listed and discussed with the attorney. Examples of damages that attorneys may not be aware of are cognitive delays in head-injured children that may require yearly psychological testing or a torn diaphragm that may have the potential to rupture repeatedly and require future surgeries. If permanent disabling injuries have resulted, a colleague may be recommended to formulate a life-care plan.

Drafts of Trial Exhibits and Demonstrative Aids

Exhibits to the jury are like the chalkboard in a classroom. The jury remembers images, diagrams, and pictures long after an expert has left the stand. Demonstrative evidence, such as wheelchair, double-lumen Hickman catheter, or suction apparatus are important. Time line maps made from the narrative chronology are effective, serving as a "picture" representation of the chronology and a useful visual aid for the jury. It is best to present this early in the testimony and then leave it on an easel for the jury to refer to throughout the proceedings. Exhibits can also include lists or charts of medications, tests, operations, treatments, complications, damages, and health care providers. Illustrations and enlarged pages of the medical record are also effective exhibits.

Collaboration with the attorney allows creative planning and development of effective exhibits. The attorney may have ideas from past trials or colleagues. The LNC knows what is available and where to get equipment and demonstrative evidence. After the ideas have been formulated, no further work is done until close to trial. Exhibits must then be created, enlarged, and mounted for the courtroom, demonstrative aids collected and prepared.

Review and Coordination of Testimony with Other Medical Witnesses

Ideally, the attorney involves the LNC early in the case to help coordinate the testimony of all the medical experts. At trial, the LNC usually testifies first to lay the foundation for the testimony of other health care professionals. This foundation allows treating physicians to amplify, supplement, and highlight specific areas or events in the medical record. All experts must understand their specific role in the outline of the medical testimony. The expert fact witness can coordinate this effort. For example, in a complicated trauma case, the nurse defines and explains anatomy of the injured areas, management of the patient in traction, the amount and frequency of pain medication, and weekly physical therapies. The trauma surgeon then explains the complicated surgery, elaborating on complications, causes and treatment, and long-lasting disabilities.

If the LNC is consulted late in the process, testimony must be tailored to existing testimony already collected by the attorney. The nurse should review all depositions to avoid redundancy or contradictions and suggest strategies for using existing testimony.

Supervision of Production of Final Exhibits and Demonstrative Evidence

The LNC reviews exhibits for correctness, simplicity, and readability at every stage of production. As the trial date draws near, all equipment should be checked for proper function. Extra supplies, such as colored markers, pointers, and easels to display the exhibits, should be gathered. Technical problems should be anticipated and backup plans formulated. All expenses for exhibits and demonstrative evidence should be preapproved by the attorney.

Practice of the Presentation

It is helpful to practice the final presentation in front of a layperson rather than an attorney, nurse, or doctor. Because testimony may have to be altered extemporaneously, concentrate on the main events of the injury. Memorizing word-for-word texts is risky, as the courtroom's climate may differ greatly from the privacy of a patient's room or the relaxed environment of classroom or office. The LNC and attorney should plan the presentation style prior to trial. Strong effective teaching in the courtroom derives from basic principles of patient education and does not differ greatly from beside teaching for patient and family.

Supervision of Exhibit Setup

The LNC should arrive early at court to assist in exhibit arrangement in the courtroom. Sitting in the jury box and witness chair before anyone arrives is recommended to become familiar with the courtroom's layout. In the witness chair, note shelf space, microphone, and distance between the attorney and the jury. Each exhibit may be placed on the easel and viewed from several juror's chairs to test readability. Verify delivery and setup of all equipment and safety of cords and wires.

Trial Testimony

The expert fact witness serves to educate the court as to the technical facts, issues, and events of the medical record. The first few minutes on the stand are critical to establish rapport with the jury. As the attorney asks questions, be attentive and establish eye contact with the jury as questions are answered. Eye contact with each juror is vital.

Listen carefully to each question, and answer only the question asked. Be articulate, factual, and to the point. Descriptions of the time line of events of the patient's hospitalization or the patient's pain and suffering should be animated, but do not bore the jury with too much detail. Use exhibits and demonstrative evidence to keep the jury interested. Be sure that every juror can see demonstrations. Show equipment as close to the jury as possible. Use everyday analogies and visual aids. Use of lay terminology is essential. Always keep the main points of the case in mind.

The opposing attorney may cross-examine the LNC. Accurate introduction of medical record evidence and clear explanations of treatment and medical terminology leave little room for questions. The opposing attorney may try to discredit or diminish the effectiveness of testimony by asking detailed questions regarding professional background to imply the LNC may not be qualified. Be prepared to discuss relevant clinical practice experience and professional positions.

Summary

LNCs undertaking to present medical record evidence testimony at trial should have an extensive background in clinical practice and teaching experience. While physicians tend to concentrate on explanations of specific medical treatments and procedures, LNCs are more likely to present a broader, more comprehensive view of the events described in the medical records which improves the court's understanding of the case.

Serving as an expert fact witness may be rewarding for nurses because it is not associated with the more adversarial, confrontational nature of nursing malpractice testimony. The testifying nurse provides the jury with an understanding of the pertinent issues in an organized, systematic, and memorable format. Opportunities for nurses to testify as expert fact witnesses are expanding as attorneys and judges are educated about its economical, educational, and strategic advantages.

References

Bogart, J. and Beerman, J. (1995). Expert fact witness: a testifying role for the legal nurse consultant, *The Journal of Legal Nurse Consulting,* 6(4).

Bibliography

Colburn, V. (1991). The nurse as expert witness: a new expanded role, *Journal of Perinatal and Neonatal Nursing,* 5(3), 16–24.

Faherty, B. L. (1991). The nurse legal consultant and disabling injuries, *Rehabilitation Nursing,* 16(1), 30–33.

Guido, G. W. (1994). Be an expert witness for critical care nursing, *MCN Clinical Issues,* 5(1), 66–70.

Hofland, S. A. L. (1990). Testifying in court: how to develop credibility with the jury, *Clinical Nurse Specialist,* 4(4), 212–216.

Iyer, P. (1996). *Nursing Malpractice,* Tucson, AZ, Lawyers and Judges Publishing Company.

Janulis, D. M. (1989). Expert witness, *Journal of Neuroscience Nursing,* 21(3), 195–197.

Murphy, E. K. (1987). The professional status of nursing: a view from the courts, *Nursing Outlook,* 35(1), 12–15.

Ogborn, M. (1995). Storytelling throughout trial, *Trial,* 31(8), 63–65.

Perry, S. E. (1992). The neuroscience nurse as an expert witness, *Journal of Neuroscience Nursing,* 24(5), 290–295.

Perry, S. E. (1992). The clinical nurse specialist as expert witness, *Clinical Nurse Specialist,* 6(1), 53–56.

Quigley, F. M. (1991). Expert testimony, *Focus on Critical Care-MCN,* 18(2), 164–165.

Quigley, F. M. (1991). Responsibilities of the consultant and expert witness, *Focus on Critical Care-AACN,* 18(3), 238–239.

Quigley, F. M. (1991). The legal basis of expert testimony, *Focus on Critical Care-MCN,* 18(4), 307–310.

Turner, N. (1995). The legal nurse consultant as a court appointed expert, *Journal of Legal Nurse Consulting,* 6(1), 12–14.

Chapter 36

Business Principles for the Nurse Expert Witness

Kathleen Martin, Karen Cepero, and Julie Bogart

Contents

Objectives

- To discuss the elements and responsibility of contracting with attorneys to serve as an expert nurse witness
- To describe key issues related to contracting with a broker or agent to provide expert services
- To name factors pertinent to determining an expert nurse's fee
- To list two methods of structuring fees
- To describe financial information that does not have to be disclosed in testimony
- To describe several methods used to collect fee

Introduction

A testifying nurse expert as an independent contractor cannot avoid the practical issues and decisions of conducting business. As an expert witness, a nurse must carefully guard credibility and integrity in professional clinical practice and testimony, but also in business practices. Details of both areas are discoverable. The nurse considering acting as an expert witness should carefully deliberate and plan ethical, defensible, practical, and legally sound business practices. Business principles for the independent contractor are described elsewhere. Issues considered here are those unique to the role of expert witness including contracting directly with the attorney, fees and collections issues, disclosure of financial information, and contracting with a broker service.

Contracting with the Attorney

Many nurse experts contract with attorneys to review cases and/or serve as expert witnesses without formal written contract. The attorney calls and interviews the expert over the phone, often having been referred by another attorney to the expert. Medical records are sent to the nurse who reviews them and reports findings over the phone or in person. The expert then sends a bill for time spent on the case and receives payment. The majority of attorneys pay their bills to experts expeditiously. However, almost every expert has had at least one difficult experience collecting payment. Such unfortunate instances have prompted some experts to require signing of formal contracts (see Appendix 36.1) or collecting large retainers, especially with out-of-city or out-of-state clients, or new clients.

During the initial contact with an attorney, the nurse expert provides a brief review of qualifications and pertinent clinical experience. The attorney usually asks about other cases for which the legal nurse consultant (LNC) has served as expert and may request a list of references of other attorneys for whom the expert has reviewed cases. The LNC should also ask how the attorney got the LNC's name, should review basic fees and retainer if required, and discuss terms or conditions of payment. A retainer may be in an amount estimated to cover the initial review of the case depending on the size of the medical records, or a flat fee typically ranging from $250.00 to $1000.00. The LNC should be direct, formal, specific, and firm in discussing payment terms to eliminate misunderstandings.

Following the phone conversation, or receipt of medical records if expected within a short period of time, the nurse expert should expeditiously send a letter to the attorney, confirming the conversation in general terms, enclosing the requested *curriculum vitae* and a fee schedule (see Appendix 36.3). The fee schedule delineates hourly rates, a list of expenses to be paid by the attorney, such as travel costs, and terms of payment.

Receipt of medical records should be acknowledged. If not received when expected, the LNC should call the attorney. If the agreed-upon retainer does not accompany the medical records, the LNC should notify the attorney and not begin review until it is received. The LNC should keep in mind that all correspondence with the attorney is discoverable if the LNC agrees to serve as expert in the case.

Once the client attorney sends the review materials with a retainer check, a contract is understood to be in existence between the two parties. The attorney has agreed to the fee schedule provided on the phone and in writing. The LNC has agreed to review and render an opinion in the case within a certain time period for the agreed-upon fee.

If the nurse expert's opinions are helpful to the attorney's case and if the nurse agrees to serve as testifying expert, the attorney may then disclose his or her name and opinions to the opposing attorney(s). An unfortunate, improper, and unethical abuse of the process occasionally occurs when an attorney names the expert without the expert's knowledge or consent. If discovered, the nurse is advised to insist on withdrawal of his or her name from the case. The nurse is also justified in invoicing the attorney for the unauthorized disclosure, as the opposing attorney was thereby prevented from contacting the expert to review the case. Disclosure also probably served the attorney's purpose. However, the nurse's credibility may be damaged by association of his or her name with an erroneous implied opinion, and compensation may not be an adequate remedy. The expert should consult an attorney to discuss appropriate actions.

Retainers

A retainer is an advance payment for future work. Most attorneys require retainers in their own practices before beginning work. A retainer serves two purposes. It formalizes the agreement and assures payment for work. Some experts ask for another advance payment when the first is exhausted and continue collecting advance payments to maintain a minimum account balance. This may be the case if they anticipate investing an extensive amount of time in a case or have not previously worked with the attorney. Generally, though, the professional relationship is based on some degree of trust that the attorney will pay for services for which the attorney contracts.

Establishing Fees

Abraham Lincoln once said "A lawyer's time and advice are his stock-in-trade." This is true of the expert nurse witness as well. The fee or hourly rate charged by the nurse expert should reflect the value of years of expertise achieved through education and practice experience. To determine an appropriate fee, the LNC may survey nurse colleagues who have served as experts, as well as other professionals with similar education and years of practice in their field. Another source is attorneys who routinely engage nurse experts to review cases. Fees range nationally from a $75.00 minimum per hour for review, and more for testimony time.

It is ill advised to quote a flat rate for a case. Quoting a fee of $600 for review of a medical record may seem reasonable at first, but unforeseen circumstances are the usual. The issues may not be as simple as the attorney described, or the record may be 2 feet high by the time missing records are collected. A rule-of-thumb often mentioned by experienced nurse experts is that it usually takes approximately 1 hour for initial review per 1 in. of medical records. Many experienced nurse experts also charge a minimum fee for review of a case equivalent to 3 or 4 hours of time even if the case review only takes 2 hours to complete. The attorney should be informed of the minimum charge before sending the records.

It is also customary to establish one base rate for all services including review of records, literature research and review, and report generation, with another higher rate for deposition and trial time. An alternative is a single rate for all services including deposition and trial time. A nurse expert may charge a base rate of anywhere from $75.00 to $150.00 per hour and $125.00 to $200.00 per hour for testimony time. A single rate charged by nurse experts range from $95.00 to $150.00 per hour. Some attorneys prefer the single rate and it simplifies record keeping and invoicing. It also eliminates the need to explain tiered rates at deposition. Rates for services of expert nurses vary by geographic location. Educational level, specialty certifications, years of clinical practice, and experience as a testifying expert should also be factored into the determination of fees.

Some nurse experts list a different rate for secretarial or transcription services, or for tasks such as simple organization and tabbing of medical records. The more multitiered the fee schedule, the more complicated the invoicing process. A recommendation to factor those kinds of services into the base rate should be considered.

It is a good idea to publish payment terms on the initial fee schedule sent to the attorney and repeat it on each invoice. If interest is charged after a designated length of time (highly recommended), the attorney client should monthly receive notice of the balance due and interest charged. If a deposition is requested and an invoice is outstanding, the expert may politely decline to appear until the invoice is paid. Often an oversight, this notification usually invokes immediate payment.

Payment for Deposition or Trial Testimony Time

Consideration may be given to requesting payment in advance for a deposition. If the case venue is out-of-the-city or town, the nurse expert should discuss this option with the sponsoring attorney when the deposition is scheduled. For the defense attorney who must submit for payment to an insurance company, the expert may be relegated to waiting for payment for a longer period of time.

Months or at least weeks ahead of a scheduled trial, the expert is given the date the case is scheduled on the court's docket. A number of cases are scheduled on the docket for the same week. Most of the cases settle before the date arrives and all but one of the remaining must be rescheduled to a later date. Because the expert must keep the calendar clear for the trial date, some may charge a fee if the case settles at the last minute or trial is rescheduled to a later date. If the case proceeds, the expert may be "on-call" waiting to testify at or away from the court venue, and usually charges for this time at the base rate or an "on-call" rate. Many experts charge a flat half day or full day fee for trial testimony based on their hourly testimony rate.

Nurse experts are paid for their time by the attorney who engages their service. The exception to this arrangement is the time the expert spends in deposition. The opposing attorney requests the expert appear and testify at deposition to discover the expert's opinions and is, therefore, responsible to pay for the expert's time at deposition. Time spent in preparation for the deposition may be paid by either side as stipulated by state statutes or mutual agreement. Prior to the deposition, the nurse expert should inquire as to how invoices should be directed and time allocated between presenting and opposing attorney(s). Following deposition, the nurse expert submits and collects payment from the attorney who took the deposition, either directly or through the sponsoring attorney. An alternative is to notify the deposing attorney ahead of time of a request for payment in full for the deposition at the time of the deposition.

Differences Between Defense and Plaintiff Attorney's Payment Methods

Most plaintiff attorneys directly pay expenses for experts. The expert submits an invoice to the attorney, and it is generally paid in a short period of time. By agreement, however, some experts submit invoices for expenses to their plaintiff clients for payment. In that case, there may be a longer time delay to payment. The nurse expert has contracted with the attorney, who is responsible for payment of invoices, rather than with his or her client. A notation to that effect can be included in the agreement letter or fee schedule. (See Appendix 36.)

Defense attorneys must submit invoices for payment to insurance companies. Unless the defense attorney pays the invoice directly out of pocket and awaits reimbursement from the insurance company, payment from defense attorneys via an insurance company may take longer simply because another (rather complex) entity is involved.

Regardless of whether directed to plaintiff or defense, invoicing should reflect a consistent policy and procedure that is clearly stated on invoices and fee schedules.

Time for Out-of-Town Travel

Out-of-town travel time (other than time for deposition) is generally figured by adding time from port to port minus sleep time, personal time, and time working on other matters. For example, an expert departs home at 3:30 p.m. arriving in

Boston for an evening dinner meeting with the attorney which ends at 8:00 p.m. The next morning the expert rises early to review materials for 1 hour before departing at 8:30 for the 9:00 a.m. deposition. The deposition lasts until 12:30 p.m. The expert goes to the airport to wait for the flight home which is delayed and departs at 4:30 p.m. While waiting at the airport and on the plane, the expert reads depositions from another case for 2 hours. The expert arrives home at 7:00 p.m. Total nontestimony hours billed for the trip are 10 hours at the base rate. The opposing attorney is billed for 3 hours at the testimony time rate. To avoid such calculations, some experts simply set a flat daily or 1-day rate for the sponsoring attorney and invoice the opposing attorney for the deposition time. The invoice may be sent if cancellation does not occur at least 48 hours prior to departure.

Expenses for Out-of-Town Travel

It is standard to charge the client attorney for expenses incurred for case review and appearance at deposition and trial. All travel expenses are billed for such items as meals, car rental, parking, or ground transportation. The nurse expert should determine the most convenient flight, make the reservations, then ask the client attorney to purchase and mail the airline ticket. The attorney should also arrange and pay for hotel accommodations for the expert. If the deposition or trial testimony is scheduled for the morning and several hours distant, the nurse expert should arrive the night before. Although this entails hotel expense for the attorney, it is important for the case as well as for the nurse expert to have a good night's sleep before testimony. If the expert drives a personal car out of town for testimony, the attorney is billed at the current IRS mileage allowance rate.

Time Logs

LNCs who keep good time records earn more than those who keep poor time records. Those who estimate tend to underestimate the actual time spent. Whatever system or method is used should be readily accessible, and time and task data easily and quickly entered. Time logs are essential for accurate billing and to satisfy the client who wants to see exactly what services he or she is paying for. Whether time is kept on paper in the case file or in a computer database, the date and time when beginning and finishing work and the category of work performed such as medical record review, literature review, or report writing should be consistently recorded. The LNC should record all time spent on telephone calls and correspondence. Any time spent for which the expert opts not to charge can be listed on the invoice as a "no-charge" item rather than leaving it off the invoice. All out-of-pocket expenses should be documented with receipts such as parking, long distance phone charges, fees for professional literature searches, photocopy charges, notebooks, etc. Some of these expenses may be considered as the cost of conducting business and factored into the expert's determination of an hourly rate. If serving as expert for the defense, it should be noted that insurance companies may restrict expenses for which they will reimburse such as secretarial or transcriptionist time. The nurse expert should inquire of the defense attorney in the beginning whether or not the insurance company pays for expenses and quote the hourly rate accordingly to accommodate those anticipated out-of-pocket expenses.

Fee Collections

Collecting payment for services performed is a necessary part of serving as an expert. The great majority of attorneys value their experts and promptly pay the invoices submitted. Those who delay payment are customarily charged interest for late payments. The nurse expert should remember that charging interest is discretionary and can be waived in certain situations. If the attorney is slow to pay, a letter or personal phone call may yield payment. To avoid a large loss, work should not continue on a case until payment is received. If the attorney declines to pay or does not respond to requests for payment, the expert should send a notice by certified mail describing impending actions that will be taken to collect the fee and attach a copy of the invoice. Those actions may include filing in small claims court, filing a complaint with the local bar association, or hiring a collection agency or attorney to pursue payment. The expert should then proceed with reasonable and cost-effective actions to collect the payment due.

Disclosure of Financial Income

At deposition, the nurse expert is generally asked about compensation rates and the amount of money he or she has been paid to date on the case in question. Another area of questioning that frequently arises during deposition is income the expert derives from testifying. Such questions usually take the form of requesting an estimate of the percentage of time and income spent on service as a testifying expert compared with other professional activities or sources of income. This is relevant in states (such as Kansas) which mandate that experts spend a certain percentage of their professional time practicing in the clinical area about which they offer opinion testimony. The expert usually does not, however, have to disclose total income or the exact amount of money he or she earns as an expert.

The Florida Supreme Court, in *Elkins v. Syken*, set criteria for seeking financial information from opposing experts. In that state, the expert may be asked about compensation for the pending case and approximate portions of professional time and percentage of income derived from expert service. The expert need not disclose income from work as an expert or total annual income. The expert may be required to specifically identify cases in which he or she testified, but may not be compelled to compile or produce nonexistent documents.

If the opposing attorney asks the expert for details of income from testimony, the LNC may agree to do so but should request the attorney pay for his or her time to search through billing records, compile, and submit the information. The request and the attorney's agreement to pay should be made on the deposition record.

Prior to a deposition, the nurse expert should inquire of the sponsoring attorney what financial information is and is not required to be disclosed in the state in which the case was filed. If opposing counsel inquires beyond disclosure requirements at deposition, the sponsoring attorney can object and/or the LNC respectfully decline to answer or to provide the information. Inquiry into the expert's personal finances is improper unless it relates to partiality. If unsure of how to respond to questions about income, the expert may request a break and discuss the issue with the sponsoring or personal attorney.

Questions or concerns about potential problems related to financial information should be discussed well ahead of time with the attorney.

Tax Returns

An attorney may request tax returns by interrogatory or at deposition to verify income derived from testimony. For most LNCs the tax returns would not yield that information since consulting income on cases in which he or she did not act as expert would also be included in business income. The LNC may explain this to the attorney and respectfully decline because the request is overly broad. If tax returns are subpoenaed, there are actions an expert can take to avoid producing them or to limit exposure of private information. Through the sponsoring attorney, the expert may file a motion to quash and/or a protective order to modify or limit disclosure. A motion to quash or modify a subpoena must show that the request is unduly burdensome, fails to allow reasonable time for compliance, or requires the expert disclose some privileged or otherwise protected material. In some cases, a subpoena may be difficult to quash because the court may find the information relevant to the subject matter. The sponsoring attorney can file a protective order limiting disclosure to only the narrowest field of information on the return such as the amount of income derived from testifying if that is specifically reported on the return. If an expert refuses to comply with the court's decision, the court may find the expert in contempt.

Attorneys will usually not pursue detailed information about financial information that is not pertinent to case issues or credibility. The LNC is wise to proactively inquire about the boundaries of such information in the state in which he or she offers testimony.

Brokers/Agents, Advertisers, and Contracts

Many national and regional companies, and independent LNCs, broker experts for attorneys. They compile names of experts (or locate an expert on request) and "sell" those names to attorneys for a fee. Brokers or agents use different methods to collect the fee for their service. Some broker services collect their fee from the attorney by adding a per-hour charge or a percentage charge to the base rate of the expert's hourly rate. For example, the expert service may add the greater of a flat $50.00 per hour or 30% of the hourly rate as their broker fee. That expert service would add $50.00 per hour to an expert's hourly rate of $100.00, or $60.00 per hour to an expert's rate of $200.00 per hour (30% of $200.00 equals $60.00). Such broker services require the expert to submit hours of work to the broker for invoicing rather than directly to the attorney. The broker, in turn, immediately pays the expert, then invoices and collects from the attorney. The obvious plus in this arrangement is that the expert does not have to wait for payment (assuming good payment practices by the broker) from the attorney, or be involved in the collection process. The broker also usually collects a retainer from the attorney which is usually forwarded to the expert with the case.

Other broker services collect a flat fee from the attorney at the time the expert's name is provided. Those fees range from $350.00 to $1,500.00 and may or may not depend on the expert's specialty or educational preparation. The charge for a family practice physician may be less than for a neurosurgeon; a general medical-surgical nurse may be less than for a certified neonatal clinical nurse specialist. These services generally do not become involved with billing or collections; once the attorney and expert are matched, their role is at an end.

Brokers may require experts to sign a contract binding them to certain rules and restrictions of the broker service. Some contracts contain a "noncircumvent" clause to prevent the expert from unfairly expropriating their clients or work. This clause says that if the broker refers the expert to an attorney, the expert must work on any subsequent cases from that attorney or firm through the broker service even if the attorney directly contacts the expert.

"Noncompete" clauses are also important to identify and understand in a contract. They may restrict the expert from working for clients (attorneys and firms) of the broker for a period of time after resigning or being discharged from the broker service. Time limits on such clauses of 1 to 2 years are common, but laws limiting time as well as geographical area restrictions vary by state.

The nurse expert should carefully read the entire contract and consult a business/contract attorney for education and advice before signing. The contract is legally binding and the broker may vigorously seek recompense for violations. Although violations of such contracts are difficult to discover and enforce, the LNC is bound ethically to adhere to any contract he or she signs. The wise LNC should ask for references of other nurses working through the broker and inquire about the amount of work referred and payment practices.

Some companies do not broker experts but merely function as middleman advertisers. They collect a fee for their service from both the expert and the attorney. The expert pays an annual membership fee to have his or her name and other information listed in a directory or catalog with other experts. The company then advertises and sells the directory/catalog to interested attorneys. The company does not screen the experts who pay to be listed or attorneys who buy the listings. They do not become involved in any way in the relationship between an attorney and expert. The expert is not required to sign a contract to be included in the directory/catalog.

Malpractice Insurance for the Expert Witness

The nurse expert should consider carrying individual professional malpractice insurance which includes errors and omissions coverage. The liability policy carried by the nurse's clinical practice employer does not provide coverage for work performed off the employer's premises or outside the scope of practice defined by the nurse's job description.

However remote, there is a possibility that a nurse could be sued for negligence in the performance of work as a testifying expert. This is unlikely if the nurse adheres to codes of ethics and standards of practice for LNCs, is meticulous, careful, truthful, and does not misrepresent credentials. It is thought provoking, though, to consider that the expert's clients are attorneys with expertise in litigation, and that professional negligence cases often represent years of work with large amounts of money at risk. An example of a situation that could trigger a malpractice lawsuit is the novice nurse expert for the plaintiff who called a defendant physician to discuss the case. The case was jeopardized and a lawsuit threatened, though fortunately not filed. Professional malpractice insurance for independent LNCs and testifying experts may be purchased through the American Association of Legal Nurse Consultants.

Terminating a Contract to Serve as Expert

A contract to serve as expert witness, whether in the form of a formal contract or by mutual acceptance of terms in letters of agreement, ethically commits the expert to complete the service through case conclusion by settlement or trial. On occasion, however, there are compelling reasons for which the nurse expert may and should withdraw from a case to which he or she has previously committed. (These reasons describe circumstances other than changes of opinions due to new information received about the case.) They include development of serious illness or impairment, identification of conflicts of interest not apparent during initial case screening, failure or refusal by the attorney to pay for the expert's work, or unprofessional, unethical, or abusive conduct by the attorney. All but the last are self-explanatory.

It is rare for attorneys to behave abusively toward their own expert but disrespect, dishonesty, harassment, or undue or inappropriate pressure to alter opinions are examples of conduct that should not be tolerated. Such abuse may cause bias and interfere with the expert's ability to enthusiastically represent his or her opinions on behalf of the attorney's client. (Consider that the attorney may also dismiss the expert from a case without so much as informing him or her of the decision no matter the reason.) The later in case progress, the more detrimental withdrawal may be to the case. If the expert has given a deposition, more problems are created by withdrawal than if withdrawal occurs before. Regardless of the reason, it is wise for the expert to seek counsel from experienced colleagues and his or her personal attorney before deciding to resign from a case because of problems with the case attorney.

To terminate the contract, the nurse expert should package all medical records, copies of depositions, and other materials and return them to the attorney with a letter informing the attorney of the inability to continue to assist with the case. An explanation may be provided but is not necessary. If unprofessional attorney conduct is the reason, it may be better left unsaid or reviewed by one's personal attorney before mailing. Proof of delivery of the package of materials by signature of the addressee should be returned and retained by the expert.

When the materials are received by the attorney, the nurse expert may expect to receive a call or correspondence from a disappointed or irate attorney who will have to locate, hire, and pay another expert to review the case. The case may be jeopardized if it is late in the process or the expert has been deposed, and legal deadlines are approaching. This is one reason why in certain cases it is not unusual for attorneys to name more than one expert of the same profession.

The nurse expert who terminates an expert contract must keep in mind that the attorney may still subpoena his or her appearance at trial. This is unlikely because the nurse would be considered a hostile witness, not necessarily helpful and perhaps damaging to the case. Opposing counsel may also subpoena the nurse expert.

Withdrawing from a case should obviously be undertaken with very serious consideration of potential consequences to the case, the attorney's client, and the nurse's reputation as an expert. At times it is unavoidable. If prompted by unprofessional attorney conduct, however, it should be undertaken as early in the case as possible and without hesitation. The nurse expert is cautioned to screen the attorneys for whom he or she agrees to serve as expert to avoid such unpleasant and difficult situations.

The Expert's Commitment

Agreement to serve as nurse expert in a legal case should not be undertaken lightly. It carries with it an ethical commitment to see the case through to the end, barring unforeseeable circumstances. The end may be 2 to 3 years after initial contact with the attorney. The nurse who wishes to serve as an expert should seek mentors with years of testifying experience for advice on how to handle the myriad of business decisions and dilemmas that may arise during the process.

References

Kishel, G. P. (1993). *How to Start, Run, and Stay in Business,* New York, John Wiley & Sons.

Market your expertise not your products (1996). *The Testifying Expert.* 4(2).

Medical-Legal Consulting (1993). *Seminar,* Tucson, AZ, Carondelet Management Institute.

Poynter, D. (1987). *The Expert Witness Handbook.* Santa Barbara, CA, Para Publishing.

Appendix 36.1
Time/Billing Record

Name of Client/Attorney: _____

Company/Law Firm: _____

Name of Patient/Case: _____

Date	Start-Stop	Total Hours	Rate	Activity	Final Total

Expenses: _____

_____

_____

Appendix 36.2
Sample Time Log

Case Name_____
Law Firm_____
Address_____
Phone_____ Fax_____

_____

SERVICES PERFORMED

Date	Type of Service	Time Spent

EXPENSES

Date	Type of Expense	Cost

Amount Owed Based on Time:

Amount Owed Based on Expenses:

Total Amount Owed: Date of Billing:

Appendix 36.3
Sample Fee Schedule

Fee Schedule

A $600.00 retainer is requested.
Base rate for services is $120.00/hr.

Within one to two weeks of initial receipt of records, a preliminary verbal opinion will be given. Written reports will be provided only at the express request of the attorney (or contractor).

OTHER FEES:

Literature review/bibliography:	$250
Attendance at depositions*:	$175/hr
Attendance at trial: (counted as a day rate)	$1,400/day
Acquisition of another/other experts/consultants:	$250

Travel time is billed at the hourly base rate. Travel expenses (hotel, airfare) are to be guaranteed by requesting attorney/firm prior to date in question.

*A fee of $700 for depositions is to be forwarded by the day prior to the deposition appointment. If the deposition is less than 4 hours, a refund will be made to the attorney.

Please call to discuss any questions regarding our services and/or fees.

Appendix 36.4
Legal Nurse Consultant Expert Witness

Fee Schedule

Work to be performed:
Research, review of charts and depositions, oral and written reports, depositions, trial preparation, travel, court testimony.

Fees:
$125/hour to $850/8 hour day maximum for work in_____
$125/hour plus expenses* for work outside of_____

*Expenses:
Actual expenses reasonably and necessarily incurred including travel, food, lodg-ing, long distance phone charges, photocopy charges at $.10/page, other costs as required (trial exhibits, etc.)

Travel:
First Class air travel or Business Class when available.

Terms:
— Billed monthly and payable net 30 days from date of invoice. An interest charge of 1.5% per month will be charged to any balance outstanding after 30 days of invoice date.
— New accounts shall be initiated with an advance payment of $375.00.
— All travel expenses shall be paid in advance.
— Fees for depositions shall be paid at time of deposition based on the anticipated length of the examination. If deposition time is longer than the anticipated length of the examination, any balance due shall be paid within 5 days receipt of the invoice in accordance with CCP 2034(i)(2).
— Fees for trials shall be paid in advance: minimum one and one half days for out of town (out of town: greater than 100 miles from_____).
— Time reserved for out of town depositions/trials will be charged unless a 48 hour cancellation notice is given.

*Payment shall be made to:*_____*(SS #*_____*)*

Appendix 36.5
Fees for Services

Payment Policy:

Nurse Expert provides attorneys with invoices periodically during a case, detailing the services provided, the time spent at each task, and any expenses incurred. Please note that expert/consultant contracts directly with attorney for services, rather than with the attorney's client whom the services are intended to benefit. Since expert/consultant has no direct or contractual relationship with attorney's clients, expert/consultant expects and appreciates prompt payment from attorney in response to invoices. Thank you for your cooperation. Should you have any questions concerning this policy or would like to make a different arrangement, please feel free to call.

Consultative Services:

- $85.00/hour for all services except,
- $25.00/hour for tasks such as organization and page numbering of medical records, typing reports, preparation of research notebooks, photocopying, etc.
- Expenses for photocopying, notebooks, library searches, parking, and long distance calls.

Expert Services:

- $350.00 retainer
- $85.00/hour for all services except,
- $25.00/hour for tasks such as organization and page numbering of medical records, typing reports, preparation of research notebooks, photocopying, etc.
- $175.00/hour for deposition or trial testimony time
- Expenses for photocopying, notebooks, library searches, parking, and long distance calls.

Life Care Planning Services:

- $1,000.00 retainer
- $85.00/hour for production of life-care plan
- $175.00/hour for deposition or trial testimony time
- Referral to qualified economist available on request at no charge
- Expenses for photocopying, notebooks, library searches, parking, and long-distance calls.

Out-of-Town Work:

- Hourly rate from port to port minus personal and sleep time.
- Hourly rate for actual work time or meeting time with attorney while at destination.
- $175.00/hour for deposition or trial testimony time
- Expenses while out of town with receipts provided include hotel, meals, airfare, parking fees, transportation to and from airport and within city, $.30/mile to drive personal car.

Location of Qualified Expert:

- $350.00 Information provided about the expert includes CV, review and testimony history, hourly rate or fees, and willingness to testify if case has merit.

Terms and Conditions:

Payment due within 60 days of receipt of invoice. Past due accounts are subject to a service charge of 1.5% per month.

Appendix 36.6
Sample Invoice

[LETTERHEAD]

DATE: 01/12/96

TO: Mr. John Smith
         Attorney at Law

FROM: Mary Jones, RN, MSN
         (S.S.#: 555-55-5555)

RE: Jane Doe V. Community Hospital

TIME (in hours)	SERVICES
6.50	Medical records review
3.00	Library research
4.50	Literature review and highlight
0.00	Telephone conference: Mr. Smith 1/5/96
0.75	Telephone conference: Mr. Smith 1/9/96

14.75 = Hourly rate @ $85/hour = $1253.75

EXPENSES:
7.50   Photocopies (75 @ $ .10/page)
TOTAL EXPENSES = 7.50

TOTAL BALANCE DUE = $1261.25

TERMS AND CONDITIONS: Balance due within 60 days. Past due accounts are subject to a service charge of 1.5% per month.

Appendix 36.7
Sample Letter Issued for Nonpayment
(sent by certified mail)

June 22, 1994

Burton R. Sands
Attorney at Law
201 North Cat Road
Clearwater, Florida 34625

Re: *Smith v. Doggins and Lizard Medical Center*

Dear Mr. Sands:

It has come to my attention that payment for my services in the above-referenced case is six months past due. I have sent notices requesting payment every month in an attempt to collect this debt. I have also left three phone messages for you which have gone unanswered.

Unfortunately, I find it is necessary to take further action. If payment for the attached invoice is not received within 10 working days, it will be necessary for this office to file a complaint with the State Bar Association and to file suit in small claims court.

If you have any questions or would like to discuss this further, please call. Otherwise I will expect to receive payment within 10 days.

Very truly yours,

Liz Vacer, RN, MSN

Appendix 36.8
Sample Contract between Attorney and Expert

THIS AGREEMENT, Made and entered into this _____, by and between _____, an attorney-at-law ("Attorney"), and _____, an expert witness ("Expert");

WHEREAS, Attorney desires to retain the professional services of Expert for the purposes of research, preparation and, if necessary, testimony in court or before an administrative board, of matters involving medical matters in the case of _____.

IT IS AGREED TO BY THE PARTIES AS FOLLOWS:

1.   Attorney hereby retains Expert to research, prepare, and, if necessary, testify regarding medical matters in said case and that the fee for research and preparation will range from $_____ to $_____, with a typical fee being $_____. Expert agrees not to charge more than $_____, for research and analysis without prior approval.

2.   Attorney agrees to pay Expert a fee of $_____ as a retainer for such services with the retainer to be applied toward total fee charged. The parties agree that no refund of the retainer will be made by Expert under any circumstances.

3.   In addition to the fee for research and preparation, Attorney agrees to pay $_____ per hour for preparation time, waiting time, and for depositions and/or testifying in court or before any administrative board, and $_____ per hour for travel time. If the beginning and ending time of the deposition and/or trial testimony are not specified, four hours will be reserved and the minimum fee will be $_____.

4.   It is agreed that if the case is settled, dismissed, or results in a mistrial prior to Expert's testifying or giving deposition, Expert shall be compensated for the per diem charges including travel time to and time spent waiting in Court or elsewhere waiting to testify or give deposition. Attorney agrees to pay Expert a scheduling fee of $200.00 for any deposition or trial canceled with 72 hours of the scheduled start of such deposition or trial.

5.   It is agreed that if more than one year passes from the date of submission of the report outlining the results of the research to the time of any testimony or deposition, Attorney will pay Expert an additional fee of one-third of the initial fee for research and preparation for an update of the analysis.

6.   Attorney agrees to accept the sole judgment of Expert as to the necessary and actual time spent in connection with the above.

7.   In the event of a retrial or appeal, if Expert's testimony is required again, an additional fee of one-third of the fee for research and preparation will be charged, in addition to the fee for travel and waiting time for testimony, and expenses.

8.   Attorney agrees to render payment to Expert within 60 days of receipt of the statement regarding such payment.

_____

Attorney

_____

Expert

Section X

The Legal Nurse Consultant's Role in the Insurance Industry

Chapter 37

The Role of the Legal Nurse Consultant in the Insurance Industry

Melanie Logenhagen

Contents

1-57444-123-X/98
© 1998 by American Association of Legal Nurse Consultants

Objectives

- To identify several different types of insurance products within the industry
- To state the requirements for employment of the LNC in the insurance industry
- To identify several professional organizations with which an LNC may be affiliated
- To identify the various roles and functions of the nurse consultant
- To define some of the available credentials that are beneficial to the nurse consultant

Introduction to Insurance Products and Lines of Business

Insurance is defined as a contract by which the insurance company (insurer) promises to pay a sum of money or give something of value to another (to either the insured or the beneficiary) in the event that the insured is injured, dies, or sustains damage as a result of particular, stated contingencies (Clarkson et al., 1992).

While there are different types of insurance products currently in existence, this chapter will focus on the those that benefit most from the contribution of the legal nurse consultant (LNC). The roles for the LNC described in this chapter are not specific to any one type of insurance product or practice, however. In fact, it is important to note that the roles described may be utilized in any number of insurance products or settings. It is the organizational structure, market, and the administrative requirements of the product that will determine the job function and role of the LNC. The following is a brief overview of the major categories of insurance products with which an LNC may be affiliated.

Accident and Health

This type of coverage provides medical benefits for illness and injury to a policyholder as described in the contract at the time of purchase. The insured is the policyholder and can either be a group or an individual. It is frequently a group with whom the insurer contracts (as is often the case with health coverage). The insurer's main duty is to the group, not the individual employee who is a member of the group. Each policy varies according to the amount of the deductible, maximum coverage, and types of illness/injuries not covered. Limits or caps are set on these types of policies and certain criteria or conditions must be met before benefits are paid. In the case of an accident policy, a causal relationship between the occurrence and injury must be shown. It must be proved that the occurrence was, in fact, an accident before any benefits are paid. In the case of health coverage, certain conditions may be excluded, or coverage may be withheld if the required preauthorizations or clearances are not first obtained by the providers involved, as in the case of HMO or PPO coverage. This is a growing market for the LNC, especially with the advent of a managed care marketplace. There is a greater-than-ever emphasis on cost and quality assurance, both of which require a sound knowledge and understanding of the health care delivery system, how it functions, and how charges and contracts are recognized.

Workers' Compensation

The basic principle underlying all state workers' compensation acts is to provide medical and wage benefits to the worker injured in the course and scope of his or her employment. When an employee is injured on the job, the case falls under the jurisdiction of the workers' compensation statute of the state in which the injured employee resides. In many states, catastrophic injuries such as spinal cord or head injuries, severe burns, amputations, or loss of sight require the injured person to have lifetime medical care and ongoing management of that care. This alone makes workers' compensation an important insurance arena for the LNC and one of the most common current areas of practice. It is important to realize that state laws differ in this area of practice and LNCs need to know and understand the laws for the state(s) in which they practice. Information about the specific benefits available under the state's Workers' Compensation Act are available by contacting the Workers' Compensation Commission in the state capital. A brief overview of the statutes is also printed by the National Chamber of Commerce.

Each state and the federal government has its own workers' compensation system. The process is as follows.

1. A job-related injury or illness occurs.
2. The employee reports the injury or illness to the employer who notifies the company's claim department or insurance representative.
3. The claims representative determines if the situation reported is compensable under the law, notifies all parties of the status of compensability, and adjudicates the claim.
4. The claim is monitored and bills are paid.

There are often disagreements between the injured worker and the insurance company as to what should be paid by the insurance carrier. When this occurs, a formal document requesting a hearing is filed with the industrial commission or industrial board that has jurisdiction over the decision. The commission is the state-appointed official who reviews every workers' compensation claim and evaluates whether or not there is a claim. A commissioner presides at a hearing and makes a ruling after the evidence from both parties is submitted. Once the claim has been accepted as a work-related injury or illness, all parties involved in the case, such as lawyers, physicians, other health care providers, must file reports to keep the commission informed of progress or lack of progress on the case. The file can be closed when the injured worker returns to work, the benefits end, or a settlement occurs.

Automobile/General Liability

This is coverage for motor vehicles and damage or liability that may occur resulting in personal injuries or property damage from the operation of an automobile. The insured is the policyholder and any other members under the policy. The claimant is the injured party. (The insured may also be an injured party and claimant.) The policy may cover damage to automobiles resulting from specific episodes or hazards and often has a monetary limit to expenses. When that monetary limit has been reached, the limit will not be exceeded. In addition, an individual may purchase "umbrella" coverage which provides additional coverage above the liability limits set forth in the original policy.

There are two categories of motor vehicle coverage: collision and comprehensive. Collision provides for coverage in the event of damage resulting from vehicular impact. Comprehensive insurance covers losses, damage, and destruction by fire, vandalism, theft, and acts of God (hail, hurricanes, trees falling onto cars, etc.). (These do not concern the LNC as they do not involve medical payments.) In addition, automobile policies may provide for the coverage of uninsured motorists, accidental death benefits, medical payment coverage, or other driver coverage (also known as an omnibus clause) which protects the vehicle's owner in the event a second or third party drives the car with permission of the owner. Automobile and liability coverage have long been practice environments for the LNC. Insurance adjusters frequently require review and analysis of the medical injuries sustained in a motor vehicle accident or under a liability policy. The LNC will often be called upon to determine the relationship of the accident to the injury and to assist in evaluating the severity and permanency of the injury in preparation for settlement or trial defense.

To determine if there is a plausible causal connection between the injury and the events associated with the accident, the LNC may be asked to research the medical literature to provide information to answer such questions as

1. Can new-onset diabetes occur as a result of head trauma?
2. Can new-onset multiple sclerosis occur as a result of trauma?
3. Can trauma aggravate preexisting degenerative changes in the spinal column?
4. How long does it take for a disk to herniate after trauma?
5. Can a preexisting cardiac arrhythmia worsen as a result of a chest injury from hitting a steering wheel?
6. Can the loss of a first trimester pregnancy occur as a result of a slip and fall?
7. Can panic disorder result in a mitral valve prolapse?
8. Can a closed head injury occur even if there is only minor damage to a car?

The LNC contributes a thorough and objective analysis of available literature which is particularly essential when claims are suspected of being fraudulent. Inadvertent payment of fraudulent claims increases the cost of insurance for all insureds.

Disability Insurance

A disability policy generally provides benefits for a covered member who is usually wholly and continuously disabled from performing an occupation he or she might ordinarily be capable of performing. An insured does not have benefits withheld if able to perform some tasks or another type of job, as it is often stipulated that the insured's activity must be related to the occupation ordinarily performed. Often the insured must be disabled in such a way that he is confined to his immediate premises (substantial not permanent confinement). Policies will specify the types of disabilities covered and not covered. Limits for coverage are set initially and coverage is generally capped at those limits set.

Malpractice (Professional Liability)

Malpractice insurance protects policyholders from malpractice claims brought against them by their patients or clients. Most often, this insurance is obtained by professionals in the following lines of work: dentists, physicians, nurses, attorneys, architects, or engineers. Any professional who is licensed to practice needs this type of insurance coverage. LNCs are vital to this area of insurance to assist the carrier in determining whether or not a deviation of a standard of care has occurred or whether or not there was performance outside of the licensed scope of practice. Detailed information on the role of the LNC in malpractice cases is provided elsewhere in this text.

Business Organization and Structure

Employee Requirements

LNCs working in the insurance industry represent a wide variety of clinical nursing specialties. Specialty clinical backgrounds in areas, such as neonatal, psychiatric, home health, emergency, rehabilitation, or critical care, provide excellent training and resource for insurance work. In the workers' compensation field, it is common to find rehabilitation, neurology, or orthopedic nurses, as a majority of workers' compensation injuries fall into one of these categories. Nurses from such specialties as operating room nursing, infectious disease, oncology, and gerontology are in increasing demand because of the social and demographic shifts in the population which generate an increasing number of issues and claims in those areas. Nurses with managerial experience or a broad experiential background are also effective LNCs in this setting; the ability to interpret a wide range of policies and procedures is a useful adjunct for insurance work. Nurses use their clinical backgrounds as a resource for understanding, identifying, and addressing a particular condition or situation, and often provide immediate interpretation and analysis of complex medical information.

Creative problem-solving skills are essential. The LNC should be a self-starter who is capable of working with little supervision. Analytical detective skills are useful in sifting through the medical facts of the case. Essential members of the insurance provider's team, LNCs with specific backgrounds are often sought because of specialty areas the carrier may frequently cover or insure. Health insurance carriers may have case management programs in place. Such programs identify and specialize in monitoring and reviewing treatment for a specific patient population with a given diagnosis. Currently, the most prevalent types of disease management programs are in the areas of orthopedics (hip and knee replacements), infectious disease (AIDS), cardiopulmonary disorders (asthma and congestive heart failure), and endocrine disorders (diabetes). Clinical specialty certifications in a given field are not essential for positions. It is generally considered sufficient to have several years of practice experience working with the target population. Continuing education in the specialty is most always viewed favorably and adds to one's professionalism and expertise. Some LNCs are employed to do basic medical interpretation and summarize occurrences. Most are utilized more effectively to perform detailed audits, analyses, and client management functions.

In addition to the clinical expertise required for a position, a minimum of 2 to 5 years of experience in that field may been specified, particularly if the type of insurance product is specialized. A current license for the state in which the office is located is required, but the LNC need not be licensed in states in which a case is being reviewed unless it is part of the job requirement that actual nursing care be rendered. Often the LNC will review a course of medical treatment or consider a request for coverage or services on a file when events have occurred in another state. These policy and insurance coverage issues can currently be addressed without the need of the LNC being licensed in the state in which the incident occurred.

Business Practices and Professional Relationships

Since most insurance carriers sell nationwide, LNCs working within an insurance company may be based in a regional local or corporate office or may work with an attorney who does insurance work. They may function primarily as health care professionals, claim specialists, case managers, benefit analysts, or in a position that combines any or all of these roles. The common denominator of all these roles is the overall goal to maximize the outcome and reduce the risk to the carrier.

The LNC's first responsibility is to be ethical and objective. The LNC is obligated to investigate and evaluate the claim properly and to inform the carrier fully of the pros and cons of the case. The insurance company's responsibility is to compensate claimants and insureds for damages covered by an insured event. It is not uncommon for the LNC to be a claimant advocate on one case, then come to the defense of the insurance company on another case. Most often, the LNC must mediate and negotiate among the claimant or patient, the health care provider, and the policyholder or group purchasing the insurance coverage. The focus of the LNC's work is to provide objective clinical analysis, interpretation, and education.

LNCs in the insurance industry often work directly with more nonclinical persons than medical or peer professionals. Terminology and attitudes common to the medical setting may not be (and are often not) appropriate for the insurance company setting. Complex clinical information and medical terminology must be "translated" into layman's terms so they may be understood by those required to do so. LNCs may go through an adjustment upon entering the unfamiliar insurance/business setting with few, if any, LNC colleagues. It is helpful to recognize that the insurance company consists of teams of individuals, just as is true in health care settings. The LNC must learn who the members of the team are and their responsibilities. The other members of the team must identify how the LNC can contribute to the work and goals of the team.

The LNC may be working with different product lines within the same company as many insurance companies have a mixed "book of business." This means that they sell and administer more than one type of insurance product at the same office location. Frequently, the offices are separated, or the office plan is laid out and structured by product line or department. Each product has its own requirements and restrictions that are product specific. In a large insurance company there may be several LNCs hired for each product line and the LNC may only work in one particular department or product division and not "cross lines." If a company is small or has limited resources, the LNC's role is usually more universal and less product specific.

Assignments may come from any number of sources. The LNC may be assigned the case from any of the following:

- The office manager who oversees the claim work flow
- The insurance adjuster for the case
- In-house counsel
- An independent case management firm

Assignments may vary in length and intensity. The level of knowledge of the individuals making the assignments may also vary. The effective LNC will educate the individuals about the role of the LNC, will anticipate the needs of the case, and will provide consistent follow-through. "Typical" types of assignments the LNC encounters are outlined in the next section.

The Roles of the Legal Nurse Consultant

The LNC has emerged as a vital actor in the insurance arena. Today, nurses often oversee the entire operational aspects of insurance medical divisions. The focus on managed care demands a thorough understanding of the various health care delivery systems. This is unique knowledge acquired through clinical and business practice. This combination allows the LNC to capitalize on the growing demand for interpretation, analysis, and management of the processes of establishing liability, coverage, appropriateness, standardization, and accountability of the medical community. Given the many different types of insurance in existence, a wide variety of opportunities exists for the LNC to apply nursing practice knowledge and skills to serve both insureds and insurers.

Claims Consultant/Adjuster

The primary responsibilities of the LNC as a claims consultant/adjuster are to investigate, evaluate, and negotiate (Kay, 1994). This includes investigating potential as well as actual claims, negotiating settlements directly with the claimant or attorney, and participating in mediation on behalf of clients. The LNC may also audit files for claim activity and monitor trials in addition to assisting defense counsel in discovery responses (Kay, 1994). Claims are investigated and evaluated by adjusters to determine their worth or merit and possible potential exposure for which a monetary reserve must be set (the process of assigning a dollar amount to the claim). Often adjusters work directly with attorneys and representatives in preparation of a settlement package that is appropriate based on their findings. They monitor the activities of the attorneys involved to make sure payment amounts are not exceeded.

Currently, many insurance adjusters have business backgrounds, but little or no medical background or experience. The LNC's clinical nursing background is a distinct asset. The LNC functions as evaluator, mediator, negotiator, consultant, and technical analyst. In most states, according to Kay, adjusters are required to pass an examination to obtain a license which is renewed every 2 years. Some states require additional continuing education credits.

Case Manager

Case management in the insurance company is primarily a service that assists clients (groups, insurers, and providers) in obtaining maximization of services and available resources and contain costs through ongoing coordination and evaluation, to assure appropriate outcome. Maximizing outcomes while containing costs is the primary goal of case management. The case manager assumes responsibility for identifying needs, planning, arranging service delivery, and monitoring service provision and outcomes (Boling, 1990). In this position, the LNC may initially meet the patient in the home for an on-site visit. The LNC evaluates the nature of the patient's clinical condition, inspects the condition of the home setting in preparation for initiation of services in order to assure that accommodations are adequate, and directly monitors and evaluates the patient's progress. Communication with health care providers such as physicians, home care companies, nursing agencies, medical equipment or infusion companies may be required. In addition, if a patient requires placement in a facility, the case manager authorizes and coordinates this admission.

The nurse case manager is a role that has emerged as a result of managed care. It has been described as the bottom-line management care delivery model that positively affects patient outcomes (patient satisfaction and achieved care), caregiver outcomes (job satisfaction), and systems outcomes (cost and productivity) (Noonan, 1996). Cost analysis, reimbursement directives, coverage provisions, and client satisfaction are constantly addressed by the case manager. These activities are frequently driven by the need for insurance companies to maximize the benefit of dollars spent on clients while keeping overall health care costs to a minimum. This is the principle behind managed care.

Overall, this position requires in-depth knowledge of the health care delivery system. It also requires the ability to match needs to resources and delivery settings, and a thorough understanding of the levels of care and intensities of service of different providers. Insurance companies generally seek nurses with several years of clinical experience in a hospital setting in addition to recent experience in home care, infusion, medical equipment management, discharge planning, or skilled facility/subacute care. A minimum of a CCM (certification in case management) is more frequently being requested by insurance employers.

Benefits Coordinator

The position of benefit coordinator primarily centers around understanding, interpreting, analyzing, and calculating an insured's benefits and making sure that (particularly in the case of a catastrophic illness) the needs match the resources (benefits) available. This position investigates the origins, conditions for, and risks associated with coverage for a group. The LNC will interface with the rating, underwriting, and marketing departments in order to establish the performance reliability and stability of an insured group. When a clinical condition of a group member is being evaluated, the LNC may seek out a medical management area or physician (usually employed full-time or as a consultant to the insurance company) for interpretation of a medical provision written into the benefit. While this position is similar to that of a case manager in matching needs to resources, it differs in that its primary focus is on the benefits rather than on the clinical condition of the patient.

In this role, greater emphasis and consideration is given to the nature of the insurance product or policy held by the insured person, the type of employer group (large group, small group), and how they are rated. Rating is based on how their premiums are calculated: are their premiums based on their own experience or is their rating pooled with other small like employers into a community type of rating? In the case of a costly or catastrophic occurrence, the group will often be contacted and informed of the nature of the episode and that there may be a direct impact upon its premiums. The group may then request that some type of extension or exception to the policy be made in order to accommodate the patient's needs (the member) while also meeting the needs of the other client (the group that purchased the coverage for the individual member).

It is then up to the benefit coordinator to identify or create a cost-effective alternative, cost out the impact (in premium dollars) to the group, and obtain its approval to the plan in the form of an additional contract or addendum to the original policy. The permission of the policyholder may also need to be obtained in order to implement the proposed plan. Any discrepancies (between the group, the policyholder, and the carrier) are negotiated. The group usually has the final say about whether the costs or savings belong directly to it. The benefit coordinator will then ensure contracts are maintained, current and accurate for the duration of the case. Frequent interfacing with the attending physician, health care providers, client and family is customary in this type of situation. In addition, the benefit coordinator will interface with the claims area in order to provide direction for claim payment in the event an exception has been arranged to make sure that charges are addressed and covered appropriately. At times, this position is incorporated into case management or claims work in a work setting. There is no special license or certification for this type of position. A background in clinical services, contracts, claims services, or case management is often sufficient.

Workers' Compensation Manager

The legal nurse consulting in the workers' compensation setting often parallels the efforts of the case manager in that the main aspects of this position focus around coordinating, implementing, and evaluating care and outcomes in order to make sure the claimant's needs are met and the goals are achieved. In the workers' compensation arena, the goal is often to get the patient back to work and this goal is frequently met. Some of the injuries or conditions dealt with in workers' compensation are difficult to manage as they focus on very subjective complaints such as pain and restriction of movement. The law and rules that guide this coverage are very strict and fairly clear. The focus is always on safety as well as minimization or management of a disability. The benefits are mandatory and defined by law, leaving less room for interpretation and possible misinterpretation.

In workers' compensation, the employer has virtually no financial obligation to a claim (no copay, no deductible, no premium sharing), which does not provide incentive for cost containment. Employer premiums are based on specific job class code insurance rates and on 3 years of loss experience information for that position. Traditionally, workers' compensation providers are reimbursed on a fee-for-service basis and fee schedules are relatively easy to circumvent. Workers' compensation is a very challenging arena that has long been a field fraught with abuse, fraud, and malingering. Because of the nature of the benefits provided, mandatory for employers to support, many individuals have falsified claims in order to be paid while not working. With the advent of managed care in the workers' compensation, this type of activity cannot easily be sustained and has diminished. There are now far too many checks and balances in the managed care system to allow for unjustified appropriation of health care resources.

Insurance companies seek nurses with experience in negotiating, claim analysis, and understanding of the compensation system. With the growth of managed care, it is possible to obtain a position with some prior managed care experience and little or no compensation background. It is not uncommon for the LNC in this role to be involved in performing on-site audits of providers to assure care billed for was in fact rendered. The LNC audits providers by surveying the medical records. Rate evaluations, negotiation of claim charges, and attending IMEs (independent medical examinations) are some of the more common activities for the LNC in this field. It may also be necessary for the LNC to perform an ergonomic evaluation of the work setting. The work site, job function, and its physical requirements are evaluated to determine if and when the client can return to work, and, if so, what if any accommodations or restrictions must be made. A vocational rehabilitation specialist may be consulted. It is then the responsibility of the LNC to convey this information to the employer and assure that the work site or job function is modified in such a way that the client may return to work. This area of practice also requires a good understanding of federal statutes and regulations such as COBRA (Consolidated Omnibus Reconciliation Act), FMLA (Family and Medical Leave Act), and the ADA (Americans with Disabilities Act).

Medical Policy Coordinator

In this position, the LNC functions as the individual who identifies a need and assists in formulating and maintaining a medical policy. This position is very different from others mentioned in this chapter. The LNC performs a primarily research and investigative function. Depending on the nature of a company's insurance benefits and the guidelines used for establishing what is or is not covered under a policy, the medical policy coordinator may often evaluate FDA guidelines. The LNC may also be in direct contact with a research group to obtain information on a particular study in progress or recently obtained outcome. Other well-established entities such as the NIH (National Institutes of Health), AHCPR (Agency for Health Care Policy and Research, a division of the Public Health Service), or other governing bodies may be frequent sources of information for writing medical policy. Medical literature searches are conducted to obtain current information on a particular topic.

The medical policy coordinator may research and write on a variety of topics, such as

- Whether or not a certain operative procedure should be covered
- Whether a procedure is performed for medical or cosmetic reasons
- Whether or not to approve non-FDA-approved items
- Whether or not certain pieces of equipment are covered
- Whether or not certain services or products are covered

The coordinator may create new medical policies or evaluate, revise, restructure, or adapt existing policies periodically, as needed, or upon request. Requests may come from a variety of sources, including medical staff, claims or underwriting staff, policyholders, or groups wanting clarification of coverage issues. The coordinator also assists in maintaining the policy manual for the division or company. A policy coordinator is often part of a team which may consist of

- A person who is able to analyze and interpret benefits (a benefit coordinator or marketing representative)
- A medical director or physician advisor to address application or clinical issues
- An attorney to assure that policies are in accordance with the product or company guidelines for operation
- A person proficient in the actual writing of policy documents

The role of the medical policy coordinator incorporates knowledge of benefits and coverage, clinical indications, the ability to interpret medical data and guidelines, and basic research and writing skills. There is no required license or certification for this type of position.

Utilization Review Coordinator

The primary role of the utilization review nurse is to evaluate the need for and appropriateness of benefits use of the individual member. This position is sometimes referred to as the "gatekeeper" or "insurance policeman." The primary responsibility of the utilization review coordinator is to assure that the applicable benefits policies or clinical guidelines that are employed by the carrier are being followed. The reviewer primarily deals with the medical provider of the service being reviewed. Reviews may be on-site (in the hospital or office setting) or over the phone. It is during the review process that decision criteria are applied and the reviewer makes a determination of medical appropriateness and whether or not to approve a service, item, or procedure.

Established bodies of principles and clinical guidelines are utilized to implement this evaluation and decision-making process. Resources such as IntenQual guidelines or Opti-Med criteria are common resources. These products provide questions and guidelines for decision making for implementing medical qualifications for needed procedures or services. In the case of patients who need to be hospitalized, often a "length of stay" is assigned with each review. For example, a knee or hip replacement may be authorized for a patient for a 3-day hospital stay with a follow-up or concurrent review needed on the third hospital day. The reviewer would then perform subsequent review(s) until the patient is discharged or the stay (in part or total) is denied for lack of medical appropriateness. This process usually provides for a right to appeal on the part of the provider. Often a medical panel or director is available to address unique or individual exceptions.

Currently, there is no license or certification required for this position. Insurance companies usually seek registered nurses with at least 2 to 3 years of current hospital experience and prefer a nurse with some background in either insurance or hospital utilization. This position frequently interfaces with the insurance company's medical staff, the patient's physician, or other health care providers.

As a nurse, the utilization review coordinator is a patient advocate. However, he or she is also expected to adhere to cost-containment goals of the company. The dichotomy may result in conflict. Because it involves denying payment for services rendered, the LNC in this role is often on the frontlines and must be able to handle a great deal of confrontation and scrutiny. The LNC must think clearly, analyze well, and apply criteria and guidelines via interpretation and review. In the event an unfavorable determination is rendered, the LNC will likely be asked to defend the decision. Therefore, decisions should always be carefully considered and based on the clinical information, provided by telephone from the provider representative or obtained directly from the medical chart (if on-site).

Risk Manager

The insurance company risk manager focuses on loss prevention and minimizing claim damages through creation of loss prevention initiatives, education, and counseling of insured health care professionals on how to prevent occurrences. The role of the risk management representative involves such duties as counseling, public speaking or performing practice assessments, telephone consultations with licensed medical professionals, and consulting with claim representatives or underwriters. In addition, the risk manager may develop educational programs or work in the publication of company educational literature. The role has a strong preventive and proactive focus.

This position requires a thorough understanding of professional and health law. Sometimes there is specialization among risk managers. Some focus on hospital risk management, while others concentrate on specific groups of professionals. In this position the LNC works as researcher, educator, and clinical analyst. The majority of nurse consultants in this position have dual degrees (RN, JD, MS, MD). Most companies require a higher level of education, as well as strong clinical and risk management experience.

Medical Malpractice (Liability) Consultant

The field of medical liability is one of the largest in which LNCs practice within the insurance industry. Most of the medical malpractice cases handled by the LNC involve one or more of the following issues:

- Delay in treatment or diagnosis
- Failure to treat properly
- Improper medical or surgical procedures
- Informed consent
- Medication error or side effect

In the malpractice insurance area, the LNC works with the claims personnel, physician reviewers, and often directly with the legal department. With a new case, the initial goal is to ascertain as quickly and as cost-effectively as possible whether or not the case is defensible. The LNC is often involved from the very beginning of a case assisting the insurance carrier or attorney with any or all of the following activities:

- Requesting review and/or client interview
- Completing medical history
- Obtaining necessary medical records
- Organizing, reviewing, and analyzing medical records
- Relaying results to the attorney (written or oral report)
- Assisting with identification of expert witnesses
- Assisting with any required clinical research

The LNC's services are invaluable during the initial screening process. A committee or similar entity within the insurance company, usually composed of claims, legal, underwriting, and executive staff, reviews cases and determines whether to settle or defend the case often based substantially on the analysis and recommendation of the LNC. If a case is correctly determined to be not worth defending, both time and money are saved in the short- and long-term for the insurance carrier, attorney, and any other parties involved. With experience, the LNC becomes very proficient in case screening and thereby more valuable to the insurance company and legal staff.

If a case is deemed worth defending, the LNC continues to perform any or all of the above-listed services as assigned, but in much more depth and detail. In addition to these activities, the LNC may aid in the deposition process by providing the attorney with information and questions to address, and may attend depositions. The LNC's expertise helps the attorney focus on what is technically and medically pertinent to a case while avoiding time spent on useless or irrelevant information.

In addition to casework on medical malpractice cases, the LNC may work directly with the carrier's medical review board or medical performance panel in the investigation phase of a claim. The LNC may be asked to research similar cases or obtain and prepare the medical record and other pertinent documents related to the issues presented in the claim for board review.

While there is no specific training or certification required to do this type of work, the attorney or carrier most often seeks solid clinical expertise and the ability to analyze and organize material thoroughly, effectively, and efficiently. The LNC must possess excellent organizational skills and be very detail oriented.

Summary

The insurance industry provides the LNC with many opportunities for professional practice, growth, and development. While some of the more highly specialized areas such as workers' compensation and risk management are a bit more difficult for the novice LNC, other areas such as utilization review, case management, and claims adjustment experience periodic growth spurts which provide opportunity for the LNC to gain entrée into insurance work. This field of work exposes the LNC to many areas of medical practice and medical/legal analysis with significant impact on the parties served. The nature of the work forces LNCs to broaden their scope of practice and thinking beyond the traditional "nurse–patient relationship." The critical thinking and problem-solving process required in the nursing profession provides a natural foundation for the LNC's practice within the insurance industry. It is almost always the LNC's health care background that the employer is seeking when hiring an LNC. During the process of mutual exchange of information between the LNC and insurance professionals, the LNC acquires the knowledge necessary to build a specialty career in the industry.

Credentials and Certifications

There are several credentials available to the LNC working in the insurance field. While none is required, obtaining specialty certification demonstrates mastery of pertinent bodies of knowledge. The more-seasoned LNC working in the insurance industry has obtained some or all of the following during the course of his or her work experience.

- CDMS: Certified Disability Management Specialist (formerly CIRS: Certified Insurance Rehabilitation Specialist)

This is a nonprofessional certificate obtained by passing an examination. Proof of 2 years of experience working with the disabled population within the disability compensation system is a requirement to be eligible for taking the exam which is offered to many professional disciplines.

- CRRN: Certified Registered Rehabilitation Nurse

This is a professional certification offered by the Association of Rehabilitation Nurses only to registered nurses. The certificate is obtained by proving two years of experience working in rehabilitation and passing the examination.

- CRC: Certified Rehabilitation Counselor

This is a professional certificate obtained by proving work experience and passing an examination. The certificate is available to master's-level rehabilitation counselors.

■ CCM: Certified Case Manager

This is a professional certification obtained by proving 2 or more years experience in case management in any number of settings (insurance, hospital, home care, etc.). Several types of professionals in addition to registered nurse, such as rehabilitation therapists and social workers, may be eligible for this certification.

Professional Organizations and Associations

The following organizations are listed to provide the reader additional resources for further information about the insurance environment. These are some of the more common organizations to which LNCs working in the insurance industry may belong. In addition, the LNC may join local and state claim associations. Attending meetings offers an excellent opportunity to learn more about the different jobs and possibilities for LNC work.

NARPS: National Association of Rehabilitation Professionals in the Private Sector, RO. 697, Brookline, MA 02146 (this organization also has local chapters).

ARN: Association of Rehabilitation Nurses, 4700 Glenview, IL. (this organization also has local chapters).

CMSA: Case Management Society of America, 8201 Cantrell Road, Suite 230, Little Rock, AR 72227

RIMS: Risk and Insurance Management Society, Inc., 205 East 42nd St., New York, NY 10017 (composed of risk managers for thousands of self-insured and insured companies).

Discussion Questions

1. Which of the following is the underlying principle of workers' compensation coverage?
   a. An illness or injury is job related
   b. It is a type of liability of coverage obtained by professionals for work-related claims
   c. It provides benefits for a member who is usually wholly and continuously disabled
2. Insurance is defined as:
   a. A contract for the provision of coverage for services, injuries, or damages as set forth in the contract
   b. A request to the carrier for payment of benefits
   c. The quantifying of an insured's or group's activity
3. Experience refers to
   a. The type of coverage an insurer may sell or handle
   b. The past performance history of injuries or accidents
   c. The analysis done for accepting risk

4. CCM, CRC, CRRN, CIRS are
   a. Insurance coverage codes
   b. Professional organizations
   c. Professional certifications
5. The LNC insurance role that most frequently deals with review of clinical activities for medical necessity and appropriateness is
   a. Case management
   b. Risk management
   c. Claim adjuster
   d. Utilization review
6. The method for comparison of like charges is referred to as
   a. Usual, reasonable, and customary
   b. Rating
   c. Utilization review
7. The insurance role that most frequently deals with reducing claim frequency and severity through education is
   a. Claim adjuster
   b. Case management
   c. Risk management
   d. Utilization review

Glossary

Assigned risk: A risk which underwriters do not wish to insure but which, because of state law or otherwise, must be insured. The coverage is assigned through a pool of handlers each taking turns.

Book of business: The specific type(s) of insurance products an insurance company might sell, such as 50% automobile, 40% workers' compensation, and 10% group life and health.

Carrier: The insurance company which "carries" the insurance.

Catastrophic loss: A loss of an extraordinarily large value.

Claim: A request to the carrier by the insured for payment of benefits under a policy.

Claimant: The individual receiving benefits.

Claim processor: Carrier's employee responsible for handling claims as they are received from patients and providers.

Claims consultant: Person designated to represent the insurance company in investigations and negotiations in order to reach an agreement on the amount of a loss or the insurer's liability.

Client: The purchaser of services.

Co-payment: A sharing in the cost of certain covered expenses on the part of the insured on a percentage basis.

Coverage: The assurance against losses provided under the terms of a policy of insurance. It is used synonymously with the term insurance or protection.

Deductible: A pre-set amount which each insured must pay toward the cost of treatment before benefits go into effect.

Exclusions: Noted services or conditions which the policy will not cover.

Experience: The past history of injuries or accidents which is used for substantiating the setting of a current premium amount.

Exposure: The maximum amount of money that an insurer could spend on one claim (often coincided with the policy limit).

Insurance: A contract for the provision of coverage for services, injuries, or damages as set forth in the conditions, types, and terms of the contract.

Insurer: The party agreeing to reimburse another party for loss by designated contingencies.

Liability: Any legally enforceable obligation. In insurance this usually is associated with a monetary value.

Limits: The amount the payer covers.

Premium: The amount of money paid to an insurer in return for insurance coverage.

Provider: The party providing services and supplies to the beneficiary.

Rating: The quantifying of an insured or group's activity (experience).

Reserves: The monies set aside by the insurance company for the future expenditures on a claim based on an educated projection.

Risk: The degree of likelihood that something will occur.

Underwriting: The analysis done for accepting insurance risk and determining the amount of insurance the company will write on each risk.

URC: Usual, customary, and reasonable: a method for determining benefits by comparing the charges of one provider to like charges of others in the same area and specialty.

Utilization review: A process of evaluation of health care based on medical necessity and appropriateness. It can include preadmission review, concurrent review, discharge planning, and retrospective review.

References

Biancett, S. S. and Flarey, O. L. (1996). Case management in an insurance setting: the role of the professional nurse, in *Case Studies in Nursing Case Management,* Aspen Publ., chap. 10, 151–168.

Boling, J. (1990). Case management. cm definition project, *The Case Manager,* Oct, 35–36.

Case management survey. (1993). *The Case Manager,* Oct./Nov./Dec., 48–50.

Connell, K. H. (1993). Career alternatives for the legal nurse consultant [feature column], *AALNC,* July, 6.

Eliot, F. (1992). The role of the case manager, *National Medical-Legal Journal,* 3(3), 1–7.

Feuer, L. (1996). Upgrade your clinical image by learning business skills, *Continuing Care,* Feb. 16–29.

Jarreau, C. (1993). Career alternatives for the legal nurse consultant [feature column], *AALNC,* July, 6.

Kay, D. I. (1994). Career alternatives for the legal nurse consultant [feature column], *AALNC,* July, 6–17.

Lashley, M. (1993). The hidden benefits of case management, *The Case Manager,* July/Aug/Sept., 78–79.

Medical Benefits, (1995, July 30) (12) 14, 1–12.

Nicolaysen, L. (1996). More than just UR, *Continuing Care,* March, 22–25.

Noonan, R. A. (1996). Case management to the rescue: managed care's progression from concept to reality; *Journal of Legal Nurse Consulting,* 7(1), 10–12.

Orr, M. J. (1993). Career alternatives for the legal nurse consultant [feature column], *AALNC,* Jan., 4.

Saber, M. A. (1993). Career alternatives for the legal nurse consultant [feature column], *AALNC,* Jan., 4.

Schaffer, C. (1996). Integration, contracting to change case management, *Continuing Care,* March, 14.

Sowers, R. (1993). Career alternatives for the legal nurse consultant [feature column], *AALNC,* April, 4.

Ziemba, T. M. (1995). Worker's Compensation: A Productive Field for LNCs, *National Medical-Legal Journal,* 6(4), 4.

Section XI

The Legal Nurse Consultant's Role in Health Care Risk Management

Chapter 38

The Legal Nurse Consultant's Role in Health Care Risk Management

Thomas B. Méndez

Contents

1-57444-123-X/98
© 1998 by American Association of Legal Nurse Consultants

Objectives

Upon completion of this chapter the reader will be able to:

- Define and apply the risk management process
- Discuss and apply the risk management techniques of Loss Control and Loss Prevention
- Identify at least four examples of events that should be reported
- Develop a tool for use in the monitoring of a claim or potential claim
- Discuss the role of the legal nurse consultant in the area of risk management.

Introduction

One of the most interesting roles for the legal nurse consultant (LNC) is providing services in the area of health care risk management. LNCs use the skills and knowledge gained from their training as nurses as well as their knowledge and experience in the area of management and administration. In addition, exposure to and involvement with accreditation and licensing bodies is of tremendous benefit. The LNCs knowledge of the legal process and system teamed with the other attributes presents a dynamic combination.

The role of the LNC in the area of risk management can be quite expansive based on his or her credentials and desires. Functions range from consultation and assistance in the practice of risk management for the entire facility to educating the staff and physicians regarding compliance with accreditation and licensing requirements. Involvement in the management of claims is another interesting and challenging area. The role in health care is not limited to hospitals, but ambulatory care centers, physician groups, managed care organizations, insurance brokers, insurance companies, as well as legal practices. In addition, home health care and long-term care are appropriate agencies for the LNC risk manager.

As health care is redefined and as the industry integrates and becomes more competitive, physicians, health care facilities, and health care systems are charged with managing costs associated with traditional liability exposures, as well as liabilities stemming from newly acquired managed care organizations. Patient satisfaction, provider productivity, and quality management are critical to success; therefore, health care entities must explore new ways to reduce direct and indirect liability exposures. Additionally, liability exposures increase the cost of health care in a "cost squeezed" industry.

The most obvious costs are those of defense and settlement of lawsuits. The costs may also substantially impact premium payments made to insuring organizations. Provider distraction, patient dissatisfaction, and "defensive" medicine are difficult to quantify, but have great impact on operating margins. They can be positively impacted by a viable risk management program.

A successful risk management program is subject to several factors such as an institution's commitment to such a program, the level of expertise of the individual charged with the responsibilities of risk management, and the availability of resources such as staff or computer support. In some institutions, the undesirable occurs when the risk management position is eliminated. Frequently, the individuals charged with risk management are delegated additional areas of responsibility, thus decreasing their involvement and impact with risk management. From this standpoint, the LNCs can be of great benefit to a health care organization by providing consultative services, performing risk assessments, developing programs, and providing staff education, all of which are a result of their experiences as clinicians, managers, administrators, and legal consultants.

Risk Management

Generally, nurses apply risk management principles without realizing it. We assess situations, make necessary changes, and determine if our changes worked. Ultimately, we attempt to protect the patients, their visitors, and our colleagues from harm. However, for the LNC to be effective, it is necessary that he or she have a basic knowledge of exactly what risk management is all about.

Most authors agree that there are several steps in the risk management process. Levick (1995) identifies four basic steps in the risk management process: (1) the identification of the sources from which losses may arise; (2) evaluation of the financial risk involved in each exposure in terms of expected frequency, severity, and impact; (3) treatment of or management of risks by elimination, reduction, or control, transfer to others, and funding through the operation of a coordinated and effective program; and (4) monitoring of risks continuously and systematically. While the terminology is somewhat different, the basics in the steps of risk management are very simple and should be very familiar to nurses: APIE or Assessment, Plan, Intervention, and Evaluation, better known as the nursing process. For the purposes of this section, identification, plan, implementation, and evaluation will be used as headings for the processes.

Identification of Risk

The identification component refers to the identification of potential or actual areas of risk. The identification of risk can be informal, such as things heard through the "grapevine" or through a formal process, such as through review of incident or occurrence reports or in committee meetings; such as safety, infection control, or quality improvement. Also, a review of relevant statutory and case law pertaining to the type of health care organization will identify current risks within similar organizations and the consequences.

Patient or family complaints or patient satisfactions surveys are excellent forms of risk identification. In addition, risks may be identified through physician or staff complaints; through committee meetings, through tracking and trending such as utilization review or quality assurance; through compliance with accreditation bodies, such as the Joint Commission on Accreditation of Healthcare Organizations (JCAHO), the National Committee on Quality Assurance (NCQA), and the Commission on Accreditation of Rehabilitation Facilities (CARF); through state or federal agencies such as the Department of Health or Occupational Safety and Health Act (OSHA); through industry trends such as development of or involvement with managed care organizations, professional organization standards, or guidelines; and through the community such as newspaper, television, or radio. Identification may also include clinical risks recognized as part of the utilization review process, policy and procedure reviews, or by quality screens or clinical pathways or care maps.

The risk identification process should be part of a formalized process and should be well defined. Responsibility for carrying out the process should be fixed and individuals or departments accountable should be identified. The risk identification process should be part of the orientation process and should be readily available to all staff. As previously noted, the review of occurrence or incident reports is very important. In addition, legal notification such as receipt of Notice of Intent (NOI) or Summons and Complaints (S&C) are considered as risk identifiers.

Confidentiality is an important element for members of the staff, especially if you want their support. Also, any information supplied should be protected from discoverability in some format. Information received can be labeled "in anticipation of litigation" or as a work product for an attorney, if the need ever arises. This may protect the information from a plaintiff's attorney.

Plan

The plan component of the risk management process is twofold: the plan as a part of the formalized process and plan of action with a compensable event. A written risk management plan is a very important part of the risk management program because it defines the risk management process. As part of this process, roles and responsibilities are assigned and authority is delineated. The plan also describes the facility's risk management activities. These activities, may range from managing the day-to-day activities such as tracking, trending, and analysis of risk management data, conducting investigations of incidents, and providing education programs to more complex processes, such as risk financing, risk transfer, management of claims, as well as involvement with defense counsel.

On the other hand, a plan of action should be developed as part of the risk management process in dealing with an identified issue. Just as with any other plan of action, the plan should include actions to be taken, responsibility assigned for carrying out the actions, time limitations, and follow-up. Plans of action should be reviewed frequently for appropriateness and compliance and revised as necessary.

Implementation

With the risk management process, implementation is a form of the treatment of a risk. There are several methods to manage risks. One method is the application of controls. In other words, you are attempting to control a risk or the severity of a risk. These controls can be applied is several ways, but two of the most common applications are to reduce the frequency of a risk or the severity of a risk. With frequency, an attempt is made at the reduction or elimination of an established number of occurrences of a risk. Frequency of falls is a common problem as well as being very expensive from a liability standpoint. For example, a health care entity has determined that falls comprise less than 5% of patient injuries per quarter. Through the identification process, it has been determined that within the first 6 months, the data indicate that the ratio of falls to patient injuries is well above the established threshold. Data collected through quality assessment, safety, and risk management are then analyzed with regard to the number of falls and a plan of action is developed as a means to reduce the frequency of events. If not already established, the development and implementation of a fall prevention program might be indicated. As part of the process, early identification of individuals with a potential for falling would be a major component. In addition, the education of staff to the fall prevention program could be a factor in the reduction of falls.

An example of the application of controls with severity could be applied to patient burns as a result of faulty electrical equipment. In such an example, the risk management process would be initiated. The plan of action would include involvement with nursing, bioengineering, plant safety, risk management, and quality assurance to determine necessary actions to control burns due to electrical equipment. A preventative maintenance (PM) program is key in this scenario and the plan of action should include close review of the PM program, the equipment maintenance records for the equipment in question, as well as the education of staff in the use of the equipment.

Evaluation

Evaluation as part of the risk management program should include not only evaluation of outcomes, but continued follow-up as indicated. We know that education is a valuable and effective tool. Relevant findings should be used as opportunities for providing staff education. For example, sharing the trending information on the problem of clotted specimens in an ongoing educational forum led to a decrease in the problem. This situation therefore reduced the frequency of blood redraws and decreased the associated risks for the patient.

Loss Control and Loss Prevention

Loss Control

Two essential components of an effective risk management program are the use of loss control and loss prevention techniques. Loss control is the application of techniques that are designed to minimize loss in a cost-effective manner. One of the most common techniques is risk avoidance. In risk avoidance, known high-risk or problem-prone areas are avoided. An example would be a hospital that has chosen not to provide obstetrical services. Generally, obstetrical services are considered high risk and/or problem prone.

Risk transfer is a further means to control risk. There are two primary techniques in risk transfer. The first technique is to purchase insurance to cover an identified risk. In a simple form, a hospital has an economic responsibility in the event of an injury to a patient, visitor, or employee. To transfer a portion of that responsibility, the facility would purchase insurance, such as general liability insurance, which would assume some or all of the risk for an amount to be paid (premium) to the insurance company.

Another risk transfer technique is a noninsurance transfer of risk, also known as contractual transfer. With this technique, the transfer of risk is effected by means of a contract, other than insurance, in which one party transfers to another legal responsibility for losses. One of the most common examples is the use of contractors who subcontract to perform certain functions. In this scenario, the subcontractors hire their own employees. The contract contains a hold-harmless clause releasing the contractor of any responsibility in the event of a loss. As a result, responsibility for the employees, by contract, transfers to the subcontractors who then assume responsibility and are obligated to pay for any losses arising from their services.

Let's complicate matters with what will be termed "crossover." A frequent use of noninsurance or contractual risk transfer would occur in the emergency department. Oftentimes, emergency departments are staffed by contract physicians. In most instances, the contractor, often an emergency physician service provider, would provide physician coverage by subcontracting with emergency physicians. With a traditional noninsurance or contractual risk transfer, the contractor would assume liability. However, as the physicians are providing direct care to patients, the liability is transferred back to the facility due to vicarious liability, hence, the term *crossover*. In most states, "vicarious liability" laws impute professional liability to the health care entity even though the individual providing the care is not a direct employee of the entity. On the bottom line, the entity has a duty to protect the patients, visitors, and employees from harm or injury. Although explained very simply, this process can be very complex and an understanding of state law dealing with such issues is necessary. Close review of insurance policies and contracts is essential as there is no margin for error. Further, this issue has not yet been settled in the managed care arena, specifically for independent practice associations (IPAs). Close attention to precedents now being established is important.

One additional risk transfer technique is the segregation of risk exposures. With this technique, risks are identified and are divided into separate areas or entities. An example would be the separation of one entity into two distinct entities or corporations. Each entity or corporation would then be responsible for its respective liabilities. This technique is seen frequently with acquisitions and mergers.

Another type of risk control is risk retention. This is accomplished through establishment of a self-insurance retention (SIR). A majority of the larger medical centers are self-insured to a certain level and then transfer a portion of the risk to the insurance carrier in an umbrella coverage plan. This provides much more independent functions for the risk manager in a self-insured setting.

Loss Prevention

Loss prevention is the proactive use of programs or activities to reduce or eliminate the chance of loss or the potential severity of a loss. Employee orientation is an excellent example of a loss-prevention mechanism. In theory, by providing employees with guidelines, policies, and procedures, etc., employees are made aware of their responsibility as well as the responsibility of the organization.

Employees are then made aware that they will be held accountable for their actions while employed at the facility. Presenting the hospital's policies and procedure on confidentiality is paramount. In addition, having the employee sign a confidentiality form provides a contract that the employee will abide by the facility's policy and procedure and that a violation of the agreement will result in disciplinary action or even termination. By providing the employee with the requirements and holding the employee accountable, there should never be an untoward event due to a violation of patient confidentiality.

A proactive safety program is also an excellent loss-prevention technique. Such a program would include active participation by the safety officer or designee in the employee orientation program. The orientation should include identification of the individual responsible for safety, the safety officer; a review of pertinent safety and security policies and procedures with emphasis on electrical and fire safety; review of the pm program including furniture as well as equipment; disaster preparedness; use of the Materials Safety Data Sheet (MSDS) manual; the employee's responsibility in the safety program; and the reporting of safety or security concerns. Frequent walking rounds or site visits are another helpful loss-prevention technique.

Annual updates for employees are encouraged. Updates should include information from risk management as well as safety and security. As noncompliance with policies and procedures or inappropriate or inadequate policies and procedures are frequently cited in case law, periodic review of policies and procedures to reflect current practice is very important. Information gleaned from quality assurance, risk management, safety and security activities, as well as patient satisfaction surveys, can provide valuable information as to actual or potential areas for exposure.

Risk Management Involvement with Other Departments

It should be obvious that communication with other departments by the risk manager is of paramount importance. This is particularly true with quality assurance, safety and security, and hospital personnel. There is a wealth of information obtained by all areas that should be shared. Data collected by quality assurance may be invaluable in the prevention of a loss particularly from patient complaints or satisfaction surveys. This also holds true for information compiled by safety and security such as product recalls, waste management, and walking rounds, as well as reports from facility and ground inspections.

The risk manager should also communicate regularly with the facility's professional staff, including physicians, midlevel practitioners, nurses, and other support staff. A daily working relationship will facilitate the early reporting of potential compensable events by the staff, as well as serve as a direct means for preventive risk management educational programs.

Other areas for information gathering include medical staff credentialing, minutes from committees such as pharmacy and therapeutics, surgical case review, and peer review. Employee-related data is also beneficial, such as employee health reports and workers' compensation reports.

Whether the various departments share common data banks or have individual data banks, information should be shared and communicated. In addition, information must be shared with those in authority such as the governing body. Application of proactive mechanisms and programs does not eliminate all risks; however, it can have a substantial positive impact on operating costs. In addition, such mechanisms and programs can be effective in improving patient care and services within an institution or organization.

Claims Management

One of the primary objectives in a claims management program is to reduce the overall number and cost of claims. This process works hand-in-hand with the risk management process as the management of claims is a process of prevention as well as resolution. Early identification of risks can act as an early warning for a potential compensable event. Just as with the risk management program, a claims management program should be a formalized process and should be readily available to staff. Development of policies and procedures are important as they delineate actions to be taken, and assign responsibility as well as accountability.

Of great importance is what should be reported. A general rule-of-thumb should be that any event that has the potential to result in injury or any event which results in an injury to a patient, visitor, or staff member should be reported. Examples of what should be reported include, but should not be limited to:

1. Cardiopulmonary or respiratory arrest with unsuccessful resuscitation, suicides, as well as unexpected deaths (non-CPR or suicide)
2. Birth-related injuries, maternal or fetal death, low Apgar at 5 minutes, infant resuscitations, fractures or dislocations, and anesthesia-related injuries
3. Unanticipated neurological or sensory deficits such as brain damage, permanent paralysis including paraplegia and quadriplegia, partial or complete loss of sight or hearing functions
4. Unanticipated systemic defects such as renal failure or sepsis
5. Burns from electrical, chemical, thermal, or radiological sources
6. Severe injuries to internal organs such as laceration of an organ, infectious process, or retention of a foreign body
7. Injuries that limit activities of daily living such as sprains, fractures, amputation, or disfigurement
8. Drug–drug or food–drug reaction as a result of use, or death from use

Those listed above constitute major events. Reporting should also include minor events such as slips and falls. In addition, staff injuries such as needle sticks or cuts should be reported. Patient or staff injuries resulting from physical altercations are also important reportable events.

A mechanism should be established for the reporting of events. There are various names for a reporting tool, such as incident report, occurrence report, quality monitoring report, etc. Ideally, the reporting mechanism is a component of the quality assurance process. Upon receipt of the reporting tool, there should be a thorough investigation of the event and an evaluation as to its potential for a claim. In the event that there is concern as to potential for a claim, the administration should be made aware of the circumstances immediately. In such circumstances, the facility's defense counsel should be notified expeditiously. The use of a Report to Attorney form is encouraged. In most instances, minor claims are investigated by the local risk manager. In the event of significant events, investigation may be determined by the defense counsel and performed by an outside agency or third-party administrator (TPA). Generally, a letter of assignment and any pertinent documents are forwarded to the defense counsel or outside claims investigator. Upon receipt, the defense counsel or outside investigator will then forward a letter of acknowledgment to the facility. In the investigation process, the risk manager will function as coordinator of all investigation activity. This will include arranging employee interviews and securing evidence.

Securing evidence is particularly important now with the Safe Medical Device Act in place. Any injury, illness, or death must be reported within 10 working days if a medical device is a factor in the event. Education and compliance of the staff are essentials.

Upon completion of the investigation, the defense counsel or TPA will provide a report of the findings as well as any recommendations for further investigation or disposition of the claim. Should additional investigation be required, periodic reports of the investigation should be provided to the facility by the defense counsel or TPA until such time as the investigation is deemed to be completed. Again, any written report must be protected from discoverability. Disposition of the claim may include offering a settlement to the claimant or proceeding to trial. In the event of a settlement, settlement authority should be defined in the risk management plan.

Included in the notification process and investigation process is notification of the facility's insurance carrier. In most instances the initial indemnity reserve is established; however, the reserve amount should be adjusted periodically to reflect findings during the investigation or discovery process. Most insurance carriers have specific reporting requirements. These requirements may include an initial evaluation of the case as well as determination on liability, damages, and settlement value. Careful monitoring of the claim or potential claim should be done by the risk manager.

Monitoring of an incident or claim can be very time-consuming. To assist in this process, the use of a mechanism or tool is helpful. Such a tool as illustrated in (Table 38.1).

Role of the Legal Nurse Consultant
Licensure and Certification

The LNC interested in this role should become well aquainted with licensing and certification requirements regarding the regulation of risk management consultants. Generally, the state board of insurance regulates licensing requirements for individuals functioning in the role of a risk management consultant. Qualification is usually obtained by examination. However, there is no consistency from state to state and some states have no requirements for licensing or certification. Some states require an individual be licensed as a consultant or advisor and, in some instances, as an agent or broker. Other states have no requirements for licensing of consultants. There are a few states that do not allow an individual to hold both an agent's or broker's license and an adviser's license.

Table 38.1

Patient or Claimant Information	Comments
Name:	
Address:	
Telephone number:	
Age:	
Social Security Number:	
Occupation:	
Employment status:	
Marital status:	
Name of spouse:	
Number, name(s) and age(s) of dependents:	
INCIDENT INFORMATION	
Date of loss or date of report:	
Description of loss or claim:	
Names, addresses and phone numbers of all personnel involved in claim:	
Names, addresses and phone numbers of all witnesses to claim:	
INDEMNITY INFORMATION	
Name, address, phone, and fax number of insurance company:	
Contact person (there may be one for policy issues and another for claim issues):	
Policy number:	
Policy period:	
Policy limits:	
Deductible:	
CLAIM INFORMATION	
Claim number (yours and insurance carriers if different):	
Codefendants(s):	
Codefendant(s) policy information:	
Defense counsel:	
Defense attorney:	
Address, phone & fax number:	
Primary Investigator:	
Address, phone, & fax number:	
Date assigned:	
Plaintiff Counsel:	
Plaintiff Attorney:	
Address, phone & fax number:	
Date of suit:	
Court number:	
Indemnity reserve:	
Expense(s) (attorney costs):	
Date established (reserve):	

Table 38.1 (continued)

Patient or Claimant Information	Comments
Documentation of any changes to reserves, the amount, date & reason for adjustments:	
Payment schedule by date, amount, & category (display running totals):	
Claim status — open or closed. If closed, by dismissal, settlement, or trial with verdict	

Texas, for example, has two requirements for individuals providing consultative services in the areas of loss control and risk management. The first is a certification with the State Board of Insurance as a Loss Control Representative. The second is a license as a risk manager. The primary distinction is the function of the job. Individuals providing services for the identification of risk for the purpose of insurance should be licensed by the Board of Insurance. Licensure requires successful completion of an examination administered by a third-party testing agency. LNCs wishing to provide services are well advised to be familiar with licensing requirements in the states they wish to consult.

There are several avenues for certification. Some insurance carriers have programs which provide courses in risk management. Upon completion, the participant is certified to have completed the course. The American Society for Health Care Risk Management (ASHRM) offers a series of modules which, upon successful completion, provide the recipient with a certification that he or she has completed the course. Completion of the course can then be applied toward diplomat or fellow status.

Formal Education

Several colleges and universities now offer undergraduate and graduate programs in risk management. Courses may be in risk management instead of, or in addition to, courses with an insurance business focus.

Risk Management

There are any number of services that the LNC may perform. As previously mentioned, the LNC may provide consultation to a facility's risk manager. In instances where a facility or entity does not have a designated risk manager, the LNC may directly perform risk management services. In addition, the LNC may function in the role of claims manager in conjunction with a facility risk manager.

The performance of risk assessments is one opportunity for the LNC. Risk assessments may be clinical in nature and focus on high-risk, problem-prone, or high-volume clinical areas. Risk assessments may include the assessment of property and casualty (P&C) as well as directors and officers (D&O) risks, depending on the expertise of the consultant.

A clinical risk assessment is usually performed as part of an on-site visit. Generally, the assessment is of high-risk, problem-prone, and high-volume areas such as perioperative, perinatal, emergency, and behavioral medicine services.

The process includes one-on-one interview of key personnel; a review of documentation including a sampling of charts; committee minutes and plans from such areas as safety, risk management, quality assurance, credentialing, and personnel files; and a walk through of the physical plant including high-risk areas.

Many consulting firms and insurance companies have tools with which to conduct the assessment. Tools are constructed from knowledge of case law, accreditation and licensing standards, and professional standards. Opportunities exist for the licensed nurse consultant to create tools to be used in nontraditional settings, such as physician group practices, substance abuse centers, and mental health clinics.

Risk assessments may be global in which a survey, or an overview, of the facility or entity is performed. Focus assessments can also be performed and are more intense in nature. Focus assessments may be performed on one particular department or service.

System analysis is another form of risk assessment. The assessment may be done on one or more system such as a quality management system and subsystems or on a particular system such as a risk management reporting system.

Staff development and education is a significant role for the LNC. Educational needs may be derived as a result of an event, as an identified need from a risk assessment, or as a plan of action as part of the monitoring and evaluation process. Many health care entities have reduced costs by the elimination of attendance at outside seminars or, in some instances, an education department. This is a prime area of opportunity for the LNC.

Client support is another avenue for the LNC. Client support may range from something as simple as being available for phone consultation to the more complex, such as the management of claims. The review of contracts and the development of a policy and procedure are other means to support the client.

Claims Management

Services provided by the LNC in the area of the management of claims are varied based on the needs of the client. One service is the review of claims for frequency, severity, and impact.

Case management service is the actual management of a case from the evaluation phase to final resolution of the case. There is involvement with the defense counsel, insurance carrier, monitoring of expenses, establishing reserves, and monitoring the evolution of the case are part of the process.

Investigation of the claim itself involves reviewing the medical records, interviewing all pertinent employees, visitors, patients, and family members. Analysis of findings are then discussed with key personnel as the decision for handling the claim is determined.

Report Preparation

Provision of services often includes the preparation of reports. Just as in the use of risk assessment tools, many consultative firms and insurance companies have specific guidelines for report writing. Just as there are various tools, there are various formats including the more expansive narrative format to summary bullet points or grid format.

Ideally, the report should identify potential or actual areas for improvement, but, as importantly, should identify areas that are being performed well. Recommendations or suggestions are generally included as part of the process. The consultant who provides documentation or references that support recommendations or suggestions is greatly appreciated. In addition, possible realistic approaches to problematic areas are also appreciated.

Remember to keep the reader in mind. Reports should be as concise as possible and not contain language that may be totally unfamiliar to the reader. Reports should also be completed in a timely manner. Follow-up by the consultant within a reasonable time after receipt of the report by the organization may have great benefits.

A word of caution. Reports should always contain a caveat explaining the position of the individual preparing the report. Most caveats include language that releases the writer of any liability as a result of the report. If possible, it is suggested that reports flow through the facility's legal counsel or be a component of the peer review or quality process to limit the potential for discovery of the document. It is also suggested that the LNC work closely with the facility risk manager or legal counsel to determine the most appropriate route.

Summary

There are many opportunities for the LNC who is interested in the area of risk management. Employment opportunities range from being an employee of an institution or organization to that of an independent consultant.

As the health care industry is in a constant state of change, the LNC is well advised to stay abreast of current trends, case law, professional standards, and accreditation and licensing requirements and guidelines. There are extensive resources to support the LNC from professional organizations to utilization of the Internet.

Glossary

Claim: Used in reference to insurance, a demand by an individual or corporation to recover, under a policy of insurance, for loss which may come within that policy.

Claims management: A mechanism that can substantially reduce the overall cost of claims.

Incident: A broad term used to describe any occurrence that is not consistent with routine hospital activities.

Loss control: A measure taken which effectively impacts risk by decreasing the chance that a loss will occur or, by reducing the severity if it does occur.

Loss prevention: A program which seeks to reduce or eliminate the chance of loss or the potential severity of a loss.

Notice of Intent: A document sent to a health care facility which puts that facility on notice that a party has initiated legal action against the facility.

Risk: Can be defined numerous ways. For this purpose, risk is a chance of loss. Risk is a variation in possible outcomes that exist in any given situation or event. Risk may include two categories: (1) *objective* — variations that exist in nature and that are the same for all individuals facing the same situation and (2) *subjective* — an individual's estimation of the objective risk.

Risk management: A process which identifies, evaluates, and takes corrective action against potential or actual risks to patients, visitors, employees or property.

Summons & Complaint (or Petition): A document that sets forth allegations against the defendant(s) that the plaintiff intends to prove. The document is formal notification and initiates the legal action against the facility. The method of instituting a legal proceeding and notification of such action to all concerned parities is regulated by the individual Rules of Civil Procedure of each state. The LNC is advised to seek legal counsel in the particular state to determine the proper legal notification process.

Reference

Levick, D. L. (1995). *Risk Management and Insurance Audit Techniques,* 3rd ed, Boston, Standard Publishing Corporation.

Suggested Reading

American Health Consultants. *Health Care Risk Management*. Atlanta, Hospitals.

American Hospital Association, (1991). *Risk Management Self-Assessment Manual,* Chicago, American Hospital Publishing.

American Hospital Association (1996). *Member Resources, Publications, and Products,* Chicago, American Hospital Publishing.

American Society for Health Care Risk Management (1996). *Mapping Your Risk Management Course in Ambulatory Care Facilities,* Chicago, American Hospital Association.

American Society for Health Care Risk Management (1996). *Mapping Your Risk Management Course in Stand-Alone Hospitals.* Chicago, American Hospital Association.

American Society for Health Care Risk Management (1992). *Strategies for Success,* Chicago, American Hospital Association.

Benson, D. S. and Miller, J. A. (1993). *AmbuQual II: An Ambulatory Quality Assessment and Quality Management System.* Indianapolis.

Defense Research Institute, Inc. *For the Defense,* Chicago, The Institute.

Harpster, J. D. and Veach, M. S., Eds., (1990). *Risk Management Handbook for Health Care Facilities,* Chicago, American Hospital Publishing.

Health Care Financing Administration. (1994). *Federal Resister: Rules & Regulations,* Dallas.

Hospitals, *The Malpractice Reporter,* New York.

Joint Commission on Accreditation of Healthcare Organizations (1996). *Accreditation Manual for Hospitals,* Chicago, The Commission.

Levick, D. L. (1995). *Risk Management and Insurance Audit Techniques,* 3rd ed., Boston, Standard Publishing Corporation.

Malpractice Reporter, *HRM Legal Review & Commentary,* Atlanta, Hospitals.

MIS Training Institute Press, Inc. *Infosecurity News,* Farmingham, MA.

National Association for Health Care Quality, *Journal of Health Care Quality,* Chicago.

National Committee for Quality Assurance (1991). *Standards for Accreditation,* Washington, D.C., The Committee.

Occupational Safety and Health Act (1996). *Standards,* Washington, D.C.

Prather, S. E., Blake, R. R., and Mouton, J. S. (1990). *Medical Risk Mmanagement,* Oradell, NJ, Medical Economics Company, Inc.

INDEX

A

AALNC, see American Association of Legal Nurse
    Consultants
Abdominal aortic aneurysm, treatment of, 282
Abortion, 91
Accident policy, 716
Accrual accounting, 594
ACNM, see American College of Nurse-Midwives
ACOG, see American College of Obstetricians
    and Gynecologists
Active euthanasia, 99
Acute risks, 115
ADA, see Americans with Disabilities Act
Administrative code, 40, 136
Administrative law, 4, 29
Administrative rulings, 40
Admission history and physical, 294
ADRs, see Adverse drug reactions
Adverse Drug Reaction Report, 372
Adverse drug reactions (ADRs), 384
Advertisers, 702
Affidavit, 639
Agency attorneys, 158
Agreed Board Order, 154
AHIMA, see American Health Information
    Management Association
AIDS, 128, 720
Air pollution, 115
Air toxics, 115
Alcohol problems, historical information regarding, 287
Allegations, 269
All-or-nothing concept, 356
Alternative dispute resolution, 530
AMA, see American Medical Association
Ambulance run reports, 53
AMC, see Association Management Center
American Academy of Pediatrics, 297
American Association of Legal Nurse Consultants
    (AALNC), 4, 275, 196
  annual conferences, 7
  by laws, 9
  chapter listing, 12–16
  Code of Ethics, 215
  decision-making body of, 6
  founding of, 5
  mentoring program, 213

  mission of, 6
  National Founding Members, 6
  National Founding Steering Committee
  Members, 5–6
  presidents, 12
American Bar Association, 8, 23
American College of Nurse-Midwives (ACNM), 459
American College of Obstetricians and Gynecologists
    (ACOG), 459
American Health Information Management Association
    (AHIMA), 123
American Institute of Chemists, 412
American Medical Association (AMA), 8, 122, 352
American Nurses Association (ANA), 8, 23, 123, 178,
    196
  Code for Nurses, 190, 215
  Code of Ethics, 185, 188
Americans with Disabilities Act (ADA), 724
American Society of Anesthesiologists, 289
ANA, see American Nurses Association
Analysis, 21
Analysis and issue identification, 201
Anecdotal reporting, 384
Anesthesia
  preoperative assessment, 289
  progressive respiratory problems after, 301
  records, 281, 289
Anoxic brain injury, 432
Anthropology, 419
Antiarrhythmics, 388
Antibiotics, 69
Anti-dumping statute, 70, 71, 76
Apgar score, 300
Arraignment, 424
Arteriosclerotic heart disease, 94
Arthroscopy scars, description of, 526
Asbestos litigation, 400
Assault, 32, 34, 424
Assessment, 21, 199, 200, 241
Asset management, past personal financial, 597
Assigned risk, 730
Assisted suicide, state statutes prohibiting, 99
Association Management Center (AMC), 7
Attendant care, 681
Attorney(s)
  adversarial, 654
  case theories, 647
  client privilege, 21

O

X